THE CANONGATE BURNS

The Canongate Burns

VOLUME I

Introduced by Andrew Noble

★

Edited by Andrew Noble
and Patrick Scott Hogg

★

CANONGATE

CLASSICS

104

First published in the UK and simultaneously in North America in 2001 as a Canongate Classic, an imprint of Canongate Books Limited, 14 High Street, Edinburgh EHI ITE.

10 9 8 7 6 5 4 3 2 1

The editors wish to acknowledge research grants from The Carnegie and Leverhulme Trusts which helped make this book possible. Andrw Noble would also like to thank the Institute for Advanced Studies in The Humanities, University of Edinburgh for a Visiting Research Fellowship in 1990.

The publishers gratefully acknowledge general subsidy from the Scottish Arts Council towards the Canongate Classics series and a specific grant towards the publication of this volume.

Typeset in Monotype Plantin by Hewer Text Ltd, Edinburgh. Printed and bound by Omnia Books Ltd, Glasgow.

British Library Cataloguing-in-Publication Data
A catalogue record for this volume
is available on request from the
British Library.

ISBN 1 84195 148 X

www.canongate.net

Contents

A NOTE ON ROBERT BURNS

Robert Burns (1759–96) entered the world on 25 January as the first of William Burnes and Agnes Brown's seven children (four boys and three girls). Originally from Kincardineshire, Burnes worked as a gardener in Ayrshire where he also leased land as a tenant farmer and built a two-roomed cottage at Alloway. Burnes was not a successful farmer and had to struggle with harsh land and demanding factors first at Mount Oliphant and then at Lochlie farm at Tarbolton. Nevertheless, he aimed to give Robert and his brother Gilbert a decent education, sending them to village schools and making arrangements for Robert to spend some of the summer months studying French and Mathematics with his former teacher as tutor. By the age of fifteen Burns was widely read in English literature and considered something of a 'prodigy' in French, but it seems likely that hard labour on the farm weakened his heart and eventually contributed to an early death.

Forming a bachelors' club and debating society at Tarbolton, young Robert became a Freemason, worked as a flax dresser in Irvine and enjoyed an active social and sexual life. He began to write poems, inspired to use Scots by the work of Robert Fergusson. His father's illness, his debts, and a court case over his rent arrears brought the poet back to Lochlie and when William Burnes died in 1784, Robert and Gilbert took up a farm at nearby Mossgiel and found themselves supporting the family. By this time Burns was involved with Betty Paton, by whom he had a daughter, and Jean Armour was also pregnant. (She was to bear him two pairs of twins before he eventually married her in 1788.) During these years (1784–6) Burns wrote some his most famous poems, including many epistles to various friends, his attacks on religious hypocrisy in 'Holy Willie's Prayer', his celebration of Rabelaisian energy in 'The Holy Fair' and 'The Jolly Beggars' and his subtle but scathing satire on social injustice 'The Twa Dogs'. Creative or not, these were difficult and exhausting years and, faced with local scandal, nervous strain, unrewarding hard labour and rising debt, Burns considered emigrating to Jamaica. The success of his first collection, *Poems, Chiefly in the Scottish Dialect* (1786) did much to change his mind.

This first 'Kilmarnock edition' sold out, it was praised by Henry Mackenzie, the most influential author and critic in Edinburgh, and a revised 'Edinburgh Edition' followed in 1787 to even greater acclaim, with an American edition published the following year.

Burns spent the winters of 1786–7 and 1787–8 in Edinburgh, lionised by society and the literary establishment, if largely misunderstood and sentimentalised by them as a 'heaven-taught ploughman'. The winter of 1788 saw the start of a sentimental correspondence with Mrs Agnes McLehose in Edinburgh, remembered as 'Clarinda' in his letters from 'Sylvander'. Despite his literary success, Burns found it difficult to get any money from his Edinburgh publisher, William Creech, and was still in need of a patron or a job. Having spent the summer months of these years touring the Borders and the Highlands, he took an interest in old Scots songs and this led to his writing, collecting and re-writing songs for Johnson's *Scots Musical Museum* (1787–1803) and *Thomson's Select Scotish Airs* (1793–1818), a major task to which he devoted himself for the rest of his life. The poet took up farming again at Ellisland in the summer of 1788, and set about training to be an Excise Officer. In the early 1790s, like Wordsworth, Coleridge and Mary Wollstonecraft, Burns supported the libertarian ideals of the French revolution. Such opinions were dangerous, however, when government informers were on the look-out for sedition and his verses to the radical press were often published either anonymously or under various pseudonyms. The farm at Ellisland was not a success, and in 1791 Burns moved to Dumfries where he took up the post of Excise Officer. These last years were times of considerable political and social unrest throughout Britain and in 1795 severe shortages and food riots broke out in Dumfries. Burns's health was as uncertain as his finances. The poet's weak heart was exacerbated by the medicines of the day and, fevered and fearing for the future of his family, he died at home on 21 July at the age of 37.

ABOUT THE EDITORS

ANDREW NOBLE is Senior Lecturer in the Department of English Studies at the University of Strathclyde. His books include *The Art of Robert Burns* edited and introduced with R.D.S. Jack (1982) and the uncollected Scottish criticism of Edwin Muir (1982). He has also edited and introduced critical studies of Robert Louis Stevenson (1983), as well as Stevenson's account of his emigrant journey, *From the Clyde to California* (1985). An authority on Scottish cinema, he has written particuarly on Bill Douglas, *A Lanternist's Account*, 1922.

PATRICK SCOTT HOGG is a native of rural Galloway and comes from a fishing family. After graduating in History (Stirling University) he took a postgraduate Diploma in Information Systems (University of Portsmouth). He returned to Scotland after a successful career in London publishing and lectured at Dumfries and Galloway College of Technology for three years. He is the author of *Robert Burns: The Lost Poems* (1997); has published essays in *The Edinburgh Review*, *The Herald* newspaper, *The Burns Chronicle* and most recently, in the American volume, *Critical Essays on Robert Burns*, edited by Prof Carol McGuirk (1998).

Acknowledgements

Patrick Scott Hogg would like to thank Dumfries and Galloway Council's Burns Bicentenary Committee, especially Shirley Bell and John Dowson, for its grant in 1995 to initiate the archival research programme. Two subsequent grants from The Carnegie Trust were also of invaluable assistance. Scott Hogg would like to repeat his gratitude expressed in *Robert Burns: The Lost Poems* (1997) to everybody who helped him. Particular thanks are due to Bobby Dalziel, John Manson and Peter Westwood and many other members of The Burns Federation. Outwith the Federation, Albert Calder and Norry Paton were sources of encouragement.

Andrew Noble would like to thank The Leverhulme Trust for a major grant, which allowed him to employ his co-editor in 1998–9 as a Research Assistant at Strathclyde University. He would also like to record his gratitude to The Institute for Advanced Studies at Edinburgh University, whose award of a Visiting Research Fellowship in 2000 gave him invaluable time and space to complete this project.

We would also record our thanks to librarians all over Britain; the most harassed were Donald Nelson and Harzara Singh of Glasgow's Mitchell Library's world-famous Burns Collection. For keying in various parts of the manuscript we received sterling help from Jordana Brown, John MacLeish, Martin Ogg and David Exley.

From the academic community Carol McGuirk, Tom Crawford, and David Daiches were consistently supportive in their sympathetic and objective scholarship. Thanks are also due to Rory Watson for his assistance and, with Cairns Craig, his editorial acceptance of the project. Of signal help was Liam McIlvanney's scholarship. His forthcoming book from Tuckwell (*The Radical Burns: Poetry and Politics in the Late Eighteenth Century*) complements and compliments this edition.

Last, but by no means least, Andrew Noble would like to thank his wife Jennifer, and Patrick Scott Hogg and his partner Helen for the patience shown in the face of this mammoth task. The last words, as always, should be the Bard's:

> Ah, gentle dames! it gars me greet,
> To think how many counsels sweet,
> How mony lengthen'd sage advices,
> The husband frae the wife despises!

'To select and arrange what ought to be published of Burns's will be no easy task, when you consider the variety of taste and opinions which obtain among men and the necessity there is for the strictest delicacy being ever kept in view. His poetry and letters were so often blended with Religion, Politics, Love, and Bawdry that the greatest care must be taken to render his thoughts and opinions consistent.'

Alexander Cunningham: The Syme-Cunningham Correspondence, *The Burns Chronicle*, 1938, XIII, p. 43.

'. . . the editing of his works was, for a full century after his death, in the hands of men temperamentally unfitted to sympathise with certain phases of his character, and incapable of frank and objective presentation of facts of which they disapproved.'

Professor J. De Lancey Ferguson, *The Letters of Robert Burns*, p. xxxix, Oxford, Clarendon Press, 1931.

Introduction

Introduction

'The very ink with which all history is written is merely fluid prejudice.'

Mark Twain, *Pudd'nhead Wilson's New Calendar*.

'I think this enlightened age, as it is called, is as much given to persecution as the most barbarous. The transportation of the Deputies and Directors is not perhaps quite so bad as that of Muir, Palmer, etc., . . . Men persecute because they love persecution and so far as I am from believing fear to be the true cause of persecution that I begin to think that fear is the only motive that ever can persuade men to suffer those who differ in opinion from them to breathe the same atmosphere with them. This is not pleasant philosophy but I am afraid it is true.'

Charles James Fox to Charles Grey, 1801.

For the first time in over two centuries we have in this single volume all Burns's *surviving* poems glossed and annotated. To do such editorial work has been for us a salutary and revealing task. What has fundamentally impressed us has been the tenacity of Burns's creative drive which, despite all obstacles, sustained a flow of over six hundred poems and songs over a period of twenty-two years. Such productivity also entailed that he constantly metamorphosed his day to day experiences into poetry. Thus, as we annotated the poems, making as much use of that other source of parallel commentary, his quite extraordinary and, arguably, still under valued letters, not only his biographical shape but an encompassing picture of the peculiarly fraught late eighteenth century emerged. As admirable, and even more surprising, is the sustained quality of his poetic achievement. If we compare him to Wordsworth or, even more pertinently, Coleridge, briefly his creative contemporaries and consistent admirers of his genius, Burns achieves a higher ratio of poetry of the first order than either of them.

All this was achieved in opposition to a series of diverse and formidable obstacles. With some few significant exceptions, Burns's biographers and editors have been, as we shall see, either anodyne or, worse, in some early instances, deliberately mendacious about the harsh physical, social and political environment in which he had to survive as a creative writer. Consequently this edition lays stress on his capacity not only to endure but poetically to overcome the multiple constraints he experienced. Textually and contextually, this edition, therefore, lays unique emphasis, partly by bringing some recently retrieved archival material to bear, on Burns's necessarily ironic and often oblique political life and poems. Consequent on such a new explication of Burns's political values and poetry, will be an exploration into the calculated and deeply successful manner in which, from the moment of his death, his achievement as a radically dissenting democratic poet was denied and suppressed. Indeed, what is revealed is the degree to which a whole segment of late-enlightenment liberal, Scottish culture of which Burns was an integral part was, as far as possible, obliterated from the national memory by reactionary forces which were quick to build on their total victory in the 1790s. Burns's corpse, as we shall see, was not the only thing consigned to the grave in 1796. It is, indeed, a signal example of the fact that the victors *do* write history.

EARLY LIFE AND LABOUR

The primary and conditioning factor of Burns's life was his experience of the often harshly brutal and almost always near impoverished nature of late-eighteenth century farm labour. We should first contemplate the physical conditions under which he had to write as a prelude to understanding the psychological and political consequences for his poetry. This has been obscured from us by the mass of sentimental, mainly nineteenth-century writing on Burns which sees him as the spokesman for a pietistic, hence politically quiescent, peasant culture.

In his quite wonderful opening stanzas to *The Vision* Burns describes himself 'half-mad, half-fed, half-sarket', portraying the fierce restrictions of work, domestic squalor and poverty in which he mainly lived. Or as he wrote from Mauchline in 1788 to Robert Cleghorn:

I am so harassed [sic] with Care and Anxiety about this farming project of mine, that my Muse has degenerated into the veriest prose-wrench that ever picked cinders or followed a Tinker. — When I am fairly got into the routine of business, I shall trouble you with a longer epistle; perhaps with some queries respecting farming: at present the world sits such a load on my mind that it has effaced almost every trace of the image of God in me.

Routine, initiated by the harsh demands of the marginal farm, so prematurely imposed on his childhood, Burns loathed.[1] He described his early life as having 'the cheerless gloom of a hermit with the unceasing moil of a galley slave'. Or, as in this letter to Mrs Dunlop of 1788 where, so characteristic of his letters, wit and despair blend:

> . . . the heart of the man, and the fancy of the poet, are the two grand considerations for which I live: if miry ridges and dirty dunghills are to engross the best part of the functions of my soul immortal, I had better been a rook or a magpie all at once & then I would not have been plagued with any ideas superior to breaking of clods & picking up grubs: not to mention Barn-door Cocks or Mallards, creatures with which I could almost exchange lives at any time.

Some sort of acute nervous disorder was the result of his attempt to become disciplined to the mechanistic demands of becoming a flax worker in Irvine, 1784. After moving to Ellisland farm near Dumfries most of his new found wealth from the Edinburgh edition went to save the family farm at Mossgiel. The dwelling at Ellisland is described by the young lawyer, Robert Ainslie, as 'ill contrived – and pretty Dirty'. Mrs Jean Burns is 'Vulgar & Common-place in a high degree – and pretty round & fat . . . a kind Body in her own way, and the husband Tolerably Attentive to her.' The poet's local associates are 'a Vulgar looking Tavern keeper from Dumfries; and his wife, more Vulgar — Mr Millar of Dalswinton's Gardiner and his Wife — and said Wife's sister — and a little fellow from Dumfries, [probably John Drummond] who had been a Clerk.'[2] Hence, the poverty and hardship of his early years, described so eloquently and bluntly to Dr John Moore, 'the clouterly appearance of my ploughboy carcase, the two extremes of which were often exposed to all the inclements of all the seasons', was still with Burns after his temporary fame and even more temporary riches beyond his Edinburgh edition of 1787.

Nor, leaving aside the problem of his vowed fidelity to a Pittite regime he loathed, were his Excise duties any escape from devouring physical drudgery: 'I am jaded to death with fatigue. For these two months or three months, on an average, I have not ridden less than two hundred miles per week.' The paper work of the Excise also ate into not only his time but his spirit:[3]

> Sunday closes the period of our cursed revenue business, & may probably keep me employed with my pen until noon. —Fine

employment for a poet's pen! There is a species of the Human genius that I call, the Ginhorse Class: what enviable dogs they are! —round, & round, & round they go— Mundell's ox that drives his cotton mill, their exact prototype— without an idea or wish beyond their circle; fat sleek, stupid, patient, quiet & contented:— while here I sit, altogether Novemberish, a damned melange of Fretfulness & melancholy; not enough of the one to rouse me to passion; nor of the other to repose me in torpor; my soul flouncing & fluttering round her tenement, like a wild Finch caught amid the horrors of winter & newly thrust into a cage.

Burns's case as medical study, symptomatically discernible in the letters and, indeed, in much of the poetry, is a grim one. If he was atypical in the extreme mood swings that seem integral to his creativity (it was specifically with Burns in mind that Wordsworth wrote in *Resolution and Independence*: 'We poets in our youth begin in gladness:/ But thereof come in the end despondency and madness.'), he was wholly typical of the age, its life expectancy and its exposure to poverty related illness.

His life, as read in his letters, is a catalogue of fractures and worsening fevers: in temporary lodgings while the farmhouse at Ellisland by Dumfries was under construction, he complained

> . . . but for some nights preceding I had slept in an apartment where the force of the wind and the rains was only mitigated by being sifted thro' numberless apertures in the windows, walls, &c. In consequence I was on Sunday, Monday, & part of Tuesday unable to stir out of bed with all the miserable effects of a violent cold.

Since medicine had so little ability to intervene, 'suffering', as Roy Porter has pertinently remarked, 'was *everyone's* lot sooner or later, low or high born'. Yet it was worse for the poor. As so often in Burns's poetry, *Death and Dr Hornbook* is a comic caricature with a savage edge to it: cholera in the clachan is not an oxymoron and crude, often lethal abortion is part of the women's lot. Further, as Porter has again remarked, the physical discrepancy between the rich and poor had deep political implications:

> The wealthier were healthier and lived longer; sexually they probably matured earlier; being taller, they literally looked down on the poor. Their lives were lived by a different clock

—for example, the poor rose, ate and slept early (lighting was costly), the rich late. The show of superiority and deference was emphasised by the encrusted rituals of bowing and scraping, head-baring, standing, curtseying, and knuckling foreheads.[4]

In Burns's poetry, then, the repressed resentment of the common people towards their propertied masters becomes articulate. His letters are also obsessively, often more overtly, preoccupied with the multiple slights he feels inflicted on his assertively independent spirit as a consequence of the social gulf between rich and poor.

This is made deeply ambivalent by the fact that as a poet it was the people of property who formed his audience and to whom he not infrequently looked for creative support. His letters, consequently, are saturated with a sort of baffled rage. This over-wrought letter to Robert Graham, Commissioner of the Scottish Board of Excise, to whom Burns's looked in vain to be a replacement patron for the deceased Earl of Glencairn, is typical of the agonies he endured concerning the imposed, impoverished inferiority of his rank:

> As I had an eye to getting on in the examiners list, if attainable by me, I was going to ask you if it would be of any service to try the service of some Great, and some *very* Great folks to whom I have the honour to be known; I mean in the way of a Treasury Warrant. —But much as early impressions have [impression (*deleted*)] given me the honour of Spectres, &c. still, I would [rather (*deleted*)] face the Arch-fiend, in Miltonic pomp, at the head of all his legions; and hear that infernal shout which blind John says: 'Tore hell's concave;' rather than crawl in, a dust-licking petitioner, before the presence of a Mighty Man, & bear [the(*deleted*)], amid all the mortifying pangs of Self-annihilation, the swelling consequence of his d-mn'd State, & the cold monosyllables of his hollow heart!

Worse, if he was to be the spokesman for the common people he had, certainly after his Ayrshire days, diminished faith that they had any sympathetic understandings of what he was writing. As he wrote in *Epistle to Hugh Parker*:

> In this strange land, this uncouth clime,
> A land unknown to prose or rhyme:
> Where words ne'er cros't the Muse's heckles,
> Nor limpit in poetic shackles:
> A land that Prose did never view it,

Except when drunk he stacher't thro' it:
Here, ambushed by the chimla cheek,
Hid in an atmosphere of reek,
I hear a wheel thrum i' the neuk,
I hear it— for in vain I leuk:
The red peat gleams, a fiery kernel
Enhusked by a fog infernal.
Here, for my wonted rhyming raptures,
I sit and count my sins by chapters;
For life and spunk like other Christians,
I'm dwindled down to mere existence:
Wi' nae converse but Gallowa' bodies,
Wi' nae kind face but Jenny Geddes.

Such absence of stimulation and response increasingly led to severe
depression. Little wonder that Coleridge was so sensitive to this
dark side of Burns. This Burns letter of 1789 to David Blair could be
confused with the prose of the English poet:

> Know you of anything worse than Gallery Bondage, a slavery
> where the soul with all her powers is laden with weary fetters of
> ever increasing weight: a Slavery which involves the mind in
> dreary darkness and almost total eclipse of every ray of God's
> image: and all this the work, the baneful doings of the arch-
> fiend known among worlds by the name of Indolence.

His initial childhood experience had led him to hope for better; like
his English Romantic peers, Burns, anti-Calvinistically, profoundly
believed that the child entered the world as uncorrupted spirit. His
own childhood anticipations of an unrestricted, public social life
were, however, soon to be disabused. The Romantic poets, of
course, long pre-date Freud in grounding the nature of the adult
self on childhood experience. Burns's self-analysis, while hardly
Wordsworthian in its outcome, is extraordinarily keen in its aware-
ness of the forces that shaped him as man and poet:

> My vicinity to Ayr was of great advantage to me.—My social
> disposition, when not checked by some modification of spited
> pride, like our catechism definition of Infinitude, was 'without
> bounds or limits'. —I formed many connections with other
> Youngkers who possessed superiour advantages; the youngling
> actors who were busy with the rehearsal of PARTS in which
> they were shortly to appear on that STAGE where, Alas! I was

destined to drudge behind the SCENES. — It is not commonly at these green years that the young Noblesse and Gentry have a just sense of the immense distance between them and their ragged Playfellows. —It takes a few dashes into the world to give the young Great man that proper, decent, unnoticing disregard for the poor, insignificant, stupid devils, the mechanics and the peasantry around him; who were perhaps born in the same village. —My young superiours never insulted the clouterly appearance of my ploughboy carcase, the two extremes of which were often exposed to all the inclemencies of all the seasons.— They would give me stray volumes of books; among them, even then, I could pick up some observations; and ONE, whose heart I am sure not even the MUNNY BE-GUM'S scenes have tainted, helped me to a little French. — Parting with these, my young friend and benefactors, as they dropped off for the east or the West Indies, was often to me a sore affliction; but I was soon called to more serious evils.— My father's generous master died; the farm proved a ruinous bargain; and, to clench the curse, we fell into the hands of a Factor who sat for the picture I have drawn of one in my tale of two dogs.—My father was advanced in life when he married; I was the eldest of seven children; and he, worn out by early hardship, was unfit for labour.—My father's spirit was soon irritated, but not easily broken.— There was a freedom in his lease in two years more, and to weather these two years we retrenched expenses.— We lived very poorly; I was a dextrous ploughman for my years; and the next eldest to me was a brother, who could drive the plough very well and help me to thrash.— A Novel-Writer might perhaps have viewed these scenes with some satisfaction, but so did not I: my indignation yet boils at the recollection of the scoundrel tyrants insolent, threatening epistles, which used to set us all in tears.

This notion of it being an essential part of democracy that one be, so to speak, 'on stage', that all men have a right to be visible in the public domain of history, a visibility the schoolboy Burns believed he had, is a concept to which we will return. If there was no economic base for this, such freedom was impossible. Burns's experience was one of the intensification of power of the land-holding class fired by the energies and methods of agrarian capitalism which were making life for many economically worse. That, in fact, the Enlightenment pressures towards democratic reform expressed through the new Freemasonry and, for him, present in the

American Revolution were being undermined by a re-energised, even more avaricious propertied class. The childhood threat of being thrown off their farm stayed with Burns. Always, for diverse reasons, a keen Bible reader no book was more pertinent to him than that of the Book of Job where he clearly discerned both his father's ill-fate and his own in that nothing they turned their hands to would prosper. His father's death saved him from debtor's prison. The trauma stayed with the son:

> I am curst with a melancholy prescience, which makes me the veriest coward, in life. There is not any exertion which I would not attempt, rather than be in a horrid situation —to be ready to call on the mountains to fall on me, & the hills to cover me from the presence of a haughty Landlord, or his still more haughty underling, to whom I owed —what I could not pay.

The creative compensation was that this fear and rage drove some of his best poetry whether, as in the cunning irony of *The Twa Dogs* or the biting, black anger of his demonic monologue about the initial stages of the Highland Clearances, *The Address of Beelzebub*. Though Burns himself was never ejected, the fear of dispossession either through debt or due to his radical beliefs, haunted him to the end. As he wrote in that marvellously reworked late song of ancestral suffering, the primal agony of not being able to feed one's children, *O That I Had Ne'er Been Married*:

> Waefu' Want and Hunger fley me
>   Glowerin by the hallan en'
> Sair I fecht them at th' door
>   But ay I'm eerie they come ben.

And come ben they did. The physical agony of his death bed, as terrible as that of his great admirer Keats, was horrendously intensified by his sense that all he would leave his wife and children were the terrible consequences of his debts. Further, that the spectre of famine, as a consequence of the war with France, was loose in the Dumfries streets:

> Many days my family, & hundreds of other families, are absolutely without one grain of meal; as money cannot purchase it. —How long the *Swinish Multitude* will be quiet, I cannot tell: they threaten daily.

That Burns should so allude to Burke's remark of the pig-sty quality of the cultural life of the French common people, a remark unforgivably burnt into the consciousness of all the British radicals of that age, implies he did not die purged of his revolutionary aspirations.

Indeed, none of his contemporaries thought he had. Ironically, it was that singular English Romantic Tory, Thomas De Quincey, who most penetratingly and passionately revealed the social vision at the heart of so much of Burns's poetry. De Quincey had no doubt that Burns was a compendium of the radical vices of the Jacobin type, the quintessence of the revolutionary personality.[5] He feared and disliked, given his disposition to traditional order, Burns's 'peculiarly wild and almost ferocious spirit of independence'. As much as his friend Charles Lamb adored the poetry, De Quincey loathed the letters which he found self-declamatory, irascible, resentful, provocative manifestations of personal and public unrest. Yet of all the English Romantics, it was De Quincey, who had himself for a time lived among the dispossessed and, indeed, had come to Scotland to take ecclesiastical refuge from his creditors, who best defined, probably because of the very contradiction between his personal experience and his political ideology, Burns's social vision:

Jacobinism —although the seminal principle of all political evil in all ages alike of advanced civilisation— is natural to the heart of man, and, in a qualified sense, may be meritorious. A good man, a high minded man, in certain circumstances, *must* be a Jacobin in a certain sense. The aspect under which Burns's Jacobinism appears is striking; there is a thought which an observing reader will find often recurring, which expresses its particular bitterness. It is this: the necessity which in old countries exists for the labourer humbly to beg *permission* that he may labour. To eat in the sweat of a man's brow, —that is bad; and that is a curse, and pronounced such by God. But when *that* is all, the labourer is by comparison happy. The second curse makes that a jest: he must sue, he must sneak, he must fawn like an oriental slave, in order to win his fellow man, in Burns's indignant words 'to give him leave to toil'. That was the scorpion thought that was forever shooting its sting into Burns's meditations, whether forward looking or backward looking; and, that considered, there arises a world of allowance for that vulgar bluster of independence which Lord Jeffrey, with so much apparent reason, charges upon his prose writings.[6]

If De Quincey finds Burns's political position paradoxical, his own is no less so. Burns's compassion, according to De Quincey, touches the nerve of the greatest evil, not work but its denial from which stems starvation and dispossession. De Quincey supports an established order which not only turns its face from such suffering but also economically promotes it. Little wonder that *King Lear* haunted the writers of the 1790s for when the hierarchical King is made destitute, he finds a form of being hitherto unimaginable to him. Thus Burns, in that early bi-lingual cry of rage against social oppression and exploitation, *A Winter's Night*, invokes Shakespeare's earlier cry of outrage:

> Poor naked wretches, whereso'er you are,
> That bide the pelting and the pityless storm!
> How shall your houseless heads, and unfed sides,
> Your looped and window'd raggedness, defend you
> From seasons such as these.

As we have seen, Burns as a farmer led a near subsistence existence which his subsequent Excise work did not financially transform. Nor did the business of poetry ease his fear of debt and the abyss into which he might fall. Only the Edinburgh edition sold in great numbers. Even here, he significantly under-earned due to the contractual conditions then prevailing between book publisher and author, which was added by William Creech's, at best, dilatory behaviour. Even then, the bulk of his earnings from the Edinburgh edition went to save the family farm at Mauchline, propping up Gilbert Burns with money he never returned. Subsequent editions made money for Creech who purchased the copyright of the Edinburgh poems and laid claim to everything Burns wrote thereafter with a merciless callousness, which saw the poet receive only a few presentation copies of the 1793 edition. The later songs he wrote for the nation and not the cash. The covert political poetry was sent to newspapers to support the radical cause and not for personal gain. He was, in any case, characteristically both reckless and generous with money.

Burns's constant stress on his own personal, political and enforced fiscal independence found everywhere in his writings, partly stems from his constant sense of rejection by his social superiors. Hence, for example, his witty, wry, characteristic account of having to make it on his own:

> 'Twas noble, Sir; 'twas like yoursel,
>   To grant your high protection;

A great man's smile ye ken fu'well
   Is ay a blest infection.—

Tho' by his banes wha in a tub
   Match'd Macedonian Sandy!
On my ain legs thro' dirt and dub,
   I independent stand ay.—

And when those legs to gude, warm kail
   Wi' welcome canna bear me;
A lee dyke-syde, a sybow tail,
   And barley-scone shall chear me.—

This brilliant comic reduction of the world of Diogenes and Alexander the Great to his own terminal fate in the Scottish countryside ironises the desperation of his own financial situation. Great men smiled seldom; one can also smile and be a villain and, thus, spread infection. When he did occasionally think that he had encountered a relationship not polluted by social condescension, as with Lord Daer or Dugald Stewart, such men shone for him in an idealised glow. He craves that such a figure should enter his life so that, ironically, the democratic poet should return to a traditional, even feudal, situation where the patron provides both imaginative and financial succour. Hence, this account of the Earl of Glencairn, whose premature death struck him to the very core of his being:

> The noble Earl of Glencairn took me by the hand today, and interested himself in my concerns, with a goodness like the benevolent BEING whose image he so richly bears.—'Oubliez moi, grand Dieu, si jamais je l'oublie!' He is a stronger proof of the immortality of the Soul than any that Philosophy has ever produced.— A mind like his can never die.— Let the Squire Hugh Logan, or Mass James Mckindlay, go into their primitive nothing.— At best they are but ill-digested lumps of Chaos, only one of them strongly tinged with bituminous particles, and sulphureous effluvia.— But my noble Patron, eternal as the heroic swell of Magnanimity and the generous throb of Benevolence shall look on with princely eye —

> 'Unhurt amid the war of elements,
> The wrecks of matter, and the crush of Worlds.'

Glencairn being so defined in terms of that key Real Whig text, Addison's *Cato* is, as we shall see, politically important. For De

Quincey, however, even the notion that Glencairn was the true patron who tested the rule of Scottish aristocratic indifference to Burns was nonsense. He saw nothing in Glencairn's activities beyond the gestural:

> Lord Glencairn is the 'patron' to whom Burns appears to have felt the most sincere respect. Yet even he —did he give him more than a seat at his dinner table? Lord Buchan again, whose liberalities are by this time pretty well appreciated in Scotland, exhorts Burns, in a tone of one preaching upon a primary duty of life, to exemplary gratitude towards a person who has given him absolutely nothing at all. The man has not yet lived to whose happiness it was more essential that he should live unencumbered by the sense of obligation; and on the other hand, the man has not lived upon whose independence as professing benefactors so many people practised, or who found so many others ready to give value to their pretences.[7]

Though Burns often reached similar depths of despairing self-prognosis about his life and career, he did make extensive and misguided attempts to replace Glencairn in his life with Robert Graham of Fintry, a Commissioner of the Scottish Board of Excise. How misguided these attempts were we have recently discovered; Graham was not only looking with increased scepticism on reports of Burns's Dumfries activities but was himself on the payroll of that vast network of paid informers reporting back to Robert Dundas about the activities of radical dissidents. The only thing Fintry is to be thanked for was that he inspired two major English language poems, *To Robt. Graham of Fintry, Esq., with a request for an Excise Division* and *To Robert Graham of Fintry, Esq.* which are masterful, creative reworking of themes initially found in Swift's perhaps greatest poem, *On Poetry: A Rhapsody.* The latter Burns poem was of such quality, in fact, that only now has it become known that for years, a fragment of it, slightly bowdlerised, has been attributed to Coleridge. As well as learning from Swift, Burns's thinking on poetry and patronage was influenced by Dr Johnson. As he wrote:

> It is often a reverie of mine, when I am disposed to be melancholy, the characters & fates of the Rhyming tribe — there is not among all the Martyrologies that ever were penned, so rueful a narrative as Johnson's *Lives of the Poets.*— In the comparative view of the Wretches, the criterion is not what they are doomed to suffer, but how they are formed to bear.

Nor does Burns's analysis of the desperate life of the late-eighteenth century poet, an age replete in prematurely terminated and self-destructive careers, yield, especially in the two Fintry poems, to the quality of Johnson's psychological and sociological grasp of what was taking place. His rhetorical style may not be ours but there is actually little self-indulgence in what he sees as his own fate and that of his immediate predecessors. This is particularly so with regard to his beloved Edinburgh predecessor, Robert Fergusson, as mentioned in *To William Simson*:

> (O *Fergusson!* thy glorious parts
> Ill suited law's dry, musty arts!
> My curse upon your whunstane hearts,
>   Ye Enbrugh Gentry!
> The tythe o' what ye waste at *cartes*
>   Wad stow'd his pantry!)

He was not to know that not only was he to share Fergusson's pains in his life but, like Fergusson he was also to be pursued beyond the grave by the vilification of genteel Edinburgh and by its master spirit, Henry Mackenzie, who never forgave Fergusson's fine parody of *The Man of Feeling* in his poem, *The Sow of Feeling*. Underneath Mackenzie's simpering mask was a malice easily provoked by slights to his vanity or, in Burns's case, if he felt the reactionary power base, which propped up his doubtful talent and his monstrous ego, endangered.

THE RADICAL BURNS

It is not inevitable that out of a background of constantly threatening poverty, a profound sense of communal economic and political dissolution, bloody international warfare on land and sea, failure to make a living after being, initially, declared a poetic genius, a revolutionary spirit will emerge. Oliver Goldsmith, a poet Burns loved, came to the political conclusion that what the age needed to restrain the greedy, fractious aristocracy was an increase in the authority of the King. Burns, however, manifestly belongs to the temporarily dominant radical British literary culture which emerged with the loss of America. Hence all his actual and epistolary connections with the English radicals: Mary Wollstonecraft, Helen Maria Williams, William Roscoe, Dr Wolcot (pen name, Peter Pindar). Hence his persistent seeking to publish in not only Edinburgh and Glasgow radical newspapers but, from the very beginning of his career, in London ones. Hence the resemblance in his

poetry's theme in image, if rarely in quality, to the outpouring of
Scottish and English radical protest poetry accompanied by his
signal influence on the dissenting Ulster radical poets. Hence the
manifest parallels, albeit they were quite unaware of each other, with
William Blake. De Quincey's definition of Burns as a Jacobin was
anything but singular among the English radicals. John Thelwall,
Wordsworth and Coleridge's political mentor, greatly admired
Burns. James Perry, editor of the anti-government *Morning Chronicle* not only published his poetry but, simultaneously, sought to hire
him and Coleridge to work in London for his newspaper. Indeed,
this was a conversational paradise lost. Politically, of course, not
only Coleridge but Wordsworth knew Burns for the revolutionary
spirit which, at that early stage of their lives, they themselves were.
In burying their own past, they were important influences in
allowing subsequent reactionary critics to deny Burns. This denial
of Burns is not the least of the offences Shelley holds against
Wordsworth in his parody of him, *Peter Bell the Third*.

Further, if we look at the pattern of Burns's career, we can quite
clearly discern his membership of politically active groups of an
increasingly radical tendency. Freemasonry at Kilwinning led to his
connections with Edinburgh's Crochallan Fencibles which, as well
as being a bawdy drinking club, was an extraordinary hot-house for
not only brilliantly rhetorical and theoretical, but practical radical
political activity. His Dumfries years led not only to his attempt to
send carronades to the French Revolutionaries but, as we now
know, to his membership of the Dumfries cell of The Friends of
the People. By this time he was not only under scrutiny by his
masters in The Excise but by Robert Dundas's extensive security
apparatus centred in Edinburgh and reporting to London. Little
wonder that after the 1793–4 Sedition Trials Burns should write:

> The shrinking Bard adown an alley sculks
> And dreads a meeting worse than Woolwich hulks
> Tho' there his heresies in Church and State
> Might well award him Muir and Palmer's fate . . .

Given the poetry and the letters with this mass of corroborative
contextual historical evidence from within and without Scotland, it
is hard to understand why not only in current Scottish popular
culture but, indeed, in significant elements of Scottish academic
culture, there is still a persistent compulsion to downplay, even
deny, the revolutionary Burns. One cannot imagine kindred spirits
like Blake or Shelley being so treated. One tangible reason for the

denial is due to the fact that we will never be able to retrieve the full
volume of radical writing in the 1790s. Key newspapers, such as *The
Glasgow Advertiser* 1795–7, are irretrievably lost. Governmental
scrutiny was intensive against radicals and the postal system mon-
itored to such a degree that communication was furtive and re-
stricted. To corroborate Burns's radicalism further, he himself was
wholly aware of this factor. As he wrote to Patrick Millar in March
1794:

—Nay, if Mr Perry, whose honor, after your character of him I
cannot doubt, if he will give me an Adress & channel by which
anything will come safe from these spies with which he may be
certain that his correspondence is beset, I will now & then send
him any bagatelle that I may write.— . . . but against the days
of Peace, which Heaven send soon, my little assistance may
perhaps fill up an idle column of a Newspaper.— I have long
had it in my head to try my hand in the way of Prose Essays,
which I propose sending into the World through the medium of
some Newspaper; and should these be worth his while, to these
Mr Perry shall be welcome; & my reward shall be, his treating
me with his paper, which, by the bye, to anybody who has the
least relish for Wit, is a high treat indeed.

In the general implosion of British radical writing culture under
governmental pressure, the loss of Burns's political writings was
particularly severe due, as we shall see, to the panic surrounding his
premature death at the darkest point of the 1790s.

While significant, however, the denial of Burns's radicalism is not
essentially based on missing texts. The denial of Burns's actual
politics is much more multiform and historically protracted than
that. As we shall see, the after-shock of the revolutionary, even
insurrectionary, activities of the 1790s was so colossal that it extended
deep into the nineteenth century. It was particularly severely felt in
Scotland. What we see, then, in Victorian Scotland is Burns, with
oceans of whisky and mountains of haggis, being converted into an
iconic national figure by a nation in almost complete denial of the
political values he stood for. Editorial and critical work inevitably
reflected this absurdity with activities which included sanitising,
suppressing and trivialising any evidence, textual and otherwise,
contrary to the travesty they were creating. Edward Dowden in his
seminal *The French Revolution and English Literature*, written at the
end of the nineteenth century, included Burns among writers so
affected. If for English radical writers, this book marked the begin-

ning of mature, objective scholarship regarding the reality of their engagement with the political issues of the 1790s, this was ignored by Scottish Burns scholars. Hugh Blair's remark that 'Burns's politics always smell of the smithy' held sway with almost all subsequent commentators. Indeed, in the early twentieth century W.P. Ker designated Burns as a Tory Unionist. Heroic efforts in the 1930s by that greatest of Burns scholars and critics, tellingly American, Professor De Lancey Ferguson, ended in bitter comments such as his attempt properly to locate Burns in history had been met in Scotland with 'passionate apathy'. Insofar as Burns was permitted to express political values, the critical strategy was either to claim that his political poems either did not meet their tests of aesthetic quality or that such poetry expressed confusion. These tactics persist. Dr James Mackay has recently noted that 'Burns's politics were . . . never less than moderately confused . . .'[8] Dr Mackay's opinion is hardly one to cause surprise since essentially his biography presents no advance on the nineteenth-century criticism of Burns but, in fact, is extensively based on and partly plagiarised from nineteenth-century published biographical sources.

Such assertions of confusion are grounded on ignorance of the radical tradition within which Burns was operating. A coherent tradition dating from the Civil War, British radical thought in the latter stages of the eighteenth century combined Scottish and English elements in alternating proportions. Burns is not to be understood as some sort of barely rational political oddity. With Blake, he is a central poet of a long established revolutionary vision. Consciously or otherwise, the vast bulk of Burns criticism has detached him from his proper intellectual, cultural and political context so that, an isolated figure, his politics can be seen as subjective, whimsical, even eccentric. In proper context, he is wholly different. Much of this, of course, smacks of a bourgeois condescension to not only Burns's class status but also the actual power of poetry itself. Poetry is not, for such minds, 'hard' knowledge. Burns himself constantly stresses the 'bedlamite' tendencies of the poetic personality but he never confused the turmoil and travails of the process of poetic productivity with the absolute perfection of the formal and linguistic nature of the poetic product. Also what we see constantly in his letters is a polemical and dialectical skill based on a wholly coherent grasp of the key intellectual issues of his age. Maria Riddell was not alone in thinking him an even greater conversationalist than poet. Never granted a public stage, his extraordinary prose suggests he would have been among the greatest in that arguably greatest of rhetorical ages.

Painful reality taught Burns economics, but he was not only aware of Adam Smith's sentimental theories but his economic ones. As he wrote of his current reading to Robert Graham in 1789:

> By and by the excise-instructions you mentioned were not in the bundle.— But 'tis no matter; Marshall in his Yorkshire, & particularly that extraordinary man, Smith, in his Wealth of Nations, find my leisure employment enough.— I could not have given any mere *man* credit for half the intelligence Mr Smith discovers in the book. I would covet much to have his ideas respecting the present state of some quarters of the world that are or have been the scenes of considerable revolutions since his book was written.

Central to the 'considerable revolutions' that had taken place was Burns's chastened experience that the manifest increase in wealth in the latter part of the century was not accompanied by any growth in equitable distribution. All boats were certainly not rising on this flood tide of new wealth. As David Cannadine has cogently pointed out there was throughout Burns's adult life an intense massification of wealth among the aristocracy both by carefully calculated pan-British marriages and their capacity to insert themselves in the burgeoning civil and military offices of a state expanding to meet its ultimate conflict with France.[9] Nor did the initially reformist middle-class, the 'stately stupidity of self-sufficient Squires or the luxuriant insolence of upstart "Nabobs"', offer the people political and financial hope. Thus in *The Heron Ballads*, Burns lifts a stone on Scottish provincial life to reveal a bourgeois world replete with sexual but mainly fiscal chicanery. His vision of the entrepreneurial personality is significantly close to John Galt. Indeed, his vision of crime and Edinburgh makes him a precursor of R.L. Stevenson. Indeed, even Stevenson never wrote anything quite of this order about his loved and loathed Edinburgh —the letter is to Peter Hill, the Edinburgh bookseller, a correspondent who always evoked his most extraordinary rhetorical salvoes:

> I will make no excuses my dear Bibliopolus, (God forgive me for murdering language) that I have sat down to write to you on this vile paper, stained with the sanguinary scores of 'thae curst horse leeches o' th' Excise'. —It is economy, Sir; it is that cardinal virtue, Prudence; so I beg you will sit down & either compose or borrow a panegyric (if you are going to borrow, apply to our friend, Ramsay, for the assistance of the author of

those pretty little buttering paragraphs of eulogiums on your
thrice-honored & never-enough-to-be-praised MAGIS-
TRACY —how they hunt down a [Shop (*deleted*)] house-
breaker with the sanguinary perseverance of a bloodhound
—how they outdo a terrier in a badger-hole, in unearthing a
resettor of stolen goods —how they steal on a thoughtless troop
of Night-nymphs as a spaniel winds the unsuspecting Covey —
or how they riot o'er a ravaged B—dy house as a cat does o'er a
plundered Mouse-nest —how they new-vamp old Churches,
aiming at appearances of Piety —plan Squares and Colledges,
to pass for men of taste and learning, &c. &c. &c. —while old
Edinburgh, like [a (*deleted*)] the doting Mother of a parcel a
rakehelly Prodigals, may sing 'Hooly & fairly,' or cry, 'Wae's
me that e'er I saw ye,' but still must put her hand in her pocket
& pay whatever scores the young dogs think proper to contract)
—I was going to say, but this damn'd Parenthesis has put me
out of breath, that you should get the manufacturer of the
tinselled crockery of magistratial reputations, who makes so
distinguished & distinguishing a figure in the Ev: Courant, to
compose or rather to compound something very clever on my
remarkable frugality; that I write to one of my most esteemed
friends on this wretched paper, which was originally intended
for the venal fist of some drunken Exciseman, to take dirty
notes in a miserable vault of an Ale-cellar.

Burns's political thought, then, is created by his perception of
political, institutional degeneration driven by individual economic
rapacity and how this might be countered by alternative forms of
justice-creating communality. The immediate question arising from
this is, of course, the question of Burns's fidelity to the British State
of which he was not only a subject but a paid civil-servant who, as
Tom Paine had also been, was bound to it by an all-encompassing
oath, which cast a shadow over the rest of his life. The Excise oath is
deeply revealing of the pressure the British State exerted:

I, ..., do swear that I do, from my Heart, Abhor,
Detest, and Abjure, as impious and heretical, that damnable
Doctrine and Position, that Princes excommunicated or de-
prived by the Pope, or any Authority of the See of Rome,
may be deposed or murdered by their Subjects, or any other
whatsoever. And I do declare, that no foreign Prince, Person,
Prelate, State or Potentate hath, or ought to have, any
Jurisdiction, Power, Superiority, Pre-eminence or Authority,

Ecclesiastical or Spiritual, within the Realm: so help me God.[10]

In part, Burns's protestations of fidelity to that state were wrung out of him as his masters in the Excise grew ever more worried about his revolutionary tendencies. In protesting fidelity, however, to the Glorious Revolution of 1688, Burns was not simply being hypocritically skin saving. That revolution had been acceptable, certainly as a stage to further democratic progress. What he and his fellow radicals believed, however, was that the trajectory of the British State with its Hanoverian monarchy was degenerately downwards. As he wrote to Mrs Dunlop in 1788:

> What you mention of the thanksgiving day is inspirational from above. —Is it not remarkable, odiously remarkable, that tho' manners are more civilised & the rights of mankind better understood, by an Augustan Century's improvement, yet in this very reign of heavenly Hanoverianism, & almost in this very year, an empire beyond the Atlantic has had its REVO-LUTION too, & for the same maladministration & legislative misdemeanours in the illustrious & sapientipetent Family of H[anover] as was complained in the tyrannical & bloody house of STUART.—

The 'Empire beyond the Atlantic' was for Burns, as Blake, a benchmark for his ideal of Republican, democratic virtue. It was the revolution that presaged the desired revolutions to come. As he wrote in *The Tree of Liberty*:

> My blessings ay attend the chiel,
>   Wha pitied Gallia's slaves, man
> And staw a branch, spite o' the Deil
>   Frae 'yont the western waves, man!

The demonic forces of reaction were for Burns, however, usually more successful in hindering and, indeed, destroying the transmission of the forces of liberty. Worse, Britain which had been because of its history the initiator and prime mover in the cause of liberty was now become the chief oppressor. In poetic terms this dialectic between a self-betraying England and a self-creating democratic America achieves its most complete expression in his *Ode for General Washington's Birthday*. This is a poem of extraordinary importance in terms of Burns's political ideas but one which his

conservative commentators have almost wholly ignored by conve-
niently drawing attention to their sense of its linguistic and formal
inadequacies caused by the poet's use of the Pindaric Ode. For
Burns himself, however, the subject of the poem was 'Liberty: you
know my honoured friend, how dear the theme is to me.' For Burns
and his fellow radicals the cause of liberty was a pan-European
phenomenon, nations were tested by the degree by which they had
gone beyond absolutism towards democracy. Most of them, as he
testifies in that brilliantly satiric tour de force and tour of Europe,
To a Gentleman who had sent a Newspaper, failed the test miserably.
It was, however, particularly painful to see England fallen from her
pre-eminent position. As he wrote in the 'Washington' poem:

> Alfred, on thy starry throne,
> Surrounded by the tuneful choir,
> The Bards that erst have struck the patriot lyre,
> And roused the freeborn Briton's soul of fire,
> No more thy England own.—
> Dare injured nations form the great design,
> To make detested tyrants bleed?
> Thy England execrates the glorious deed!
> Beneath her hostile banners waving,
> Every pang of honor braving,
> England in thunder calls— 'The Tyrant's cause is mine!'
> That hour accurst, how did the fiends rejoice,
> And hell thro' all her confines raise the exulting voice,
> That hour which saw the generous the English name
> Linkt with such damned deeds of everlasting shame!

For Burns an England so fallen, inevitably dragged Scotland down
with her. On occasion he could be defiantly nationalistic:

> You know my national prejudices. —I have often read &
> admired the *Spectator, Adventurer, Rambler, & World*, but
> still with certain regret that they were so thoroughly and
> entirely English.— Alas! Have I often said to myself, what
> are all the boasted advantages which my country reaps from a
> certain Union, that can counterbalance the annihilation of her
> independence, & even her very Name! . . .

Unlike many of his educated compatriots, the Anglo-British empire
did not look to Burns a good deal for Scotland. He saw Scots sucked
into the deadly wars of empire. He also saw the degeneration of
Scottish leadership with Scots as sycophantic Westminster politi-

cians and bullies back home among their countrymen with Henry
Dundas, the quintessence of these vices, as his enemy incarnate. At
his bleakest, as in *Ode on General Washington's Birthday*, Burns's
perceived Scotland, despite her heroic history of asserting her
freedom, lost beyond resurrection:

> Thee, Caledonia, thy wild heaths among,
> Famed for the martial deed, the heaven-taught song,
>> To thee, I turn with swimming eyes.—
>> Where is that soul of Freedom fled?
>> Immingled with the mighty Dead!
> Beneath the hallowed turf where WALLACE lies!
> Hear it not, Wallace, in thy bed of death!
>> Ye babbling winds in silence sweep;
>> Disturb not ye the hero's sleep,
>> Nor give the coward secret breath.—
> Is this the ancient Caledonian form,
> Firm as her rock, resistless as her storm?
> Shew me that eye which shot immortal hate,
>> Blasting the Despot's proudest bearing:
> Shew me that arm which, nerved with thundering fate,
>> Braved Usurpation's boldest daring!
>> Dark-quenched as yonder sinking star,
>> No more that glance lightens afar;
> That palsied arm no more whirls on the waste of war.

Opposed to such national pessimism, he also perceived a resurrected
not morbid Scotland with himself as National Bard writing, a sort of
Yeatsian precursor, a historically derived national mytho-poetry. As
he wrote to Alex Cunningham in March 1791: '—When political
combustion ceases to be the object of Princes & Patriots, it then, you
know becomes the lawful prey of Historians and Poets.—' He knew
the explosively, for him, liberating forces locked up in Scottish
history. Sir Walter Scott knew them, too, and was terrified of them.
Burns, however, proceeded to create poetic time-bombs as in *Scots
Wha Hae*, where the subtext is an attack on the Pittite policies of
oppression against Scottish radicals in the Scots vernacular and the
words of the French Revolutionaries, making the Tennis Court
Oath to do or die, come from the mouths of fourteenth-century
Scottish soldiers. It may be questionable history but its purpose is to
detect semi-mythical antecedents in the Scottish past as precursors
for the reintegrated, resurrected nation. William Wallace and, to a
lesser extent, Robert Bruce were the obvious candidates:

What a poor, blighted, rickety breed and the virtues & charities when they take their birth from geometrical hypothesis & mathematical demonstration? And what a vigorous Offspring are they when they owe their origin to, and are nursed with the vital blood of a heart glowing with the noble enthusiasm of generosity, benevolence and Greatness of soul? The first may do very well for those philosophers who look on the world of man as one vast ocean and each individual as a little vortex in it whose sole business and merit is to absorb as much as it can in its own center (*sic*); but the last is absolutely and essentially necessary when you would make a Leonidas, a Hannibal, an Alfred, or a WALLACE.—

What Burns was attempting was a Scottish variant of the manner in which his English radical contemporaries were retrieving the English past. As Stephen C. Behrendt has remarked, 'Oppositional Radical rhetoric frequently sought to politicise the masses by linking their interests with ancient British (Saxon) traditions of individual and collective liberty ostensibly preserved in the House of Commons but increasingly imperilled by self-serving initiatives of the aristocracy and the monarchy.'[11] In an age whose rapacious entrepreneurial activities increasingly atomised society, Wallace, then, was the heroic selfless embodiment of the spirit of Scottish community. This looking to the past for virtuous political models and heroic embodiment of these models is, of course, characteristic of the seventeenth and eighteenth-century republican imagination with, of course, the virtuous pantheon to be derived from the classic republics of Greece and Rome. Like Shakespeare, with little Latin and less Greek, Burns certainly knew that central Real Whig text, Addison's *Cato* and he did also draw witty parallels between the reformist Scots of his own era and their classical predecessors:

> Erskine, a spunkie Norland billie;
> True Campbells, Frederick and Illay;
> An' Livinstone, the bauld Sir Willie;
>   An' monie ithers,
> Whom auld Demosthenes or Tully
>   Might own for brithers.

In this discussion of republican tendencies, an immediate difficulty presents itself regarding Burns's Jacobinism. As Hugh Miller remarked in the nineteenth century: 'The *Jacobite* of one year who addressed verses to the reverend defenders of the beauteous Stuart and composed *the Chevalier's Lament* had become in the next the uncompromising Jacobin who wrote *A Man's a Man for a' That*.' In actual fact there is no chronological transition in Burns from Jacobite to Jacobin; these themes intermingle throughout. Nor are they essentially contradictory. Miller's problem arises, as so many misunderstandings of Burns, from his belief that what he is dealing with is confusion unique to Burns. While Burns's personal life pursued a self-aware, sometimes chaotic, zigzag course, his political ideation was not similarly eccentric. Miller, however, does not understand how radical culture as a whole integrated the apparently opposing element of Jacobitism into itself. As Fintan O'Toole has cogently remarked in dealing with a similar apparent self-contradiction in the Irish dramatist and Whig politician, R.B. Sheridan:

> At first sight, there may seem to be a contradiction between the Jacobite tinge of Sheridan's political ancestry and the radical Whiggism to which he was now attaching himself. But by the time Sheridan became conscious of public life, the vestiges of Jacobitism had become, paradoxically, a few stray threads in the banners of the radical Whigs. Rather paradoxically, Tory blue became the colour of Wilkes's supporters. *The Public Advertiser* which published the Junius Letters also published Jacobite propaganda. Later, a number of prominent former Jacobites, including Sir Thomas Gasgoigne, Frances Plowden and Joseph Ritson, became adherents of the radical Whig, Charles James Fox. Sir Frances Burndett's family had come out for Bonnie Prince Charlie in the '45. The apparent conservatism of Jacobitism, its hankering after an increasingly mythic utopia in the past, was not really out of tune with the language and sentiments of the radicals. As Paul Kleber Monod puts it 'the illusion that a "golden age" might have existed at some time in the past fascinated radicals . . .' The old promises of unity and moral regeneration continued to appeal to the imagination of the English radicals even after the Stuart cause collapsed.[12]

Against Hanoverian triumphalism, misfortune, then, made strange political bedfellows. Also, like Sheridan, Burns's sense of Jacobitism was familial. His family were not rooted in Ayrshire; his father had come from the North-East Jacobite redoubt. Indeed, Burns claimed that in 1715 they had been 'out'. As he wrote in 1789 to Lady Winifred Maxwell Constable:

. . . with your ladyship I have the honor to be connected by one of the strongest and most endearing ties in the whole Moral world —Common Sufferers in a cause where even to be unfortunate is glorious, the cause of Heroic Loyalty! Though my Fathers had not illustrious Honours and vast properties to hazard in the contest; though they left their humble cottages only to add so many units to the unnoted croud that followed their leaders; yet what they could they did, and what they had they lost; with unshaken firmness and unconcealed Political Attachments, they shook hands with Ruin for what they esteemed the cause of their King and their Country.—

This language, and the inclosed verses, are for your Ladyship's eyes alone.— Poets are not very famous for their prudence; but as I can do nothing for a Cause which is nearly no more, I do not wish to hurt myself.

Excise officers, as part of their routine duty post-1745, were expected to compile and deliver to Edinburgh, a list of all known Jacobite sympathisers in their area. This remained true until the death of Charles Edward Stuart in Rome the year after Burns wrote his dedicatory *Birthday Ode* to the exiled Stuart. Though he thought Jacobitism in practical terms a spent force, Burns knew it still had enough vitality to get him into trouble with his Hanoverian masters, thus he did not sign his Jacobite songs. Also it provided for him an image of Scottish self-loyalty which he increasingly believed was lacking in the contemporary nation replete with individuals variedly on the make at home and abroad. Nor did he perceive authoritarian kingship and consequent petrified social hierarchy as a solution to the nation's ills. What he did fear, and this in his last years brought him ever closer to the views of Charles James Fox and the Scottish Foxite Whigs, was that a massification under Pitt of Hanoverian monarchical power was taking place. Thus as early as 1787, at the very moment he was seeking to enter The Excise, he did not only diamond cut these lines on a Stirling window but subsequently published them in an Edinburgh newspaper thinly disguised with the initials R.B.

HERE Stewarts once in triumph reign'd,
And laws for Scotland's weal ordain'd;
But now unroof'd their Palace stands,
Their sceptre's fall'n to other hands;
Fallen indeed, and to the earth,
Whence grovelling reptiles take their birth.—

The injur'd STEWART-line are gone,
A Race outlandish fill their throne;
An idiot race, to honor lost;
Who knows them best despise them most.

Indeed, the appeal of the Stewarts to his imagination was a mixture of empathy for their suffering and displacement, as contrast gainers against the loathed Hanoverians and, not least, the aesthetic tradition they represented. They may have had something of the knight about them but, like the devil, they also had all the best tunes:

By the bye, it is singular enough that the Scottish Muses were all Jacobites. I have paid more attention to every description of Scots songs than perhaps any body living has done, I do not recollect one single stanza, or even the title of the most trifling Scots air, which has the least panegyrical reference to the families of Nassau or Brunswick; while there are hundreds satirizing them. This may be thought no panegyric on the Scots Poets, but I mean it as such. For myself, I would always take it as a compliment to have it said, that my heart ran before my head. And surely the gallant but unfortunate house of Stewart, the kings of our fathers for so many heroic ages, is a theme much more interesting than an obscure beef-witted insolent race of foreigners whom a conjuncture of circumstances kickt up into power and consequence.

If the unmerited rise of the Hanoverians excited his rage, the fall of the executed or exiled Stewarts caught his sympathy. Tudor England's conduct towards Scotland proved as inflammatory to him as that of the contemporary Hanoverians; 'What a rock-hearted, perfidious Succubus was that Queen Elizabeth! —Judas Iscariot was a sad dog to be sure, but still his demerits sink into insignificance, compared with the doings of infernal Bess Tudor.' This vision of Mary Queen of Scots or Bonnie Prince Charlie is not, however, an inversion of Burns's democratic principles. He viewed them, especially the Prince, as Shakespeare viewed Lear. As he wrote: 'A poor, friendless wand'rer may claim a sigh,/ Still more if that Wand'rer were royal.' If experience of Jacobite defeat and its 'Heroic Loyalty' created social parity between himself and Lady Winifred, it made brothers of a kind between himself and the fallen Prince who was not only an outcast but also the father of an illegitimate child. People so fallen from their proper station into obscurity and poverty constantly preoccupied his imagination and filled his poetry. In con-

templating Pitt's fall from power in 1789, he compared his plight
with that of Nebuchadnezzar. Had he known what was to transpire,
he might well have wished that Pitt had indeed gone out to grass. He
also saw in the fate of the common supporters of the Jacobite cause a
grievous expulsion not simply from their ancestral home but into
Miltonic hyperspace:

> . . . the brave but unfortunate Jacobite Clans who, as John
> Milton tells us, after their unhappy Culloden in Heaven, lay
> 'nine times the space that measures day and night,' in oblivious
> astonishment, prone-weltering on the fiery surge.

This inspired casting of the Highlanders as the fallen angels of
Paradise Lost is not only a general expression of Burns's conceited
genius for creatively amalgamating diverse elements but a particular
example of his constant, synergic ability to fuse not only Scottish
and English poetic elements but also, with regard to radical political
philosophy, to be indebted to both English and Scottish sources as
means of energising his political poetry and thought. Consider, for
example, this little known poem, *On Johnson's Opinion of Hampden*;

> FOR shame!
> Let Folly and Knavery
>   Freedom oppose:
> 'Tis suicide, Genius,
>   To mix with her foes.

Greatly admiring of and influenced by Dr Johnson's *Lives of the Poets*,
wherein he saw so many of his own pains, Burns was provoked into this
remark by Johnson's acerbic Tory aside that John Hampden was 'a
zealot of rebellion'. Hampden, due to his struggles with Charles I, was
an exemplary, indeed iconic figure for Scottish as well as English
radicals. Indeed, not only did Burns but all radical thought, as it
developed throughout the eighteenth century, was an amalgam of
intermingling Scottish and English traditions. As is demonstrated in
Caroline Robbins's seminal work, *The Eighteenth-Century Common-
wealthmen* (1957), eighteenth-century radical political philosophy
was a functional construction made from diverse elements. As John
Dinwiddy has cogently remarked:

> The traditions or discourses on which they drew, and to some
> of which their conceptions of revolution were related, were
> numerous and diverse. They included 'Commonwealth' or

'Country' ideology, the myth of the ancient constitution, millennial religion, natural-rights theory, American republicanism, French Jacobinism, Irish insurrectionalism. Some of them were quite closely linked to one another both historically and conceptually, as American republicanism was to Country ideology. Others, such as historic rights and natural rights were theoretically more distinct; but none the less they were often treated in practise as mutually reinforcing rather than competing modes of argument, and radicals moved to and fro between them without any great regard for logical consistency.[13]

From what has already been said and from our consequent textual analyses of individual political poems, this description fits Burns like a glove. His ideas are absolutely in the mainstream of eighteenth-century radicalism; it is not his beliefs but, like John Milton or William Blake, the quality of his poetic genius that makes him exceptional.

Should there still be any doubt about Burns's debt to eighteenth-century radical thought, consider, for example, these extracts from *Cato's Letters* published through the early 1720s and, tellingly, jointly English and Scottish authored:

> There is nothing moral in Blood or in Title, or in Place; Actions only, and the Causes that produce them are moral. He therefore is best that does best. Noble blood prevents neither Folly, nor Lunacy, nor Crimes, but frequently begets or promotes them: And Noblemen, who act infamously, derive no honour from virtuous Ancestors whom they dishonour. A Man who does base Things, is not noble or great, if he do little Things: A sober Villager is a better Man than a debauched Lord; an honest Mechanick than a Knavish Courtier.[14]

It is of course no accident that the poet's closest friend during his period at Ellisland, Robert Riddell, a highly respected Whig polemicist, wrote under the pen name *Cato*, Or, again from *Cato's Letters*, on the rapacious cupidity and the political consequences of the aristocratic and propertied classes at home and abroad:

> They will be ever contriving and forming wicked and dangerous Projects, to make the People poor, and themselves rich; well knowing the Dominion follows Property; that where there are Wealth and Power, there will always be crowds of servile Dependents; and that, on the contrary, Poverty dejects the

Mind, fashions it to Slavery, and renders it unequal to any generous Undertaking, and incapable of opposing any bold Usurpation. They will squander away the Publick Money in wanton Presents to Minions, and their Creatures of Pleasure or of Burthern, or in Pensions to mercenary and worthless Men and Women, for vile Ends and traiterous Purposes.

They will engage their Country in ridiculous, expensive, fantastical Wars, to keep the Minds of Men in continual Hurry and Agitation, and under constant Fears and Alarms, and, by such means, deprive them both of Leisure and Inclination to look into publick Miscarriages. Men, on the contrary, will, instead of such Inspection, be disposed to fall into all Measures offered, seemingly, for their Defence, and will agree to every wild Demand made by those who are betraying them.[15]

If this, as it should, sounds familiar so to is the stress that, with Lockean contractuality, power should reside not with a corrupt elite but with the people:

The first principles of Power are in the People; and all the Projects of Men in Power ought to refer to the People, to aim solely at their good, and end in it: And who will ever pretend to govern them without regarding them, will soon repent it. Such Feats of Errantry may do perhaps in *Asia*: but in the countries where the people are free, it is Madness to hope to rule them against their Wills. They will know, that Government is appointed for their Sakes, and will be saucy enough to expect some Regard and some from their own Delegates.[16]

While there is some doubt about Aberdonian Thomas Gordon's commitment to the Right Whig cause after his joint-authorship of *The Independent Whig* and *Cato's Letters*, he is certainly the forefather of a stream of Scots who went south to fill prominent and powerful positions in English radical circles. We need to modify the notion that Scottish writers going south, from giants like Smollett to minnows like Mallett (Malloch), were simply on the make by being hyper-patriotic propagandists in the forging of the Anglo-British Empire. Thus, for example we have the expatriate radical careers of Gilbert and Peter Stuart, Thomas Hardy, Secretary of the London Corresponding Society, James Perry (Pirie), editor of *The Morning Chronicle*, Dr Alexander Geddes, radical Catholic priest, poet and religious contributor to *The Analytical Review* and James Oswald, who not only, like a significant number of Scots, went to France, but died in the Vendée fighting for the revolutionary army. Certainly, if they were to emerge from historical darkness, their political values and consequent rhetoric would also help to return Burns to his appropriate cultural, political context. We need also to understand the headlong flight of poets and writers such as James Thomson Callander, James Kennedy and James 'Balloon' Tytler, mainly westward to America in the wake of the 1793/4 Treason trials, to see parallels between their lesser political poetry to that of Burns.[17] The absence of these radicals voices serves to diminish appreciation of the iron grip Dundas had in suffocating dissent by means not only of the prostitution of the Scottish legal system but because that system was inadequate in terms of defining treasonable behaviour. As John Thelwall, the great English radical and intimate friend of Coleridge and Wordsworth, in the 1790s, wrote:

> It is a protest against an alarming threat held out —not by the sovereign —not by the legislature but by Mr Secretary Dundas. —He alone it was who had the audacity to threaten the violation and subversion of those yet remaining laws that guarantee Englishmen an impartial trial by Jury of their country, and to substitute in their place, the arbitrary tyrannical practices of the Court of Justiciary in Scotland.[18]

Perhaps the single greatest source of reformative change affecting Burns, was, however, within Scotland itself and had its origin in that charismatic Ulsterman, Francis Hutcheson and his professorial tenure at Glasgow University. His tradition ended in the 1790s with Professor John Millar whose cosmopolitan scholarship, integrity and passionate commitment to democratic reformation was lost in the vortex of repression. His 1796 *Letter of Crito: On the Causes, Objects and Consequences of the Present War*, dedicated to his friend Charles James Fox, published along with John McLaurin's (Lord Dreghorn) anti-war poetry in Edinburgh's *The Scots Chronicle*, both confirm Burns's rhetoric and experiences in the same decade. They also signal the tragic death of Hutcheson's aspirations for not only Scotland but the still festering sore of the Irish problem. While we do not know if Burns read Hutcheson, there can be no doubt of his teaching's proximity to the poet's own values:

> In every form of government the people has this right of defending themselves against the abuse of power . . . the people's right of resistance is unquestionable.

But when there's no other way of preserving a people; and when their governors by their perfidious frauds have plainly forfeited their right; they may justly be divested of their power, and others put into their places, or a new plan of power established.

Nor does this doctrine of the right of resistance in defence of the rights of a people, naturally tend to excite seditions and civil wars. Nay they have been more frequently occasioned by the contrary tenets. In all ages there has been too much patience in the body of the people, and too stupid a veneration for their princes or rulers; which for each one free kingdom or state has produced many monstrous herds of miserable abject slaves or beasts of burden, rather than civil polities of rational creatures, under the most inhuman and worthless masters, trampling upon all things human and divine with the uttmost effrontery.[19]

Such Hutchesonian values would, in any case, have percolated down to Burns through his connection to Glasgow-trained New Licht clergy in Ayrshire. This entails that the wonderful anti-Auld Licht satires of the early Ayrshire period are not provincial storms in a tea cup but a variant on the intense British struggle by reforming religion to shake off the theocratic control of both the Trinitarian Anglican and, in Scotland, the reactionary Presbyterian churches whose vision of the innately sinful, fallen nature of man renders impossible a reformative, never mind utopian, politics. At the heart of the poetry of Burns and Blake is this preoccupation with removing the absolute political power given to the reactionary state by the teaching of what they saw as a perverted institutional Christianity. Burns's *Address to the Deil* is profoundly different in language and tone from Blake but not in essential purpose and meaning. Had he been aware of his true English peer he would have been transfixed by such Blakean lines:

> . . . & the purpose of the Priests & Churches
> Is to impress on men the fear of death; to teach
> Trembling & fear, terror, constriction; abject selfishness.
> Mine is to teach Men to despise death & to go on
> In fearless majesty annihilating Self . . .   (*Milton*, 11. 37–41)

As Richard Rorty has written,

> The Romantics were inspired by the successes of antimonarchist
> and anticlericalist revolutions to think that the desire for some-

thing to obey is a symptom of immaturity. These successes made it possible to envisage building a new Jerusalem without divine assistance, thereby creating a society in which men and women would lead the perfected lives which had previously seemed possible only in an invisible, immaterial, post-mortem paradise. The image of progress towards such a society —horizontal progress, so to speak— began to take the place of Platonic or Dantean images of vertical ascent. History began to replace God, Reason and Nature as the source of human hope.[20]

This accounts, too, for the religio-mythical compatibility of Burns and Blake in that both are obsessed with those transgressive figures who destroy the institutional, regressive corruption of the established world in the name of a new earthly heaven. Blake is the more extreme and mythopoetic. Burns never similarly defines Blake's transgressive Christ as discovered in *The Everlasting Gospel*. But both are preoccupied with not only the heroic, vitalising figure of 'Blind John's' Satan but with the problematic figure of Job. Cynthia Ozick[21] has commented on Job:

> Like the noblest of prophets he assails injustice; and still he is unlike them. They accuse the men and women who do evil; their targets are made of flesh and blood. It is human transgression they hope to mend. Job seeks to rectify God. His is an ambition higher, deeper, vaster, grander than theirs; he is possessed by a righteousness more frenzied than theirs; the scale of his justice-hunger exceeds all that precedes him . . . he can be said to be the consummate prophet. And at the same time he is the consummate violator. If we are to understand him at all, if we are rightly to enter into his passions at the pinnacle, then we ought to name him prophet; but we may not. Call him, instead, antiprophet —his teaching, after all, verges on atheism: the rejection of God's power. His thesis is revolution.

Both Burns's poetry and prose are saturated with the deeply varied ways he employed his early exposure to the sermon and his life-long, intense reading of the Bible. No story affected him more deeply than that of Job's.

Liam McIlvanney, one of a tiny minority of the legion of Burns commentators to have sympathetic knowledge of Burns's true politics, traces in a particularly fine article, 'Presbyterian Radicalism and the Politics of Robert Burns', a similarly long tradition of radical political gestation from a more distinctively Scottish point of view. He highlights the ambivalence at the heart of Burns's relationship to Presbyterianism thus:

> . . . it remains unfortunate that Burns's run-ins with the kirk have obscured the extent to which his own political philosophy is grounded in his religious inheritance. His politics are shaped by two complimentary strands of Presbyterian thought: on the one hand, the New Light, with its subjection of all forms of authority to the tribunal of individual reason: on the other, the traditional contractarian political theory long associated with Presbyterianism. These influences are evident in Burns's repeated avowal of 'revolution' principles in his support for the American Revolution and, above all, in his satirical attacks on political corruption. The whole framework of assumption on which Burns's political satires rest recalls the contractarian principles of Presbyterian thought: that authority ascends from below; that government is a contract, and political power a trust; and that even the humblest members of society are competent to censure their governors. That Burns deplored certain aspects of Calvinism —its harsh soteriology, its emphasis on faith over works— should not blind us to his sincere identification with the Presbyterian political inheritance:

> The Solemn league and Covenant
>   Now brings a smile, now brings a tear.
> But sacred Freedom, too, was theirs;
>   If thou'rt a slave, indulge thy sneer.[22]

Burns, of course, was not the only Scotsman to embrace such radical ideals. We cannot properly understand his life and much of his poetry if we do not understand the degree to which his personal relationships and affiliations were directed towards and driven by seeking out similarly politically sympathetic groups and individuals. It was the Lodge friends and patrons who eased his path towards Edinburgh; that so politically riven city which was to prove so disastrous to him in both life and death. Without, as all his generation, fully understanding the political causes of what happened in the capital, the ever astute Edwin Muir put his finger on the events of his sensational first extended visit to the capital as the cause of Burns's subsequent accelerating decline:

> It was after his first trip to Edinburgh that his nature, strongly built and normal, disintegrated. He had hoped, in meeting the

first shock of his astonishing triumph in the capital, that an escape was at last possible from the life of hardly maintained poverty which as a boy he had foreseen and feared. He left Edinburgh recognising that there was no reprieve, that hardship must sit at his elbow to the end of his days. Fame had lifted him on the point of an immediate pinnacle; now the structure had melted away and, astonished, he found himself once more in his native county, an Ayrshire peasant. Some fairy had set him for a little in the centre of a rich and foreign society; then calmly and finally, she had taken it from under his feet. There is hardly another incident in literary history to parallel this brief rise and setting of social favour, and hardly one showing the remorselessness of fortune in the world. The shock told deeply on Burns, working more for evil than the taste for dissipation which he was said to have acquired from the Edinburgh aristocracy.[23]

Given Muir's lack of knowledge of the covert political forces operating on Burns, this is well said. It does, however, underestimate the extraordinary degree to which Burns, in the midst of his Edinburgh triumph, was conscious not only of its transience but the darkness to follow. As he wrote to Robert Ainslie on 16th December 1786:

> You will very probably think, my honoured friend, that a hint about the mischievous nature of intoxicated vanity may not be unreasonable, but, alas! You are wide of the mark. Various concurring circumstances have raised my fame as a poet to a height which I am absolutely certain I have not merits to support; and I look down on the future as I would into the bottomless pit.

He realised that his Edinburgh fame was largely based on the temporary social novelty of a ploughman writing poetry. He also probably realised that his Preface to the Kilmarnock Poems was, as we shall see, a brilliant confidence trick on a willingly gullible genteel Scottish audience, for which a price had to be paid. In the same month he wrote, even more particularly and precisely, to Rev William Greenfield about the consequences of Edinburgh:

> Never did Saul's armour sit so heavily on David when going to encounter Goliath, as does the encumbering robe of public notice with which the friendship and patronage of some 'names

dear to fame' have invested me. I do not say this in the ridiculous idea of seeming self-abasement, and affected modesty. I have long studied myself and I think I know pretty exactly what ground I occupy, both as a man, & a poet; and however the world or a friend may sometimes differ from me in that particular, I stand for it, in silent resolve with all the tenaciousness of Property. I am willing to believe that my abilities deserved a better fate than the veriest shades of life; but to be dragged forth, with all my imperfections on my head, to the full glare of learned and polite observation, is what, I am afraid, I shall have bitter reason to repent I mention this to you, once for all, merely, in the Confessor style, to disburthen my conscience, and that 'When proud Fortune's ebbing tide recedes' you may hear me witness, when my bubble of fame was at its highest, I stood unintoxicated, with the inebriating cup in my hand. Looking forward, with rueful resolve, to the hastening time when the stroke of envious Calumny, with all the eagerness of vengeful triumph, should dash it to the ground.

Mozarts seem inevitably to have their Salieris. The treachery that Burns so accurately predicted for himself was also to be understood as not only psychologically motivated resentment of genuine creativity, but also essentially driven by political ideology. As the 1793–4 Sedition Trials revealed, Edinburgh was a politically schismatic society. This was not so apparent in 1789 and Burns's contacts with two utterly contrasting groups has never been fully understood in terms of the consequent conflicting politics or the terrible personal consequences for the poet of this division.

Initially, Burns was lauded by two utterly contrasting groups. He was a member of the boozy, boisterous, in many instances brilliant, radical, reformist club, The Crochallan Fencibles. He was also taken up, mildly patronised, by the aesthetically, politically and religiously conformist pro-Hanoverian group led by Henry Mackenzie and Hugh Blair. What has never been understood is not only how partisan to their own causes both groups were but, indeed, the degree to which, as the political scene darkened in the 1790s, they were sucked into active participation either towards not simply reform but insurrection on the radical side and covert anti-revolutionary activity on the government side. Of such undeclared civil war, Burns was among the chief victims.

Despite some excellent work by John Brims and Elaine MacFarland we still fall considerably short of understanding the fraught complexity of the extent and intensity of radical protest in Scotland in the 1790s. One consequence of this, of course, has been the contextually impoverished state of Burns criticism. Most of it has been written with the political dimension quite absent. Nor does space here allow anything like the necessary explication of the complex nature of that political culture. What can be said, however, is that most Scottish history seriously underestimates certainly the quantity and, arguably, the quality of radical opposition prevalent in Scotland which became genuinely divisive due to the American War of Independence.

It was that war which created that group so essential to understanding both Burns's political affiliations and what happened to him, The Crochallan Fencibles. The name was a deliberate parody of the loyalist militia groups springing up in opposition to the American cause. What the American war engendered in the radical, reformist side of Edinburgh can be gauged by the invited open letter of Dr Richard Price in 1784, 'To the Secretary of the Committee of Citizens of Edinburgh':

> God grant that this spirit might increase till it has abolished all despotic governments and exterminated the slavery which debased mankind. This spirit first rose in America (it soon reached Ireland) it has diffused itself in some foreign countries, and your letter informs me that it is now animating Scotland.[24]

Ingenuously, late eighteenth-century radicals had a kind of millennial vision of history as an American initiated domino game of collapsing crowns. For a time the reform of a particularly undemocratic Scotland seemed a distinct possibility. The bumpers, bawdy songs and personal badinage which Burns enlisted for with the Fencibles in their howff in Anchor Close was part of what must have seemed the initial stages of an ill-disguised victory celebration. The Fencibles were of course typically a heavy drinking culture. It was not, however, the most erotically inflamed of Scotland's men's clubs. Public masturbation was not on the agenda. Certainly, as camouflage, it was this side of the club's activities to which Burns confessed. He did not always publicly make the connection between libidinal energy and radical politics. Thus he wrote to Mrs Dunlop:

> You may guess that the convivial hours of men have their mysteries of wit and mirth, and I hold it a piece of contemptible baseness to detail the sallies of thoughtless merriment, or the orgies of accidental intoxication to the ear of cool sobriety or female delicacy.

Or, as he wrote in conclusion to a brilliant extended parody of *The Revelation of St John the Divine* in a letter to William Chalmers in December, 1786, that he had never seen 'as many wild beasts as I have seen since I came to Edinburgh.' Burns's own stressing of the social wildness of the Fencibles may have been a deliberate camouflage for the actual reality of their political beliefs and activities. Intellectually, they were an astonishing bunch. William Smellie, commissioned as 'Hangman', not only edited the first *Encyclopaedia Britannica* but had written much of it. Of all Burns's lost letters, those to Smellie would possibly have been of the most profound political importance. They were destroyed by Smellie's biographer, Robert Kerr, with an insouciance that we chillingly recognise as seminal for the manner in which Burns's texts were to be treated not only in the hyper-respectable nineteenth century: 'Many letters of Burns to Mr. Smellie which remained being totally unfit for publication, and several of them containing severe reflections on many respectable people still in life, have been burnt.' Smellie was also the author of a *Philosophy of Natural History* which postulated that the most highly refined, developed human consciousness was incompatible with the world. James 'Balloon' Tytler was an even more extraordinary polymath. As Burns wrote in November 1788 to Mrs Dunlop:

> Those marked T, are the work of an obscure, tippling but extraordinary body of the name of Tytler: a mortal, who though he drudges about Edinburgh as a common printer, with leaky shoes, a sky-lighted hat, & knee buckles as unlike as George-by-the-grace-of-God, & Solomon-the-son-of-David, yet that same unknown drunken Mortal is author and compiler of three-fourths of Elliot's pompous Encyclopaedia Brittanica.

Poet, song-writer, polymath, Scotland's first balloonist and eventually so politically active that he fled Scotland in 1793 to Belfast and then volunteered to return to Scotland to promote insurrection:

> . . . he was to traverse Scotland as a *Highland Piper*. He learned the tongue and was to have gone from town to town to organise a General Insurrection, from there to the South of Ireland (Cork), hence to Paris to enlist the French.[25]

To Tytler's extreme irritation, this mission did not take place. Like many others of his creed and generation, his journey was to be westwards to American safety. An almost equally irascible, restless spirit was Dr Gilbert Stuart who had so upset genteel Edinburgh with his writings in Smellie's *Edinburgh Magazine and Review* that he had to seek employment in London thus initiating the long tradition of Scots radicals forced South. Obviously extremely important in the Fencibles was the legal profession. Of a considerable number of lawyers, the most prominent was Henry Erskine, Dean of the Faculty of Advocates and brother of the even greater radical lawyer Thomas. It was Henry Erskine's fall at the hands of the Robert Dundas faction in the election for Dean of Faculty in 1795 that Burns turned into, in January 1796, a bitterly witty song about the loss of the men of merit and worth to the reactionary loyalists.

> In your heretic sins may live and die,
>   Ye heretic Eight and thirty
> But accept, ye Sublime Majority,
>   My congratulations hearty.
> With your Honors and a certain King,
>   In your servants this is striking—
> The more incapacity they bring,
>   The more they're to your liking.

This, then, was the intimate company Burns was keeping. Nor did he only wholly share their politics but was an active participant not only in terms of his contributions to the radical press, but in actually attempting to send carronades, captured from the smuggling brig *Rosamund* as part of his excise duties, to the French revolutionaries. It is little wonder that even during his first Edinburgh visit his relationships with genteel, conformist, pro-Hanoverian society were strained. How strained we can see, for example, in the fury of his riposte to Mrs McLehose when a Mrs Stewart had checked him over his seditious anti-Hanoverian lines on the Stirling window:

> I have almost given up the excise idea —I have just been now to wait on a great person, Miss N—'s friend, Mrs. Stewart. — Why will great people not only deafen us with the din of their equipage, and dazzle us with their fastidious pomp, but they must also be so very dictatorially wise? I have been questioned like a child about my matters, and blamed and schooled for my Inscription on Stirling window. Come, Clarinda—'Come, curse me Jacob; come, defy me Israel!'

Yet he needed his enemy's patronage. He did join the Excise. Blair and Mackenzie, with their mixture of lachrymose and evangelical values, expressed a faith not so much of a suffering Christ as a quiescently accepting Christ as exemplar to a politically similarly quiescent, hence an apolitical, common people. As Blake wrote: 'Pity would be no more, if we did not make someone poor.' They were, however, able to open doors to publishing connections and offer mainly ill-received poetic advice. In the name of rules and decency, they were always trying to get Burns to tidy up his, to them, unruly act. This had almost no effect other than to irritate the Bard. As he wrote to Greenfield:

> . . . I stumbled on two Songs which I here enclose you as a kind of curiosity to a Professor of the Belle lettres de la Nature: which allow me to say, I look upon as an additional merit of yours: a kind of bye Professorship, not always to be found among the systematic Fathers and Brothers of scientific Criticism.

These tensions were also not confined to matters aesthetic and linguistic. Unlike Heathcliff, Burns was not the brute, sub-literate, threat, that dark erotic stranger, which haunted the bourgeois imagination of the period. They were faced with someone hyper-literate, fecundly allusive to a degree far beyond their powers in canonical literary and biblical tradition, who could not only talk their pants off but, it was feared, those of their wives and daughters too. Command of language was directly related to a fixed hierarchical social order; Burns threatened social anarchy by the very nature of his poetic, rhetorical potency. It offered them some security to classify him as a class-bound 'heaven-taught ploughman' rather than great poet.

REPUTATION: CRITICS, BIOGRAPHERS AND BOWDLERISERS
Even more than Henry Dundas, Henry Mackenzie was probably the most sustained, malign influence on Burns's reputation. He may initially have genuinely wanted to help the poet. He also almost certainly sensed a bandwagon that his self-importance would not allow him *not* to join. As Donald Low has remarked, however, the nature of Mackenzie's praise was to be in the long term confining and destructive:

> . . . his was a disastrously inaccurate essay in criticism which gave rise to endless distortion of Burns's poetry. The whole tendency of Mackenzie's encomium was to emasculate *Poems*. He paid lip-service to humour and satire, but found them too

embarrassing to discuss: introduced a comparison with Sha-
kespeare, only to withdraw it at once: repeatedly shrank from
Burns's characteristic self-expression and fell back on general-
isations. He apologised for the language in which the poet did
his best work, and concentrated on the poems of sentiment in
English. This was to sacrifice truth, and therefore also Burns's
long-term interests as a poet, for instant acclaim.[26]

From the beginning Mackenzie's deeply influential aesthetic stric-
tures were socially and politically motivated. Hence Burns is turned
into a safe sentimentalist rather than, like Pope or Swift, a turbulent,
dissenting satirist of the established, corrupt order. He is a naïve
exception rather than, in terms of both poetry and politics, the most
knowing of men. Burns was as formally naïve in poetic tradition as
Mozart was in musical tradition. They were both examples of
creative pieces of ground, as Blake suggests, born spaded and
seeded. It was socially unacceptable for Mackenzie to grant Burns
such potency. As an extension of this, he had to define Burns as a
naïve innocent, coming from peasant origins. Mackenzie also down-
grades the actual vernacular language of that world with its elements
which bespoke the raw pleasures, pains and, indeed, turbulent
discontents of the common people. If there was genuine ambiva-
lence in Mackenzie's attitude to Burns at the beginning of their
relationship, it did not survive the poet's death. In his résumé of the
careers of Scotland three great eighteenth-century poets, Ramsay,
Fergusson and Burns, the first is praised for his achievement of
prudent respectability. The latter two are not:

Fergusson, dissipated and drunken, died in early life, after
having produced poems faithfully and humorously describing
scenes of Edinburgh and somewhat of blackguardism. Burns
originally virtuous, was seduced by dissipated companions, and
after he got into the Excise addicted himself to drunkenness,
tho' the rays of his genius sometimes broke through the mist of
his dissipation: but the habit had got too much power over him
to be overcome and it brought him, with a few lucid intervals, to
an early grave. He unfortunately during the greatest part of his
life had called and thought dissipation *spirit*, sobriety and
discretion a *want of it*, virtues too shabby for a man of genius.
His great admiration of Fergusson showed his propensity to
coarse dissipation.
    . . . How different was the fate of *Burns* compared with that of a
Poet in birth, in Education, and many other circumstances like

him, tho' I do not arrogate to him so much creative genius, *Allan Ramsay*. He came into notice in a Station as mean as Burns, had no advantage over him in Birth, Connections, or any other circumstances independent of his own genius alas: it was the Patronage and Companionship which Burns obtained, that changed the colour of his later life: the patronage of dissipated men of high rank, and the Companionship of clever, witty, but dissipated men of lower rank. The notice of the former flattered his vanity, and in some degree unsettled his from an anecdote to be immediately mentioned he seemed to mingle with the most amiable feelings —but the levity of his Patrons and his associ- ates Dwelt on the Surface of his Mind and prompted some of his Poetry which offended the serious, and lost him better friends than those which that poetry had acquired —Dugald Stewart who first introduced him to me, told me latterly, that his Conduct and Manners had become so degraded that decent persons could hardly take any notice of him.[27]

Given Fergusson's sweet, convivial personality and the terrible nature of his incarcerated death, Mackenzie's vicious pursuit of him beyond the grave beggars belief. In the history of poetic biographies, Ian Hamilton has remarked that Burns was the first poet to be character assassinated. Given Mackenzie's treatment of Fergusson, however, we would have to grant Fergusson unhappy precedence. Mackenzie tainted, wrongly, both their reputations with, at best, alcoholic tendencies. This alleged addiction was then implied to lead to other forms of licence where, certainly in Burns's case, sexual promiscuity was on the charge sheet.

This demonisation of Burns is not to be understood, however, without it being placed in its proper political context. The Mac- kenzie who penned these personal attacks was the same man who was writing fervid anti-revolutionary polemics in *The Edinburgh Herald* during 1790–1 under the pen name 'An Old Tradesman' and again in 1793, in *The Caledonian Mercury*, under the pen name 'Brutus' to prove that all was for the best in the best of all worn torn, economically distressed Hanoverian worlds. As spokesperson for the old regime he believed that strong government would 'save the people from that worst enemy of purely democratic states – the people themselves'.[28] The pinnacle of his loyalty is the 1792 *A Review of the Principal Proceedings of the Parliament of 1784*, a defense of William Pitt, when Pitt's pro-reformist views of 1784 were being thrown back in his face by radicals. Retrospectively referring to that pamphlet Mackenzie described the ideological clash of the 1790's as an 'epidemic insanity . . . which set up certain idols, under the names of Liberty, Equality and The Rights of Man'.[29] Pitt personally thanked Mackenzie for his loyal defence, and basking in such praise, he replied 'My Opinion, Sir, of you as a Minister I hold only in common with the Millions around me.'[30] (Letter 93, To William Pitt, March 1792). These 'millions' were not so loyal, as Mackenzie informed George Home on 26th March 1792:

> There is a Spirit of Sedition gone forth, of which it is very difficult to tell the Extent, but even if not so considerable as some timid people fear, so restless, so busy, so zealous, as to be truly alarming to every considerate Man. I forget the Calculation made of the numbers of Manufactures in England, but we all know it is very great. Of these I believe I may say a Majority, but assuredly a great part, are determined enemies to the present Order of things[31] . . .

Theatre goers, as Mackenzie records, were among this swelling radical 'enemy' and in one incident he tells Home, open conflict erupted between radicals and loyalists at London's Haymarket theatre when the revolutionary song 'Ca Ira' was demanded by reformers, but chanted down by loyalist calls for 'God Save the King'. Similar tensions spread to the provincial theatres, including Dumfries and an unidentified informer reported to the Excise that Burns was in the reformist mob. Mackenzie goes on in the same letter to condemn Scottish academics: 'From my Communication with Men of Letters here, I can perceive that they are generally on the side of the Malcontents'.[32] Fanatically partisan, status obsessed, politically scared, Mackenzie so hated his reforming and radical political enemies that he could not speak their names. To do so would give them a credibility he utterly sought to deny. For Mackenzie the radical was equivalent to the bestial. This is why in Mackenzie and the subsequent Tory criticism he inspired always described Burns as surrounded by destructive groups of unnamed degenerates in Edinburgh and, even worse, Dumfries.

It should further be understood that Burns was not a unique case for such treatment. The heavily subsidised, reactionary literary, magazine and newspaper culture put together by Pitt and Dundas specialised in trashing the radical literary enemy by varied forms of abuse based on the relationship of personal licentiousness to consequent political anarchy if these people were to succeed. For example, Mary Wollstonecraft with whom Burns corresponded received treatment even worse than his, as a promiscuous woman she was even more reprehensible than a randy ploughman. Engrossed in destroying the careers of any radical sympathisers, Mackenzie boasted to the ultra-loyalist George Chalmers, in March 1793:

> One thing Mr Young suggests as never yet thought of, which however was thought of here, and enforced in two short Articles in the Newspapers by myself, at the very opening of this Business, namely the resolution of not employing Jacobin Tradesmen, which had a very excellent Effect in this Town. . . . contrary to my Expectations, the War has I think done good in this Country, given a Sort of Impulse to the good Part of the Community . . .[33]

An ever-willing anti-reform propagandist, Mackenzie helped organise the Scottish distribution of a vicious attack, printed by the same George Chalmers, on Tom Paine as a degenerate, dangerous individual. The black art of character assassination, well established before the death of Burns, won rich patronage for the loyal Mackenzie, appointed Comptroller of Taxes in Scotland in 1799.

The degree of Mackenzie's vindictiveness and his stress of the later Dumfries years, also alert us to one of the most pervasive and politically wilfully misconceived of myths surrounding Burns. Indeed, so pervasive that it has even penetrated the normally sceptical consciousness of Professor T.M. Devine who has recently written of 'the public recantation of such celebrated supporters of the radical cause as Robert Burns'.[34] This alleged recantation stems from one misinterpreted, truncated song, *The Dumfries Volunteers*. It avoids all the substantial poetic evidence of the Dumfries years to the contrary; not least *Extempore* [on the Loyal Natives' *Verses*]:

> Ye true 'Loyal Natives', attend to my song,
> In uproar and riot rejoice the night long:
> From envy and hatred your corps is exempt:
> But where is your shield from the *darts of contempt*?

The poem catches perfectly both Burns's contempt for the British cause under the war-mongering Pitt and the political company he was keeping in the bitterly politically factionalised little town from which he kept sending out not only radical poems to politically sympathetic London, Edinburgh and Glasgow newspapers, but, as his doctor William Maxwell had, weapons to the French. All this, of course, at ferocious risk to, at best, his Excise position as he was scrutinised by his rightly suspicious masters. This, too, accounts for his attempts in the last years to get free of the claustrophobic cockpit of Dumfries to the relatively safer, because larger Glasgow area where, even more than Edinburgh, Scottish history has still chronically underestimated the depth of a radical opposition to Pitt's war policy so great that Burke brought it up in the House.

If Burns had made any public recantation, Mackenzie and his ilk would have shouted it from the house-tops. That there was none accounts not only for the intensity of Mackenzie's malice but also for what we now know about his activities not only as literary propagandist but practically on behalf of the government. The nature of Mackenzie's key role in the government's scrutiny of Burns and the subsequent creation of a literary, psychological context by which to sanitise the poetry we now know from the archives of Edinburgh University. Here we have discovered letters from Robert Heron requesting payments from Robert Dundas via Henry Mackenzie for espionage services rendered:

> My Lord . . . Five or six years since, I, too boldly introduced myself to your Lordship, by suggesting that it was requisite to counteract from the Press, the effects of those seditious associations and seditious writings which were then busily corrupting the political sentiments of the people of this country . . . you were pleased not to disapprove the ingeniuness and honesty of my wishes and intentions. I was, in consequence of this condescending goodness of your Lordship, noticed by the Committee of the Association for the Defence of the Constitution, which was soon after formed. Under the direction —particularly of Mr Mackenzie, Lord Glenlee and Mr Campbell, I was employed to write several little articles for the newspapers, and for other occasions, in order to oppose the malignant efforts of sedition . . .
> . . . The Committee had, with sufficient liberality, already paid my petty services with the sum of thirty pounds . . . Your Lordship, within a short time, munificently sent me no less than fifty pounds.[35]

The core of these services involved his exploitation of a relationship built up with Burns in Edinburgh. Worse, on the poet's death he rushed to print with a memoir of the poet which was to prove ruinously influential for both Burns and his poetry.

Heron was too talented to be a mere hack. When he was the Rev. Hugh Blair's assistant he had met Burns in Edinburgh. Heron maintained the relationship and en route to his native Galloway made a point of visiting the poet. The often prescient Bard recorded a visit from Heron to Ellisand thus:

The ill-thief blaw the Heron south!
And never drink be near his drouth!
He tald myself, by work o' mouth,
          He'd take my letter;
I lippened to the chief in trough,
          And bade nae better.—

But aiblins honest Master Heron
Had at the time some dainty *Fair One*,
To ware his theologic care on,
          And holy study:
And tired o' Sauls to waste his lear on,
          E'en tried the *Body*.—

Burns got the scale of the betrayal wrong; it was infinitely in excess of a non-delivered letter to Dr Blacklock. The devil of his political enemies really had blown Heron south. Behind Heron's black-gowned clerical front, Burns also keenly observed his capacity for chronic alcoholic and sexual dissipation. A familiar of the debtor's prison, Heron was to die prematurely, again imprisoned for debt, in Newgate in 1807.

Along with the new factual evidence of the Mackenzie/Heron connection, it might have been deduced both from Heron's slavish taking of Mackenzie tactics against Burns to a biographical extreme and his equally slavish eulogy to his patron's critical prowess. This is Heron's account of Mackenzie's contribution, via his *Lounger* magazine article, to Burns's initial Edinburgh success:

That criticism is now known to have been composed by HENRY MACKENZIE Esq, whose writings are universally admired for an *Addisonian* delicacy and felicity of wit and humour, by which the CLIO of the *Spectator* is more than rivalled; for a wildly tender pathos that excites the most ex-quisite vibrations of the finest chords of sympathy in the human heart, for a lofty, vehement, persuasive eloquence, by which the immortal *Junius* has sometimes perhaps been excelled and often almost equalled![36]

Heron's biographical memoir was not the occasion of his first writing about Burns. In 1793 he published a travel book where he created a contrast on the poet's not so much varied talents as antipathetic ones as expressed in the difference between *The Cotter's Saturday Night* and *Tam o' Shanter*. The latter is initially admitted as a masterpiece but this is then significantly qualified: 'Burns seems to have thought, with Boccacce and Prior, that some share of indelicacy was a necessary ingredient in a Tale. Pity that he should have debased so fine a piece, by any things, — having even the remotest relation to obscenity'. This kind of Mackenzie-initiated sentimentalism was the seminal language of nineteenth-century political pietism which would become, mainly though *Blackwood's*, the dominant mode of Scottish Toryism. Burns had to be converted into the pietistic poet of a quiescent common people. Whether they were properly reading its concluding stanzas, *The Cotter's Saturday Night* became the Ark of the Covenant for the Scottish upper and middle-classes as, increasingly anxious about the fetid, brutal potentially insurrectionary common life of the new emergent industry-based (coal, iron, tobacco, weaving) towns, they sought the politically calming notion of pastoral, god-fearing peace reigning in the Scottish countryside. Heron is a seminal figure in the concoction of this fantasy:

> The whole books of the sacred scriptures are continually in the hands of almost every peasant. And it is impossible, that there should not be some souls among them, awakened to the divine emotions of genius, by that rich assemblage which these books present, of almost all that is interesting in incidents, or picturesque in imagery, or affectingly sublime or tender in sentiments and character. It is impossible that those rude rhymes, and the simple artless music with which they are accompanied, should not excite some ear to fond perception of the melody of verse. That Burns had felt these impulses will appear undeniably certain to whoever shall carefully peruse his 'Cotter's Saturday Night'; or shall remark with nice observation, the various fragments of *scripture* sentiment, of *scripture* *imagery*, of *scripture* language, which are scattered throughout his works.[37]

Of course, Heron knew as well as anyone that the bulk of Burns poetry neither sociologically confirmed this view and expressed anything but personal or popular quiescence in the face of the established order. To deal with this what he did was sycophantically flesh out the bones of Mackenzie's account of the dead poet. Apparently more in sorrow than anger, Heron constructed the myth of Burns as betrayer of his own earliest spiritual impulses because he lacked 'that steady VIRTUE , without which even genius in all its omnipotence is soon reduced to paralytic imbecility, or to manic mischievousness'. Thus Burns's life becomes a melodrama where he always surrendered to those elements in himself which inevitably took him into increasingly bad company.

> The *bucks* of Edinburgh accomplished, in regard to BURNS, that in which the *boors* of Ayrshire had failed. After residing some months in Edinburgh, he began to estrange himself . . . from the society of his graver friends. Too many of his hours were now spent at the tables of persons who delighted to urge conviviality to drunkenness, in the tavern, in the brothel, on the lap of the woman of pleasure. He *suffered* himself to be surrounded by a race of miserable beings who were proud to tell that they had been in company with BURNS, and had seen Burns as loose and as foolish as themselves. He was not yet irrecoverably lost to temperance and moderation, but he was already almost too much captivated with their wanton rivals, to be ever more won back to a faithful attachment to *their* more sober charms. He now began to contract something of new arrogance in conversation. Accustomed to be among his favourite associates . . . *the cock of the company*, he could scarcely refrain from indulging in similar freedom and dictatorial decision of talk, even in presence of persons who could less patiently endure his presumption.[38]

Here the suppressed rage of sentimental, genteel Edinburgh wells up. The people's poet had no right to his creative superiority of language. Hence is evolved the fiction of the unstable genius who falls away from his prudent, real friends and into evil company and, by his sinful depravity, betrays not only his better self but the sanctified common people whom he represents. In Burke's great shadow, a Scottish conservatism is forged which converts the dialectic of opposing secular political systems to one which, on the conservative side, has divine sanction as embodying the inherent nature of reality. By definition, opposition to this is implicitly evil. Burns is a sinner (he *suffers* but for the wrong things), with even a hint of anti-Christ. As with Mackenzie's account, the speed of Burns's descent accelerates in Dumfries. He has crosses to bear, admittedly, but they are not properly borne:

In the neighbourhood were other gentlemen occasionally ad-
dicted, like Burns, to convivial excess, who, while they admired
the poet's talents, and were charmed with his licentious wit,
forgot the care of his real interests in the pleasure in which they
found in his company, and in the gratification which the plenty
and festivity of their tables appeared evidently to afford him.
With these gentlemen, while disappointments and disgusts
continued to multiply upon him in his present situation, he
persisted to associate every day more and more eagerly. His
crosses and disappointments drove him every day more into
dissipation, and his dissipation tended to enhance whatever was
disagreeable and by degrees, into the boon companion of mere
excisemen, spend his money lavishly in the ale house, could
easily command the company of BURNS. The care of his farm
was thus neglected, Waste and losses wholly consumed his little
capital.[39]

As with Edinburgh and The Crochallan Fencibles, the political
nature of Burns's affiliations in Dumfries, is not identified. What
Heron is mainly referring to here is that Real Whig bibulous bear of
a man, Robert Riddell. As we now know, Burns was the middle-man
responsible for Riddell's political essays being published under the
pen-name Cato. What, of course, Heron does not narrate is the story
of the collapse of Burns's political hopes under ferocious govern-
mental pressure but a moral fable whereby, in its terminal stage, the
sinner is driven to misanthropic blackness. The peculiar fevered
tearing apart of Burns's body, the agony of night sweats and pain
wracked joints, is seen as both a consequence of his heavy drinking
where, in fact, his rapidly deteriorating health made his tolerance to
alcohol ever less. Or, psychosomatically, his bodily agony is seen as a
punishing consequence of his sins. In actual fact, a convincing case
has been made that medically what was tearing Burns's body apart
in these last terrible months was brucellosis caught from infected
milk, although it is generally thought he died of rheumatic heart
disorder.[40] That alcoholic fornicator Heron, has a quite different
'spiritual' diagnosis:

Nor, amidst these agonising reflections, did he fail to look, with
an indignation half invidious, half contemptuous, on those, who,
with moral habits not more excellent than his, with powers of
intellect far inferior, yet basked in the sunshine of fortune, and
were loaded in the wealth and honours of the world, while *his*
follies could not obtain pardon, nor his wants an honourable

supply. His wit became, from this time, more gloomy sarcastic; and his conversation and writings began to assume something of a tone misanthropical malignity, by which they had not been before, in any eminent degree, distinguished. But, with all these failings; he was still that exalted mind which had raised above the depression of its original condition, with all the energy of *the lion, pawing to set free his hinder limbs from the yet encumbering earth*: he still appeared *not less than an archangel ruined!*[41]

Whether this 'archangel' image is knowingly derived from the genuine addict, S.T. Coleridge, the heroic but defeated lion fits perfectly Heron's sentimentally disguised assassination. Scottish sentimentalists have a penchant for weeping at the gravesides of their victims. Burns's long-term friend, William Nicol, had other thoughts concerning the death of his once rampantly *alive* friend. As he wrote almost immediately after Burns's death to John Lewars:

> . . . it gives me great pain to see the encomiums passed upon him, both in the Scottish and English news-papers are mingled with the reproaches of the most indelicate and cruel nature. But stupidity and idiocy delight when a great and immortal genius falls; and they pour forth their invidious reflections, without mercy, well knowing that the dead Lion, from whose presence they formerly scudded away with terror, and at whose voice they trembled through every nerve, can devour no more.
>
> The fanatics have now got it into their heads, that dreadful bursts of penitential sorrow issued from the breast of our friend, before he expired. But if I am not much mistaken in relation to his firmness, he would disdain to have his dying moments disturbed with sacerdotal gloom, like sacerdotal howls. I knew he would negotiate with God alone, concerning his immortal interests.[42]

Without the leonine Bard there to protect his manuscripts, the nature of his precipitous, premature death left his papers in disorder. Given that his death coincided exactly with the peak of the scrutiny, censorship and penal repression of the understandably Francophobic Pitt/Dundas security-state such disorder was heavily amplified by his literary executors, mainly anxiety-driven radicals, hiding, dispersing or, at worst, destroying his dissident writings. Some alleged friends, minor Judases like Robert Ainslie, also wished to retrieve their letters or mangle and censor those of the poet's that they had in their possession.

In his magisterial editorial work of the 1930s, De Lancey Ferguson calculated that 25% of Burns's epistolary output was irretrievably lost. The poetry undoubtedly suffered similar depredations. There was the difficulty of identifying texts pseudonymously and anonymously published in radical London, Edinburgh and Glasgow newspapers. It seems certain that a key notebook of late, unpublished poems did go to William Roscoe but vanished without trace in 1816. Further, many of the central political poems (e.g. *Address of Beelzebub* and the *Ode on General Washington's Birthday*) appeared erratically and fortuitously in the course of the nineteenth century. A burning of political and erotic material in the 1850s at Lesmahagow by Mr Greenshields (of the stamps fame) may not have been the last instance of genteel Scotland deciding to save the poet's reputation from himself.

The two men immediately involved in dealing with the manuscripts were the poet's Dumfries friend John Syme who enlisted a mutual friend, Alexander Cunningham, to help in dealing with the papers and to make an appeal for funds to aid the truly impoverished family. In Edinburgh, enthusiasm had 'cooled with the corpse' and Ayrshire proved equally miserly. For such virulent Scotophobes as Hazlitt and Coleridge, this treatment of the nation's bard gave further evidence, if evidence were needed, of the treacherous, mean-spiritedness of the Scots. As Coleridge wrote in 1796:

> Is thy Burns dead?
> And shall he die unwept, and sink to earth
> 'Without the meed of one melodious tear'?
> Thy Burns, and Nature's own beloved bard,
> Who to the 'Illustrious of his native Land
> So properly did look for patronage'
> Ghost of Macenas! Hide thy blushing face!
> They snatched him from the sickle and the plough—
> To gauge ale-firkins.

To be fair to the committee of executors set up in Dumfries, the situation was not only complex but carried real danger with it. Also given the political spirit of the age, much of the material could not be made public far less profitably so. As Ian Hamilton has written:

> The Dumfries executors' committee had already done some preliminary sifting and, fearing piracies, had advertised for any Burns material that was in private hands. The mass of the papers they found at the poet's house was in 'utter confusion'

but it took no more than a glance to determine that much of the
collection ought probably to be destroyed: 'viz. Such as may
touch on the most private and delicate matters relative to female
individuals'. When, in August, a bonfire was arranged, Syme
was more hesitant: 'Avaunt the sacrilege of destroying them
and shutting them forever from the light: But on the other
hand, can we bring them into the light?' On this occasion, only a
few 'unimportant' notes and cards were burnt.[43]

As well as sexually intimate indiscretions, went political ones. Such
were safer out of Scotland given that, comparatively, it was a more
politically controlled environment than England.

Establishment Scots were even more zealous than their English
masters in hunting down treason in a more demographically con-
trolled environment. The radical English connection that Burns
most prided himself on, indeed his intention had been to visit him,
was William Roscoe of Liverpool. Roscoe, the centre of a vast web of
radical connections was poet, historian and financier. His friend was
a Scottish doctor and part-time scholar, Dr James Currie. Currie's
initial response to receiving the papers is replete with the personal
and textual terrible harm of which he was to be both initiator and
chief agent:

> My dear Syme: Your letter of the 6th January reached me on the
> 12th, and along with it came the remains of poor Burns. I
> viewed the large and shapeless mass with astonishment! Instead
> of finding . . . a selection of his papers, with such annotations as
> might clear up any obscurities . . . I received the complete
> sweepings of his drawers and of his desk . . . even to the copy
> book on which his little boy had been practising writing. No
> one had given these papers a perusal, or even an inspection . . .
> the manuscripts of a man of genius . . . were sent, with all their
> sins on their head, to meet the eye of an entire stranger.[44]

Why Currie, a man of allegedly radical political persuasion quite at
odds with Heron's toadying Toryism was, indeed, complicit with
Heron's account of Burns will probably remain not fully explicable.
The most generous explanation is that Currie, given the spirit of the
times, produced a work designed to sell to a conformist, bourgeois
public in order to gain as much money as possible for the bereft
family. The good doctor, however, went well beyond cosmetic
surgery. Himself plagued by alcoholic tendencies, he was working
in 1797 on a pseudo scientific paper 'Observations on the Nature of

Fever and on the Effects of Opium, Alcohol and Inanition'. Burns's later letters, replete with confessions of savagely black depressions and not a few severe hangovers were grist to Currie's diagnostic mill. Worse, one addiction led to another:

> His temper now became more irritable and gloomy, he fled from himself into society, often of the lowest kind. And in such company that part of the convivial scene, in which wine increases sensibly and excites benevolence, was hurried over, to reach the succeeding part, over which uncontrolled passion generally presided. He who suffers from pollution of inebriation, how shall he escape other pollution? But let us refrain from the mention of errors over which delicacy and humanity draw the veil.[45]

As Ian Hamilton has remarked: 'This then was the autopsy report: alcoholic poisoning plus maybe a touch of venereal disease had killed off Scotland's greatest poet'. Nor was Currie finished with delivering his patient into the hands of his enemies. Currie enunciated the notion that the poet, of his very nature, was susceptible to addiction. Too sensitive, the poet would always find the world on the margin of the tolerable. Again Burns's letters supplied Currie with significant evidence for this point of view. For example, this brilliant letter of August 1790 on the essential incompatibility of the poet and the world:

> It is often a reverie of mine, when I am disposed to be melancholy, the characters and fates of the Rhyming tribe. There is not among all the Martyrologies that were ever penned, so rueful a narrative as Johnson's Lives of the Poets. In the comparative view of Wretches, the criterion is not what they are doomed to suffer, but how they are formed to bear. Take a being of our kind: give him a stronger imagination and more delicate sensibility, which will ever between them engender a more ungovernable set of Passions, than the usual lot of man: implant in him an irresistible impulse to some idle vagary, such as, arranging wild flowers in fantastical nosegays, tracing the grasshopper (sic) to his haunt by the chirping song, watching the frisks of little minnows in the sunny pool, or haunting after the intrigues of wanton butterflies —in short, send him adrift after some wayward pursuit which shall eternally mislead him from the paths of Lucre; yet curse him with a keener relish than any man living for the pleasures that only

Lucre can bestow; lastly, fill up the measure of his woes, by bestowing on him a spurning sense of his own dignity; and you have created a wight nearly as miserable as a Poet.

Since Currie edited this letter, there is little wonder about from where his principal biographical evidence comes. Further, he had used for his template that most indulgent of defences of the libertine poet, Dr Johnson's *Life of Savage*. Steeped in Burns's confessional letters, it was not difficult for Currie to articulate the poet's frequent despairing self-diagnosis of his own tumultuous mood swings and lack of volition. Certainly from Ellisland onwards, the poet became increasingly prone to depression. As he wrote to Mrs Dunlop in June 1789:

> Will you take the effusions, the miserable effusions, of low spirits, just as they flow from their bitter spring? I know not of any particular cause for this worst of all my foes besetting me; but for some time my soul has been beclouded with a thickening atmosphere of evil imaginations and gloomy presages.

All trouble, therefore, is located by Currie within Burns; he is an endogenous depressive rather than a reactive one. Yet, he had so much to react against. Ellisland was the last in an unbroken line of fiscal farm traps. After Edinburgh he felt profoundly deprived of creative company. His body was signalling premature dissolution accelerated by the physical and mental grind of his Excise duties. Also to someone so politically attuned he must have had an overbearing awareness of the darkening political scene as a wheel on which his personal and public hopes were to be brutally broken. Currie, setting the programme for all of nineteenth-century biographers and, indeed, most twentieth-century ones, paid no real attention to these grim external forces. Burns was for Currie destructively committed to his irrational, even fallen, self:

> His understanding was equal to the other powers of his mind, and his deliberate opinions were singularly candid and just; but like other men of great and irregular genius, the opinions which he delivered in conversation were often the offspring of temporary feelings, and widely different from the calm decisions of his judgement. This was not merely true respecting the character of others, but in regard to some of the most important points of human speculation.[46]

From this Currie deduced a Burnsian dialectic 'in which virtue and passion had been at perpetual variance'. Fuelled by alcohol, passion had achieved overwhelming, self-destructive victory. Inevitably, intentionally this diagnosis destroys the poetry as much as the poet. Currie creates a situation in which, from now on, any conformist critical hack can and, indeed, did have the prescriptive power to censor any of Burns's poetry not conforming to that respectability which was the first line of defence of conservative political correctness. The political poet becomes a malcontented unstable neurotic, not an incisive diagnostician of manifest ills in the body politic.

There is some evidence, both contextual and textual, that Currie politically knew very well what he was up to. De Quincey had always loathed the Liverpool coterie to which Currie belonged to as a group of narcissistic radicals who were, particularly in the case of Burns, deeply condescending, at best, to the alleged object of their shallow affections. He particularly hated Currie as the physician who was 'unable to heal himself'. His 1801 account of this group is charged with shocked outrage at the gross indifference of these mendacious friends of the people who were deaf to the pain that he, as a Tory, could feel all too clearly:

> I had for ever ringing in my ears, during that summer of 1801, those groans that ascended to heaven from his [Burns's] over-burthened heart those harrowing words, 'To give him leave to toil', which record almost as a reproach to the ordinances of God and I felt that upon him, amongst all the children of labour, the primal curse had fallen heaviest and sunk deepest. Feelings such as these I had the courage to express; a personal compliment, or so, I might now and then hear; but all were against me on the *matter*. Dr Currie said 'Poor Burns! Such notions had been his ruin'; Mr Sheperd continued to draw on the subject some scoff or groan at Mr Pitt and the Excise . . . Mr Clarke proposed that I should write a Greek inscription for a cenotaph which he was to erect in his garden to the memory of Burns; and so passed away the solitary protestation on behalf of Burns's jacobinism, together with the wine and the roses, and the sea-breezes of that same Verton, in that same summer of 1801 . . . three men who remain at the most of all who in these convivial meetings held it right to look down upon Burns as one whose spirit was rebellious overmuch against the institutions of man, and jacobinal in a sense which 'men of property' and master manufacturers will never brook, albeit democrats by profession.[47]

With friends like these, Burns's reputation hardly needed the legion of newspaper and magazine owning enemies whose overt Toryism gave them reason to destroy it. How deep Currie's radicalism had ever been is impossible to judge. Better men than he had become apostates to the radical cause.[48] It is hard not to believe that he knew what he was doing as he linked, albeit obliquely, Burns's alleged degeneration with political turpitude. He also had that classic bad doctor's ability to confuse mental or moral symptoms with physical ones:

> As the strength of the body decays, the volition fails; in proportion as the sensations are soothing and gratified, the sensibility increases; and morbid sensibility is the parent of indolence, because, while it impairs the regulating power of the mind, it exaggerates all the obstacles to exertion. Activity, perseverance, and self-command, and the great purposes of utility, patriotism, or of honourable ambition, which had occupied the imagination, die away in fruitless resolutions, or in feeble efforts.[49]

It is little wonder that Coleridge, irretrievably addicted to laudanum, called Currie's book 'a masterly specimen of philosophical biography'. He was so symptomatic of Currie's account that he must have felt as if struck by a cross-bow bolt from the blue. It is, however, most certainly *not* Burns. Further, the allusion to patriotism gives Currie's game away. It is an unequivocal linking of Burns with insurrectionary, hence definably degenerate, forces.

Not content, however, with rendering Burns's personality a suitable case for mistreatment, Currie followed exactly Heron's critical criteria for sifting the acceptable, sentimental chaff from the troublesome, satirical wheat. The literary analysis is an attack on the poetry as effective as the wholly related attacks on the Bard's character. Behind both psychological and aesthetic repudiation lie, of course, the real but unnamed political reasons. Burns's employment of the vernacular was the primary, obvious place of attack:

> The greater part of his earlier poems are written in the dialect of his country, which is obscure, if not unintelligible to Englishmen, and which though adheres more or less to the speech of almost every Scotsman, all the polite and ambitious are now endeavouring to banish from their tongues as well as their writings. The use of it in composition naturally therefore calls up ideas of vulgarity to the mind. These singularities are

increased by the character of the poet, who delights to express himself with a simplicity that approaches to nakedness, and with an unmeasured energy that often alarms delicacy, and sometimes offends taste. Hence in approaching him, the first impression is perhaps repulsive: there is an air of coarseness about him which is with difficulty reconciled with our established notions of poetical excellence.[50]

Along with such fundamental creative castration went covert politically motivated readings of these two satirical masterpieces with which Burns deliberately opened the Kilmarnock edition. That wickedly irreverent dialogue, *The Twa Dogs*, is defined, absurdly, as Burns's plan 'to inculcate a lesson of contentment on the lower classes of society by showing that their superiors are neither much better nor happier than themselves.' The quite extraordinary postscript to *The Author's Earnest Cry and Prayer* with its terrible national images of the Highland soldier slaughtered in the service of an alien Hanoverian cause and 'Mother Scotland' as an incontinent crone, are described as purely humorous. Currie, in fact, set a tactical fashion for conservative criticism of Burns to laugh, damagingly, in the wrong places. Needless to say, one poem floats free of the clarty waters occupied by the bulk of the achievement:

> . . . the representation of these humble cottagers forming a wider circle round their hearth and uniting in the worship of God, is a picture most affecting of any which the rural muse has ever presented to the view. Burns was admirably adapted to this delineation. . . . The Cotter's Saturday Night is tender and moral, it is solemn and devotional, and rises at length into a strain of grandeur and sublimity which modern poetry has not surpassed. The noble sentiments of patriotism with which it concludes correspond with the rest of the poem. In no age or country have the pastoral muses breathed such elevated accents, if the 'Messiah' of Pope be excepted, which is indeed a pastoral in form only. It is to be regretted that Burns did not employ his genius on other subjects of the same nature which the manners and customs of Scottish peasantry would have amply supplied.[51]

Praise, indeed, but praise granted at the price of near complete distortion. Currie's misreading of the last two stanzas of the poem apart, this post-Burkean account of a peasant world of piety, humility and hence, hierarchical loyalty is used as the criterion

by which the rest of Burns's poetry is not only judged but con-
demned.

In his 1808 review of Cromek's *Reliques* in *The Edinburgh Review*
Jeffrey also expresses inordinate enthusiasm for this, indeed, ex-
ceptional poem: 'The exquisite description of *The Cotter's Saturday
Night* affords, perhaps, the finest example of this sort of pathetic. Its
whole beauty cannot indeed be discerned but by those whom
experience has enabled to judge of the admirable fidelity and
completeness of the picture.' This review of Jeffrey's is absolutely
seminal to an understanding of the image of Burns and his poetry
which was to dominate the nineteenth century and, indeed, elements
of it still persist into the twenty-first. As well as Jeffrey's legally
fine-honed intellect he was from 1802 to 1829 the editor of *The
Edinburgh Review*. This magazine having freed itself from reviewing
as a mere vehicle for the book trade was not only independent but, in
terms of payment to contributors, unprecedently wealthy. Ironi-
cally, it was a Whig magazine, which was on political issues almost
uniformly reformative. Hence its support of Catholic emancipation
and its attacks on the sale of army commissions, flogging in the
British Navy and Army and the Test and Corporations Act. So
exceptional were its fiscal and intellectual powers that, with the
subsequent Tory *Blackwood's*, it unprecedently, if temporarily,
moved the locus of British critical intelligence from London to
Edinburgh. It was from such a position of unparalleled authority
that Jeffrey, with near total success, decided to contain, if necessary
by emasculation and vilification, what he perceived to be the threat
of the revolutionary impetus of Burns as man and poet. Jeffrey's
arguments derived from Currie but even, in some instances, ex-
ceeding the latter's account are not to be understood in literary
terms without understanding the politics that underlay the aes-
thetics.[52] Like all men of his class, the French terror had bitten into
his soul. Evidence real or invented of a common people diligently,
culturally, passively loyal was everywhere sought. Burns had con-
sequently to be fitted to the procrustean bed of their political
anxieties and phobias. Hence this account of the degree to which
Burns and the Scottish peasantry exceed all others in educated,
hence, conformist virtue:

> We shall conclude with two general remarks — the one na-
> tional, the other critical. The first is, that it is impossible to read
> the productions of Burns, along with his history, without
> forming a higher idea of the intelligence, taste, and accomplish-
> ments of the peasantry, than most of those in the higher ranks

are disposed to entertain . . . it is evident . . . that the whole
family, and many of their associates, who have never emerged
from the native obscurity of their condition, possessed talents,
and taste, and intelligence, which are little suspected to lurk in
those humble retreats. His epistles to brother poets, in the rank
of farmers and shopkeepers in the adjoining villages, — the
existence of a book-society and debating club among persons of
that description, and many other incidental traits in his
sketches of his youthful companions, — all contribute to show,
that not only good sense, and enlightened morality, but litera-
ture and talents for speculation, are far more generally diffused
in society than is generally imagined; and that the delights and
the benefits of these generous and humanizing pursuits, are by
no means confined to those whom leisure and affluence have
courted to their enjoyment. That much of this is peculiar to
Scotland, and may be properly referred to our excellent in-
stitutions for parochial education, and to the natural sobriety
and prudence of our nation, may certainly be allowed . . . It is
pleasing to know, that the sources of rational enjoyment are so
widely disseminated; and, in a free country, it is comfortable to
think, that so great a proportion of the people is able to
appreciate the advantages of its condition, and fit to be relied
on in all emergencies where steadiness and intelligence is
required.[53]

As analysis, this is, of course, an inversion of the cultural and
political truth. The common readers of the Scottish late eighteenth
century, especially key groups like the weavers, were more likely to
be reading Tom Paine than anything else. Also, given that Burns's
'carnivalesque' poetry is the quintessence of dissidence against the
prevailing church and state, it is not easy to see how it can be
squared with the pacific vision of the lower orders. What Jeffrey did
was to use his enormous authority to impose a crude binary division
on Burns's poetry so that we have the 'good' acceptable poet as
opposed to the 'bad' rejected one. Among other things this involved
him in reinventing the Scottish vernacular tradition with that
'bletherin' bitch's' unique capacity for reductive, derisory satire,
acute psychological insight, and often bitter realism, transformed
into a mode suitable for historical and psychological regressive
nostalgia. The Kailyard begins here:

We beg leave too, in passing, to observe, that this Scotch is not
to be considered as a provincial dialect, the vehicle only of

rustic vulgarity and rude local humour. It is the language of a whole country, — long an independent kingdom, and still separate in laws, character and manners. It is by no means peculiar to the vulgar; but is the common speech of the whole nation in early life, — and with many of its most exalted and accomplished individuals throughout their whole existence; and, if it be true that, in later times, it has been, in some measure, laid aside by the more ambitious and aspiring of the present generation, it is still recollected, even by them, as the familiar language of their childhood, and of those who were the earliest objects of their love and veneration. It is connected, in their imagination, not only with the olden times which is uniformly conceived as more pure, lofty and simple than the present, but also with all the soft and bright colours of remembered childhood and domestic affection. All its phrases conjure up images of childhood innocence and sports, and friendships which have no pattern in succeeding years. Add to all this, that it is the language of a great body of poetry, with which almost all Scotchmen are familiar; and, in particular, of a great multitude of songs, written with more tenderness, nature and feeling, than any other lyric compositions that are extant, and we may perhaps be allowed to say, that the Scotch is, in reality, a highly poetical language; and that it is an ignorant, as well as an illiberal prejudice, which would seek to confound it with the barbarous dialects of Yorkshire or Devon.[54]

Opposed to this, was the dissident Burns who had, as man and poet, to be condemned to outer darkness as quickly as possible. While Currie could grant Burns's satirical poetry some virtue, Jeffrey could conceive of nothing in it but the malign manifestations of the poet's personality:

The first is, the undisciplined harshness and acrimony of his invective. The great boast of polished life is the delicacy, and even the generosity of its hostility, —that quality which is still the characteristic as it is that denomination of a gentleman, — that principle which forbids us to attack the defenceless, to strike the fallen, or malign the slain, —and enjoins us, in forging the shafts of satire, to increase the polish exactly as we add to their keenness or their weight . . . His ingenious and amiable biographer has spoken repeatedly in praise of his talents for satire, —we think, with a most unhappy partiality. His epigrams and lampoons appear to us, one and all, unworthy of him; —offensive from their extreme coarseness and violence, —and contemptible from their want of wit or brilliancy. They seem to have been written, not out of playful malice or virtuous indignation, but out of fierce and ungovernable anger. His whole raillery consists in railing; and his satirical vein displays itself chiefly in calling names and in swearing.[55]

In fact Jeffrey's criticism of Burns is overwhelmingly *ad hominem*. The poet is seen as the great transgressor in terms of his multiple morbid and impolite discontents. He is a threat, not least a sexual threat ('his complimentary effusions to ladies of the higher rank, is forever straining them to the bosom of her impetuous votary') to the desired, indeed, necessary order of things. Burns, in fact, is corrupted by the Romantic, revolutionary spirit of the age with its absolute moral dispensation for the self-anointed man of genius:

> But the leading vice in Burns's character, and the cardinal deformity of all his productions, was his contempt or affectation of contempt for prudence, decency and regularity; and his admiration of thoughtlessness, oddity and vehement sensibility; his belief, in short, in the dispensing power of genius and social feeling, in all matters of morality and common sense. This is the very slang of the worst German plays, and the lowest of our out of town-made novels; nor can anything be more lamentable, than that it should have found a patron in such a man as Burns, and communicated to a great part of his productions a character of immortality, at once contemptible and hateful.[56]

Granted the applicability of contempt and hate for his poetry, Jeffrey returns to the fallible, fallacious nature of a man who, having forgotten the ordinary duties of life, loses himself in various forms of self-absorbed licentiousness:

> It requires no habit of deep thinking, nor anything more, indeed, than the information of an honest heart, to perceive that it is cruel and base to spend in vain superfluities, that money which belongs of right to the pale industrious tradesman and his famishing infants; or that it is a vile prostitution of language, to talk of that man's generosity or goodness of heart, who sits raving about friendship and philanthropy in a tavern, while his wife's heart is breaking at her cheerless fireside, and his children pining in solitary poverty.[57]

This, of course, is derived from the language of *The Anti-Jacobin* of the previous decade with its insistent connection of exaggerated moral fallibility, especially sexual, with political anarchy. (*The Anti-Jacobin* of 1797 looked forward to an emergent generation of loyalist Tory poets to emulate and surpass the 'bards of Freedom' of the 1790s, with their 'wood-notes wild'. This latter description was, of course, on Burns's waxen seal.) Character assassination was and, indeed, is an essential establishment weapon. Jeffrey's intemperate indulgence in it gave open season to varied lesser talents as that for the first two decades of the nineteenth century memoir writers and biographers of Burns outdid each other in denigrating him. Such personal denigration always carried within it the connection between his varied irresponsible, dissolute behaviour and his revolutionary politics. Here again, Jeffrey provides the model:

> This pitiful cant of careless feeling and eccentric genius, accordingly, has never found much favour in the eyes of English sense and morality. The most signal effect which it ever produced, was on the muddy brains of some German youth, who left college in a body to rob on the highway, because Schiller had represented the captain of a gang as so very noble a creature. But in this country, we believe, a predilection for that honourable profession must have proceeded this admiration of the character. The style we have been speaking of, accordingly, is now the heroics only of the hulks and the house of correction; and has no chance, we suppose, of being greatly admired, except in the farewell speech of a young gentleman preparing for Botany Bay.[58]

This brutal allusion to the horrendous events of 1793–4 which manifested the criminal breakdown of the Scottish legal system with Braxfield as front-man for the Dundas clan demonstrates the depths of vindictive fear in Jeffrey's heart for radicalism. Hence Burns himself is to be spared nothing:

> It is humiliating to think how deeply Burns has fallen into this debasing error. He is perpetually making a parade of his thoughtlessness, inflammability and imprudence, and talking with much complacency and exultation of the offence he has occasioned to the sober and correct part of mankind. The odious slang infects almost all his prose, and a very great proportion of his poetry; and is, we are persuaded, the chief if not only the source of the disgust with which, in spite of his

genius, we know that he is regarded by many very competent and liberal judges.[59]

Jeffrey then, condescendingly, lets Burns wriggle, if not escape from, the hook on which he has impaled him:

> His apology, too, we are willing to believe, is to be found in the original lowness of his situation, and the slightness of his acquaintance with the world. With his talents and powers of observation, he could not have seen much of the beings who echoed this raving, without feeling for them that distrust and contempt which would have made him blush to think he had ever stretched over them the protecting shield of genius.[60]

The alleged naïvety inherent in inferior social status has forever haunted Burns criticism and commentary. Jeffrey's attempt to detach Burns from radical, Romantic connections was as successful as it was erroneous. Wordsworth's *Lyrical Ballads* and *The Edinburgh Review* appeared simultaneously and it was Jeffrey's intention, from the magazine's inception, to do as much harm to Wordsworth's poetic reputation as possible because he saw inherent in it a perverse democratic tendency which really was a manifestation of culturally and politically regressive tendencies. In Jeffrey there is, in fact, contempt and fear of the lower classes as not only threatening political disruption but of dragging civilised achievement backwards. Jeffrey feared that the adult condition which he believed his society had attained might be lost in the childish state inherent in socially inferior persons. One of his most repeated protests against the Romantics, Wordsworth in particular, was that their poetic diction was both an expression of and invitation to such regression. Infantilism was its essential mode of speech and society was thereby threatened. Wordsworth, linguistically, offended the law of literary progress:

> But what we do maintain is, that much of the most popular poetry in the world owes its celebrity chiefly to the beauty of its diction; and no poetry can be long or generally acceptable, the language of which is coarse, inelegant, or infantine.
> . . . the new poets are just as great borrowers as the old; only that, instead of borrowing from the more popular passages of their illustrious predecessors, they have preferred furnishing themselves from vulgar ballads and plebian nurseries.[61]

Given this principle, it was absolutely necessary for Jeffrey to detach Burns from any possibility of his poetry being infected by Wordsworth. It was not really his Europhobic attitude to Schiller's *The Robbers* but his attitude to Wordsworth in whom he discerned the dangerous source of aesthetic, psychological and political contagion. Thus he wrote:

> . . . the followers and patrons of that new school of poetry, against which we have thought it our duty to neglect no opportunity of testifying. Those gentlemen are outrageous for simplicity; and we beg leave to recommend to them the simplicity of Burns. He has copied the spoken language of passion and affection, with infinitely more fidelity than they have ever done . . . but he has not rejected the help of elevated language and habitual associations, nor debased his composition by an affectation of babyish interjections, and all the puling expletives of an old nursery maid's vocabulary. They may look long enough among his nervous and manly lines, before they find . . . any stuff about dancing daffodils and sister Emmelines . . . with what infinite contempt the powerful mind of Burns would have perused the story of Alice Fell and her duffle coat . . . Let them contrast their own fantastical personages of hysterical schoolmasters and sententious leech-gatherers, with the authentic rustics of Burns's 'The Cotter's Saturday Night', and his inimitable songs . . . Though they will not be reclaimed from their puny affectations by the example of their learned predecessors, they may, perhaps, submit to be admonished by a self-taught and illiterate poet, who drew from Nature far more directly than they can do, and produced something so much like the admired copies of the masters whom they have abjured.[62]

Not the least of the consequences of Jeffrey's obsessive fear and contempt and what he, initially and derogatorily, named as the Lake School, was a blindness, which this edition supplementing recent modern scholarship seeks to rectify, about the actual relationship of Wordsworth to Burns. As Wordsworth wrote in *At the Grave of Burns*, 1803: Seven Years After His Death:

> I mourned with thousands, but as one
> More deeply grieved, for He was gone
> Whose light I hailed when first it shone,
>   And showed my youth
> How Verse may build a princely throne
>   On humble truth.

What enraged Jeffrey was not simply the belief that the aesthetically highest art should engage with the socially lowest class, it was the radical political commitment behind that poetry. Aesthetically, linguistically to deny any possible connection between the English Wordsworth and the Scottish Burns was to deny a radical Scottish political poetry. In the 1790s Burns (especially in the Kilmarnock Edition) and Wordsworth were creatively preoccupied with precisely the same economic and political issues. Hence Wordsworth's retrospective account of *Guilt And Sorrow, or Incidents Upon Salisbury Plain*, is not only, as we shall see, related to Burns's *A Winter's Night*, but could be read as a summary of the Scottish poet's political sympathies and preoccupations at exactly the same period:

> During the latter part of the summer of 1793, having passed a month in the Isle of Wight, in view of the fleet which was then preparing for sea off Portsmouth at the commencement of the war, I left the place with melancholy forebodings. The American war was still fresh in memory. The struggle which was beginning, and which many thought would be brought to a speedy close by the irresistible arms of Great Britain being added to those of the Allies, I was assured in my own mind would be of a long continuance, and productive of distress and misery beyond all possible calculation. This conviction was pressed upon me by having been a witness during a long residence in revolutionary France, of the spirit which prevailed in that country. After leaving the Isle of Wight, I spent two days in wandering on foot over Salisbury Plain . . .
>
> The monuments and traces of antiquity, scattered in abundance over that region, led me unavoidably to compare what we know or guess of those remote times with certain aspects of modern society, and with calamities, principally those consequent upon war, to which, more than other classes of men, the poor are subject.[63]

Jeffrey's example opened the floodgates to a tide of abuse, denigration, innuendo which constantly made the connection between licentious character flaws and radical politics. In a gallantly unsuccessful attempt to stop this, an Edinburgh lawyer, Alexander Peterkin, brought out in 1815 *A Review of the Life of Robert Burns, and of Various Criticisms of his Character and Writings*. As well as mounting a lucid empirical case for the defence, he enlisted Gilbert Burns, James Gray of the Edinburgh High School, Alexander Findlater of the Excise and George Thomson, song publisher, to testify to Burns's actual practices as family man and gauger. In a controlled rage against what he considered a simian caricature of the poet, derived from 'the drivelling fanaticism' of right-wing politics, Peterkin wrote:

> We hold the adversaries of Burns to be aggressors; misguided, we are inclined to think, and ready, we trust, in charity, to renounce their errors on satisfactory proof, that they have been misinformed, or have misconstrued the conduct and writing of Burns. But by their public and voluntary assertions and reflections of an injurious tendency, they have, successively, thrown down the gauntlet to every Scotchman who takes an interest in the honour of his country, of its literature, and of human nature . . . from the system of reitered critical preaching, which has become fashionable in all the recent publications about Burns . . . remaining uncontradicted and unexposed, we are afraid that future biographers, might be misled by longer silence, and adopt declamatory ravings as genuine admitted facts. The most celebrated literary journal of which Britain can boast, and of which, as Scotchmen, we are proud, began the cry; all the would-be moralists in newspapers, magazines, and reviews, have taken it up, and have repeated unauthenticated stories as grave truths: at length these have found a resting-place in large and lasting volumes.[64]

Given the quantity and quality of the vilification of Burns as documented in Peterkin (not least Walter Scott's anonymous, execrable account in *The Quarterly Review*), Burns might have vanished from view perhaps beyond resurrection. What his critics also offered him, moreover, was celebrity on their terms. The bibulous, gustatory junketings which became ritualised in the Burns Supper began in the first decade of the nineteenth century with Jeffrey presiding. Burns was thus both for a period simultaneously radical scapegoat and sentimental national icon. To misquote Edwin Muir, he was the real Bard of a false nation. As the political anxieties calmed, the sentimental Burns of corrupt national imagining could occupy centre stage. He was a multi-purpose deity. The amnesia purging of Burns's radical politics, meant the nation could forget the actual events of the 1790s when not only Burns, but a generation of enlightened Scottish writers, political idealists and academics were driven into internal psychological exile or exile in England, France, Australia and America.

The subsequent Victorian Burns cult was bizarrely multicausal.[65] The anglophobic Professor John Wilson (Christopher North) harangued a crowd of 40,000 at the opening of the Burns mausoleum. The body was exhumed three times in the nineteenth century partly to seek phrenological confirmation of his genius. As with 'Ossian' MacPherson and John Home, Burns was seen as a titanic national poet fit to face down Shakespeare. This compensatory cultural account, partly derived from Scotland's lack of real political power, quite missed the point that Burns had much more of a creative relationship with Wordsworth, Blake, Shelley and the still disgraced Byron, quite absent from his relationship to his bourgeois Scottish apostles. Carlyle, that anti-democratic antithesis of everything the reforming humanism of the Enlightenment stood for, discovered in Burns a Scottish peasant who, like himself, had made good. Indeed, forgetting the bitter marginalised reality of Burns's premature death, Scotland saw in him the archetype of the 'lad o' pairts', the man whose sheer talent brings him to the top. Also, a society locked into the squalid suffering and mortality of the horrors of urban industrialization read Burns as a pseudo-pastoral antidote to everyday reality. As Richard J. Finlay has cogently put it:

> The important point to emphasise here is that . . . for most of the nineteenth century his work was used to give credence to *laissez-faire* liberalism. Burnsian notions of freedom and liberty and the dignity of mankind were ideally suited to Scottish middle-class self-perception and the erection of statues in his honour throughout the country reinforced the belief that talent was God-given and not the preserve of noble birth. The achievement of Burns's rise from lowly birth was something that all Scots could aspire to emulate . . . Burns could be used to promote notions that the dignity of hard work, the perseverance of toil and calm stoicism in the face of adversity were values that were intrinsic to Scottish society.
>
> Burns was praised for inculcating family values. According to Rosebery, Burns 'dwells repeatedly on the primary sacredness of the home and the family, the responsibility of fatherhood and marriage'. The vision of family life in 'The Cotter's Saturday Night' was an antidote to the widespread unease about moral degeneracy in the sprawling slums of urban Scotland. He was likewise praised for making respectable the old Scottish songs which contained language that was crude and vulgar and unfit for genteel company. Burns transformed the baseness of Scottish society into something sublime.[66]

Or as Lord Rosebery put it in his conception of an entirely apolitical poet:

> *A Man's A Man for A' That* is not politics — it is the assertion of the rights of humanity in a sense far wider than politics. It erects all mankind; it is the character of self-respect . . . it cannot be narrowed into politics. Burns's politics are indeed nothing but the occasional overflow of his human sympathy into past history and current events.

Hollow rhetorical misrepresentation disguised as eulogy, Rosebery's straw man cum icon is hoisted free of the contextual political events and ideals that helped forge the democratic anthem. Distortion and abuse of the dead artist's memory is the theme of Patrick Kavanagh's marvellous poem *A Wreath for Tom Moore's Statue*, dealing with the small minded betrayals and corruptions of Irish society to its artists. It catches better than anything what was done to Burns during the nineteenth century:

> They put a wreath upon the dead
> For the dead will wear the cap of any racket,
> The corpse will not put his elbows through his jacket
> Or contradict the words some liar has said.
> The corpse can be fitted out to deceive—
> Fake thoughts, fake love, fake ideal,
> And rogues can sell its guaranteed appeal,
> Guaranteed to work and never come alive.
> The poet would not stay poetical
> And his humility was far from being pliable,
> Voluptuary tomorrow, today ascetical,
> His morning gentleness was the evening's rage.
> But here we give you death, the old reliable
> Whose white blood cannot blot the respectable page.[67]

As well as the particularly Scottish virulent, conformist forces controlling the response to both Burns's reputation and writings, Burns was also a victim, as most eighteenth-century writers of substance, of a pronounced shift of the boundary of sexual acceptability in nineteenth-century Anglo-American culture. *Gulliver's Travels* is expurgated and on such as Smollett and Sterne the library key is firmly turned. Writing about Mozart, in several respects Burns's kindred spirit, Saul Bellow noted that:

The nineteenth century gave us an interregnum of puritanism.
I have often thought that 'repression' and 'inhibition' as de-
scribed by Freud refer to a temporary shift of 'moral' emphasis.
Students of English literature are familiar with this move from
the open sensuality of Fielding and Laurence Sterne to Victor-
ian prudery ('propriety') in Dickens or Trollope. Rousseau's
Confessions or Diderot's *Les Bijoux Indiscrets* confirm this . . .
Seventy years ago, my Russian immigrant uncles, aunts, and
cousins were still speaking freely and colourfully about bodily
functions and things sexual — 'country matters', as Shakespeare
called them in *Hamlet*. (Such lewd double entendres are com-
mon in his plays, specialists in Tudor and Stuart literature have
collected them.) Bawdry has a long pedigree. Conversation in
the courts of Elizabeth and James I was not what we came later
to call 'respectable'.[68]

Of course, Eros may have been driven underground in the Victorian
world. He could not be obliterated. Prostitution and pornography
flourished and Burns himself became a set text for the elbow-
nudging male smoking room.

It is, however, this sort of respectability that, in part, conditions
Matthew Arnold's influential view of Burns. Despite his virtuous
courage in opposing the crass, material philistine Victorian world,
Arnold's ethnic prescriptions for literature were not happy ones.
Having designated, indeed invented, Celtic literature as fey and
ethereal, he saw in Burns's Scottish writing, the very opposite of
this, as often nauseatingly tangible. Thus he wrote in November,
1879:

I have been reading Chaucer a great deal, the early French
poets a great deal, and Burns a great deal. Burns is a beast with
splendid gleams, and the medium in which he lived, Scotch
peasants, Scotch Presbyterianism, and Scotch drink, is repul-
sive. Chaucer on the other hand pleases me more and more, and
his medium is infinitely superior.[69]

This epistolary remark, he fleshed out in *The Study of Poetry*:

We English turn naturally, in Burns, to the poems in our own
language, because we can read them easily; but in real poems we
have not the real Burns.

The real Burns is of course in his Scotch poems. Let us say
that much of his poetry, a poetry dealing perpetually with

Scotch drink, Scotch religion, and Scotch manners, a Scotch-
man's estimate is apt to be personal. A Scotchman is used to
this world of Scotch drink, Scotch religion, and Scotch man-
ners; he has a tenderness for it; he meets its poet half way. In
this tender mood he reads pieces like the 'Holy Fair' or
'Halloween'. But this world of Scotch drink, Scotch religion,
and Scotch manners is against a poet and not for him, when it is
not a partial countryman who reads him; for in itself it is not a
beautiful world, and no one can deny that it is of advantage to a
poet to deal with a beautiful world. Burns's world of Scotch
drink, Scotch religion, and Scotch manners, is often a harsh,
a sordid, a repulsive world; even the world of his 'The Cotter's
Saturday Night' is not a beautiful world. No doubt a poet's
criticism of life may have such truth or power that it triumphs
over its world and delights us.[70]

In one respect Arnold simply represents the consequences of the
insistent Scottish claims for exclusive possession of Burns. Arnold,
with a vengeance, locates him in a brutally circumscribed ethnic
world. In another respect, Arnold is quite wildly wrong. He assumes
Burns as a naïve realist, almost a poetic pig in clover in a Scottish
sty, whereas Burns was a political satirist of the very elements,
especially Hebraic spiritual and material hypocrisy, which Arnold
himself attacks. Worse, he disconnects Burns, partly linguistically,
from the radical *British* fraternity of the 1790s to which he belongs.
Burns's accent and examples are Scottish; his themes and insights
are comparable to Blake. Despite Edward Dowden's *The French
Revolution and English Literature* (1897) which reintegrates Burns
with his English peers, Arnold's authority caused damage so severe
that elements of it still exist. It may indeed have influenced the even
more authoritative figure of T.S. Eliot, that provincial American
who so yearned for Arnoldian metropolitan status, so that he saw in
Burns the last flare-up of a subsequently redundant Scottish tradi-
tion, rather than a poet who used that tradition to write some of the
greatest radical poetry of the late eighteenth century. Given of
course, Eliot's monarchical, High Anglican tendencies, it was not
in his interest to see in the Scottish literary tradition such virile,
dissident flexibility.[71]

By the latter part of the nineteenth century and with the em-
bryonic stirring of Modernism, the roots of the later self-defined
Scottish Renaissance Movement, a crucial problem for Scottish
creative writers was whether Burns could be exhumed as a creative
force from under the growing mountains of verbiage, false history

and commercial artefacts. The initial movement in this direction came from R.L. Stevenson with his acutely attuned antennae both to contemporary world literature and to the Scottish tradition. Along with that went a peculiar, even psychic, identification with Robert Fergusson and associated fellow-feeling with Burns. He also grasped the degree to which Burns was indebted to Fergusson. Hence his haunted, near death retrospective of Edinburgh's 'three Robins':

> Burns alone has been just to his promise: follow Burns, he knew best, he knew whence he drew fire — from the poor, white-faced, drunken, vicious boy that raved himself to death in the Edinburgh madhouse. Surely there is more to be gleaned about Fergusson, and surely it is high time the task was set about . . . We are three Robins who have touched the Scots lyre this last century. Well the one is the world's, he did it, he came off, he is for ever: but I and the other — ah! What bonds we have — born in the same city: both sickly, both pestered one nearly to madness, one to the madhouse with a damnatory creed . . . and the old Robin, who was before Burns and the flood, died in his acute, painful youth and left the models of the great things that were to come . . . you will never know, nor will any man, · how deep this feeling is; I believe Fergusson lives in me.[72]

Despite the genuine intensity of this feeling, Stevenson felt the task of resurrection of Fergusson and Burns beyond him. The Calvinist and genteel claustrophobia of Edinburgh which he believed had destroyed his namesake was something, with Joycean acumen, from which he fled into ever geographically further exile. Before doing so, however, he diagnosed in his earliest journalistic writings the remarkably over-inflated literary culture that infected Victorian Scotland in general and Burns's false reputation in particular. Rather than Arnold's vision of the Scots retreating north of the Tweed, clutching to their bosoms their shibboleth poet, Stevenson, with much more literary sociological realism, saw the Scots as enormously successful commercial exporters and exploiters of a pseudo-national literary tradition. While the more mature Stevenson would not have adhered to these disparaging remarks about Burns's vernacular poetry, his sense of national literary narcissism did not abate:

> It is somewhat too much the fashion to pat Scotch literature on the back. Inhabitants of South Britain are pleased to commend

verses, which, short of a miraculous gift of tongues, it is morally impossible they should comprehend. It may interest these persons to learn that Burns wrote a most difficult and crude patois . . . there are not so very many people alive in Scotland who could read his works without a furtive reference to the margin . . . any Englishman need not be ashamed to confess he can make nothing out of the vernacular poems except a raucous gibberish — which is the honest belief of the present reviewer, is about the measure of his achievement. It is partly to this that we must attribute the exaggerated favour of 'The Cotter's Saturday Night', by no means one of his best poems, but one of the most easily understood . . .

But even the least intelligent condescension of the South Briton is better than the hysterical praise with which Mr Grant Wilson bedaubs his native literature . . . Wilson thinks that Burns spoke 'with too much extravagance' when he called *The Gentle Shepherd* 'the most glorious poem ever written'. . . this barbarous gallimaufry or hotch-potch of indiscriminate laudation does not come fairly to the boil, until we hear that Falconer's 'Shipwreck' placed its author 'in the front rank of Scottish poets' . . . Was there ever such an irreverent hurly-burly of names, such a profane morris-dance of great men and little poetasters? Whaur's Wullie Shakespeare noo?[73]

At the end of this assault on the unfortunate James Grant Wilson, we also find this remark on Burns:

A point of curiosity is the rest of Burns's *Ode* about *Washington*, some lines of which appear already in his Correspondence. It is a very poor performance, but interesting as another testimony to the profound sympathy of Burns for all democratic movements. Why does Mr. Wilson tell us no more about the history of the piece.[74]

Or, indeed, why did Stevenson, given his brilliantly innovative essay on Walt Whitman in *Familiar Studies of Men and Books*, not himself write about the democratic Burns. Partly perhaps because when talking about Scottish subjects he was infected by a sort of internalized Calvinism so that the empathy he could extend to Villon and Baudelaire (he was preoccupied with both these anarchic French spirits) could not be replicated for Burns who, like Hazlitt, he declared a sexually out-of-bounds bounder.[75]

A second wave was to follow Stevenson in the wake of the First

World War. The British imperial economic and political project was damaged beyond repair, as correctly interpreted by the tiny Scottish avant garde, and it was felt that Scotland needed to be reconnected to its roots. Obstacles to this were the travesty of Celticism present in the sentimental tartanisation of the nation. 'Out of the Celtic twilight', as MacDiarmid wrote, 'and into the Gaelic sun'. Another cultural, political phenomenon as destructive to what the avant garde considered vital to a resurrected Scotland was the Burns phenomenon now incorporated into The Burns Federation. Between the avant garde and the established Burnsians there was no co-operation and, indeed, relations were soon to turn to active hostility. Catherine Carswell's honest, passionate biography of Burns was met with a bullet sent through the post to her. Written from her Lawrentian influenced position of a reintegrative instinctual and erotic vision, such open discussion of the poet's sexual nature was unacceptable. By far the greatest of all Burns's scholars the American John De Lancey Ferguson, as his correspondence with Mrs Carswell shows, was met not with open hostility but a marked lack of co-operation from the Federation regarding his magisterial edition of the poet's letters. His subsequent biography, the fine *The Pride and the Passion*, was met with, as he ruefully put it, 'passionate apathy'. Presbyterian Tory-Unionism would not release its death grip on a poet to whom, unlike Sir Walter Scott, it had absolutely no claim. Edwin Muir, while not personally empathetic to Burns as a poet, concisely summed up what he perceived as an end-game for Burns and Scotland. The occasion for Muir's observations was the unveiling of a new statue to Burns with that bastion of 'socialism', Ramsay McDonald, making the oration:

> The symbolism implicit in this scene is quite casual and involuntary. The churchyard could hold only a certain number of people; the 'platform party' (in Scotland one is always hitting against platform parties) was naturally chosen from the more well-to-do admirers of the poet: landlords, baronets, and officers in the British army. Objectively one can see that, Scotland being what it is, a ceremony in honour of its greatest poet should just take this form and no other. But at the same time one is driven to ask what can have happened to Burns since his death to make him now the implicit property of the middle and upper classes, when he was the property of the poor man at the beginning. This change may be briefly described by saying that Holy Willie, after being the poet's butt, has now become the keeper of his memory . . .

Burns set the world in a roar of laughing at the people who now unveil statuary in his honour. Why is it that they are so kind to his kail and potatoes?

One reason for this is that the figure of Burns has become quite vague, and that the vaguer he becomes the more universally he pleases his countrymen. His words no longer mean anything.[76]

Muir then turns to an exemplary example of this vagueness by dealing with MacDonald's eulogy to Burns. At this time Scottish society was in a state of political unrest, although somewhat different from the 1790s. There existed, however, a similar pattern of economic breakdown, profiteering and war weariness though the revolutionary cloud on the horizon was Russia, not France. Muir quotes MacDonald's maunderings on Burns as revolutionary whereby 'Burns's revolution, was a revolution in soul, a revolution in being, a revolution in manliness, a revolution in humanity'. That is, of course, a revolution whereby everything except economic power and social justice are effectively changed. With his customary lucidity, Muir pointed out how the events of the darkening 1930s cast their shadow on the then contemporary interpretations of the 1790s:

I think I have said enough to show that Burns has been ostentatiously but securely swallowed and digested by Holy Willie during the century and a bit since his death. Burns was not the revolutionist who Mr. MacDonald makes him out to be, but he was an honest writer. And though he was a revolutionist, he showed his sympathy with the French Revolution in a quite practical way, without stopping to consider whether it was a mere revolution in circumstance or a revolution in soul. We cannot imagine the Burns whose statue Mr. MacDonald unveiled sending arms even to the constitutional government of Spain against the expressed wishes of the established order, as the living Burns did to the leaders of the French revolution against a similar prohibition. Something has happened to him since his death, and it is what happens to all writers after their death, no matter what they have written. It may not be true that all writers reflect the economic ideology of the society in which they live — I do not think it is — but it does seem to be true that their writings are finally and in the long run made to reflect that ideology, by a process of elimination and transformation, until the most influential classes in society can finally put their seal

on the result. This necessity for social elimination and trans-
formation probably accounts for Mr. MacDonald's sharply
condemnatory but vague references to Burns's recent biogra-
phers (he could only have meant Mrs. Catherine Carswell's
plain-spoken and entirely sympathetic *Life*). For an honest
biography helps to destroy the imposed image and to undo
careful work of social transformation.[77]

Muir, of course, was not to know that in 1993, Tony Blair, then
Shadow Home Secretary, toasted the 'Immortal Memory' in the
Edinburgh Central constituency (we are reliably informed by a still
enraged Old Labour source) without mentioning Burns at all.

One would have anticipated that Hugh MacDiarmid, bourgeois
Scotland's worst nightmare, with his celebration of John Maclean,
Lenin and his intended book on Red Clydeside would have been
prolix on the parallels between the 1790s and 1930s. With his early
involvement in the Independent Labour Party (I.L.P.), he was,
overtly and expansively, a far more politically committed writer
than Muir. Even so, he rarely mentions Scottish culture's constant,
mendacious denial of Burns as a democratic revolutionary. He was,
however, constantly caustic about the literary implications of the
Burns cult and how it had diverted attention not only from Burns's
poetry but poetry *per se* into a morass of biographical, antiquarian
trivia. As he wrote:

> Those who love poetry best today, and understand best its
> nature and function, have least to say of Burns as poet. To the
> quest for increased facilities of human self-expression —to the
> evolution of the art of poetry— Burns contributes nothing. It is
> almost exclusively in non-literary circles, amongst people who
> seldom read poetry of any kind, that Burns is still enthusias-
> tically acclaimed as a great poet. . . . Burns the satirist is
> another matter. And the Burns of the verses that are not to
> be found in the expurgated editions —those little lewd revela-
> tions which enable us to discern in him (sed longe intervallo) a
> forerunner of James Joyce.[78]

Burns, for MacDiarmid, had a Janus-face. He saw him, by analogy
with Joyce, as a proto-modernist capable of literary innovation and
the changing of human consciousness. But he also saw him as a
redundant poet not entirely irresponsible for the sterile cult created
in his name. As MacDiarmid grew older, culminating in his dreadful
polemic, *Burns Today and Tomorrow* (1958), the latter view pre-

vailed. Initially, however, he thought that he could not only co-opt Burns but the Burns Federation into his programme for his version of radical, revolutionary change. Hence the sestet of this appalling sonnet *To Duncan McNaught, LLD., J.P., President of the Burns Federation*, written in 1923:

> Burns International! The mighty cry
> Prophetic of eventual brotherhood
> Rings still, imperative to be fulfilled.
> M'Naught, who follows you must surely try
> To take his stand, where living, Burns had stood
> Nor save on this foundation can he build.[79]

This grimly bad version of third-rate post-Miltonic Wordsworth was addressed to Dr McNaught who had distinguished himself by declaring that, 'After Burns became a Government official he was a shorn Samson whose duty was to be "silent and obey"; and his daily realisation of his dependant position dampened his energies and restrained the free action of his powers'. This was not propitious and led MacDiarmid to remark that, 'The same type of mind that quite unjustly vilified Burns is now most busily engaged in quite unnecessarily white-washing him'. By 1934, however, he had lost hope of the Burns Federation as a revolutionary agent for change, and indeed increasingly saw it as the antithesis of everything Burns stood for and what Scotland had been and should become:

> What an organization the World Federation of Burns Clubs could have been — could even yet become — if it were animated with the true spirit of Burns and fulfilling a programme based on his essential motives applied to crucial contemporary issues as he applied them while he was living to the crucial issues of his own time and generation! What a true Scottish Internationale that would be —what a culmination and crown of Scotland's role in history, the role that has carried Scotsmen to every country in the world and given them radical leadership every-where they went![80]

What obsessed MacDiarmid was not simply the need to galvanise his retarded nation but to put it at the very vanguard of what he perceived as a quantum, science-driven evolution in human con-sciousness. What he was faced with was an actual situation where the global network of Burns Clubs provided locations for the transmission, not of innovative consciousness, but of the worst aspects of sentimental banality. Within Scotland, things were even worse:

> It is an organisation designed to prevent any further renais-
> sance of the Scottish spirit such as he himself encompassed, and
> in his name it treats all who would attempt to renew his spirit
> and carry on his work on the magnificent basis he provided as
> he himself was treated in his own day — with obloquy and
> financial hardship and all the dastardly wiles of suave Angli-
> cized time servers . . .
>
> It has produced mountains of rubbish about him — to
> effectively bury the dynamic spirit — but not a single good
> critical study . . .
>
> It has failed . . . to get Burns or Scottish literature or the
> Scottish language to which Burns courageously and rightly and
> triumphantly reverted from English, taught in Scottish schools.
>
> Its gross betrayal of the Scots language — its role as a lying
> agent of the Anglicizing process Burns repudiated — was well
> seen in its failure to support the great new Scots dictionaries.
>
> . . . the need to follow his lead at long last is today a thousand
> times greater than when he gave it.
>
> We can — if we will . . . We can still affirm the fearless
> radical spirit of the true Scotland. We can even yet throw off the
> yoke of all the canting humbug in our midst. We can rise and
> quit ourselves like men and make Scotland worthy to have had a
> Burns — and conscious of it; and we can communicate that
> consciousness powerfully to the ends of the earth.
>
> . . . if we don't, if we won't, the Burns cult will remain a
> monstrous monument to the triumph of his enemies.[81]

What appears about this time in MacDiarmid's poetry is the image of Burns as a latter day Christ crucified by his cultish followers. This is best known from *A Drunk Man Looks at the Thistle*. Less well known is this disturbing English sonnet, *They Know Not What They Do*:

> Burns in Elysium once every year
> Ceases from intercourse and turns aside
> Shorn for a day of all his rightful pride,
> Wounded by those whom yet he holds most dear.
> Chaucer he leaves, and Marlowe, and Shakespeare,
> Milton and Wordsworth —and he turns to hide
> His privy shame that will not be denied,

And pay his annual penalty of fear.
But Christ comes to him there and takes his arm.
'My followers too,' He says, 'are false as thine,
True to themselves and ignorant of Me,
Grieve not thy fame seems so compact of harm;
Star of the Sot, Staff of the Philistine
—Truth goes from Calvary to Calvary!'[82]

MacDiarmid saw Burns as an incomplete revolutionary when com-
pared to Byron, Baudelaire and (by implication) MacDiarmid
himself:

He was intimidated in the most insidious fashion by the existing
order of things . . . The pity about Burns is that he never got
beyond good and evil. If he had been able to kick the traces over
completely his potential genius might have been liberated —as
was Gaugin's for instance, when he ceased to be a stockbroker
and reverted to savagery. Burns went in the opposite direction
—from genius to 'gauger'.[83]

This concept of an early Modernist, definably post-Nietzschean
Burns, MacDiarmid may have derived from a little known poem by
Swinburne (a poet he admired), *Burns: An Ode* (1896):

And Calvin, night's prophetic bird,
Out of his home in hell was heard
Shrieking; and all the fens were stirred
    Whence plague is bred;
Can God endure the scoffer's word?
    But God was dead.[84]

Not only does the poem personify Burns within terms of late
nineteenth-century atheism and, perhaps expectedly, finds him
inferior to Chaucer, but also, quite unexpectedly, it sees him as
inferior to Dunbar:

But Chaucer's daisy shines a star
Above his ploughshare's reach to mar,
And mightier vision gave Dunbar
    More strenuous wing
To hear around all sins that are
    Hell dance and sing.

Ironically, MacDiarmid's slogan 'Not Burns, but Dunbar' may have been derived from an English source. What is certain, however, is that it was not Burns but Byron whom he saw as the quintessence of Scottish literary and associated virtues:

> Byron will come to his own yet in his own country, however. Scotland is shedding its super-imposed and unnatural religiosity. Unlike English literature Scottish literature remains amoral — full of illimitable potentialities, unexplored, let alone unexhausted, in the Spenglerian sense. And Byron was beyond all else a Scottish poet — the most nationally typical of Scottish poets, not excluding Burns. He answers — not to the stock conceptions, the grotesque Anglo-Scottish Kailyard travesty, of Scottish psychology — but to all the realities of our dark, difficult, unequal and inconsistent national temper.[85]

Implicit in MacDiarmid's concept of Byron as the essential Scottish writer, is the notion that he is also definably the pure, uncompromised revolutionary spirit. This is hardly borne out by either history or biography. Was the mine-owning self-dramatising aristocrat ever under the cosh in the way Burns was? Is individual nihilism of the Byron, Baudelaire variety the necessary prelude to utopian change? MacDiarmid seems not to have read Dostoevsky deeply enough to have understood that Russian's genius in tracing the demonically possessed connection between such nihilism and social catastrophe. In fact, MacDiarmid, as hierarchically preoccupied as Ezra Pound, was, at best, antipathetic to the universal democratic revolution of the late eighteenth century.[86] His revolution was predicated on a quantum leap in human consciousness to be made by a scientifically attuned, necessarily tiny *avant garde*. Iain Crichton Smith thought that this position destroyed him as a poet, committing his later poetry to versified, programmatic propaganda for his science-manual saturated version of beyond the human.[87] That is why he loathed Burns's *A Man's A Man*, seeing in it not a profound statement of fraternity but only crassly self-indulgent sentimentality. According to MacDiarmid, the real Scottish tradition, manifest in Byron, would return Scots to their hard, pristine selves, purged of the cloying psychological excesses and political corruptions of an imposed, Anglicised identity.

The failure to claim Byron for Scottish literature — the deference paid to English standards of taste in that and other 'Scottish' anthologies — is a characteristic of the Anglicisation

of Scotland. All the natural perspectives of Scottish literature
are arbitrarily manipulated in the light of entirely false inter-
pretations of Scottish character. The type of people who are
constrained to whitewash Burns are naturally anxious to dis-
avow Byron — whom it would be impossible to 'puritanise' . . .
He stands outwith the English literary tradition altogether. He
is alien to it and not to be assimilated. English literature . . . has
developed moral limitations — a quality of censorship which
renders it impossible to naturalise certain attitudes of life,
certain tendencies in expression . . .[88]

MacDiarmid's capacity for intellectual absolutism, albeit frequently
self-contradictory, has the ideological danger inherent in literary
criticism of thesis-driven misreading. There is no little irony in the
fact that it is an Englishman, W.H. Auden, who made a much more
convincing distinction between Burns and Byron and, in so doing,
makes one of the most acute critical remarks about the essence of
Burns's genius:

At the beginning of the Romantic age stand two writers of
Light Verse who were also major poets, Burns and Byron, one a
peasant the other an aristocrat. The former came from a
Scottish parish which, whatever its faults of hypocrisy and
petty religious tyranny, was a genuine community where the
popular tradition in poetry had never been lost. In consequence
Burns was able to write directly and easily about all aspects of
life, the most serious as well as the most trivial. He is the last
poet of whom this can be said. Byron, on the other hand, is the
first writer of Light Verse in the modern sense. His success lasts
as long as he takes nothing very serious; the moment he tried to
be profound and 'poetic' he fails. However much they tried to
reject each other, he was a member of 'Society', and his poetry
is the result of his membership. If he cannot be poetic, it is
because smart society is not poetic.[89]

MacDiarmid's nationalist essentialism offers a heady, narcissistic
appeal. If, however, history should be written about relationships
between states not about mythically essential nations, literary his-
tory has constantly to concern itself with the inherent, ongoing
dialogue between literatures. This is why Burns and the 1790s have
been so misunderstood. Jeffrey wanted all relationships between
Burns and the English Romantics, especially Wordsworth, termi-
nated because the Scots were naturally loyal. MacDiarmid inverts

the terms of the equation, the Scots are innate radicals and the English inherent constitutionalists, but he too achieves the same end in divorcing Scottish and English writing. This, particularly, in the 1790s is nonsense. Albeit in differently accented voices, Blake and Burns are deeply compatible, just as Cowper and Burns are. That savagely funny, neglected English satirist and friend of James Perry of *The Morning Chronicle*, Professor Richard Porson, produced polemics in a Scots-styled stanza that could, to the untrained eye, be easily mistaken for Burns. Wordsworth in particular, but almost all English radical writers of that decade, knew exactly what politics were inherent in Burns's poetry. Indeed they were influenced by his example as man and poet. Equally, Burns along with the innate strengths of his native vernacular and the profound influence of Fergusson in particular, creatively plundered Shakespeare, Milton, the Tory Augustans, the Eighteenth-century Novel, and his sentimental English and Irish (Goldsmith) contemporaries to create a unique synthesis. As Thomas Preston has notably remarked in viewing Burns through the highly rewarding perspective of Bakhtin:

> Burns's poetry offers a gold mine of contestation among Scottish, English, classic, European, and non-European matters — a wondrous intertextuality of quotations, traditions, dictions, idioms, dialects, languages, meanings. His texts do not produce, I suggest, the agonistic of conflicted tongues heard by Thomas Crawford nor the Smollettian dialect of synthesized literary traditions sought by Carol McGuirk. Instead they orchestrate a polyphony of voices contesting languages, literary traditions, and cultures. Burns's poetic project is dialogical through and through, internally within and between poems and externally within and between Scottish and other cultures. It scripts a future Scottish national culture that is inherently diverse — an imagined community whose lack of uniformity would appal Tobias Smollett, whose last and dying years, despite his anglicizing in aid of a sublated British culture, nevertheless were spent, perhaps fittingly, outside of Britain. Kenneth Simpson has written the most persuasively, I think, of Burns's varying roles and poses, a poetic strategy he considers a reflection of the protean eighteenth-century Scot undergoing the dissociation of sensibility caused by the Union. Burns, he thinks, 'became trapped behind the roles he so readily created'. I would suggest instead that these roles register the rich profusion of personal and cultural possibilities, opportunities,

and identities made available to both individuals and Scottish society by the dialogic — indeed postmodern — world Burns's poetic project scripts. This paper serves merely to suggest the many possibilities for exploration that Burns's dialogism offers. Alan Bold misleadingly argues that Burns 'looked back in ecstasy and did not take the future of Scotland into account'. It can be argued that dominant Scottish discourse since the Union has instead looked back in ecstasy while enacting the literati's rather than Burns's implied national script, and this possibility may cause some subconscious guilt that the 'great tartan monster' and the annual Burns Supper orgies seek to absolve. If this is so, tartanry and toasts to the 'Immortal Memory' yet also serve to keep alive the possibility of attending to Burns's script.[90]

Preston's essay is a deeply perceptive and provocative argument in favour of Burns creating a sort of healthily open, dialogically en-ergised Scottish literature which was in opposition to the integration of Scottish writing into the standardised language, envisaged by such as the Irishman Thomas Sheridan and advocated by Edmund Burke and James Boswell, of the Anglo-British empire. Burns knew and loathed the power and accent of the Scots who served that imperium: 'Thou Eunuch of language—Thou Englishman who was never south of the Tweed—Thou servile echo of fashionable barbarisms'. Henry Dundas would be the prime example of that category though he, according to a jealous Boswell, had hardly the capacity to put pen to paper. Preston's account requires only the modification that the relationship with English literature in the 1790s was not only dia-logical but collusive in that these writers were seeking a republican reorientation of the British state through the resurrected democratic nationalism of its English, Scottish, Irish parts. The failure of this ambition is, as we shall see, tragically embodied in *Ode for General Washington's Birthday*. Though, as Preston notes, two hundred years later we seem to be entering similar territory. It is the primary impulse behind this edition, then, to make Burns available to a contemporary Scottish consciousness that is hopefully more openly responsive to the man, his values and, above all, his poetry than has largely been the case over the last two centuries.

Notes

1 See John Strawhorn, 'Farming in 18th-century Ayrshire', in *Collections of the Ayrshire Archeological and Natural History Society*, 2nd Series, III (1955), pp. 136–73.

2 See J. De Lancey Ferguson *The Pride and the Passion* (New York: Oxford University Press, 1939), p. 114.

3 See John Brewer, *The Sinews of Power: War, Money and the English State 1688–1783* (London: Routledge, 1989), pp. 101–14.

4 Roy Porter, *The Pelican Social History of Britain: English Society in the Eighteenth Century* (London: Penguin, 1982), p. 30.

5 Robert Morrison, 'Red De Quincey', *The Wordsworth Circle*, Vol. 28, 1998, pp. 131–6.

6 Donald Low, *Robert Burns: The Critical Heritage* (London: Routledge, 1974), pp. 421–30.

7 *Ibid.*, p. 429.

8 James Mackay, *RB: A Biography of Robert Burns* (Edinburgh Mainstream, 1992), p. 519.

9 David Cannadine, 'The Making of the British Upper Class' in *Aspects of Aristocracy* (London: Penguin, 1994), pp. 9–36.

10 John Keane, *Tom Paine: A Political Life* (London: Bloomsbury, 1995), p. 54.

11 See Stephen C. Behrendt, *Romanticism, Radicalism and the Press* (University of Nebraska, 1997), p. 14.

12 Fintan O'Toole, *A Traitor's Kiss: The Life of Richard Brinsley Sheridan* (London: Granta, 1997), pp. 31–2.

13 J.R. Dinwiddy, 'Conceptions of Revolution in the English Radicalism of the 1790s' in *Radicalism and Reform in Britain, 1780–1850*, ed. H.T. Dickinson, (London: The Hambledon Press, 1992,) p. 169.

14 John Trenchard and Thomas Gordon, 'Cato's Letters' in *The English Libertarian Heritage*, ed. David L. Jacobson (San Francisco: Fox & Wilkes, 1994), p. 42.

15 *Ibid.* pp. 53–4.

16 *Ibid.* p. 63.

17 Michael Durey, *Transatlantic Radicals and the Early American Republic* (University of Kansas, 1997), pp. 50–79. *The Life and Letters of Alexander Wilson*, ed. Clark Hunter (Philadelphia, American Philosophical Society, 1983).

18 John Thelwall, *The Politics of English Jacobinism*, ed. Gregory Claeys (Pennsylvania State U.P., 1995), p. 40.

19 See Francis Hutcheson, *Short Introduction*, 5th edn (Philadelphia, 1799), pp. 289–92.

20 Richard Rorty, 'Afterword: Pragmatism, Pluralism and Postmodernism' in *Philosophy and Social Hope* (London: Penguin, 1999), p. 265.

21 Cynthia Ozick, 'From the *Book of Job*', (New York: Vintage Spiritual Classics, 1998), pp. xx–xxi.

22 *Love and Liberty*, ed. K.G. Simpson (Edinburgh: Tuckwell Press, 1997), p. 179.

23 Edwin Muir, 'Robert Burns' in *Edwin Muir: Uncollected Scottish Criticism*, ed. Andrew Noble (London/New York, 1982), p. 183.

24 Roger Fechner, 'Burns and American Liberty' in *Love and Liberty*, p. 278.

25 E.W. McFarlane, *Ireland and Scotland in the Age of Revolution* (Edinburgh University Press, 1994), p. 136.

26 *The Critical Heritage*, p. 16.

27 Henry Mackenzie, 'Three Scottish Poets' in *The Anecdotes and Egotisms of Henry Mackenzie*, ed. H.W. Thompson (Oxford University Press, 1927), pp. 150–2.

28 *Literature and Literati: The Literary Correspondence and Notebooks of Henry Mackenzie*, Vol. 2, 'Letters 1766–1827', ed. Horst W. Drescher, (Frankfurt, 1989), p. 358.

29 *Ibid.*, p. 358.

30 *Ibid.*, p. 172.

31 *Ibid.*, p. 74.

32 *Ibid.*, p. 175.

33 *Ibid.*, p. 178.

34 T.M. Devine, *The Scottish Nation 1700–2000* (London: The Penguin Press, 1999), p. 215.

35 Edinburgh University Library, Laing Collection, II, folio 269. Two other Heron letters in folio 500–501.

36 Robert Heron, *A Memoir of the Life of the Late Robert Burns* (Edinburgh, 1797). Reprinted in Hans Hecht, *Robert Burns: The Man and His Work* (London: William Hodge & Co., 1936), pp. 335–6.

37 *Ibid.*, p. 326.

38 *Ibid.*, pp. 338–9.

39 *Ibid.*, pp. 344–5.

40 Ian Hamilton, 'The Frailties of Robert Burns' in *Keepers of the Flame: Literary Estates and the Rise of Biography* (Boston/London: Faber & Faber, 1992), p. 101.

41 *A Memoir of the Life of Robert Burns*, p. 346.

42 Edinburgh University Library, Laing Collection, III, folio 586.

43 'The Frailties of Robert Burns', p. 93.

44 Quoted in R.D. Thornton, *James Currie: The Entire Stranger & Robert Burns* (Edinburgh: Oliver & Boyd, 1963), p. 358.

45 'The Frailties of Robert Burns', p. 98.

46 'The Frailties of Robert Burns', p. 101.

47 Low, *The Critical Heritage*, p. 431.

48 In 1793, Currie had written a Francophile, abrasively anti-Pitt pamphlet under the pseudonym, 'Jasper Wilson'. In consequence he considered American exile and lived in terror of disclosure. See Chapter 9, 'Dissenter' in Thornton's *The Entire Stranger*.

49 'The Frailties of Robert Burns', p. 97.

50 Low, *The Critical Heritage*, p. 152.

51 *Ibid.*, p. 144.

52 Andrew Noble, 'Versions of Scottish Pastoral' in *Order in Space and Society: Architectural Form and Its Context in the Scottish Englightenment*, ed. Thomas Marcus (Edinburgh: Mainstream, 1982), pp. 288–91.

53 Low, *Critical Heritage*, p. 194.

54 *Ibid.*, pp. 186–7.

55 *Ibid.*, p. 181.

56 *Ibid.*, p. 182.

57 *Ibid.*, p. 183.

58 *Ibid.*, p. 183.

59 *Ibid.*, pp. 183–4.

60 *Ibid.*, p. 181.

61 *Ibid.*, p. 180.

62 *Ibid.*, p. 195.

63 While this, revealingly, was not published till 1842 it was written between 1793 and 1794. This is the Advertisement to *Guilt and Sorrow or Incidents Upon Salisbury Plain. Poetical Works of Wordsworth* (Oxford University Press, 1956), pp. 18–19.

64 *The life and Works of Robert Burns*, as originally ed. by James Currie, to which is prefixed a review of its life of Burns and of various criticisms of his character and writings (Edinburgh: Macredie, Skelly and Muckersy, 1815), p. vii.

65 Andrew Noble, 'Burns and Scottish Nationalism', in *Burns Now* (Edinburgh: Canongate Academic, 1994), pp. 167–92.

66 'The Burns Cult and Scottish Identity in the Nineteenth and Twentieth Centuries' in *Love and Liberty*, p. 72.

67 *Patrick Kavanagh: Selected Poems* (London: Penguin, 1996) pp. 70–1. While Moore was not of Burns's militant spirit we are now also realising the degree to which his songs are coded expressions of the bloodier Irish political turmoil of the 1790s and arguably, an embryonic assertion of new national forces. See Matthew Campbell 'Thomas Moore's Wild Song: The 1821 Irish Melodies'. *Bullán*, Vol. v. No. 2, pp. 83–104.

68 Saul Bellow, 'Mozart: An Overture' in *It All Adds Up* (London, Secker and Warburg, 1994), pp. 9–10.

69 Matthew Arnold, Letter of November 1879, quoted in *Selected Poems and Prose*, ed. Miriam Allott (London: Everyman, 1991), p. 295.

70 *Ibid.*, 262–3.

71 T.S. Eliot, 'Was there a Scottish Literature?', *The Athenaeum*, No. 4657, 1st Aug. 1919, pp. 680–1.

72 Letter 2315, *The Letters of Robert Louis Stevenson*, Vol. 7, ed. Booth and Mehew (Yale University Press, 1995). p. 110.

73 R.L. Stevenson 'Review of *The Poets and Poetry of Scotland*', ed. James Grant Wilson, *The Academy*, 12 Feb., 1876, p. 30.

74 *Ibid.*, p. 31.

75 For Stevenson's profound ambivalence to Burns see Letter 635, Vol. 1, *The Letters of Robert Louis Stevenson*. In the same volume (Letter 424) there is a project for not only a book about Ramsay, Fergusson and Burns, but a book that would use Villon as context. He never really synthesised his Scottish roots with his Francophilia.

76 Edwin Muir, 'Burns and Holy Willie' in *Edwin Muir: Uncollected Scottish Criticism* (London/New York: Vision, 1982), pp. 189–90.

77 *Ibid.*, pp. 191–2.

78 'Burns and Baudelaire' in *Hugh MacDiarmid: The Raucle Tongue*, ed. Calder, Murray, Riach (Manchester: Carcanet, 1996), p. 69.

79 *The Complete Poems of Hugh MacDiarmid*, Vol. 2, ed. Grieve and Aitken (London: Penguin, 1985), p. 1224.

80 'The Burns Cult', in *Hugh MacDiarmid: Selected Prose*, ed. Riach (Manchester: Carcanet, 1992), p. 82.

81 *Ibid.*, p. 84. MacDiarmid's most sustained polemic against the Burns Federation and Cult can be found in *Burns Today and Tomorrow* (Edinburgh: Castle Wynd Printers Ltd, 1959).

82 *The Complete Poems of Hugh MacDiarmid*, Vol. 1, pp. 693–4. This can be compared to the much more in your face 'Your Immortal Memory, Burns!', pp. 77–9.

83 'Burns and Baudelaire', pp. 70–1.

84 'Robert Burns' in *A Channel Passage, and Other Poems* (London, 1904).

85 'The Neglect of Byron' in *The Raucle Tongue*, Vol. 1, p. 77.

86 Some qualification for this is to be found in *Burns Today and Tomorrow* where MacDiarmid does address the politics of the 1790s and compares the French and Russian Revolutions, pp. 105–10.

87 Iain Crichton Smith, 'The Golden Lyric' in *Towards the Human* (Edinburgh: Macdonald, 1986), pp. 176–91.

88 'The Neglect of Byron', p. 76.

89 W.H. Auden, 'Light Verse' in *The English Auden: Poems, Essays and Dramatic Writings 1927–1939* (London: Faber & Faber, 1977), p. 367.

90 'Contrary Scriptings: Implied National Narratives in Burns and Smollett' in *Love and Liberty*, p. 213.

Editorial Policy and Practice

As we have seen in our Introduction, nineteenth-century editors were seriously remiss, with varied degrees of ignorance and prejudice, in providing a proper context for the poems and the politically fractious culture out of which they emerged. One could simply not expect any knowledgeable enthusiasm for a revolutionary, democratic Burns given the victory of the British Old Regime during the ideological war of the 1790s, so complete was it that it virtually wiped the radical struggle from national memory. Towards the end of the century, the Henley–Henderson edition of 1896 brought Burns editorship to a nadir by combining Henley's rampant right-wing jingoism with a deliberate policy of 'correcting' the poet's spelling, punctuation and stresses according to modern standards. Burns's distinctive habit of spelling place and proper names in capitals, italicising idioms and ironies and his use of long dashes are virtually all purged from their edition. This constant, careless editorial meddling seriously disrupts the intelligible rhythm of the poems by an accelerated 'streamlining' of the reading process so that the poet's voice is significantly diminished.

In the twentieth century we had the heroic scholarship of the American, Professor J. De Lancey Ferguson, with his edition of the letters. This, as his correspondence with Catherine Carswell shows,[1] was achieved with, at best, the non-cooperation of the then Scottish Burns establishment. Despite his great scholarly virtues, De Lancey Ferguson was not sufficiently equipped in either the political history of ideas or comparative Romantic scholarship to provide the letters and their recipients with the literary and political context needed to bring Burns into fuller focus, although he did begin down this road with his last essay, the largely unknown but brilliant critique on previous editorship, *They Censored Burns*.[2] Sadly, Oxford's expensive re-edition of the letters in 1985 arguably achieved its most significant addition by appending Professor G. Ross Roy's name as editor.

The three-volume Oxford edition of *Burns: Songs and Poems* (1968) by James Kinsley, is by far the most important edition of the poems. He lists a formal number of 605 poems and songs within the canon. However, several works are counted by him under a number with sub-categories, 100A, 100B, and so on. This means he accepts 621 poems, songs and fragments to the canon. This is increased further by the poems within Kinsley's *Dubia* section – those works he could not properly date in terms of composition. Hence, the overall Kinsley total is around 630, with a few marked as 'probably' authentic.

There is, however, among his extensive, indeed, apparently exhaustive quarrying of Burns's poetry for the poet's quite enormous range of allusion to English, Scottish, Folk and, not least, Biblical sources, a degree of exhibitonist erudition. One really doubts that even so much a poet's poet as Burns (the very reverse of the limited ploughman) had access to such esoteric texts. Given that qualification, this new edition is everywhere marked by Kinsley's scholarly presence. As with Carol McGuirk's excellent *Robert Burns: Selected Poems* (Penguin, 1993), we have everywhere tried to acknowledge our specific debts. While Kinsley is almost Olympian in erudition, the same cannot be said of his degree of detachment. Though less obviously so, his edition carries many of the omissions and prejudices of nineteenth-century scholars. Kinsley, essentially, was a conservative eighteenth-century scholar with neither patience for nor understanding of Romantic radical poetics. It may be that such wilful obscuritanism in Kinsley is part of a much larger pattern prevailing in British literary criticism. David Norbrook, in a recent study of seventeenth-century English poetry[3] argues that there is an in-built, repressive prejudice in our national literary criticism to prefer a royalist over a republican poetics. He comments that the memory of republican poetry had been 'kept at bay by a *cordon sanitaire* of defensive ridicule'. The parallel between the bloody crucible of the mid-seventeenth century and the political tumult of the 1790s should be obvious from our introduction with relevance to Burns and Scotland and what was subsequently done to him.

In his Warton lecture to the British Academy on 23 January 1974, Kinsley summarised what he had learned from his work on Burns. Thus he wrote:

> Indeed, the deep spring of his finest poetry was not literary at all – not even the vernacular tradition – but what he called his 'social disposition'; a heart 'completely tinder and . . . eternally lighted up by some Goddess or other' and a 'strong appetite for sociability' . . . This appetite led him often into 'scenes of swaggering riot and roaring dissipation' . . . It also gave him

the chance and capacity to see the rustic society about him with the sympathy and critical clarity of a Breughel; to write some of the most natural and generous verse letters in the language; and give to the world some of its best songs.[4]

The implications of his bizarre conclusions are not those to induce confidence in his editorial vision or practices, coming from an editor whose perhaps over-laden commentary annotates the extraordinary degree of Burns's allusiveness to other poetry. From the evidence of his poetry and letters he is about as unliterary as James Joyce. Indeed, from further remarks, it would seem Kinsley's intention was to keep Burns's poetry marginalised on the rural farm, isolated from his English contemporaries and de-politicised.

Dr James Mackay's 1993 edition, endorsed by the Burns Federation, parasitically plunders Kinsley's volume 3 annotations (often presenting them as his own, without acknowledgement) and, to make matters worse, reproduces the worst Burns text available, that of the corrupted Henley–Henderson edition. Mackay enlarges the Burns canon to around 650 works, without explanation. He does not number each poem, so the increase is not noticeable. He includes works *omitted* by Kinsley and *excludes* work Kinsley accepted. In the appendix he asserts that Kinsley 'attempted to define the canon for all time, listing 632 poems and songs which were incontrovertibly the work of Burns'. He then states that all of the poems in Kinsley's *Dubia* section are shown *not to be* from Burns, although most of these are printed by Mackay as genuine. The net effect is to leave the Burns canon confused.

The essential purpose of this edition, therefore, has been to update Burns, by recontextualising him into the 1790s where he was a central creative Scottish figure. As our commentaries try to show, he was also a central figure in British radical consciousness and widely admired in that circle. His poetry and rhetoric is only properly understood as an inspired Scottish variant amid the creative language of that period for he shared the sense that generation had of being in a sort of historical cyclotron where, accelerating to breaking point, their initial Utopian hopes were eventually reduced to 'dark despair' by the tyranny and fear inspired by Pitt's government. In a recent article 'Beware of Reverence: Writing and Radicalism in the 1790s', Paul O'Flinn refers to the:

. . . extraordinary explosion of radical writing from the early 1790s, a period probably unmatched in British history for its intellectual daring and its moral courage. The conventional and

surely correct explanation for this phenomenon is that it re-
presents the cultural articulation of a unique conjuncture in
Western history, the years that saw the American Revolution of
1776, the French Revolution of 1789 and, in Britain, the
onslaught of the Industrial Revolution.[5]

The real 'onslaught' was more the British elite's hysterical reaction
to the effects of the French Revolution. This was a war between
democratic reformist forces and conservatism which the latter over-
whelmingly won. The effect was to pervert the development of the
Industrial Revolution, displace and effectively destroy the Scottish
Enlightenment, silence and crush the voice of dissent, for at least a
generation.

This was largely achieved through the tyrannical spy network
overseen in Scotland by Robert Dundas and in London by Henry
Dundas and key Home Office personnel, including a Mr John
Spottiswood, a London based Scottish lawyer. Spottiswood dis-
pensed the Secret Service funds from London to John Pringle,
Sheriff Depute of Edinburgh on a regular basis from December
1792 onwards. A bill for £1000 was paid on 8 February, 1793 and
during the first quarter of the year £975 had been spent on secrect
service 'spying' activities. Out of this total the poet's apparent *loyal*
patron, Robert Graham of Fintry, as we commented in the Intro-
duction, was paid £26.6s.od.[6] Burns's fear of persecution at the
close of 1792 is no isolated case. The cases of Tytler and Muir are
already mentioned, but less known is the case of Professor Richard-
son of Glasgow University, who had a personal letter intercepted by
the government. He wrote, 'I tread on dangerous ground. Many
things may be said which cannot be written . . . there is not a literary
man in Glasgow with whom I can speak freely on the topic of the
times'[7] Even the poet's friend William Dunbar, the 'Colonel' of the
Crochallan Fencibles, was suspected of being a radical Jacobin. In a
letter to a friend, Alexander Brodie, Dunbar pleaded for his job and
pledged his allegiance to the crown, constitution and personal
loyalty to the Lord Advocate, Robert Dundas.[8] We have tried to
integrate as much as possible of this political material into our poetic
commentary.

Thus, the structure of this edition, rather than chronological,
represents not simply the sequence in which Burns's poetry came
into the public domain, but, initially, the way he chose creatively to
reveal himself in the work published in his lifetime under his own
name. Hence, the Kilmarnock is followed by the two Edinburgh
editions. The first Edinburgh edition added 15 new poems and 8

new songs to the canon. The 1793 edition added several more, including *Tam o'Shanter* which, given that William Creech had purchased the poet's copyright, earned Burns merely a few 'presentation copies' of his own works. The 1793 edition was re-printed in 1794 without addition.

Our next section, the songs published in the poet's lifetime, mostly in James Johnson's *Scots Musical Museum*, include many Jacobite songs that were printed anonymously. For the benefit of the reader, we have included many of the tunes to the better known songs. The importance of Scottish traditional music, particularly fiddle-based slow airs, to Burns's lyrics, cannot be overestimated, given his extraordinary debt to musicians and music collectors of the period. However, Burns's debt to traditional song is also extensive as our notes reveal and it is in this section, particularly songs merely improved by Burns, where the genre of traditional song and the Burns canon tend to blur and overlap. Like a grand mural tapestry, traditional Scottish folk song from the eighteenth century was effectively rewoven by Burns with a mixture of his own and older lyrics.

We then move to the Anonymous and Pseudonymous section, where, like almost all the radical writers of that darkening decade, he had deliberately to disguise his identity. We hope we have shown, with painstaking archival research and detailed textual analyses, the way in which poems, especially those recovered from *The Edinburgh Gazetteer*, stylistically, linguistically and thematically match his other known ones. Ten of the poems printed here derive from Patrick Scott Hogg's *Robert Burns: The Lost Poems* (1997). Despite the over-heated, largely media-driven debate on the appearance of that book, it has stood up extremely well to proper academic scrutiny. Only two of Scott Hogg's discoveries have been found to be certainly not by Burns. These poems we now know came from the pen of the extraordinary Dr Alexander Geddes, a radical Roman Catholic priest (Burns knew and adored his uncle, John Geddes, Roman Catholic Bishop of Dunkeld). Geddes is at the top of the list of radical Scots to be retrieved from the abyss of the 1790s into which they vanished from the national memory. Geddes was a polymath. He was at the cutting edge of the new German inspired Higher Biblical Criticism. He was an intimate of Coleridge and, arguably, an influence on Blake's Biblical views. He was co-editor of the radical house-journal of the period, *The Analytical Review*. He not only went to France but read a celebratory ode written in Latin to the National Assembly.

The two Geddes poems identified by our then colleague at

the University of Strathclyde, Gerald Carruthers, are *Exhortatory Ode to the Prince of Wales on Entering his 34th Year* and *Ode for the Birthday of C.J. Fox*. The Burns/Geddes connection will be dealt with in detail with regard to particular, relevant poems in the following commentary. What should be stressed is that the retrieval of Geddes will be an enormously strong element in supporting this edition's argument for a pervasive literary and radical Scottish political culture at the end of the eighteenth century.

Scott Hogg's initial case and that of this edition has also been enormously strengthened by the discovery of Professor Lucyle Werkmeister's magisterial work on the radical press in the 1790s and, in particular, her two articles on the politically necessary complex but extensive relations between Burns and the London press. Why her work was ignored is problematic. Certainly it stems in part from a sort of Scottish psychological and political conservatism that has led to Burns being detached from his radical peers. We have tried in our poetic commentary to renew these connections with Burns and the English Romantics. He is not understandable without an awareness of advanced Romantic scholarship as is recently discoverable in such books as E.P. Thompson's *The Romantics: England in Revolutionary Age* (London: Merlin Press, 1998) or Kenneth Johnston's *The Hidden Wordsworth* (London: Norton, 1998).

In the Posthumous section, virtually half of this volume, we have tried to pinpoint the incalculable degree to which, after his death, Burns's work was hidden away, destroyed or even burned. The fact that such an enormous number of poems, many of the highest quality and importance, only surfaced after his death and that destruction of texts carried on for such a long period of time, is overwhelming proof of the enormous censorship he had, in life and death, to endure. For example the page torn from volume three of the *Interleaved Scots Musical Museum* with the song title *The Lucubrations of Henry Dundass, May* 1792, probably revealed Burns's satirical treatment of Dundas's clumsy and authoritarian action to cripple Borough reform, which resulted in street riots in Edinburgh and burning effigies of Dundas being paraded around the city. That such censorship has carried over into the twenty-first century is clear from a recent discovery of a private collection of transcripts to Burns's letters to Robert Ainslie which remain unpublished.

The final section *The Merry Muses of Caledonia* presents those bawdy songs known to have been written or improved by Burns, which, for so long, were the private amusement of smoking-room 'gentlemen' who sought to protect the general public from this earthy trait of the vital Burns. The volume closes with an appendix of as-yet undetermined and rejected works.

Andrew Noble
Patrick Scott Hogg

Notes

1 Catherine Carswell, Letters, Mitchell Library, Glasgow, MS 53.
2 Prof. J. De Lancey Ferguson, 'They Censored Burns', in *Scotland's Magazine*, Vol. 51, January 1955, pp. 29–30.
3 David Norbrook, *Writing The English Republic: Poetry, Rhetoric and Politics 1627–1660*, Cambridge, 1999.
4 James Kinsley, Warton Lecture to the British Academy, 23 January 1974, printed by the British Academy, 1985.
5 Paul O'Flinn, in *Writing and Radicalism*, ed. Lucas (London: Longman), 1996, pp. 84–101.
6 See Laing MS. 500, ff.404–5. Additional letters Fintry to Robert Dundas, exist in Laing II, 500/f.734, f.747, f.751, ff.753–7, f.1076, f.1084.
7 RH 2/4/65f.84–5.
8 Laing II, 500, f.544.

PART ONE
The Kilmarnock Edition
1786

APRIL 14th, 1786
PROPOSALS,
FOR PUBLISHING BY SUBSCRIPTION,

SCOTCH POEMS,

BY ROBERT BURNS.

The work to be elegantly Printed in One
Volume, Octavo, Price, stitched *Three*
Shillings.

As the Author has not the most distant
Mercenary view in Publishing, as soon as so
many Subscribers appear as will defray the
necessary Expense, the Work will be sent to
the Press.

'Set out the brunt side o' your shin,
For pride in *Poets* is nae sin;
Glory's the Prize for which *they* rin,
And *Fame's* their jo;
And wha blaws best the Horn shall win:
And wharefare no?'

RAMSAY.

The following trifles are not the production of the Poet, who, with
all the advantages of learned art, and perhaps amid the elegancies
and idleness of upper life, looks down for a rural theme, with an eye
to Theocrites or Virgil. To the Author of this, these and other
celebrated names their countrymen are, in their original languages,
'A fountain shut up' and, a 'book sealed'. Unacquainted with the
necessary requisites for commencing Poet by Rule, he sings the
sentiments and manners, he felt and saw in himself and his rustic
compeers around him, in his and their native language. Though a
Rhymer from his earliest years, at least from the earliest impulses of
the softer passions, it was not till very lately, that the applause,
perhaps the partiality, of Friendship, wakened his vanity so far as to
make him think any thing of his was worth showing; and none of the
following works were ever composed with a view to the press. To

amuse himself with the little creations of his own fancy, amid the toils and fatigues of a laborious life; to transcribe the various feelings, the loves, the griefs, the hopes, the fears, in his own breast; to find some kind of counterpoise to the struggles of a world, always an alien scene, a task uncouth to the Poetical mind; these were his motives for courting the Muses, and in these he found Poetry to be its own reward.

Now that he appears in the public character of an Author, he does it with fear and trembling. So dear is fame to the Rhyming tribe, that even he, an obscure, nameless Bard, shrinks aghast, at the thought of being branded as 'an impertinent blockhead, obtruding his nonsense on the world; and because he can make a shift to jingle a few doggerel, Scotch rhymes together, looks upon himself as a Poet of no small consequence forsooth'.

It is an observation of that celebrated Poet [Shenstone], whose divine Elegies do honour to our language, our nation, and our species, that 'Humility has depressed many a genius to a hermit, but never raised one to fame'. If any Critic catches at the word genius, the Author tells him, once for all, that he certainly looks upon himself as possest of some poetic abilities, otherwise his publishing in the manner he has done, would be a manoeuvre below the worst character, which, he hopes, his worst enemy will ever give him: but to the genius of a Ramsay, or the glorious dawning of the poor, unfortunate Ferguson, he with equal unaffected sincerity, declares, that, even in his highest pulse of vanity, he has not the most distant pretensions. These two justly admired Scotch Poets he has often had in his eye in the following pieces; but rather with a view to kindle at their flame, than for servile imitation.

To his Subscribers, the Author returns his most sincere thanks. Not the mercenary bow over a counter, but the heart-throbbing gratitude of the Bard, conscious how much he is indebted to Benevolence and Friendship, for gratifying him, if he deserves it, in that dearest wish of every poetic bosom – to be distinguished. He begs his readers, particularly the Learned and the Polite, who may honour him with a perusal, that they will make every allowance for Education and Circumstances of Life: but, if after a fair, candid, and impartial criticism, he shall stand convicted of Dulness and Nonsense, let him be done by, as he would in that case do by others – let him be condemned, without mercy, to oblivion.

R.B.

Nature's Bard

First published on the front page of the Kilmarnock edition, 1786.

The Simple Bard, unbroke by rules of Art,
He pours the wild effusions of the heart:
And if inspir'd, 'tis Nature's pow'rs inspire;
Her's all the melting thrill, and her's the kindling fire.
                                        Anonymous.

The Kilmarnock edition begins with four lines supposedly from an anonymous poet, wholly appropriate to the image Burns wished to project to his readers. They are, in all probability, his own composition. In his *Preface*, Burns coyly suggests that he does not have 'all the advantages of learned art' in poetry – when, in fact, he is a master craftsman in poetic form and metre. He goes on to explain that his poetry is the product of Nature's influence on him. This projected persona is captured perfectly in the quatrain. The possibility that Burns wrote these lines was first suggested by the highly distinguished American scholar, Professor Carol McGuirk, in her excellent *Robert Burns: Selected Poems* (Penguin, 1993). A search of known anonymous poetry for the 18th century did not trace a potential author other than Burns. The lines are a hand-in-glove portrayal of Burns's self-projection of himself as a poet.

The Twa Dogs: A Tale

First printed in the Kilmarnock edition, 1786.

'Twas in that place o' *Scotland's* isle	
That bears the name of auld King COIL,	old, Kyle
Upon a bonie day in June,	bonny
When wearing thro' the afternoon,	
5 *Twa Dogs*, that were na thrang at hame,	two, not busy, home
Forgather'd ance upon a time.	met by chance, once

The first I'll name, they ca'd him *Caesar*,	called
Was keepet for his Honor's pleasure:	kept
His hair, his size, his mouth, his lugs,	ears
10 Shew'd he was nane o' Scotland's dogs;	none
But whalpet some place far abroad,	pupped
Whare sailors gang to fish for Cod.	where, go

His locked, letter'd, braw brass-collar
Shew'd him the *gentleman* an' *scholar*;
15 But tho' he was o' high degree,
The fient a pride na pride had he;   fiend, no
But wad hae spent an hour caressan,   would have
Ev'n wi' a Tinkler-gipsey's *messan*;   mongrel
At *Kirk* or *Market*, *Mill* or *Smiddie*,   smithy
20 Nae tawtied *tyke*, tho' e'er sae duddie, matted cur, so ragged
But he wad stan't, as glad to see him,   would have stood
An' stroan't on stanes an' hillocks wi' him. pissed, stones

The tither was a *ploughman's collie*,
A rhyming, ranting, raving billie,   fellow/character
25 Wha for his friend an' comrade had him, who
And in his freaks had *Luath* ca'd him,
After some dog in *Highland Sang*,[1]
Was made lang syne, Lord knows how lang. long ago

He was a gash an' faithfu' *tyke*,   wise, dog
30 As ever lap a sheugh or dyke!   leapt, ditch, stone wall
His honest, sonsie, baws'nt face   friendly, white marks
Ay gat him friends in ilka place;   always got, every
His *breast* was white, his touzie *back*   shaggy
Weel clad wi' coat o' glossy black;   well covered
35 His gawsie tail, wi' upward curl,   fine/full
Hung owre his hurdies wi' a swirl.   over, buttocks

Nae doubt but they were fain o' ither,   no, fond of each other
And unco pack an' thick thegither;   kept secrets/confidential
Wi' social *nose* whyles snuff'd an' snowcket; whiles, sniffed
40 Whyles mice an' moudiewurks they howcket; whiles, moles, dug for
Whyles scour'd awa' in lang excursion,   whiles, long
An' worry'd ither in *diversion*;
Till tir'd at last wi' monie a farce,   many
They sat them down upon their arse,
45 An' there began a lang digression   long
About the *lords o' the creation*.

CAESAR
I've aften wonder'd, honest *Luath*,   often
What sort o' life poor dogs like you have;

1 Cuchullin's dog in Ossian's *Fingal*, R.B.

An' when the *gentry's* life I saw,
50   What way poor bodies liv'd ava.   at all

Our *Laird* gets in his racked rents,   extortionate
His coals, his kane, an' a' his stents: payments in kind, dues
He rises when he likes himsel;
His flunkies answer at the bell;   servants
55   He ca's his coach; he ca's his horse;   calls
He draws a bonie, silken purse,   carries
As lang's my *tail*, whare thro' the steeks,   long as, where, stiches
The yellow, letter'd *Geordie* keeks.   guinea (King's head) peeps

Frae morn to een it's nought but toiling,   from, evening, nothing
60   At baking, roasting, frying, boiling;
An' tho' the gentry first are steghan,   cramming
Yet ev'n the *ha' folk* fill their peghan   hall (servants), stomach
Wi' sauce, ragouts, an sic like trashtrie,   such like rubbish
That's little short o' downright wastrie: wastage
65   Our *Whipper-in*, wee, blastit wonner,   small, blasted wonder
Poor, worthless elf, it eats a dinner,
Better than onie *Tenant-man*   any
His Honor has in a' the lan':   all the land
An' what poor *Cot-folk* pit their painch in,   put, paunch
70   I own it's past my comprehension.

LUATH

Trowth, *Caesar*, whyles they're fash'd eneugh: sometimes, bothered
A *Cotter* howckan in a sheugh,   farm labourer, digging, ditch
Wi' dirty stanes biggan a dyke,   stones, building, stone wall
Bairan a quarry, an' sic like,   clearing, such
75   Himsel, a wife, he thus sustains,
A smytrie o' wee duddie weans,   number, small ragged children
An' nought but his han'-daurk, to keep   hands' work
Them right an' tight in *thack an' raep*.   snug, thatch, rope

An' when they meet wi' sair disasters,   sore
80   Like loss o' health or want o' masters,
Ye maist wad think, a wee touch langer,   most would, longer
An' they maun starve o' cauld and hunger: should, cold
But how it comes, I never kend yet,   knew
They're maistly wonderfu' contented;   mostly
85   An' buirdly chiels, an' clever hizzies,   stout lads, girls
Are bred in sic a way as this is.   such

CAESAR
But then to see how ye're neglecket,   neglected
How huff'd, an' cuff'd, an' disrespecket!   scolded, slapped, disrespected
Lord man, our gentry care as little
90   For *delvers*, *ditchers*, an' sic cattle;   labourers, diggers, such
They gang as saucy by poor folk,   go, smugly
As I wad by a stinkan brock.   would, badger

I've notic'd, on our Laird's *court-day*,[2]
(An' monie a time my heart's been wae),   many, sad
95   Poor tenant bodies, scant o' cash,   short of money
How they maun thole a *Factor's* snash:[3]   would suffer, abuse
He'll stamp an' threaten, curse an' swear
He'll *apprehend* them, *poind* their gear;   seize & sell their goods
While they maun staun', wi' aspect humble,   must stand
100 An' hear it a', an' fear an' tremble!   all

I see how folk live that hae riches;   have
But surely poor-folk maun be wretches!   must

LUATH
They're nae sae wretched's ane wad think: not so, as one would
Tho' constantly on poortith's brink,   poverty's
105 They're sae accustom'd wi' the sight,   so
The view o't gies them little fright.   gives

Then chance an' fortune are sae guided,   so
They're ay in less or mair provided;   always, more
An' tho' fatigu'd wi' close employment,
110 A blink o' rest's a sweet enjoyment.

The dearest comfort o' their lives,
Their grushie weans an' faithfu' wives;   thriving children
The *prattling things* are just their pride,
That sweetens a' their fire-side.

115 An' whyles twalpennie worth o' *nappy*   sometimes, ale
Can mak the bodies unco happy: folk, very

2 The quarterly Circuit Court that travelled around the towns and counties
of Scotland.
3 The title of Factor is that of an Estate manager, who, in the West of
Scotland, cleared many 'cottars' from large estates during the late 18th
century.

They lay aside their private cares,
To mind the Kirk an' State affairs;
They'll talk o' *patronage* an' *priests*,

120 Wi' kindling fury i' their breasts,
Or tell what new taxation's comin,
An' ferlie at the folk in LON'ON.   wonder

As bleak-fac'd Hallowmass returns,   festival of All-Saints
They get the jovial, rantan *Kirns*,   harvest homes

125 When *rural life*, of ev'ry station,
Unite in common recreation;
Love blinks, Wit slaps, an' social Mirth
Forgets there's *Care* upo' the earth.

That *merry day* the year begins,

130 They bar the door on frosty win's;   winds
The nappy reeks wi' mantling ream,   ale, foaming froth
An' sheds a heart-inspiring steam;
The luntan pipe, an' sneeshin mill,   smoking, snuff box
Are handed round wi' right guid will;   good

135 The cantie, auld folks, crackan crouse,   jolly old, chatting, cheerful
The young anes rantan thro' the house —   one, running
My heart has been sae fain to see them,   so content
That I for joy hae *barket* wi' them.   have barked

Still it's owre true that ye hae said   over, have

140 Sic game is now owre aften play'd;   such a, over often
There's monie a creditable *stock*   many
O' decent, honest, fawsont folk,   respectable
Are riven out baith root an' branch,   thrown out by force, both
Some rascal's pridefu' greed to quench,

145 Wha thinks to knit himsel the faster   who
In favor wi' some *gentle Master*,
Wha, aiblins thrang a *parliamentin'*,   who, maybe crowd
For *Britain's guid* his saul indentin' —   good, soul engaged

CAESAR
Haith, lad, ye little ken about it: an exclamation, know

150 *For Britain's guid*! guid faith! I doubt it.   good
Say rather, gaun as PREMIERS lead him: go
An' saying *aye* or *no* 's they bid him:
At Operas an' Plays parading,
Mortgaging, gambling, masquerading:

155 Or maybe, in a frolic daft,
    To HAGUE or CALAIS takes a waft,
    To mak *a tour* an' tak a whirl,
    To learn *bon ton*, an' see the worl'.   Fr. good breeding

    There, at VIENNA or VERSAILLES,
160 He rives his father's auld entails;   splits, old
    Or by MADRID he taks the rout,   road
    To thrum guittarres an' fecht wi' *nowt*;   strum, guitars, fight with cattle
    Or down *Italian Vista* startles,   courses
    Whore-hunting amang groves o' myrtles: among
165 Then bowses drumlie *German-water*,   drinks muddy
    To mak himsel look fair an' fatter,
    An' clear the consequential sorrows,
    Love-gifts of Carnival Signioras.
    For Britain's guid! for her destruction!
170 Wi' dissipation, feud an' faction!

    LUATH
    Hech man! dear sirs! is that the gate   way
    They waste sae monie a braw estate!   so many
    Are we sae foughten an' harass'd   so troubled
    For gear ta gang that gate at last!   wealth to go

175 O would they stay aback frae courts,   away from
    An' please themsels wi' countra sports,   country
    It wad for ev'ry ane be better,   would, every one
    The *Laird*, the *Tenant*, an' the *Cotter*!
    For thae frank, rantan, ramblan billies,   those, lads
180 Fient haet o' them's ill-hearted fellows;   few of them are
    Except for breakin o' their timmer,   timber
    Or speakin lightly o' their *Limmer*,   mistress
    Or shootin of a hare or moor-cock,
    The ne'er-a-bit they're ill to poor folk.

185 But will ye tell me, master Caesar,
    Sure *great folk's* life's a life o' pleasure?
    Nae cauld nor hunger e'er can steer them,   no cold, touch
    The vera thought o't need na fear them.   very, not

    CAESAR
    Lord, man, were ye but whyles whare I am,   whiles where
190 The *Gentles*, ye wad ne'er envy them!   would

It's true, they need na starve or sweat,   *not*
Thro' Winter's cauld, or Simmer's heat;   *cold, summer's*
They've nae sair-wark to craze their banes,   *no sore work, bones*
An' fill *auld-age* wi' grips an' granes: *old-age, gripes & groans*
195   But *human bodies* are sic fools,   *such*
For a' their Colledges an' Schools,
That when nae *real* ills perplex them,   *no*
They *mak* enow themsels to vex them;
An' ay the less they hae to sturt them,   *always, have, fret*
200   In like proportion, less will hurt them.

A countra fellow at the pleugh,   *country, plough*
His *acre's* till'd, he's right eneugh;   *well enough*
A countra girl at her wheel,   *country*
Her *dizzen's* done, she's unco weel;   *dozens (yarn), very well*
205   But Gentlemen, an' Ladies warst,
Wi' ev'n down *want o' wark* they're curst: *work*
They loiter, lounging, lank an' lazy;
Tho' deil-haet ails them, yet uneasy: *nothing*
Their days insipid, dull an' tasteless;
210   Their nights unquiet, lang an' restless.   *long*

An' ev'n their sports, their balls an' races,
Their galloping thro' public places,
There's sic parade, sic pomp an' art,   *such*
The joy can scarcely reach the heart.

215   The *Men* cast out in *party-matches*,   *compete*
Then sowther a' in deep debauches;   *patch up*
Ae night they're mad wi' drink an' whoring,   *one*
Niest day their life is past enduring.   *next*

The *Ladies* arm-in-arm in clusters,
220   As great an' gracious a' as sisters;   *all*
But hear their *absent thoughts* o' ither,
They're a' run deils an' jads thegither.   *downright, together*
Whyles, owre the wee bit cup an' platie,   *whiles, over, plate*
They sip the *scandal-potion* pretty;
225   Or lee-lang nights, wi' crabbet leuks   *live-long, bad tempered looks*
Pore owre the devil's *pictur'd beuks*;   *over, books (playing cards)*
Stake on a chance a farmer's stackyard,
An' cheat like onie *unhang'd blackguard*.   *any, villain*

There's some exceptions, man an' woman;
230   But this is Gentry's life in common.

By this, the sun was out o' sight,
An' darker gloamin brought the night;   fading twilight
The *bum-clock* humm'd wi' lazy drone;   beetle
The kye stood rowtin i' the loan;   cattle, lowing, field
235 When up they gat, an' shook their lugs,   got, ears
Rejoic'd they were na *men*, but *dogs*;   not
An' each took aff his several way,   went his different
Resolv'd to meet some ither day.   other

Burns lived with animals, wild and domestic, in conditions of intimacy which few of us in this twenty-first century can easily appreciate. This poem, as much of his poetry, is filled with an empathetic, hence, detailed knowledge of them. The collie and the Newfoundland are sportively present to us. Throughout his writing there are also frequent, often obliquely political analogies, made between the lots of animals and men.

The genesis of this poem was his own collie, Luath, who, his brother tells us, was 'killed by some wanton cruelty of some person the night before my father's death'. This extraordinary witty, seminal poem is the result of his original intention to write, for the sinisterly murdered Luath, *Stanzas to the Memory of a Quadruped Friend* (Currie, Vol. 3, p. 386).

His wholly deliberate choice of opening The Kilmarnock edition with this particular poem is mockingly ironic. In that volume, he had no sooner come on stage with his highly successful self-promoting prose remarks about his poetic ploughman's pastoral naïvety, than he immediately delivers a poetic performance of not only formidable linguistic and double-voiced dramatic subtlety but one which is eruditely allusive to earlier Scottish and English poetry. Indeed, it would be, as in ll. 26–28, an extremely odd ploughman who would not only name his dog from a character in Macpherson's *Ossian* but also allude to that simmering controversy. Also both the octosyllabic verse and the dialogue form are derived from his beloved predecessor, Robert Fergusson's *The Mutual Complaint of Plainstanes and Causey, in their Mother Tongue*.

While the poem formally and linguistically is not indebted to English poetry, the content certainly is. As William Empson (*Some Versions of Pastoral*, 1935) and Raymond Williams (*The City and Country*, 1975) have revealed, English poetry from the sixteenth century had been preoccupied with the nature and representation of country life as a reflection of the quarrel between largely conservative poets and their aristocratic patrons due to the disruptive evolution in the life of the common people caused by the accelerating participation by the

aristocratic master class in agrarian capitalism. The greatest state-
ment of this theme, as we shall see Burns demonstrably knew in his
own *A Winter's Night*, is Shakespeare's *King Lear*. The consistently
cogent McGuirk in discussing this poem locates its tap-roots in
Augustan convention, especially Pope's *Moral Epistles*. Burns also
had, of course, the endorsement of his views from contemporary
sources such as Goldsmith, particularly *The Deserted Village*.
Although they diverged totally about the role of the monarchy, Burns
and Goldsmith were also part of that rising late eighteenth-century
tide of patriotic feeling about the 'Frenchified' degeneration of the
British aristocracy as increasingly they squandered their ill-gotten
agrarian rents in European fleshpots. (See Gerald Newman, *The Rise
of English Nationalism*, London, 1987.) Hence that quite wonderfully
sophisticated section, comparable to anything in Augustan satire,
from ll. 149–170 where Caesar describes into what The Grand Tour
has degenerated. This brilliantly echoes Fergusson's pronouncedly
anti-aristocratic lines from *Hame Content*:

> Some daft chiel reads, and takes advice
> The chaise is yokit in a trice;
> Awa drives he like huntit deil,
> And scarce tholes time to cool his wheel,
> Till he's Lord ken how far awa,
> At Italy, or Well o' Spaw,
> Or to Montpelier's safer air;
> For far off fowls hae feathers fair.
>   There rest him weel; for eith can we
> Spare mony glakit gouks like he;
> They'll tell whare Tibur's water's rise;
> What sea receives the drumly prize,
> That never wi' their feet hae mett
> The marches o' their ain estate.

Stimulated by Fergusson, then, this dramatic dialogue, domesti-
cates in the Scottish vernacular this great English poetic quarrel
with a rapacious land-owning class. What further intensified this in
Burns is that from childhood he had been exposed to both brutal-
ising toil and chronic economic anxiety. Ll. 95–100 do, in fact, seem
to refer to actual events on the family farm at Lochlea of which he
wrote: 'my indignation yet boils at the recollection of the scoundrel
tyrant's insolent threatening epistles which he used to set us all in
tears' (Letter 137). As Burns's subsequent poetry reveals, this early
trauma about debt, bankruptcy and possible homelessness was to be

a subject of inflammatory repetition. Also, as much of his later poetry, the poem is filled with telling detail about the harsh, exposed, exhausting nature of farm work in the late eighteenth century as opposed to the pampered sloth of the aristocracy. Indeed, as in ll. 89–90, such brutal work leads to a Swiftian vision of the bestialisation of the common people: 'Lord man, our gentry care as little/For *delvers, ditchers* and sic cattle'.

Burns's strategy in the poem of course is to create through the dogs a kind of comic brio, which, at a primary level, disguises the poem's incisive documentation and its anti-establishment values. Further, he does not do the ideologically obvious thing by creating an oppositional dialogue between the people's collie and the master's newly fashionable Newfoundland. Caesar is not so much a traitor to his class as a natural democrat who will put his nose anywhere as a possible prelude to even more intimate entanglements. It is he who really spills the beans about the condition of the working people and the lifestyle of their masters. In Luath's speeches, especially ll. 103–38, we find the roots of Burns's vision of the nobility of the common people which is to recur throughout his poetry though, at times, especially in 'The Cotter's Saturday Night', somewhat questionably.

Scotch Drink

First printed in the Kilmarnock edition, 1786.

> *Gie him strong drink until he wink,*
> *That's sinking in despair;*
> *An' liquor guid to fire his bluid,*
> *That's prest wi' grief an' care:*
> *There let him bowse, and deep carouse,*
> *Wi' bumpers flowing o'er,*
> *Till he forgets his loves or debts,*
> *An' minds his griefs no more.*

Solomon's Proverbs, xxxi. 6, 7.I.
A paraphrase from Hugh Blair's *The Grave*, p. 8.

Let other Poets raise a frácas
'Bout vines, an' wines, an' drucken *Bacchus*,   drunken
An' crabbed names an' stories wrack us,   torment
     An' grate our lug: vex, ears
5   I sing the juice *Scotch bear* can mak us,   drink, barley
     In glass or jug.

O thou, my MUSE! guid auld SCOTCH DRINK!   good old
Whether thro' wimplin worms thou jink,   winding, frisk
Or, richly brown, ream owre the brink,   froth over
      In glorious faem,   foam
Inspire me, till I *lisp* an' *wink*,
      To sing thy name!

Let husky Wheat the haughs adorn,   hollows
An' Aits set up their awnie horn,   oats, bearded
An' Pease an' Beans, at een or morn,
      Perfume the plain:
Leeze me on thee, *John Barleycorn*,   blessing on thee
      Thou king o' grain!

On thee aft Scotland chows her cood,   often, chews, cud
In souple scones, the wale o' food!   soft, pick
Or tumbling in the boiling flood
      Wi' kail an' beef;   greens
But when thou pours thy strong *heart's blood*,
      There thou shines chief.

Food fills the wame, an' keeps us livin;   belly
Tho' life's a gift no worth receivin,
When heavy-dragg'd wi' pine an' grievin;
      But oil'd by thee,
The wheels o' life gae down-hill, scrievin,   go, careering
      Wi' rattlin glee.   noisy joy

Thou clears the head o' doited Lear,   muddled knowledge
Thou cheers the heart o' drooping Care;
Thou strings the nerves o' Labor-sair,   sore
      At's weary toil;
Thou ev'n brightens dark Despair
      Wi' gloomy smile.

Aft, clad in massy, siller weed,   often clothed
Wi' Gentles thou erects thy head;
Yet, humbly kind, in time o' need,
      The *poorman's* wine:
His wee drap parritch, or his bread,   drop, porridge
      Thou kitchens fine.

Thou art the life o' public haunts;
But thee, what were our fairs and rants?   *without, merry-makings*
45 Ev'n goodly meetings o' the saunts,   *saints*
          By thee inspir'd,
When, gaping, they besiege the *tents*,
          Are doubly fir'd.

That *merry night* we get the corn in,
50 O sweetly, then, thou reams the horn in!
Or reekin on a *New-Year-mornin*   *steaming*
          In cog or bicker,   *bowl, jug*
An' just a wee drap *sp'ritual burn* in,   *small drop*
          An' *gusty sucker*!   *tasty sugar*

55 When Vulcan gies his bellys breath,   *gives, bellows*
An' Ploughmen gather wi' their graith,   *gear*
O rare! to see thee fizz an' fraeth   *bubble and froth*
          I' the lugget caup!   *two-handled jug*
Then *Burnewin* comes on like Death   *blacksmith*
60   At ev'ry chap.   *stroke*

Nae mercy, then, for airn *or* steel: *no, iron*
The brawnie, bainie, Ploughman-chiel,   *sturdy, boney, fellow*
Brings hard owrehip, wi' sturdy wheel,   *over hip*
          The strong forehammer,
65 Till block an' studdie ring an' reel,   *anvil*
          Wi' dinsome clamour.

When skirlin weanies see the light,   *squalling infants*
Thou maks the gossips clatter bright.   *makes, chatter, cheerfully*
How fumbling coofs their dearies slight;   *fools*
70   Wae worth the name!   *woe betide*
Nae Howdie gets a social night,   *no midwife*
          Or plack frae them.   *coin*

When neebors anger at a plea,   *neighbours*
An' just as wud as wud can be,   *mad/wild*
75 How easy can the *barley-bree*   *-brew*
          Cement the quarrel!
It's ay the cheapest Lawyer's fee,
          To taste the barrel.

Alake! that e'er my *Muse* has reason,
To wyte her countrymen wi' treason!   blame/charge
But mony daily weet their weason   many, wet their throat
     Wi' liquors nice,
An' hardly, in a winter season,
     E'er spier her price.   ask

80 (line number)

Wae worth that *Brandy*, burnin trash!   woe to
Fell source o' monie a pain an' brash!   sickness
Twins mony a poor, doylt, drucken hash,   (deprives many,
     O' half his days;   weary drunken fellow)
An' sends, beside, auld *Scotland's* cash   old
     To her warst faes.   worst foes

85, 90 (line numbers)

Ye Scots, wha wish auld Scotland well,   who, old
Ye chief, to you my tale I tell,
Poor, plackless devils like *mysel*,   penniless
     It sets you ill,
Wi' bitter, dearthfu' *wines* to mell,   meddle
     Or *foreign gill*.

95 (line number)

May *Gravels* round his blather wrench,   stones, bladder
An' *Gouts* torment him, inch by inch,
Wha twists his gruntle wi' a glunch   who, mouth, grumble
     O' sour disdain,
Out owre a glass o' *Whisky-punch*   over
     Wi' honest men!

100 (line number)

O *Whisky*! soul o' plays an' pranks!
Accept a *Bardie's* gratefu' thanks!
When wanting thee, what tuneless cranks
     Are my poor Verses!
Thou comes — they rattle i' their ranks
     At ither's arses!

105 (line number)

Thee, *Ferintosh*! O sadly lost!
Scotland lament frae coast to coast!   from
Now colic-grips, an' barkin hoast   coughing hoarse
     May kill us a';
For loyal *Forbes' Chartered boast*
     Is taen awa!   taken away

110 (line number)

115 Thae curst horse-leeches o' th' Excise,   those
    Wha mak the *Whisky stills* their prize!   who make, stills
    Haud up thy han', *Deil*! ance, twice, thrice!   hold, hand, once
        There, seize the blinkers!   rascals/spies
    An' bake them up in brunstane pies   brimstone
120   For poor damn'd *Drinkers*.

    Fortune! if thou'll but gie me still   give
    Hale breeks, a scone, an' *Whisky gill*,   whole breeches
    An' rowth o' *rhyme* to rave at will,   abundance/store
        Tak a' the rest,
125 An' deal't about as thy blind skill
        Directs thee best.

Though not quite in the manner of his contemporary, William Blake, Burns found *The Bible* a constant source of inspiration and allusion. This vernacularisation of *Proverbs* with which he introduces the poem is characteristic of his delight in the often excessively erotic, violent and, in this case, alcoholic tales he found in *The Old Testament*. Such use of *The Bible* was not the least of his anti-clerical weapons. Nor was it the least of his offences against Hugh Blair and the pietistic critical sensibilities of genteel Edinburgh.

A copy of *Scotch Drink* was sent to Robert Muir in March, 1786, having been apparently written sometime in the preceding winter. This celebratory 'hymn' to the virtues of the national drink again owes its genesis and tone to the bibulous gaiety which pulses through Robert Fergusson's poetry. In particular it is related to Fergusson's *Caller Water* and *A Drink Eclogue* with its disputation between Brandy and Whisky. As in Fergusson's poems, whisky is ever the vital, democratising, somewhat chauvinistic heart's blood of the nation, energising and socialising everybody with whom it comes into contact. The sad exception is the impotent, cuckolded husband of ll. 67–72.

In ll. 102–8 Burns also associates whisky with the power to energise his own poetic creativity so that the quality of his verses catches up with those of his poetic competitors. We cannot know to what degree alcohol was a creative stimulant for Burns, though certainly some of his most extraordinary letters are self-confessedly written with well-plied glass in hand. See, for example, Letter 506 to Alexander Cunningham.

The reference in l. 109 to Ferintosh as Kinsley tells us, is that this Cromarty Firth whisky had been exempted from duty after 1695 in reparation for damage to the estates of Forbes of Culloden, the

owner of the distillery, by the Jacobites in 1689. Forbes' loss of this
privilege in 1785 drove the price of whisky up.

The penultimate stanza's consignment of the Excise to the fires of
hell for their still-breaking activities must have caused Burns sub-
sequent guilty grief. The Excise was the most hated and efficient
arm of a state that had nothing to do with welfare and everything to
do with intrusive, punitive taxation. Had he known it, Burns would
have wholeheartedly agreed with Blake that 'Lawful Bread, Bought
with Lawful Money, & a Lawful Heaven, seen thro' a Lawful
Telescope, by means of a Lawful Window Light! The Holy Ghost,
& whatever cannot be Taxed, is Unlawful & Witchcraft'.

The Author's Earnest Cry and Prayer
To The Scotch Representatives In The House of Commons[1]
First printed in the Kilmarnock edition, 1786.

> *Dearest of distillation! last and best —*
> *— How art thou lost! —*
>> Parody on Milton.

Ye Irish lords, ye *knights* an' *squires*,
Wha represent our BRUGHS an' SHIRES,   who, burghs
An' doucely manage our affairs   prudently
    In *Parliament*,
5 To you a simple Bardie's pray'rs
    Are humbly sent.

Alas! my roupet *Muse* is haerse!   husky, hoarse
Your Honors' hearts wi' grief 'twad pierce,   it would
To see her sittan on her arse
10   Low i' the dust,
And scriechan out prosaic verse,   screeching
    An' like to brust!   burst

Tell them wha hae the chief direction,   who have
Scotland an' *me's* in great affliction,
15 E'er sin' they laid that curst restriction   ever since
    On AQUAVITAE   whisky/water-of-life
An' rouse them up to strong conviction,
    An' move their pity.

1 This was written before the Act anent the Scotch Distilleries of session 1786;
for which Scotland and the Author return their most grateful thanks. R.B.

Stand forth, an' tell yon PREMIER YOUTH
20   The honest, open, naked truth:
Tell him o' mine an' Scotland's drouth,   thirst
          His servants humble:
The muckle devil blaw you south,   great, blow
          If ye dissemble!

25   Does onie *great man* glunch an' gloom?   any, growl, grumble
Speak out, an' never fash your thumb!   trouble yourself
Let *posts* an' *pensions* sink or soom   swim
          Wi' them wha grant 'em: who
If honestly they canna come,   cannot
30   Far better want 'em.   lack them

In gath'rin votes you were na slack;   not lazy
Now stand as tightly by your tack:
Ne'er claw your lug, an' fidge your back,   scratch your ear, shrug
          An' hum an haw;
35   But raise your arm, an' tell your crack   tale
          Before them a'.

Paint Scotland greetan owre her thrissle;   weeping, over, thistle
Her *mutchkin stowp* as toom's a whissle;   pint-pot, empty as a whistle
An' damn'd *Excise-men* in a bustle,
40   Seizin a *Stell*,   still
Triumphant, crushan't like a mussel,
          Or laimpet shell.   limpet

Then on the tither hand present her,   other
A blackguard *Smuggler* right behint her,
45   An' cheek-for-chow, a chuffie *Vintner*   cheek-by-jowl, fat faced
          Colleaguing join, —
Pickin her pouch as bare as Winter   pocket
          Of a' kind coin.

Is there, that bears the name o' SCOT,
50   But feels his heart's bluid rising hot,   blood
To see his poor auld Mither's *pot*   old mother's
          Thus dung in staves,   broken in pieces
An' plunder'd o' her hindmost groat,   last coin
          By gallows knaves?

55 Alas! I'm but a nameless wight,
Trode i' the mire out o' sight!
But could I like MONTGOMERIES fight,
         Or gab like BOSWELL,   talk
There's some *sark-necks* I wad *draw* tight,   shirt-necks, would
60   An' tye some *hose* well.   tie

God bless your Honors! can ye see't,
The kind, auld, cantie Carlin greet,   old, jolly, wife weep
An' no get warmly to your feet,
         An' gar them hear it,   make
65 An' tell them wi' a patriot-heat,   Scottish passion
         Ye winna bear it?   will not

Some o' you nicely ken the laws,   know
To round the period an' pause,
An' with rhetoric clause on clause
70   To mak harangues;
Then echo thro' Saint Stephen's wa's   Parliament's walls
         Auld Scotland's wrangs.   old, wrongs

Dempster,[1] a true blue Scot I'se warran;   I'll warrant
Thee, aith-detesting, chaste *Kilkerran*;[2]   oath
75 An' that glib-gabbet Highland Baron,   quick-tongued
         The Laird o' *Graham*;[3]
An' ane, a chap that's damn'd auldfarran,   one, shrewd
         Dundass[4] his name:

Erskine,[5] a spunkie Norland billie;   spirited Northern young man
80 True Campbells, *Frederick* an' *Ilay*;[6]
An' Livistone, the bauld *Sir Willie*;[7]   bold
         An' mony ithers,   many others
Whom auld Demosthenes or Tully[8]   old
         Might own for brithers.   brothers

1 George Dempster, mentioned in *The Vision*.
2 Sir Adam Ferguson.
3 James Graham, Son of the Duke of Montrose.
4 Henry Dundas, Viscount Melville.
5 Thomas Erskine, M.P., brother of Henry Erskine.
6 Frederick Campbell and Ilay Campbell.
7 Sir William Cunninghame of Livingston.
8 Classical rhetorical orators – colloquial for Cicero.

85 Thee sodger Hugh, my watchman stented,[9]   *soldier, assigned (M.P.)*
    If Bardies e'er are represented;
    I ken if that your sword were wanted,   *know*
            Ye'd lend your hand;
    But when there's ought to say anent it,   *about*
90   Ye're at a stand.

    Arouse my boys! exert your mettle,
    To get auld Scotland back her *kettle*!   *old, whisky still*
    Or faith! I'll wad my new pleugh-pettle,   *wager, plough scraper*
            Ye'll see't or lang,   *before long*
95 She'll teach you, wi' a reekan whittle,   *smoking knife*
            Anither sang.   *another song*

    This while she's been in crankous mood,   *fretful*
    Her *lost Militia* fir'd her bluid;   *blood*
    (Deil na they never mair do guid,   *not, more, good*
100   Play'd her that pliskie!)   *trick*
    An' now she's like to rin red-wud   *run stark mad*
            About her *Whisky*.

    An' Lord! if ance they pit her till't,   *once, put her to it*
    Her tartan petticoat she'll kilt,   *tuck up*
105 An' durk an' pistol at her belt,   *blade*
            She'll tak the streets,
    An' rin her whittle to the hilt,   *run her knife, handle*
            I' the first she meets!

    For God-sake, Sirs! then speak her fair,
110 An' straik her cannie wi' the hair,   *stroke, carefully*
    An' to the *Muckle House* repair,   *great Parliament*
            Wi' instant speed,
    An' strive, wi' a' your Wit an' Lear,   *knowledge*
            To get remead.

115 Yon ill-tongu'd tinkler, *Charlie Fox*,[10]   *gypsy*
    May taunt you wi' his jeers an' mocks;
    But gie him't het, my hearty cocks!   *give him it hot*
            E'en cowe the cadie!   *subdue, rascal*
    An' send him to his dicing box
120   An' sportin lady.

    9 Hugh Montgomerie, Earl of Eglinton.
    10 Leader of the Whig Opposition.

Tell yon guid bluid of auld *Boconnock's*,[11]   good blood, old
I'll be his debt twa mashlum bonnocks,   mixed meal bannocks
An' drink his health in auld *Nanse Tinnock's*[12] old
      Nine times a-week,
125 If he some scheme, like tea an' winnocks,   windows
      Wad kindly seek.   would

Could he some *commutation* broach,
I'll pledge my aith in guid braid Scotch,   oath, good broad
He needna fear their foul reproach   need not
130   Nor erudition,
Yon mixtie-maxtie, queer hotch-potch,   mixed up
      The *Coalition*.

Auld Scotland has a raucle tongue;   old, rough
She's just a devil wi' a rung;   bludgeon
135 An' if she promise auld or young   old
      To tak their part,
Tho' by the neck she should be strung,
      She'll no desert.

And now, ye chosen FIVE AND FORTY,
140 May still your Mither's heart support ye;   mother's
Then, tho' a Minister grow dorty,   haughty
      An' kick your place,
Ye'll snap your fingers, poor an' hearty,
      Before his face.

145 God bless your Honors, a' your days,
Wi' sowps o' kail and brats o' claes,   sups of broth, coarse cloth
In spite o' a' the thievish kaes,   jackdaws
      That haunt St. *Jamie's*!   parliament
Your humble Bardie sings an' prays,
150   While *Rab* his name is.

POSTSCRIPT
Let half-starv'd slaves in warmer skies,
See future wines, rich-clust'ring, rise;

11 An allusion to William Pitt's grandfather, Robert.
12 A worthy old Hostess of the Author's in *Mauchline*, where he sometimes
studies Politics over a glass of guid auld *Scotch Drink*. R.B.

Their lot auld Scotland ne'er envies,   old
    But, blythe and frisky,
155 She eyes her freeborn, martial boys
    Tak aff their Whisky.   drink down

What tho' their Phoebus kinder warms,   sun
While Fragrance blooms and Beauty charms!
When wretches range, in famish'd swarms,
160   The scented groves,
Or hounded forth, *dishonor* arms
    In hungry droves.

Their *gun's* a burden on their shouther;   shoulder
They downa bide the stink o' *powther*;   do not, gun powder
165 Their bauldest thought's a hank'ring swither   boldest, uncertain doubt
    To stan' or rin,
Till skelp – a shot – they're aff, a' throw'ther, crack, off, pell-mell
    To save their skin.

But bring a SCOTCHMAN frae his hill,   from
170 Clap in his cheek a *Highlan* gill,   gill (measure)
Say, such is royal GEORGE'S will,
    An' there's the foe!
He has nae thought but how to kill   no
    Twa at a blow.   two

175 Nae cauld, faint-hearted doubtings tease him;   no cold
Death comes, wi' fearless eye he sees him;
Wi' bluidy han' a welcome gies him;   bloody hand, gives
    An' when he fa's,   falls
His latest draught o' breathin lea'es him   leaves
180   In faint huzzas.

Sages their solemn een may steek   eyes, close
An' raise a philosophic reek,   smoke
An' physically causes seek,
    In *clime* an' *season*;
185 But tell me *Whisky's* name in Greek:
    I'll tell the reason.

SCOTLAND, my auld, respected Mither!   old, mother
Tho' whyles ye moistify your leather,   moisten, vagina

Till whare ye sit on craps o' heather	crops
190 Ye tine your dam,	lose your water
Freedom and whisky gang thegither,	go together
Tak aff your dram!	raise up your glass

The extended title which conveys the notion of self-mocking very minor prophetic biblical lamentation and political tract is given, by the parodic use in Milton, an added impulse to see the poem, despite its manifest political content, as laughing and lightweight. Surely the poet, unlike Adam for Eve, is not grieving for a fallen Scotland (*Paradise Lost*, Book IX, ll. 896–901)? The political, economic occasion for the poem was the Wash Act brought in by English pressure in 1784 to prevent what they considered preferential treatment to the Scottish distilling industry. This had not only severe effects on the Scottish whisky industry but was in breach of the terms of the Union and, for Burns, another symptom of the London Parliament's, at best, indifference to Scottish needs. By the time the poem appeared the injustice seemed, as Burns's footnote suggests, to have been corrected: 'This was wrote before the Act anent the Scotch Distilleries of session 1786; for which Scotland and the Author return their most grateful thanks.'

In February, 1789, the matter flared up again. On this occasion Burns chose for the second time to send a pseudonymous letter to the *Edinburgh Evening Courant* on the 9th February. The occasion for his first letter had been his request for compassion for the fallen House of Stuart along with his risky defence of the American Revolution as akin to the British events of 1688. This second letter was signed John Barleycorn and purports, remarkably, to be written on behalf of the Scottish Distillers to William Pitt who, at the time of composition, appears to be about to fall from power due to the Regency Bill as an antidote to the King's madness. The letter is based on the Scottish Distillers' alleged mutual sense of falling with Pitt from power and prosperity to exclusion and poverty. There is also an extraordinary parallel made with King Nebuchadnezzar which is implicitly to be read as Burns's own sense of sharing Pitt's exile. The letter also repeats the poem's allegations of political injustice to Scotland:

> But turn your eyes, Sir, to the tragic scenes of our fate. An ancient nation that for many ages had gallantly maintained the unequal struggle for independence with her much more power-ful neighbour, at last agrees to a union which should ever after make them one people. In consideration of certain circum-stances, it was solemnly covenanted that the Former should

always enjoy a stipulated alleviation of her share of the public burdens, particularly in that branch of the revenue known by the name of the Excise.

This just priviledge has of late given great umbrage to some invidious powerful individuals of the more potent half of the Empire, and they have spared no wicked pains, under insidious pretexts to subvert, what they yet too much dreaded the spirit of their ancient enemies openly to attack.

By this conspiracy we fell; nor did we alone suffer, our Country was deeply wounded. A number of, we will say it, respectable characters largely engaged in trade where we were not only useful but absolutely necessary to our Country in her dearest interest; we, with all that was near and dear to us, were sacrificed without remorse, to the Infernal Deity of Political Expediency (Letter, 311).

Burns's second intrusion into *The Courant* is as seriously meant in national and political terms as his first. The poem, also invoking Pitt, depends on laughter but the comic tone is one that both covertly asserts Burns's satirising superiority to his subject and his ability to give tangible witness to the economic distresses caused by the whisky tax. As well as the machinations of the London Parliament and the betrayals of Scotland therein by her forty-five Commons representatives , he also speculates on the degree to which available Scottish talent could be employed to the Nation's benefit. Not least, running through the poem, are insinuations of ancestral Scottish violence resurrecting itself again to put right political injustice.

The poem begins with the ironic comment that, whilst Irish Lords were allowed to represent Scotland in Parliament, the elder sons of Scottish Peers were not. He then craftily invokes his coarse, arse-in-the-dust muse. As well as the tactical self-denigration of his muse, this allows the poet to distance himself in the wings, putting the muse centre stage. But, at l. 55, this somewhat transparent mask drops and he speaks, again, ironically, self-denigratorily, as himself.

Ll. 13–54 invoke the muse to have the courage to tell the truth about establishment censure by revealing the social dereliction caused by the related excesses of the Excisemen and the Smugglers. He also looks to specifically Ayrshire heroes (See *The Vision*) such as the military Montgomery and the writerly Boswell to save Mother Scotland from dereliction. We get the first suggestion of reactive violence (ll. 59–60), with a vengeful image of choking restriction perpetrated by the poet on his nation's enemies.

The poem is, thus, both an analysis of post-Union Scottish

distress and a thesis about Scottish resurrection based on the available Scottish greatness. In a letter he wrote to Bruce Campbell on November 13th, 1788 he included the poem which he hoped would be passed to James Boswell, thus procuring him an introduction to the great writer:

There are few pleasures my late will-o'-wisp character has given me, equal to that of having seen many of the extraordinary men, the heroes of Wit and Literature in my Country; and as I had the honour of drawing my first breath in almost the same Parish with Mr Boswell, my pride Plumes itself on the connection. To crouch in the train of meer, stupid Wealth & Greatness, except where the commercial interests of worldly Prudence find their account in it, I hold to be Prostitution in any one that is not born a Slave; but to have been acquainted with a man such as Mr Boswell, I would hand down to my Posterity, as one of the honours of their Ancestor (Letter 284).

Boswell received and endorsed the letter (13th Nov 1788, 'Mr Robert Burns the Poet expressing very high sentiments of me') but made no attempts to meet Burns. Burns's need for redemptive Scottish Heroes, ancestral and contemporary, certainly chose the wrong man in that sycophantic, anglophile prose genius. Also this poem's programme puts together a misalliance of talents who Burns then thought were the rhetorical equals of Demosthenes and Tully, whose eloquence would cause the triumph of Scotland at Saint Stephens, the then site of Parliament. Ll. 73–81 list the candidates allegedly worthy of this task.

That this élite legal, political corps would co-operate to save Scotland was to prove for Burns the wildest of hopes. By 1795, as his brilliant poem *The Dean of Faculty* reveals, Scotland was tearing itself apart with the brilliant radical Henry Erskine outvoted and ejected from office by Robert Dundas. Henry Dundas, as Pitt's ferociously repressive Home Secretary, was running a fatwah against his radical countrymen.

From ll. 85–100 we have images of Scottish outrage spilling into weapons bearing anarchy with echoes of recent Jacobite incursion. Pitt, auld Boconnocks, is praised for his new methods of taxation. 'Commutation' (l. 121) refers to his 1784 Commutation Act which diverted tax from tea to windows. Fox, at this time is still for Burns merely a licentious nuisance. After another invocation of Scottish capacity for violence, he ends by requesting the 45 MPs to support their Nation. His actual hopes of their doing so is summed up in a brilliantly ironic last stanza where he envisages these pursy placemen subsisting on the diet and in the rags of Scottish peasantry among the temptations of St James's in London.

This level of irony is sustained in the quite brilliantly subtle seven-stanza Postscript which Burns adds to the poem. Carol McGuirk suggests that this should be read as the Poet's first address to Parliament. On the face of it, derived from Enlightenment theories that national character is the product of climate and environment, the poem seems to be a celebration of Scottish machismo and militarism over the cowardice inherent to the wine drinking peasantry of warmer climes. This apparent celebration of Scottish militarism is, however, immediately, devastatingly undercut. Ll. 163–74 are an astonishingly compressed denunciation of the savage, self-destructive consequences to the *unaware* Highlanders of their post-Culloden integration into British Imperial armies. Equally dark for Scotland is the fact that the feminine part of the nation (ll. 181–3) has degenerated to an incontinent crone. Thus, the ultimate toast (ll. 185–6) is the blackest irony.

N.B. Stanza 15 here is not included in Kinsley. There is also a variation in the last stanza.

The Holy Fair

First printed in the Kilmarnock edition, 1786.

> *A robe of seeming truth and trust*
> *Hid crafty observation;*
> *And secret hung, with poison'd crust,*
> *The dirk of defamation:*
> *A mask that like the gorget show'd,*
> *Dye-varying on the pigeon;*
> *And for a mantle large and broad,*
> *He wrapt him in Religion.*

Tom Brown, *Hypocrisy A-La-Mode.*

Upon a simmer *Sunday morn,*	summer
When Nature's face is fair,	
I walked forth to view the corn,	
An' snuff the callor air:	fresh
5 The rising sun, owre GALSTON Muirs,	over, moors
Wi' glorious light was glintan;	
The hares were hirplan down the furs,	hobbling with uneven speed, furrows
The lav'rocks they were chantan	larks
Fu' sweet that day.	full

10 As lightsomely I glowr'd abroad,
        To see a scene sae gay,   *so*
    Three *hizzies*, early at the road,   *young wenches*
        Cam skelpan up the way.   *came hurrying*
    Twa had manteeles o' dolefu' black,   *two, mantles*
15   But ane wi' lyart lining;   *one, grey*
    The *third*, that gaed a wee aback,   *went, behind*
        Was in the fashion shining
            Fu' gay that day.   *full*

    The *twa* appear'd like sisters twin,   *two*
20   In feature, form, an' claes;   *clothes*
    Their visage — wither'd, lang an' thin,   *long*
        An' sour as onie slaes: *any sloes*
    The *third* cam up, hap-step-an'-lowp,   *hop-step-and-leap*
        As light as onie lambie, —   *any lamb*
25 An' wi' a curchie low did stoop,   *curtsey*
        As soon as e'er she saw me,
            Fu' kind that day.

    Wi' bonnet aff, quoth I, 'Sweet lass,   *off*
        I think ye seem to ken me;   *know*
30 I'm sure I've seen that bonie face,   *pretty*
        But yet I canna name ye. — '   *cannot*
    Quo' she, an' laughin as she spak,   *spoke*
        An' taks me by the hands,
    'Ye, for my sake, hae gi'en the feck   *have given, bulk*
35   Of a' the *ten commands*
            A screed some day.   *rip*

    'My name is FUN — your cronie dear,   *friend*
        The nearest friend ye hae;   *have*
    An' this is SUPERSTITION here,
40   An' that's HYPOCRISY.
    I'm gaun to Mauchline *Holy Fair*,   *going*
        To spend an hour in daffin: *larking/playing*
    Gin ye'll go there, yon runkl'd pair,   *if, wrinkled*
        We will get famous laughin
45   At them this day.'

    Quoth I, 'Wi' a' my heart, I'll do't;
        I'll get my Sunday's sark on,   *shirt*
    An' meet you on the holy spot;
        Faith, we'se hae fine remarkin!'   *we'll have*

50 Then I gaed hame at crowdie-time,   went, breakfast/gruel
        An' soon I made me ready;
    For roads were clad, frae side to side,   filled
        Wi' monie a wearie body,   many
            In droves that day.

55 Here farmers gash, in ridin graith,   smart, gear
        Gaed hoddan by their cotters;   went jogging, farm workers
    There swankies young, in braw braid-claith,   strapping fellows, fine broadcloth
        Are springan owre the gutters.   jumping over
    The lasses, skelpan barefit, thrang,   hastening barefoot, crowded
60   In silks an' scarlets glitter;
    Wi' *sweet-milk cheese*, in monie a whang,   many, large slice
        An' *farls*, bak'd wi' butter,   cakes
            Fu' crump that day.   hard or crisp

    When by the *plate* we set our nose,   collection plate
65   Weel heapèd up wi' ha'pence,
    A greedy glowr *Black-bonnet* throws,   stare, Church elder
        An' we maun draw our tippence.   must give
    Then in we go to see the show:
        On ev'ry side they're gath'ran;
70 Some carryin dails, some chairs an' stools,   bench planks
        An' some are busy bleth'ran   talking gossip
            Right loud that day.

    Here, stands a shed to fend the show'rs,   ward off
        An' screen our countra Gentry;   country
75 There *Racer Jess*, an' twa-three whores,   two or three
        Are blinkan at the entry.
    Here sits a raw o' tittlan jads,   giggling girls
        Wi' heavin breasts an' bare neck;
    An' there a batch o' *Wabster lads*,   group of weavers
80   Blackguardin frae Kilmarnock,   mischief making from
            For fun this day.

    Here some are thinkan on their sins,
        An' some upo' their claes;   clothes
    Ane curses feet that fyl'd his shins,   one, soiled, shoes/feet
85   Anither sighs an' prays: another
    On this hand sits a Chosen swatch,   sample
        Wi' screw'd-up, grace-proud faces;
    On that, a set o' chaps, at watch,
        Thrang winkan on the lasses   busy
90   To *chairs* that day.

O happy is that man an' blest!
    Nae wonder that it pride him!   no
Whase ain dear lass, that he likes best,   whose own
    Comes clinkan down beside him!   sitting quickly
95   Wi' arm repos'd on the *chair back*,
    He sweetly does compose him;
Which, by degrees, slips round her *neck*,
    An's loof upon her *bosom*,   hand
        Unkend that day.   unnoticed

100   Now a' the congregation o'er
    Is silent expectation;
For Moodie speels the holy door,   reaches
    Wi' tidings o' damnation:
Should *Hornie*, as in ancient days,   the Devil
105   'Mang sons o' God present him;
The vera sight o' Moodie's face,   very
    To's ain *het hame* had sent him   to his own hot home
        Wi' fright that day.

Hear how he clears the points o' Faith
110   Wi' rattlin and thumpin!
Now meekly calm, now wild in wrath,
    He's stampan, an' he's jumpan!   stomping
His lengthen'd chin, his turn'd-up snout,
    His eldritch squeel an' gestures,   unearthly squeal
115   O how they fire the heart devout,
    Like cantharidian plaisters   blister-producing plasters
        On sic a day!   such

But hark! the *tent* has chang'd its voice;
    There's peace an' rest nae langer;   no longer
120   For a' the *real judges* rise,
    They canna sit for anger: cannot
Smith opens out his cauld harangues,   cold
    On *practice* and on *morals*;
An' aff the godly pour in thrangs,   off, groups
125   To gie the jars an' barrels   give
        A lift that day.   to drink

What signifies his barren shine,
    Of *moral pow'rs* an' *reason;*
His English style, an' gesture fine
130   Are a' clean out o' season.

Like SOCRATES or ANTONINE,
    Or some auld pagan heathen,   old
The *moral man* he does define,
    But ne'er a word o' *faith* in
135   That's right that day.

In guid time comes an antidote   good
    Against sic poison'd nostrum;   such, preaching
For Peebles, frae the water-fit,   from, mouth of the river
    Ascends the *holy rostrum*:
140 See, up he's got the Word o' God,
    An' meek an' mim has view'd it,
While COMMON-SENSE has taen the road,
    An' aff, an' up the *Cowgate*[1]
        Fast, fast that day.

145 Wee Miller niest, the Guard relieves,   next
    An' Orthodoxy raibles,   recites by rote
Tho' in his heart he weel believes,   well
    An' thinks it auld wives' fables: old
But faith! the birkie wants a *Manse*:   fellow
150   So, cannilie he hums them;   carefully he humbugs
Altho' his *carnal* Wit an' Sense
    Like hafflins-wise o'ercomes him   almost half-wise
        At times that day.

Now butt an' ben the Change-house fills,   every corner of the Ale House
155   Wi' *yill-caup* Commentators: ale cup
Here's crying out for bakes an' gills,   biscuits
    An' there the pint-stowp clatters;   pint-jug slams
While thick an' thrang, an' loud an' lang,   crowded, long
    Wi' *Logic* an' wi' *Scripture*,
160 They raise a din, that, in the end   noise
    Is like to breed a rupture
        O' wrath that day.

Leeze me on Drink! it gies us mair   my blessings, gives, more
    Than either School or Colledge;
165 It kindles Wit, it waukens Lear,   wakens learning
    It pangs us fou o' Knowledge: crams, full

1 A street so called, which faces the *tent* in *Mauchline*. R.B.

Be't *whisky-gill* or *penny wheep*,   small beer costing a penny
    Or onie stronger potion,   any
It never fails, on drinkin deep,
170   To kittle up our *notion*,   enliven spirits
      By night or day.

The lads an' lasses, blythely bent
    To mind baith *saul* an' *body*,   both soul
Sit round the table, weel content,   well
175   An' steer about the *Toddy*:   stir
On this ane's dress, an' that ane's leuk,   one's, look
    They're makin observations;
While some are cozie i' the neuk,   cosy, corner
    An' formin *assignations*
180   To meet some day.

But now the Lord's ain trumpet touts,   own, sounds
    Till a' the hills are rairan,   roaring back the echo
And echoes back return the shouts;
    Black Russell is na spairan: not sparing
185 His piercin words, like Highlan' swords,
    Divide the joints an' marrow;
His talk o' Hell, whare devils dwell,   where
    Our vera 'Sauls does harrow'[2]   very souls
      Wi' fright that day.

190 A vast, unbottom'd, boundless *Pit*,
    Fill'd fou o' *lowan brunstane*,   full, flaming brimstone
Whase ragin flame, an' scorchin heat,   whose
    Wad melt the hardest whun-stane!   would, whinstone
The *half-asleep* start up wi' fear,
195   An' think they hear it roaran;   roaring
When presently it does appear,
    'Twas but some neebor *snoran*   neighbour, snoring
      Asleep that day.

'Twad be owre lang a tale to tell,   over long
200   How monie stories past;   many
An' how they crouded to the yill,   crowded, ale
    When they were a' dismist;

2 Shakespeare's *Hamlet*, R.B. [Act I, Sc. 5].

How drink gaed round, in cogs an' caups,   went, wooden jugs, cups
    Amang the furms an' benches;   among, a row of seats
205 An' *cheese* an' *bread*, frae women's laps,   from
    Was dealt about in lunches,
        An' dawds that day.   large pieces

In comes a gausie, gash *Guidwife*,   jolly, smart, good-
    An' sits down by the fire,
210 Syne draws her *kebbuck* an' her knife;   then, cheese
    The lasses they are shyer:
The auld *Guidmen*, about the *grace*,   old, good-
    Frae side to side they bother;   from
Till some ane by his bonnet lays,   one, cap
215   An' gies them't, like a *tether*,   gives, rope
        Fu' lang that day.   long

Waesucks! for him that gets nae lass,   Alas!, no
    Or lasses that hae naething!   have nothing
Sma' need has he to say a grace,
220   Or melvie his braw claithing!   dirty with meal, fine clothes
O *Wives*, be mindfu', ance yoursel,   once
    How bonie lads ye wanted;   handsome
An' dinna for a *kebbuck-heel*   do not, hard cheese rind
    Let lasses be affronted
225   On sic a day!   such

Now *Clinkumbell*,[3] wi' rattlan tow,   noisy pull
    Begins to jow an' croon;   swing, toll
Some swagger hame the best they dow,   home, can
    Some wait the afternoon.
230 At slaps the billies halt a blink,   a dyke gap, young lads
    Till lasses strip their shoon: take off, shoes
Wi' *faith* an' *hope*, an' *love* an' *drink*,
    They're a' in famous tune
        For crack that day.   talk

235 How monie hearts this day converts   many
    O' Sinners and o' Lasses!
Their hearts o' stane, gin night, are gane   stone, come, gone
    As saft as onie flesh is: soft, any

3 The Bell Ringer.

There's some are fou o' *love divine*;   full
240   There's some are fou o' *brandy*;   full
An' monie jobs that day begin,   many
May end in *Houghmagandie*   sexual intercourse
Some ither day.   other

This celebration of the sensual capacity of the Scottish people to
resist the worst rhetorical excesses of their clerical masters was
written in 1785 and revised in early 1786 for the Kilmarnock edition.
As McGuirk notes it is a direct descendent of Fergusson's *Leith
Races* which itself descends from Milton's *L'Allegro* and the nine-
line Scottish medieval 'brawl' poem:

I dwall amang the caller springs
    That weet the Land o' Cakes,
And aften tune my canty strings
    At bridals and late-wakes.
They ca' me Mirth; I ne'er was kend
    To grumble or look sour,
But blyth was be to lift a lend,
    Gif ye was sey my pow'r
        An' pith this day.

Fergusson's poem is, of course, the celebration of a purely secular
occasion; Burns is writing a more complex religious satire. Crawford
(*Burns, A Study of the Poems and Songs*, p. 69) places the occasional
poem accurately in the long Covenanter-originated Scottish tradi-
tion of open-air preaching. This specific event held in Mauchline in
1785 gathered together an audience of 2000 (four times the Mauch-
line population) of whom 1200 were communicants. Gilbert re-
corded that his brother was witness to this and had personal
knowledge of the preachers he so incisively satirises.

Burns takes his epigraph from *Hypocrisy A-La-Mode*, a play
written in 1704 by Tom Brown. That gale of liberal, satirical,
enlightened laughter that runs through eighteenth-century English
literature, especially Henry Fielding, as it attempts to sweep away
institutionalised religious hypocrisy also blows powerfully through
Burns's writings. He is the major Scottish variant on this anti-
clerical Enlightenment project. His Scotland, however, was a dar-
ker, more theocratically-controlled state than almost anywhere else
in Europe. In his early writing, as here, he senses victory over the
savage forces of religious repression. Later, his mood was to darken
as he despaired of the unbreakable grip Calvin's damnation had on
the Scottish psyche and, hence, body politic.

This early poem has, however, the comic optimism of Fielding's *Tom Jones* rather than the demonic repression of Blake's *The Songs of Experience*. The roaring flames of hell here (ll. 190–8) are merely the snores of a fellow pew-member. Unlike Macbeth, who tragically meets three witches on the moor, our comic narrator meets only two, Superstition and Hypocrisy, but their gorgeous sister Fun is an immediately victorious Cinderella and her spirit drives the whole poem. If not promiscuous, Fun is a decidedly erotic young lady as are the young women running barefoot, to save their shoes, towards the thronging excitement and carrying gifts which might be for the satisfaction of appetites other than those of the stomach. Indeed, the whole poem is infused with the way in which the people convert the 'Occasion', so clerically defined, into an opportunity for their multiple, but especially sexual, appetites:

> O happy is that man an' blest!
> Nae wonder that it pride him!
> Whase ain dear lass, that he likes best,
> Comes clinkan down beside him!

This echo of *Psalm 46* also alerts us to the fact that the rhetorical world of these preachers breeds sexual ills. For example, in l.116, 'cantharidian plaisters' were poultices made from the aphrodisiac Spanish fly.

Burns's assault on the various masters of pulpit oratory names names in a way that ensured there would be a severe backlash against him. 'Sawney' Moodie, with his old-time, 'Auld-Licht' undiluted gospel of damnation, is first on stage (ll. 100–17). Moodie (1728–99) was minister of Riccarton near Kilmarnock. He is followed by the 'New Licht' George Smith (d. 1823), minister of Galston. McGuirk subtly argues that while Burns is criticising Smith's rhetorical banality, he is more intent on satirising the congregation whose appetite for hell-fire preaching excludes the life of actual good-works. Smith's position is then assaulted by William Peebles of Newton-upon-Ayr (1753–1826) who, further inflaming the malign passions of the congregation, drives Common Sense, a central value of the new, more liberal Christianity, from the field. He is succeeded by Alexander Miller (d. 1804) whose professional self-seeking rebounded against him when the parishioners of Kilmaurs subsequently attempted to stop him getting that charge due, he claimed, to the effects of ll. 145–54. The worst is saved to the last. 'Black' John Russel (c. 1740–1817) was then minister at Kilmarnock. Subsequently minister at Cromarty, Hugh Miller (*My Schools and*

Schoolmasters) testified to his capacity to terrify, indeed, traumatise his congregation.

Along with such manifestations of theocratic control Burns adds some more overt political commentary. 'Racer Jess' is Janet Gibson (d. 1813), who is the daughter of Poosie Nansie, mine hostess of *Love and Liberty*, is with her like-inclined companions strategically placed beside the laird's tent. In the same stanza, the '*Wabster* lads/ Blackguarding from Kilmarnock' probably belong to the weaving community which was deeply and dissidently radical.

The poem moves from a celebration of alcohol (ll. 163–71) and the triumph of this earthy spirit over the one of false sanctimony to a triumphant assertion, implicit throughout the poem, of spontaneous eroticism. The experienced women may already be dealing out more than bread and cheese but, assignations made, loss of virginity happily looms at the poem's end. As Edwin Muir wrote, regarding the 'sordid and general tyranny' of the kirk session: 'it is only necessary to say that the time-honoured Scottish tradition of fornication triumphantly survived all its terrors' (*John Knox*, 1930, pp. 306–7).

Address to the Deil

First printed in the Kilmarnock edition, 1786.

> *O Prince! O Chief of many thronèd pow'rs!*
> *That led th' embattl'd seraphim to war —*
>   Milton.

	O Thou! whatever title suit thee —	
	Auld Hornie, Satan, Nick, or Clootie —	old, cloven-hoofed
	Wha in yon cavern grim an' sootie,	who, filled with soot
	Clos'd under hatches,	
5	Spairges about the brunstane cootie,	splashes, brimstone dish
	To scaud poor wretches!	scald
	Hear me, *auld Hangie*, for a wee,	old hangman, while
	An' let poor *damnèd bodies* be;	
	I'm sure sma' pleasure it can gie,	give
10	Ev'n to a *deil*,	devil
	To skelp an' scaud poor dogs like me	hit/slap, scald
	An' hear us squeel!	

Great is thy pow'r an' great thy fame;
Far kend, an' noted is thy name;   known
15 An' tho' yon *lowan heugh's* thy hame,   moaning, hollow, home
        Thou travels far;
An' faith! thou's neither lag, nor lame,   backward
        Nor blate nor scaur.   bashful, afraid

Whyles, ranging like a roarin lion,   sometimes
20 For prey, a' holes an' corners tryin;
Whyles, on the strong-wing'd Tempest flyin,
        Tirlan the *Kirks*;   stripping – attacking
Whyles, in the human bosom pryin,
        Unseen thou lurks.

25 I've heard my rev'rend *Graunie* say,   grannie
In lanely glens ye like to stray;   lonely
Or, where auld ruin'd castles grey   old
        Nod to the moon,
Ye fright the nightly wand'rer's way
30   Wi' eldritch croon.   unearthly eerie moan

When twilight did my *Graunie* summon,   grannie
To say her pray'rs, douce, honest woman!   sober/prudent
Aft yont the dyke she's heard you bumman,   away beyond
        Wi' eerie drone;
35 Or, rustlin, thro' the boortries coman,   alder trees coming
        Wi' heavy groan.

Ae dreary, windy, winter night,   one
The stars shot down wi' sklentan light,   slanting
Wi' you mysel, I gat a fright: got
40   Ayont the lough,   beyond, loch
Ye, like a *rash-buss*, stood in sight,   bunch of rushes
        Wi' waving sugh: moan

The cudgel in my nieve did shake,   fist
Each bristl'd hair stood like a stake;
45 When wi' an eldritch, stoor *quaick, quaick*,   unearthly harsh, duck quack
        Amang the springs,   among
Awa ye squatter'd like a *drake*,   away, a noisy take-off
        On whistling wings.

Let *Warlocks* grim, an' wither'd *Hags*,
50 Tell how wi' you, on ragweed nags,   ragwort
  They skim the muirs an' dizzy crags,   moors, high peaks
      Wi' wicked speed;
  And in kirk-yards renew their leagues,
      Owre howket dead.   over those raised from the grave

55 Thence, countra wives, wi' toil an' pain,   country
  May plunge an' plunge the *kirn* in vain;   churn
  For Och! the yellow treasure's taen   taken
      By witching skill;
  An' dawtit, twal-pint *Hawkie's* gaen   petted, 12-pint cow has gone
60   As yell's the Bill.   dry, bull

  Thence, mystic knots mak great abuse
  On *Young-Guidmen*, fond, keen an' croose;   husbands, over confident
  When the best *warklum* i' the house,   work-tool, penis
      By cantraip wit,   magic/evil
65 Is instant made no worth a louse,
      Just at the bit.   stopped before ejaculation

  When thowes dissolve the snawy hoord,   thawes, snowy hoard
  An' float the jinglin icy boord,   water's surface
  Then, *Water-kelpies* haunt the foord,   imaginary water-spirits, ford
70   By your direction,
  An' nighted Trav'llers are allur'd
      To their destruction.

  An' aft your moss-traversing *Spunkies*   often, bog-, demons
  Decoy the wight that late an' drunk is: fellow
75 The bleezan, curst, mischievous monkies
      Delude his eyes,
  Till in some miry slough he sunk is,   dirty hole
      Ne'er mair to rise.   more

  When MASONS' mystic *word* an' *grip*
80 In storms an' tempests raise you up,
  Some cock or cat your rage maun stop,   shall
      Or, strange to tell!
  The *youngest Brother* ye wad whip   would
      Aff straught to *Hell*.   off straight

85   Lang syne in *Eden's* bonie yard,   long ago
     When youthfu' lovers first were pair'd,
     An' all the Soul of Love they shar'd,
          The raptur'd hour,
     Sweet on the fragrant flow'ry swaird,   grassy edge
90   In shady bow'r:

     Then you, ye auld, snick-drawing dog!   old, sly door opener
     Ye cam to Paradise incog,   came, disguised
     An' play'd on man a cursed brogue   trick
          (Black be your fa'!),   fall
95   An' gied the infant warld a shog,   gave, world, shake
         'Maist ruin'd a'.   almost

     D'ye mind that day when in a bizz   flurry/bustle
     Wi' reeket duds, an' reestet gizz,   smoky clothes, scorched wig
     Ye did present your smoutie phiz   smutty face
100   'Mang better folk;
     An' sklented on the *man of Uzz*   squinted at Job
         Your spitefu' joke?

     An' how ye gat him i' your thrall,   got, spell
     An' brak him out o' house an' hal',   broke
105   While scabs an' blotches did him gall,
         Wi' bitter claw;
     An' lows'd his ill-tongu'd wicked *Scawl* —   slackened, scolding wife
         Was warst ava?   worst of all

     But a' your doings to rehearse,
110   Your wily snares an' fechtin fierce,   fighting
     Sin' that day MICHAEL did you pierce
         Down to this time,
     Wad ding a *Lallan* tongue, or *Erse*,   would, beat, Lowland Scots, Irish
         In Prose or Rhyme.

115   An' now, auld *Cloots*, I ken ye're thinkan,   old, know
     A certain Bardie's rantin, drinkin,
     Some luckless hour will send him linkan,   hurrying
         To your black pit;   Hell
     But, faith! he'll turn a corner jinkin,   dodging
120   An' cheat you yet.

But fare-you-weel, auld *Nickie-ben*!   old
O wad ye tak a thought an' men'!   would, mend
Ye aiblins might — I dinna ken —   perhaps, do not know
    Still hae a *stake*:   have
125 I'm wae to think upo' yon den,   sad
    Ev'n for your sake.

Burns mentions to John Richmond on 17th February 1786 that he had recently completed this poem. It is normally dated to the winter of 1785–6. A poem of this length Burns might have turned out quickly, so it is probably one of the fruits of his intense writing campaign leading to publication of the Kilmarnock edition.

This poem is now generally accepted as a relatively light-weight piece of near comic knockabout as Burns mocks the allegedly fast-fading figure of the Devil from his hitherto central role in Scottish theology and folk-lore. In his essay 'Robert Burns, Master of Scottish Poetry' (*Uncollected Scottish Criticism*, ed. Noble (London), pp. 199–200), Edwin Muir analyses this poem as the centre-piece of his persuasive argument that during the eighteenth century enlightened, improving, secularising Scotland had lost both its theological passion and its sense of supernatural mystery integral to its older poetry:

. . . two centuries of religious terrors had faded under the touch of reason and enlightenment, and the mysterious problems of election and damnation, had turned into amusing doggerel:

    O Thou wha in the Heavens dost dwell,
    Wha, as it pleases best thysel';
    Sends ane to heaven and ten to hell,
        A' for thy glory,
    And no for any guid or ill
        They've done afore thee!

Calvinism, once feared as a power or hated as a superstition, became absurd under the attack of common reason. The growing powers of the Enlightenment encouraged the change in the universities, the churches, in popular debate, and among the people. The ideas of liberty and equality did their part; Scotland became a place where a man was a man for a' that; the new humanistic attitude to religion led people to believe that 'The hert's aye the pairt aye that mak's us richt or wrang.' The story of the Fall became a simple story of human misfortune to two young people whose intentions had been so good, 'Lang syne in Eden's bonnie yard'.

> Then you, ye auld sneck-drawing dog!
> Ye cam to Paradise incog.
> And played on a man a curse brogue
>   (Black be your fa!)
> An' gled the infant world a shog
>   Maist ruined a'.

Muir further thinks that this new enlightened poetry is, with 'something of Voltaire's contes and Bernard Shaw's plays', witty but lightweight, even, relative to the old poetry, superficial. There are two related fundamental miscomprehensions in Muir's account. First, the power of folklore is present in the poem though not, say, as we find its direct intrusion as in the great Scottish Ballad tradition, so beloved by Muir, but in Burns's ambivalent treatment of it. As he wrote to Dr Moore:

> I sometimes keep a sharp look-out in suspicious places; and though nobody can be more sceptical in these matters than I, yet it often takes an effort of Philosophy to shake of these idle terrors (Letter 125).

What we see in this particular poem from ll. 5–84 is no simple send-up of foolishly atavistic folk-superstition. Not only is Burns intent on anthropologically recording, as in *Halloween*, the customs and beliefs of his rural community but, as in *Tam o' Shanter*, conveying the still 'eerie' potency of that world. (See Edward J. Cowan, 'Burns and Superstition', *Love and Liberty*, pp. 229–37.) He is also, as usual, making salacious jokes inspired by the bottomless well of sexual metaphor supplied to him by folk-tradition. Hugh Blair wanted ll. 61–6 deleted as 'indecent' because they depend on the identification of lume/loom with the penis. (See *BC*, 1932, p. 95.)

Muir, however, is absolutely wrong in thinking that it is the diminished power of Calvinism on the Scottish psyche that leads to the poem's, to him, lightweight tone. This is a particularly weird error in Muir, who more than any other figure in a profoundly anti-Calvinist, Scottish Renaissance group believed that Knox (of whom he actually wrote a biography) had not lost his sadistic, disintegrating grip on the Scottish soul. Further, that Scottish reintegration meant a return to catholic, European humanism.

Burns is certainly partly laughing at the Devil in the poem's opening sequences (ll. 1–24) by the reductive ridicule of reducing the devil's energies to being devoted to the poet's petty transgressions. The Devil, however, is not for his own sake being laughed out of court. Burns's poetic wit is in direct proportion to his most potent enemies. The enemy here is not the devil but those who seek demonically to control mankind in his name. For their power structure to remain intact the Devil could not be allowed to become a laughing matter. This is why, even more than the more personally abusive clerical satires, this poem caused such an outcry. As Carol McGuirk finely writes:

> A ringing blow in Burns's quarrel with the Auld Licht, this satire caused a major local scandal. Several of the anonymous contributors to *Animadversions*, James Maxwell's compilation of evangelical attacks on Burns (Paisley, 1788), saw this poem as final proof of Burns's evil values. Alexander ('Saunders') Tait of Tarbolton, a mantua-maker and tailor who considered himself Burns's equal as a satirist, also seized upon this as Burns's most shocking poem, publishing his attack in 1790.
>
> Burns intended it to shock, and so structures the poem round what any Auld Licht partisan would see as a heretical statement of Arminianism: the deil's long-ago invasion of Eden only 'almost' 'ruined all' for Adam and Eve (1. 96): the stain of sin is not ineradicable and even Satan (if he wished) could 'tak a thought' and mend = change and receive forgiveness. Burns's 'deil' is neither the sadistic demon of Auld Licht sermons nor the tragic hero Milton's Satan considered himself to be. A rather forlorn and unsuccessful mischief-maker, his smudged ('smoutie') face ashy from brimstone and his plots against humanity invariably thwarted, the deil is addressed more or less as just another 'poor, damned body'. The poet is dramatising his rejection of predestination. The Arminians had challenged Calvinist 'election' (salvation through grace alone, not human effort) but Burns focuses on its corollary—repudiation, a doctrine that insisted that the reprobated are eternally cast away from grace, whatever their benighted individual efforts to be (and do) good. Burns, by contrast, announces that he considers himself salvageable (ll. 119–20) – and if 'a certain Bardie' can be saved, then there must be hope for a mere devil. The poet is paying a backhanded compliment to his own sinfulness as he mocks the Auld Licht. No one – not even the deil – is all bad and forever incapable of change, the poem argues with a cheerful perversity that enraged the Auld Licht. A more orthodox point is also made: hope of heaven is more likely to convert sinners than fear of damnation. (pp. 233–4)

The Death and Dying Words of Poor Mailie,
The Author's Only Pet Yowe: An Unco Mournfu' Tale
First printed in the Kilmarnock edition, 1786.

As MAILIE, an' her lambs thegither, together
Was ae day nibblin on the tether, one day, chewing
Upon her cloot she coost a hitch, hoof, looped
An' owre she warsl'd in the ditch: over, floundered
5 There, groanin, dying, she did ly,
When *Hughoc* he cam doytan by. walking/staggering

Wi' glowrin een, an' lifted han's staring eyes
Poor *Hughoc* like a statue stan's;
He saw her days were near hand ended,
10 But, wae's my heart! he could na mend it! woe, not
He gaped wide, but naething spak. nothing spoke
At length poor *Mailie* silence brak: — broke

'O thou, whase lamentable face whose
Appears to mourn my woefu' case!
15 My *dying words* attentive hear,
An' bear them to my *Master* dear.

'Tell him, if e'er again he keep
As muckle gear as buy a *sheep*, much money
O, bid him never tie them mair, more
20 Wi' wicked strings o' hemp or hair!
But ca' them out to park or hill, call/drive
An' let them wander at their will:
So may his flock increase, an' grow
To *scores* o' lambs, an' *packs* o' woo'!

25 'Tell him, he was a Master kin', kind
An' ay was guid to me an' mine; good
An' now my *dying* charge I gie him, give
My helpless *lambs*, I trust them wi' him. with

'O, bid him save their harmless lives,
30 Frae dogs, an' tods, an' butchers' knives! from, foxes
But gie them guid cow-milk their fill, give, good
Till they be fit to fend themsel; themselves
An' tent them duely, e'en an' morn, tend
Wi' taets o' *hay* an' ripps o' *corn*. small amounts, handfuls

35　'An' may they never learn the gaets,　　　　　*ways*
　　Of ither vile, wanrestfu' *Pets* —　　　　　*other, restless*
　　To slink thro' slaps, an' reave an' steal,　　　*gaps in dykes*
　　At stacks o' pease, or stocks o' kail.　　　　*plants*
　　So may they, like their great *forbears*,
40　For monie a year come thro' the sheers:　　　*many*
　　So *wives* will gie them bits o' bread,　　　　*give*
　　An' *bairns* greet for them when they're dead.　*children cry*

　　'My poor *toop-lamb*, my son an' heir,　　　　*tup/male*
　　O, bid him breed him up wi' care!　　　　　*with*
45　An' if he live to be a beast,
　　To pit some havins in his breast!　　　　　*conduct*
　　An' warn him, what I winna name,　　　　　*would not*
　　To stay content wi' *yowes* at hame;　　　　*ewes*
　　An' no to rin an' wear his cloots,　　　　　*run, hooves*
50　Like other menseless, graceless brutes.　　　*unmannerly*

　　'An' niest, my *yowie*, silly thing;　　　　*next, ewekin/female baby*
　　Gude keep thee frae a *tether string*!　　　　*from*
　　O, may thou ne'er forgather up,　　　　　*make friends*
　　Wi' onie blastet, moorland *toop*;　　　　　*any, blasted/damned*
55　But ay keep mind to moop an' mell,　　　　*always, nibble & mix*
　　Wi' sheep o' credit like thysel!

　　'And now, *my bairns*, wi' my last breath,
　　I lea'e my blessin wi' you baith:　　　　　*leave, with, both*
　　An' when you think upo' your Mither,　　　*mother*
60　Mind to be kind to ane anither.　　　　　*one another*

　　'Now, honest *Hughoc*, dinna fail,　　　　*do not*
　　To tell my Master a' my tale;
　　An' bid him burn this cursed *tether*,
　　An' for thy pains thou'se get my blather.'　　*thou will, bladder*

65　This said, poor *Mailie* turn'd her head,
　　An' clos'd her een amang the dead!　　　　*eyes, among*

This poem fuses an actual experience at Lochlea, subsequently recorded by Gilbert Burns, with Burns's awareness of the tradition of comic animal monologue as integral to the eighteenth-century Scottish vernacular revival. As Burns noted, Hughoc was an actual neighbouring herdsman though, in reality, the sheep was freed from the strangling tether and survived. Its 'poetic' death is necessary to the comic pathos of the poem. The literary tradition of burlesquing animal poetry commenced with William Hamilton of Gilbertfield (c. 1665–1751) whose rhetorical greyhound's death-speech parodies Blind Harry's *Wallace*. Burns would also be aware of the so-influential Robert Fergusson's very funny parody of Henry Mackenzie's *The Man of Feeling* (1771) with his Milton-burlesquing *The Sow of Feeling* (1773). As we saw in the Introduction, Mackenzie never forgave Fergusson's lachrymose porcine parody. The tone of Burns's poem is more subtle since the mother's dying warnings to her children, particularly against keeping the wrong sexual company, are a mixture of his satirising snobbery and prudery with genuine sympathy towards a mother's natural, protective love. Burns, indeed (see *Address to a Young Friend*), often displayed a genuine paternal care, which revealed a desire to preserve his varied dependants from the dangers inherent in his own licentious excesses.

Poor Mailie's Elegy

First printed in the Kilmarnock edition, 1786.

Lament in rhyme, lament in prose,
Wi' saut tears tricklin down your nose;   salt
Our *Bardie's* fate is at a close,
    Past a' remead!   remedy
5 The last, sad cape-stane of his woes;   coping stone(final weight)
    Poor *Mailie's* dead!

It's no the loss of warl's gear,   worldly goods
That could sae bitter draw the tear,   so
Or mak our *Bardie*, dowie, wear   drooping/gloomy
10   The mourning weed:
He's lost a friend an' neebor dear   neighbour
    In *Mailie* dead.

Thro' a' the toun she trotted by him;   town
A lang half-mile she could descry him;   long
15 Wi' kindly bleat, when she did spy him,
    She ran wi' speed:
A friend mair faithfu' ne'er cam nigh him,   more, came near
    Than *Mailie* dead.

I wat she was a *sheep* o' sense,   wot
20 An' could behave hersel wi' mense: tact/grace
    I'll say't, she never brak a fence,   broke
        Thro' thievish greed.
    Our *Bardie*, lanely, keeps the spence   parlour
        Sin' *Mailie's* dead.

25 Or, if he wanders up the howe,   glen
    Her livin image in *her yowe*   ewe
    Comes bleatin till him, owre the knowe,   over the hill edge
        For bits o' bread;
    An' down the briny pearls rowe   roll
30   For *Mailie* dead.

    She was nae get o' moorlan tips,   not born from
    Wi' tawted ket, an' hairy hips;   matted fleece
    For her forbears were brought in ships,
        Frae 'yont the TWEED: from beyond
35 A bonier *fleesh* ne'er cross'd the clips   fleece, sheep shears
        Than *Mailie* dead.

    Wae worth the man wha first did shape   woe befall
    That vile, wanchancie thing — a *raep*!   dangerous, rope
    It maks guid fellows girn an' gape,   makes good, facial contortion
40   Wi' chokin dread;
    An' *Robin's* bonnet wave wi' crape   mourning
        For *Mailie* dead.

    O a' ye *Bards* on bonie DOON!
    An' wha on AIRE your chanters tune!   who, Ayr, bagpipes
45 Come, join the melancholious croon
        O' *Robin's* reed!
    His heart will never get aboon!   above/over
        His *Mailie's* dead!

This was probably written in 1785–6 as a companion piece for
publication with the preceding Mailie monologue. Again the tone
of the poem is mixed. Burns employs the six-line Standard Habbie
used in vernacular eighteenth-century elegy while partly parodying
the content of these poems. His most specified source is probably
Fergusson's *Elegy on the Death of Mr David Gregory* with its
repetitive end-line 'Sin Gregory's dead'. He is also partly sending
up his own emotions. This is emphasised by the recent discovery

from a London saleroom catalogue for May 1962 of an hitherto unknown last stanza:

> She was nae get o' runted rams,
> Wi' woo' like goat's an' legs like trams;
> She was the flower o' Fairlee lambs,
>   A famous breed:
> Now Robin, greetin', chows the hams
>   O' Mailie dead.

This peasant practicality would have been too much for his genteel audience. On the other hand, there is real affection for its pedigree beauty. This was the man who was still surrounding himself with pet sheep at Ellisland. Further, as in his mouse poem, the lives of men and beasts are both brutally intruded upon not only by lethal elemental forces but by human-inspired, cruel economic and political forces. The accidentally throttled beast has its more sinister legally garrotted human counterpart:

> Wae worth the man wha first did shape
> That vile chancie thing – a rape!
> It maks guid fellows girn an' gape,
>   Wi' chokin dread . . .

Epistle to James Smith

First printed in the Kilmarnock edition, 1786.

Friendship, mysterious cement of the soul!
Sweet'ner of Life, and solder of Society!
I owe thee much.

– BLAIR

Dear Smith, the sleest, pawkie thief,	slyest, cunning
That e'er attempted stealth or rief!	robbery/plunder
Ye surely hae some warlock-breef	have, wizard-spell
Owre human hearts;	over
For ne'er a bosom yet was prief	proof
Against your arts.	
For me, I swear by sun an' moon,	
And ev'ry star that blinks aboon,	above
Ye've cost me twenty pair o' shoon,	shoes
Just gaun to see you;	going
And ev'ry ither pair that's done,	other
Mair taen I'm wi' you.	more taken

That auld, capricious carlin, *Nature*,　　　hag
To mak amends for scrimpit stature,　　　make, stunted
15　She's turn'd you off, a human-creature
　　　　On her *first* plan;
And in her freaks, on ev'ry feature
　　　　She's wrote *the Man*.

Just now I've taen the fit o' rhyme,　　　taken
20　My barmie noddle's working prime,　　　excited head/brain
My fancy yerket up sublime,　　　pulled together
　　　　Wi' hasty summon:
Hae ye a leisure-moment's time　　　have
　　　　To hear what's comin?

25　Some rhyme a neebor's name to lash;　　　neighbour
Some rhyme (vain thought!) for needfu' cash;
Some rhyme to court the countra clash,　　　country gossip
　　　　An' raise a din;
For me, an *aim* I never fash;　　　think of
30　　　　I rhyme for *fun*.

The star that rules my luckless lot,
Has fated me the russet coat,　　　poor man's coat
An' damn'd my fortune to the groat;　　　smallest coin
　　　　But, in requit,　　　as compensation
35　Has blest me with a *random-shot*
　　　　O' countra wit.　　　country

This while my notion's taen a sklent,　　　taken a turn/bend
To try my fate in guid, black *prent*;　　　good, print
But still the mair I'm that way bent,　　　more
40　　　　Something cries, 'Hoolie!　　　halt
I red you, honest man, tak tent!　　　warn, heed
　　　　Ye'll shaw your folly:　　　show

'There's ither Poets, much your betters,　　　other
Far seen in *Greek*, deep men o' *letters*,　　　well versed
45　Hae thought they had ensur'd their debtors,　　　have
　　　　A' future ages;
Now moths deform, in shapeless tatters,
　　　　Their unknown pages.'

Then farewell hopes o' Laurel-boughs
50 To garland my poetic brows!
Henceforth, I'll rove where busy ploughs
    Are whistling thrang;   *busily/at work*
An teach the lanely heights an' howes *lonely hills and dales*
    My rustic sang.   *song*

55 I'll wander on, wi' tentless heed   *carefree*
How ne er-halting moments speed,
Till Fate shall snap the brittle thread;
    Then, all unknown,
I'll lay m with th' *inglorious dead*,
60   rgot and gone!

But w eath, begin a tale?
Just n e living sound an' hale;   *strong*
Then t maintop croud the sail,   *crowd*
    ave *Care* o'er-side!
65 And larg before Enjoyment's gale,
      tak the tide.

This life, sae far's I understand,   *so*
Is a' enchanted fairy-land,
Where Pleasure is the Magic-wand,
70   That, wielded right,
Maks Hours like Minutes, hand in hand, *makes*
    Dance by fu' light.

The *magic-wand* then let us wield;
For, ance that five-an'-forty's speel'd, *once, climbed/reached*
75 See, crazy, weary, joyless, Eild,   *old age*
    Wi' wrinkl'd face,
Comes hostin, hirplan owre the field, *coughing, limping over*
    Wi' creepin pace.

When ance *life's day* draws near the gloamin, *once, twilight*
80 Then fareweel vacant, careless roamin; *farewell*
An' fareweel chearfu' tankards foamin,
    An' social noise:
An' fareweel dear, deluding Woman,
    The joy of joys!

85 O *Life!* how pleasant, in thy morning,
Young Fancy's rays the hills adorning!
Cold-pausing Caution's lesson scorning,
   We frisk away,
Like school-boys, at th' expected warning,
90   To joy an' play.

We wander there, we wander here,
We eye the *rose* upon the brier,
Unmindful that the *thorn* is near,
   Among the leaves;
95 And tho' the puny wound appear,
   Short while it grieves.

Some, lucky, find a flow'ry spot,
For which they never toil'd nor swat;   sweated
They drink the *sweet* and eat the *fat*,
100   But care or pain;   without
And haply eye the barren hut
   With high disdain.

With steady aim, some Fortune chase;
Keen Hope does ev'ry sinew brace;
105 Thro' fair, thro' foul, they urge the race,
   And seize the prey:
Then cannie, in some cozie place,   quietly, snug
   They close the *day*.

And others, like your humble servan',
110 *Poor wights!* nae rules nor roads observin,   no
To right or left eternal swervin,
   They zig-zag on;
Till, curst with Age, obscure an' starvin,
   They aften groan.   often

115 Alas! what bitter toil an' straining —
But truce with peevish, poor complaining!
Is Fortune's fickle *Luna* waning?
   E'en let her gang!   go
Beneath what light she has remaining,
120   Let's sing our Sang.   song

My pen I here fling to the door,
And kneel, ye *Pow'rs*, and warm implore,
'Tho' I should wander *Terra* o'er,   world
      In all her climes,
125 Grant me but this, I ask no more,
      Ay rowth o' rhymes.   abundant

'Gie dreeping roasts to *countra Lairds*,   give dripping, country
Till icicles hing frae their beards;   hang from
Gie fine braw claes to fine *Life-guards*   give, handsome clothes
130   And *Maids of Honor*;
And yill an' whisky gie to *Cairds*,   ale, give, tinkers
      Until they sconner.   are sick of it

'A *Title*, DEMPSTER merits it;
A Garter gie to WILLIE PIT;   symbol of Knighthood, give
135 Gie Wealth to some be-ledger'd Cit,   give, accounting citizen
      In cent per cent;
But give me real, sterling Wit,
      And I'm content

'While ye are pleas'd to keep me hale,   healthy
140 I'll sit down o'er my scanty meal,
Be't *water-brose* or *muslin-kail*,   gruel, meatless broth
      Wi' cheerfu' face,
As lang's the Muses dinna fail   long, do not
      To say the grace.'

145 An anxious e'e I never throws   eye
Behint my lug, or by my nose;   behind, ear
I jouk beneath Misfortune's blows   dodge/duck
      As weel's I may;   well as
Sworn foe to *sorrow*, *care*, and *prose*,
150   I rhyme away.

O ye douce folk that live by rule,   serious/sober
Grave, tideless-blooded, calm an' cool,   no rise & fall of passions
Compar'd wi' you — O fool! fool! fool!
      How much unlike!
155 Your hearts are just a standing pool,
      Your lives, a dyke!   stone wall

Nae hair-brained, sentimental traces   no
In your unletter'd, nameless faces!
In *arioso* trills and graces
160   Ye never stray;
But *gravissimo*, solemn basses
           Ye hum away.

Ye are sae *grave*, nae doubt ye're *wise*;   so, no
Nae ferly tho' ye do despise   no wonder
165 The hairum-scairum, ram-stam boys,   wild, headlong
           The rattling squad:
I see ye upward cast your eyes —
           Ye ken the road!   know

Whilst I — but I shall haud me there,   hold
170 Wi' you I'll scarce gang *ony where* —   go any
Then, *Jamie*, I shall say nae mair,   no more
           But quat my sang,   quit, song
Content wi' YOU to mak a *pair*,   make
           Whare'er I gang.   go

James Smith (1765–1823) was initially a linen-draper in Mauchline
who eventually emigrated to Jamaica after his business partnership
in printing near Linlithgow collapsed. He was younger brother to
one of the 'Mauchline Belles'. Smith is the recipient of several
letters from Burns.

   This is the first of a series of epistles written by Burns to either
Ayrshire intimates or intended intimates. This phase of his life,
energised by Masonic membership, is intensely social and, as we
will see in *The Vision*, a central aspiration, despite so many influ-
ences to the contrary, was to put creative tap-roots into Ayrshire soil
and anoint himself the Bard of its fertile but, as yet, poetically fallow
terrain. Historically this meant, beginning with Wallace, a resurrec-
tion of Ayrshire heroes. In terms of his own life he looked to
surround himself with fraternal like-minded spirits. Hence this
sequence of significant poetic epistles to James Smith, David Sillar,
Gavin Hamilton, John Lapraik, William Simpson and John Rankin.

   The epistolary form derives, of course, from classical poetry and
was heavily used in Augustan verse, most happily by Pope. The
genre had been domesticated, however, by an exchange of epistles
between Alan Ramsay and William Hamilton of Gilbertfield which
were instrumental in reactivating Scottish vernacular poetry in the
eighteenth century. As McGuirk has noted, these epistles were 'a

means of interchange between patriotic Scots poets' which 'also incorporated Horatian themes: country pleasure, disdain of 'greatness', praise of friendship, discussion of current issues and (especially) the state of Scottish poetry'. The proper use of the genre entails a degree of creative, technical parity between the correspondents. This was denied Burns, but his desire for the comforts of a poetic coterie was so strong that he often seriously overemphasised the talents of his correspondents. Sillars, for example, was a fine fiddler but a less than mediocre poet. Lapraik very likely plagiarised the song for which he achieved local fame. Later in life Burns was to show absolutely no patience with poetic inferiors who clung to his coat-tail in terms of social identity but not creative ability. He was as *creatively* hierarchical as Swift or Pope.

While the surface and formal, linguistic energy of these early Ayrshire epistles is cheerful and, even, boisterous, almost all of them are marked with a degree of black anxiety about not only the external social, economic and political forces acting on his achieving identity and recognition as a true poet but the often anarchic, even chaotic, internal forces which, while creatively necessary, were incompatible with the prudence and self-restraint necessary for a secure existence. Or, as he brilliantly defined it, in *The Vision*:

> Had I to guid advice but harket,
> I might, by this, hae led a market,
> Or strutted in a Bank and clarket
>   My Cash-Account;
> While here, half-mad, half-fed, half-sarket,
>   Is a' th' amount.

This epistle was written in the winter of 1785–6. Smith was (ll. 163–74) a key member of the 'ram-stam boys'. This testosterone charged group, especially Gavin Hamilton, were in constant conflict with the ministry. Burns's comment on Smith being small but perfectly formed (ll. 13–18) may be partly a response to clerical condemnation of his friend. The extent of Smith's friendship also extended to Jean Armour. Burns was to order from Smith, then a partner in a Calico works, his first present for Jean: ' 'tis my first present to her since I have irrevocably called her mine, and I have a kind of whimsical wish to get it from an old and much valued friend of hers and mine, a Trusty Trojan, on whose friendship I count myself possessed on a life-rent lease' (Letter 237). The 'Trusty Trojan' was his sole Mauchline friend as the dispute with the Armour family deepened.

McGuirk ('Loose Canons: Milton and Burns, Artsong and Folksong', *Love and Liberty*, pp. 317–20) has drawn attention to parallels between this poem and Milton's *Lycidas* as a poem which not only 'addresses issues of friendship and bereavement, fame and obscurity, poetic immortality and premature death' but also includes a harsher satire on corrupt religiosity (ll. 151–68) and on the capricious, lethal intrusions of blind fate into human life.

The central dialectic of the poem is based on Burns's chronic anxiety, equally pervasive in his letters, about the problematic nature of forging a poetic identity for himself. At this particular point in his life he was considering trying 'fate in guid, black prent' and the poem charts his disbelief that even the printed page will grant him the laurel bow of poetic immortality so that the poem celebrates the compensatory, rural, russet-coated anonymous rhyming funster (ll. 31–6). The black star of ill-luck, his sense of being under a Job-like curse, is, however, not so easily dismissed. The pervasive melancholy of Gray's *Elegy Written in a Country Churchyard* alluded to in ll. 59–60, 'I'll lay me with th' inglorious dead,/Forgot and gone!' suggests also Gray's line 'Some mute inglorious Milton here may rest' as his own fate. Also, as in contemporary English sentimental poetry, Burns makes the equation between the inability of the poet to become socially visible with the similar fate of the mass of the common people not to appear as individually identifiable in the stream of history. Thus the poem links Burns the invisible poet, with not only Burns the impoverished, unknown farmer but the mass of the people who are neither to be identified nor rewarded by history. Life is appallingly ill-divided between the poor and the over-rewarded rich (ll. 127–38). Dempster (l. 133) known as 'Honest George' Dempster was a Whig M.P. for Forfar Burghs 1761–90 and an agricultural improver. Pitt, at this stage in his prime-ministerial career, was the object of Burns's approval; it was he in the darkening 1790s, not Burns, who was to change political identity. As well as this fatalistic sense in the poem of political and economic forces too strong to be resisted, Burns in ll. 109–14 mentions his own Shandean proclivities for eccentric forward motion wholly unconducive to making a prosperous, if not a poetic, life.

A Dream

First printed in the Kilmarnock edition, 1786.

Thoughts, words, and deeds, the Statute blames with reason;
But surely Dreams *were ne'er indicted Treason.*

On reading, in the public papers, the Laureate's Ode with the other parade of June 4th, 1786, the Author was no sooner dropt asleep, than he imagined himself transported to the Birth-day Levee; and, in his dreaming fancy, made the following Address: —

GUID-MORNIN to your MAJESTY!
    May Heaven augment your blisses,
On ev'ry new *Birth-day* ye see,
    A humble Poet wishes!   (changed from *Bardie* in 1793)
5 My Bardship here, at your Levee,
    On sic a day as this is,   such
Is sure an uncouth sight to see,
    Amang thae Birth-day dresses   among they
      Sae fine this day.   so

10 I see ye're complimented thrang,   busily
    By monie a *lord* an' *lady*;   many
'God Save the King' 's a cuckoo sang   song
    That's unco easy said ay: mighty
The *Poets*, too, a venal gang,
15   Wi' rhymes weel-turn'd an' ready,   well-
Wad gar you trow ye ne'er do wrang,   would make, think,wrong
    But ay unerring steady,
      On sic a day.   such

For me! before a Monarch's face,
20   Ev'n *there* I winna flatter;   will not
For neither Pension, Post, nor Place,
    Am I your humble debtor:
So, nae reflection on YOUR GRACE,   no
    Your Kingship to bespatter;
25 There's monie *waur* been o' the Race,   many worse
    And aiblins *ane* been better   maybe one
      Than You this day.

'Tis very true, my sovereign King,
    My skill may weel be doubted;   *well*
30 But *Facts* are chiels that winna ding,   *fellows, will not be upset*
    And downa be disputed: *cannot*
Your *royal nest*, beneath *Your* wing,
    Is e'en right reft and clouted,   *torn & patched*
And now the third part o' the string,
35   An' less, will gang about it   *go*
        Than did ae day.   *one*

Far be't frae me that I aspire   *from*
    To blame your Legislation,
Or say, ye wisdom want, or fire
40   To rule this mighty nation:
But faith! I muckle doubt, my SIRE,   *much*
    Ye've trusted 'Ministration
To chaps wha in a *barn* or *byre*   *who*
    Wad better fill'd their station,
45   Than *courts* yon day.

And now Ye've gien auld *Britain* peace,   *given old*
    Her broken shins to plaister;   *plaster*
Your sair taxation does her fleece,   *sore*
    Till she has scarce a tester: *sixpence*
50 For me, thank God, my life's a *lease*,   *a tenant farm lease*
    Nae *bargain* wearin faster,   *no*
Or faith! I fear, that, wi' the geese,
    I shortly boost to pasture   *must*
        I' the craft some day.

55 I'm no mistrusting *Willie Pit*,
    When taxes he enlarges,
(An' *Will's* a true guid fallow's get,   *good, breed*
    A Name not Envy spairges),   *bespatters*
That he intends to pay your *debt*,
60   An' lessen a' your *charges*;
But, God sake! let nae *saving fit*   *no*
    Abridge your bonie *Barges*   *handsome*
        An' *Boats* this day.

Adieu, my LIEGE! may Freedom geck   *sport*
65   Beneath your high protection;
An' may Ye rax Corruption's neck,
    And gie her for dissection!   *give*

But since I'm here I'll no neglect,
    In loyal, true affection,
70 To pay your QUEEN, wi' due respect,
    My fealty an' subjection
        This great Birth-day.

Hail, *Majesty most Excellent*!
    While Nobles strive to please Ye,
75 Will Ye accept a Compliment,
    A simple Bardie gies Ye?   gives
Thae bonie Bairntime, Heav'n has lent,   that pretty brood
    Still higher may they heeze Ye   hoist
In bliss, till Fate some day is sent,
80   For ever to release Ye
        Frae Care that day.   from

For you, young Potentate o' Wales,
    I tell your *Highness* fairly,
Down Pleasure's stream, wi' swelling sails,
85 I'm tauld ye're driving rarely;   told, unusually well
But some day ye may gnaw your nails,
    An' curse your folly sairly,   sorely
That e'er ye brak *Diana's pales*,   break
    Or rattl'd dice wi' *Charlie*
90   By night or day.

Yet aft a ragged *Cowte's* been known,   colt
    To mak a noble *Aiver*;   make, old horse
So, ye may doucely fill a Throne,   soberly
    For a' their clish-ma-claver: gossip
95 There, Him at *Agincourt* wha shone,   who
    Few better were or braver;
And yet, wi' funny, queer Sir John,[1]
    He was an unco shaver   a great madcap
        For monie a day.   many

100 For you, right rev'rend Osnaburg,
    Nane sets the *lawn-sleeve* sweeter,   none, becomes
Altho' a ribban at your lug   ribbon, ear
    Wad been a dress compleater: would

1 Sir John Falstaff, Vide Shakespeare. R.B.

As ye disown yon paughty dog,   proud
105   That *bears* the Keys of Peter,
Then swith! an' get a *wife* to hug,
         Or trowth, ye'll stain the *Mitre*   in truth
              Some luckless day.

Young, royal TARRY-BREEKS, I learn,
110   Ye've lately come athwart her;
A glorious *Galley*, stem an' stern
         Weel rigg'd for *Venus barter*;[2]   well
But first hang out that she'll discern
         Your *hymeneal Charter*;
115 Then heave aboard your *grapple-airn*,   grappling iron
         An', large upon her *quarter*,
              Come full that day.

Ye, lastly, bonie blossoms a',
         Ye *royal Lasses* dainty,
120 Heav'n mak you guid as weel as braw,   good, well, fair
         An' gie you *lads* a-plenty: give
But sneer na *British-boys* awa!   not, away
         For Kings are unco scant ay,   greatly scarce
An' German-gentles are but *sma*',   small
125   They're better just than *want ay*
              On onie day.   any

God bless you a'! consider now,
         Ye're unco muckle dautet;   greatly fussed over
But ere the *course* o' life be through,
130   It may be bitter sautet: salted
An' I hae seen their *coggie* fou,   have, plate full
         That yet hae tarrow't at it;   shown reluctance
But or the *day* was done, I trow,   believe
         The laggen they hae clautet   bottom, have scraped
135   Fu' clean that day.

Byron must have read this with admiration; he himself never wrote anything funnier or, amidst the laughter, landed on the Hanoverians, he also so loathed, so many palpable hits. Describing it as a 'dream' allows Burns, as in the headquote, to claim its non-serious nature and intent. It also, of course, allows him direct, deadly access as 'humble poet' into the royal birthday levee.

2 Alluding to the Newspaper account of a certain royal Sailor's Amour. R.B.

George's birthday on 4th June 1786 had been celebrated by the laureate, Thomas Warton with a Pindaric ode. Burns's almost immediate response to this sycophantic work enabled him to insert the poem into the Kilmarnock edition. These were not the sentiments of a complicit 'heaven taught ploughman' and Mrs Dunlop was quick to warn him as to the commercial consequences of such satire. On 26th February 1787 she wrote to him urging that *A Dream* should be excluded from the second edition:

> I ought to have told you that numbers at London are learning Scots to read your book, but they don't like your address to the King, and say it will hurt the sale of the rest. Of this I am no judge. I can only say there is no piece . . . I would vote to leave out, tho' several where I would draw my pen over the lines, or spill the ink glass over a verse. (*Robert Burns and Mrs Dunlop*, ed. William Wallace (London: 1898), p. 11)

Burns's response was peremptory and unyielding:

> Your criticisms, Madam I understand very well, and could have wished to have pleased you better. You are right in your guesses that I am not very amenable. Poets, much my superiors, have so flattered those who possessed the adventitious qualities of wealth and power that I am determined to flatter no created being, either in prose or verse, so help me God. I set as little by kings, lords, clergy, critics, &c as all these respectable Gentry do by my Bardship. I know what I may expect from the world, by and by, illiberal abuse and contemptuous neglect: but I am resolved to study the sentiments of a very respectable Personage, Milton's Satan – Hail horrors! Hail infernal world!

> I am happy, Madam, that some of my favourite pieces are distinguished by you're particular approbation. For my DREAM which has unfortunately incurred your loyal displeasure, I hope in four weeks time or less to have the honour of appearing, at Dunlop, in it's defence in person (Letter 98).

It is hard to see what sort of convincing defence Burns could have mounted concerning the danger to his incipient poetic career with regard to the flagrantly disloyal, anti-Hanoverian elements of this poem. Beginning with the general weakened fiscal state of the nation resulting from the disastrously lost American war and

Pitt's subsequent punitive taxation policies and naval cuts (ll. 60–2) with an inverted political order where the lowest types are at the top of the government, Burns launches into a highly specific assault on the varied cupidities and promiscuities of what he consistently perceived as an irretrievably dysfunctional family of German upstarts. L. 26 contrasts the virtues of Charles Edward Stuart.

The treatment of the King and Queen is mild compared to that doled out to their children. Driven by infantile, Oedipal rage, the Prince of Wales, had flung himself into the grossly licentious world of whoring and gambling of 'Charlie' Fox's opposing Whigs. Brilliantly, ironically, Burns (ll. 91–9) compresses an allusion to post-Falstaffian redemption to *this* Prince of Wales. The ploughman poet, tellingly, feels he needs to explain this reference to *Henry IV* to his cultivated audience. The 'right rev'rend Osnaburg' is Frederick Augustus (1763–1827) who was 'elected' to the bishopric of Asnaburg in Westphalia by his father, George III, in 1764. He added to this clerical distinction by taking up with Letita Derby, the ex-mistress of Rann the highwayman. The 'Royal TARRY-BREEKS' (l. 109) is another prodigally gifted son, Prince William (1765–1837), who became William IV in 1830. He had become naughtily, nautically involved with Sarah Martin, daughter of the commissioner of the Portsmouth dockyard. This naval encounter may have been derived from what Kinsley describes as the 'ingenious model' in Robert Sempill's *Ballat Maid Upoun Margaret Fleming, callit the Fleming Bark in Edinburgh*, which was modernised in Ramsay's *The Ever Green* (1724). Similar metaphors of dropped tackle and predatory boarding parties can also be found in Donne, followed by Pope.

Burns claims that his knowledge of this particular incident came from a newspaper. It is probable that most of this kind of information so came to him. Unlike Wordsworth, who was wholly averse to what he saw as such vulgar contemporary contaminants, Burns belongs to an earlier satirical tradition. He not only throve on journalistic gossip, but could transmute it, like Byron, into great poetry. He also refers warmly to Hogarth and the whole world of eighteenth-century political caricature had undoubtedly a strong influence on him, perhaps not yet fully appreciated. The King also had five daughters (ll. 118–126) who were, needless to say, not noted for their beauty, unlike their chronic constipation.

The Vision
Duan First[1]
First printed in the Kilmarnock edition, 1786.

The Sun had clos'd the *winter-day*,
The Curlers quat their roaring play,   quit
And hunger'd Maukin taen her way,   hare, taken
    To kail-yards green,   kitchen-gardens
5 While faithless snaws ilk step betray   snows each
    Whare she has been.   where

The Thresher's weary *flingin-tree*,   flailing
The lee-lang day had tired me;   live-long
And when the Day had clos'd his e'e   eye
10   Far i' the West,
Ben i' the *Spence*, right pensivelie,   back, parlour
    I gaed to rest.   went

There, lanely by the ingle-cheek,   lonely, fire side
I sat and ey'd the spewing reek,   smoke
15 That fill'd, wi' hoast-provoking smeek,   cough, smoke
    The auld clay biggin;   old, building
An' heard the restless rattons squeak   rats
    About the riggin.   roof

All in this mottie, misty clime,   dusty specks
20 I backward mus'd on wasted time:
How I had spent my *youthfu' prime*,
    An' done naething,   nothing
But stringing blethers up in rhyme,   nonesense stories
    For fools to sing.

25 Had I to guid advice but harket,   good, listened
I might, by this, hae led a market,   have
Or strutted in a bank and clarket   clarked
    My *Cash-Account*:
While here, half-mad, half-fed, half-sarket,   half-clothed
30   Is a' th' amount.

---

1 Duan, a term of Ossian's for the different divisions of a digressive Poem. See his *Cath-Loda*, Vol. 2. of M'Pherson's Translation. R.B.

I started, mutt'ring blockhead! coof!   fool
An' heav'd on high my wauket loof,   horny palm/hand
To swear by a' yon starry roof,
    Or some rash aith,   oath
35 That I, henceforth, would be *rhyme-proof*
    Till my last breath —

When click! the *string* the *snick* did draw;   door latch
And jee! the door gaed to the wa';   went, wall
And by my ingle-lowe I saw,   fire-flame
40   Now bleezan bright,
A tight, outlandish *Hizzie*, braw,   girl
    Come full in sight.

Ye need na doubt, I held my whisht;   not doubt, said nothing
The infant aith, half-form'd, was crusht;   oath/pledge
45 I glowr'd as eerie's I'd been dusht,   stared, touched
    In some wild glen;
When sweet, like *modest Worth*, she blusht,
    And stepped ben.   inside

Green, slender, leaf-clad *Holly-boughs*   leaf-clothed/covered
50 Were twisted, gracefu', round her brows;
I took her for some SCOTTISH MUSE,
    By that same token;
And come to stop those reckless vows,
    Would soon been broken.

55 A 'hair-brain'd, sentimental trace'
Was strongly marked in her face;
A wildly-witty, rustic grace
    Shone full upon her;
Her *eye*, ev'n turn'd on empty space,
60   Beam'd keen with *Honor*.

Down flow'd her robe, a *tartan* sheen,   bright
Till half a leg was scrimply seen;   barely
And such a *leg*! my bonie JEAN
    Could only peer it;   equal
65 Sae straught, sae taper, tight an' clean   so, straight, so
    Nane else came near it.   no-one

Her *Mantle* large, of greenish hue,
My gazing wonder chiefly drew;
Deep *lights* and *shades*, bold-mingling, threw
70   A lustre grand;
And seem'd, to my astonish'd view,
        A *well-known* Land.

Here, rivers in the sea were lost;
There, mountains to the skies were tosst;
75 Here, tumbling billows mark'd the coast,
        With surging foam;
There, distant shone *Art's* lofty boast,
        The lordly dome.

Here, DOON pour'd down his far-fetch'd floods;
80 There, well-fed IRWINE stately thuds: beats/churns
Auld hermit AIRE staw thro' his woods,   Ayr, stole/steals
        On to the shore;
And many a lesser torrent scuds   races along
        With seeming roar.

85 Low, in a sandy valley spread,
An ancient BOROUGH rear'd her head;
Still, as in *Scottish Story* read,
        She boasts a *Race*
To ev'ry nobler virtue bred,
90   And polish'd grace.

[By stately tow'r, or palace fair,
Or ruins pendent in the air,
Bold stems of Heroes, here and there,
        I could discern;
95 Some seem'd to muse, some seem'd to dare,
        With feature stern.

My heart did glowing transport feel,
To see a Race[2] heroic wheel,
And brandish round the deep-dy'd steel
100   In sturdy blows;
While, back-recoiling, seem'd to reel
        Their Suthron foes.   English

2 The Wallaces. R.B.

His COUNTRY'S SAVIOUR,[3] mark him well!
Bold RICHARDTON'S[4] heroic swell;
105   The Chief on Sark[5] who glorious fell
          In high command;
And *He* whom ruthless Fates expel
          His native land.

There, where a sceptr'd *Pictish*[6] shade
110   Stalk'd round his ashes lowly laid,
I mark'd a martial Race, pourtray'd
          In colours strong:
Bold, soldier-featur'd, undismay'd,
          They strode along.

115   Thro' many a wild, romantic grove,[7]
Near many a hermit-fancy'd cove
(Fit haunts for Friendship or for Love
          In musing mood),
An *aged Judge*, I saw him rove,
120   Dispensing good.

With deep-struck, reverential awe,[8]
The learned *Sire* and *Son* I saw:
To Nature's God, and Nature's law,
          They gave their lore;
125   This, all its source and end to draw,
          That, to adore.

3 William Wallace.
4 Adam Wallace of Richardton, cousin to the immortal Preserver of Scottish Independence.
5 Wallace Laird of Craigie, who was second in Command, under Douglas Earl of Ormond, at the famous battle on the banks of Sark, fought anno 1448. That glorious victory was principally owing to the judicious conduct and intrepid valour of the gallant Laird of Craigie, who died of his wounds after the action. R.B.
6 Coilus King of the Picts, from whom the district of Kyle is said to take its name, lies buried, as tradition says, near the family-seat of the Montgomeries of Coilsfield, where his burial place is still shown. R.B.
7 Barskimming, the seat of the Lord Justice Clerk. R.B.
8 Catrine, the seat of the late Doctor, and present Professor [Dugald] Stewart. R.B. His father was Matthew Stewart, also Professor of Moral Philosophy at Edinburgh.

BRYDON'S brave Ward I well could spy,[9]
Beneath old SCOTIA'S smiling eye;
Who call'd on Fame, low standing by,
130   To hand him on,
Where many a Patriot-name on high,
     And Hero shone].

The final seven stanzas, enclosed above in square brackets, were added in the Edinburgh edition, 1787.

Duan Second

With musing-deep, astonish'd stare,
I view'd the heavenly-seeming *Fair*;
A whisp'ring *throb* did witness bear
     Of kindred sweet,
5 When with an elder Sister's air
     She did me greet.

'All hail! *my own* inspired Bard!
In me thy native Muse regard!
Nor longer mourn thy fate is hard,
10   Thus poorly low!
I come to give thee such reward,
     As we bestow.'

'Know, the great *Genius* of this land
Has many a light, aerial band,
15 Who, all beneath his high command,
     Harmoniously,
As *Arts* or *Arms* they understand,
     Their labors ply.

'They SCOTIA'S Race among them share:
20 Some fire the *Sodger* on to dare;
Some rouse the *Patriot* up to bare
     Corruption's heart;
Some teach the *Bard*, a darling care,
     The tuneful Art.

9 Colonel Fullerton. R.B.

25 'Mong swelling floods of reeking gore,   smoking
   They, ardent, kindling spirits pour;
   Or, 'mid the venal Senate's roar,
        They, sightless, stand,
   To mend the honest *Patriot-lore*,
30   And grace the hand.

   'And when the Bard, or hoary Sage,
   Charm or instruct the future age,
   They bind the wild Poetic rage
        In energy;
35 Or point the inconclusive page
        Full on the eye.

   'Hence, FULLARTON, the brave and young;[10]
   Hence, DEMPSTER'S zeal-inspirèd tongue;[11]
   Hence, sweet, harmonious BEATTIE sung[12]
40   His "Minstrel lays";
   Or tore, with noble ardour stung,
        The *Sceptic's* bays'.

   'To lower Orders are assign'd
   The humbler ranks of Human-kind,
45 The rustic Bard, the lab'ring Hind,
        The Artisan;
   All chuse, as various they're inclin'd,
        The various man.

   'When yellow waves the heavy grain,
50 The threat'ning *Storm* some strongly rein,
   Some teach to meliorate the plain,
        With *tillage-skill*;
   And some instruct the Shepherd-train,
        Blythe o'er the hill.

55 'Some hint the Lover's harmless wile;
   Some grace the Maiden's artless smile;
   Some soothe the Lab'rer's weary toil
        For humble gains,
   And make his *cottage-scenes* beguile
60   His cares and pains.

10 William Fullerton.
11 George Dempster, M.P. (1732–1818)
12 Dr James Beattie (1735–1803).

'Some, bounded to a district-space,
Explore at large Man's *infant race*,
To mark the embryotic trace
    Of *rustic Bard*;
65 And careful note each op'ning grace,
      A guide and guard.

'*Of these am I* — COILA my name;
And this district as mine I claim,
Where once the *Campbells*, chiefs of fame,
70   Held ruling pow'r:
I mark'd thy embryo-tuneful flame,
      Thy natal hour.

'With future hope I oft would gaze,
Fond, on thy little early ways;
75 Thy rudely caroll'd, chiming phrase,
    In uncouth rhymes;
Fir'd at the simple, artless lays
      Of other times.

'I saw thee seek the sounding shore,
80 Delighted with the dashing roar;
Or when the *North* his fleecy store
    Drove thro' the sky,
I saw grim Nature's visage hoar,
      Struck thy young eye.

85 'Or when the deep green-mantled Earth
Warm-cherish'd ev'ry floweret's birth,
And joy and music pouring forth
    In ev'ry grove;
I saw thee eye the gen'ral mirth
90   With boundless love.

'When ripen'd fields and azure skies
Call'd forth the *Reaper's* rustling noise,
I saw thee leave their ev'ning joys,
    And lonely stalk,
95 To vent thy bosom's swelling rise,
      In pensive walk.

'When *youthful Love*, warm-blushing, strong,
Keen-shivering, shot thy nerves along,
Those accents grateful to thy tongue,
100   Th' adored *Name*,
I taught thee how to pour in song
        To soothe thy flame.

'I saw thy pulse's maddening play,
Wild-send thee Pleasure's devious way,
105 Misled by Fancy's *meteor-ray*,
        By Passion driven;
But yet the *light* that led astray
        Was *light* from Heaven.

'I taught thy manners-painting strains
110 The *loves*, the *ways* of simple swains,
Till now, o'er all my wide domains
        Thy fame extends;
And some, the pride of *Coila's* plains,
        Become thy friends.

115 'Thou canst not learn, nor can I show,
To paint with *Thomson's* landscape glow;
Or wake the bosom-melting throe
        With *Shenstone's* art;
Or pour, with *Gray*, the moving flow
120   Warm on the heart.

'Yet, all beneath th'unrivall'd Rose,
The lowly Daisy sweetly blows;
Tho' large the forest's Monarch throws
        His army shade,
125 Yet green the juicy Hawthorn grows
        Adown the glade.

'Then never murmur nor repine;
Strive in thy *humble sphere* to shine;
And trust me, not *Potosi's* [13] *mine*,
130   Nor *King's regard*,
Can give a bliss o'ermatching thine,
        A *rustic Bard*.

13 Commenting on 'Potosi's mine' (in Bolivia, South America) to Peter Hill, Burns wrote: 'these glittering cliffs of Potosi where the all-sufficient, all powerful Deity, WEALTH, holds his immediate court of joys and pleasures' (Letter 325).

'To give my counsels all in one:
Thy *tuneful flame* still careful fan;
135 Preserve *the dignity of Man*,
        With Soul erect;
And trust the UNIVERSAL PLAN
        Will all protect.

'*And wear thou this*' — She solemn said,
140 And bound the *Holly* round my head:
The polish'd leaves and berries red
        Did rustling play;
And, like a passing thought, she fled
        In light away.

The poem is structured in two 'Duans' which Burns tells us in his footnote is a term derived from Macpherson's *Ossian* where it signifies different sections within a digressive poem. This may have been slightly exhibitionistic, given that contemporary Edinburgh's enthusiasm for the 'Highland' poem was so great that it was even subject to balletic theatrical performance. The games he played with the local literati were, however, usually of a deeper kind. A constant adopter, and adapter of a catholic range of earlier poetic forms, what Burns may be doing here is taking a formal structural device from Macpherson in order to deliver an *inverted* content. In *The Vision* we have not a poet melancholically wandering in a ghostly landscape littered with the Celtic-warrior dead, a culture irretrievably lost, but a virile poet celebrating an Ayrshire landscape energised by the power and beauty of its rivers and its organic, living connection with its heroic dead. The intrusion of the supernatural in this poem is not elegiac but consoling and celebratory. The Second Duan, indeed, not only reassures the poet about the nature and success of his creative career but integrates this individual success into an efflorescent Ayrshire, a land full of land-owning local heroes whose varied talents are benevolently directed to the nation's common good. Here the optimistic energies and anticipations of the Scottish Enlightenment *seem* to be yielding a rich harvest.

This poem has always been deeply controversial. Daiches (pp. 134–7) sees the poem as broken-backed with the anglicised, literati-pleasing second Duan betraying the vernacular brilliance of the first. Crawford in an extended treatment of the poem sees it as one of Burns's most complete masterpieces with the stanzas xiv-xviii of the second Duan achieving 'a unity of the personal and elemental of the sort we associate with poets like Shakespeare and Yeats'. Nor does he think Burns was involved in any kind of sycophancy:

> To regard these stanzas as flattery of the local nobility and nothing more would be to misunderstand Burns's intention completely. *The Vision* is the work, above all others, in which Burns shows himself aware of the contemporary national renaissance: a movement which, in many spheres of life, from agricultural improvement to moral philosophy, was led by the most energetic and forward-looking of the landed gentry. (pp. 182–92)

The Vision, then, is an extraordinarily ambitious poem, which attempts to resolve, in a related fashion, the poet's personal crisis-ridden anxieties with those of the nation and perceives a happy-ending for both. That it has such national as well as personal aspirations is partly deducible from its main source which was a forgery also entitled *The Vision* which Ramsay alleged as being translated in 1524 from a fourteenth-century Latin text dealing with a warrior spirit appearing before the depressed narrator who is agonised by John Baliol's appeasement to England's King Edward. McGuirk writes (p. 209) that 'Ramsay's "sact" bears a thistle and a prophecy of Scottish history; "Coila" bears holly and a prophecy of Burns's poetic destiny.' Coila, however, also bears a prophecy of a revived Scotland and it is here that lies the poem's main difficulty and, indeed, final failure.

The largely successful, vernacular first Duan is one of the most beautiful and moving in all Burns's poetry. The varied movements of men and beasts through a winterscape lead to arguably the best, most compressed of all accounts by Burns of the toll of farm life on him with its exhausting labour and its rat infested restricted living space culminating in the chronic, constant pressure of poverty and his volatile inadequacy in making a prudent living in the face of it. This bitter introspection is tangibly present to us and it is typical of Burns that such detailed realism is always a prelude to the entry, usually partly comical, of the supernatural into his poetry. Hence the appearance of his holly-crowned, gorgeously-legged Muse. Initially, at least the legs, this may have been based on Bess Paton but she was replaced by another evidently leggy beauty, Jean Armour. Dazzlingly beautiful in herself, this divine woman, mystically, projects the beauty of Ayrshire (ll.62–72). This celebration of Ayrshire's spirit of place metamorphoses to celebration of the historical nation where, happily, Ayrshire's virtues converge with those of Scotland as a whole in Burns's archetypal Scottish hero,

William Wallace. Not the least of Mrs Dunlop's attractions for
Burns was as descendant of Wallace. This is one of several poems,
which confirm his early wish (Letter 55) 'to be able to make a Song
on his equal to his merits'. Hence Burns's own footnotes outlining
the unbroken lineage of Wallace to the present. Kinsley considers
that ll. 107–8 refer to Mrs Dunlop's eldest son Craigie, who became
bankrupt in 1783. He died in England in 1786. This, it should be
noted, is hardly the stuff of epic but the all too common experience
of the economically deeply unstable world of eighteenth-century
incipient capitalism.

Quite atypical of Burns, however, this poem is concerned not with
the destructive, often disruptive late eighteenth-century forces of
social and economic change but it is an optimistic, partly Utopian,
vision or, indeed, dream of a resurrected Ayrshire/Scotland by virtue
of the *top-down* activities of a liberal progressive land-owning and
professional élite. Thus we have not epic heroes drawn up for battle
but a list of new men of virtue who tangibly seem, in varied ways, to
be delivering the reformative Scottish Enlightenment project. Thus
ll. 109–14 celebrate the patriotic, military valour of the Montgom-
eries of Coylfield. This is no distant hero-worship, however, as
Burns was on fraternal terms with James Montgomerie in the
merged Tarbolton Masonic Lodge in 1781. L. 115 refers to Barskim-
ming, the home of the improving Sir Thomas Miller, Bt. (1717–89).
His steam-boat innovating brother Patrick Miller (1731–1815) of
Dalswinton let Ellisland to Burns in 1788. Thomas Miller had an
extremely successful legal career. As Lord Barskimming he became
Lord Justice Clerk in 1766 and, as Lord Glenlee, Lord President of
the Court of Session in 1788. He seems the antithesis of the terrible
Lord Braxfield who was to run amok in the political trials of the
1790s: 'Though well aware that offended justice required satisfac-
tion, he knew that the vilest criminal was entitled to a fair and
dispassionate trial. . . he never uttered a harsh or taunting word'
(Ramsay of Ochtertyre, *Scotland and Scotsmen in the Eighteenth
Century*, l. 343–50.) Ll. 121–6 deal with the noted Professor of
Mathematics at Edinburgh Matthew Stewart and his even more
celebrated son Dugald (1753–1828) who was a tangible friend to
Burns in Edinburgh. As Burns wrote to Mrs Dunlop (Letter 152A)
of this exceptional man: 'It requires no common exertion of good
sense and Philosophy in persons of elevated rank to keep a friendship
properly alive with one much their inferior.' The letter continues as
an act of homage to Stewart's innate democratic virtues. Ll. 127–32
refer to William Fullerton, diplomat, politician, soldier and agri-
cultural improver who accepted Burns's advice on the care of cattle

and to whom in 1791 the poet sent songs and poems (Letters, 472, 474). Unlike the absentee, Europhile, aristocratic degenerates of *The Twa Dogs* who, in Fergusson's lines, '. . . never wi' their feet hae mett/The marches o' their ain estate' these men are tangible assets to Ayrshire and Scotland. Further Burns enjoys support and degrees of intimacy with the best of them. There are, indeed, significant grounds for national optimism.

The second Duan is devoted to Coila's monologue in which she pours a cornucopia of promised gifts not only on the head of her chosen poet but over all Ayrshire by dint of the aid of her accompanying spirits (perhaps derived from *The Rape of the Lock*). In this very non-Burnsian happily hierarchical society, each is given according to his needs. Regarding the 'embryonic' Burns she gives a detailed account of the growth of the poet. Pre-Wordsworth, Burns believed that the child was father of the creative man. As a sort of angelic counsellor, she offers soothing solutions to the anxieties which, with varying intensity, preoccupied him concerning the nature of his poetic career. Ll. 235–40 are particularly memorable in dealing with the central, crucial problem in all Burns's poetry and thought concerning the rights of the instinctual self as opposed to imposed conformity. He knew libidinal energy was essential to his art; he was never certain whether it was not only a predatory force for others but, finally, also a self-destructive one. Coila also, in a poem concerned with Scotland's political independence, deals with his properly modest but worthy relationships to English poetry (ll. 247–8). Finally, l. 259 she reassures him that his true role as rustic poet more than compensates for the lack of money and fame. Crowning him with her holly she triumphantly asserts that:

> To give my counsels all in one,
> They tuneful-flame still careful fan;
> Preserve the *dignity of Man*,
>   With Soul erect
> And trust the Universal Plan
>   Will all protect.

Partly energised by his experience, social and intellectual, with Free Masonry this is a pre-Whitmanian dream of progressive, enlightened social and political virtue and not the thing itself. Ayrshire, of which Burns himself is the best witness, was a deeply frictive culture marked by severe economic instability even for the prosperous and much poverty for the rest. It was also subject to extreme clerical bigotry. The aesthetic stresses we feel in the second Duan derive

from the forced, if not false, historical vision Burns here unchar-
acteristically adopts. There is, of course, the problem, significantly
discussed in Issac Kramnick's *Republicanism and Bourgeois Radic-
alism: Political Ideology in Late Eighteenth-Century England and
America* (Cornell U.P.: 1990), as to whether such reformists could
deliver their partly practical, partly Utopian project. They were not
to be given the opportunity. By the mid 1790s these progressives
were, with their poet laureate, in the deepest of trouble as Burkean
derived hierarchy and economics brutally reinherited the world.
Dugald Stewart like his fellow Whig academics was suspiciously
confined. At least, unlike the octogenarian Thomas Reid, he was not
roughed up. The admired James Beattie (1735–1803), whose *The
Minstrel* influenced Wordsworth, and, as ll. 123–6 state, allegedly
defeated David Hume's atheism, relapsed, like James Boswell, into
a semi-hysterical Toryism to the degree of involving himself in
drinking bouts with the frequently besotted Henry Dundas.

Halloween

First published in the Kilmarnock edition, 1786

Yes! let the Rich deride, the Proud disdain,
The simple pleasures of the lowly train:
To me more dear, congenial to my heart,
One native charm, than all the gloss of art.
                              GOLDSMITH.

'The following poem will, by many readers, be well enough under-
stood; but for the sake of those unaquainted with the manners and
traditions of the country [region] where the scene is cast, notes are
added, to give some account of the principal charms and spells of
that night, so big with prophecy to the peasantry of the west of
Scotland. The passion of prying into futurity makes a striking part
of the history of human nature in its rude state, in all ages and
nations; and it may be some entertainment to a philosophic mind, if
any such honour the author with a perusal, to see the remains of it,
among the more unenlightened in our own.'

To this headnote, Burns defines Halloween thus: 'Is thought to be
a night when Witches, Devils, and other mischief-making beings,
are all abroad on their baneful, midnight errands: particularly, those
aerial people, the fairies, are said, on that night, to hold a grand
anniversary.'

R.B.

Upon that *night*, when Fairies light
    On *Cassilis Downans*[1] dance,
Or owre the lays, in splendid blaze,   *over, fields*
    On sprightly coursers prance;
5 Or for *Colean* the rout is taen,   *Culzean, taken*
    Beneath the moon's pale beams;
There, up the *Cove*[2], to stray and rove,
    Amang the rocks and streams
        To sport that night:

10 Amang the bonie winding banks,
    Where Doon rins, wimplin, clear;   *runs, winding*
Where BRUCE[3] ance ruled the martial ranks,   *once*
    An' shook his *Carrick* spear;
Some merry, friendly, country-folks
15   Together did convene,
To *burn* their nits, an' *pou* their stocks,   *nuts, pull*
    An' haud their *Halloween*   *hold*
        Fu' blythe that night.

The lassies feat, an' cleanly neat,   *trim*
20   Mair braw than when they're fine;   *more fair*
Their faces blythe fu' sweetly kythe   *show*
    Hearts leal, an' warm, an' kin':   *loyal, kind*
The lads sae trig, wi' wooer-babs   *so spruce, love-knots*
    Weel-knotted on their garten;   *well, garters*
25 Some unco blate, an' some wi' gabs   *very shy, chatting up*
    Gar lasses' hearts gang startin   *make, go beating*
        Whyles fast at night.   *sometimes*

Then, first an' foremost, thro' the kail,   *cabbage-plot*
    Their *stocks*[4] maun a' be sought ance;   *shall, once*
30 They steek their een, an' grape an' wale   *close, eyes, grope, choose*
    For muckle anes, an' straught anes.   *big ones, straight ones*

1 Cassilis Downans – Certain little, romantic, rocky, green hills, in the
neighbourhood of the ancient seat of the Earls of Cassilis. R.B.
2 A noted cavern near Colean [Culzean] House, called the Cove of Colean;
which, as well as Cassilis Downans, is famed, in country story, for being a
favourite haunt of the fairies. R.B.
3 The famous family of that name, the ancestors of ROBERT, the great
Deliverer of his country, were Earls of Carrick. R. B.
4 The first ceremony of Halloween, is, pulling each a *Stock*, or plant of kail.
They must go out, hand in hand, with eyes shut, and pull the first they meet

Poor hav'rel *Will* fell aff the drift,   half-witted, lost the way
 An' wandered thro' the *Bow-kail*,   cabbage
An' pow't, for want o' better shift,   pulled
35 A *runt*, was like a sow-tail,   small cabbage stalk
   Sae bow't that night.   so bent

Then, straught or crooked, yird or nane,   straight, dirt, none
 They roar an' cry a' throu'ther;   pell-mell
The vera *wee-things*, toddlin, rin   very children, run
40 Wi' stocks out-owre their shouther: -over, shoulder
An' gif the *custock's* sweet or sour,   if, pith
 Wi' joctelegs they taste them;   knives
Syne coziely, aboon the door,   then, comfortably, above
 Wi' cannie care, they've plac'd them   gentle
45   To lye that night.   lie

The lasses staw frae 'mang them a',   stole, from, among them all
 To pou their *stalks o' corn*;[5]   pull
But *Rab* slips out, an' jinks about,   dodges
 Behint the muckle thorn: large
50 He grippet *Nelly* hard an' fast;   gripped
 Loud skirl'd a' the lasses;   screamed
But her *tap-pickle* maist was lost,   top amount mostly
 Whan kiutlan in the *Fause-house*[6]   when cuddling, corn drier
   Wi' him that night.

with: its being big or little, straight or crooked, is prophetic of the size and shape of the grand object of all their Spells – the husband or wife. If any *yird*, or earth, stick to the root, that is *tocher*, or fortune; and the taste of the *custoc*, that is, the heart of the stem, is indicative of the natural temper and disposition. Lastly, the stems, or to give them their ordinary appellation, the *runts*, are placed somewhere above the head of the door; and the Christian names of the people whom chance brings into the house, are, according to the priority of placing the runts, the names in question. R.B.
5 They go to the barnyard, and pull each, at three several times, a stalk of oats. If the third stalk wants the 'top-pickle', that is, the grain at the top of the stalk, the party in question will come to the marriage bed anything but a Maid. R.B.
6 When the corn is in a doubtful state, by being too green or wet, the stack-builder, by means of old timber, &c., makes a large apartment in his stack, with an opening in the side which is fairest exposed to the wind: this he calls a 'Fause-house'. R.B.

55   The auld Guidwife's weel-hoordet *nits*[7]   old, good-, well-hoarded nuts
       Are round an' round divided,
  An' monie lads' an' lasses' fates   many
       Are there that night decided:
  Some kindle couthie, side by side,   warm comfortably
60   An' *burn* thegither trimly;   together
  Some start awa wi' saucy pride,   away
       An' jump out-owre the chimlie   -over, fireplace
          Fu' high that night.

  Jean slips in twa, wi' tentie e'e;   two, watchful eye
65   Wha 'twas, she wadna tell;   who, would not
  But this is *Jock*, an' this is *me*,
       She says in to hersel:
  He bleez'd owre her, an' she owre him,   over
       As they wad never mair part;   would, more
70 Till fuff! he started up the lum,   chimney
       And *Jean* had e'en a sair heart   sore
          To see't that night.

  Poor *Willie*, wi' his *bow-kail runt*,   cabbage stalk
       Was *burnt* wi' primsie *Mallie*;   prudish
75 An' *Mary*, nae doubt, took the drunt,   no, huff
       To be compar'd to *Willie*:
  Mall's nit lap out, wi' pridefu' fling,   nut leaped
       An' her ain fit, it burnt it;   own foot
  While *Willie* lap, an' swoor by *jing*,   jumped, swore with conviction
80   'Twas just the way he wanted
          To be that night.

  Nell had the *Fause-house* in her min',   corn drying structure
       She pits hersel an' *Rob* in;   puts
  In loving bleeze they sweetly join,   heat/flame
85   Till white in ase they're sobbin: ashes
  Nell's heart was dancin at the view;
       She whisper'd *Rob* to leuk for't: tasted
  Rob, stownlins, prie'd her bonie mou,   stealthily, kissed, mouth
       Fu' cozie in the neuk for't,   snugly, corner
90   Unseen that night.

7 Burning the nuts is a favourite charm. They name the lad and lass to each particular nut, as they lay them in the fire, and acccordingly as they burn quietly together, or start from beside one another, the course and issue of the Courtship will be. R.B.

But *Merran* sat behint their backs,   Marion
    Her thoughts on *Andrew Bell*;
She lea'es them gashan at their cracks,   gabbing, conversation
    An' slips out by hersel:
95 She thro' the yard the nearest taks,
    An' to the *kiln* she goes then,
An' darklins grapet for the *bauks*,   darkness, groped, cross-beam
    And in the *blue-clue*[8] throws them,   yarn
        Right fear't that night.

100 An' ay she *win't*, an' ay she swat,   winded, sweated
    I wat she made nae jaukin;   bet, no delay
Till something *held* within the *pat*,   pot/kiln
    Guid Lord! but she was quakin!   shaking
But whether 'twas the *Deil* himsel,
105   Or whether 'twas a *bauk-en'*,   end of a beam
Or whether it was *Andrew Bell*,
    She did na wait on talkin   not
        To spier that night.   inquire/find out

Wee Jenny to her Graunie says,   grandmother
110   'Will ye go wi' me, Graunie?
I'll *eat the apple*[9] at the *glass*,
    I gat frae uncle Johnie:'   got, from
She fuff't her pipe wi' sic a lunt,   puffed, such, smoke
    In wrath she was sae vap'rin,   so, agitated
115 She notic't na an aizle brunt   not, cinder, burnt
    Her braw, new, worset apron   good, worsted/twisted yarn
        Out thro' that night.

'Ye little Skelpie-limmer's-face!   hussy
    I daur ye try sic sportin,   dare, such
120 As seek the *Foul Thief* onie place,   any
    For him to spae your fortune: foretell

8 Whoever would, with success, try this spell must strictly observe these
directions: Steal out all alone, to the kiln, and, darkling, throw into the *pot* a
clew of blue yarn; wind it in a new clew off the old one; and, towards the
latter end, something will hold the thread: demand *Wha hauds?*, i.e. Who
holds? And answer will be returned from the kiln-pot, by naming the
Christian and Sirname of your future Spouse. R.B.
9 Take a candle and go alone to a looking glass; eat an apple before it, and
some traditions say, you should comb your hair all the time; the face of your
conjugal companion, *to be*, will be seen in the glass, as if peeping over your
shoulder. R.B.

Nae doubt but ye may get a *sight*!   no
   Great cause ye hae to fear it;   have
For monie a ane has gotten a fright,   many, one
   An' liv'd an' died deleeret,   delerious/insane
125
         On sic a night.   such

'Ae Hairst afore the *Sherra-moor*,   one harvest before
   I mind't as weel's yestreen,   well as yesterday
I was a gilpey then, I'm sure   young girl
   I was na past fyfteen: not
130
The Simmer had been cauld an' wat,   summer, cold, wet
   An' *Stuff* was unco green;   corn
An' ay a rantan Kirn we gat,   rollicking, harvest, got
   An' just on *Halloween*
135
        It fell that night.

'Our *Stibble-rig* was *Rab M'Graen*,   leader of the reapers
   A clever, sturdy fallow;   fellow
His Sin gat *Eppie Sim* wi' wean,   son, got, child
   That lived in Achmachalla:
140
He gat *hemp-seed*,[10] I mind it weel,   got, well
   An' he made unco light o't;
But monie a day was *by himsel*,   many
   He was sae sairly frighted   so sorely
        That vera night.'

145
Then up gat fechtan *Jamie Fleck*,   got fighting
   An' he swoor by his conscience,   swore
That he could *saw hemp-seed* a peck;   sow
   For it was a' but nonsense:
The auld guidman raught down the pock,   old good-, reached, bag
150
   An' out a handfu' gied him;   gave
Syne bad him slip frae 'mang the folk,   then, bade, from
   Sometime when nae ane see'd him,   no one, sees
        An' try't that night.

10 Steal out unperceived and sow a handful of hemp-seed, harrowing it with anything you can conveniently draw after you. Repeat, now and then – 'Hemp-seed I saw [sow] thee, hemp-seed I saw thee; and him (or her) that is to be my true love, come after me and pou thee'. Look over your left shoulder, and you will see the appearance of the person invoked, in the attitude of pulling hemp. Some traditions say, 'Come after me, and shaw thee', that is, show thyself; in which case, it simply appears. Others omit the harrowing, and say, 'Come after me, and harrow thee.' R.B.

He marches thro' amang the stacks, _among_
155   Tho' he was something sturtan; _staggering_
The *graip* he for a *harrow* taks, _garden-fork_
    And haurls at his curpan; _drags, rear_
And ev'ry now and then, he says,
    'Hemp-seed I saw thee, _sow_
160 An' her that is to be my lass
    Come after me, an' draw thee
        As fast this night.'

He whistl'd up *Lord Lenox' March*,
    To keep his courage cheery;
165 Altho' his hair began to arch, _stand with fear_
    He was sae fley'd an' eerie; _so frightened_
Till presently he hears a squeak,
    An' then a grane an' gruntle; _groan, grunt_
He by his shouther gae a keek, _shoulder gives, look_
170   An' tumbl'd wi' a wintle _somersault_
        Out-owre that night. _over_

He roar'd a horrid murder-shout,
    In dreadfu' desperation!
An' young an' auld come rinnan out, _old, running_
175   An' hear the sad narration:
He swoor 'twas hilchin *Jean M'Craw*, _halting_
    Or crouchie *Merran Humphie* — _hunchback_
Till stop! she trotted thro' them a';
    An' wha was it but *Grumphie* _who, the pig_
180   Asteer that night? _moving about_

Meg fain wad to the *Barn* gaen, _content, would have gone_
    To *winn three wechts o' naething*;[11] _dry corn, baskets, nothing_
But for to meet the Deil her lane, _all alone_
    She pat but little faith in: _put_

11 This charm must likewise be performed unperceived and alone. You go to the barn, and open both doors, taking them off the hinges if possible; for there is danger that the being that is about to appear may shut the doors, and do you some mischief. Then take that instrument used in winnowing the corn, which in our country-dialect we call a 'wecht', and go through all the attitudes of letting down corn against the wind. Repeat it three times, and the third time, an apparition will pass through the barn, in at the windy door, and out at the other, having both the figure in question, and the appearance or retinue, marking the employment or station in life. R.B.

185 She gies the herd a pickle nits,   gives, shepherd, few
         An' twa red-cheeket apples,   two, -cheeked
     To watch, while for the *Barn* she sets,   goes
         In hopes to see *Tam Kipples*
             That vera night.   very

190 She turns the key wi' cannie thraw,   gentle, twist
         An' owre the threshold ventures;   over
     But first on *Sawnie* gies a ca',   Satan, gives, call
         Syne bauldly in she enters: once boldly
     A *ratton* rattl'd up the wa',   rat, wall
195   An' she cry'd, Lord preserve her!
     An' ran thro' midden-hole an' a',   dung-hole
         An' pray'd wi' zeal and fervour
             Fu' fast that night.

     They hoy't out *Will*, wi' sair advice;   urged, sore
200   They hecht him some fine braw ane;   promised, fine one
     It chane'd the *Stack* he *faddom't thrice*,[12]   fathomed
         Was timmer-propt for thrawin: wood stacked, support
     He taks a swirlie, auld *moss-oak*   twisted, old
         For some black gruesome Carlin;   old hag
205 An' loot a winze, an' drew a stroke,   cursed, swiped
         Till skin in blypes cam haurlin   shreds, peeling
             Aff's nieves that night.   off his fists

     A wanton widow *Leezie* was,
         As cantie as a kittlen;   lively, kitten
210 But Och! that night, amang the shaws,   among, large leaves & branches
         She gat a fearfu' settlin!   got, severely unsettled
     She thro' the whins, an' by the cairn,   gorse bushes
         An' owre the hill gaed scrievin;   over, went careering
     Whare *three Lairds' lands met at a burn*,[13]   where
215   To dip her *left sark-sleeve* in   shirt-
             Was bent that night.

12 Take an opportunity of going, unnoticed, to a 'bear-stack' [stack of bere
or bigg, a kind of barley] and fathom it three times round. The last fathom of
the last time, you will catch in your arms the appearance of your future
conjugal yolk-fellow. R.B.
13 You go out, one or more, for this is a social spell, to a south-running
spring, or rivulet, where 'three Lairds' lands' meet, and dip your left shirt-
sleeve. Go to bed in sight of a fire, and hang your wet sleeve before it to dry.
Ly awake, and sometime near midnight, an apparition, having the exact
figure of the grand object in question, will come and turn the sleeve, as if to
dry the other side of it. R.B.

Whyles owre a linn the burnie plays,   whiles over, waterfall, burns falls
    As thro' the glen it wimpl't;   meandered
Wyles round a rocky scaur it strays,   jutting rocky edge
220   Whyles in a wiel it dimpl't;   whiles eddy
W. yles glitter'd to the nightly rays,   reflected
    Wi' bickerin, dancin dazzle;   running fast
Whyles cookit underneath the braes,   whiles hid
    Below the spreading hazel
225   Unseen that night.

Amang the brachens, on the brae,   ferns, hillside
    Betw en her an' the moon,
The Deil r else an outler Quey,   stray young cow
    Ga⁺ n' gae a croon: got, gave, moan
230 Poor I   eart maist lap the hool;   almost leaped, sheath
    N   ock-height she jumpet,   lark-flying level, jumped
But m.   , an' in the *pool*   missed a foot
    Ou   re the lugs she plumpet   -over, ears, plummeted
            Wi' a plunge that night.

235 In order, on the clean hearth-stane,   -stone
    The *Luggies*[14] three are ranged;   dishes
And ev'ry time great care is taen   taken
    To see them duly changed:
Auld uncle *John*, wha *wedlock's joys*,   old, who
240   Sin *Mar's-year*[15] did desire,   since
Because he gat the toom dish thrice,   got, empty
    He heav'd them on the fire
            In wrath that night.

Wi' merry sangs, an' friendly cracks,   songs, conversation
245   I wat they did na weary;   know, not
And unco tales, an' funnie jokes,   wondrous
    Their sports were cheap an' cheary:

14 Take three dishes, put clean water in one, foul water in another, leave the third empty; blindfold a person and lead him to the hearth where the dishes are ranged; he (or she) dips the left hand: if by chance in the clean water, the future husband (or wife) will come to the bar of Matrimony a Maid; if in the foul, a widow; if in the empty dish, it foretells with equal certainty, no marriage at all. It is repeated three times, and every time the arrangement of the dishes is altered. R.B.

15 Mar's-year: This was the year 1715, when the 11th Earl of Mar, John Erskine (1675–1732) spear-headed the Jacobite revolt to proclaim the Stuart Pretender King.

Till *butter'd Sow'ns,*[16] wi' fragrant lunt,   sour oat pudding, steam
    Set a' their gabs a-steerin;   tongues, wagging
250 Syne, wi' a social glass o' strunt,   whisky
    They parted aff careerin   off/away
        Fu' blythe that night.

Mackay's edition omits the poet's detailed notes to this work. They serve to assist the general reader in understanding the superstitious rural beliefs associated with Halloween. Due to the broad Scots language of the poem and its description of various superstitious rituals associated with peasant belief, much of the poem is unintelligible without the poet's notes as in the Kilmarnock edition. Kinsley (no. 73) gives the notes but without indicating that they are Burns's. The prose explanations of Burns reveal another example of his extraordinary talent for turning prose into poetry within the body of *Halloween*.

The Auld Farmers New-year Morning Salutation to his Auld Mare, Maggie
on giving her the accustomed ripp of corn to hansel in the new-year
First printed in the Kilmarnock edition, 1786.

A *Guid New-Year* I wish thee, Maggie!
Hae, there's a ripp to thy auld baggie: handful, stomach
Tho' thou's howe-backit now, an' knaggie,   hollow-backed, knobbly
    I've seen the day
5 Thou could hae gaen like onie staggie,   have gone, any colt
    Out-owre the lay.   -over, lea

Tho' now thou's dowie, stiff, an' crazy,   drooping
An' thy auld hide as white's a daisie,   old
I've seen thee dappl't, sleek an' glaizie,   glossy
10   A bonie gray:
He should been tight that daur't to *raize* thee, dared, excite
    Ance in a day.   once

16 Sowens, with butter instead of milk, to them, is always the Halloween Supper. R.B.

Thou ance was i' the foremost rank,   *once*
A *filly* buirdly, steeve, an' swank;   *strong, trim, stately*
15   An' set weel down a shapely shank   *well, leg*
        As e'er tread yird;   *earth*
An' could hae flown out-owre a stank   *have, -over, ditch*
        Like onie bird.   *any*

It's now some nine-an'-twenty year
20   Sin' thou was my *Guidfather's Meere*;   *good-, mare*
He gied me thee, o' tocher clear,   *gave, dowry*
        An' fifty mark;   *a coin worth 13s 4d*
Tho' it was sma', 'twas *weel-won* gear,   *small, well-won money*
        An' thou was stark.   *strong*

25   When first I gaed to woo my *Jenny*,   *went*
Ye then was trottan wi' your Minnie: *mother*
Tho' ye was trickie, slee, an' funnie,   *difficult, sly*
        Ye ne'er was donsie;   *mischievous*
But hamely, tawie, quiet, an' cannie,   *homely, placid, docile*
30   An' unco sonsie.   *very good-natured*

That day, ye pranc'd wi' muckle pride,   *great*
When ye bure hame my bonie *Bride*:   *bore/carried home*
An' sweet an' gracefu' she did ride,
        Wi' maiden air!
35   KYLE-STEWART I could bragged wide,   *boasted the district over*
        For sic a *pair*.   *such*

Tho' now ye dow but hoyte and hobble,   *can, limp, stumble*
An' wintle like a saumont-coble,   *twist, salmon-boat*
That day, ye was a jinker noble,   *runner*
40   For heels an' win'!   *wind*
An' ran them till they a' did wauble,   *wobble*
        Far, far behin'!

When thou an' I were young and skiegh,   *proud/fiery*
An' *Stable-meals* at Fairs were driegh,   *tedious*
45   How thou wad prance, an' snore, an' scriegh,   *would, snort, whinny*
        An' tak the road!
Town's-bodies ran, an' stood abiegh,   *out of the way*
        An' ca't thee mad.   *called*

When thou was corn't, an' I was mellow,   fed
50 We took the road ay like a Swallow:
At *Brooses* thou had ne'er a fellow,   a horse race at a wedding
        For pith an' speed;
But ev'ry tail thou pay't them hollow,   beat
        Whare'er thou gaed.   went

55 The sma', droop-rumpl't, hunter cattle   small, short-rumped
Might aiblins waur't thee for a brattle;   perhaps beat, short race
But *sax Scotch mile* thou try't their mettle,   six
        An' gar't them whaizle: made, wheeze
Nae whip nor spur, but just a wattle   no, stick
60   O' saugh or hazle.   willow, hazel

Thou was a noble *Fittie-lan'*,   back left-hand plough horse
As e'er in tug or tow was drawn!
Aft thee an' I, in aught hours' gaun,   often, any, going
        On guid March-weather,   good
65 Hae turn'd *sax rood* beside our han'   have, six quarter acres
        For days thegither.   together

Thou never braing't, an' fetch't, an' flisket;   rushed, stalled, kicked
But thy *auld tail* thou wad hae whisket,   old, would have lashed
An' spread abreed thy weel-fill'd *brisket*,   across to, breast
70   Wi' pith an' pow'r;
Till sprittie knowes wad rair't, an' risket,   tough slopes were climbed
        An' slypet owre.   dreeled over

When frosts lay lang, an' snaws were deep,   long, snows
An' threaten'd *labour* back to keep,
75 I gied thy *cog* a wee bit heap   gave, feed bag
        Aboon the timmer: above the rim
I ken'd my *Maggie* wad na sleep   knew, would not
        For that, or Simmer.   summer

In *cart* or *car* thou never reestet;   rested
80 The steyest brae thou wad hae fac't it;   steepest hill, would have
Thou never lap, an' sten't, an' breastet,   leaped, reared
        Then stood to blaw;   puff for air
But just thy step a wee thing hastet,   a little shortened
        Thou snoov't awa.   pushed away

85   My Pleugh is now thy *bairn-time* a',   my plough-team is your offspring
    Four gallant brutes as e'er did draw;
    Forbye sax mae I've sell't awa,   six more, sold away
        That thou hast nurst: nursed
    They drew me thretteen pund an' twa,   thirteen pound, two
90   The vera warst.

    Monie a sair daurk we twa hae wrought,   many, sore day's work, two, have
    An' wi' the weary warl' fought!   world
    An' monie an *anxious day* I thought   many
        We wad be beat!   would
95   Yet here to *crazy Age* we're brought,
        Wi' something yet.

    An' think na, my auld trusty *Servan*',   not, old
    That now perhaps thou's less deservin,
    An' thy *auld days* may end in starvin;   old
100   For my last fow,   bushel
    A heapet *Stimpart*, I'll reserve ane   heaped, 8th of a bushel
        Laid by for you.

    We've worn to crazy years thegither;   together
    We'll toyte about wi' ane anither;   totter, one another
105   Wi' tentie care I'll flit thy tether   heedful, change
        To some hain'd rig,   reserved ground
    Whare ye may nobly rax your leather   stretch your body
        Wi' sma' fatigue.

Inevitably, in that now forever lost agrarian world, of all the deep bonds between man and beast, those with horses were the most intimate and profound. Burns's extraordinary empathy with his horses is everywhere present in his writing and is exemplified by his often naming them as expression of the current state of his own feelings. Thus, for example, the quixotic Rosinante or the disruptively comic, stool-throwing, anti-clerical Jenny Geddes. If Wordsworth needed the rhythmical stimulation of walking to write poetry, Burns discovered more varied, energised rhythms in the saddle. His Excise horse he named Pegasus, that mythical winged icon of poetical creativity. In a sense, however, all his horses had contained these magical energies as can be seen in those astonishing lines (ll. 17–44) of *The Epistle to Hugh Parker*.

    The horse honoured here is not a flyer of that kind, though her young power had allowed her eventually to outpace the lightweight hunters of the gentry in an actual and, hence, political victory. The poem is a deeply moving, heavily vernacularised, monologue by the old man as he parallels the life of his mare and himself. Not the least of Burns's intentions in the poem is to document the sheer, brutal harshness of the work conditions man and horse had to overcome in order to survive. McGuirk postulates that in part the poem is drawn from Burns's memories of his father. The poem was probably written in January 1786.

The Cotter's Saturday Night
Inscribed to R. Aiken, Esq.
First published in the Kilmarnock edition, 1786.

Let not Ambition mock their useful toil,
Their homely joys, and destiny obscure;
Nor Grandeur hear, with a disdainful smile,
The short and simple annals of the Poor.
GRAY.

My lov'd, my honor'd, much respected friend!
    No mercenary Bard his homage pays;
With honest pride, I scorn each selfish end,
    My dearest meed, a friend's esteem and praise:
5 To you I sing, in simple Scottish lays,
    The *lowly train* in life's sequester'd scene;
The native feelings strong, the guileless ways,
    What Aiken in a *Cottage* would have been;
Ah! tho' his worth unknown, far happier there I ween!   trust

10 November chill blaws loud wi' angry sugh;   blows, whistling wind
    The short'ning winter-day is near a close;
The miry beasts retreating frae the pleugh;   dirty, from, plough
    The black'ning trains o' craws to their repose: crows
The toil-worn COTTER frae his labour goes,   from
15   *This night* his weekly moil is at an end,   toil/drudgery
Collects his *spades*, his *mattocks*, and his *hoes*,   a two-mouthed pick
    Hoping the *morn* in ease and rest to spend,
And weary, o'er the moor, his course does hameward bend. homeward

At length his lonely *Cot* appears in view,   cottage
20   Beneath the shelter of an aged tree;
Th' expectant wee-things, toddlan, stacher through   children, totter
    To meet their *Dad*, wi' flichterin noise and glee.   fluttering

His wee bit ingle, blinkan bonilie,   fire, burning nicely
   His clean hearth-stane, his thrifty *Wifie's* smile,   fireside, wife's
25 The *lisping infant*, prattling on his knee,
   Does a' his weary kiaugh and care beguile,   anxiety
And makes him quite forget his labor and his toil.

Belyve, the *elder bairns* come drapping in,   by-and-by, kids, dropping
   At *Service* out, amang the Farmers roun';   among, round
30 Some ca' the pleugh, some herd, some tentie rin   work, shepherd,
                                       attentively run

   A cannie errand to a neebor town: private, neighbour
Their eldest hope, their *Jenny*, woman-grown,
   In youthfu' bloom, Love sparkling in her e'e,   eye
Comes hame, perhaps, to shew a braw new gown,   home, show, fine
35   Or deposite her sair-won penny-fee,   sore-, wages
To help her *Parents* dear, if they in hardship be.

With joy unfeign'd, *brothers* and *sisters* meet,
   And each for other's weelfare kindly spiers: welfare, inquires
The social hours, swift-wing'd, unnotic'd fleet;
40   Each tells the uncos that he sees or hears.   news
The *Parents partial* eye their hopeful years;
   Anticipation forward points the view;
The *Mother*, wi' her needle and her sheers,   scissors
   Gars auld claes look amaist as weel's the new;   makes old clothes,
                                       almost, well
45 The *Father* mixes a' wi' admonition due.

Their Master's and their Mistress's command
   The *youngkers* a' are warned to obey;   youngsters all
And mind their labors wi' an eydent hand,   diligent
   And ne'er, tho' out o' sight, to jauk or play: fool around
50 'And O! be sure to fear the LORD always!   always

And mind your *duty*, duly, morn and night!
Lest in temptation's path ye gang astray,   go
   Implore His counsel and assisting might:
They never sought in vain that sought the LORD aright.'

55 But hark! a rap comes gently to the door;
   Jenny, wha kens the meaning o' the same.   who knows
Tells how a neebor lad came o'er the moor,   neighbour
   To do some errands, and convoy her hame.   home

The wily Mother sees the *conscious flame*
    Sparkle in *Jenny's* e'e, and flush her cheek;   eye
With heart-struck anxious care, enquires his name,
    While *Jenny* hafflins is afraid to speak;   almost/partly
Weel-pleas'd the mother hears, it's nae wild,   no
    worthless *Rake*.

With kindly welcome, *Jenny* brings him ben;   inside
    A *strappan youth*, he takes the Mother's eye;
Blythe *Jenny* sees the *visit's* no ill taen;   taken
    The Father cracks of horses, pleughs, and kye.   talks, ploughs, cattle
The *youngster's* artless heart o'erflows wi' joy,
    But blate and laithfu', scarce can weel behave;   shy, hesitating, well
The Mother, wi' a woman's wiles, can spy   cunning
    What makes the *youth* sae bashfu' and sae grave;   so
Weel-pleas'd to think her *bairn's* respected like the   well-, child's,
    lave.   the others

O happy love! where love like this is found:
    O heart-felt raptures! bliss beyond compare!
I've pacèd much this weary, *mortal round*,
    And sage EXPERIENCE bids me this declare —
'If Heaven a draught of heavenly pleasure spare,
    One *cordial* in this melancholy *Vale*,
'Tis when a youthful, loving, *modest* Pair,
    In other's arms, breathe out the tender tale
Beneath the milk-white thorn that scents the ev'ning gale.'

Is there, in human form, that bears a heart —
    A wretch! a villain! lost to love and truth!
That can, with studied, sly, ensnaring art,
    Betray sweet *Jenny's* unsuspecting youth?
Curse on his perjur'd arts! dissembling, smoothe!
    Are *Honor*, *Virtue*, *Conscience*, all exil'd?
Is there no Pity, no relenting Ruth,   sorrow
    Points to the Parents fondling o'er their Child?
Then paints the *ruin'd Maid*, and *their* distraction wild?

But now the Supper crowns their simple board,
    The halesome *Porritch*, chief o' SCOTIA'S food;   wholesome porridge
The soupe their *only Hawkie* does afford,   drink/milk, cow
    That, 'yont the hallan snugly chows her cood;   beyond, partition,
        chews

95   The *Dame* brings forth, in complimental mood,
         To grace the lad, her weel-hain'd kebbuck, fell;

                                         well-matured cheese, tasty
     And aft he's prest, and aft he ca's it guid;   often, asked, calls, good
         The frugal *Wifie*, garrulous, will tell,   wife
     How 'twas a towmond auld, sin' Lint was i' the bell.

                                      12 months old, flax, flower

100   The chearfu' Supper done, wi' serious face,
         They, round the ingle, form a circle wide;
     The sire turns o'er, wi' patriarchal grace,
         The big *ha'-Bible*, ance his *Father's* pride. hall Bible, once
     His bonnet rev'rently is laid aside,
105   His *lyart haffets* wearing thin and bare;   grey sidelocks
     Those strains that once did sweet in ZION glide,
         He wales a portion with judicious care,
     '*And let us worship GOD!*' he says, with solemn air.

     They chant their artless notes in simple guise,
110   They tune their hearts, by far the noblest aim;
     Perhaps *Dundee's* wild-warbling measures rise,
         Or plaintive *Martyrs*, worthy of the name;
     Or noble *Elgin* beets the heaven-ward flame,   fans
         The sweetest far of SCOTIA'S holy lays:
115   Compar'd with these, *Italian trills* are tame;
         The tickl'd ears no heart-felt raptures raise;
     Nae unison hae they, with our CREATOR'S praise.   no, have

     The priest-like Father reads the sacred page,
         How *Abram* was the Friend of God on high;
120   Or, *Moses* bade eternal warfare wage
         With *Amalek's* ungracious progeny;
     Or, how the *royal Bard* did groaning lye
         Beneath the stroke of Heaven's avenging ire;
     Or *Job's* pathetic plaint, and wailing cry;
125   Or rapt *Isaiah's* wild, seraphic fire;
     Or other *Holy Seers* that tune the *sacred lyre*.

     Perhaps the *Christian Volume* is the theme:
         How *guiltless blood* for *guilty* man was shed;
     How He, who bore in Heaven the second name,
130   Had not on Earth whereon to lay His head;

How His first *followers* and *servants* sped;
   The *Precepts sage* they wrote to many a land:
How *he*, who lone in *Patmos* banishèd,
   Saw in the sun a mighty angel stand,
135 And heard great *Bab'lon's* doom pronounc'd by Heaven's command.

Then kneeling down to HEAVEN'S ETERNAL KING,
   The *Saint*, the *Father*, and the *Husband* prays:
Hope 'springs exulting on triumphant wing,'[1]
   That *thus* they all shall meet in future days,
140   There, ever bask in *uncreated rays*,
     No more to sigh or shed the bitter tear,
Together hymning their CREATOR'S praise,
     In *such society*, yet still more dear;
While circling Time moves round in an eternal sphere.

145 Compar'd with this, how poor Religion's pride,
   In all the pomp of *method*, and of *art*;
When men display to congregations wide
   Devotion's ev'ry grace, except the *heart*!
The POWER, incens'd, the Pageant will desert,
150   The pompous strain, the sacerdotal stole;
But haply, in some *Cottage* far apart,
     May hear, well-pleas'd, the language of the Soul,
And in His *Book of Life* the Inmates poor enroll.

Then homeward all take off their sev'ral way;
155   The youngling *Cottagers* retire to rest: youthful
The Parent-pair their *secret homage* pay,
   And proffer up to Heaven the warm request,
That 'He who stills the *raven's* clam'rous nest,
     'And decks the *lily* fair in flow'ry pride,
160 'Would, in the way His *Wisdom* sees the best,
     'For *them* and for their *little ones* provide;
'But, chiefly, in their hearts with *Grace Divine* preside'.

From Scenes like these, old SCOTIA'S grandeur springs,
   That makes her lov'd at home, rever'd abroad:

1 Pope's *Windsor Forest*, R.B.

165 Princes and lords are but the breath of kings,
       'An honest man's the noble work of GOD';[2]
     And *certes*, in fair Virtue's heavenly road,   verily
       The *Cottage* leaves the *Palace* far behind;
     What is a lordling's pomp? – a cumbrous load,
170   Disguising oft the *wretch* of human kind,
     Studied in arts of Hell, in wickedness refin'd!

     O SCOTIA! my dear, my native soil!
       For whom my warmest wish to Heaven is sent!
     Long may thy hardy sons of *rustic toil*
175   Be blest with health, and peace, and sweet content!
     And O! may Heaven their simple lives prevent
       From *Luxury's contagion*, weak and vile!
     Then, howe'er *crowns* and *coronets* be rent,
       A *virtuous Populace* may rise the while,
180 And stand a wall of fire around their much-lov'd ISLE.

     O THOU! who pour'd the *patriotic tide*,
       That stream'd thro' WALLACE'S undaunted heart,
     Who dar'd to, nobly, stem tyrannic pride,
       Or *nobly die*, the second glorious part:
185 (The Patriot's GOD, peculiarly Thou art,
       His *friend, inspirer, guardian*, and *reward*!)
     O never, never SCOTIA'S realm desert;
       But still the *Patriot*, and the *Patriot-bard*
     In bright succession raise, her *Ornament* and *Guard*!

As Kinsley noted (Vol. III, p. 112): 'What appealed to Burns
contemporaries . . . was the naturalism and the moral tone of *TC's
SN*. *The English Review* (Feb. 1787) thought it the best poem in the
Kilmarnock book, offering 'a domestic picture of rustic simplicity,
natural tenderness, and innocent passion that must please every
reader whose feelings are not perverted'. As Henry Mackenzie's and
Robert Heron's reviews show (See Low, *The Critical Heritage*),
conformist Scots were only too eager to build up such English
pieties.
    Unfazed that a 'heaven-taught' ploughman should be so canoni-
cally allusive, we find, embryonically in these Tory sentimentalists,
the enormous Victorian enthusiasm for a poem which seemed,

2 Pope's *Essay on Man*, R.B.

under the growing threat of the anarchic urban, industrial crowd, to offer the security and succour of a pietistically all-accepting rural folk. (See Andrew Noble, 'Some Versions of Scottish Pastoral: The Literati and the Tradition' in *Order in Space and Society*, ed. Markus (Edinburgh, 1982), pp. 263–310.

Twentieth-century critics have mainly been less easy with the poem. In his masterly reading Daiches compares it unfavourably to Fergusson's formally Spenserian precursor, *The Farmer's Ingle*. Compared to Fergusson's consistent vernacular, Daiches finds the language and voice uneven in the Burns poem. The problem Daiches believes is that, beginning with its initial homage to Robert Aitken: 'What Aitken in a Cottage would have been;/Ah! tho' his worth unknown, far happier there I ween', a most unlikely tale, the poem is muddled, in parts, especially the ruined maid sequence, by Burns too consciously looking over his shoulder to please genteel Edinburgh.' As he further notes:

> There is probably no poem of Burns in which the introduction of an artificial personality has spoiled a potentially fine work to the extent that it has in *The Cotter's Saturday Night*. The main trouble is that the poet has kept shifting his attitude, and with it his diction, between several incompatible positions. He is at one and the same time the sympathetic, realistic observer; at still another he is the sophisticated moralist acting as a guide showing off his rustic character for the benefit of a sentimental, genteel audience (p. 149).

Daiches is also rightly concerned with the semi, if not wholly, detached nature of the last two stanzas: 'But he overdoes the patriotic note, and in his final stanza seems to forget altogether the real theme of his poem.' Perhaps subconsciously, Burns did realise that some of the poem was complicit with values he detested and this invocation of a national, contractually governed common people was his attempt to deny some of the sentiments which preceded his inevitably inorganic conclusion. Certainly he is echoing the national spirit of Fergusson's *The Farmer's Ingle*:

> On sicken food has mony doughty deed
>   By Caledonia's ancestors been done;
> By this did mony wright fu' weirlike bleed
>   In brulzies frae the dawn to set o' sun:

'Twas this that brac'd their gardies stiff and strang
        That bent the deidly yew in antient days,
Laid Denmark's daring sons on yird alang,
        Gar'd Scottish thristles bang the Roman bays;
For near our crest their heads they doughtna raise.

It would be hard to overestimate Fergusson's influence in both
national style and substance on Burns. From Fergusson, albeit often
more elegiacally expressed, come the sense of the food, drink, music
and personages that make up the Scottish spirit. Burns also under-
stood that Fergusson was, if covertly, a profoundly political poet.
Like himself, Fergusson was socially displaced because he also
existed in a hierarchical world between masters and men. Their
political poetry, then, had to be ironic, oblique, comically masked.
In defining Fergusson as 'bauld and slee' (bold and sly) Burns,
knowingly, defined himself. As we have already seen, Fergusson's
brilliant *Hame Content: A Satire* with its denunciation of those
Europhiliac, decadent aristocrats who will not remain responsibly at
home was put, in *The Twa Dogs*, to equally brilliant use. These lines
from the same Fergusson poem should remind us simultaneously of
the relatively uneven failure of *The Cotter's Saturday Night* and the
greatness in representing the harshness, beauty and injustice in the
life of the common people found in so much of Burns's other poetry,
significantly due to Fergusson's influence on him:

Now whan the Dog-day heats begin
To birsel and to peel the skin,
May I lie streetkit at my ease,
Beneath the caller shady trees,
(Far frae the din o' Borrowstown,)
Whar water plays the haughs bedown,
To jouk the simmer's rigor there,
And breath a while the caller air
'Mang herds, an' honest cotter fock
That till the farm and feed the flock;
Careless o' mair, wha never fash
To lade their kist wi' useless cash
But thank the gods for what they've sent
O' health eneugh, and blyth content,
An' pith, that helps them to stravaig
Owr ilka cleugh and ilka craig,
Unkend to a' the weary granes
That aft arise frae gentler banes,

On easy-chair that pamper'd lie,
Wi' banefu' viands gustit high,
And turn and fald their weary clay,
To rax and gaunt the live-lang day.

To a Mouse
On Turning Her Up in Her Nest with the Plough
November 1785

First printed in the Kilmarnock edition, 1786.

Wee, sleekit, cowrin, tim'rous *beastie*,   small, sleek
O, what a panic's in thy breastie!   breast
Thou need na start awa sae hasty,   away, so
    Wi' bickering brattle!   hasty, scurry
5 I wad be laith to rin an' chase thee,   would, loath, run
    Wi' murdering *pattle*!   a wooden plough-scraper

I'm truly sorry Man's dominion
Has broken Nature's social union,
An' justifies that ill opinion
10   Which makes thee startle
At me, thy poor, earth-born companion
    An' *fellow mortal*!

I doubt na, whyles, but thou may thieve;   not, sometimes
What then? poor beastie, thou maun live!   must
15 A *daimen icker* in a *thrave*   one ear of corn in 24 sheaves
    'S a sma' request;
I'll get a blessin wi' the lave,   remainder
    An' never miss't!

Thy wee-bit *housie*, too, in ruin!   small, house/nest
20 Its silly wa's the win's are strewin!   walls, winds
An' naething, now, to big a new ane,   nothing, build, new one
    O' foggage green!   thick winter grass
An' bleak *December's win's* ensuin,   winds
    Baith snell an' keen!   both bitter, biting cold

25 Thou saw the fields laid bare an' waste,
An' weary *Winter* comin fast,
An' cozie here, beneath the blast,   cosy
    Thou thought to dwell,
Till crash! the cruel *coulter* past   plough blade
30   Out thro' thy cell.

That wee bit heap o' leaves an' stibble,   *small, stubble*
Has cost thee monie a weary nibble!   *many*
Now thou's turned out, for a' thy trouble,
          But house or hald,   *without, holding*
35   To thole the Winter's *sleety dribble*,   *endure, drizzle*
          An' *cranreuch* cauld!   *hoar-frost cold*

But Mousie, thou art no thy lane,   *not alone*
In proving *foresight* may be vain:
The best-laid schemes o' *Mice* an' *Men*
40   Gang aft agley,   *go often wrong*
An' lea'e us nought but grief an' pain,   *leave*
          For promis'd joy!

Still thou art blest, compared wi' me!
The *present* only toucheth thee:
45   But Och! I backward cast my e'e,
          On prospects drear!
An' *forward*, tho' I canna *see*,   *cannot*
          I *guess* an' *fear*!

Formally, this is a companion to that other creaturely masterpiece, *To a Louse*. McGuirk defines them as both belonging to 'Horatian satire, linking an *exemplum* of observed experience with a final *sententia* or maxim' (p. 223). In terms of content, however, the two poems, presumably deliberately, could not be more different. The hypothermic mouse, houselessly unprotected, has the ice of winter penetrating its fast fading heart. The hyperactive louse, pulsing with grotesque energy and intentions, foresees a comfortable head-high residence.

This is truly one of the great animal poems of the Sentimental canon fit to stand with Fergusson's great goldfinch and butterfly poems and Smart's cat poem. The destructive ploughman poet's guilt and empathy for the creature are wholly realised as is the sense of the inherent relationship of all created things. It is, seriously, *The Ancient Mariner* in miniature.

Crawford, in a very fine reading of the poem, rescued it from its daisy-like sentimental reputation particularly by stressing the subtle political analogy in the poem between mice and peasant suffering similar, perhaps fatal, decanting in that age of agrarian revolution. As Crawford remarks:

The mouse becomes more than any animal; she is a symbol of the peasant, or rather of the 'poor peasant' condition. On a careful

reading of the fifth stanza, the lines 'Till crash! the cruel coulter
past/out thro' thy cell' affect us with all the terror of Blake's 'dark
Satanic mills'. The coulter is in reality Burns's equivalent of the
mills – part of the metaphorical plough of social change that
breaks down the houses of both Lowland and Highland cotters.
This is not to claim that the poem is allegorical in any crude or
literal sense. The mouse does not 'stand for' the mother of 'The
Cotter's Saturday Night' or the Highland 'hizzies' whom Beel-
zebub thought should be 'lessoned' in Drury Lane, but she
belongs to the same world as these others and gains an extra
dimension from those emotions whose intensity arises from the
depth and power of Burns's own contemplation of human
wretchedness and exploitation. (pp. 166–7)

It was written in the early winter of 1785.

Epistle to Davie, a Brother Poet

First printed in the Kilmarnock edition, 1786.

While winds frae aff BEN-LOMOND blaw,	from off, blow (north wind)
And bar the doors wi' drivin' snaw,	snow
And hing us owre the ingle,	*sit around*/over, fireplace
I set me down to pass the time,	
5 And spin a verse or twa o' rhyme,	two
In hamely, *westlin* jingle:	western
While frosty winds blaw in the drift,	blow
Ben to the chimla lug,	right, chimney bottom/fire
I grudge a wee the *Great-folk's* gift,	little
10 That live sae bien an' snug:	so comfortable
I tent less, and want less	care for
Their roomy fire-side;	
But hanker, and canker,	
To see their cursed pride.	
15 It's hardly in a body's pow'r,	
To keep, at times, frae being sour,	from
To see how things are shar'd;	
How *best o' chiels* are whyles in want,	people, often
While *Coofs* on countless thousands rant,	fools, make merry/riot
20 And ken na how to ware't;	know not, spend
But DAVIE, lad, ne'er fash your head,	trouble
Tho' we hae little gear;	have, wealth

We're fit to win our daily bread,
   As lang's we're hale and fier: _long as, whole, vigorous_
25   'Mair spier na, nor fear na,'[1]   _don't ask more, nor fear_
      Auld age ne'er mind a feg;   _old, fig_
   The last o't, the warst o't,   _worst_
      Is only but to beg.

To lie in kilns and barns at e'en,
30 When banes are craz'd, and bluid is thin, _bones, blood_
     Is, doubtless, great distress!
   Yet then _content_ could make us blest;
   Ev'n then, sometimes, we'd snatch a taste
      Of truest happiness.
35 The honest heart that's free frae a'   _from all_
     Intended fraud or guile,
   However Fortune kick the ba',   _ball – whatever misfortunes_
     Has ay some cause to smile;   _always_
   And mind still, you'll find still,
40   A comfort this nae sma';   _not small_
      Nae mair then, we'll care then, _no more_
      Nae _farther_ can we _fa'_.   _no, fall_

What tho', like Commoners of air,   _owners of air, not land_
We wander out, we know not where,
45   But either house or hal'?   _without house or hall_
   Yet _Nature's_ charms, the hills and woods,
   The sweeping vales, and foaming floods,
      Are free alike to all.
   In days when Daisies deck the ground,
50 And Blackbirds whistle clear,
   With honest joy our hearts will bound,
     To see the _coming_ year:
     On braes when we please then,   _hillsides_
      We'll sit an' _sowth_ a tune; _hum_
55   Syne _rhyme_ till 't we'll time till 't, _then_
      An' sing 't when we hae done. _have_

It's no in titles nor in rank: _not_
It's no in wealth like _Lon'on Bank_,   _not, London_
   To purchase peace and rest.
60 It's no in makin muckle, _mair_: _making much, more_
   It's no in books, it's no in Lear,   _wisdom_
     To make us truly blest:

1 Ramsay, R.B.

If happiness hae not her seat   has
　　An' centre in the breast,
65 We may be wise, or *rich*, or *great*,
　　But never can be *blest*:
　　　Nae treasures nor pleasures   no
　　　　　Could make us happy lang;   long
　　　The *heart* ay 's the part ay   always is
70 　　　　　That makes us right or wrang.   wrong

Think ye, that sic as *you* and *I*,   such
Wha drudge and drive thro' wet and dry,   who
　　Wi' never ceasing toil;
Think ye, are we less blest than they,
75 Wha scarcely tent us in their way,   who, notice
　　As hardly worth their while?
Alas! how oft, in haughty mood,
　　GOD's creatures they oppress!
Or else, neglecting a' that's guid,   good
80 　　They riot in excess!
　　　Baith careless and fearless   both
　　　　　Of either Heaven or Hell;
　　　Esteeming and deeming
　　　　　It a' an idle tale!

85 Then let us chearfu' acquiesce,
Nor make our scanty Pleasures less
　　By pining at our state:
And, even should Misfortunes come,
I here wha sit hae met wi' some,   who, have
90 　　An 's thankfu' for them yet,
They gie the wit of *Age to Youth*;   give
　　　They let us ken oursel;   know ourselves
They make us see the naked truth,
　　The *real* guid and ill: good
95 　　　Tho' losses and crosses
　　　　　Be lessons right severe,
　　　There's *Wit* there, ye'll get there,
　　　　　Ye'll find nae other where.   no

But tent me, DAVIE, *Ace o' Hearts*!   take heed
100 (To say aught less wad wrang the *cartes*,   anything, would wrong, cards
　　And flatt'ry I detest)
This life has joys for you and I;

And joys that riches ne'er could buy,
    And joys the very best.
105 There's a' the *Pleasures o' the Heart*,
    The *Lover* an' the *Frien'*;   friend
Ye hae your MEG, your dearest part,   have
    And I my darling JEAN!
    It warms me, it charms me
110   To mention but her *name*:
    It heats me, it beets me,   enraptures
        And sets me a' on flame!

O all ye *Pow'rs* who rule above!
O THOU whose very self art *love*!
115   THOU know'st my words sincere!
The *life blood* streaming thro' my heart,
Or my more dear *Immortal part*,
    Is not more fondly dear!
When heart-corroding care and grief
120   Deprive my soul of rest,
Her dear idea brings relief
        And solace to my breast.
    Thou BEING, All-seeing,
        O hear my fervent pray'r!
125   Still take her, and make her
        THY most peculiar care!

All hail! ye tender feelings dear!
The smile of love, the friendly tear,
    The sympathetic glow!
130 Long since, this world's thorny ways
Had number'd out my weary days,
    Had it not been for you!
Fate still has blest me with a friend
    In every care and ill;
135 And oft a more *endearing* band,
    A tye more tender still.   tie
    It lightens, it brightens
        The tenebrific scene,   darkening/depressive
    To meet with, and greet with
140   My DAVIE or my JEAN!

O, how that *Name* inspires my style!
The words come skelpin' rank an' file,   rattling/running
    Amaist before I ken!   almost, know

The ready measure rins as fine,   runs
45 As *Phoebus* and the famous *Nine*
      Were glowran owre my pen.   looking over
My spavet *Pegasus* will limp,   lame, leg joint problems
      Till ance he's fairly het;   once, hot
And then he'll hilch, an' stilt, an' jimp,   hobble, limp, jump
50   And rin an unco fit;   run, rapid pace
      But least then, the beast then
        Should rue this hasty ride,
      I'll light now, and dight now   wipe clean
        His sweaty, wizen'd hide.   withered

David Sillar (1760–1830) was one of several recipients of Burns's Ayrshire epistolary poetry whom the Bard certainly overestimated poetically if not personally. Sillar had a mixed career as failed teacher then grocer but eventually inherited the family farm, Spittleside, Tarbolton and died a rich Irvine magistrate. This is the very reverse of the life of shared deprivation outlined for him and Burns himself in this poem. A good fiddler and composer (he composed the music to Burns's *The Rosebud*), he published his less than mediocre *Poems* at Kilmarnock in 1789. His proximity to Burns can be gauged by ll. 114–17 where, as in Sterne, rugged, biological reality constantly penetrates the surface of fine feeling. The poem is a technically formidable example of Burns's employment of Alexander Montgomerie's *The Cherry and the Slae* measure which James VI defined as one example of 'cuttit and broken verse, quhairof new formes daylie inuentit' (*Poems*, STS, l. 82). Burns is, however, hardly ever given to technique for its own sake. As Daiches has remarked (p. 163), the poem is remarkable for its ability to mould the process of thought to such complex form. However, the nature of this thought itself is more questionable. The exposed multiple, tangible distresses of penury are expressed with extraordinary power throughout the poem as is the sense of chronic injustice between rich and poor. The compensations of poverty are less credible. Edwin Muir was particularly unhappy with 'The heart ay's the part ay, /That makes us right or wrang.' Nor do the notions of compensatory and sexual harmony ring wholly true. Daiches in discussing stanza three, with its extraordinary initial delineation of the life of the beggars, defends the poem against such a sense of disparity between the desperate life it presents and the possible compensation for such a life thus:

> Here the poet is not posturing for the benefit of the Edinburgh gentry, but letting the poem work itself easily into a lively

expression of careless, cheerful view of life. The theme is a
mood rather than a philosophy, a mood of defiance of the rich
and happy acceptance of easygoing poverty. To seek for pro-
fundity of ethical thought here would be to miss the point of the
poem, which seeks to capture a transitory state of mind rather
than to state general principles (p. 163).

Arguably, rather than refuting it, this repeats the poem's own
inadequacy. Daiches, however, also considers that, after stanza
seven, the poem falters badly. 'Tenebrific' (l. 138) is the poet's
neologism and not, certainly, the happiest of touches. The irresis-
tible, Pegasian flood of language in the last stanza is a quite
remarkable self-analysis of Burns in the grip of creativity.

The Lament
Occasioned by the Unfortunate Issue
of a Friend's Amour
First printed in the Kilmarnock edition, 1786.

Alas! how oft does Goodness wound itself,
And sweet Affection prove the spring of Woe!
                              HOME.

   O thou pale Orb, that silent shines
      While care-untroubled mortals sleep!
   Thou seest a *wretch* who inly pines,
      And wanders here to wail and weep!
5 With Woe I nightly vigils keep,
      Beneath thy wan, unwarming beam;
   And mourn, in lamentation deep,
      How *life* and *love* are all a dream!

   I joyless view thy rays adorn
10   The faintly-marked, distant hill;
   I joyless view thy trembling horn
      Reflected in the gurgling rill.
   My fondly-fluttering heart, be still!
      Thou busy pow'r, Remembrance, cease!
15 Ah! must the agonizing thrill
      For ever bar returning Peace?

No idly-feign'd, poetic pains
    My sad, lovelorn lamentings claim:
No shepherd's pipe — Arcadian strains;
20   No fabled tortures quaint and tame.
The *plighted faith*, the *mutual flame*,
    The *oft-attested Pow'rs above*,
The *promis'd Father's tender name*,
    These were the pledges of my love!

25 Encircled in her clasping arms,
    How have the raptur'd moments flown!
How have I wished for Fortune's charms,
    For her dear sake, and her's alone!
And, must I think it! is she gone,
30   My secret heart's exulting boast?
And does she heedless hear my groan?
    And is she ever, ever lost?

Oh! can she bear so base a heart,
    So lost to Honour, lost to Truth,
35 As from the *fondest lover* part,
    The *plighted husband* of her youth?
Alas! Life's path may be unsmooth!
    Her way may lie thro' rough distress!
Then, who her pangs and pains will soothe,
40   Her sorrows share, and make them less?

Ye winged Hours that o'er us past,
    Enraptur'd more the more enjoy'd,
Your dear remembrance in my breast
    My fondly treasur'd thoughts employ'd.
45 That breast, how dreary now, and void,
    For her too scanty once of room!
Ev'n ev'ry *ray* of *Hope* destroy'd,
    And not a *Wish* to gild the gloom!

The morn, that warns th' approaching day,
50   Awakes me up to toil and woe;
I see the hours in long array,
    That I must suffer, lingering slow:
Full many a pang, and many a throe,
    Keen Recollection's direful train,
55 Must wring my soul, ere Phoebus, low,
    Shall kiss the distant western main.

And when my nightly couch I try,
    Sore-harass'd out, with care and grief,
My toil-beat nerves and tear-worn eye
60   Keep watchings with the nightly thief:
Or, if I slumber, Fancy, chief,
    Reigns, haggard-wild, in sore affright:
Ev'n day, all-bitter, brings relief
    From such a horror-breathing night.

65 O! thou bright Queen, who, o'er th' expanse
    Now highest reign'st, with boundless sway!
Oft has thy silent-marking glance
    Observ'd us, fondly-wand'ring, stray!
The time, unheeded, sped away,
70   While Love's *luxurious pulse* beat high,
Beneath thy silver-gleaming ray,
    To mark the mutual-kindling eye.

Oh! scenes in strong remembrance set!
    Scenes, never, never to return!
75 Scenes if in stupor I forget,
    Again I feel, again I burn!
From ev'ry joy and pleasure torn,
    Life's weary vale I wander thro';
And hopeless, comfortless, I'll mourn
80   *A faithless woman's broken vow*!

Written in the rhyming format of Ramsay's *Ever-Green*, this expresses the poet's deep anguish at the forced break-up of his relationship with Jean Armour. He informed Dr Moore, after causing a stir among the Ayrshire clergy by circulating a copy of *Holy Willie's Prayer*, that:

> Unluckily for me, my idle wanderings led me, on another side, point-blank within the reach of their heaviest metal. – This is the unfortunate story alluded to in my printed poem, *The Lament*. 'Twas a shocking affair, which I cannot bear yet to recollect; and had very nearly given [me] one or two of the principal qualifications for a place among those who have lost the chart and mistake the reckoning of Rationality. – I gave up my part of the farm to my brother . . . (Letter 125)

Burns told Mrs Dunlop of his vexation at Jean being taken away by her family and their 'detestation of my guilt of being a poor devil, not only forbade me her company & their house, but on my rumoured West Indian voyage, got a warrant to incarcerate me in jail till I should find security in my about-to-be Paternal relation' (Letter 254). The closing line would suggest that Burns blamed Jean Armour as 'faithless' to him, although she was as much the victim of her parents' extreme action as Burns.

Kinsley notes two minor influences from Blair's poem *The Grave* and Goldsmith's popular *The Deserted Village* (Vol. III, no. 93, p. 1174). The poem could easily be mistaken for an early work of Samuel Taylor Coleridge, given lines such as '. . . I nightly vigils keep,/ Beneath thy wan, unwarming beam; /And mourn, in lamentation deep, /How life and love are all a dream!' It is an arguably underrated English poem.

Despondency: An Ode

First printed in the Kilmarnock edition, 1786.

Oppress'd with grief, oppress'd with care,
A burden more than I can bear,
   I set me down and sigh;
O Life! Thou art a galling load,
5   Along a rough, a weary road,
To wretches such as I!
Dim-backward, as I cast my view,
   What sick'ning Scenes appear!
What Sorrows *yet* may pierce me thro',
10   Too justly I may fear!
    Still caring, despairing,
       Must be my bitter doom;
    My woes here shall close ne'er
       But with the *closing tomb*!

15 Happy ye sons of Busy-life,
Who, equal to the bustling strife,
   No other view regard!
Ev'n when the wishèd *end's* denied,
Yet while the busy *means* are plied,
20   They bring their own reward:
Whilst I, a hope-abandoned wight,
   Unfitted with an *aim*,
Meet ev'ry sad returning night
   And joyless morn the same.

25   You, bustling and justling,
                        Forget each grief and pain;
                    I, listless yet restless,
                        Find ev'ry prospect vain.

                How blest the Solitary's lot,
30   Who, all-forgetting, all-forgot,
                    Within his humble cell —
                The cavern, wild with tangling roots —
                Sits o'er his newly-gather'd fruits,
                    Beside his crystal well!
35   Or haply to his ev'ning thought,
                    By unfrequented stream,
                The *ways of men* are distant brought,
                    A faint-collected dream:
                        While praising, and raising
40   His thoughts to Heav'n on high,
                        As wand'ring, meand'ring,
                            He views the solemn sky.

                Than I, no *lonely Hermit* plac'd
                Where never human footstep trac'd,
45   Less fit to play the part;
                The *lucky moment* to improve,
                And just to stop, and just to move,
                    With *self-respecting* art:
                But ah! those pleasures, Loves, and Joys,
50   Which I too keenly taste,
                        The *Solitary* can despise,
                    Can want and yet be blest!
                        He needs not, he heeds not
                            Or human love or hate;
55   Whilst I here, must cry here
                            At perfidy ingrate!

                O enviable early days,
                When dancing thoughtless Pleasure's maze,
                    To Care, to Guilt unknown!
60   How ill exchang'd for riper times,
                To feel the follies or the crimes
                    Of others, or my own!
                Ye tiny elves that guiltless sport,
                    Like linnets in the bush,

65 Ye little know the ills ye court,
        When Manhood is your wish!
            The losses, the crosses
                That *active man* engage;
            The fears all, the tears all
70   Of dim declining *Age*!

While this poem can be dated to the time of his estrangement from
Jean Armour (see *The Lament*), it is also symptomatic of the bouts of
depression, which, as their external causes increased, plagued his
adult life. With masochistic logic he defines himself as a chronically
displaced person with neither the opposing talents of the material
man of business nor the spiritual hermit to locate himself appro-
priately in the world. The biographical letter of August 1787 to Dr
Moore is another example of Burns turning prose, this time his
marvellous own, into poetry:

> – The great misfortune of my life was never to have an aim –. I
> had felt early some stirrings of Ambition, but they were the
> blind gropins [*sic*] of Homer's Cyclops round the walls of his
> cave: I saw my father's situation entailed on me perpetual labor.
> – The only two doors by which I could enter the fields of
> fortune were, the most niggardly economy, or the little chican-
> ing art of bargain-making: the first is so contracted an aperture,
> I never could squeeze myself into it; the last, I always hated the
> contamination of the threshold. – Thus, abandoned of [every
> (deleted)] aim or view in life; with a strong appetite for socia-
> bility, as well from native hilarity as from a pride of observation
> and remark; a constitutional hypochondriac taint which made
> me fly solitude; add to all these incentives to social life, my
> reputation for bookish knowledge, a certain wild, logical talent,
> and a strength of thought something like the rudiments of good
> sense, made me generally a welcome guest; so 'tis no great
> wonder that always "where two or three were met together,
> there was I in the midst of them" (Letter 125).

The semi-vacuous self of this poem is further pervaded by chronic
guilt and, in the last stanza, a sense of childhood uncomprehending
of the losses and crosses that await the adult. If this sounds more the
agonised Coleridge than Burns, this is not accidental. An admirer of
Burns's innovative prosody: 'Bowles, the most tender and, with the
exception of Burns, *the only always-natural poet* in our Language'
(Low, *Critical Heritage*, p. 108), Coleridge also identified pro-
foundly with this dark side of the Scottish poet.

As George Dekker makes clear in *Coleridge and the Literature of Sensibility* (London, 1978), Burns's *Despondency: An Ode* was a seminal tonal and thematic influence on Coleridge's *Dejection: An Ode*. It is perhaps a case of it taking one to know one. Equally the manically protean self-mocking, self-making tone is a common factor in both poets' letters. Presumably it was not this quality which caused that inspired Scottish talent spotter, James Perry (Pirie) (1756 – 1821) to attempt to lure both men to come to London to work for his radically-inclined *Morning Chronicle*. If anything Coleridge's often also disguised contributions to the paper in the early 1790s are at least as dissidently radical as Burns's.

Man Was Made to Mourn: A Dirge

First printed in the Kilmarnock edition, 1786.
Tune: Peggy Bawn

When chill November's surly blast
    Made fields and forests bare,
One ev'ning, as I wand'red forth
    Along the banks of AIRE,   Ayr
5   I spy'd a man, whose aged step
    Seem'd weary, worn with care,
His face was furrow'd o'er with years,
    And hoary was his hair.

Young stranger, whither wand'rest thou?
10   Began the rev'rend Sage;
Does thirst of wealth thy step constrain,
    Or youthful Pleasure's rage?
Or haply, prest with cares and woes,
    Too soon thou hast began
15 To wander forth, with me to mourn
    The miseries of Man.

The Sun that overhangs yon moors,
    Out-spreading far and wide,
Where hundreds labour to support
20   A haughty lordling's pride:
I've seen yon weary winter-sun
    Twice forty times return;
And ev'ry time has added proofs,
    That Man was made to mourn.

25 O Man! while in thy early years,
　　　　How prodigal of time!
Mis-spending all thy precious hours,
　　　　Thy glorious, youthful prime!
Alternate Follies take the sway,
30　　　　Licentious Passions burn;
Which tenfold force gives Nature's law,
　　　　That Man was made to mourn.

Look not alone on youthful Prime,
　　　　Or Manhood's active might;
35 Man then is useful to his kind,
　　　　Supported is his right:
But see him on the edge of life,
　　　　With Cares and Sorrows worn;
Then Age and Want, Oh! ill-match'd pair!
40　　　　Shew Man was made to mourn!

A few seem favourites of Fate,
　　　　In Pleasure's lap carest;
Yet think not all the Rich and Great
　　　　Are likewise truly blest:
45 But Oh! what crouds in ev'ry land,
　　　　All wretched and forlorn,
Thro' weary life this lesson learn,
　　　　That Man was made to mourn.

Many and sharp the num'rous Ills
50　　　　Inwoven with our frame!
More pointed still we make ourselves
　　　　Regret, Remorse, and Shame!
And Man, whose heav'n-erected face,
　　　　The smiles of love adorn,
55 Man's inhumanity to Man
　　　　Makes countless thousands mourn!

See yonder poor, o'erlabour'd wight,
　　　　So abject, mean, and vile,
Who begs a brother of the earth
60　　　　To give him leave to toil;
And see his lordly *fellow-worm*
　　　　The poor petition spurn,
Unmindful, tho' a weeping wife
　　　　And helpless offspring mourn.

65   If I'm design'd yon lordling's slave,
          By Nature's law design'd,
     Why was an independent wish
          E'er planted in my mind?
     If not, why am I subject to
70   His cruelty, or scorn?
     Or why has Man the will and pow'r
          To make his fellow mourn?

     Yet let not this too much, my Son,
          Disturb thy youthful breast:
75   This partial view of human-kind
          Is surely not the *last*!
     The poor, oppressed, honest man
          Had never, sure, been born,
     Had there not been some recompence
80   To comfort those that mourn!

     O Death! the poor man's dearest friend,
          The kindest and the best!
     Welcome the hour my aged limbs
          Are laid with thee at rest!
85   The great, the wealthy fear thy blow,
          From pomp and pleasure torn;
     But, Oh! a blest relief to those
          That weary-laden mourn!

This was written sometime during the summer of 1785. It is entered in the *FCB* under August 1785. In his commentary on l. 5 of this poem Kinsley remarks that a 'meeting with a didactic sage is common in eighteenth-century poetry down to the time of Wordsworth. Burns's immediate model was apparently the white-haired "grateful form" encountered "on distant heaths beneath autumn skies" by Shenstone (*Elegies*, vii)'. It is characteristic of Kinsley that as a commentator on Burns's poems his eye is always fixed on the rear-view mirror hardly ever the road ahead. His commentary is eruditely, densely allusive to Burns's sources; he rarely has anything to say about Burns's seminal capacity to influence others, especially if the influence is of a political nature. Burns profoundly influenced Wordsworth. This poem, with its mixture of the elemental and political pains of existence, is probably the single best example of that influence. The depth of Burns's political passion in the poem can be gauged from Gilbert's account of its genesis when he noted that several of his brother's poems were written to 'bring forward some favourite sentiment of the author. He used to remark to me, that he could not well conceive a more mortifying picture of human life, than a man seeking work. In casting about in his mind how the sentiment might be brought forward, the elegy *Man was Made to Mourn* was composed' (Currie, iii. 384). Ll. 57–64 are this sentiment turned into poetry.

Mary Jacobus is particularly astute in her awareness of the degree to which Wordsworth creativity derived from the Scottish poet's sense of the terrible injustices of the rampant agrarian revolution. As she remarks:

> *The Last of the Flock* confronts, not death, but destitution – the plight of the labouring poor. Burns's *Man was Made to Mourn: A Dirge* was clearly in Wordsworth's mind during the spring of 1798, and its lament for the human condition shapes his poem (*Tradition and Experiment in Wordsworth's Lyrical Ballads 1798* (Oxford: 1976), p. 202).

Wordsworth's *Simon Lee, the Old Huntsman* is, if anything, even closer to Burns's dirge. Simon Lee, a tragic version of Tam Sampson, is faced with not only the increasingly severe symptoms of geriatric decline but the brutal redundancy of, no longer useful, being cast into helpless destitution. This combination of age and political injustice exactly follows Burns and his poem is deliberately echoed in the last lines of Wordsworth's:

> I've heard of hearts unkind, kind deeds
> With coldness still returning;
> Alas! The gratitude of men
> Hath oftener left me mourning.

The Dirge is also echoed in Wordsworth's *Lines Written in Early Spring*: 'Have I not reason to lament/ What man has made of man?', (ll. 23–4). The Leech Gatherer in *Resolution and Independence*, a poem in which Burns (ll. 45–9) makes an unnamed appearance, is also partly derived from the Dirge. Wordsworth's poem perhaps postulates a more spiritual consolation than Burns's Dirge with its vision of that ultimate and absolute democratic equaliser, Death itself.

Winter, a Dirge

Tune: MacPherson's Farewell
First printed in the Kilmarnock edition, 1786.

The Wintry West extends his blast,
    And hail and rain does blaw;
Or, the stormy North sends driving forth
    The blinding sleet and snaw: snow
5 While, tumbling brown, the Burn comes down,
    And roars frae bank to brae: from
While bird and beast in covert, rest,
    And pass the heartless day.

'The sweeping blast, the sky o'ercast,'[1]
10   The joyless *winter-day*,
Let others fear, to me more dear
    Than all the pride of May:
The Tempest's howl, it *soothes* my soul,
    My *griefs* it seems to join;
15 The leafless trees my fancy please,
    Their *fate* resembles mine!

Thou POW'R SUPREME, whose mighty Scheme
    These *woes* of mine fulfill,
Here, firm I rest, they *must* be best,
20   Because they are *Thy* Will!
Then all I want (Oh, do Thou grant
    This one request of mine!):
Since to *enjoy* Thou dost deny,
    Assist me to *resign*.

This song is 'The eldest of my printed pieces' Burns told Dr Moore
(Letter 125). In the *FCB* the poet records the influence upon him of
Nature during the most inclement of winter weather: 'There is
scarcely any earthly object gives me more – I don't know if I should
call it pleasure, but something which exalts me, something which
enraptures me – than to walk in the sheltered side of a wood or high
plantation, in a cloudy winter day, and to hear a stormy wind
howling among the trees & raving o'er the plain. – It is my best
season for devotion . . .' The imagery of winter desolation cast in a

1 Dr Young, R.B.

melancholy vein runs through the poetry of Burns as a motif for individual loss, or resignation to a person's fate.

A Prayer, in the Prospect of Death

First printed in the Kilmarnock edition, 1786.

O THOU unknown, Almighty Cause
    Of all my hope and fear!
In whose dread Presence, ere an hour,
    Perhaps I must appear!

5   If I have wander'd in those paths
    Of life I ought to shun;
As *Something*, loudly, in my breast,
    Remonstrates I have done.

Thou know'st that Thou hast formed me,
10   With Passions wild and strong;
And list'ning to their witching voice
    Has often led me wrong.

Where human *weakness* has come short,
    Or *frailty* stept aside,
15   Do Thou, ALL-GOOD, for such Thou art,
    In shades of darkness hide.

Where with *intention* I have err'd,
    No other plea I have,
But, *Thou art good*; and Goodness still
20   Delighteth to forgive.

This was almost certainly composed while the poet was at Irvine during the winter of 1781. The original title is, according to the copy in the *FCB*, 'A Prayer when fainting fits and other alarming symptoms of a pleurisy or some other dangerous disorder, which indeed still threatens me, first put Nature on the alarm'. Writing to his father, 27th December, 1781, Burns revealed his gloomy illness: 'The weakness of my nerves has so debilitated my mind that I dare not, either review past events, or look forward into futurity; for the least anxiety, or perturbation in my breast, produces most unhappy effects on my whole frame . . . I am quite transported at the thought that ere long, perhaps very soon, I shall bid an eternal adieu to all the pains, & uneasiness & disquietudes of this weary life; for I assure you I am heartily tired of it' (Letter 4). The poem is partly derived from the content of Pope's *Universal Prayer*, although the form is that of the Scottish metrical psalms.

To a Mountain Daisy
On Turning One Down, with the Plough, in April, 1786
First printed in the Kilmarnock edition, 1786.

	Wee, modest, crimson-tipped flow'r,	small
	Thou's met me in an evil hour;	
	For I maun crush amang the stoure	must, among, dust
	Thy slender stem:	
5	To spare thee now is past my pow'r,	
	Thou bonie gem.	pretty
	Alas! it's no thy neebor sweet,	not, neighbour
	The bonie *Lark*, companion meet!	handsome
	Bending thee 'mang the dewy weet!	wet
10	Wi' spreckl'd breast,	
	When upward-springing, blythe, to greet	
	The purpling East.	
	Cauld blew the bitter-biting *North*	cold
	Upon thy early, humble birth;	
15	Yet cheerfully thou glinted forth	
	Amid the storm,	
	Scarce rear'd above the *Parent-earth*	
	Thy tender form.	
	The flaunting *flow'rs* our Gardens yield,	
20	High shelt'ring woods and wa's maun shield;	walls shall
	But thou, beneath the random bield	shelter
	O' clod or stane,	turf, stone
	Adorns the histie *stibble-field*,	dry, stubble
	Unseen, alane.	alone
25	There, in thy scanty mantle clad,	
	Thy snawie bosom sun-ward spread,	snow white
	Thou lifts thy unassuming head	
	In humble guise;	
	But now the *share* uptears thy bed,	ploughshare/blade
30	And low thou lies!	

Such is the fate of artless Maid,
Sweet *flow'ret* of the rural shade!
By love's simplicity betray'd,
    And guileless trust;
35 Till she, like thee, all soil'd, is laid
    Low i' the dust.

Such is the fate of simple Bard,
On Life's rough ocean luckless starr'd!
Unskilful he to note the card   chart
40   Of *prudent Lore*,   wisdom
Till billows rage, and gales blow hard,
    And whelm him o'er!

Such fate to *suffering Worth* is giv'n,
Who long with wants and woes has striv'n,
45 By human pride or cunning driv'n
    To Mis'ry's brink;
Till, wrench'd of ev'ry stay but HEAV'N,
    He, ruin'd, sink!

Ev'n thou who mourn'st the *Daisy's* fate,
50 *That fate is thine* — no distant date;
Stern Ruin's *plough-share* drives elate,
    Full on thy bloom,
Till crush'd beneath the *furrow's* weight
    Shall be thy doom!

Henry Mackenzie, a frequent kiss of death for twentieth-century critical taste, waxed as eloquently about this poem as 'The Cotter's Saturday Night':

> I have seldom met with an image more truly pastoral than that of the lark in the second stanza. Such strokes as these mark the pencil of the poet, which delineates Nature with the precision, yet with the delicate colouring of beauty and taste. (Low, *Critical Heritage*, p. 69).

Burns's own account of the poem in a letter to John Kennedy in April 1786 seems to suggest that he had produced a mawkish poem compatible with Mackenzie's cloying response:

I have here . . . inclosed a small piece, the very latest of my productions. I am a good deal pleased with some sentiments in it myself, as they are just the native querulous feelings of a heart which, as the elegantly melting Gray says, "Melancholy has marked for her own" (Letter 27).

Certainly this is what Daiches (pp. 154–6) believes and he is also correct in saying that the inherent danger of sentimentality in animal poetry is even more extreme when dealing with plant life. Burns (Letter 56) could certainly descend to terrible bathos in this branch of his endeavours as he not infrequently set out his sentimentally-baited traps for socially superior women: 'Even the hoary Hawthorn twig that shot across the way, what heart at such a time, must have been interested in its welfare, and wished it to be preserved from the rudely browsing cattle, or the withering eastern Blast?'

This poem, however, is not self-promotingly narcissistic. Nor is it a mere piece of lyric natural description as Mackenzie, probably deliberately, certainly imperceptively, remarked. It is as political as its 'Mouse' and 'Louse' companion pieces. Like the mass of men, the daisy has to eke out its dangerously exposed existence outwith the walled security of the aristocratic garden flowers. The specific analogies of the daisy with the human world are all recurrent archetypes of suffering in Burns's imagination: the sexually violated women; the imprudently overwhelmed poet; the Job-like, ruined but honest farmer. The poem has a dark, even apocalyptic tone partly derived from Young's *Night Thoughts*, IX, ll. 167–8: 'Stars rush; and final ruin fiercely drives/her ploughshare o'er creation!' which Burns amends to 'Stern Ruin's *plough share* drives elate'. It is definably sentimental but in the honourable sense that the senti-mental poetry of the late eighteenth century, at its best, embodies a tragically irreconcilable sense that the great Enlightenment impulse towards the recognition of all human worth will not lead to a just, fearless democratic society. In 1802, his radicalism diminished, Wordsworth wrote his *To the Daisy*. It is, not least in metrical form, significantly influenced by Burns's version:

Methinks that there abides in thee
Some concord with humanity,
Given to no other flower I see
The forest through.

To Ruin

First printed in the Kilmarnock edition, 1786.

All hail! inexorable lord!
At whose destruction-breathing word,
    The mightiest empires fall!
Thy cruel, woe-delighted train,
5 The ministers of Grief and Pain,
    A sullen welcome, all!
    With stern-resolv'd despairing eye,
I see each aimed dart;
For one has cut my *dearest tye*,
10   And quivers in my heart.
    Then low'ring and pouring,
      The *Storm* no more I dread;
    Tho' thick'ning and black'ning
      Round my devoted head.

15 And thou grim Pow'r, by Life abhorr'd,
While Life a *pleasure* can afford,
    Oh! hear a wretch's pray'r!
No more I shrink appall'd, afraid;
I court, I beg thy friendly aid,
20   To close this scene of care!
When shall my soul, in silent peace,
    Resign Life's *joyless day*?
My weary heart its throbbings cease,
    Cold-mould'ring in the clay?
25   No fear more, no tear more
      To stain my lifeless face,
    Enclasped and grasped
      Within thy cold embrace!

This was probably written in the winter of 1781–2. This melancholic work in the bob-wheel stanza of the old Scots poem *The Cherry and the Slae*, reveals the poet's holistic view that a God of Nature influences both the pleasure and the woes of life from the fall of historic Empires to individual experience. It is a distinctive brush-stroke of Burns to move from universal comment to a specific incident. The hardship of eighteenth-century rural existence on a leased farm, particularly during winter periods, energises the poem. The subtext is the poet's rejection by a lover who is believed to be Alison Begbie.

Epistle to a Young Friend May, 1786

First printed in the Kilmarnock edition, 1786.

I lang hae thought, my youthfu' friend,   long have
    A Something to have sent you,
Tho' it should serve nae ither end   no other
    Than just a kind memento;
5 But how the subject-theme may gang,   go
    Let time and chance determine;
Perhaps it may turn out a Sang;   song
    Perhaps, turn out a Sermon.

Ye'll try the world soon, my lad;
10   And, ANDREW dear believe me,
Ye'll find mankind an unco squad,   strange crowd
    And muckle they may grieve ye: much
For care and trouble set your thought,
    Ev'n when your end's attained;
15 And a' your views may come to nought,
    Where ev'ry nerve is strained.

I'll no say, men are villains a':
    The real, harden'd wicked,
Wha hae nae check but *human law*,   who have no
20   Are to a few restricked;   restricted
But, Och, mankind are unco weak   very
    An' little to be trusted;
If *Self* the wavering balance shake,
    It's rarely right adjusted!

25 Yet they wha fa' in Fortune's strife,   who fall
    Their fate we should na censure,   not
For still, th' *important end* of life
    They equally may answer:
A man may hae an *honest heart*,   have
30   Tho' Poortith hourly stare him;   poverty, look over him
A man may tak a neebor's part,   neighbour's
    Yet hae nae *cash* to spare him.   have no

Ay free, aff han', your story tell,   always, off hand/casual
    When wi' a bosom crony;   close friend
35 But still keep something to yoursel
    Ye scarcely tell to ony: any

Conceal yoursel as weel's ye can   well as
    Frae critical dissection: from
But keek thro' ev'ry other man   look
40   Wi' sharpen'd, sly inspection.

The *sacred lowe* o' weel-plac'd love,   flame, well-
    Luxuriantly indulge it;
But never tempt th' *illicit rove*,
    Tho' naething should divulge it: nothing
45 I waive the quantum o' the sin,
    The hazard of concealing;
But, Och! it hardens a' *within*,
    And petrifies the feeling!

To catch Dame Fortune's golden smile,
50   Assiduous wait upon her;
And gather gear by ev'ry wile   worldly goods, skill
    That's justify'd by Honor:
Not for to *hide* it in a *hedge*,   not to be a miser
    Nor for a *train-attendant*;   not for showy wealth
55 But for the glorious privilege
    Of being *independent*.

The *fear o' Hell's* a hangman's whip
    To haud the wretch in order;   hold
But where ye feel your *Honour* grip,
60   Let that ay be your border: always
Its slightest touches, instant pause —
    Debar a' side-pretences;   consider no distraction
And resolutely keep its laws,
    Uncaring consequences.

65 The great CREATOR to revere
    Must sure become the *Creature*;
But still the preaching cant forbear,
    And ev'n the rigid feature:
Yet ne'er with Wits prophane to range
70   Be complaisance extended;
An *atheist-laugh's* a poor exchange
    For *Deity offended*!

When ranting round in Pleasure's ring,   *making merry/fun*
          Religion may be blinded;
75   Or if she gie a *random-fling*,   *give*
          It may be little minded;
     But when on Life we're tempest-driv'n,
          A Conscience but a canker —   *peevishness*
     A correspondence fix'd wi' Heav'n
80   Is sure a noble *anchor*!

     Adieu, dear, amiable youth!
          Your *heart* can ne'er be wanting!
     May Prudence, Fortitude, and Truth,
          Erect your brow undaunting!
85   In *ploughman phrase*, 'GOD send you speed,'
          Still daily to grow wiser;
     And may ye better reck the *rede*,   *heed the advice*
          Than ever did th' *Adviser*!

This was written for his friend Robert Aitken's son Andrew and was
finished in May, 1786. Robert Aitken is the legal hero of *Holy
Willie's Prayer*. Prudent counsellor is not the most probable of
Burns's multiple roles. The problems implicit in the poem are
highlighted by a deeply cautionary letter sent four years later to
his younger brother William who was moving from Newcastle to
London to pursue his career as a saddler:

> Now that you are setting out from that place, put on manly
> resolve, & determine to persevere; and in that case you will less
> or more be sure of success. – One or two things allow me to
> particularize to you. – London swarms with worthless wretches
> who prey on their fellow-creatures' thoughtlessness or inex-
> perience. – Be cautious in forming connections with comrades
> and companions. – You can be pretty good company to your-
> self, & you cannot be too shy of letting any body know you
> farther than to know you as a Sadler. – Another caution; I give
> you great credit for you [sic] sobriety with respect to that
> universal vice, Bad Women . . . – Whoring is a most ruinous
> expensive species of dissipation; is spending a poor fellow's
> money with which he ought clothe and support himself noth-
> ing? Whoring has ninety-nine chances in a hundred to bring on
> a man the most nauseous & excruciating diseases to which
> Human nature is liable; are disease & an impaired constitution
> trifling considerations? All this is independent of the crimin-
> ality of it (Letter 391).

This, from a man so addicted to women, should not be seen simply as massive hypocrisy. From as yet unpublished sources, Burns does seem to have suffered the venereal self-disgust of the so infected. More importantly, as in such Romantic libertine figures centrally present in the life and work of Mozart, Boswell, Byron and Pushkin, there exists, as a result of such serial fornication, a sense of self-punitive, guilty emptiness. Or, as it is brilliantly, vernacularly, put here:

> I wave the quantum o' the sin,
> The hazard of concealing;
> But Och! It hardens a' within,
> And petrifies the feeling.

R.L. Stevenson diagnosed this element in Burns and wrote him off because of it (*Familiar Studies of Men and Books*). G.K. Chesterton, more perceptively objective about the Scottish context, wrote in a brilliant foreword to A.A. Thomson's profoundly bad *The Burns We Love* (London: 1931):

> Nor is it true to say, as some have said, that this self-reproach was merely of the morbid or mawkish sort. So far from being mawkish and morbid, it could sometimes be both acrid and coarse. He really had a sense of something grotesque and even grovelling in his own orgies; of something of farce and bathos about the bad ending of so many of his love stories; a sense of being hooted from heaven with a sort of harsh laughter. In a word, he had a realistic as well as a romantic strain in him; and it is not altogether his fault that the national legend of his has become almost entirely romantic, to the extent of often forgetting how far his own view of himself was realistic (p. 5–6).

As well as the dangers, physical and moral, of sexual excess, Burns, in both the letter to William and in this poem, defines prudence as a necessary form of self- preservation in a world so variedly hostile. In a deeply perceptive essay, 'The Dialectics of Morality', Steven R. McKenna defines the question of necessary prudence as being a core problem in Burns's writings. In support of this thesis he identifies ll. 33–40 as a vernacular paraphrase of Polonius's cautionary speech to his son, Laertes in *Hamlet*, Act I, Scene iii. In extending these *Hamlet* parallels he finally reads the epistle as reaching for a kind of middle way of individual conscience, which avoids the one extreme of sadistically repressive conformity and the other of anarchic self-destruction. Burns himself appears to have understood how his repressed early life was partly responsible for his potentially self-destructive response to rigidly imposed order. As McKenna comments:

> Honour and self-protection are the issues here, and they form essential elements of this scene in the play, for Laertes in his long-winded, cautionary advice to his sister Ophelia regarding her relationship with Hamlet tells her she 'must fear' Hamlet, his greatness and his will. Says he, 'Fear it, Ophelia, fear it, my dear sister . . ./ Be wary then; best safety lies in fear' (I. 3.33, 42). A similar sentiment pervades Polonius's advice to her later in the scene: Hamlet's vows are to be held suspect that her honour is at stake. When taken together, these issues are a call to trust no one but oneself and to fear the power of others. And these are fundamental themes in Burns's 'Epistle to a Young Friend'. As in the case of Shakespeare's play, Burns's advice preaches an essential mistrust of the world, hence leads to a stultifying and isolating philosophy of life. Leaving aside the very possibility that Burns may be engaging in a bit of tongue-in-cheek irony with the epistle, the philosophy upon which it is premised is a matter of crime and punishment, and this takes two forms. First, insofar as religion and, broadly speaking, morality are concerned, fear particularly as something that can be manipulated by institutions and powers beyond the individual's control, is that which key 'To haud the wretch in order' as Burns says (l. 58). The second fear, and for Burns apparently the more important of the two, is the fear of self-punishment. In other words, one's sense of honour and integrity appears to be paramount, superseding potentially the 'fear o' hell' (l. 57). This is not to say Burns thumbs his nose at God, for stanzas nine and ten he sees the natural necessity of 'the Creature' revering the 'Creator'. Rather, this aspect of his epistle centres squarely on pitting the individual and conscience in opposition to formalised, institutionalised dogma. As he says, '. . . still the preaching cant forbear, / And ev'n the rigid feature' (67–8). Thus, in this case, organised religion is not the solution but rather the problem. Another case of churches built to please the priest, to bestow upon the ecclesiastical class the power to control people's lives. In the face of this, Burns posits the apparently radical notion that one's conscience should be one's guide (See *Love and Liberty*, p. 159).

On a Scotch Bard
Gone to the West Indies
First printed in the Kilmarnock edition, 1786.

A' Ye wha live by sowps o' drink,   who, mouthfuls
A' ye wha live by crambo-clink,   who, doggerel verse
A' ye wha live and never think,   who
    Come, mourn wi' me
5 Our *billie's* gien us a' a jink,   friend, given, the slip
    An' owre the Sea.   over

Lament him a' ye rantan core,   merry crowd
Wha dearly like a random-splore;   who, frolic
Nae mair he'll join the *merry roar*,   no more
10   In social key;
For now he's taen anither shore,   taken another
    An' owre the Sea!   over

The bonie lasses weel may wiss him,   handsome, well, wish
And in their dear *petitions* place him:
15 The widows, wives, an' a' may bless him
    Wi' tearfu' e'e;   eye
For weel I wat they'll sairly miss him   well I trust/know, sorely
    That's owre the Sea!   over

O Fortune, they hae room to grumble!   have
20 Hadst thou taen aff some drowsy bummle,   taken off, bungler
Wha can do nought but fyke an' fumble,   who, fuss
    'Twad been nae plea;   it would have, no
But he was gleg as onie wumble,   keen-eyed, gimlet (phallus)
    That's owre the Sea!   over

25 Auld, cantie KYLE may weepers wear,   old, cheerful, mourning cuffs
An' stain them wi' the saut, saut tear: salt, salt
'Twill mak her poor auld heart, I fear, old
    In flinders flee;   splinters fly
He was her *Laureat* monie a year,   poetic champion, many
30   That's owre the Sea!   over

He saw Misfortune's cauld *Nor-west*   cold, north-
Lang-mustering up a bitter blast;   long-
A Jillet brak his heart at last,   broke
        Ill may she be!
35   So, took a berth afore the mast,
        An' owre the Sea!   over

To tremble under Fortune's cummock,   rod
On scarce a bellyfu' o' *drummock*,   stomachful, meal & water
Wi' his proud, independent stomach,
40   Could ill agree;
So, row't his hurdies in a *hammock*,   rolled, hips/buttocks
        An' owre the Sea!   over

He ne'er was gien to great misguidin,   given
Yet coin his pouches wad na bide in;   pockets would not stay
45   Wi' him it ne'er was *under hidin*,
        He dealt it free: gave it away
The *Muse* was a' that he took pride in,
        That's owre the Sea!   over

Jamaica bodies, use him weel,   folk, well
50   An' hap him in a cozie biel: shelter, cosy place
Ye'll find him ay a dainty chiel,   friendly fellow
        An' fou o' glee: full of good nature
He wad na wrang'd the vera *Deil*,   would not wrong, very Devil
        That's owre the Sea!   over

55   Fareweel, my *rhyme-composing billie*!   farewell, friend
Your native soil was right ill-willie: ill-willed
But may ye flourish like a lily,
        Now bonilie!
I'll toast you in my hindmost *gillie*, last   gill (whisky)
60   Tho' owre the Sea!   over

There is unresolved critical contention about the reality of Burns's
plan to immigrate to Jamaica. Kinsley writes (Vol. III, p. 1176):

> The spirit of *On a Scotch Bard*, though sturdily more cheerful
> than that of the letters, hardly justifies Daiches's view that
> Burns was never serious about emigrating (pp. 95, 189). He was
> volatile, and ready to shift to extremes; he was capable of
> representing his misfortunes as tragic or comic, as occasions
> for dependency or from a display of swaggering courage. 'I have

heard Wordsworth praise the ready flow of verse in this poem,' says Cunningham (1834, II. 288), 'and recite with much emotion the eighth and ninth stanza'.

Facts would seem to be on Kinsley's side. The poet's letters are detailed about the voyage. The ship's delay seems to have prevented the journey. What is not in doubt is the degree of tormented uncertainty underlying the poetry of that period. He did want to be the rooted, celebrated Bard of Kyle. The bitter fracas with Jean Armour's family had, however, thrown him into the merciless path of his Auld Licht enemies. He wrote to Dr Moore that:

> I had for some time been skulking from covert under all the terrors of a Jail; as some ill-advised, ungrateful people had uncoupled the merciless legal Pack at my heels (Letter 125).

The writ was taken out by Mr Armour, Jean's father (Letter 254). Even in October 1786, after the Kilmarnock edition, he could still write:

> . . . the consequences of my follies, which may perhaps make it impracticable to stay at home . . . I have some time been pining under secret wretchedness . . . the pang of disappointment, the sting of pride, with some wandering stabs of remorse, which never fail to settle on my vitals like vultures . . . My gaiety is the madness of an intoxicated criminal under the hands of the executioner (Letter 53).

Despite the moment of deeply ill-judged self-pity with the denigration of Jean (ll. 34–5) as mere jilt, the poem is fuelled, if not quite by the 'madness of an intoxicated criminal' then certainly by the wild energy of a partly comic revenge fantasy on his often betraying fellow countrymen and women who, in his absence, will certainly bitterly discover what they have lost. Exile and cunning but not silence are part of *this* national poet's repertoire.

It should also be noted that this is, deliberately, not straight biography. The poem's tone and content are wittily distanced by being the monologue of an unnamed but sympathetic poet narrator. This poet, addressing his impoverished fellow poets, turns Burns's particular case into a general view, as in Goldsmith, of the penurious state of the poetic career in the late eighteenth century. Wordsworth's perceptive admiration for its linguistic and metrical virtues probably extended to a mutual sympathy for this theme.

A Dedication to Gavin Hamilton, Esq

First printed in the Kilmarnock edition, 1786.

EXPECT na, Sir, in this narration,   not
A fleechan, fleth'ran *Dedication*,   wheedling, flattering
To roose you up, an' ca' you guid,   praise, call, good
An' sprung o' great an' noble bluid,   blood
5   Because ye're surnam'd like *His Grace*,[1]
Perhaps related to the race:
Then, when I'm tired — and sae are *ye*,   so
Wi' monie a fulsome, sinfu' lie,   many
Set up a face, how I stop short,
10 For fear your modesty be hurt.

This may do — maun do, Sir, wi' them wha   shall, who
Maun please the Great-folk for a wamefou;   must, bellyful
For me! sae laigh I need na bow,   so low, not
For, LORD be thankit, *I can plough*;
15 And when I downa yoke a naig,   do not/cannot, horse
Then, LORD be thanket, *I can beg*;
Sae I shall say, an' that's nae flatt'rin,   so, not
It's just *sic Poet* an' *sic Patron*.   such a

The Poet, some guid Angel help him,   good
20 Or else, I fear, some *ill ane* skelp him!   one, beat
He may do weel for a' he's done yet,   well
But only — he's no just begun yet.

The Patron (Sir, ye maun forgie me,   must forgive
I winna lie, come what will o' me)   will not
25 On ev'ry hand it will allow'd be,
He's just — nae better than he should be.   no

I readily and freely grant,
He downa see a poor man want;   would not
What's no his ain he winna tak it;   own, will not
30 What ance he says, he winna break it;   once, will not
Ought he can lend he'll no refus't,
Till aft his guidness is abus'd;   often, goodness

1 The Duke of Hamilton.

And rascals whyles that do him wrang,   *sometimes, wrong*
Ev'n *that*, he does na mind it lang;   *not, long*
35   As Master, Landlord, Husband, Father,
He does na fail his part in either.   *not*

But then, nae thanks to him for a' that   *no*
Nae *godly symptom* ye can ca' that;   *no, call*
It's naething but a milder feature   *nothing*
40   Of our poor, sinfu', corrupt Nature:
Ye'll get the best o' moral works,
'Mang black *Gentoos*, and Pagan *Turks*,   *Indians, Hindus*
Or Hunters wild on *Ponotaxi*,   *Cotopaxi in Ecuador*
Wha never heard of Orthodoxy.   *who*
45   That he's the poor man's friend in need,
The GENTLEMAN in word and deed,
It's no thro' terror of Damnation:
It's just a carnal inclination,
[And Och! that's nae regeneration].²

50   Morality, thou deadly bane,   *poison*
Thy tens o' thousands thou hast slain!
Vain is his hope, whase stay an' trust is   *whose*
In *moral* Mercy, Truth, and Justice!

No — stretch a point to catch a plack;   *farthing/coin*
55   Abuse a Brother to his back;
Steal thro' the *winnock* frae a whore,   *window from*
But point the rake that taks the *door*;
Be to the Poor like onie whunstane,
And haud their noses to the grunstane;   *hold, grindstone*
60   Ply ev'ry art o' *legal* thieving;
No matter — stick to *sound believing*.

Learn three-mile pray'rs, an' half-mile graces,
Wi' weel-spread looves, an' lang, wry faces;   *well-, palms, long*
Grunt up a solemn, lengthen'd groan,
65   And damn a' Parties but your own;
I'll warrant then, ye're nae Deceiver,   *no*
A steady, sturdy, staunch *Believer*.

2 This line was omitted in the 1787 edition.

O ye wha leave the springs o' Calvin,
For *gumlie dubs* of your ain delvin!   muddy puddles, own digging
70 Ye sons of Heresy and Error,
Ye'll *some day* squeel in quaking terror,
When Vengeance draws the sword in wrath,
And in the fire throws the *sheath*;
When Ruin, with his sweeping *besom*,
75 Just frets till Heav'n commission gies him;   gives
While o'er the *Harp* pale Misery moans,
And strikes the ever-deep'ning tones,
Still louder shrieks, and heavier groans!

Your pardon, Sir, for this digression:
80 I maist forgat my *Dedication*;   almost forgot
But when Divinity comes 'cross me,
My readers still are sures me.

So, Sir, you see 'twas nae daft vapour;   no
But I maturely thought it proper,
85 When a' my works I did review,
To *dedicate* them, Sir, to YOU:
Because (ye need na tak' it ill)   not take it badly
I thought them something like *yoursel*.

Then patronize them wi' your favor,   howling
90 And your Petitioner shall ever —
I had amaist said, *ever pray*,   almost
But that's a word I need na say;   not
For prayin, I hae little skill o't,   have
I'm baith dead-sweer, an' wretched ill o't;   both loath, sick of it
95 But I'se repeat each poor man's *pray'r*,   I'll
That kens or hears about you, Sir —   knows

'May ne'er Misfortune's gowling bark   howling
Howl thro' the dwelling o' the CLERK!
May ne'er his gen'rous, honest heart,
100 For that same gen'rous spirit smart!
May Kennedy's far-honor'd name
Lang beet his hymeneal flame,   long fan
Till Hamiltons, at least a diz'n,   dozen
Are frae their nuptial labors risen: from
105 Five bonie Lasses round their table,
And sev'n braw fellows, stout an' able,   fine, sturdy

To serve their King an' Country weel,   well
By word, or pen, or pointed steel!
May Health and Peace, with mutual rays,
110   Shine on the ev'ning o' his days;
Till his wee, curlie *John's* ier-oe,   small, great-grandchild
When ebbing life nae mair shall flow,   no more
The last, sad, mournful rites bestow!'

I will not wind a lang conclusion,   long
115   With complimentary effusion;
But, whilst your wishes and endeavours
Are blest with Fortune's smiles and favours,
I am, Dear Sir, with zeal most fervent,
Your much indebted, humble servant.

120   But if, which Pow'rs above prevent,
That iron-hearted Carl, *Want*,   fellow/old man
Attended, in his grim advances,
By *sad mistakes*, and *black mischances*,
While hopes, and joys, and pleasures fly him,
125   Make you as poor a dog as I am,
Your *humble servant* then no more;
For who would humbly serve the Poor?
But, by a poor man's hopes in Heav'n!
While recollection's pow'r is giv'n,
130   If, in the vale of humble life,
The victim sad of Fortune's strife,
I, thro' the tender-gushing tear,
Should recognise my *Master dear*,
If friendless, low, we meet together,
135   Then, sir, your hand — my FRIEND and BROTHER!

Gavin Hamilton (1751–1805) was a Mauchline writer (solicitor) who
was one of Burns's closest friends and one of the few professional
men to whom the poet was tangibly indebted. He, as landlord, sub-
leased Mossgiel to Robert and Gilbert to save them from their
father's bankruptcy and was also to the fore in supporting publica-
tion of the Kilmarnock edition. Like Burns he, too, fell foul of the
malign forces of local Calvinism and it was his dispute with William
Fisher over alleged breaches of Church discipline on Hamilton's
part which was the cause of the quite wonderful *Holy Willie's
Prayer*. We, as well as Burns, are, consequently, deeply in his debt.
    Thus the poem reflects these two principal issues: Burns's gra-

titude to an honest good-hearted man (a type he constantly evoked but rarely found) and the fanatical power of Calvinism to control through the creation of diabolic terror and its by-product of malignant hypocrisy. Ll. 53–66 are particularly eloquent on this subject. Hamilton not only provides in this poem the image of the appropriate patron but his singular example leads to a larger digression (ll. 37–48) on the global manifestations of The Enlightenment's belief of the good-hearted natural man as opposed to the vicious, rebarbative provincials who control Ayrshire. For Burns's knowledge of the Philosophes see Ian S. Ross's 'Burns and the 'Siècles des Lumières' (*Love and Liberty*, pp. 217–28).

Hugh Blair wished ll. 67–77 omitted on the grounds that: 'The poem will be much better without it, and it will give offence by the ludicrous views of punishments of Hell'. Kinsley remarks that 'for once he may have been right' but on the evidence Kinsley cites from Calvin's own statutes regarding the inherent, eternal corruption of the non-elect, it is hard to agree with him. There is also a pro-Byronic self-referential flippancy in the poem (ll. 78–81) as well as moments of darkness and how one might respond to the collapse of creative and social hopes.

For Gavin Hamilton, Esq.
First printed in the Kilmarnock edition, 1786.

The poor man weeps — here Gavin sleeps,
        Whom canting wretches blam'd;
But with *such as he*, where'er he be,
        May I be sav'd or damn'd.

For notes on Gavin Hamilton, see *A Dedication to Gavin Hamilton*.

To a Louse
On Seeing One on a Lady's Bonnet at Church
First printed in the Kilmarnock edition, 1786.

HA! whare ye gaun, ye crowlan ferlie!	where, going, crawling wonder
Your impudence protects you sairly:	very well
I canna say but ye strunt rarely	cannot, strut confidently
Owre *gauze* and *lace*,	over
5 Tho' faith, I fear ye dine but sparely	eat little
On sic a place.	such

Ye ugly, creepan, blastet wonner,   blasted wonder
Detested, shunn'd by saunt an' sinner,   saint
How daur ye set your fit upon her —   dare, foot
10   Sae fine a *Lady*!   so
Gae somewhere else and seek your dinner   go
          On some poor body.

Swith, in some beggar's haffet squattle: away!, temples, squat
There ye may creep, and sprawl, and sprattle,   scramble
15 Wi' ither kindred, jumping cattle,   other
          In shoals and nations;
Whare *horn* nor *bane* ne'er daur unsettle   where, bone (comb), dare
          Your thick plantations.

Now haud you there, ye're out o' sight,   hold
20 Below the fatt'rels, snug an' tight,   ribbon-ends
Na, faith ye yet! ye'll no be right,   no, confound you
          Till ye've got on it,
The vera tapmost, tow'ring height   very topmost
          O' *Miss's bonnet*.   hat

25 My sooth! right bauld ye set your nose out,   bold
As plump an' grey as onie grozet: any gooseberry
O for some rank, mercurial rozet,   mercury pasted rosin
          Or fell, red smeddum,   deadly powder
I'd gie ye sic a hearty dose o't,   give
30   Wad dress your droddum!   would, backside

I wad na been surpris'd to spy   would not
You on an auld wife's *flainen toy*;   old flannel cap
Or aiblins some bit duddie boy,   perhaps, small ragged
          On 's *wylecoat*;   flannel vest
35 But Miss's fine *Lunardi*, fye!   balloon-shaped hat
          How daur ye do't?   dare

O *Jenny*, dinna toss your head,   do not
An' set your beauties a' abroad!   abroad
Ye little ken what cursèd speed   know
40   The blastie's makin!   damned thing's
Thae *winks* an' *finger-ends*, I dread,
          Are notice takin!

O wad some Pow'r the giftie gie us   *would, gift give*
To *see oursels as ithers see us*!   *others*
45 It wad frae monie a blunder free us,   *would from many*
     An' foolish notion:
What airs in dress an' gait wad lea'e us,   *would leave*
     An' ev'n Devotion!

If perceptible animal motion in *To a Mouse* is reduced to a drift towards cold death, the louse's world is charged with manic upward mobility. Its achieved goal is the very top of the refined Jenny's Lunardi bonnet. These height of fashion bonnets derived from the shape of the Lunardi balloon flown over Edinburgh by Burns's Crochallan Fencible comrade, James 'Balloon' Tytler in 1784. The Italian aeronaut Vincenzo Lunardi made several flights in Scotland in the following year. The church service which combines strict social regimentation with, for the prosperous, fashionable display, becomes the occasion for the louse to traverse the class barrier with a vengeance leaving behind its accustomed world of greasy, dirty flannel for that of gauze and lace. Burns's own ambivalent but constant attraction for the world of women of a superior class (cloyingly obvious with Mrs McLehose and frenzied with regard to Maria Riddell) perhaps provides the poem with its dynamism and profound sense of satirical social contrast. Kinsley calls the poem a 'minor triumph of whimsy' but David Craig surely comes nearer the truth when he comments:

> *To a Louse* isn't radical in a usual or obvious sense. The point is that Burns's radicalism pervades his imagination through and through. The least domestic item reminds him of the hunger and shortages of poor folk, the unfeeling above-it-all stance of the well-to-do, the need to expose the shame of finery and what was then called rank. For Burns, the louse is an underdog and all his complicity is with it (ll. 9–16). Already the louse has come to stand for all the dispossessed and propertyless who one day will come and squat in the big houses when the upper class nightmare of a jacquerie comes to pass. The beauty of this poem is that it insinuates its radical challenge to the unequal nature of class society into a perfectly observed comic scene. The social point makes itself. It is the kind of piece we need when answering the usual conservative objection that radical litera- ture tends to blaze and tub-thump ('The Radical Literary Tradition', *The Red Paper on Scotland*, ed. Gordon Brown (Edinburgh University Publications Board: 1975), pp. 292–3).

Craig's is both a brilliant insight into this poem and a salutary reminder of the fact that Burns as poet is necessarily preoccupied with varied oblique strategies for his radical politics. As a writer he was a smuggler not an Excise man. It should also remind us not to read 'O wad some Pow'r the giftie gie us/*to see oursels as ithers see us*!' as a piece of sententious sentimentality but Burns's two line demolition of Adam Smith's concept of the creation of internalised spectator in his *Theory of Moral Sentiments* as a form of secular conscience adequate to controlling our materialism and social pretentiousness.

Epistle to J. Lapraik:
An Old Scotch Bard, April 1, 1785
First printed in the Kilmarnock edition, 1786.

WHILE briers an' woodbines budding green,
And Paitricks scraichin loud at e'en,   partridges screeching
An' morning Poossie whiddin seen,   hare scudding
     Inspire my Muse,
5 This freedom, in an *unknown* frien'   friend
     I pray excuse.

On Fasteneen we had a rockin,   Shrove Tuesday, meeting
To ca' the crack and weave our stockin;   call the conversation
And there was muckle fun and jokin,   much
10   Ye need na doubt;   not
At length we had a hearty yokin,   set-to
     At *sang about*.

There was *ae sang*, amang the rest,   one
Aboon them a' it pleas'd me best,   above
15 That some kind husband had addrest
     To some sweet wife:
It thirl'd the heart-strings thro' the breast,   thrilled
     A' to the life.

I've scarce heard ought describ'd sae weel,   anything, so well
20 What gen'rous, manly bosoms feel;
Thought I, 'Can this be *Pope* or *Steele*,
     Or *Beattie's* wark?'   work
They tald me 'twas an odd kind chiel   told, chap or person
     About *Muirkirk*.

25   It pat me fidgean-fain to hear't,   put, tingling/excited
      An' sae about him there I spier't;   so, asked
      Then a' that kent him round declar'd,   all, knew
            He had *ingine*;   genius
      That nane excell'd it, few cam near't,   none, came
30   It was sae fine: so

      That set him to a pint of ale,
      An' either douce or merry tale,   sober
      Or rhymes an' sangs he'd made himsel,   songs
            Or witty catches,
35   'Tween Inverness and Teviotdale,
            He had few matches.

      Then up I gat, an' swoor an aith,   got, swore an oath
      Tho' I should pawn my pleugh an' graith,   plough and harness
      Or die a cadger pownie's death,   hawker pony's
40   At some dyke-back,   beind a stone wall
      A *pint* an' *gill* I'd gie them *baith*,   give, both
            To hear your crack.   conversation

      But, first an' foremost, I should tell,
      Amaist as soon as I could spell,   almost
45   I to the *crambo-jingle* fell;   rhyming
            Tho' rude an' rough,
      Yet crooning to a body's sel,   humming, self
            Does weel eneugh.   well enough

      I am nae *Poet*, in a sense;   no
50   But just a *Rhymer* like by chance,
      An' hae to Learning nae pretence;   have, no
            Yet, what the matter?
      Whene'er my Muse does on me glance,
            I jingle at her.

55   Your Critic-folk may cock their nose,
      And say, 'How can you e'er propose,
      You wha ken hardly *verse* frae *prose*,   who know, from
            To mak a *sang*?'   make
      But by your leaves, my learned foes,
60   Ye're maybe wrang.

What's a' your jargon o' your Schools,
Your Latin names for horns an' stools?
If honest Nature made you *fools*,
   What sairs your Grammers?   serves
65 Ye'd better taen up *spades* and *shools*, shovels
   Or *knappin-hammers*.   stone-breaking

 A set o' dull, conceited Hashes, dunderheads/fools
Confuse their brains in *Colledge-classes*!
They *gang in* Stirks, and *come out* Asses, go
70   Plain truth to speak;
An' syne they think to climb Parnassus then
   By dint o' Greek!

Gie me ae spark o' Nature's fire, one
That's a' the learning I desire;
75 Then, tho' I drudge thro' dub an' mire puddle
   At pleugh or cart, plough
My Muse, tho' hamely in attire,
   May touch the heart.

O for a spunk o' ALLAN'S glee, spark
80 Or FERGUSSON'S, the bauld an' slee, sly
Or bright LAPRAIK'S, my friend to be,
   If I can hit it!
That would be *lear* eneugh for me, learning enough
   If I could get it.

85 Now, sir, if ye hae friends enow, have, enough
Tho' *real friends* I b'lieve are few;
Yet, if your catalogue be fow, full
   I'se no insist;
But, gif ye want ae friend that's true, if, one
90   I'm on your list.

I winna blaw about *mysel*, will not boast
As ill I like my fauts to tell; faults
But friends, an' folks that wish me well,
   They sometimes roose me; praise
95 Tho', I maun own, as monie still shall, many
   As far abuse me.

There's ae *wee faut* they whyles lay to me,   one small fault, whiles
I like the lasses — Gude forgie me!   God forgive
For monie a Plack they wheedle frae me   many a coin, get from
100   At dance or fair:
Maybe some *ither thing* they gie me,   other, give
        They weel can spare.   well

But MAUCHLINE Race or MAUCHLINE Fair,
I should be proud to meet you there;
105 We'se gie ae night's discharge to *care*,   we will give one
        If we forgather;   get together
And hae a swap o' *rhymin-ware*,   have
        Wi' ane anither.   one another

The *four-gill chap*, we'se gar him clatter,   four-gill cup, we will make
110 An' kirs'n him wi' reekin water;   christen
Syne we'll sit down an' tak our whitter,   then, draught
        To chear our heart;
An' faith, we'se be *acquainted* better
        Before we part.

115 Awa ye selfish, warly race,   worldly
Wha think that havins, sense, an' grace,   who, manners
Ev'n love an' friendship should give place
        To *catch-the-plack*!   hunt for coin/money
I dinna like to see your face,   do not
120   Nor hear your crack.   conversation

But ye whom social pleasure charms,
Whose hearts the *tide of kindness* warms,
Who hold your *being* on the terms,
        'Each aid the others,'
125 Come to my bowl, come to my arms,
        My friends, my brothers!

But to conclude my lang epistle,
As my auld pen's worn to the grissle,   old, stump of a quill
Twa lines frae you wad gar me fissle,   two, from, would make me tingle
130   Who am, most fervent,
While I can either sing, or whissle,   whistle
        Your friend and servant.

The recipient of this epistle was John Lapraik (1727–1807) who was
postmaster at Muirkirk when he received it after a life of fiscal

mischance which had involved him in the Ayrshire Bank failure of 1773, so losing his farm at Dalfarn, and concluded with his imprisonment for debt in Ayr in 1785. Diverting himself with poetry in prison and observing Burns's success, he published *Poems on Several Occasions* (1788). Inevitably sympathetic to a man whose fiscal record only slightly exceeded the misfortunes of his own family, Burns may have over-responded to the alleged Lapraik song, *When I Upon Thy Bosom Lean*, he heard sung at a rural gathering. It has been strongly suggested by J.L. Hempstead (*BC*, February, 1994, pp. 94–101) that this song, initially published in *The Weekly Magazine*, was plagiarised. Burns revised the song for inclusion in the S.M.M. and in his interleaved copy remarked that Lapraik was 'a worthy, facetious old fellow' who 'often told me that he composed (the song) one day when his wife had been fretting o'er their misfortunes'.

Certainly the associations in this epistle of the 'facetious' Lapraik as *creatively* comparable to Pope, Steele, Beattie, Ramsay and Fergusson are hyperbolic in the extreme. Perhaps unconsciously Burns is projecting his own influences onto the older man. It also adds irony, of course, the proto-Wordsworthian pastoral poet Burns here celebrates in the stanza beginning 'Gie me ae spark o' Nature's fire' does so in a line which McGuirk (p. 205) notes, contains deliberate associations with these two earlier well-known rural non-sophisticates, Sterne and Pope. Certainly it allows Burns to make merry with rule-constipated academic poets and, another old-enemy, those rigidly and successfully, quite unlike himself and Lapraik, making money. The celebration of social pleasures also involves, as so often the case, in ll. 97–101 witty sexual innuendo.

Second Epistle to J. Lapraik
April 21, 1785
First printed in the Kilmarnock edition, 1786.

While new-ca'd kye rowte at the stake	new driven cattle, low
An' pownies reek in pleugh or braik,	ponies, snort, plough, harrow
This hour on e'enin's edge I take,	
To own I'm debtor	
5 To honest-hearted, auld LAPRAIK,	old
For his kind *letter*.	

Forjesket sair, with weary legs,   jaded, sore
Rattlin the corn out-owre the rigs,   out-over, ridges
Or dealing thro' amang the naigs   dealing out food among ponies
10   Their ten-hours' bite,
My awkart Muse sair pleads and begs,   awkward, sore
          I would na write.   not

The tapetless, ramfeezl'd hizzie,   feckless, worn-out girl
She's saft at best an' something lazy: soft
15   Quo' she: 'Ye ken we've been sae busy   know, so
          This month an' mair,   more
That trowth, my head is grown right dizzie,
          An' something sair.'   sore/aching

Her dowf excuses pat me mad;   dull, put
20   'Conscience,' says I, 'ye thowless jad!   lazy
I'll write, an' that a hearty blaud,   screed
          This vera night;   very
So dinna ye affront your trade,   do not
          But rhyme it right.

25   'Shall bauld·LAPRAIK, the *king o' hearts*,
Tho' mankind were a *pack o' cartes*,   cards
Roose you sae weel for your deserts,   praise, so well
          In terms sae friendly;   so
Yet ye'll neglect to shaw your parts   show
30   An' thank him kindly?'

Sae I gat paper in a blink,   so, got
An' down gaed *stumpie* in the ink: went
Quoth I, 'Before I sleep a wink,
          I vow I'll close it:
35   An' if ye winna mak it clink,   will not make
          By Jove I'll prose it!'

Sae I've begun to scrawl, but whether   so
In rhyme, or prose, or baith thegither,   both together
Or some hotch-potch that's rightly neither,
40   Let time mak proof;
But I shall scribble down some blether   chit-chat
          Just clean aff-loof.   off the cuff

My worthy friend, ne'er grudge an' carp,
Tho' Fortune use you hard an' sharp;
45 Come, kittle up your *moorland harp*   tickle
       Wi' gleesome touch!
Ne'er mind how Fortune *waft an' warp*;
       She's but a bitch.

She's gien me monie a jirt an' fleg,   given, many, jerk, scare
50 Sin' I could striddle owre a rig;   straddle over
But, by the Lord, tho' I should beg
       Wi' lyart pow,   grey head
I'll laugh an' sing, an' shake my leg,   dance
       As lang's I dow!   long as I can

55 Now comes the *sax an twentieth simmer*   six, summer
I've seen the bud upo' the timmer,   woods/trees
Still persecuted by the limmer   jade
       Frae year to year;   from
But yet, despite the kittle kimmer,   fickle gossip
60   *I, Rob, am here.*

Do ye envy the *city-gent*,
Behint a kist to lie an' sklent,   counter, cheat
Or purse-proud, big wi' cent per cent,   counting money
       An' muckle wame,   large belly
65 In some bit *Brugh* to represent   borough
       A *Bailie's* name?   town magistrate

Or is't the paughty feudal *Thane*,   haughty
Wi' ruffl'd sark an' glancing cane,   shirt, shining
Wha thinks himsel nae *sheep-shank bane*,   who, himself no, bone
70   But lordly stalks;
While caps an' bonnets aff are taen,   off, taken
       As by he walks?

'O Thou wha gies us each guid gift!   who gives, good
Gie me o' *wit* an' *sense* a lift,   give
75 Then turn me, if *Thou* please, *adrift*
       Thro' Scotland wide;
Wi' *cits* nor *lairds* I wadna shift,   citizens, would not
       In a' their pride!'

Were this the *charter* of our state,
80   'On pain o' *hell* be rich an' great,'
Damnation then would be our fate,
          Beyond remead;
But, thanks to *Heav'n*, that's no the gate
          We learn our *creed*.

85   For thus the royal *Mandate* ran,
When first the human race began:
'The social, friendly, honest man,
          Whate'er he be,
'Tis *he* fulfils *great Nature's plan*,
90   And none but *he*.'

O *Mandate* glorious and divine!
The followers o' the ragged Nine —   the Muses
Poor, thoughtless devils! yet may shine
          In glorious light;
95   While sordid sons o' Mammon's line
          Are dark as night!

Tho' here they scrape, an' squeeze, an' growl,
Their worthless neivefu' of a *soul*   fistful
May in some *future carcase* howl,
100   The forest's fright;
Or in some day-detesting *owl*
          May shun the light.

Then may LAPRAIK and BURNS arise,
To reach their native, kindred skies,
105   And *sing* their pleasures, hopes an' joys,
          In some mild sphere;
Still closer knit in friendship's ties,
          Each passing year!

As further proof of Wordsworth's passionate enthusiasm for Burns's poetry, Alan Cunningham recollects hearing him recite this epistle 'with commendations. . . pointing out as he went the all but inimitable ease and happiness of thought and language. He remarked, however, that Burns was either fond of out-of-the-way sort of words, or that he made them occasionally in his fits of feeling and fancy'. Other than Cowper, Burns's English peers rarely complained about vernacular difficulty though 'forjesket' and 'tapetless', not to mention 'ram-feezl'd' may have been a linguistic bridge too far. It is interesting that well into the nineteenth century the, by then, deeply reactionary Wordsworth should have so responded to so politically radical a poem. Not only (ll. 7–12) does Burns record the brutal cost of farm work to his creativity, but the bulk of the poem is a cry of defiant, satirical rage against the old land-owning classes and the newly emerging bourgeoisie. Those 'Cits' who are equally castigated by Oliver Goldsmith and Charles Churchill. Burns brilliantly inverts the prosperous's use of 'economic Calvinism' to control the poor by showing what the real political would be in an inversion worthy of Blake:

Were this the *charter* of our state
'On pain o' hell to be rich an' great',
Damnation then would be our fate,
    Beyond remead;
But, thanks to *Heav'n*, that's no the gate
    We learn our creed.

Again, like Blake (ll. 85–90) he invoked the spirit of divinely natural democracy so that this poem becomes a splendid prelude to the later, more overtly political *A Man's a Man* and the American section of *Ode for General Washington's Birthday*. Thus Burns would enrol fully armed in Edinburgh's dissident Crochallan Fencibles.

    The poem concludes with an extraordinary image of the poor but poetically creative inheriting Heaven, with Mammon's sordid sons suitably rewarded for their bestial conduct to their fellow human beings.

To William Simson, Ochiltree,
May 1785
First printed in the Kilmarnock edition, 1786.

I GAT your letter, winsome Willie;	got
Wi' gratefu' heart I thank you brawlie;	handsomely
Tho' I maun say't, I wad be silly	shall, would
And unco vain,	mighty
5 Should I believe, my coaxin billie,	fellow
Your flatterin strain.	

But I'se believe ye kindly meant it,   I'll
I sud be laith to think ye hinted   should be loath
Ironic satire, sidelins sklented,   squinted sideways
10   On my poor Musie;
Tho' in sic phraisin terms ye've penn'd it,   such wheedling
        I scarce excuse ye.

My senses wad be in a creel,   would
Should I but dare a *hope* to speel,   climb
15   Wi' *Allan*, or wi' *Gilbertfield*,
        The braes o' fame;   slopes
Or *Fergusson*, the writer-chiel,   fellow
        A deathless name.

(O *Fergusson*! thy glorious parts
20   Ill suited law's dry, musty arts!
My curse upon your whunstane hearts,   whinstone
        Ye Enbrugh Gentry!
The tythe o' what ye waste at *cartes*   tenth, cards
        Wad stow'd his pantry!)   would have stored

25   Yet when a tale comes i' my head,
Or lasses gie my heart a screed —   give
As whyles they're like to be my dead,   whiles, death
        (O sad disease!)
I kittle up my *rustic reed*;   tickle, pipe
30   It gies me ease.   gives

Auld COILA, now, may fidge fu' fain,   tingle with delight
She's gotten *Bardies* o' her ain,   own
Chiels wha their chanters winna hain,   fellows who, will not spare
        But tune their lays,
35   Till echoes a' resound again
        Her weel-sung praise.   well-sung

Nae *Poet* thought her worth his while,   no
To set her name in measur'd style;
She lay like some unkend-of isle   unknown
40   Beside *New Holland*,
Or whare wild-meeting oceans boil   where
        Besouth *Magellan*.   to the south of

Ramsay an' famous *Fergusson*
Gied *Forth* an' *Tay* a lift aboon;   gave, above
45 *Yarrow* an' *Tweed*, to monie a tune,   many
    Owre Scotland rings;   over
While *Irwin, Lugar, Aire*, an' *Doon*   old spelling of Ayr
    Naebody sings.   nobody

Th' *Illissus, Tiber, Thames*, an' *Seine*,
50 Glide sweet in monie a tunefu' line: many
But, *Willie*, set your fit to mine,   foot (in music timing)
    An' cock your crest!
We'll gar our streams and burnies shine   make, burns
    Up wi' the best.

55 We'll sing auld COILA'S plains an' fells,   Coila/Kyle, Ayrshire
Her moors red-brown wi' heather bells,
Her banks an' braes, her dens an' dells,   slopes, hill sides, glens
    Whare glorious WALLACE   where
Aft bure the gree, as story tells,   often took victory
60   Frae Suthron billies.   from English people

At WALLACE' name, what Scottish blood
But boils up in a spring-tide flood?
Oft have our fearless fathers strode
    By WALLACE' side,
65 Still pressing onward, red-wat-shod,   shoes soaked in blood
    Or glorious dy'd!

O sweet are COILA's haughs an' woods,   hollows
When lintwhites chant amang the buds,   linnets, among
And jinkin hares, in amorous whids,   sporting, silent running
70   Their loves enjoy,
While thro' the braes the cushat croods   slopes, pidgeon coos
    With wailfu' cry!

Ev'n winter bleak has charms to me,
When winds rave thro' the naked tree;
75 Or frosts on hills of *Ochiltree*
    Are hoary gray;
Or blinding drifts wild-furious flee,
    Dark'ning the day!

    O NATURE! a' thy shews an' forms
80 To feeling, pensive hearts hae charms!   have
    Whether the summer kindly warms,
        Wi' life an' light;
    Or winter howls, in gusty storms,
        The lang, dark night!   long

85 The *Muse*, nae *Poet* ever fand her,   no, found
    Till by himsel he learn'd to wander,
    Adown some trottin burn's meander,   running
        An' no think lang: long
    O, sweet to stray, an' pensive ponder
90   A heart-felt sang!   song

    The warly race may drudge an' drive,   worldly
    Hog-shouther, jundie, stretch, an' strive; shoulder push, jostle
    Let me fair NATURE's face descrive,   describe
        And I, wi' pleasure,
95 Shall let the busy, grumbling hive
        Bum owre their treasure.   hum over

    Fareweel, 'my rhyme-composing' brither! farewell, brother
    We've been owre lang unkenn'd to ither: too long unknown, other
    Now let us lay our heads thegither,   together
100   In love fraternal:
    May *Envy* wallop in a tether,   swing on a rope
        Black fiend, infernal!

    While Highlandmen hate tolls an' taxes;
    While moorlan' herds like guid, fat braxies; good, sheep carcases
105 While Terra Firma, on her axis,
        Diurnal turns;
    Count on a friend, in faith an' practice,
        In ROBERT BURNS.

POSTSCRIPT
    My memory's no worth a preen: pin
    I had amaist forgotten clean,   almost
    Ye bade me write you what they mean   bid
        By this *new-light*,[1]
5 'Bout which our herds sae aft hae been   flocks so often
        Maist like to fight.   most

1 A cant-term for those religious opinions which Dr Taylor of Norwich has
defended so strenuously. –R.B.

In days when mankind were but callans;   striplings
At *Grammar, Logic,* an' sic talents,   such
They took nae pains their speech to balance,   no
10   Or rules to gie;   give
But spak their thoughts in plain, braid Lallans, spoke, broad vernacular
        Like you or me.

In thae auld times, they thought the *Moon*,   those old
Just like a sark, or pair o' shoon,   shirt, shoes
15 Wore by degrees, till her last roon   round
        Gaed past their viewin;   went
An' shortly after she was done,
        They gat a new ane.   got, one

This past for certain, undisputed;
20 It ne'er cam i' their heads to doubt it,
Till chiels gat up an' wad confute it,   chaps got, would
        An' ca'd it wrang;   called, wrong
An' muckle din there was about it,   much
        Baith loud an' lang.   both, long

25 Some *herds,* weel learn'd upo' the beuk,   well, Book (Bible)
Wad threap auld folk the thing misteuk;   would, maintain old, mistook
For 'twas the *auld moon* turn'd a newk   old, corner
        An' out o' sight.
An' backlins-comin to the leuk,   backwards, look
30   She grew mair bright.   more

This was deny'd, it was affirm'd;
The *herds* and *hissels* were alarm'd;   shepherds, flocks
The rev'rend gray-beards rav'd an' storm'd,
        That beardless laddies   young men
35 Should think they better were inform'd
        Than their auld daddies.   old fathers

Frae less to mair, it gaed to sticks;   from, more, went
Frae words an' aiths, to clours an' nicks;   from, oaths, bumps, cuts
An' monie a fallow gat his licks,   many, fellow got, punishment
40   Wi' hearty crunt;   blow
An' some, to learn them for their tricks,
        Were hang'd an' brunt.   burned

This game was play'd in monie lands,   many
    An' *auld-light caddies* bure sic hands,   lackeys bore such
45 That faith, the *youngsters* took the sands   fled
        Wi' nimble shanks,   legs
    Till *Lairds* forbade, by strict commands,
        Sic bluidy pranks.   such bloody

    But *new-light herds* gat sic a cowe,   got such a terror
50 Folk thought them ruin'd stick-an-stowe;   completely
    Till now, amaist on ev'ry *knowe*   almost, hill or hillock
        Ye'll find ane placed;   one
    An' some, their *New-Light* fair avow,
        Just quite barefac'd.

55 Nae doubt the *auld-light flocks* are bleatan;
    Their zealous herds are vex'd and sweatan;
    Mysel, I've even seen them greetan   crying
        Wi' girnan spite,   snarling
    To hear the *Moon* sae sadly lie'd on   so
60   By word an' write.

    But shortly they will cowe the louns!   terrify, rascals
    Some *auld-light herds* in neebor touns   neighbour towns
    Are mind't, in things they ca' *balloons*,   call
        To tak a flight,   take
65 An' stay ae month amang the *Moons*   one, among
        An' see them right.

    Guid observation they will gie them;   good, give
    An' when the *auld Moon's* gaun to lea'e them,   old, going, leave
    The hindmost *shaird*, they'll fetch it wi' them,   fragment
70   Just i' their pouch;
    An' when the *new-light* billies see them,   people
        I think they'll crouch!

    Sae, ye observe that a' this clatter   so, talk
    Is naething but a 'moonshine matter';   nothing
75 But tho' dull *prose-folk* Latin splatter   speak
        In logic tulzie,   quarrel
    I hope we, *Bardies*, ken some better   know
        Than mind sic brulzie.   such a brawl

William Simpson (1758–1815) was a Glasgow University graduate
who taught at Ochiltree and later at Cumnock. His relationship with
Burns was initiated by sending him a now lost verse epistle praising

Burns's anti-clerical satire, *The Holy Tulzie*. Burns was, of course, always looking for allies in his guerrilla warfare with the forces of Auld-Licht Calvinism. The attack, almost surreal, on crazed theology provides the poem's postscript. The bulk of the poem is, however, like its longer contemporary, *The Vision*, taken up with Burns's self-placing in the lineage of great Scottish poets and Ayrshire's topography and heroic dead. L. 9, 'Ironic satire, sidelins sklented' is of particular note because it is of the quintessence of Burns's own poetic strategy as a satirist since he was socially disempowered from full frontal assault on his enemies.

He celebrates his great eighteenth century vernacular predecessors, Ramsay, Hamilton of Gilbertfield but above all his wholly beloved Robert Fergusson to whom, as soon as he got to Edinburgh, he paid for a tombstone for his unmarked grave. Ironically Fergusson's fate at the hands of genteel Edinburgh (ll. 19–24) was to be a sorry prelude to his own.

Burns's genteel contemporaries thought his pastoral poetry imitatively conventional. John Logan wrote to Henry Mackenzie: 'Mr Burns is a clever fellow, a Man of Observation, and a Country Libertine, but I am much mistaken if he has anything of the Penseroso in his character' (Low, *Robert Burns: The Critical Heritage*, p. 79). Actually, Burns's intense intimate rural realism they shied away from; the harsh life of man and beast is not what they wished to countenance. Burns himself would not have disavowed the libertine. L. 29. 'I kittle up my *rustic reed*' arguably endorses his opinion that erotic and creative energy were always synergetic for him: in this case, ejaculatively so.

As in *The Vision* the poem looks forward to a Bardic celebration of Ayrshire, in this case as a poetic-newfoundland. Wordsworth when he came to pay pilgrimage to the poet to whom he owed so much was perturbed that Burns had not creatively, unlike himself, lifted his eyes unto the hills. The Arran Mountains were for the English poet disturbingly above Burns's line of vision. Burns is, however, like MacDiarmid a poet given to water music:

> The Muse nae Poet ever fand her,
> Till by himself he learn'd to wander,
> Adown some trottin burn's meander. . . .

Thus Coila's (Ayrshire's) rivers are to receive the poetic celebration given already to bardically celebrated Scottish and European streams. So, too, is Ayrshire's archetypal hero, William Wallace. Wallace haunts Burns's poetry and letters. A biography of Wallace was one of the first things he read: 'the story of Wallace poured a Scottish prejudice in my veins which will boil along there till the floodgates of life shut in eternal rest' (See Letters 55, 78, 125). Burns hoped that Wallace's example would energise the struggle for freedom of his own generation. More darkly, he perhaps came to associate Scotland's dismembered hero with his own fate. As in all these early Ayrshire epistles a compensatory natural freedom is celebrated in the face of the greedy (Mandevillism) of the prosperously secure (ll. 90–6).

The poem's Postscript is a deeply comic account of the controversy between Auld and New Licht Theology in terms of the analogy of a quarrel between the old and new thought about the nature of the moon. Ancestral thought believed that the moon, when it waned, was discarded and replaced by a completely new one in the sky. The Auld Lichts cling to this unscientific cosmology. The traditionalists then decide to set off into space in a balloon to prove their case empirically. There is controversy regarding how much Swift Burns knew. Certainly they were, for different reasons, both profoundly displaced persons which allowed them to view eccentrically worlds to which they never fully belonged and which they agonisingly saw as suffused with inequity and iniquity. Certainly also, as in this balloon fantasy, Burns is distinctively Swiftian in his send-up of the madness of scientific hyper-rationalism. Burns, as he footnotes, is also defending the theology of 'Dr Taylor of Norwich (1722)' whose tract *The Scripture Doctrine of Original Sin Proposed to Free and Candid Examination* (1740) provided the foundation for liberalising 'New Licht' doctrine.

Epistle to John Ranken,
Enclosing Some Poems
First printed in the Kilmarnock edition, 1786.

O rough, rude, ready-witted RANKEN,	
The wale o' cocks for fun an' drinkin!	pick/choice
There's monie godly folks are thinkin'	many
Your *dreams*[1] and tricks	
5 Will send you, Korah-like, a-sinkin	
Straught to Auld Nick's.	straight, old, the Devil

[1] A certain humorous dream of his was then making a noise in the world. R.B.

Ye hae sae monie cracks an' cants,   have so many stories & jokes
And in your wicked drucken rants,   drunken babble
Ye mak a devil o' the *Saunts*,   saints
10   An' fill them fou';   drunk
And then their failings, flaws, an' wants
   Are a' seen thro'.

Hypocrisy, in mercy spare it!
That *holy robe*, O dinna tear it!   do not
15 Spare 't for their sakes, wha aften wear it — who often
   The lads in *black*;   robes
But your curst wit, when it comes near it,
   Rives 't aff their back.   rips, off

Think, wicked Sinner, wha ye're skaithing: who, slighting
20 It's just the *Blue-gown* badge an' claithing clothing
O' *Saunts*; tak that, ye lea'e them naething saints, take, leave, nothing
   To ken them by,   know
Frae ony unregenerate Heathen,   from any
   Like you or I.

25 I've sent you here some rhyming ware items of poetry
A' that I bargain'd for, an' mair;   more
Sae, when ye hae an hour to spare,   so, have
   I will expect,
Yon *Sang*² ye'll sen 't, wi' cannie care, song, send it, cautious
30   And no neglect.

Tho' faith, sma' heart hae I to sing: little, have
My Muse dow scarcely spread her wing: can
I've play'd mysel a bonie *spring*,   pleasant tune
   An' *danc'd* my fill!
35 I'd better gaen an' sair't the King   gone, served
   At Bunker's Hill.

'Twas ae night lately, in my fun,   one
I gaed a rovin wi' the gun,   went
An' brought a *Paitrick* to the *grun*', partridge, ground
40   A bonie *hen*;   pretty
And, as the twilight was begun,
   Thought nane wad ken.   none would know

2 A *Song* he had promised the author.

The poor, wee thing was *little hurt*;
I *straikit* it a wee for sport,   stroked, a little
45   Ne'er thinkan they wad fash me for't;   would, trouble
          But, Deil-ma-care!
      Somebody tells the *Poacher-Court*   Kirk Session
          The hale affair.   whole

      Some auld, us'd hands had taen a note,   old, taken
50   That *sic a hen* had got a *shot*;   such
      I was suspected for the plot;
          I scorn'd to lie;
      So gat the whissle o' my groat,   got, played a losing game
          An' pay't the *fee*.

55   But by my *gun*, o' guns the wale,   pick/choice
      An' by my *pouther* an' my *hail*.   gunpowder
      An' by my *hen*, an' by her *tail*,
          I vow an' swear!
      The Game shall Pay, owre moor an' *dail*,   over
60   For this, niest year!   next

      As soon's the *clockin-time* is by,   egg-hatching
      An' the *wee pouts* begun to cry,   small chicks
      Lord, I'se hae sportin by an' by   I'll have
      For my *gowd guinea*;   gold
65   Tho' I should herd the *buckskin* kye   American cattle/slaves
          For 't, in Virginia!   in America

      Trowth, they had muckle for to blame!   in truth, much
      'Twas neither broken wing nor limb,
      But twa-three *draps* about the *wame*,   two-, (sperm), belly
70   Scarce thro' the *feathers*;
      An' baith a *yellow George* to claim   both, gold guinea
          An' *thole* their *blethers*!   suffer, gossip

      It pits me ay as mad's a hare;   puts/makes, always
      So I can rhyme nor write nae mair;   no more
75   But *pennyworths* again is fair,   a paid bargain
          When time's expedient:
      Meanwhile I am, respected Sir,
          Your most obedient,
              Robt. Burns.

John Rankin (d. 1810) was a tenant farmer in Adamhill, Tarbolton. He was friendly with Burns in the Lochlea years. His sister Margaret was, appropriately, the first wife of John Lapraik since both Lapraik and Rankin belonged to that anarchic, anti-clerical 'ram-stam' Ayrshire group. The specific occasion of the poem is Burns's 'allegorical' account of his impregnation of Betty Paton resulting in the birth of an illegitimate daughter represented in terms of the poacher and his gun. Hugh Blair was first uncomprehending and then horrified as understanding slowly dawned: 'The description of shooting the hen is understood, I find, to convey an indecent meaning tho' in reading the poem. . . I took it literally, and the indecency did not strike me. But. . . the whole poem ought undoubtedly to be left out of the new edition' (J. De Lancey Ferguson, 'Burns and Hugh Blair', *Modern Language Notes*, xlv (1930), 441–3). It was not in the least of Burns's resistances to Blair that he kept the poem in.

L. 5. is a direct reference to *Numbers* xvi, 29–33, again demonstrating the range of Burns's allusive grasp of the Bible. The initial part of the poem, especially ll. 13–18, is an attack on the clergy akin to Blake's *Songs of Experience*. These holy devils reassert themselves later in the poem as 'the Poacher-Court' kirk session which punished apprehended fornicators by putting them on black-gowned display.

While this Ayrshire epistle is much less concerned than the others with Burns's anxieties about his ability to create for himself a poetic career in such a hostile environment, American allusions betray doubts about both the worth of his creativity and its capacity to earn him a living. Thus ll. 35–6, 'I'd better gaen an' sair't the King/At Bunker's Hill' is, given both the fate of British arms and Burns's espousal of the American cause, a particularly self-denigrating remark. Troubling in a different way are ll. 65–66, 'Tho' I should herd the *buckskin* kye/For 't in Virginia!' which are arguably the least politically correct lines the Bard wrote. He is, of course, referring to his intended emigration as escape from Ayrshire's cloying fiscal and clerical restraints to become a 'poor Negro-driver' (Letter 125). On the other hand, he went on to write *The Slave's Lament*, praised by Maya Angelou because of its grasp not only of the substance but the very rhythm of Black American experience.

The Rigs o Barley
or It was upon a Lammas Night
First printed in the Kilmarnock edition, 1786.
Tune: Corn Rigs are Bonie

It was upon a Lammas night,   harvest festival
    When corn rigs are bonie,   ridges/rows
Beneath the moon's unclouded light,
    I held awa to Annie: away
5   The time flew by, wi' tentless heed;   carefree
    Till, 'tween the late and early,
Wi' sma' persuasion she agreed
    To see me thro' the barley.

Chorus
10   Corn rigs, an' barley rigs,
    An' corn rigs are bonie:
I'll ne'er forget that happy night,
    Amang the rigs wi' Annie.

The sky was blue, the wind was still,
15   The moon was shining clearly;
I set her down, wi' right good will,
    Amang the rigs o' barley:
I ken't her heart was a' my ain;   knew
    I lov'd her most sincerely;
20   I kiss'd her owre and owre again,   over
    Amang the rigs o' barley.
Corn rigs, &c.

I lock'd her in my fond embrace;
    Her heart was beating rarely:
25   My blessings on that happy place,
    Amang the rigs o' barley!
But by the moon and stars so bright,
    That shone that hour so clearly!
She ay shall bless that happy night   always
30   Amang the rigs o' barley.
Corn rigs, &c.

I hae been blythe wi' comrades dear;   have
    I hae been merry drinking;
I hae been joyfu' gath'rin gear;   making money
35   I hae been happy thinking:
But a' the pleasures e'er I saw,
    Tho' three times doubl'd fairly —
That happy night was worth them a',
    Amang the rigs o' barley.
40   Corn rigs, &c.

This joyful reminiscence of love has been one of the poet's most
popular songs, perfectly matching his lyric to traditional music. The
poem's Annie is supposed to be John Rankine's daughter. (See
Epistle to John Ranken).

Composed in August –
Westlin Winds
First printed in the Kilmarnock edition, 1786.
Tune: Port Gordon

Now westlin winds and slaught'ring guns   from the west
    Bring Autumn's pleasant weather;
The moorcock springs on whirring wings
    Amang the blooming heather:
5 Now waving grain, wide o'er the plain,
    Delights the weary Farmer;
The moon shines bright, as I rove at night
    To muse upon my Charmer.

The Paitrick lo'es the fruitfu' fells,   partridge, loves
10   The Plover lo'es the mountains;
The Woodcock haunts the lanely dells,   lonely
    The soaring Hern the fountains;   heron
Thro' lofty groves the Cushat roves,   wood pigeon
    The path o' man to shun it;
15 The hazel bush o'erhangs the Thrush,
    The spreading thorn the Linnet.

Thus ev'ry kind their pleasure find,
    The savage and the tender;
Some social join, and leagues combine,
20   Some solitary wander:

Avaunt, away! the cruel sway,
    Tyrannic man's dominion!
The Sportsman's joy, the murd'ring cry,
    The flutt'ring, gory pinion!

25 But, PEGGY dear, the ev'ning's clear,
    Thick flies the skimming swallow,
The sky is blue, the fields in view
    All fading-green and yellow:
Come let us stray our gladsome way,
30   And view the charms o' Nature;
The rustling corn, the fruited thorn,
    And ilka happy creature.   *every*

We'll gently walk, and sweetly talk,
    While the silent moon shines clearly;
35 I'll clasp thy waist, and, fondly prest,
    Swear how I lo'e thee dearly: *love*
Not vernal show'rs to budding flow'rs,
    Not Autumn to the Farmer,
So dear can be as thou to me,
40   My fair, my lovely Charmer!

In August 1785, the first 8 lines were copied into the poet's *First Commonplace Book*. That version is not the final polished work. It reads:

Now breezy win's and slaughtering guns
    Bring Autumn's pleasant weather;
And the muir-cock springs on whirring wings
    Amang the blooming heather:
Now waving crops, with yellow tops.
    Delights the weary Farmer;
An' the moon shines bright, when I rove at night
    To muse on Jeanie Armour.

This early version is included in the printed Sales Catalogue of the London auction house, Puttock & Simpson, 1862, printed by R. Bigmore, Mitchell Library Collection.

It appears in SMM, no. 351, 1792 and later in SC, with a minor textual ammendment by Thomson, who characteristically softens the opening line from 'slaught'ring guns' to 'sportsmen's guns'. An early manuscript copy was sold in London, May, 1862, with different text from the final published song, suggesting that the poet improved the lyric considerably prior to the 1786 edition. Although begun around

1775, the song bears the mark of the mature poet during the winter of 1785–6. The Peggy referred to is Margaret Thompson of Kirkoswald. Burns told Dr Moore of his rapture with her, '. . . stepping out to the garden one charming noon, to take the sun's altitude, I met with my Angel "Like Prosperine gathering flowers, / Herself a fairer flower". [Milton's *Paradise Lost*, Book IV, line 269.] It was vain to think of doing any more good at school . . . I did nothing but craze the faculties of my soul about her, or steal out to meet her . . .' (Letter 125). The modern folk singer Dick Gaughan enhances the old music with a haunting re-tuned guitar (DAGDAD) pick style. Gaughan does not miss the dark, forceful condemnation, 'tyrannic man's dominion' whose 'murdering, gory pinion' claims to be sport being interwoven amid a song of love and nature.

From Thee Eliza

First printed in the Kilmarnock edition, 1786.
Tune: Gilderoy

From thee, ELIZA, I must go,
    And from my native shore:
The cruel fates between us throw
    A boundless ocean's roar;
5   But boundless oceans, roaring wide
    Between my Love and me,
They never, never can divide
    My heart and soul from thee.

Farewell, farewell, ELIZA dear,
10   The maid that I adore!
A boding voice is in mine ear,
    We part to meet no more!
But the latest throb that leaves my heart,
    While Death stands victor by,
15 That throb, ELIZA, is thy part,
    And thine that latest sigh!

This song appears to have been composed just prior to publication in 1786, when the poet considered a plan of emigration to Jamaica. However, possible exile may have occurred to Burns at an earlier stage in his life, given that he informs Dr Moore that the song was already written by the time he was twenty-three years old (Letter 125). The heroine, 'my quondam Eliza' (Letter 113) may be Elizabeth

Miller of Mauchline, although Mackay (1993) suggests an earlier acquaintance, Elizabeth Gebbie (1762–1823), as an alternative.

The Farewell to The Brethren of St James's Lodge, Tarbolton

Tune: Good-Night, and Joy be wi' You A'
First printed in the Kilmarnock edition, 1786.

Adieu! a heart-warm, fond adieu;
    Dear Brothers of the *mystic tye*!   fellow Masons
Ye favour'd, ye *enlighten'd* Few,
    Companions of my social joy!
5 Tho' I to foreign lands must hie,   speed
    Pursuing Fortune's slidd'ry ba',   slippery ball
With melting heart and brimful eye,
    I'll mind you still, tho' far awa.   away

Oft have I met your social Band,
10 And spent the cheerful, festive night;
Oft, honour'd with supreme command,
    Presided o'er the *Sons of light*:
And by that *Hieroglyphic* bright,
    Which none but *Craftsmen* ever saw!
15 Strong Mem'ry on my heart shall write
    Those happy scenes when far awa.   away

May Freedom, Harmony, and Love,
    Unite you in the *grand Design*,
Beneath th' Omniscient Eye above,
20   The glorious ARCHITECT Divine!
That you may keep th' *unerring line*,
    Still rising by the *plummet's law*,
Till *Order* bright completely shine,
    Shall be my Pray'r when far awa.   away

25 And *YOU* farewell! whose merits claim
    Justly that *highest badge* to wear:
Heav'n bless your honour'd, noble Name,
    To MASONRY and SCOTIA dear!   Muse of Scotland
A last request permit me here,
30   When yearly ye assemble a',
One *round*, I ask it with a *tear*,
    To him, *the Bard, that's far awa.*   away

The poet became an ordinary member of the Freemason movement in October 1781. He became Depute Master of the St James's lodge on 27th July 1784, where his oratorial skills in debate and discussion were clearly acknowledged. This song was written for his brother masons of the St James's lodge as the Kilmarnock edition was going to press. Burns used his influential contacts within the Ayrshire masonic movement to further his poetic career, particularly in selling the Kilmarnock and Edinburgh editions. Moreover, many of the leading Whigs and radicals of this period who were sympathetic to the poet's outspoken values, were brother masons.

Epitaph on a Henpecked Squire

First printed in the Kilmarnock edition, 1786.

As father Adam first was fool'd,
    A case that's still too common,
Here lies a man a woman rul'd:
    The Devil ruled the woman.

This was aimed at William Campbell and his wife, Lilias Campbell, of Netherplace who lived near Mauchline. This and the following two epigrams were dropped from the Edinburgh edition. Scott Douglas's comment on this is typical of reactionary conservativism, devoid of humour: 'Burns had a strong aptitude for producing these smart and often very biting things' (Vol. 1, p. 128).

Epigram on Said Occasion

First printed in the Kilmarnock edition, 1786.

O Death, had'st thou but spar'd his life,
    Whom we this day lament!
We freely wad exchanged the *wife*,   would
    An' a' been weel content.   well

Ev'n as he is, cauld in his graff,   cold, grave
    The swap we yet will do't;
Tak thou the carlin's carcase aff,   off/away
    Thou'se get the *saul o' boot*.   soul, as well

This also relates to William Campbell of Netherplace.

Another

First printed in the Kilmarnock edition, 1786.

One Queen Artemisa, as old stories tell,
When depriv'd of her husband she lovèd so well,
In respect for the love and affection he'd show'd her,
She reduc'd him to dust and she drank up the Powder.

But Queen Netherplace, of a diff'rent complexion,
When call'd on to order the fun'ral direction,
Would have *eat* her dead lord, on a slender pretence,
Not to show her respect, but — *to save the expense.*

When first printed, it was not possible for general readers to identify the satirical target of this epigram; the name 'Netherplace' was merely a line of asterisks beginning with the letter 'N'. For notes on William Campbell of Netherplace and his wife, see *Epitaph on a Henpecked Squire*. This was omitted from the Edinburgh edition.

On a Celebrated Ruling Elder

First printed in the Kilmarnock edition, 1786.

Here Sowter Hood, in Death does sleep;   cobbler
   To Hell, if he's gane thither,   gone that way
Satan, gie him thy gear to keep;   give
   He'll haud it weel thegither.   hold, well together

Composed during the poet's Tarbolton period, on William Hood, whose surname was marked by asterisks in the 1786 publication. Dated in the *First Commonplace Book* for April, 1784, under the title *Epitaph for William Hood, senr., in Talbolton*. Hood was a shoemaker.

On a Noisy Polemic

First printed in the Kilmarnock edition, 1786.

Below thir stanes lie Jamie's banes;   these stones, bones
   O Death, it's my opinion,
Thou ne'er took such a bleth'ran bitch,   talkative
   Into thy dark dominion.

It is believed this was written on James Humphrey (1755–1844) who, in the Scots idiom, was a blether – he talked too much and with little intelligence. It is alleged from folklore, perhaps garnished by Cromek and later Cunningham, that Humphrey's claim to fame in his old age was that Burns targeted him with these lines.

On Wee Johnie

Hic jacet *wee* Johnie

First printed in the Kilmarnock edition, 1786.

Whoe'er thou art, O reader, know,
   That Death has murder'd Johnie,
An' here his body lies fu' low —   full
   For saul he ne'er had onie.   soul, any

This is thought to be on John Wilson (d. 1839) who was a school-master and session clerk in Tarbolton, although Mackay asserts that the object was the Reverend John Kennedy of Ochiltree.

For the Author's Father

First printed in the Kilmarnock edition, 1786.

O ye whose cheek the tear of pity stains,
Draw near with pious rev'rence, and attend!
Here lie the loving Husband's dear remains,
The tender Father, and the gen'rous Friend.

The pitying Heart that felt for human Woe,
The dauntless heart that fear'd no human Pride;
The Friend of Man, to vice alone a foe;
For 'ev'n his failings lean'd to Virtue's side'.

William Burn[es]s died, 13th February, 1784, at Lochlie. He is clearly the role model of manly worth and virtue which permeates the poetry and letters of Burns, an honest, hard working, honour-able and noble provider who struggled against poverty, ill health and in his final year, the harshness of winter. In eight lines Burns describes his father as tender, generous, compassionate, dauntless – a man who did not cowe in deference to the 'pride' of the landed Gentry – a friend to manly virtue, a religious opponent to immoral behaviour and a person whose 'failings' were probably due to his religious beliefs. L. 8 is from Goldsmith's *The Deserted Village*, l. 164.

   It is remarkable that the extent of denigratory politically moti-vated malice expended on Burns for two decades after his death extended to examine even his father's misfortunes and consider them as symptomatic of a hidden moral flaw. Outraged by the character assassination of the poet 'under the dagger of literary patriots', Alexander Peterkin in his 1816 re-edition of Currie's edition (see Introduction) bitterly wrote of a particularly mendacious life by an alleged friend of the poet, Mr Walker of Perth:

> No better illustration can be given of this unsatisfactory style of biography, than the 'suspicion' which is excited against the unspotted worth of William Burn[es]s, the poet's father. We are instructed by a philosophical reverie, that the misfortunes of that worthy man *must probably* have arisen from some radical defect in his own character or conduct, since uniform mischance, it is assumed, always implies as much! How silly and cruel are such insinuations? God knows, there are many pressed down in adversity for life, without the slightest cause existing in their conduct or personal characters. We have known individuals possessing every quality that we can conceive of human worth, destined, like William Burn[es]s, to drink deeply in the cup of affliction—to struggle through life with poverty and disappointment and sorrow; and to descend, like him, into the grave with few other consolations than the prospects beyond it. The cause of William Burn[es]s's uniform misfortune is very obvious to an ordinary observer: He had not money: that was his defect. And the want of capital alone fettered him to all the disasters which he experienced in his affectionate anxiety to keep his family around him in their tender years. There is no occasion for a refinement in speculation, when a fact stands manifestly in view sufficient to account for occurrences.

If Burns's father had Jacobite leanings, he gave his son through Murdoch an education in the key-texts, especially Addison, of the English Real Whigs which, though deliberately anti-Auld Licht Calvinism, stressed austere independence in thought and behaviour. In this sense, Gilbert, chaste and conformist, was much more his father's son than Robert. What this elegy does not, understandably, reveal is the tension and conflict between father and son. Thus in Letter 125, Burns records his attendance at a country dancing school against his father's wishes: 'from that instance of rebellion he took a kind of dislike to me, which I believe was one cause of that dissipation which marked my future years!' All Romantic literature, familial and political, pulses with oedipal conflict.

For an innovative study of Burns's father's educational influence on him, see Liam McIlvanney's *Burns the Radical: Poetry and Politics in Late Eighteenth-century Scotland* (Tuckwell Press, 2001).

For Robert Aiken, Esq.

First printed in the Kilmarnock edition, 1786.

Know thou, O stranger to the fame
Of this much lov'd, much honour'd name!
(For none that knew him need be told),
A warmer heart Death ne'er made cold

'The Cotter's Saturday Night' is dedicated to Robert Aitken (1739–1807), an intimate friend and correspondent of Burns who was a lawyer in Ayr. Only Aitken's initials were given in the publication to preserve anonymity.

A Bard's Epitaph

First printed in the Kilmarnock edition, 1786.

Is there a whim-inspired fool,
Owre fast for thought, owre hot for rule,   over/too
Owre blate to seek, owre proud to snool,   over, shy, tamely submit
      Let him draw near;
5 And owre this grassy heap sing dool,   over, sadly/lament
      And drap a tear.   drop

Is there a Bard of rustic song,
Who, noteless, steals the crowds among,
That weekly this area throng,
10   O, pass not by!
But with a frater-feeling strong,   brother-feeling
      Here, heave a sigh.

Is there a man, whose judgment clear
Can others teach the course to steer,
15 Yet runs, himself, life's mad career
      Wild as the wave,
Here pause — and, thro' the starting tear,
      Survey this grave.

The poor Inhabitant below
20 Was quick to learn and wise to know,
And keenly felt the friendly glow
      And *softer flame*;
But thoughtless follies laid him low,
      And stain'd his name!

25   Reader, attend — whether thy soul
      Soars Fancy's flights beyond the pole,
      Or darkling grubs this earthly hole,
              In low pursuit,
      Know, prudent, cautious, *self-controul*
30   Is Wisdom's root.

This is the final work of the Kilmarnock edition. It is a strangely sombre ending to such a virile collection. After writing an actual epitaph for his father and an apparent one for Robert Aitken, he then writes his own. His sense of the symmetry of the Kilmarnock edition may be partly responsible for this. Having begun by celebrating in *Nature's Bard* a formally unrestricted poet galvanised by nature's energy, he ends by elegising the (self) image of a poet brought to disaster by the promiscuity of both his creative mind and randy body combined with a complete lack of prudence. One of the sources for the poem is the Epitaph for the young country poet Gray placed at the end of *Epitaph Written in a Country Churchyard*. That poem, with its ineradicably melancholic sense that historical invisibility is the common fate for people of worth, talent, even and especially, poetic genius, 'some mute, inglorious Milton', was seminal for Burns. It has also been suggested that Burns thought of another deathly piece, *Elegy on the Death of Robert Ruisseaux*, to end the volume. As we shall see, that poem is essentially an account of the external pressures that brought 'Ruisseaux' (the French for streams, i.e. burns) low. Here, however, he chooses to take upon himself the alleged burden of his self-defined failure.

While Victorian editors had no trouble with a concluding poem of such self-denigratory didacticism, it has been either forgotten or peremptorily dismissed by most modern commentators. Daiches (pp. 150–1) sees the poem as manifesting the symptoms of *The Cotter's Saturday Night* and thus spoiled by 'a combination of Scots literary influences and an exhibitionism directed at the literati and their tastes'. He further notes that it employs 'a Scots literary form' but is 'otherwise English in inspiration and timidly genteel in attitude'. In actual fact, the first stanza, puzzlingly, is wholly vernacular. There was one near contemporaneous reader, however, over whom the poem had an extraordinary, almost magnetic, attraction. Wordsworth must have felt that, in some psychic way, *he* was the 'Bard of rustic song' summoned to the graveside. In his 1803 Scottish tour he and Dorothy went to Burns's graveside which caused him to write three complex, fraught poems: *At the Grave of Burns 1803; Thoughts Suggested the Day Following, on the Banks of the Nith, Near the Poet's Residence; To the Sons of Burns, After Visiting the Grave of their Father.* The degree to which Wordsworth was troubled by these poems is partly manifested in their publishing history. The first two did not appear till 1842; only the third appeared close to the event in 1807. Stanzas two and eight of the first poem intensely catch the 'frater-feeling strong' that Wordsworth had for Burns:

> And have I then thy bones so near,
> And thou forbidden to appear?
> As if it were thyself that's here
>   I shrink with pain;
> And both my wishes and my fear
>   Alike are vain.

> . . . True friends though diversely inclined:
> But heart with heart and mind with mind,
> Where the main fibres are entwined,
>   Through Nature's skill,
> May even by contraries be joined
>   More closely still.

Describing this as a 'weird little Gothic lyric', Kenneth R. Johnston, *The Hidden Wordsworth* (N.Y./London: 1998), p. 799 asks 'where, exactly, is the "here" of line 3? Does it point to Burns's corpse under the sod or to Wordsworth's identification with it; or is he imagining that he himself is Burns standing on his own grave?' This, remember, is from the most self-composed of poets. George Dekker in *Coleridge and the Literature of Sensibility* (London: 1978), p. 67 gives this convincing answer to this complex identification:

> The career of Burns . . . offered a lesson that Wordsworth . . .
> could apply immediately to his own life. So different to Burns
> in most essentials, Wordsworth cannot have failed to notice a
> few striking parallels between his current experience and that of
> the Ayrshire peasant. He suffered from the same mysterious
> chest and headaches that presaged Burns's early dissolution; he
> too had been long prevented from marrying by untoward
> circumstances; and he was a man with 'Jacobin' sympathies
> to live down.

Burns, then, for Wordsworth is both the beloved creative brother and also the dark, dangerous stranger who embodied his own shadowy inner-self, a self passionate to the point of sexual and radical political violence, which after about 1800 he, conservatively, increasingly denied. For some understanding of the psychological, literary and creative ambivalence of Wordsworth towards Burns see Andrew Noble's 'Wordsworth and Burns: The Anxiety of Being Under the Influence', *Critical Essays on Robert Burns*, ed. McGurk (N.Y., 1998), pp. 49–62.

There is, literally, a final testimony to this deeply ambivalent relationship. In *A Bard's Epitaph* the poem is based on a series of interrogative requests as the poet appropriate to mourning his deceased brother-poet. Wordsworth was haunted by these questions because they seemed directed at his own poetic ambitions and hidden anxieties about his inner passions. Wordsworth's *A Poet's Epitaph* is also based on a series of questions as to the sort of person (statesman, lawyer, soldier, priest, merchant, scientist) appropriate to the act of mourning. As Kenneth Johnston has remarked (pp. 86–7): 'Both poems are indebted to the pastoral tradition of one shepherd piping a lament at the grave of another. But Burns invoked this tradition mainly to distinguish his poems from it: 'The following trifles are not the production of the Poet, who, with all the advantages of learned art, and perhaps amid the elegancies and idlenesses of upper life, look down for a rural theme, with an eye to Theocritus or Vergil.' This, the lead sentence of Burns's preface, helped prepare the way for Wordsworth's great preface of 1800.' This is undoubtedly part of the reason that the necessary mourner in Wordsworth's Epitaph is not simply the poet but *a russet-coated* poet who, not only in costume but in nature, is unmistakably, in his mixture of frailties and genius, Burns himself:

> But who is He, with modest looks
> And clad in homely russet brown?
> He murmurs near the running brooks
> A music sweeter than their own.
>
> He is retired as noontide dew,
> Or fountain in a noon-day grove;
> And you must love him, ere to you
> He will seem worthy of your love.
>
> The outward shows of sky and earth,
> Of hill and valley, he has viewed;
> And impulses of deeper birth
> Have come to him in solitude.

In common things that round us lie
Some random truths he can impart,—
The harvest of a quiet eye
That broods and sleeps on his own heart.

But he is weak; both Man and Boy,
Hath been an idler in the land;
Contented if he might enjoy
The things which others understand.

—Come hither in thy hour of strength;
Come, weak as is a breaking wave!
Here stretch thy body at full length;
Or build thy house upon this grave.

PART TWO

The Edinburgh Edition
1787

Dedication to the Noblemen and Gentlemen of the Caledonian Hunt

My Lords And Gentlemen,

A SCOTTISH BARD, proud of the name, and whose highest ambition is to sing in his Country's service, where shall he so properly look for patronage as to the illustrious Names of his native Land; those who bear the honours and inherit the virtues of their Ancestors? The Poetic Genius of my Country found me as the prophetic bard Elijah did Elisha – at the *plough*; and threw her inspiring *mantle* over me. She bade me sing the loves, the joys, the rural scenes and rural pleasures of my native Soil, in my native tongue: I tuned my wildness, artless notes, as she inspired. — She whispered me to come to this ancient metropolis of Caledonia, and lay my Songs under your honoured protection: I now obey her dictates.

Though much indebted to your goodness, I do not approach you, my Lords and Gentlemen, in the usual stile of dedication, to thank you for past favours; that path is so hackneyed by prostituted Learning, that honest Rusticity is ashamed of it. —Nor do I present this Address with the venal soul of a servile Author, looking for a continuation of those favours: I was bred to the Plough, and am independent. I come to claim the common Scottish name with you, my illustrious Countrymen; and to tell the world that I glory in the title. —I come to congratulate my Country, that the blood of her ancient heroes still runs uncontaminated; and that from your courage, knowledge, and public spirit, she may expect protection, wealth and liberty. —In the last place, I come to proffer my warmest wishes to the Great Fountain of Honour, the Monarch of the Universe, for your welfare and happiness.

When you go forth to waken the Echoes, in the ancient and favourite amusements of your Forefathers, may Pleasure ever be of your party; and may Social-joy await your return! When harassed in courts or camps with the justlings of bad men and bad measures, may the honest consciousness of injured Worth attend your return to your native Seats; and may Domestic Happiness, with a smiling welcome, meet you at your gates! May Corruption shrink at your kindling indignant glance; and may tyranny in the Ruler and licentiousness in the People equally find you an inexorable foe!

    I have the honour to be,
        With the sincerest gratitude and highest respect,
                MY LORDS AND GENTLEMEN,
            Your most devoted humble servant,
                ROBERT BURNS.
                   EDINBURGH *April* 4. 1787

Death and Doctor Hornbook:
A True Story
First printed in the Edinburgh edition, 1787.

SOME books are lies frae end to end,	from
And some great lies were never penn'd:	
Ev'n Ministers, they hae been kenn'd,	have been known
In holy rapture,	
5 A rousing whid, at times, to vend,	lie
And nail't wi' Scripture.	
But this that I am gaun to tell,	going
Which lately on a night befel,	occurred
Is just as true's the Deil's in hell	
10 Or Dublin city:	
That e'er he nearer comes oursel	ourselves
'S a muckle pity.	it is, great
The Clachan yill had made me canty,	village ale, jolly
I was na fou, but just had plenty;	not drunk
15 I stacher'd whyles, but yet took tent ay	staggered whiles, was careful
To free the ditches;	
An' hillocks, stanes, an' bushes kend ay	stones, knew always
Frae ghaists an' witches.	from ghosts
The rising Moon began to glowr	stare/glow
20 The distant *Cumnock* hills out-owre;	out-over
To count her horns, wi' a' my pow'r	
I set mysel,	
But whether she had three or four,	
I cou'd na tell.	could not
25 I was come round about the hill,	
And todlin down on *Willie's mill*,	walking sprightly
Setting my staff wi' a' my skill,	with all
To keep me sicker;	steady
Tho' leeward whyles, against my will,	at tmes
30 I took a bicker.	unbalanced run
I there wi' *Something* does forgather,	meet
That pat me in an eerie swither;	put, ghostly dread
An awfu' scythe, out-owre ae shouther,	across one shoulder

Clear-dangling, hang;
35 A three-tae'd leister on the ither   three pronged spear, other
Lay, large an' lang.   long

Its stature seem'd lang Scotch ells twa;   long, 37 inches, two
The queerest shape that e'er I saw,
For fient a wame it had ava;   hardly a belly at all
40   And then its shanks,   legs
They were as thin, as sharp an' sma'   small
As cheeks o' branks.   parts of a horse bridle

'Guid-een,' quo' I; 'Friend! hae ye been mawin,   good evening, have you, mowing
When ither folk are busy sawin?'[1]   other, sowing
45 It seem'd to mak a kind o' stan',   make, stand
But naething spak;   nothing spoke
At length, says I: 'Friend! whare ye gaun?   where, going
Will ye go back?'

It spak right howe: 'My name is *Death*,   spoke, hollow
50 But be na' fley'd.' — Quoth I, 'Guid faith,   not frightened
Ye're may be come to stap my breath;   stop
But tent me, billie;   heed, comrade
I red ye weel, tak care o' skaith,   counsel you well, injury
See, there's a gully!'   large knife

55 'Gudeman,' quo' he, 'put up your whittle,   blade/knife
I'm no design'd to try its mettle;
But if I did, I wad be kittle   would be inclined
To be mislear'd,   mischievous
I wad na mind it, no that spittle   would not
60   Out-owre my beard.   out-over

'Weel, weel!' says I, 'a bargain be't;
Come, gie's your hand, an' say we're gree't;   give me, agreed
We'll ease our shanks, an' tak a seat: legs, take
Come, gie's your news!   give me
65 This while ye hae been monie a gate,   many
At monie a house.[2]   many

1 This recounter happened in seed-time 1785. R.B.
2 An epidemical fever was then raging in that country. R.B.

'Ay, ay!' quo' he, an' shook his head,
'It's e'en a lang, lang time indeed   even a long, long
Sin' I began to nick the thread
70   An' choke the breath:
Folk maun do something for their bread,   must
          An' sae maun *Death*.   so must

'Sax thousand years are near hand fled
Sin' I was to the butching bred,   since
75   An' monie a scheme in vain's been laid,   many
          To stap or scar me;   stop, scare
Till ane Hornbook's ta'en up the trade,[3]   one, taken up
          And faith! he'll waur me.   surpass me

'Ye ken *Jock Hornbook* i' the Clachan,   know, village
80   Deil mak his king's-hood in a spleuchan!   make his scrotum, tobacco-pouch
He's grown sae weel acquaint wi' *Buchan*,[4]   so well
          And ither chaps,   other
The weans haud out their fingers laughin,   children hold
          An' pouk my hips.   poke/prod

85   'See, here's a scythe, an' there's a dart,
They hae pierc'd monie a gallant heart;   have, many
But Doctor *Hornbook* wi' his art
          An' cursed skill,
Has made them baith no worth a fart,   both
90   Damn'd haet they'll kill!   damn all/nothing

''Twas but yestreen, nae farther gane,   no, gone
I threw a noble throw at ane;   one
Wi' less, I'm sure, I've hundreds slain;
          But Deil-ma-care!
95   It just played dirl on the bane,   went tinkle on the bone
          But did nae mair.   no more

'*Hornbook* was by wi' ready art,
An' had sae fortify'd the part,   so
That when I look'd to my dart,
100   It was sae blunt,   so
Fient haet o't wad hae pierc'd the heart   little of it would have
          Of a kail-runt.   cabbage stalk

3 This Gentleman, Dr Hornbook, is, professionally, a brother of the
sovereign Order of the Ferula; but, by intuition and inspiration, is at once
an Apothecary, Surgeon, and Physician. R.B.
4 Buchan's Domestic Medicine. R.B.

'I drew my scythe in sic a fury,   such
I near-hand cowpit wi' my hurry,   almost, toppled
105   But yet the bauld *Apothecary*
          Withstood the shock;
I might as weel hae try'd a quarry   well have
          O' hard whin-rock

'Ev'n them he canna get attended,   cannot
110   Altho' their face he ne'er had kend it,   known
Just shit in a kail-blade an' send it,   cabbage leaf
          As soon's he smells't,
Baith their disease, and what will mend it,   both
          At once he tells't.

115   'And then a' doctor's saws and whittles,   all
Of a' dimensions, shapes, an' mettles,   all
A' kinds o' boxes, mugs, and bottles,
          He's sure to hae;   have
Their Latin names as fast he rattles
120   As A B C.

'Calces o' fossils, earths, and trees;   bone meal
True Sal-marinum o' the seas;   salt-water
The Farina of beans an' pease,   vegetable meal
          He has't in plenty;
125   Aqua-fontis, what you please,   fresh water
          He can content ye.

'Forbye some new, uncommon weapons,
Urinus Spiritus of capons;   urine
Or Mite-horn shavings, filings, scrapings,
130   Distill'd *per se*;
Sal-alkali o' Midge-tail-clippings,   salt
          And monie mae.'   many more

'Waes me for *Johnie Ged's Hole* now,'[5]   woe is
Quoth I, 'if that thae news be true!   these
135   His braw calf-ward whare gowans grew   fine grazing plot, where daisies
          Sae white and bonie,   so
Nae doubt they'll rive it wi' the plew: no split, plough
          They'll ruin *Johnie*!'

5 The grave-digger. R.B.

The creature grain'd an eldritch laugh,   groaned, unearthly
140   And says: 'Ye needna yoke the pleugh,   need not, plough
Kirkyards will soon be till'd eneugh,   enough
    Tak ye nae fear: no
They'll a' be trench'd wi monie a sheugh   all, with many, ditch
    In twa-three year.

145   'Whare I kill'd ane, a fair strae-death   where, one, straw
By loss o' blood, or want o' breath,
This night I'm free to tak my aith,   take my oath
    That *Hornbook's* skill
Has clad a score i' their last claith,   clothed, clothes
150   By drap an' pill.   drop/potion

'An honest Wabster to his trade,   weaver
Whase wife's twa nieves were scarce weel-bred,   whose, two fists, well-bred
Gat tippence-worth to mend her head,   got tuppence
    When it was sair;   sore
155   The wife slade cannie to her bed,   crept quietly
    But ne'er spak mair.   spoke more

'A countra Laird had taen the batts,   country, taken colic
Or some curmurring in his guts,   commotion
His only son for *Hornbook* sets,
160   An' pays him well,
The lad, for twa guid gimmer-pets,   two good pet-ewes
    Was Laird himsel.

'A bonie lass, ye kend her name —   know
Some ill-brewn drink had hov'd her wame,   swollen her stomach
165   She trusts hersel, to hide the shame,
    In *Hornbook's* care;
Horn sent her aff to her lang hame   off, long home/grave
    To hide it there.

'That's just a swatch o' *Hornbook's* way,   sample
170   Thus goes he on from day to day,
Thus does he poison, kill, an' slay,
    An's weel paid for't;   and is well
Yet stops me o' my lawfu' prey,
    Wi' his damn'd dirt!

175   'But, hark! I'll tell you of a plot,
      Tho' dinna ye be speakin o't;
      I'll nail the self-conceited Sot,
          As dead's a herrin:
      Niest time we meet, I'll wad a groat,   *next, wager fourpence*
180   He gets his fairin!'   *reward*

      But just as he began to tell,
      The auld kirk-hammer strak the bell   *old, struck*
      Some wee short hour ayont the *twal*,   *beyond twelve*
          Which raised us baith: *both, made us stand up*
185   I took the way that pleas'd mysel,
          And sae did *Death*.   *so*

Currie (iii. 32) reports Gilbert Burns as recording the origin of the poem thus: 'written early in the year 1785. The Schoolmaster of Tarbolton parish, to eke out its scanty subsistence allowed to that useless class of men, had set up a shop of grocery goods. Having accidentally fallen upon some medical books, and become almost hobby-horsically attached to the study of medicine, he had added the sale of few medicines to his little trade . . . and advertised that 'Advice would be given in common disorders at the shop gratis'. This schoolmaster was John Wilson (c. 1751–1839) who compounded his other errors by boasting at a Masonic meeting in Burns's presence of his medical prowess. The poet's hatchet, unimpaired, unlike Death's scythe, did the following job on him. Extraordinarily, either because of innocence, or given the other evidence, gross stupidity, Wilson bore the poet no ill will over this. The poem did him no harm and when he was removed from Tarbolton School, he wrote to the poet for help and Burns considerately replied (Letter 420). He subsequently became a prosperous session clerk in Govan. See J.C. Ewing *BC*, 1941, pp. 31–9 for his biography.

    The poem involves two narratives. First that of the poet who on meeting with Death surrenders the narrative to an even more thickly vernacular voice, which, with splendid irony, laments the loss of a six-thousand-year career of mayhem to Hornbook's more lethal talents. With his ambivalence about folk-myth, Burns, jokingly, inserts footnotes which give the appearance of tying the poem into the mundane, everyday world. Hornbook's name is taken from the hornbook used in Scottish schools whereby lettered pieces of parchment were savingly inserted between a wooden back and a transparent bone front. Hence, too, the joke (l. 120) of his rattling of the A B C. As well as Wilson's illiterate incompetence derived from a fragile knowledge of Buchan's *Domestic Medicine*, there is, amongst the wit, a wider sense of how exposed these communities were to illness and death, not least the child-aborting girl (ll. 163–8), by a mixture of, at best, useless folk-remedies and sheer general lack of adequate medical knowledge, professional or otherwise.

The Brigs o Ayr
Inscribed to John Ballantine, Esq., Ayr
First printed in the Edinburgh edition, 1787.

[Sir, Think not with a mercenary view
Some servile Sycophant approaches you.
To you my Muse would sing these simple lays
To you my heart its grateful homage pays,
5   I feel the weight of all your kindness past,
But thank you not as wishing it to last:
Scorn'd be the wretch whose earth-born grov'lling soul
Would in his *ledger-hopes* his Friends enroll.
Tho' I, a lowly, nameless, rustic Bard,
10   Who ne'er must hope your goodness to reward,
Yet man to man, Sir, let us fairly meet,
And like Masonic Level, equal greet.
How poor the balance! Ev'n what Monarch's plan,
Between two noble creatures such as Man.
15   That to your Friendship I am strongly tied
I still shall own it, Sir, with grateful pride,
When haply roaring seas between us tumble wide.

Or if among so many cent'ries waste,
Thro the long vista of dark ages past,
20   Some much-lov'd honor'd name a radiance cast,
Perhaps some Patriot of distinguish'd worth,
I'll match him if My Lord will please step forth.
Or Gentleman and Citizen combine,
And I shall shew his peer in Ballantine:
25   Tho' honest men were *parcell'd* out for sale,
He might be shown a sample for the hale.]   whole

The simple Bard, rough at the rustic plough,
Learning his tuneful trade from ev'ry bough;

The chanting linnet, or the mellow thrush,
30   Hailing the setting sun, sweet, in the green thorn bush,
The soaring lark, the perching red-breast shrill,
Or deep-ton'd plovers grey, wild-whistling o'er the hill;
Shall he, nurst in the Peasant's lowly shed,
To hardy Independence bravely bred,
35   By early Poverty to hardship steel'd,
And train'd to arms in stern Misfortune's field,
Shall he be guilty of their hireling crimes,
The servile, mercenary Swiss of rhymes?
Or labour hard the panegyric close,
40   With all the venal soul of dedicating Prose?
No! though his artless strains he rudely sings,
And throws his hand uncouthly o'er the strings,
He glows with all the spirit of the Bard,
Fame, honest fame, his great, his dear reward.
45   Still, if some Patron's gen'rous care he trace,
Skill'd in the secret to bestow with grace;
When Ballantine befriends his humble name,
And hands the rustic Stranger up to fame,
With heartfelt throes his grateful bosom swells,
50   The godlike bliss, to give, alone excels.

'Twas when the stacks get on their winter-hap,   wrapping
And thack and rape secure the toil-won crap;   thatch & rope, crop
Potatoe-bings are snugg'd up frae skaith   -heaps, from damage
O' coming Winter's biting, frosty breath;
55   The bees, rejoicing o'er their summer toils,
Unnumber'd buds' an' flowers' delicious spoils,
Seal'd up with frugal care in massive, waxen piles,
Are doom'd by Man, that tyrant o'er the weak,
The death o' devils, smoor'd wi' brimstone reek: smothered, smoke
60   The thund'ring guns are heard on ev'ry side,
The wounded coveys, reeling, scatter wide;
The feather'd field-mates, bound by Nature's tie,
Sires, mothers, children, in one carnage lie:
(What warm, poetic heart but inly bleeds,
65   And execrates man's savage, ruthless deeds!)
Nae mair the flower in field or meadow springs;   no more
Nae mair the grove with airy concert rings,   no more
Except perhaps the Robin's whistling glee,
Proud o' the height o' some bit half-lang tree;   -long/half-sized tree
70   The hoary morns precede the sunny days;

Mild, calm, serene, widespreads the noontide blaze,
While thick the gossamour waves wanton in the rays.

'Twas in that season, when a simple Bard,
Unknown and poor, simplicity's reward,
75   Ae night, within the ancient brugh of *Ayr*,   one, borough
By whim inspir'd, or haply prest wi' care,
He left his bed, and took his wayward rout,   route
And down by *Simpson's*[1] wheel'd the left about:
(Whether impell'd by all-directing Fate,
80   To witness what I after shall narrate;
Or whether, rapt in meditation high,
He wander'd forth, he knew not where nor why.)
The drowsy *Dungeon-Clock*[2] had number'd two,
And *Wallace Tower*[2] had sworn the fact was true:
85   The tide-swoln Firth, with sullen-sounding roar,   swollen
Through the still night dash'd hoarse along the shore:
All else was hush'd as Nature's closed e'e;
The silent moon shone high o'er tower and tree:
The chilly frost, beneath the silver beam,
90   Crept, gently-crusting, o'er the glittering stream.

When, lo! on either hand the list'ning Bard,
The clanging sugh of whistling wings is heard;   rustle
Two dusky forms dart thro' the midnight air,
Swift as the *Gos*[3] drives on the wheeling hare;
95   Ane on th' *Auld Brig* his airy shape uprears,   one, old
The ither flutters o'er the *rising piers*:   other

Our warlock Rhymer instantly descry'd   wizard
The Sprites that owre the *Brigs of Ayr* preside.   over
(That Bards are second-sighted is nae joke,   no
100 And ken the lingo of the sp'ritual folk;   know, language
Fays, spunkies, kelpies, a', they can explain them,   fairies, will-o-wisps,
                                               water spirits
And ev'n the vera deils they brawly ken them).   very devils, well know
Auld Brig appear'd of ancient Pictish race,   old
The vera wrinkles Gothic in his face: very
105 He seem'd as he wi' Time had warstl'd lang,   wrestled long

1 A noted tavern at the Auld Brig end. R.B.
2 The two steeples. R.B. [plus the Wallace Tower]
3 The gos-hawk, or falcon. R.B.

Yet, teughly doure, he bade an unco bang.   *stubborn, surprisingly robust*
New Brig was buskit in a braw new coat,   *dressed, fine*
That he, at *Lon'on*, frae ane *Adams* got;   *from one*
In's hand five taper staves as smooth's a bead,   *in his*
110   Wi' virls an' whirlygigums at the head.   *rings, flourishes*
The Goth was stalking round with anxious search,
Spying the time-worn flaws in ev'ry arch;
It chanc'd his new-come neebor took his e'e,   *neighbour, eye*
And e'en a vex'd and angry heart had he!   *even*
115   Wi' thieveless sneer to see his modish mien,
He, down the water, gies him this guid-een —   *gives, good evening*

AULD BRIG
I doubt na, frien', ye'll think ye're nae
     sheep-shank,   *person of little importance*
Ance ye were streekit owre frae bank to bank!   *once, stretched over from*
But gin ye be a Brig as auld as me,   *once/if, old*
120   Tho' faith, that date, I doubt, ye'll never see;
There'll be, if that day come, I'll wad a boddle,   *bet a half-farthing*
Some fewer whigmeleeries in your noddle.   *whims, head*

NEW BRIG
Auld Vandal! ye but show your little mense,   *old, decorum*
Just much about it wi' your scanty sense;
125   Will your poor, narrow foot-path of a street,
Where twa wheel-barrows tremble when they   *two*
     meet,
Your ruin'd, formless bulk o' stane an' lime,   *stone*
Compare wi' bonie *Brigs* o' modern time?   *handsome*
There's men of taste would tak the *Ducat stream*,[4]   *take*
130   Tho' they should cast the vera sark and swim,   *very shirt*
E'er they would grate their feelings wi' the view
O' sic an ugly, Gothic hulk as you.   *such*

AULD BRIG
Conceited gowk! puff'd up wi' windy pride!   *fool*
This monie a year I've stood the flood an' tide;   *many*
135   And tho' wi' crazy eild I'm sair forfairn,   *old age, sore, worn out*
I'll be a *Brig* when ye're a shapeless cairn!   *pile of stones*
As yet ye little ken about the matter,   *know*
But twa-three winters will inform ye better.   *two-*

4 A noted ford, just above the old brig. R.B.

When heavy, dark, continued, a'-day rains   all-day
140   Wi' deepening deluges o'erflow the plains;
When from the hills where springs the brawling *Coil*,
Or stately *Lugar's* mossy fountains boil,
Or where the *Greenock* winds his moorland course,
Or haunted *Garpal*[5] draws his feeble source,
145   Arous'd by blustering winds an' spotting thowes,   thaws
In monie a torrent down the snaw-broo rowes;   many, snow-brew rolls
While crashing ice, borne on the roaring speat,   spate/flood
Sweeps dams, an' mills, an' brigs, a' to the gate;
And from *Glenbuck*[6] down to the *Ratton-Key*,[7]
150   Auld *Ayr* is just one lengthen'd, tumbling sea;   old
Then down ye'll hurl, deil nor ye never rise!   devil
And dash the gumlie jaups up to the pouring skies.   muddy splashes
A lesson sadly teaching, to your cost,
That Architecture's noble art is lost!'

NEW BRIG

155   Fine *architecture*, trowth, I needs must say't o't!   in truth
The Lord be thankit that we've tint the gate o't!   lost, way/skill
Gaunt, ghastly, ghaist-alluring edifices,   ghost-
Hanging with threat'ning jut, like precipices;
O'er-arching, mouldy, gloom-inspiring coves,
160   Supporting roofs, fantastic, stony groves:
Windows and doors, in nameless sculptures drest,
With order, symmetry, or taste unblest;
Forms like some bedlam Statuary's dream,
The craz'd creations of misguided whim;
165   Forms might be worshipp'd on the bended knee,
And still the *second dread Command*[8] be free:
Their likeness is not found on earth, in air, or sea!
Mansions that would disgrace the building taste
Of any mason reptile, bird or beast,
170   Fit only for a doited Monkish race,   stupid/muddled
Or frosty maids forsworn the dear embrace,
Or Cuifs of later times, wha held the notion,   fools, who

5 The banks of *Garpal Water* is one of the few places in the West of
Scotland, where those fancy-scaring beings, known by the name of Ghaists,
still continue pertinaciously to inhabit. R.B.
6 The source of the river of Ayr. R.B.
7 A small landing-place above the large key. R.B.
8 This allusion is to the Second Commandment, that there should not be a
likeness of Heavenly things on earth.

That sullen gloom was sterling true devotion:
Fancies that our guid Brugh denies protection, good borough
175   And soon may they expire, unblest with resurrection!

AULD BRIG
O ye, my dear-remember'd, ancient yealings,   contemporaries
Were ye but here to share my wounded feelings!
Ye worthy *Proveses*, an' mony a *Bailie*,   Provosts, many
Wha in the paths o' righteousness did toil ay;   who
180   Ye dainty *Deacons*, an' ye douce *Conveeners*,
To whom our moderns are but causey-cleaners; street-
Ye godly *Councils*, wha hae blest this town;   who have
Ye godly brethren o' the sacred gown
Wha meekly gie your *hurdies* to the *smiters*;   give, buttocks
185   And (what would now be strange), *ye godly Writers*;
A' ye douce folk I've borne aboon the broo,   prudent, above, water
Were ye but here, what would ye say or do!
How would your spirits groan in deep vexation
To see each melancholy alteration;
190   And, agonising, curse the time and place
When ye begat the base, degen'rate race!
Nae langer Rev'rend Men, their country's glory, no longer
In plain, braid Scots hold forth a plain, braid story;   broad
Nae langer thrifty Citizens, an' douce,   no longer, prudent
195   Meet owre a pint, or in the Council-house: over
But staumrel, corky-headed, graceless Gentry, half-witted/silly
The herryment and ruin of the country;   destruction
Men, three-parts made by Tailors and by Barbers,
Wha waste your weel-hain'd gear on damn'd   who, well-saved wealth
    new Brigs and *Harbours*!

NEW BRIG
200   Now haud you there! for faith ye've said enough,   hold
And muckle mair than ye can mak to through. much more, make good
As for your Priesthood, I shall say but little,
Corbies and *Clergy* are a shot right kittle: ravens, difficult to shoot
But, under favour o' your langer beard,   longer/older age
205   Abuse o' Magistrates might weel be spar'd;   well
To liken them to your auld-warld squad,   old-world
I must needs say, comparisons are odd.
In Ayr, *Wag-wits* nae mair can hae a handle   scandal-mongers, no more, have
To mouth 'A Citizen,' a term o' scandal:
210   Nae mair the Council waddles down the street, no more

In all the pomp of ignorant conceit;
Men wha grew wise priggin owre hops an'   who, haggling over
   raisins,
Or gather'd lib'ral views in Bonds and Seisins;
If haply Knowledge, on a random tramp,   walk
215 Had shor'd them with a glimmer of his lamp,   threatened
And would to Common-sense for once betray'd them,
Plain, dull Stupidity stept kindly in to aid them.

What farther clishmaclaver might been said,   nonsense
What bloody wars, if Sprites had blood to shed,
220 No man can tell; but, all before their sight,
A fairy train appear'd in order bright:
Adown the glittering stream they featly danc'd:
Bright to the moon their various dresses glanc'd:
They footed o'er the wat'ry glass so neat,
225 The infant ice scarce bent beneath their feet:
While arts of Minstrelsy among them rung,
And soul-ennobling Bards heroic ditties sung.

O, had *M'Lauchlan*,[9] thairm-inspiring Sage,   catgut-/musical
Been there to hear this heavenly band engage,
230 When thro' his dear *Strathspeys* they bore with Highland rage;
Or when they struck old Scotia's melting airs,
The lover's raptured joys or bleeding cares;
How would his Highland lug been nobler fir'd,   ear
And ev'n his matchless hand with finer touch inspir'd!
235 No guess could tell what instrument appear'd,
But all the soul of Music's self was heard;
Harmonious concert rung in every part,
While simple melody pour'd moving on the heart.

The Genius of the Stream in front appears,
240 A venerable Chief advanc'd in years;
His hoary head with water-lilies crown'd,
His manly leg with garter tangle bound.
Next came the loveliest pair in all the ring,
Sweet Female Beauty hand in hand with Spring;

9 A well-known performer of Scottish music on the violin. R.B. Wallace
(1896) records that James M'Lauchlan originated from the Highlands, was
once footman to a Laird at Inverary, then moved to Ayrshire as part of a
fencible regiment where he found a patron for his musical talent in Hugh
Montgomerie, Coilsfield, later Earl of Eglintoun.

245 Then, crown'd with flow'ry hay, came Rural Joy,
     And Summer, with his fervid-beaming eye:
     All-cheering Plenty, with her flowing horn,
     Led yellow Autumn wreath'd with nodding corn;
     Then Winter's time-bleach'd locks did hoary show,
250 By Hospitality, with cloudless brow.
     Next follow'd Courage, with his martial stride,
     From where the *Feal*[10] wild-woody coverts hide:
     Benevolence, with mild, benignant air,
     A female form, came from the towers of *Stair*:
255 Learning and Worth in equal measures trode,
     From simple *Catrine*, their long-lov'd abode:
     Last, white-rob'd Peace, crown'd with a hazel wreath,
     To Rustic Agriculture did bequeath
     The broken, iron instruments of Death,
260 At sight of whom our Sprites forgat their kindling wrath.

The opening passage (ll. 1–26) in brackets are generally not printed as an integral part of this poem. However, given that they and the body of the poem are dedicated to John Ballantine (1743–1812), they are included. They first appeared in the *BC*, 1926, pp. 61–2 but the original manuscript of ll. 1–26 is now lost.

The poem was composed in late 1786 after the contruction of the New Bridge of Ayr started in May 1786. John Ballantine, a friend of Robert Aitken, was Dean of the Guild of Stone Masons and took charge of construction with Alexander Steven. The architect was Robert Adam (1728–92) of London. Ballantine was a banker and merchant. He owned Castlehill estate near Kilmarnock and in 1787 was appointed Provost of Ayr. Through an initial introduction from Robert Aitken, Ballantine became a keen patron of Burns and promised to assist him with a financial guarantee for a proposed second Kilmarnock edition, advising Burns to publish in Edinburgh. Ballantine took delivery of 100 copies of the Edinburgh edition for Ayrshire subscribers. There are 13 recorded letters by Burns to Ballantine, two being no more than brief scribbled notes. As both Daiches and Crawford have pointed out, the poem lacks both formal and linguistic integration due to its being a 'mixtie, maxtie' amalgam of Fergusson's vernacular dialogue and Thomson's socially celebratory poetry. The dialectic between tradition and modernity was a convention that never really energised Burns in this poem. Crawford (1933–9) is both informative and perhaps too generous to it.

10 A tributary of the river Ayr, near Coilsfield.

The Ordination

For sense, they little owe to frugal Heav'n:
To please the mob they hide the little giv'n.

First printed in the Edinburgh edition, 1787.

Kilmarnock Wabsters, fidge an' claw,   weavers, fidget/twitch, scratch
    An' pour your creeshie nations;   greasy
An' ye wha leather rax an' draw,   who, stretch
    Of a' denominations;
5 Swith! to the *Laigh Kirk*,[1] ane an' a',   away!/haste!, one
    An' there tak up your stations;
Then aff to *Begbie's*[2] in a raw,   off/away, row
    An' pour divine libations
        For joy this day.

10 Curst Common-sense, that imp o' hell,
    Cam in wi' *Maggie Lauder;*[3]
But Oliphant[4] aft made her yell,   often
    An' Russell[5] sair misca'd her: sore
This day M'Kinlay[6] taks the flail,   for thrashing corn/whip
15   An' he's the boy will blaud her!   slap
He'll clap a *shangan* on her tail,   cleft stick
    An' set the bairns to daud her   children, hit
        Wi' dirt this day.

Mak haste an' turn King David owre,   metrical psalms, over
20   An' lilt wi' holy clangor;   sing
O' double verse come gie us four,   give
    An' skirl up the *Bangor*:   a popular church tune
This day the Kirk kicks up a stoure,   dust/noise
    Nae mair the knaves shall wrang her,   no more, wrong
25 For Heresy is in her pow'r,
    And gloriously she'll whang her   punish
        Wi' pith this day.

1 The Leigh Kirk in Kilmarnock.
2 A tavern, later named the Angel Hotel, in Kilmarnock, across the bridge over the Marnock Water.
3 Alluding to a scoffing ballad which was made on the admission of the late Reverend and worthy Mr L—. to the Laigh Kirk. R.B.
4 Rev. James Oliphant, an 'Auld Licht' minister of Kilmarnock's High Church.
5 Rev. John Russell – took over from Oliphant in 1774.
6 Rev. James Mackinlay [spelt M'Kinlay by Burns in a letter, no. 21], whose ordination was opposed by 'New Licht' moderates.

Come, let a proper text be read,
　　An' touch it aff wi' vigour,　　　　　　　off
30　How graceless *Ham*[7] leugh at his Dad,　laughed
　　Which made *Canaan* a nigger;
Or *Phineas*[8] drove the murdering blade
　　Wi' whore-abhorring rigour;
Or *Zipporah*,[9] the scauldin jad,　　　　scolding hussy
35　　　Was like a bluidy tiger　　　　　　bloody
　　　　I' th' inn that day.　　　　　　in the

There, try his mettle on the Creed,
　　And bind him down wi' caution,
That *Stipend* is a carnal weed
40　　He taks but for the fashion;　　　　takes
And gie him o'er the flock to feed,　　　give
　　And punish each transgression;
Especial, *rams* that cross the breed,　the fornicators
　　Gie them sufficient threshin,　　　give, beating
45　　　Spare them nae day.　　　　　no

Now auld Kilmarnock, cock thy tail,　　old, stick up
　　An' toss thy horns fu' canty;　　　merrily
Nae mair thou'lt rowte out-owre the dale,　no more, roar, -over
　　Because thy pasture's scanty;
50　For lapfu's large o' *gospel kail*　　armfuls, greens
　　Shall fill thy crib in plenty,
An' *runts* o' *grace*, the pick an' wale,　cabbage-stocks, choice
　　No gien by way o' dainty,　　　　not given
　　　But ilka day.　　　　　　　every

55　Nae mair by *Babel's streams* we'll weep　no more
　　To think upon our *Zion*;
And hing our fiddles up to sleep,　　　hang
　　Like baby-clouts a-dryin　　　　cloth
Come, screw the pegs wi' tunefu' cheep,　fiddle pegs, chirp/notes
60　　And o'er the thairms be tryin;　　strings
Oh, rare! to see our elbucks wheep,　elbows jerk/jig
　　And a' like lamb-tails flyin
　　　Fu' fast this day!

7 Genesis, Ch. IX, verse 22. R.B.
8 Numbers, Ch. XXV, verse 8. R.B.
9 Exodus, Ch. IV, verse 25. R.B.

Lang, *Patronage*, wi' rod o' airn,   iron
65   Has shor'd the Kirk's undoin;   threatened
As lately *Fenwick*, sair forfairn,   sore distressed
        Has proven to its ruin:
Our Patron, honest man! *Glencairn*,
        He saw mischief was brewin;
70 An' like a godly, elect bairn,   child/person
        He's waled us out a true ane,   picked, one
                And sound this day.

Now Robertson[10] harangue nae mair,   no more
        But steek your gab for ever;   shut, mouth
75 Or try the wicked town of Ayr,
        For there they'll think you clever;
Or, nae reflection on your lear,   no, wisdom/learning
        Ye may commence a Shaver;   barber
Or to the *Netherton* repair,
80   An' turn a Carpet-weaver
                Aff-hand this day.   off-/at once

Mutrie[11] and you were just a match,
        We never had sic twa drones: such two
Auld *Hornie* did the *Laigh Kirk* watch,   old Devil
85   Just like a winkin baudrons,   cat
And ay he catch'd the tither wretch,   other
        To fry them in his caudrons;
But now his Honor maun detach,   shall
        Wi' a' his brimstone squadrons,
90   Fast, fast this day.

See, see auld Orthodoxy's faes   old, foes
        She's swingein thro' the city!   flogging/whipping
Hark, how the nine-tail'd cat she plays!   whip
        I vow it's unco pretty: mighty/very
95 There, Learning, with his Greekish face,
        Grunts out some Latin ditty;
And Common-Sense is gaun, she says,   going
        To mak to *Jamie Beattie*   make
                Her plaint this day.

10 Rev. John Robertson, a moderate colleague of Mackinlay.
11 Rev. John Mutrie, Minister of the Laigh Kirk prior to Mackinlay.

100   But there's Morality himsel,
          Embracing all opinions;
      Hear, how he gies the tither yell   gives, other
          Between his twa companions!   two
      See, how she peels the skin an' fell,   fleshy tissue under the skin
105   As ane were peelin onions!   one
      Now there, they're packèd aff to hell,   off/away
          An' banish'd our dominions,
              Henceforth this day.

      O happy day! rejoice, rejoice!
110   Come bouse about the porter!   drink/pass around
      Morality's demure decoys
          Shall here nae mair find quarter: no more
      Mackinlay, Russell, are the boys
          That Heresy can torture;
115   They'll gie her on a rape a hoyse,   give, rope, hoist
          And cowe her measure shorter   cut/crop
              By th' head some day.

      Come, bring the tither mutchkin in,   other, pint
          And here's — for a conclusion —
120   To ev'ry *New Light*[12] mother's son,
          From this time forth, Confusion:
      If mair they deave us wi' their din   more, deafen
          Or Patronage intrusion,
      We'll light a spunk, and, ev'ry skin   match
125   We'll run them aff in fusion   off
              Like oil, some day.

'I have been very busy with the Muses since I saw you,' Burns wrote to Richmond on 17 February, 1786, 'and have composed among several others, The Ordination, a poem on Mr M'Kinlay's being called to Kilmarnock' (Letters, 21). Prior to its appearance in the Edinburgh edition the poem was, in the form of Ayrshire samizdat, locally available under the pen-names of 'Rob Rhymer' or 'Ruisseaux'. The latter being a play on Rousseau and the French word for streams or (Scottish) burns. Thus Burns's pseudonymous, covert satirical career, a rehearsal for the darker, more dangerous world of the 1790s, was with him from the beginning. When it appeared in

12 New Light is a cant phrase in the West of Scotland for those religious opinions which Dr Taylor of Norwich has defended so strenuously. R.B.

The Edinburgh, the names of his specific 'Auld Licht' targets were identified only by the first, capital letter of their surname. These men were tangible and powerful enemies. As Daiches has commented, the specific, proper named detail of the poem, as in the similarly undervalued *Holy Fair* and the other early ecclesiastical satires, creates difficulties of contextual retrieval for the modern reader. This poem is certainly worth the difficulty and Burns's own footnotes are of considerable help. While not achieving the manically, perhaps demonically, inspired level of *Holy Willie's Prayer* or *The Address of Beelzebub*, it shares with these poems Burns's savage, post-Swiftian power of destroying one's enemies by ironically assuming their voice, person and values and, hence, to the mad, destructive conclusions inherent in them. In many respects it is a darker version of *The Holy Fair*. It shares with that poem the same sense of the fanatical, 'Auld Licht' Calvinism on Scottish consciousness with its power of denigratory pulpit rhetoric. This poem, however, goes beyond tongue lashing into tangible sadism as a mode of clerical control. The image of the whip recurs through the poem. See, for example, ll. 43–5, partly autobiographical from his own kirk-punished fornication, and ll. 91–4. From the second stanza the poem is saturated in vengeful violence as the mode of 'Auld Licht' doctrinaire control. This pervasive, perverted violence extends to the hanging image of ll. 113–17 and the burning one of the poem's conclusion.

A note by Burns to the poem reveals his knowledge of the history of 'Auld Licht' fanaticism which surrounded this particular Kilmarnock charge. In it he refers to a 'scoffing ballad' written when the 'New Licht' Mr Lindsay had been inducted in 1764. Maggie Lauder of l. 11 was Lindsay's wife and had been the Earl of Glencairn's housekeeper. On this occasion, however, Glencairn had submitted to 'Auld Licht' pressure and appointed one of their own. Glencairn, whom Burns was to idealise as his patron, was not yet known to the poet. In his 1896 edition of the poems, William Wallace gives evidence of the reality of 'Auld Licht' violence in 1764: 'The violence of the people was so extreme at the attempted induction of Mr. Lindsay as to put an effectual stop to the proceedings. . . . The clergy dispersed in terror. . . Three young men. . . were whipped through the streets' (p. 153, fn.1).

As well as 'Auld Licht' violence Burns brilliantly ironises their self-congratulatory Biblically derived singing and pulpit rhetoric as their 'New Licht' moderate and 'commonsensical' enemies are everywhere put to flight. Both the cacophonous singing and choice of texts in ll. 19–36 are in form and content the reverse of Christian love. Kinsley, as uneasy perhaps with Burns as an ecclesiastical satirist as a political one, totally misreads this stanza when he remarks: 'But the texts proposed are all indecorous' (Vol. III, p. 1165). The image, both megalomaniac and self-pitying (ll. 55–6) of the 'Auld Lichts' having undergone a Babylonish captivity is quite marvellous. Also Burns points to the fact that while they hated Patronage, the power of the landowner to appoint the minister (see Galt's more muted, ironic treatment of this theme from a different point of view in *Annals of the Parish*), these creatures of pure spirit were not averse to the material prosperity the acquisition of a Manse would bring. Ll. 46–54 celebrate their new-found prosperity. Burns revelled in plucking from *The Old Testament* anecdotes suffused with sex and violence to expose and embarrass the hypothetically pious.

Ll. 39–40 provided an excuse for this acquisitiveness as accepted in the fashionable way that tobacco is accepted. Nor are they averse to (l. 118) alcohol. As in all ecclesiastical satires, as in Blake, varied, savage, devouring, punitive appetites are located behind hypocritical masks. L. 99 refers to James Beattie (1735–1803) who was in his day a major figure as the alleged proponent of Common Sense philosophy and, thereby, the antidote to Humean scepticism. He was also author of the influential 'Spenserian' poem *The Minstrel*; or, *The Progress of Genius* (1771–4) admired by the not easily impressed Wordsworth.

The Calf

First printed in the Edinburgh edition, 1787.

To the Rev. Mr James Stephen, on his text, Malachi, IV, Verse 2 –
'And ye shall go forth, and grow up, like CALVES of the stall.'

Right, Sir! your text I'll prove it true,	
Tho' Heretics may laugh;	
For instance, there 's yoursel just now,	yourself
God knows, an unco *Calf*!	great

5	And should some Patron be so kind,	
	As bless you wi' a kirk,	give his own church
	I doubt na, Sir, but then we'll find	not
	You're still as great a *Stirk*.	young bullock

But, if the Lover's raptur'd hour
10   Shall ever be your lot,
Forbid it, ev'ry heavenly Power,
      You e'er should be a *Stot*!   young bullock

Tho', when some kind, connubial Dear
      Your But-an-ben adorns,   small house
15 The like has been that you may wear
      A noble head of *horns*.

And, in your lug, most reverend James,   ear
      To hear you roar and rowte,   rant/bellow
Few men o' sense will doubt your claims
20   To rank among the *Nowte*.   cattle

And when ye're number'd wi' the dead,
      Below a grassy hillock,
With justice they may mark your head —
      'Here lies a famous *Bullock*!'

This *jeu d'esprit* was composed after a challenge by Gavin Hamilton
that Burns could not produce a poem on the subject of the Rev.
James Stephen's sermon at Mauchline on Sunday 3rd September
1786 'in a given time' (Letter 46). Hamilton was to miss the sermon
and asked Burns for a poem on the visiting minister's sermon.
Originally only four stanzas, as read to Hamilton by Burns and so
winning his bet, a further two were added that evening.

The publication of this work in the Edinburgh edition obviously
omitted the name of the kirk minister. A pamphlet publication of the
poem had been circulated, presumably without the poet's knowl-
edge, which included *The Calf*; *The Unco Calf's Answer*; *Virtue to a
Mountain Bard*; and *The Deil's Answer to his Vera Worthy Frien
Robert Burns*. Later in 1786 another anonymous work appeared
called *Burns' Calf Turned a Bull; Or Some Remarks on His Mean and
Unprecedented Attack on Mr S —*. Steven's identity did not remain
anonymous, although unnamed by Burns. The poet was attacked as
irreligious and associated with the Devil. Even by the late 19th
century Scott Douglas attacks the poet for his verses: 'very clever,
but recklessly severe; for the author could have no personal dislike to
this victim of his satirical propensity' (Vol. I, p. 155). The Rev.
Stephen, who later worked in London and ended up in Kilwinning,
bore the nickname of 'the calf' thereafter. It is highly probable that if
Burns had not been attacked in the doggerel pamphlet poems over
this work, the minister's identity would not have been made public.

Address to the Unco Guid
or The Rigidly Righteous
First printed in the Edinburgh edition, 1787.

My Son, these maxims make a rule,	
An' lump them ay thegither:	together
The Rigid Righteous is a fool,	
The Rigid Wise anither;	another
The cleanest corn that e'er was dight	sifted
May hae some pyles o' caff in;	have, piles, chaff
So ne'er a fellow-creature slight	
For random fits o' daffin.	

Burns's Paraphrase of Solomon
(*Eccles*. vii. 16).

	O YE wha are sae guid yoursel,	you who, so good
	Sae pious and sae holy,	so
	Ye've nought to do but mark and tell	nothing
	Your Neebours' fauts and folly!	neighbours' faults
5	Whase life is like a weel-gaun mill,	whose, well going
	Supplied wi' store o' water,	
	The heapet happer's ebbing still,	heaped hopper
	An' still the clap plays clatter!	clapper of a Mill, moving grain.
	Hear me, ye venerable Core,	group
10	As counsel for poor mortals,	
	That frequent pass douce Wisdom's door	sober
	For glaikit Folly's portals;	careless/stupid
	I, for their thoughtless, careless sakes	
	Would here propone defences,	
15	Their donsie tricks, their black mistakes,	hapless/unlucky
	Their failings and mischances.	
	Ye see your state wi' theirs compared,	
	And shudder at the niffer,	comparison
	But cast a moment's fair regard,	
20	What makes the mighty differ;	
	Discount what scant occasion gave,	
	That purity ye pride in,	
	And (what's aft mair than a' the lave)	oft more, remainder
	Your better art o' hidin.	

25 Think, when your castigated pulse
        Gies now and then a wallop,   gives, violent beat
    What ragings must his veins convulse,
        That still eternal gallop:
    Wi' wind and tide fair i' your tail,
30   Right on ye scud your sea-way   move fast
    But, in the teeth o' baith to sail,   both
        It maks an unco leeway.   uncommon

    See Social-life and Glee sit down,
        All joyous and unthinking,
35 Till, quite transmugrify'd, they're grown
        Debauchery and Drinking:
    O, would they stay to calculate
        Th' eternal consequences;
    Or your more dreaded hell to state,
40   Damnation of expenses!

    Ye high, exalted, virtuous Dames,
        Ty'd up in godly laces,
    Before ye gie poor *Frailty* names,   give
        Suppose a change o' cases;
45 A dear-lov'd lad, convenience snug,
        A treach'rous inclination —
    But, let me whisper i' your lug,   ear
        Ye're aiblins nae temptation.   maybe no

    Then gently scan your brother Man,
50   Still gentler sister Woman;
    Tho' they may gang a kennin wrang,   go a little wrong
        To step aside is human:
    One point must still be greatly dark,
        The moving *Why* they do it;
55 And just as lamely can ye mark,
        How far perhaps they rue it.

    Who made the heart, 'tis *He* alone
        Decidedly can try us,
    He knows each chord its various tone,
60   Each spring, its various bias:
    Then at the balance let's be mute,
        We never can adjust it;
    What's *done* we partly may compute,
        But know not what's *resisted*.

The date of the poem is uncertain. Prose sentiments very similar to those of the poem are to be found in the *FCB* for March 1784. It may also, with its emphasis on sexual transgression, in particular, female frailty, relate to Betsy Paton and Jean Armour in 1786. In the CB we find the following entry:

> I have often observed . . . that every man even the worst, have something good about them . . . Let any of the strictest char-acter for regularity of conduct among us, examine impartially how many of his virtues are owing to constitution and educa-tion; how many vices he has never been guilty of, not from any care or vigilance, but from want of opportunity . . . how much he is indebted to the World's good opinion, because the world does not know all; I say any man who can thus think, will scan the failings, nay the faults and crimes of mankind around him, with a brother's eye.

From this young man's somewhat sententious, self-conscious prose, this vivid, knowingly witty, anti-Pharisaical poem emerges. Burns invokes the true spirit of charitable religion against the hypocritical, repressed and repressive, 'unco guid'. Thus his own epigraph against the 'Rigid Righteous' and the 'Rigid Wise' is taken from *Ecclesiastes*, vii.16: 'Be not righteous over much; neither make thyself over wise: why shouldst thou destroy thyself.' Thus against the absolutist judgment inherent in Calvinism he propounds the compassion of a Christ who was implicitly opposed to those judge-mentally throwing stones at adulterous women (*John*: 3–7). The translation of *Ecclesiastes* into vernacular Scots constitutes, as The First Psalm, an original work in its own right.

   While not as obsessed as William Blake with Christ not as lawmaker but lawbreaker (*The Marriage of Heaven and Hell* and *The Everlasting Gospel*), Burns does not see in him a spirit not only charitable and empathetic but insurrectionary against conventional social piety. Hence, like himself, a keeper of unconventional company.

Tam Samson's[1] Elegy

First printed in the Edinburgh edition, 1787.

'An honest man's the noblest work of God.'
Alexander Pope.

	Has auld Kilmarnock seen the Deil?	old, Devil
	Or great M'Kinlay[2] thrawn his heel?	hurt his ankle
	Or Robertson[3] again grown weel	well/healthy
	To preach an' read?	
5	'Na, waur than a'!' cries ilka chiel,	no, worse, every one
	'*Tam Samson's* dead!'	
	Kilmarnock lang may grunt an' grane,	long, groan
	An' sigh an' sab, an' greet her lane,	sob, cry alone
	An' cleed her bairns, man, wife an' wean,	clothe, children, child
10	In mourning weed;	
	To Death she's dearly pay'd the kane,	rent in kind
	Tam Samson's dead!	
	The Brethren o' the mystic *level*	masons
	May hing their head in woefu' bevel,	hang, down/slope
15	While by their nose the tears will revel,	
	Like ony bead;	any
	Death's gien the Lodge an unco devel,	given, terrible blow
	Tam Samson's dead!	
	When Winter muffles up his cloak,	
20	And binds the mire like a rock;	
	When to the loughs the Curlers flock,	lochs
	Wi' gleesome speed,	
	Wha will they station at the cock? —	who, mark
	Tam Samson's dead!	

1 When this worthy old Sportsman went out last muir-fowl season, he supposed it was to be, in Ossian's phrase, 'the last in his fields'; and expressed an ardent wish to die and be buried in the muirs. On this hint the author composed his Elegy and Epitaph. R.B.

2 A certain Preacher, a great favourite with the Million. *Vide The Ordination*, stanza 2. R.B.

3 Another Preacher, and equal favourite with the Few, who was at that time ailing. For him, see also *The Ordination*, stanza 9. R.B.

25 He was the king of a' the Core,   company of curlers
    To guard, or draw, or wick a bore,   curling terms
    Or up the rink like *Jehu* roar
        In time o' need;
    But now he lags on Death's *hog-score*,   a line across the curling ice
30   Tam Samson's dead!

    Now safe the stately Sawmont sail,   salmon
    And Trouts bedropp'd wi' crimson hail,   spots
    And Eels weel-kend for souple tail,   well-known, supple
        And Geds for greed,   pike (fish)
35 Since, dark in Death's *fish-creel* we wail   fish-basket
        Tam Samson dead!

    Rejoice, ye birring Paitricks a';   whirring partridges
    Ye cootie Moorcocks, crousely craw;   leg-feathered, boldly crow
    Ye Maukins, cock your fud fu' braw,   hares, tail, fine well
40   Withoutten dread;   without
    Your mortal Fae is now awa',   foe, away
        Tam Samson's dead!

    That woefu' morn be ever mourn'd
    Saw him in shootin graith adorn'd,   gear/clothes
45 While pointers round impatient burn'd,
        Frae couples freed;   from
    But, Och! he gaed and ne'er return'd!   went
        Tam Samson's dead!

    In vain Auld-age his body batters;   old-
50 In vain the Gout his ankles fetters;   ankles
    In vain the burns cam down like waters,   came
        An acre-braid!   broad/wide
    Now ev'ry auld wife, greetin, clatters: old, crying, exclaims
        'Tam Samson's dead!'

55 Owre mony a weary hag he limpit,   over, many, moss, limped
    An ay the tither shot he thumpit,   always, other, he hit
    Till coward Death behind him jumpit,   jumped
        Wi' deadly feide;   feud/rage
    Now he proclaims, wi' tout o' trumpet,   blast
60   Tam Samson's dead!

When at his heart he felt the dagger,
He reel'd his wonted bottle-swagger,
But yet he drew the mortal trigger,
    Wi' weel-aim'd heed;   *well-aimed*
65 'Lord, five!' he cry'd, an owre did stagger; *over*
    Tam Samson's dead!

Ilk hoary Hunter mourn'd a brither;   *each, brother*
Ilk Sportsman-youth bemoan'd a father;   *each*
Yon auld gray stane, amang the heather,   *the old grey stone, among*
70   Marks out his head;
Whare *Burns* has wrote, in rhyming blether, *where, nonsense*
    Tam Samson's dead!

There, low he lies in lasting rest;
Perhaps upon his mould'ring breast
75 Some spitefu muirfowl bigs her nest,   *builds*
    To hatch an' breed:
Alas! nae mair he'll them molest!   *no more*
    Tam Samson's dead!

When August winds the heather wave,
80 And Sportsmen wander by yon grave,
Three volleys let his memory crave,
    O' pouther an' lead,   *(gun) powder*
Till Echo answer frae her cave,   *from*
    Tam Samson's dead!

85 Heav'n rest his saul, whare'er he be!   *soul, where'er*
Is th' wish o' mony mae than me: *many more*
He had twa fauts, or maybe three,   *two faults*
    Yet what remead?
Ae social, honest man want we: *one*
90   Tam Samson's dead!

THE EPITAPH
Tam Samson's weel-worn clay here lies,   *well-*
    Ye canting Zealots, spare him!
If Honest Worth in heaven rise,
    Ye'll mend or ye win near him.   *before, get*

PER CONTRA

95   Go, Fame, an' canter like a filly   young horse
     Thro a' the streets an' neuks o' *Killie*,[4]   alleys/closes, Kilmarnock
     Tell ev'ry social, honest billie   person
          To cease his grievin,
     For yet, unskaith'd by Death's gleg gullie,   sharp knife
100   *Tam Samson's leevin!*   living

If Mark Twain believed that reports of his death had been greatly
exaggerated, Burns builds this boisterous poem on a similar joke.
Beginning with a dig at the propensity for theatrical clamour in two
of his 'Auld Licht' clerical enemies, also savaged in *The Ordination*,
Burns runs a declamatory 'headline' through the poem with his
multi-voiced proclamations of Tam Sampson's death whereby men,
animals, birds, fish and Death itself join the chorus. Tam's en-
ormous vigour for field sports is echoed in the vocal, mixed response
to his alleged demise; hardly surprisingly the creaturely victims of
his energetic skill are ecstatic. Thomas Sampson (1722–95) was a
nurseryman, sportsman and Freemason (ll. 13–18) in Kilmarnock.
His poetic immortalisation stems from a combination of his
eccentric strength of character and Burns's access to the form
and theme of the eighteenth-century Scots comic elegiac tradition
with specific relation to Robert Semphill of Beltree's *Piper of
Kilbarchan*. Burns's celebration of his aged hunter-killer is unchar-
acteristic of his general attitude to hunting where, so much of the
poetry of the late eighteenth century is suffused with it, the suffering
and destruction of creaturely life is dominant. Here this is controlled
partly by the comic convention and also possibly by the fact that
Tam is an honest man of the people and not a bloodsport-aristocrat.
The Epitaph (ll. 91–4) is another attack on the sanctimoniously
judgemental and the *Per Contra* (ll. 95–100) which undercuts the
previous ebullient statements of grief may have resulted from Alan
Cunningham's story (ii. 235) that Burns wrote it in response to
Sampson's protest that 'I'm no dead yet. . . I'm worth ten dead
fowk'. Kinsley pertinently refers here to Ramsay's *To my Friends in
Ireland, who on a report of my death,. . . Elegies*, ll. 5–6 (*Works*, STS,
ii, 203):

          Dight your Een, and cease your grieving,
          ALLAN's hale, and well, and living . . .

4 Killie is a phrase the country-folks sometimes use for the name of a certain
town in the West. R.B.

A Winter Night

First printed in the Edinburgh edition, 1787.

Poor naked wretches, wheresoe'er you are,
That bide the pelting of this pityless storm!
How shall your houseless heads and unfed sides,
Your loop'd and window'd raggedness, defend you
From seasons such as these?
                                        SHAKESPEARE.

When biting *Boreas*, fell and doure,   the North wind, keen, hard
Sharp shivers thro' the leafless bow'r;
When *Phoebus* gies a short-liv'd glow'r,   the Sun, gives, stare
        Far south the lift,   horizon/sky
5   Dim-dark'ning thro' the flaky show'r,
        Or whirling drift.

Ae night the Storm the steeples rocked,   one
Poor Labour sweet in sleep was locked,
While burns, wi' snawy wreeths up-choked,   with snowy
10   Wild-eddying swirl,
Or, thro' the mining outlet bocked,   vomited
        Down headlong hurl.

List'ning the doors an' winnocks rattle,   windows
I thought me on the ourie cattle,   shivering
15 Or silly sheep, wha bide this brattle   who endure, noise
        O' winter war,
And thro the drift, deep-lairing, sprattle,   scramble
        Beneath a scar.   jutting rock (for shelter)

Ilk happing bird, wee, helpless thing!   each hopping
20 That, in the merry months o' spring,
Delighted me to hear thee sing,
        What comes o' thee?
Whare wilt thou cow'r thy chittering wing,   where
        An' close thy e'e?   eye

25 Ev'n you, on murd'ring errands toil'd,
Lone from your savage homes exil'd,
The blood-stain'd roost and sheep-cote spoil'd,
        My heart forgets,
While pityless the tempest wild
30   Sore on you beats.

Now *Phoebe*, in her midnight reign,   the Moon
Dark-muffl'd, view'd the dreary plain;
Still crouding thoughts, a pensive train,   crowding
   Rose in my soul,
35 When on my ear this plaintive strain,
    Slow-solemn, stole —

'Blow, blow, ye Winds, with heavier gust!
'And freeze, thou bitter-biting Frost!
'Descend, ye chilly, smothering Snows!
40 'Not all your rage, as now, united shows
   'More hard unkindness unrelenting,
   'Vengeful malice, unrepenting,
'Than heaven-illumin'd Man on brother Man bestows!

'See stern Oppression's iron grip,
45 'Or mad Ambition's gory hand,
'Sending, like blood-hounds from the slip,
  'Woe, Want, and Murder o'er a land!
'Ev'n in the peaceful rural vale,
'Truth, weeping tells the mournful tale,
50 'How pamper'd Luxury, Flatt'ry by her side,
   'The parasite empoisoning her ear,
   'With all the servile wretches in the rear,
'Looks o'er proud Property, extended wide;
   'And eyes the simple, rustic Hind,
55 'Whose toil upholds the glitt'ring show,
   'A creature of another kind,
'Some coarser substance, unrefin'd,
'Plac'd for her lordly use, thus far, thus vile, below!'

'Where, where is Love's fond, tender throe,
60 'With lordly Honor's lofty brow,
   'The pow'rs you proudly own?
'Is there, beneath Love's noble name,
'Can harbour, dark, the selfish aim,
   'To bless himself alone!
65 'Mark Maiden-Innocence a prey
   'To love-pretending snares,
   'This boasted Honor turns away,
   'Shunning soft Pity's rising sway,

'Regardless of the tears and unavailing pray'rs!
70   'Perhaps this hour, in Mis'ry's squalid nest,
        'She strains your infant to her joyless breast,
'And with a mother's fears shrinks at the rocking blast!

            'Oh ye! who, sunk in beds of down,
        'Feel not a want but what yourselves create,
75   'Think, for a moment, on his wretched fate,
            'Whom friends and fortune quite disown!
'Ill-satisfy'd, keen nature's clam'rous call,
        'Stretch'd on his straw, he lays himself to sleep,
            'While through the ragged roof and chinky wall,
80   'Chill, o'er his slumbers piles the drifty heap!
'Think on the Dungeon's grim confine,
'Where Guilt and poor Misfortune pine!
'Guilt, erring Man, relenting view!
'But shall thy legal rage pursue
85   'The Wretch, already crushed low
        'By cruel Fortune's undeservèd blow?
'Affliction's sons are brothers in distress;
'A Brother to relieve, how exquisite the bliss!'

I heard nae mair, for *Chanticleer*   no more
90   Shook off the pouthery snaw,   powdery snow
And hail'd the morning with a cheer,
        A cottage-rousing craw.   crow

But deep this truth impress'd my mind —
        Thro' all His works abroad,
95   The heart benevolent and kind
        The most resembles GOD.

Given that in successful poetry form and content are always mutually expressive, this poem has been seen as a puzzling failure because of its apparently disparate elements. Beginning with an epigraph from *King Lear*, the poem moves to five vernacular stanzas in the 'Habbie Simpson' form brilliantly detailing the impact of a stormy winter night on the exposed beasts and birds. We then, in standard English, having another linking 'Habbie Simpson' stanza which introduces an internal voice which, in the form of a Pindaric Ode, presents a hellish vision of a society overwhelmed by corruption and predatory sexuality manifest in the relation of the aristocratic rich to the destitute poor. Finally, the poem switches back to

two 'Habbie Simpson' vernacular stanzas which reassuringly sug-
gest the whole thing should be viewed as a dream from which we
have wakened to find ourselves in the presence of a benevolent God.

On the face of it this seems a 'mixtie maxie' well beyond *The Brigs
of Ayr*. However, the thread of *King Lear* leads us through this
apparent maze. In the Kilmarnock edition Burns has already used
Shakespearean allusion with telling effect in, for example, *A Dream/
Henry IV* and *Epistle to a Young Friend/Hamlet*. Despite making no
comment on the *Lear* epigraph Kinsley picks up this and another
bitter Shakespearean echo in ll. 37–43 of *A Winter Night*:

Blow, blow ye Winds, &c. Cf. King Lear, III.ii, 1–9, 'Blow
windes . . . all germaines spill at one/That makes ingrateful
Man; the song in *As You Like It*, II.vii:

Blow, blow, thou winter winde,
Thou art not so unkinde, as mans ingratitude . . .
Freize, freize, thou bitter skie that does not
Bight so night as benefitts forgot . . .

Unfortunately, however, Kinsley, despite his enormous erudition
expressed in the allusory density he brings to Burns's poetry,
consistently identifies Burns's relationship to other writers in an
apolitical way. In the 1790s, *King Lear* was the most politically
loaded and relevant of Shakespeare's plays. First, it was, given a
contemporarily, if transiently, mad king on the throne, another mad
one could not be provocatively put on stage. Second, what is
revealed in *King Lear* is the utter failure of an allegedly patriarchal
ruling class so demonically selfish that, in a hellish, a hallucinatory
night scene, the terrible condition of the common people is revealed
in their uprooted homelessness, naked hunger and alienated grief
bordering on madness.

King Lear, at the heart of Shakespeare's darkness, reveals what
happens when 'natural' man becomes a *creature* of unbridled pre-
datory, libidinous appetites. In Burns's 'night' poem the animals
are, as always, empathetically treated, and, unlike the wolfish
humanity of the Pindaric section, even the barn-robbing vernacular
fox is seen more as victim than villain.

It is further characteristic of Kinsley that having not explored this
sort of poetic terrain, he further denies such an obvious political
reading by means of arguments based on aesthetic deficiency. He
describes this particular instance of his sense of Burns's chronic
general incapacity to write in the Pindaric form thus:

Burns's strophes have rhythmical strength—though that is not always sustained—rather than exalted energy; his images are too predictable, his diction too conventional. The success of the opening scene, in his familiar style . . . only emphasized his failure to rise above the commonplace in the Pindaric part.

Two things need to be said about this. First, if Burns failed with the Pindaric Ode he was not alone in this. As Geoffrey Hartman noted: 'The sublime or greater or Pindaric ode flourished in the eighteenth century like a turgid weed.' (*The Fate of Reading* (Chicago: 1975), p. 138.) The criticism levelled at Burns by Kinsley could be easily replicated dealing with Coleridge's dissident poetry of the 1790s with its terminal, apocalyptic sense of communal breakdown due to established economic, military violence unchecked by either the duty or compassion of the ruling class.

Kinsley has no patience with Burns's radically dissenting poetry because he is wilfully ignorant of its radical context. He makes little of Burns's multiple connections with other radical writers of the period or, as in the case of Dr Walcot (Peter Pindar), a still deeply underestimated political satirist, he dismisses him, quite ignoring Burns's own high evaluation of him (Letter 578) with a crass Boswellian put-down: 'a contemptible scribbler (who), having disgraced and deserted the clerical character . . . picks up in London a scanty livelihood by scurrilous lampoons under a feigned name (Vol. III p. 1423)'. Missing the unjustly forgotten, if lesser, radical writers, Kinsley compounds his mistake by not perceiving how close the now canonical Romantic poets were in theme and form to Burns in the mid-1790s. As well as the now better-understood complexity of Wordsworth's relationship to Burns, we should contemplate the proximity of Coleridge to Burns as political satirist and commentator (Perry, as noted, wanted them both on the London staff of *The Morning Chronicle*) and poet of the mid-1790s' radical apocalypse. Consider, for example, Coleridge's *Fire, Famine, and Slaughter* with its ferocious, catastrophic sense of the consequences of the unnamed Pitt's policies in Ireland and against the French Revolution by supporting the monarchists in the terrible civil war raging in the Vendée. This poem, written the year after Burns's death, is not subjective hysteria but at the core of a national nightmare of unrewarded blood, toil and tears. Coleridge was horrified by the Scottish sedition trials of 1793–4 and hated and feared 'brazen-faced' Dundas, but it was Pitt ('Letters four do form his name') for whom, in this poem, he reserved his most savage assault:

Slau. Letters four do form his name—And who sent you?
Both. The same! the same!
Slau. He came by stealth, and unlocked my den,
And I have drunk the blood since then
Of thrice three hundred thousand men.
Both. Who bade you do't?
Slau. The same! the same!
Letters four do form his name.
He let me loose, and cried Halloo!
To him alone the praise is due.
Fam. Thanks, sister, thanks! the men have bled,
Their wives and their children faint for bread.
I stood in a swampy field of battle;
With bones and skulls I made a rattle,
To frighten the wolf and carrion-crow
And the homeless dog—but they would not go.
So off I flew: for how could I bear
To see them gorge their dainty fare?
I heard a groan and a peevish squall,
And through the chink of a cottage-wall—
Can you guess what I saw there?
Both. Whisper it, sister! in our ear.
Fam. A baby beat its dying mother:
I had starved the one and was starving the other!
Both. Who bade you do't?
Fam. The same! the same!
Letters four do form his name.
He let me loose, and cried, Halloo!
To him alone the praise is due.
Fire. Sisters! I from Ireland came!
Hedge and corn-fields all on flame,
I triumph'd o'er the setting sun!
And all the while the work was done,
On as I strode with my huge strides,
I flung back my head and I held my sides,
It was so rare a piece of fun
To see the sweltered cattle run
With uncouth gallop through the night,
Scared by the light of his own blazing cot
Was many a naked Rebel shot:
The house-stream met the flame and hissed,
While crash! fell in the roof, I wist,
On some of those old bed-rid nurses,

That deal in discontent and curses.
Both. Who bade you do't?
Fire. The same! the same!
Letters four do spell his name.
He let me loose, and cried Halloo!
To him alone the praise is due.
All. He let us loose, and cried Halloo!
How shall we yield him honour due?
Fam. Wisdom comes with lack of food.
I'll gnaw, I'll gnaw the multitude,
Till the cup of rage o'erbrim:
They shall seize him and his brood—
Slau. They shall tear him limb from limb!
Fire. O thankless beldames and untrue!
And this is all that you can do
For him, who did so much for you?
Ninety months he, by my troth!
Hath richly catered for you both;
And in an hour would you repay
An eight years' work?—Away! away!
I alone am faithful! I
Cling to him everlastingly.

As noted, the instigator of this barbarism ('Letters four do form his name') is William Pitt. As we shall see in the *Anonymous & Pseudonymous* section, the multiple consequences of Pitt's warmongering were to become also the objects of Burns's satire in the 1790s. Not even he was, however, prepared to speak so directly about Irish matters as Coleridge. Ireland was, in fact, the epicentre of the intended radical insurrection of the 1790s, trying and failing to provoke similar militant resistance in England and Scotland. In 1798 30,000 dissident Irish were to pay with their lives at Wicklow. (See Roger Wells, *Insurrection: The British Experience, 1795–1803* (Gloucester: 1983).)

Like Burns, Coleridge's poetry is impregnated with Biblical allusion; not least *Revelations*. Like Burns he also saw in *King Lear* another text which strengthened his sense of apocalypse now. As he wrote of III.iv., Lear's despair and growing madness in the storm:

What a world's convention of agonies! Surely never was such a scene conceived before or since. Take it but as a picture for the eye only, it is more terrific than any a Michelangelo inspired by a Dante could have conceived, and none but a Michelangelo could have executed. Or let it have been uttered to the blind, the howlings of convulsed nature would seem converted into the voice of conscious humanity.

The 'howlings of convulsed nature' is what *Fire, Famine and Slaughter, A Winter Night* and *Guilt and Sorrow*; or *Incidents upon Salisbury Plain* are about. Further, these convulsions are elemental *and* political. Writing to John Thelwall, one of the chief radicals of the day and a keen enthusiast for Burns's poetry, Coleridge remarked that he would send him *Guilt and Sorrow* from the as yet unknown Wordsworth who 'thinks that the lines from 364 to 375 & from 403 to 428 the best in the Volume—indeed worth all the rest— And this man is a Republican & at least a *Semi*-atheist.—' Indeed the poem is so radical that it was not published in full till 1842. Its dreadful nightscape is replete with the economically uprooted and militarily press-ganged, in Hazlitt's bitter term, the redundant part of the population. Mary Jacobus had found echoes of *King Lear* in it but it is surely a *Lear* partly mediated through Burns's *A Winter's Night*; a world where animals but not men have a place to lay their heads. Even more singular is Wordsworth's evolution of Burns's theme of guilt in the poem: 'Think on the dungeon's grim confine . . . By cruel Fortune's undeserved blow?'

A final fact about this interpretation of *A Winter's Night* is that Burns chose, as we shall see in the *Anonymous & Pseudonymous* section in *The Gentleman's Magazine* for August 1794, to update the poem and print it under a new title, *Humanity: An Ode*. It is partially identified by his initials and is stripped of its vernacular opening and its falsely consolatory vernacular ending with some other significant changes to the intervening Pindaric poem. Burns must have felt its scream of rage even more politically relevant to 1794 than to 1787. Thus, ironically, the poem which was arguably its partial genesis, reappears the year following *The Female Vagrant* section of *Guilt and Sorrow*.

Stanzas Written in Prospect of Death
First published in the Edinburgh edition, 1787.

Why am I loth to leave this earthly scene?
　　Have I so found it full of pleasing charms?
Some drops of joy with draughts of ill between;
　　Some gleams of sunshine mid renewing storms:

5   Is it departing pangs my soul alarms?
          Or Death's unlovely, dreary, dark abode?
    For guilt, for guilt, my terrors are in arms;
          I tremble to approach an angry GOD,
    And justly smart beneath his sin-avenging rod.

10 Fain would I say, 'Forgive my foul offence!'
          Fain promise never more to disobey;
    But, should my Author health again dispense,
          Again I might desert fair Virtue's way;
    Again in Folly's path might go astray;
15   Again exalt the brute and sink the man;
    Then how should I for Heavenly Mercy pray,
          Who act so counter Heavenly Mercy's plan?
    Who sin so oft have mourn'd, yet to temptation ran?

    O Thou, Great Governor of all below! —
20   If I may dare a lifted eye to Thee,
    Thy nod can make the tempest cease to blow,
          Or still the tumult of the raging sea:
    With that controuling pow'r assist ev'n me,
          Those headlong furious passions to confine;
25 For all unfit I feel my pow'rs to be,
          To rule their torrent in th' allowed line;
    O, aid me with Thy help, *Omnipotence Divine*!

The title is normally *Stanzas on the Same Occasion*, to follow *A Prayer, in the Prospect of Death*. Composition is thus during the same period, or as the poet was recuperating from illness. The Stair Ms. has the title 'Misgivings of Despondency on the Approach of the Monarch of the Grave'. It is clearly evident in these early illness-inspired works that Burns employed his introspective thoughts in trying to comprehend the tensions between his own impulsive character traits and what he deemed the proper religious behaviour expected in the wider society. It is hard to disagree with Daiches that this and the following four poems, 'show Burns writing in conventional neo-classic English with no spark of genius or originality' (p. 218). He may have retrieved these very early, orthodoxly pious poems simply to pad out the Edinburgh edition. Or, it may have been as cover against the persistent complaints of the Hugh Blairites against his, at best, deeply unorthodox sallies into *Old Testament* exegesis.

Prayer: O Thou Dread Power

Lying at a Reverend Friend's House one Night, the author left the
following verses in the room where he slept: -

First printed in the Edinburgh edition, 1787.

O Thou dread Pow'r, who reign'st above!
    I know Thou wilt me hear;
When for this scene of peace and love,
    I make my pray'r sincere.

5   The hoary Sire — the mortal stroke,
    Long, long be pleas'd to spare:
To bless his little filial flock,
    And show what good men are.

She, who her lovely Offspring eyes
10   With tender hopes and fears,
O bless her with a Mother's joys,
    But spare a Mother's tears!

Their hope, their stay, their darling youth,
    In manhood's dawning blush;
15 Bless him, Thou God of love and truth,
    Up to a Parent's wish.

The beauteous, seraph Sister-band,
    With earnest tears I pray,
Thou know'st the snares on every hand,
20   Guide Thou their steps alway.

When soon or late they reach that coast,
    O'er Life's rough ocean driven,
May they rejoice, no wand'rer lost,
    A Family in Heaven!

As the subtitle records, the poet composed and left these verses in
the home of the Rev. Dr George Lawrie (1722–99), who was
minister at Loudon, near Galston (by Kilmarnock). Currie quotes
confirmation of this (Vol. III, p. 386) from Gilbert Burns who states
that his brother first heard the spinnet played at Dr Lawrie's home
when he visited there a few months after the publication of the
Kilmarnock edition in the Autumn of 1786. George Lawrie's son
Archibald became a friend of Burns.

Paraphrase of the First Psalm
First printed in the Edinburgh edition, 1787.

The man, in life wherever plac'd,
    Hath happiness in store,
Who walks not in the wicked's way,
    Nor learns their guilty lore!

5 Nor from the seat of scornful Pride
    Casts forth his eyes abroad,
But with humility and awe
    Still walks before his GOD.

That Man shall flourish like the trees
10   Which by the streamlets grow;
The fruitful top is spread on high,
    And firm the root below.

But he whose blossom buds in guilt
    Shall to the ground be cast,
15 And like the rootless stubble tost
    Before the sweeping blast.

For why? that GOD the good adore
    Hath giv'n them peace and rest,
But hath decreed that wicked men
20   Shall ne'er be truly blest.

A summation of the sentiments in the First Psalm placed in rhyme, this work is generally dated from the 1781–2 period. While mainly employing Biblical language, Burns neatly employs some 18th century phraseology to give the verses a contemporary context. The terms 'guilty lore', 'scornful pride', 'stubble', 'sweeping blast' and 'truly blest' are not found in the original Psalm.

A Prayer,
Under the Pressure of Violent Anguish
First printed in the Edinburgh edition, 1787.

O Thou Great Being! what Thou art,
    Surpasses me to know:
Yet sure I am, that known to Thee
    Are all Thy works below.

5   Thy creature here before Thee stands,
    All wretched and distrest;
Yet sure those ills that wring my soul
    Obey Thy high behest.

Sure Thou, Almighty, canst not act
10   From cruelty or wrath!
O, free my weary eyes from tears,
    Or close them fast in death!

But if I must afflicted be,
    To suit some wise design;
15 Then, man my soul with firm resolves
    To bear and not repine!

In the *FCB*, dated March 1784, the poet introduces this poem: 'There was a certain period of my life that my spirit was broke by repeated losses and disasters, which threatened, and indeed effected the utter ruin of my fortune. My body too was attacked by that most dreadful distemper, a Hypochondria, or confirmed Melancholy: in this wretched state, the recollection of which makes me yet shudder, I hung my Harp on the Willow trees, except in some lucid intervals, in one of which I composed the following.'

The Ninetieth Psalm Paraphrased
First printed in the Edinburgh edition, 1787.

O Thou, the first, the greatest friend
    Of all the human race!
Whose strong right hand has ever been
    Their stay and dwelling-place!

5   Before the mountains heav'd their heads
          Beneath Thy forming hand,
    Before this ponderous globe itself
          Arose at Thy command:

    That Power which rais'd and still upholds
10   This universal frame,
    From countless, unbeginning time
          Was ever still the same.

    Those mighty periods of years,
          Which seem to us so vast,
15 Appear no more before Thy sight
          Than yesterday that's past.

    Thou giv'st the word; Thy creature, man,
          Is to existence brought;
    Again Thou say'st, 'Ye sons of men,
20   'Return ye into nought!'

    Thou layest them with all their cares
          In everlasting sleep;
    As with a flood Thou tak'st them off
          With overwhelming sweep.

25 They flourish like the morning flow'r,
          In beauty's pride array'd;
    But long ere night, cut down, it lies
          All wither'd and decay'd.

Yet another example of the poet's versified religious inculcation.
For all the critical attacks on Burns in Ayrshire by some elements of
the clergy prior to his successful poetic career, works like this reveal
his in-depth knowledge of Biblical subjects and his keen ability to
interpret and paraphrase Biblical text. In the strict social stratifica-
tion of 18th century society, members of the peasantry were meant
to follow religious dictates, not question or debate them as Burns
did. As the poet wryly recorded, 'ambitious of shining in conversa-
tion parties on Sundays between sermons, funerals, &c. used in a
few years more to puzzle Calvinism with so much heat and indis-
cretion that I raised a hue and cry of heresy against me which has not
ceased to this hour' (Letter 125).

To Miss Logan
With Beattie's *Poems*
A New Year's Gift January 1, 1787
First printed in the Edinburgh edition, 1787.

Again the silent wheels of time
    Their annual round have driv'n,
And you, tho' scarce in maiden prime,
    Are so much nearer Heav'n.

5 No gifts have I from Indian coasts
    The infant year to hail;
I send you more than India boasts
    In *Edwin's* simple tale.

Our Sex with guile, and faithless love
10   Is charg'd, perhaps too true;
But may, dear Maid, each Lover prove
    An *Edwin* still to you.

Miss Susan Logan was the younger sister of Major William Logan
of Park, a friend of Mrs Dunlop and the recipient of a copy of
Beattie's *Poems* sent by Burns from Edinburgh.

Address to a Haggis
First printed in *The Caledonian Mercury*, 20th December 1786.

Fair fa' your honest, sonsie face,	good luck to, cheerful
Great Chieftain o' the Puddin-race!	
Aboon them a' ye tak your place,	above
Painch, tripe, or thairm:	paunch, guts
5 Weel are ye wordy of a *grace*	well
As lang 's my arm.	long as

The groaning trencher there ye fill,	
Your hurdies like a distant hill,	buttocks
Your *pin* wad help to mend a mill	skewer would
10 In time o' need,	
While thro' your pores the dews distil	
Like amber bead.	

His knife see Rustic-labour dight,   wipe
An' cut ye up wi' ready slight,   skill
15   Trenching your gushing entrails bright,
        Like onie ditch;   any
And then, O what a glorious sight,
        Warm-reekin, rich!   -steaming

Then, horn for horn, they stretch an' strive: eating with a horn-spoon
20   Deil tak the hindmost, on they drive,   devil take the slowest
Till a' their weel-swall'd kytes belyve   well-swollen stomachs eventually
        Are bent like drums;
Then auld Guidman, maist like to rive,   old, goodman, most, burst
        Bethankit hums.

25   Is there that owre his French *ragout*,   over
Or *olio* that wad staw a sow,   would, fill up/bloat
Or *fricassee* wad mak her spew   would make, throw up
        Wi' perfect sconner,   disgust
Looks down wi' sneering, scornfu' view
30   On sic a dinner?   such

Poor devil! see him owre his trash,   over
As feckless as a wither'd rash,   feeble, rush
His spindle shank a guid whip-lash,   thin leg, good
        His nieve a nit;   fist, nut
35   Thro' bluidy flood or field to dash,   bloody
        O how unfit!

But mark the Rustic, *haggis-fed*,   country man
The trembling earth resounds his tread,
Clap in his walie nieve a blade,   place, firm fist
40   He'll make it whissle;   whistle/cutting through air
An' legs, an' arms, an' heads will sned   cut off
        Like taps o' thrissle.   tops of thistle

Ye Pow'rs wha mak mankind your care,   who make
And dish them out their bill o' fare,
45   Auld Scotland wants nae skinking ware,   old, no watery
        That jaups in luggies;   splashes in bowls
But, if ye wish her gratefu' prayer,
        Gie her a *Haggis*!   give

Subject to endless repetition as *the* indispensable Burns Supper
party-piece, this poem has probably been heard far too often for its
own good. It is, however, arguably more subtly knowing and

dissident than first appears. The poem as we have it was completed in Edinburgh in December 1786. There is, however, evidence that the last verse was composed first in the house of John Morrison, a Mauchline cabinetmaker, and was used as a free-standing grace. This is the first-recorded version of the last stanza:

> Ye Pow'rs wha gie us a' that's gude
> Still bless auld Caledonia's brood,
> Wi' great John Barleycorn's heart's bluid
>   In stoups or luggies;
> And on our boards, that King o' food
>   A gude Scotch Haggis.

A peasant dish compounded of meat left-overs, oatmeal, spices, offal, all packed in a sheep's stomach, Burns portrays the haggis as causative of the virility of the Scottish common people. Literally virility as in ll. 7–9 the haggis's vast buttock-like shape culminated in a pronounced phallic-like pin. It did provoke in those who partook of it Breughel-like orgiastic appetites. It also gave stomach for battle with its echo from Fergusson's *The Farmer's Ingle*, ll. 37–45:

> On sicken food has mony a doughty deed
>   By Caledonia's ancestors been done;
> By this did mony wight fu' weirlike bleed
>   In brulzies, &c.

An enthusiast, albeit with certain well-defined parameters, for Burns as poet-recorder of Scottish peasant life, this poem caused Kinsley not a little unease: 'But the *Address* is not merely a burlesque poem, or a piece of convivial genre-poetry like its antecedent, Fergusson's *Caller Oysters*. Through it there runs an assertion, more than half-serious, of peasant virtue and strength, expressed in harsh, violent diction and in images of slaughter'. The nearest analogy to what Burns is doing here are ll. 85–102 of *The Author's Earnest Cry and Prayer*.

Address to Edinburgh
First printed in the Edinburgh edition, 1787.

Edina! *Scotia's* darling seat!
    All hail thy palaces and tow'rs,
Where once beneath a Monarch's feet,
    Sat Legislation's sov'reign pow'rs!

5 From marking wildly-scatt'red flow'rs,
       As on the banks of *Ayr* I stray'd,
   And singing, lone, the ling'ring hours,
       I shelter in thy honor'd shade.

   Here Wealth still swells the golden tide,
10   As busy Trade his labours plies;
   There Architecture's noble pride
       Bids elegance and splendour rise;
   Here Justice, from her native skies,
       High wields her balance and her rod;
15 There Learning, with his eagle eyes,
       Seeks Science in her coy abode.

   Thy Sons, *Edina*, social, kind,
       With open arms the Stranger hail;
   Their views enlarg'd, their lib'ral mind,
20   Above the narrow, rural vale:
   Attentive still to Sorrow's wail,
       Or modest Merit's silent claim;
   And never may their sources fail!
       And never Envy blot their name!

25 Thy Daughters bright thy walks adorn,
       Gay as the gilded summer sky,
   Sweet as the dewy, milk-white thorn,
       Dear as the raptur'd thrill of joy!
   Fair Burnet strikes th' adoring eye,
30   Heav'n's beauties on my fancy shine;
   I see the *Sire of Love* on high,
       And own His work indeed divine!

   There, watching high the least alarms,
       Thy rough, rude Fortress gleams afar;
35 Like some bold Vet'ran, grey in arms,
       And mark'd with many a seamy scar:
   The pond'rous wall and massy bar
       Grim-rising o'er the rugged rock,
   Have oft withstood assailing War,
40   And oft repell'd th' Invader's shock.

With awe-struck thought, and pitying tears,
　　I view that noble, stately Dome,
Where *Scotia's* kings of other years,
　　Fam'd heroes! had their royal home:
45　Alas, how chang'd the times to come!
　　　Their royal Name low in the dust!
Their hapless Race wild-wand'ring roam!
　　Tho' rigid Law cries out, 'twas just!

Wild-beats my heart, to trace your steps,
50　　Whose ancestors, in days of yore,
Thro' hostile ranks and ruin'd gaps
　　Old *Scotia's* bloody lion bore:
Ev'n *I* who sing in rustic lore,
　　Haply *my Sires* have left their shed,
55　And fac'd grim Danger's loudest roar,
　　Bold-following where your Fathers led!

Edina! *Scotia's* darling seat!
　　All hail thy palaces and tow'rs,
Where once, beneath a Monarch's feet,
60　　Sat Legislation's sov'reign pow'rs!
From marking wildly-scatt'red flow'rs,
　　As on the banks of *Ayr* I stray'd,
And singing, lone, the ling'ring hours,
　　I shelter in thy honour'd shade.

The artificial English of this poem written not long after Burns's arrival in Edinburgh late in 1786 has achieved a degree of notoriety not least stemming from David Daiches' witty put-down:

> The 'Address to Edinburgh' was a 'duty' poem, written in December as a more or less official expression of gratitude to the city which had received him so hospitably; it too was published in the *Caledonian Mercury*, so that the Edinburgh public could see he had done his duty by the city. It is a frigid, artificial poem in stilted neoclassic English. Edinburgh is hailed as '*Edina*! *Scotia's* darling seat!' and the firm of Edinburgh plumbers and sanitary engineers who in a later generation adopted the name 'Edina' for their version of a necessary but hardly poetic kind of seat were demonstrating, if somewhat crudely, a real critical insight (p. 215).

Certainly the Thomsonian theme and style of the burgeoning vision of wealth, architecture and culture fails to convince. Nor does the specific praise of Lord Monboddo's daughter, Miss Burnett in l. 29 quite corroborate the epistolary fantasy version of this young lady, who actually bore a close resemblance to her physically unprepossessing father: 'the heavenly Miss Burnett, daughter of Lord Monboddo, at whose house I have had the honour to more than once. – There has not been anything nearly like her, in all the combinations of Beauty, Grace and Goodness the Great Creator has formed, since Milton's Eve on the first day of her existence' (Letter 68). The 'Sire of Love' (l. 31) is Coelus, begetter of Venus and, indeed, Burns was in thrall to that sky-god during his Edinburgh sojourn with a sexual voracity bordering on erotomania. Recent evidence indicates an involvement with another working-class woman and another illegitimate child as well as with Jenny Clow. Simultaneously he was besieging Mrs McLehose ('Clarinda') with a sentimental campaign of pious eroticism and in communication with Margaret (Peggy) Chalmers whom he had notions of marrying and who appears, even more than Maria Riddell, capable of sympathetic comprehension, if not reciprocation, of the Bard's deepest creative urges. The multiple, diverse, divisive nature of Burns's sexual desires at this period must surely also correspond to similar tensions in his social and cultural life. Edinburgh, as Daiches suggests, was hospitable to him, but in divided and temporary ways. The cosseted 'Stranger' pays his thanks but (ll. 21–4) at the very least, questions the longevity of this charitable celebration. His erstwhile sentimental supporters of genteel Edinburgh, especially Henry Mackenzie, were, of course, to indulge in posthumous, envious character assassination.

The poem's topographical reading of the city is also interesting. Before proceeding to a celebration of the splendours of the New Edinburgh, ll. 3–4 mark the physical disintegration of the Scottish court and parliament. While the Castle is seen (ll. 33–40) as a tangible bastion of self-defending, Scottish independence, the poem is much more concerned with the deserted Holyrood Palace as manifesting the fall of the Stuarts in whom Burns found both the public manifestation of a disintegrated Scotland and private expressions of his own sense of life as displaced, if not exiled, grief. Ll. 53–6 invoke his own family's coming-out in the 1715. Indeed, while it will be subsequently far better expressed, the essence of Burns's Jacobitism is to be found in this poem.

Thus a poem which apparently is a slight act of obeisance to Edinburgh actually obscures darker anxieties about the true state of the Scottish body politic. Indeed, utterly contradicting Walter Scott, it does not present a paradigm of burgeoning Scottish post-Union evolution but a sense of national loss at the heart of this city as symbol of the national spirit.

John Barleycorn: A Ballad[1]

Tune: Lull Me Beyond Thee

First printed in the Edinburgh edition, 1787.

There was three kings into the east,
  Three kings both great and high,
And they hae sworn a solemn oath   have
  John Barleycorn should die.

5   They took a plough and plough'd him down,
  Put clods upon his head,   lumps of grassy soil/turf
And they hae sworn a solemn oath   have
  John Barleycorn was dead.

But the cheerful Spring came kindly on,
10   And show'rs began to fall;
John Barleycorn got up again,
  And sore surpris'd them all.

The sultry suns of Summer came,
  And he grew thick and strong,
15 His head weel arm'd wi' pointed spears,   with
  That no one should him wrong.

The sober Autumn enter'd mild,
  When he grew wan and pale;
His bending joints and drooping head
20   Show'd he began to fail.

His colour sicken'd more and more,
  He faded into age;
And then his enemies began
  To show their deadly rage.

1 This is partly composed on the plan of an old song known by the same name. R.B.

25   They've taen a weapon long and sharp,   taken
         And cut him by the knee;
    Then ty'd him fast upon a cart,   tied
         Like a rogue for forgerie.

    They laid him down upon his back,
30   And cudgell'd him full sore;   smashed
    They hung him up before the storm,
         And turn'd him o'er and o'er.

    They filled up a darksome pit
         With water to the brim,
35   They heaved in John Barleycorn,
         There let him sink or swim.

    They laid him out upon the floor,
         To work him farther woe,
    And still, as signs of life appear'd,
40   They toss'd him to and fro.

    They wasted, o'er a scorching flame
         The marrow of his bones;
    But a Miller us'd him worst of all,
         For he crush'd him between two stones.

45   And they hae taen his very heart's blood,   have taken
         And drank it round and round;
    And still the more and more they drank,
         Their joy did more abound.

    John Barleycorn was a hero bold,
50   Of noble enterprise,
    For if you do but taste his blood,
         'Twill make your courage rise.

    'Twill make a man forget his woe;
         'Twill heighten all his joy;
55   'Twill make the widow's heart to sing,
         Tho' the tear were in her eye.

    Then let us toast John Barleycorn,
         Each man a glass in hand;
    And may his great posterity
60   Ne'er fail in old Scotland.

Composition is generally dated to around 1785, although Kinsley believes it was written earlier. In the *FCB* Burns writes, 'John Barleycorn. – A Song, to its own Tune. I once heard the old song that goes by this name, sung; and being very fond of it, and remembering only two or three verses of it viz the 1st, 2nd and 3rd, with some scraps which I have interwoven here and there in the following piece', June 1785. Kinsley probably over-stresses the importance of the myth of the Corn Spirit still prevalent in the 18th century as the 'kernel' theme of this song, the notion that the 'old man of vegitation' is driven out of the corn at threshing time to inhabit the fields, then returns to be the spirit of the next crop (Vol. III, p. 1017). Low is probably right in assuming Burns had read or heard the chapbook song of 1781, the allegory of drink titled *The Whole Trial and Indictment of Sir John Barleycorn, Knt., A Person of Noble Birth and Extraction . . . Being Accused of Several Misdemeanours . . . killing some, wounding others, and bringing thousands to Beggary* (p. 82). The song celebrates both the positive social influence of whisky as a prompt to friendship and waves the national flag of Scotland in the name of John Barleycorn in the final stanzas. It is a record of events, from seedtime to harvest, on till the brewing and consumption of whisky. For Burns, John Barleycorn is a hero, not a villain.

When Guilford Good
or Ballad on the American War
Tune: Gillicrankie *or* The Earl of Glencairn's.
Printed in the Edinburgh edition, 1787.

When *Guilford* good our Pilot stood,[1]		
An' did our hellim thraw, man,	helm turn
Ae night, at tea, began a plea,[2]	one
Within *America*, man:	
5 Then up they gat the maskin-pat,	got, tea-pot
And in the sea did jaw, man;	dash
An' did nae less, in full Congress,	no
Than quite refuse our law, man.	

1 Frederick, Lord North (1732–92).
2 The Boston tea party of 1773.

Then thro' the lakes *Montgomery* takes,[3]
10   I wat he was na slaw, man;   *wot, not slow*
Down *Lowrie's Burn* he took a turn,   *St Lawrence river*
      And *Carleton* did ca', man:[4]   *call*
But yet, whatreck, he at *Quebec*   *what matter*
      Montgomery-like did fa', man,   *fall*
15 Wi' sword in hand, before his band,
      Amang his en'mies a', man.   *among, all*

Poor *Tammy Gage* within a cage[5]
      Was kept at *Boston-ha'*, man;   *hall*
Till *Willie Howe* took o'er the knowe[6]   *hill edge*
20   For *Philadelphia*, man:
Wi' sword an' gun he thought a sin
      Guid Christian bluid to draw, man;   *good, blood*
But at *New-York* wi' knife an' fork
      Sir Loin he hacked sma', man.[7]   *small*

25 *Burgoyne* gaed up, like spur an' whip,[8]   *went*
      Till *Fraser* brave did fa', man;[9]   *fall*
Then lost his way, ae misty day,   *one*
      In *Saratoga* shaw, man.   *wood*
Cornwallis fought as lang's he dought,[10]   *long as he could*
30   An' did the Buckskins claw, man;   *colonists*
But *Clinton's* glaive frae rust to save,[11]   *sword, from*
      He hung it to the wa' man.   *wall*

Then *Montague*, an' *Guilford* too,[12]
      Began to fear a fa', man;   *fall*
35 And *Sackville* doure, wha stood the stoure[13] *obstinate, who fought*
      The German Chief to thraw, man: *thwart*

3 Richard Montgomery.
4 Guy Carleton.
5 General Gage (1721–88), Governor of Massachusetts.
6 Sir William Howe (d. 1814).
7 This alludes to the seizure of rebel cattle by the Hudson, at Peekskill, 1776.
8 Sir John Burgoyne (1722–92).
9 Brigadier Simon Fraser.
10 Charles Conrnwallis (1738–1805).
11 Sir Henry Clinton (1738–95).
12 John Montague, Earl of Sandwich.
13 Lord George Sackville (1716–85) who was at Culloden with the Duke of Cumberland.

For Paddy *Burke*, like ony Turk,[14]   any
    Nae mercy had at a', man;   no, all
An' *Charlie Fox* threw by the box,[15]
40   An' lows'd his tinkler jaw, man.   let loose, gypsy mouth

Then *Rockingham* took up the game;[16]
    Till Death did on him ca', man;   call
When *Shelburne* meek held up his cheek,[17]
    Conform to Gospel law, man:
45 Saint Stephen's boys, wi' jarring noise,   M.P.'s, loud
    They did his measures thraw, man;   thwart/turn
For *North* an' *Fox* united stocks,
    An' bore him to the wa', man.   wall

Then Clubs an' Hearts were Charlie's cartes,   cards
50   He swept the stakes awa', man,   away
Till the Diamond's Ace, of *Indian* race,   Fox's East India Bill
    Led him a sair *faux pas*, man: sore
The Saxon lads, wi loud placads,   cheers
    On *Chatham's Boy* did ca', man;[18]   call
55 An' Scotland drew her pipe an' blew:
    'Up, Willie, waur them a', man!'   worst

Behind the throne then *Grenville's* gone,[19]
    A secret word or twa, man;   two
While slee *Dundas* arous'd the class[20]   sly
60   Be-north the Roman wa', man: wall
An' *Chatham's* wraith, in heav'nly graith,   ghost, garments
    (Inspired Bardies saw, man),
Wi' kindling eyes, cry'd, 'Willie, rise!
    Would I hae fear'd them a', man!'   have

65 But, word an' blow, *North, Fox,* and *Co.*
    Gowff'd *Willie* like a ba', man,   golfed, ball
Till *Suthron* raise an' coost their claise   rose, cast their clothes
    Behind him in a raw, man: naked

14 Edmund Burke (1727–97) ; alluding to his Irish origin.
15 Charles James Fox (1749–1806), Whig Leader.
16 The Marquis of Rockingham, Charles Watson Wentworth (1730–82).
17 The Earl of Shelbourne (1737–1805).
18 William Pitt, the Younger (1759–1806).
19 William Wyndham (1759–1834) Lord Grenville.
20 Henry Dundas (1742–1811), Secretary of State for Scotland.

An' *Caledon* threw by the drone,   bagpipe sound
70   An' did her whittle draw, man;   knife
An' swoor fu' rude, thro' dirt an' bluid,   swore full, blood
        To mak it guid in law, man.   good

Though he did not risk publishing it in the Kilmarnock edition, this is Burns's first political poem. It is, thus, seminal in several important ways. For the first time it brings not only the world of late eighteenth-century British but international politics before the wickedly reductive court of Burns's Scottish vernacular energies. Second, it demonstrates for the first time his astonishing powers of compressed narrative. Here he records in a mere nine stanzas not only the genesis of the American War of Independence and politically significant campaigns in that war but also the extreme disruption provoked in British politics by the loss of America. Third, it signals his acutely self-endangering ambition, from his marginal social position, to comment politically on the world of kings and counsellors. As he was soon to write:

But Politics, truce! we're on dangerous ground;
        Who knows how the fashions may alter:
The doctrines today that are loyalty sound,
        Tomorrow may bring us a halter.

Further, that this is a *song* with its thumping ('man') alternate line repetition entails that he desires maximum public exposure for it. This engenders a triple-headed problem that would increasingly preoccupy him. Would he be allowed to publish it? What final strategies might he employ to disguise the explosive nature of the material? If such strategies, most frequently that of the smiler with the knife, were impossible, how might he get such explosive political material into the political realm without disclosing his authorship?

This song emphasises the first of these problems. He had some thought of placing it in the Kilmarnock edition. He then consulted his Whig patron, the Earl of Glencairn, subsequently writing to his Masonic associate in the Canongate Lodge, Henry Erskine:

I showed the enclosed political ballad to my Lord Glencairn, to have his opinion whether I should publish it; as I suspect my political tenets, such as they are, may be rather heretical in the opinion of some of my best friends. I have a few first principles in Religion and Politics which, I believe, I would not easily part with; but for the etiquette of, by whom, in what manners &c. I would not have a dissocial word about it with any one of God's creatures, particularly an honoured Patron, or a respected Friend (Letter 70).

That he might upset Glencairn and Erskine, Whig sympathisers with the American cause, seems odd until we consider his treatment of the parliamentarian Rockingham Whigs, Fox and Burke, in the latter part of the poem. He did certainly, however, upset the Tory pro-Hanoverian Edinburgh establishment. It was of this poem that, according to Lockhart (Vol. I, p. 205), Hugh Blair remarked 'Burns's politics always smell of the smithy'. His card was thus marked from the outset.

This snooty disdain for the allegedly sooty is, embryonically, that pervasive state of mind which, consciously and otherwise, has so successfully sought to exclude Burns as socially inferior poet, no matter his political intelligence, from commenting on his alleged betters. With regard to American affairs, as we have seen in the Introduction, Burns was passionately pro-American. Further, by denying this political element in Burns, Blair was also disguising the strong pro-American republican culture in Edinburgh which Burns knew about both by his membership of the Crochallan Fencibles and his avaricious reading of the Edinburgh press. Alfred A. Kline in a stimulating Columbia University doctorate written as long ago as 1953, *The English Romantics and the American Republic: An Analysis of the Concept of America in the Work of Blake, Burns, Wordsworth, Coleridge, Byron and Shelley* is deeply salutary in two respects. In general terms, it reminds us of the political company which Burns's poetry keeps. Blake's *America*, for example, though mythopoetically distinct from Burns's, is profoundly similar in content. Central to Wordsworth's *Guilt and Sorrow* or *Incidents Upon Salisbury Plain* (See commentary on *A Winter Night*) is a hellish vision of the American war as recalled by the returned widowed vagrant of one of the dead British redcoats who, revealingly, became termed in that conflict, 'bloody-backs': 'dog-like wading at the heels of War . . . a cursed existence with the brood/ That lap, their very nourishment, their brother's blood'.

Kline also provides evidence of the degree to which radical elements in Edinburgh were attracted to the American cause. Thus Richard Price's *Letter to the Secretary of the Committee of Citizens in Edinburgh, The Scots Magazine* (April, 1784), comments:

God grant that this spirit may increase till it has abolished all despotic government and exterminated the slavery which debase mankind. This spirit first rose in America – it soon reached Ireland – it has diffused itself in some foreign countries, and your letter informs me that it is now animating Scotland (p. 179).

As we saw in the Introduction, Price was influential for Burns. In January 1791 we find (Letter 430) Burns ordering from Peter Hill Dr Price's *Dissertations on Providence, Prayer, Death & Miracles*. Whether Burns also read Price's subtle, balanced *Observations an the Importance of the American Revolution and the Means of Making It A Benefit to the World* is uncertain. What is certain is that he would have agreed with its provocative sentiments (See *Richard Price: Political Writings*, ed. D.O. Thomas, Cambridge: 1991). Kline also quotes Professor W.P. Ker, whose scholarship led him to define Burns as a Tory Unionist, saying 'Burns must have read the newspapers . . . and *The Scots Magazine* with extraordinary care', to which Kline adds that this included back issues. Thus the first part of this poem is again dependent on Burns transmuting newspaper prose into poetry, as, indeed, is the latter part dealing with the political shambles in Britain consequent to the American defeat.

The first stanza deals with the good Guilford, the Prime Minister, and Lord North, whose wrecking seamanship led to the loss of North America. After the inception of the war by the taxation policy leading to the Boston Tea Party, Burns narrates the campaign leading up to the Americans' ('Buckskins') culminating in victory with Cornwallis's surrender at Yorktown, 10th October 1781 with Clinton unable to break though from New York to relieve him.

The second stanza deals with a double pronged American attack in 1775 into Canada against Quebec and Montreal. What is of particular significance is that the second-in-command of the Montreal force was Richard Montgomery, one of the Montgomerys of Coylfield celebrated by Burns in his eulogy to the greatness sprung from Ayrshire soil in *The Vision*. Montreal surrendered to Montgomery who then set down 'Lowrie's Burn' to support Arnold at Quebec, where he was killed in the assault. What, of course, Burns is implying is the heroism of not just a Scottish but an Ayrshire martyr dying for the American cause.

The third stanza deals with the passive General Gage being replaced by Sir William Howe who, despite his victories over the Americans at Bunker Hill and near Philadelphia could not change the course of the war. Despite his deep reservations at spilling American blood, Howe's army 'butchered' three thousand colonists and captured many cattle at Peerskill Fort on the Hudson in November 1776.

The fourth stanza narrates the triumph of American arms. General Burgoyne advancing into Albany in the autumn of 1777 was forced to surrender to an American army three times his size at Saratoga on 17th October. Simon Frazer (another Scottish hero) was killed at the battle of Freeman's Farm.

The defeat in America was of such catastrophic proportions that it threw the British political system into extreme factionalism, especially given George III's hatred of the Whigs in general and Fox in particular. Added to this there was the problem of making peace with France, combined with the matter of India and the East India Company and the chronic Irish problem. This produced spasmodically rapid changes of administration based on the unlikeliest of alliances, in particular that between North and Fox. What is poetically astonishing about this, is that Burns, from a provincial viewpoint at the beginning of his poetic career, can compress the roller-coaster clamour of St Stephen's (then the site of Parliament) into a mere five stanzas. Undoubtedly he was aided by not only the newspapers but the cartoons. As for example, L.G. Mitchell (in *Charles James Fox*, London, 1992) notes:

> True, some cartoons appeared showing Fox as Cromwell or Carlo Khan, riding down Leadenhall St on the back of an Indian elephant but others portrayed him as the new Demosthenes or as the 'Champion of the People'. Against anti-Coalition songs must be set images showing Pitt, riding the white horse of Despotic Hanover, battling with Fox, sitting aside the British Lion . . . Hitherto, these two young men had jointly been the hope of the reformers. Now, they were opponents and shackled by alliances to non-reformers. Which of them would prove to be the long-term friend of reformers had to be debated at public meetings all over England, and the divisions set up at these assemblies fatally harmed the reform movement as a whole. Christopher Wyvill opted for Pitt, declaring that Fox wished to change our limited Monarchy into a mere Aristocratic Republic. William Mason thought that all politics would be corruption if 'Charles Fox had the Indies at his disposal' (pp. 68–9).

Mitchell's lucid remarks should also alert us to the fact that Burns's political responses to British party politics, often represented as eccentric and quixotic, were based on the national dilemma between the relative potential of Fox and Pitt to deliver reform. Fox, with his swarthy, 'tinkler jaw' remained, to a degree, oportunistic and licentious. Pitt, to many, including Burns, at this time looked the more reforming politician. Certainly Burns was not one of the 'inspired Bardies' when he wrote this. He was not to know how catastrophically his and Scotland's support for 'Willie' Pitt and, far worse, 'slee' Dundas was to rebound on them both. Compared to the political opportunism of the age, Burns is, however, a figure of profound stability. Who could, for example, switch positions more than 'Paddy' Burke? As we shall see this exclusive identification of Burke by his Irish forename diminutive is tellingly to reappear in the recently recovered poem *The Dagger* (see Anonymous and Pseudonymous Section).

My Nanie, O

Tune: My Nanie, O
First published, Edinburgh, 1787.

Behind yon hills where Stinchar flows[1]   those
   'Mang moors an' mosses many, O,
The wintry sun the day has clos'd,
   And I'll awa to Nanie, O.

5 The westlin wind blaws loud an' shill,   shrill
   The night's baith mirk and rainy, O;   both, dark
But I'll get my plaid an' out I'll steal,   cloth garment
   An' owre the hill to Nanie, O.   over

My Nanie's charming, sweet, an' young;
10   Nae artfu' wiles to win ye, O: no
May ill befa' the flattering tongue   befall
   That wad beguile my Nanie, O!   would

Her face is fair, her heart is true,
   As spotless as she's bonie, O;
15 The op'ning gowan, wat wi' dew,   flower, wet
   Nae purer is than Nanie, O.

A country lad is my degree,
   An' few there be that ken me, O;   know
But what care I how few they be,
20   I'm welcome ay to Nanie, O.   always

1 Burns, at the suggestion of George Thomson, allowed the name of the river to be changed from Stinchar to Lugar.

My riches a's my penny-fee,   paltry wages
    An' I maun guide it cannie, O;   will, careful
But warl's gear ne'er troubles me,   world's
    My thoughts are a', my Nanie, O.

25 Our auld Guidman delights to view   old, goodman
    His sheep an' kye thrive bonie, O;   cattle
But I'm as blythe that hauds his pleugh,   holds, plough
    An' has nae care but Nanie, O.

Come weel come woe, I care na by,
30   I'll tak what Heav'n will send me, O:
Nae ither care in life have I,   other
    But live, an' love my Nanie, O.

The date of composition is uncertain, although an early draft is written in the *FCB*, April 1784. Mrs Begg claimed the poet's father saw and liked the song. Given that he died in February 1784, that would suggest composition sometime during the early 1780s. The heroine of the song has been invariably named as Agnes Sherriff of Kilmarnock, or Agnes Fleming, daughter of a Tarbolton tenant farmer. Burns saw the song as 'pastoral simplicity' with a 'dash of our native tongue' (Letter 511). The song was also printed in SC, 1793, then in S.M.M. (1803), no. 580.

Green Grow the Rashes, O

Tune: Green Grow the Rashes, O
First printed in the Edinburgh edition, 1787.

Chorus
Green grow the rashes, O;
    Green grow the rashes, O;
The sweetest hours that e'er I spend,
    Are spent among the lasses, O.

5 There's nought but care on ev'ry han',   nothing, hand
    In ev'ry hour that passes, O:
What signifies the life o' man,
    An' 'twere na for the lasses, O.   if it were not
      Green grow &c.

The war'ly race may riches chase,   worldly
10   An' riches still may fly them, O;
An' tho' at last they catch them fast,
     Their hearts can ne'er enjoy them, O.
         Green grow &c.

But gie me a cannie hour at e'en,   give, quiet, evening
     My arms about my Dearie, O;
15   An' war'ly cares, an' war'ly men,   worldly
     May a' gae tapsalteerie, O!   topsy-turvy
         Green grow &c.

For you sae douce, ye sneer at this,   so prudent
     Ye're nought but senseless asses, O: nothing
The wisest Man the warl' e'er saw,   world
20   He dearly lov'd the lasses, O.
         Green grow &c.

Auld Nature swears, the lovely dears
     Her noblest work she classes, O:
Her prentice han' she try'd on man,   hand
     An' then she made the lasses, O.

This song also featured in S.M.M. in 1787, number 77. It was
composed, bar the final verse, in 1784 and is recorded in the *FCB*,
dated August, where the song follows a lengthy prose commentary
on 'the two Grand Classes' of men, the 'Grave and the Merry'. The
song is a fine example of the poet's early skill, developed by his tutor
Murdoch, in writing out lines of poetry from his own prose. Having
written out his observations on the two main classifications of men,
the poet introduces the song: 'I shall set down the following
fragment which, as it is the genuine language of my heart, will
enable any body to determine which of the Classes I belong to'. A
further verse, developing this theme, but replacing the power of
Nature with God, is recorded by Low (p. 106) from the MSS, Lady
Stair's House, Edinburgh):

Frae Man's ain side God made his wark
     That a' the lave surpasses O
The Man but lo'es his ain heart's bluid
     Wha dearly lo'es the lasses O.

Again Rejoicing Nature Sees

Tune: Johnny's Grey Breeks
First printed in the Edinburgh edition, 1787.

Again rejoicing Nature sees
 Her robe assume its vernal hues,
Her leafy locks wave in the breeze
 All freshly steep'd in morning dews.

Chorus[1]
5 And maun I still on Menie[2] doat,   must, dote
  And bear the scorn that's in her e'e! eye
For it's jet, jet-black, an' it's like a hawk,
  An' it winna let a body be! will not

In vain to me the cowslips blaw,   blow
10 In vain to me the vi'lets spring; violets
In vain to me in glen or shaw,   wood
  The mavis and the lintwhite sing.
  And maun I still &c.

The merry Ploughboy cheers his team,
  Wi' joy the tentie Seedsman stalks, careful
15 But life to me 's a weary dream,
  A dream of ane that never wauks. one, wakes
  And maun I still &c.

The wanton coot the water skims,
  Amang the reeds the ducklings cry, among
The stately swan majestic swims,
20 And ev'ry thing is blest but I.
  And maun I still &c.

The Sheep-herd steeks his faulding slap, shuts, sheep-fold gate
  And owre the moorlands whistles shill, shrill
Wi' wild, unequal, wand'ring step
  I meet him on the dewy hill.
  And maun I still &c.

1 This chorus is part of a song composed by a gentleman in Edinburgh, a particular friend of the Author's. R.B.
2 Menie is the common abbreviation of Marianne. R.B.

25   And when the lark, 'tween light and dark,
       Blythe waukens by the daisy's side,   wakens
   And mounts and sings on flittering wings,
       A woe-worn ghaist I hameward glide.   ghost, homeward
       And maun I still &c.

   Come Winter, with thine angry howl,
30   And raging bend the naked tree;
   Thy gloom will soothe my cheerless soul,
       When Nature all is sad like me!
       And maun I still &c.

The title of this is merely 'Song' in Kinsley (no. 138). In the Mackay edition it is given as *And Maun I Still on Menie Doat*, being the first line of the chorus (p. 266). The chorus, though, was written by a friend of the poet's, as admitted by Burns in his notes when published in 1787; the first line written by Burns is given here as the title, 'Again rejoicing Nature sees'. In verse five, Mackay has changed the original 'shill' to 'shrill', changing the older word for its modern meaning, a word Burns did not employ. He further omits the poet's note indicating he did not write the chorus.

The Gloomy Night is Gathering Fast

Tune: Roslin Castle
First printed in the Edinburgh edition, 1787.

   The gloomy night is gath'ring fast,
       Loud roars the wild inconstant blast,
   Yon murky cloud is filled with rain,
       I see it driving o'er the plain;
5   The Hunter now has left the moor,
       The scatt'red coveys meet secure,
   While here I wander, prest with care,
       Along the lonely banks of *Ayr*.

   The Autumn mourns her rip'ning corn
10   By early Winter's ravage torn;
   Across her placid, azure sky,
       She sees the scowling tempest fly:
   Chill runs my blood to hear it rave,
       I think upon the stormy wave,
15   Where many a danger I must dare,
       Far from the bonie banks of *Ayr*.   bonny

'Tis not the surging billows' roar,
    'Tis not that fatal, deadly shore;
Tho' Death in ev'ry shape appear,
20   The Wretched have no more to fear:
But round my heart the ties are bound,
    That heart transpierc'd with many a wound;
These bleed afresh, those ties I tear,
    To leave the bonie banks of *Ayr*.

25 Farewell, old *Coila's* hills and dales,
    Her heathy moors and winding vales;
The scenes where wretched Fancy roves,
    Pursuing past unhappy loves!
Farewell my friends! farewell my foes!
30   My peace with these, my love with those —
The bursting tears my heart declare,
    Farewell, my bonie banks of *Ayr*.

This was composed in the late Autumn of 1786 when the problems
of the poet's personal life still prompted him to think of emigrating
from Scotland. To Dr Moore Burns explained that this was to be his
final parting song to his friends and homeland (Letter 125). Personal
vexations are evident in the final couplets, referring to a last farewell
of 'friends!' and 'foes!' It is clearly the case that in the poet's
thoughts of sailing to Jamaica he held concerns that a winter journey
by sea could be perilous on 'the stormy wave, /Where many a danger
I must dare'.

No Churchman am I

Tune: Prepare, my dear Brethren
The final song of the Edinburgh edition, 1787.

No Churchman am I for to rail and to write,
No Statesman nor Soldier to plot or to fight,
No sly man of business contriving a snare,
For a big-belly'd bottle's the whole of my care.

5 The Peer I don't envy, I give him his bow;
I scorn not the Peasant, tho' ever so low;
But a club of good fellows, like those that are here,
And a bottle like this, are my glory and care.

Here passes the Squire on his brother — his horse;
10   There Centum per Centum, the Cit with his purse,   *citizen*
But see you the Crown, how it waves in the air,   *coins*
There a big-belly'd bottle still eases my care.

The wife of my bosom, alas! she did die;
For sweet consolation to church I did fly;
15   I found that old Solomon proved it fair,
That a big-belly'd bottle's a cure for all care.

I once was persuaded a venture to make;
A letter inform'd me that all was to wreck;
But the pursy old landlord just waddled up stairs,   *focused on money*
20   With a glorious bottle that ended my cares.

'Life's cares they are comforts'[1]— a maxim laid down
By the Bard, what d'ye call him, that wore the black gown;
And faith I agree with th' old prig to a hair;
For a big-belly'd bottle's a heav'n of care.

A STANZA ADDED IN A MASON LODGE
Then fill up a bumper and make it o'erflow,
And honours Masonic prepare for to throw:
May ev'ry true Brother of the Compass and Square   *Masonic instruments*
Have a big-belly'd bottle, when harass'd with care!

The poet was entered an apprentice member of the Freemasons'
Lodge at Tarbolton in 1781 and composed this song, fully aware that
the tune formed part of Masonic culture, entitled *The Freemasons'
March* (Aird's collection of *Airs*, 1782). An earlier version of the
tune, 1730, was known as *Freemasons' Health* (Low, p. 84). Com-
position is assumed to be sometime in the winter of 1783–4, although
earlier editors place it in the 1781–2 period. Kinsley records that a
political stanza was suppressed in 1787 which alluded to William
Pitt and the governmental inquiry into Warren Hastings, which
would make the later date accurate. A song with the line 'And a big-
bellied bottle's a mighty good thing' was published in 1751, then
again in a collection owned by Burns in 1783, *A Select Collection of
English Songs*. The song was also printed in S.M.M. no. 587, 1803.
The quotation from Edward Young's *Night Thoughts*, 'Life's cares
they are comforts' is taken from Part II, l. 160.

1 Young's *Night Thoughts*. R.B.

PART THREE

The Edinburgh Edition
1793

Written in Friar's Carse Hermitage,

First printed in the Edinburgh edition, 1793.
On the Banks of Nith – Dec 1788.

Thou whom chance may hither lead,
Be thou clad in russet weed,
Be thou deckt in silken stole,
Grave these counsels on thy soul.

5   Life is but a day at most,
Sprung from night, in darkness lost:
Hope not sunshine ev'ry hour,
Fear not clouds will always lour.

     As Youth and Love with sprightly dance
10 Beneath thy morning star advance,
Pleasure with her siren air
May delude the thoughtless pair;
Let Prudence bless Enjoyment's cup,
Then raptur'd sip and sip it up. –

15   As thy day grows warm and high,
Life's meridian flaming nigh,
Dost thou spurn the humble vale?
Life's proud summits would'st thou scale?
Check thy climbing step, elate,
20 Evils lurk in felon-wait:
Dangers, eagle-pinioned, bold,
Soar around each cliffy hold;
While cheerful Peace, with linnet song,
Chants the lowly dells among.

25   As the shades of ev'ning close,
Beck'ning thee to long repose;
As life itself becomes disease,
Seek the chimney-nook of Ease.
There ruminate with sober thought;

30   On all thou'st seen, and heard, and wrought;
    And teach the sportive Younkers round,
    Saws of experience, sage and sound:
    Say, man's true, genuine estimate,
    The grand criterion of his fate,
35   Is not, Art thou high or low?
    Did thy fortune ebb or flow?
    Did many talents gild thy span?
    Or frugal Nature grudge thee one?
    Tell them, and press it on their mind,
40   As thou thyself must shortly find,
    The smile or frown of awful Heav'n,
    To Virtue or to Vice is giv'n.
    Say, to be just, and kind, and wise,
    There solid self-enjoyment lies;
45   That foolish, selfish, faithless ways,
    Lead to be wretched, vile, and base.

      Thus, resign'd and quiet, creep
    To the bed of lasting sleep;
    Sleep, whence thou shall ne'er awake,
50   Night, where dawn shall never break,
    Till Future Life, future no more,
    To light and joy the good restore,
    To light and joy unknown before.

    Stranger, go! Heav'n be thy guide!
55   Quod the Beadsman of Nith-side.

This is generally described as the first poetical production to flourish from the friendship of Burns and his nearest neighbour at Ellisland, Captain Robert Riddell (1755–94). Riddell owned the Friar's Carse estate and was well known as an antiquarian, musician and outspoken Whig. Riddell contributed several radical polemical essays to various newspapers of the period, one being the essay signed Cato sent by Burns to *The Edinburgh Gazetteer* in December 1792 (Letter 530). Riddell built the small hermitage, situated almost one mile from Ellisland, on the banks of the river Nith and provided the poet with a key, allowing him to use it whenever he desired. The hermitage is still extant, although it was re-built in the twentieth century. Scott Douglas records that he visited the site and found it in ruins in the latter part of the 19th century.

    Kinsley gives two versions of this poem. He presents the first early draft as the main poem, then prints the final polished version as a secondary work, titled 'Altered from the Foregoing – Dec – 1788', no. K223B. Although there are significant differences between the two versions, Burns only printed the final edition in 1793. He did not publish the early draft. It appeared as a separate poem in 1801 with Dr Currie's second edition of the poems of Burns. The version given here is the final draft, updated by Burns in December 1788 and published in 1793.

The earliest version found its way into print via an unauthorised source. Burns remarked to David Blair (a Birmingham Gunmaker) in August 1789, 'I know nothing how the Publishers could get it, but as I had given several copies to my friends, it has found its way, I suppose, thro' the well-meant, though blameable officiousness of some of them. – I have a little altered, and, I think, improved that poem . . .' (Letter 360). Kinsley mentions another unsanctioned publication in the *Glasgow Weekly Miscellany*, for 31st November 1791, which may have been forwarded by Robert Riddell. The final version is, as Burns comments, the superior work.

Elegy on Captain Matthew Henderson
A Gentleman who Held the Patent for his Honours Immediately from Almighty God!

First printed in the *Edinburgh Magazine*, August 1790, prior to publication in the Edinburgh edition, 1793.

> *But now his radiant course is run,*
> *For Matthew's course was bright:*
> *His soul was like the glorious sun*
> *A matchless, Heavenly light.*
> BURNS.

O DEATH! thou tyrant fell and bloody!	
The meikle Devil wi' a woodie	great, halter
Haurl thee hame to his black smiddie,	trail, home, smithy
O'er hurcheon hides,	hedgehog
5 And like stock-fish come o'er his studdie	strike, anvil
Wi' thy auld sides!	old
He's gane! he's gane! he's frae us torn,	gone, gone, from
The ae best fellow e'er was born!	one
Thee, Matthew, Nature's sel' shall mourn	self
10 By wood and wild,	
Where, haply, Pity strays forlorn,	
Frae man exil'd.	from

Ye hills, near neebors o' the starns,   *neighbours, stars*
That proudly cock your cresting cairns;   *display*
15 Ye cliffs, the haunts of sailing yearns,   *eagles*
       Where Echo slumbers,
Come join, ye Nature's sturdiest bairns,   *children*
       My wailing numbers.

Mourn, ilka grove the cushat kens;   *every, wood-pigeon knows*
20 Ye hazelly shaws and briery dens;   *woods, hollows*
Ye burnies, wimplin down your glens,   *rivulets, winding*
       Wi' toddlin din,   *trickling noise*
Or foaming, strang, wi' hasty stens,   *strong, leaps/churns*
       Frae lin to lin.   *from, waterfall*

25 Mourn little harebells o'er the lea;   *hill edge*
Ye stately foxgloves fair to see;
Ye woodbines hanging bonilie,
       In scented bowers;
Ye roses on your thorny tree,
30   The first o' flowers.

At dawn, when every grassy blade
Droops with a diamond at his head,
At even', when beans their fragrance shed,
       I' th' rustling gale,
35 Ye maukins whiddin through the glade,   *hares, skipping*
       Come join my wail.

Mourn, ye wee songsters o' the wood;
Ye grouse that crap the heather bud;   *crop/eat*
Ye curlews calling thro' a clud;   *cloud*
40   Ye whistling plover;
And mourn, ye whirring paitrick brood;   *partridge*
       He's gane for ever!   *gone*

Mourn, sooty coots, and speckled teals;   *black*
Ye fisher herons, watching eels;
45 Ye duck and drake, wi' airy wheels
       Circling the lake:
Ye bitterns, till the quagmire reels,
       Rair for his sake.   *roar*

Mourn, clam'ring craiks at close o' day,   corncrakes
50   'Mang fields o' flow'ring clover gay;
And when you wing your annual way
          Frae our cauld shore,   from, cold
Tell thae far warlds, wha lies in clay,   they, worlds, who
          Wham we deplore.   what

55   Ye houlets, frae your ivy bower,   from
In some auld tree, or eldritch tower,   old, haunted
What time the moon, wi' silent glowr,   glower/stare
          Sets up her horn,
Wail thro' the dreary midnight hour
60   Till waukrife morn.   wakeful

O rivers, forests, hills, and plains!
Oft have ye heard my canty strains: cheery/joyful
But now, what else for me remains
          But tales of woe?
65   And frae my een the drapping rains   eyes, dropping
          Maun ever flow.   must/shall

Mourn, Spring, thou darling of the year!
Ilk cowslip cup shall kep a tear: each, catch
Thou, Simmer, while each corny spear   summer
70   Shoots up its head,
Thy gay, green, flowery tresses shear,
          For him that's dead.

Thou, Autumn, wi' thy yellow hair,
In grief thy sallow mantle tear;
75   Thou, Winter, hurling thro' the air
          The roaring blast,
Wide o'er the naked world declare
          The worth we've lost.

Mourn him, thou Sun, great source of light!
80   Mourn, Empress of the silent night!
And you, ye twinkling starnies bright,   little stars
          My Matthew mourn;
For through your orbs he's taen his flight,   taken
          Ne'er to return.

85   O Henderson! the man! the brother!
    And art thou gone, and gone for ever?
    And hast thou crost that unknown river,   crossed
        Life's dreary bound?
    Like thee, where shall I find another,
90   The world around?

    Go to your sculptur'd tombs, ye Great,
    In a' the tinsel trash o' state!
    But by thy honest turf I'll wait,
        Thou man of worth!
95   And weep the ae best fellow's fate   one/very
        E'er lay in earth.

THE EPITAPH
STOP, passenger! — my story's brief,
    And truth I shall relate, man;
    I tell nae common tale o' grief —   no
100   For Matthew was a great man.

    If thou uncommon merit hast,
        Yet spurn'd at Fortune's door, man,
    A look of pity hither cast —
        For Matthew was a poor man.

105 If thou a noble sodger art,   soldier
        That passest by this grave, man,
    There moulders here a gallant heart —
        For Matthew was a brave man.

    If thou on men, their works and ways,
110   Canst throw uncommon light, man,
    Here lies wha weel had won thy praise —   who well
        For Matthew was a bright man.

    If thou, at Friendship's sacred ca'   call
        Wad life itself resign, man,   would
115 Thy sympathetic tear maun fa' —   must fall
        For Matthew was a kind man.

    If thou art staunch without a stain,
        Like the unchanging blue, man,
120 This was a kinsman o' thy ain —   own
        For Matthew was a true man.

If thou hast wit, and fun, and fire,
    And ne'er guid wine did fear, man,   good
This was thy billie, dam, and sire —   comrade
    For Matthew was a queer man.   roguish

125   If onie whiggish, whingin' sot,   any, whining
    To blame poor Matthew dare, man,
May dool and sorrow be his lot!   woe/sadness
    For Matthew was a rare man.

Kinsley gives the following biographical details: 'Matthew Henderson (1737–88) of Tannochside was a lieutenant in the Earl of Home's regiment, and later held a civil service post in Edinburgh. He was an acquaintance of Boswell's, one of a 'genteel, profligate society who live like a distinct nation in Edinburgh, having constant recruits coming and going' (*Boswell in Search of a Wife 1766–1769*, ed. Brady and Pottle, 1957, p. 125). Henderson was also a Mason and an antiquarian. He was forced by his convivial extravagance to sell his property, and when Burns met him in 1787 he was subsisting on a pension. He was buried in Greyfriars churchyard on 27 November 1788. What Kinsley fails to mention is that Henderson was a member of that dissident, reformist, pro-American, drouthy group, The Crochallan Fencibles. Thus in habits, interests and politics, this was a man after the Bard's own heart. In the copy of the letter he sent to Dugald Stewart he reported that Henderson:

> . . . was an intimate acquaintance of mine; and of all Mankind I ever knew, he was one of the first. . . for a nice sense of honour, a generous contempt for the adventitious distinctions of Men, and sterling tho' sometimes outré Wit. – The inclosed Elegy has pleased me beyond any of my late poetic efforts. – Perhaps 'tis 'the memory of the joys that are past,' and a friend who is no more that biases my criticism. – It is likewise, ever since I read your Aiken on the poetic uses of Natural history, a favourite study of mine, the characters of the Vegetable and the manners of the Animal kingdom. – I regret much that I cannot have your strictures on this Poem. – How I have succeeded on the whole – if there is any incongruity in the imagery – or whether I have not omitted some apt rural paintings altogether (Letter 410).

The poem has all the energy of Burns's elegy for Tam Sampson without, alas, the happy ending. The poet invokes landscape, fish, animals, the seasons, the sun and stars, the very grass itself into a hyperbolic chorus of pathetic fallacy which emerges from a synthesis of his readings in late eighteenth-century natural philosophy

and his creative extension of the powerful elegiac poetry found in
Ramsay and Fergusson, particularly in the latter's *Elegy On the
Death of Scots Music*, ll. 13–18 (*Poems*, STS, ii, 38):

> Mourn ilka nymph and ilka swain,
> Ilk sunny hill and dowie glen;
> Let weeping streams and Naiads drain
>   Their fountain head;
> Let echo swell the dolefu' strain,
>   Since music's dead.

Crawford, in a fine reading of this poem (pp. 211–16), sees in it a
synergetic fusion of earlier eighteenth-century Scottish and English
elegiac elements and also recognises, appropriate to Henderson's
character, the pronounced democratic politics of the piece:

> Since all of Burns is in the background of this elegy, it is not the
> least surprising that the last stanza should have political and
> moral undertones, drawing its main effect from the sharp
> dichotomy of the plebian's simple turf and the elaborate graves
> of the upper classes (ll. 91–6). The quiet rumination of Gray's
> *Elegy* has taken on a Scottish tinge and become imbued with the
> Honest Man's indignation against his aristocratic opponents.
> Even at his most traditional and writing an elegy, Burns could
> not avoid all trace of social criticism. It is only his very worst
> poems that are completely innocuous.
>   *The Epitaph* which concludes the elegy proper is only super-
> ficially divided from the sixteen stanzas that precede it. In
> reality, it develops all the democratic implications of 'thy
> honest turf' and 'Thou man of worth' until it becomes like
> the second half of a diptych: taken together, the two parts
> constitute the complete poem.

Lament of Mary Queen of Scots
on the Approach of Spring

First printed in the Edinburgh edition, 1793.

Now Nature hangs her mantle green
     On every blooming tree,
And spreads her sheets o' daisies white
     Out o'er the grassy lea:
5 Now Phoebus cheers the crystal streams,
     And glads the azure skies;
But nought can glad the weary wight
     That fast in durance lies.

Now laverocks wake the merry morn,   larks
10   Aloft on dewy wing;
The merle, in his noontide bow'r,   blackbird
          Makes woodland echoes ring;
The mavis wild wi' monie a note,   thrush, many
          Sings drowsy day to rest:
15   In love and freedom they rejoice,
          Wi' care nor thrall opprest.

Now blooms the lily by the bank,
          The primrose down the brae;   hillside
The hawthorn's budding in the glen,
20   And milk-white is the slae: sloe
The meanest hind in fair Scotland
          May rove their sweets amang;   among
But I, the Queen of a' Scotland,   all
          Maun lie in prison strang!   must, strong

25   I was the Queen o' bonie France,   beautiful
          Where happy I hae been;   have
Fu' lightly rase I in the morn,   rose
          As blythe lay down at e'en: evening
And I'm the sovereign of Scotland,
30   And mony a traitor there;   many
Yet here I lie in foreign bands,
          And never-ending care.

But as for thee, thou false woman!
          My sister and my fae,   foe
35   Grim vengeance yet shall whet a sword   wet
          That thro' thy soul shall gae!   go
The weeping blood in woman's breast
          Was never known to thee;
Nor th' balm that draps on wounds of woe   drops
40   Frae woman's pitying e'e.   from, eye

My son! my son! my kinder stars
          Upon thy fortune shine!
And may those pleasures gild thy reign,
          That ne'er wad blink on mine!   would
45   God keep thee frae thy mother's faes,   from, foes
          Or turn their hearts to thee:
And where thou meet'st thy mother's friend,
          Remember him for me!

O soon, to me, may Summer suns
50   Nae mair light up the morn!   no more
Nae mair, to me, the Autumn winds   no more
        Wave o'er the yellow corn!
And in the narrow house o' death
        Let Winter round me rave;
55 And the next flowers, that deck the Spring,
        Bloom on my peaceful grave.

Composed in the early summer of 1790, the poem was sent to several
correspondents of Burns, including Mrs Graham of Fintry, who was
addressed as follows: 'Whether it is that the story of our Mary
Queen of Scots has a peculiar effect on the feelings of a Poet, or
whether in the enclosed ballad I have succeeded beyond my usual
poetic success, I know not; but it has pleased me beyond any late
effort of the Muse' (Letter 402). It is a ballad that mixes Scots and
English with a dash of simple antiquated phraseology, particularly
the use of 'glads', then 'glad' in the first stanza, and the rare
description for a blackbird, a 'merle' in the second stanza. Set as
spoken by Queen Mary, the highly descriptive narrative perfectly
complements the mournful despair of Mary.

To Robert Graham of Fintry, Esq.

First printed in the Edinburgh edition, 1793.

Late crippled of an arm, and now a leg,
About to beg a *pass* for leave to beg;
Dull, listless, teas'd, dejected, and deprest,
(Nature is adverse to a cripple's rest);
5   Will generous Graham list to his Poet's wail?   listen
(It soothes poor Misery, hearkening to her tale),
And hear him curse the light he first surveyed,
And doubly curse the luckless rhyming trade?

Thou, Nature, partial Nature! I arraign;
10 Of thy caprice maternal I complain:
The lion and the bull thy care have found,
One shakes the forests, and one spurns the ground:
Thou giv'st the ass his hide, the snail his shell,
Th' envenomed wasp, victorious, guards his cell;
15 Thy minions, kings defend, control, devour,
In all th' omnipotence of rule and power;

Foxes and statesmen, subtile wiles ensure;
The cit and polecat stink, and are secure;
Toads with their poison, doctors with their drug,
20   The priest and hedgehog in their robes, are snug;
Ev'n silly woman has her warlike arts,
Her tongue and eyes, her dreaded spear and darts.

But, Oh! thou bitter step-mother and hard,[1]
To thy poor, fenceless, naked child — the Bard!
25   A thing unteachable in world's skill,
And half an idiot too, more helpless still;
No heels to bear him from the opening dun;
No claws to dig, his hated sight to shun;
No horns, but those by luckless Hymen worn,
30   And those, alas! not Amalthea's horn:
No nerves olfact'ry, Mammon's trusty cur,
Clad in rich Dulness' comfortable fur; —
In naked feeling, and in aching pride,
He bears th' unbroken blast from ev'ry side:
35   Vampyre booksellers drain him to the heart,
And scorpion critics cureless venom dart: —

Critics! — appalled, I venture on the name —
Those cut-throat bandits in the paths of fame:
Bloody dissectors, worse than ten Monroes!
40   He hacks to teach, they mangle to expose: —

His heart by causeless wanton malice wrung,
By blockheads' daring into madness stung;
His well-won bays, than life itself more dear,
By miscreants torn, who ne'er one sprig must wear;
45   Foiled, bleeding, tortur'd in th' unequal strife,
The hapless Poet flounders on thro' life;
Till fled each hope that once his bosom fired,
And fled each Muse that glorious once inspired,

1 In adapted form, lines 17–36 are found erroneously attributed to Samuel
Taylor Coleridge in the Oxford edition of Coleridge, under the Latin title
'Habent Sua Fata – Poetae'. See p. 587, Appendix 1, 'First Drafts, Early
Versions'. The lines were found in a Coleridge letter, dated January 1796.
They were first ascribed to Coleridge in Cottle's *Early Recollections* (1839).
Coleridge evidently identified strongly with Burns's view on critics and the
fate of poets. It is surely a compliment to Burns's ability to write verse in
English that this piece has been mistakenly attributed to one of England's
finest poets.

Low-sunk in squalid, unprotected age,
50   Dead even resentment for his injured page,
He heeds or feels no more the ruthless Critic's rage!

So, by some hedge, the generous steed deceased,
For half-starv'd snarling curs a dainty feast;
By toil and famine wore to skin and bone,
55   Lies, senseless of each tugging bitch's son.

O Dulness! portion of the truly blest!
Calm sheltered haven of eternal rest!
Thy sons ne'er madden in the fierce extremes
Of Fortune's polar frost, or torrid beams.
60   If mantling high she fills the golden cup,
With sober selfish ease they sip it up:
Conscious the bounteous meed they well deserve,
They only wonder 'some folks' do not starve.
The grave sage hern thus easy picks his frog,
65   And thinks the mallard a sad worthless dog.
When Disappointment snaps the clue of hope,
And thro' disastrous night they darkling grope,
With deaf endurance sluggishly they bear,
And just conclude that 'fools are fortune's care.'
70   So, heavy, passive to the tempest's shocks,
Strong on the sign-post stands the stupid ox.

Not so the idle Muses' mad-cap train,
Nor such the workings of their moon-struck brain;
In equanimity they never dwell,
75   By turns in soaring heaven, or vaulted hell.

I dread thee, Fate, relentless and severe,
With all a Poet's, husband's, father's fear!
Already one strong hold of hope is lost,
Glencairn, the truly noble, lies in dust;
80   (Fled, like the sun eclips'd as noon appears,
And left us darkling in a world of tears:)
O hear my ardent, grateful, selfish pray'r! —
Fintry, my other stay, long bless and spare!
Thro' a long life his hopes and wishes crown,
85   And bright in cloudless skies his sun go down!
May *bliss domestic* smooth his private path;
Give energy to life; and soothe his latest breath,
With many a filial tear circling the bed of death!

Robert Graham (1749–1815) was the 12th Laird of Fintry, although he was forced to sell most of his estate in 1780. Burns met him during his Highland tour at Athole House, August 31st, 1787. In the same year, Fintry was made a Commissioner on the Board of Excise in Scotland. In terms of poetry, the consequence of this relationship was four poems over a three-year period: *To Robert Graham of Fintry Esq., with a request for an Excise Division* (1788); *To Mr Graham of Fintry, On being appointed to my Excise Division* (1789); *Epistle to Robert Graham of Fintry on the Election for the Dumfries string of Boroughs* (1790) and *To Robert Graham of Fintry, Esq.* (1791). The third poem, as we shall see, is a somewhat risky political satire. The other three all are preoccupied with patronage. The second is deeply sycophantic; a sort of inversion of all Burns's many assertions in his prose and poetry of creative independence at all costs. The other two are fragments of a bigger, incomplete project on the nature of the poet and poetry arising from a mixture of personal observation as found in his earlier vernacular epistles and his reading of, ironically, the dark *Tory* pessimistic prescriptions of the fate of the poet in society found in Dr Johnson's *Lives of the Poets*, Pope's *Moral Epistles* and, not least, Swift's great poem *On Poetry: A Rapsody*. The mixture is further leavened by his awareness, from the latter part of the eighteenth century, of the degree of psychological and economic incompatibility of the poetic personality (Fergusson, Gray, Cowper, Churchill, for example) with the world. Burns chose to publish only this, the last and best of the four 'Fintry' poems. Prior to the poetry, Burns wrote to Fintry within a few months of meeting him at Athole House regarding an entry to the Excise:

> When I had the honour of being introduced to you at Athole House, I did not think so soon of asking a favour from you. When Lear, in Shakespeare asked old Kent why he wished to be in his service, he answered 'Because you have that in your face that I would fain call master!' For, some such reason, sir, do I now solicit your patronage (Letter 172).

Given Burns's use of *King Lear* in *A Winter's Night*, this might seem the most sycophantic betrayal of his normal attitude to social dependency. On the other hand, Burns's soul did yearn, as with Glencairn and Lord Daer, for aristocrats of benevolent integrity. It is possible, too, traumatised by the loss of Glencairn that, on the rebound, he partly subconsciously projected onto Fintry's personality what he had experienced with the former patron. He was also in

severe fiscal straits, with all the consequent anxieties of that situa-
tion.

As well as his direct approaches to Fintry regarding the limited
security an Excise post would offer him, the first and fourth poems
are a method of educating Fintry in the difficult, perhaps impos-
sible, task of poetic existence. Obliquely, therefore, the poems
insinuate the necessity of Fintry's support. Also, the money worries
ran unstoppably on. This poem was written at a time of particular
pecuniary stress. As well as his own family, he had another illegi-
timate child to provide for. The £400 for the Edinburgh edition
had been swallowed up in a loan to Gilbert for Mossgiel where the
older brother maintained their mother and sisters. The rest had
gone into the bottomless pit of stocking Ellisland. His simulta-
neously injured leg must have been the last straw. Thus he wrote to
Fintry on October 6th, 1791:

> — Along with two other Pieces, I inclose you a sheetful of
> groans, wrung from me in my elbow chair, with one unlucky leg
> on a stool before me.— I will make no apology for addressing it
> to *you*: I have no longer a *choice* of Patrons: the noble Glencairn
> is no more!
>   . . . I thought to have mentioned some Excise ideas that your
> late goodness has put in my head, but it so like the sorning
> impudence of a sturdy beggar, that I cannot do it.— It was
> something in the way of an Officiating job.—With the most
> ardent wish that you may be rewarded by HIM who can do it,
> for your generous patronage to a man, who, tho' feelingly
> sensible of it, is quite unable to repay it . . .

Victorian commentators tended to accept Fintry's benevolence at
the value Burns here places on it. Thus Scott Douglas (p. 342)
quoting Professor Wilson ('Christopher North'):

> Of all Burns's friends the most efficient was Graham of Fintry.
> To him he owed exciseman's diploma—settlement as a gauger
> in a district of ten parishes, when he was a gudeman at Ellis-
> land—translation as a gauger to Dumfries—support against
> insidious foes, despicable, yet not to be despised, with rumour
> at their head—vindication at the Excise Board—a temporary
> supervisorship—and, though he knew not of it, security from
> dreaded degradation on his death bed.

Wilson, because he was so aware of the savage social discontents of
the nineteenth century, was only too eager to represent the Burns/

Fintry relationship in the most positive light. Despite his fiscal needs and functional abilities as an Exciseman, Burns was never promoted. Nor, as Wilson suggests, was it unfounded political rumour that Fintry was benevolently dealing with. Fintry was no neutral. From our recent archival research Fintry did, in fact, receive payments from the government's secret service fund for activities against individuals in the radical movement from 1793 to 1796. (See Laing Ms. collection, II, folio 500, pp. 404–5, Edinburgh University Library.) For example, the payment of £26.6 shillings is dated April, 1793, itemised for Graham of Fintry and paid out of the 'account of Secret Service': payments were made initially to John Pringle, Sherriff Depute of the County of Edinburgh, from the administrator of spies in London, Mr John Spottiswood, a Scot with a Scottish estate, who worked directly for Henry Dundas. There are also in the archive several letters from Fintry, to inter-alia, Robert Dundas on curbing radical activity and placing these loyal to the government in public posts and sinecures. From this it is possible to speculate that, rather than looking after Burns, Fintry was keeping him dependent and cornered in Dumfries. Burns himself, of course, was desperate to have the Excise move him to the more radically sympathetic West of Scotland.

Nor does Wilson's meliorism begin to explain the known course of events. The general tenor of the fifteen extant letters of Burns to Fintry is friendly, sometimes even frank. However, the pattern is totally disrupted in December, 1792 in Burns's near hysterical response to reports that he was about to be investigated for alleged sedition/treason due to both his writing and public behaviour. On the very last day of that year, he wrote to Fintry thus:

I have been surprised, confounded & distracted by Mr Mitchel, the Collector, telling me just now, that he has received an order from your Honble Board to enquire into my political conduct, & blaming me as a person disaffected to Government.—Sir, you are a Husband—& a father—you know what you would feel, to see the much-loved wife of your bosom, & your helpless, prattling little ones, turned adrift into the word, degraded & disgraced from a situation in which they had been respectable and respected, & left [without (*deleted*)] almost without the necessary support of a miserable existence.—Alas, Sir! must I think that such, soon, will be my lot! And from the damned, dark insinuations of hellish, groundless Envy too!—I believe, Sir, I may aver it, & in the sight of Omnipotence, that I would not tell a deliberate Falsehood, no, not though even worse horrors, if worse can be, than those I have mentioned, hung over my head; & I say, that the allegation, whatever villain has made it, is a LIE! To the British Constitution, on Revolution principles, next after my God, I am most devoutly attached!—

You, Sir, have been much & generously my Friend—Heaven knows how warmly I have felt the obligation, how gratefully I have thanked you.—Fortune, Sir, has made you powerful, & me impotent; has given you patronage, & me dependance.—I would not for my *single Self* call on your Humanity; were such my insular, unconnected situation, I would despise the tear that now swells in my eye—I could brave Misfortune, I could face Ruin: for at the worst, 'Death's thousand doors stand open;' but, Good God! the tender concerns that I have mentioned, the claims & ties that I, at this moment, see & feel around me, how they ennerve Courage, & wither Resolution! To your patronage, as a man of some genius, you have allowed me a claim; & your esteem, as an honest Man, I know is my due: to these, Sir, permit me to appeal; & by these may I adjure you to save me from that misery which threatens to overwhelm me, & which, with my latest breath I will say it, I have not deserved.—

Pardon this confused scrawl.—Indeed I know not well what I have written.— (Letter 528)

This is not so out of control as it seems. As well as alluding 'death's thousand doors' from Blair's *The Grave*, his reference to 'the British Constitution, on Revolution principles next after my God', is an escape clause since the establishment Tories and Whig radicals interpreted the constitutional settlement of the Glorious Revolution wholly differently. The former group saw it as perfectly formed and finished. The latter saw it as the embryo for indefinite reformative change. This first letter to Fintry was followed on 5th January by a more considered point by point rebuttal of the charges against him. He repeats his defence of the British Constitution. He denies his involvement in a Dumfries theatrical disturbance where the singing of the national anthem was overwhelmed by the provocative French revolutionary song, *Ça ira*. He claims to have weaned himself of his French affiliations after an imperial France's annexation of Savoy and an invasion of Holland's rights. What is, however, most relevant to his subsequent anonymous radical poetry is his disclaimer of all knowledge of Captain Johnston, the publisher of the dissenting *Edinburgh Gazetteer*.

Of Johnston, the publisher of the Edinr. Gazetteer, I know nothing.—One evening in company with four or five friends, we met with his prospectus which we thought manly and independant; & I wrote to him, ordering his paper for us.— If you think that I act improperly in allowing his Paper to come addressed to me, I shall immediately countermand it.—I never so judge me, God wrote a line of prose for the Gazetteer in my life.

The key word here, of course, is *prose*. It is also a defence based on the letter not the spirit of his previous communication with Captain Johnston. As he wrote to Johnston on 13th November, 1792, describing the magazine as 'the first Composition of the kind in Europe':

Go on, Sir! Lay bare, with undaunted heart & steady hand, that horrid mass of corruption called Politics & State-Craft. Dare to draw in their native colors these
'Calm, thinking VILLAINS who no faith can fix'
whatever be the shiboleth (sic) of their pretended Party
(Quotation from Pope's *The Temple of Fame*, l. 410).

As to the poem itself, its genesis can be dated from a letter to Mrs Dunlop written three years before the poem was sent to Fintry:

I began a Work lately, but what that work may be, I am totally ignorant.—As Young says, ' 'Tis nonsense destined to be future sense.'—I sent you a fragment of it by my last: take the following rough Sketch of the intended beginning, & let me know your opinion of the lines— The Poet's Progress, An embryotic Poem in the womb of futurity (ll. 9–55, quoted).

Thus far only have I proceeded, & perhaps I may never again resume the subject.—I must mention one caution to you, Madam, with respect to these verses; I have a remote idea that I may one day use them as instruments of vengeance, & consequently I will hide them like a Conspirator's dagger (Letter 281).

Burns, indeed, as political poet is the archetypal smiler with a knife. This poem, however, has no specific targets but is a general analysis of the multi-displaced poetic personality. Kinsley was innately hostile to Burns's incursions into such Augustan linguistically and thematically derived terrain. The poem, then, has never had the attention it deserves. This is literally true, as Hogg discovered that ll. 17–36 of Burns's poem were compressed by Coleridge into a twelve-line verse and sent in a letter to Josiah Wade at Bristol *circa* February 10, 1796. These lines appear in the Oxford Coleridge under the title *Habent Sunt Fata Poetae* and are wrongly defined as a sonnet by Molly Lefebre in her *Samuel Taylor Coleridge: A Bondage of Opium* (London: 1977), p. 175. Here is Coleridge's compressed version:

> The Fox, and Statesman subtile wiles ensure,
> The Cit, and Polecat stink and are secure:
> Toads with their venom, Doctors with their drug,
> The Priest, the Hedgehog, in their robes are snug!
> 5   Oh, Nature! cruel step-mother, and hard,
> To thy poor, naked, fenceless child the Bard!
> No Horns but those by luckless Hymen worn,
> And those, (alas! alas!) not Plenty's Horn!
> With naked feelings, and with aching pride,
> 10   He bears th' unbroken blast on every side!
> Vampire Booksellers drain him to the heart,
> And Scorpion Critics cureless venom dart!

The problem of plagiarism in Coleridge is notorious though in this case, a private letter, he was not obviously trying to pass the Burns lines off as his own. What it does demonstrate, however, is not only the relevance Coleridge felt Burns's perceptions had for his own awareness of his situation as poet but the degree to which Burns was self-consciously, creatively aware of the chronic social, political, critical and economic dilemma of poetry since the early part of the eighteenth century. Carol McGuirk, always eruditely atuned to the resonances of canonical English poetry in Burns, notes with regard to this poem that 'among the sources for ll. 56–71, with their imagery of blissful folly and triumphant Dulness are Pope's *Dunciad* and Swift's . . .*Tale of a Tub*.' It is problematic as to how much of Swift Burns knew. Both were peculiarly displaced men: Burns by reason of class and Swift more by ethnicity. The psychological traumas of this were creatively compensated for in the terms of the manner in which their consequent detached, disguised personas could, with varied laughter, undermine the madness of institutionalised power especially in both its monarchical and Presbyterian states. It also seems from the textual evidence highly probable that this Burns poem is partly based on a reading of what Swift himself considered

his greatest poem, *On Poetry: A Rapsody*. Here is the opening of
Swift:

All Human Race wou'd fain be *Wits*
And Millions miss, for one that hits
Young's universal Passion, *Pride*,
Was never known to spread so wide.
5   Say *Britain*, cou'd you ever boast,—
Three *Poets* in an Age at most?
Our chilling Climate hardly bears
A *Sprig* of Bays in Fifty Years:
While ev'ry Fool his Claim alledges,
10   As if it grew in common Hedges.
What Reason can there be assign'd
For this Perverseness in the Mind?
Brutes find out where their Talents lie:
A *Bear* will not attempt to fly:
15   A founder'd *Horse* will oft debate,
Before he tries a five-barr'd Gate:
A Dog by Instinct turns aside,
Who sees the Ditch too deep and wide.
But *Man* we find the only Creature,
20   Who, led by *Folly*, fights with *Nature*;
Who, when *she* loudly cries, *Forbear*,
With Obstinacy fixes there;
And, where his *Genius* least inclines,
Absurdly bends his whole Designs.
25   Not *Empire* to the Rising-Sun
By Valour, Conduct, Fortune won;
Nor highest *Wisdom* in Debates
For framing Laws to govern States;
Nor Skill in Sciences profound,
30   So large to grasp the Circle round;
Such heavenly Influence require,
As how to strike the *Muses Lyre*.
            Not Beggar's Brat, on Bulk begot;
Nor Bastard of a Pedlar Scot;
35   Nor Boy brought up to cleaning Shoes,
The Spawn of *Bridewell*, or the Stews;
Nor Infants dropt, the spurious Pledges
Of *Gipsies* littering under Hedges,
Are so disqualified by Fate
40   To rise in *Church*, or *Law*, or *State*,

As he, whom *Phebus* in his Ire
Hath *blasted* with poetick Fire.
      What hope of Custom in the *Fair*,
      While not a soul demands your Ware?
45   Where you have nothing to produce
      For private Life, or publick Use?
      Court, City, Country want you not;
      You cannot bribe, betray, or plot.
      For Poets, Law makes no Provision:
50   The Wealthy have you in Derision.
      Of State-Affairs you cannot smatter,
      Are awkward when you try to flatter.

Both poems are obsessed with the dysfunctional role of the poet in a world where everything else is functionally placed. While Burns is more inclined to place the problem in the innate character of the poet, he is wholly complicit with Swift's analysis of a creative environment warped by the decline of aristocratic patronage, the corrupting effects of the new commercial, book-selling world and the institutionalisation of a rule-bound, pretentious criticism. Burns was a political radical but he is also as hierarchical and élitist as Tory Swift or Pope in his notion that the waters of the Helicon were increasingly polluted by usurping pseudo-poets. As he wrote to Mrs Dunlop: 'Besides, my success has encouraged such a shoal of ill-spawned monsters to crawl into public notice under the title of Scots Poets, that the very term, Scots poetry, borders on the burlesque'. Nor does he, despite Kinsley, suffer in the depth of the quality of his analysis with Swift.

L.7 again echoes Burns's obsession with the sufferings and response of Job. 'Amalthea's horn' (l. 30) was the horn of Zeus's nurse-goat which became a cornucopia unlike the more probably worn cuckold horns of the married (Hymen is the goddess of marriage) poet. Ll. 39–40 brilliantly extend a medical joke probably triggered by Pope's reference in *Imitations of Horace*, Ep.II.ii, l. 70 where he refers to James Monro, the physician of Bedlam: 'Sure I should want Care of ten *Munroes*'. Burns's Monro is Alexander Munro (1733–1817) part of a great Edinburgh medical dynasty who took up that city's first chair in surgery in 1777 in a world of amputation without anaesthetics.

Lament for James, Earl of Glencairn

First printed in the Edinburgh edition, 1793.

The wind blew hollow frae the hills,   *from*
    By fits the sun's departing beam
Look'd on the fading yellow woods
    That wav'd o'er Lugar's winding stream;
5 Beneath a craigy steep, a Bard,   *craggy precipice*
    Laden with years, and meikle pain,   *much*
In loud lament bewail'd his lord,
    Whom Death had all untimely ta'en.   *taken*

He lean'd him to an ancient aik,   *oak*
10   Whose trunk was mould'ring down with years;
His locks were bleached white with time,
    His hoary cheek was wet wi' tears;
And as he touch'd his trembling harp,
    And as he tun'd his doleful sang,   *song*
15 The winds, lamenting thro' their caves,
    To echo bore the notes alang!   *along*

'Ye scatter'd birds that faintly sing
    The reliques of the vernal quire;
Ye woods that shed on a' the winds
20   The honours of the aged year!
A few short months, and glad and gay,
    Again ye'll charm the ear and e'e;   *eye*
But nocht in all revolving time   *nothing*
    Can gladness bring again to me.

25 'I am a bending aged tree,
    That long has stood the wind and rain;
But now has come a cruel blast,
    And my last hold of earth is gane: *gone*
Nae leaf o' mine shall greet the spring,   *no*
30   Nae simmer sun exalt my bloom;   *no*
But I maun lie before the storm,   *must*
    And ithers plant them in my room.   *others*

'I've seen sae monie changefu' years,   *so many*
    On earth I am a stranger grown:
35 I wander in the ways of men,
    Alike unknowing and unknown:

Unheard, unpitied, unreliev'd,
    I bear alane my lade o' care,   *alone, load*
For silent, low, on beds of dust,
40   Lie a' that would my sorrows share.   *all*

'And last (the sum of a' my griefs!)   *all*
    My noble master lies in clay;
The flower amang our barons bold,   *among*
    His country's pride, his country's stay:
45 In weary being now I pine,
    For a' the life of life is dead,
And hope has left my aged ken,   *orbit*
    On forward wing for ever fled.

'Awake thy last sad voice, my harp!
50   The voice of woe and wild despair!
Awake! resound thy latest lay —
    Then sleep in silence evermair!   *evermore*
And thou, my last, best, only friend,
    That fillest an untimely tomb,
55 Accept this tribute from the Bard
    Thou brought from Fortune's mirkest gloom.   *darkest*

'In Poverty's low barren vale,
    Thick mists, obscure, involv'd me round;
Though oft I turn'd the wistful eye,
60   Nae ray of fame was to be found: *no*
Thou found'st me, like the morning sun
    That melts the fogs in limpid air,
The friendless Bard and rustic song
    Became alike thy fostering care.

65 'O why has Worth so short a date?
    While villains ripen grey with time;
Must thou, the noble, gen'rous, great,
    Fall in bold manhood's hardy prime!
Why did I live to see that day?
70   A day to me so full of woe!
O had I met the mortal shaft
    Which laid my benefactor low!

'The bridegroom may forget the bride,
  Was made his wedded wife yestreen; yesterday evening
75 The monarch may forget the crown
  That on his head an hour has been;
The mother may forget the child
  That smiles sae sweetly on her knee; so
But I'll remember thee, Glencairn,
80   And a' that thou hast done for me!'

James Cunningham (1748–91), 14th Earl of Glencairn was Burns's most important actual and potential patron. His premature death, dying at Falmouth on 30th January, 1791, after, like Henry Fielding, an unsuccessful winter in the Portuguese sun to regain his health, was a blow from which Burns never recovered. Burns went into deep mourning and for the Kilmarnock funeral proposed to 'cross the country and steal among the croud, to pay a tear to the last sight of my ever-revered Benefactor' (Letters 438, 439 467).

Despite De Quincey's scepticism about all Burns's patrons, Glencairn does seem to have been of tangible support. The letter of introduction that Burns carried to Edinburgh from Dalrymple of Orangefield, his wife was the Earl's sister, was sufficient to persuade Glencairn, an enthusiast for the Kilmarnock edition, that his Ayrshire compatriot deserved his influential support. Due to Glencairn, the aristocratic Caledonian Hunt subscribed to a man, making the first Edinburgh edition a runaway success.

There is a particular warmth in the three extant letters from Burns to Glencairn. Like Lord Daer, Glencairn appears to have been one of those very few Whig Friends of the People, who, theoretically politically sympathetic, were not driven by condescending egotism and anti-Tory ambition and not real commitment to the common people. Unlike, say, the Riddells, there is little ambivalence in Burns towards Glencairn as the following anecdote from Kinsley reveals:

Glencairn was the only nobleman who offended the poet's social sensibilities without incurring irrational abuse. On one occasion in Edinburgh, says Burns, he showed 'engrossing attention . . . to the only blockhead at table, as there was none but his Lordship, the Dunderpate and myself, that I was within half a point of throwing down my gage of contemptuous defiance, but he shook my hand and looked so benevolently good at parting – God bless him! Though I should never see

him more, I shall love him until my dying day! I am pleased to
think I am so capable of throes of gratitude, as I am miserably
deficient in some other virtues' (2CPB, p. 5).

It is, of course, absolutely typical of Kinsley that satirical dissent
from Burns's socially inferior position always tends to the irrational.
Kinsley had neither adequate knowledge nor sympathy for the
radical politics of the late eighteenth century. Thus he does not
bring to our attention the fact that Glencairn was a Foxite, support-
ing the India Bill, or, more crucially, that he possibly belonged to
that still largely submerged radical network so that the spy-admin-
istrator, Home Office Under-Secretary Spottiswood, dared to 'send
Sheriffs against. . . such an august personage as the Earl of Glen-
cairn' (See Robert Thornton's *William Maxwell to Robert Burns*,
John Donald, Edinburgh: 1979, p. 65).

Like his *Lament for Mary, Queen of Scots*, the regular ballad-like
metre (two sets of long-line couplets broken into tetrameters) is
formally the reverse of MacPherson's Ossianic epic. The tone and
language of the poem, including Biblical echoes, as Kinsley notes, to
Ecclesiastes and *Job*, is, however, deliberately pervaded by the tone
and verbal imagery of that work. To some extent, though the poem
grows increasingly personal, this simultaneously distances Burns
from his pain and invokes enormous Ossianic power of a world
irretrievably lost and existing only in Bardic lament.

Lines, Sent to Sir John Whiteford
with the Foregoing Poem
First printed in the Edinburgh edition, 1793.

Thou, who thy honour as thy God rever'st,
Who, save thy *mind's reproach*, nought earthly fear'st,
To thee this votive off'ring I impart,
The tearful tribute of a broken heart.
The *Friend* thou valued'st, I the *Patron* lov'd;
His worth, his honour, all the world approv'd.
We'll mourn till we too go as he has gone,
And tread the shadowy path to that dark world unknown.

Sir John Whitefoord (1734–1803) was a friend of James Cunning-
ham, Earl of Glencairn. Burns composed these brief lines in October
1791. Whitefoord's reply, written from Maybole, 16th October
1791, in acknowledgement of the *Lament* and lines addressed to

himself, remarked 'Let us cherish this hope for our departed friend, and moderate our grief for that loss we have sustained, knowing he cannot come to us, but we may go to him'. (See Scott Douglas's edition, Vol. I, p. 348 headnote.)

Prose Introduction to Tam O' Shanter

Prompted by the antiquarian Francis Grose, a friend of Robert Riddell of Glenriddell, Burns was asked to provide any ghost stories concerning Alloway church that might be utilised in Francis Grose's forthcoming book on Scottish antiquities. The result was a prose recollection, eventually honed into the comic-epic masterpiece, *Tam O'Shanter*. The poet's remarkable ability to translate prose into poetry is apparent in examining his comments to Grose and because they provide the genesis of the poem, we give them here as introduction:

Among the many Witch Stories I have heard relating to Alloway Kirk, I distinctly remember two or three. Upon a stormy night, amid whirling squalls of wind and bitter blasts of hail, in short on such a night as the devil would chuse to take the air in, a farmer or farmer's servant was plodding and plashing homeward with his plough-iron on his shoulder, having been getting some repairs on them at a neighbouring smithy. His way lay by the Kirk of Aloway, and being on the anxious look-out in approaching a place so well known to be a favourite haunt of the devil and the devil's friends and emissaries, he was struck aghast by discovering through the horrors of the storm and stormy night, a light, which on his nearer approach, plainly shewed itself to proceed from the haunted edifice. Whether he had been fortified from above on his devout supplication, as is customary with people when they suspect the immediate presence of Satan; or whether, according to another custom, he had got courageously drunk at the smithy, I will not pretend to determine; but so it was that he ventured to go up to, nay into the very kirk. As good luck would have it, his temerity came off unpunished. The members of the infernal junto were all out on some midnight business or other, and he saw nothing but a kind of kettle or caldron, depending from the roof, over the fire, simmering some heads of unchristened children, limbs of executed malefactors, &c. for the business of the night. It was, in for a penny in for a pound, with the honest ploughman: so without ceremony he unhooked the caldron from off the fire, and pouring out the damnable ingredients, inverted it on his head, and carried it fairly home, where it remained long in the family a living evidence of the truth of the story.

Another story which I can prove to be equally authentic was as follows. On a market day in the town of Ayr, a farmer from Carrick, and consequently whose way lay by the very gate of Alloway Kirk-yard in order to cross the river Doon at the old bridge, which is about two or three hundred yards further on than the said gate, had been detained by his business, till by the time he reached Alloway, it was the wizard hour, between night and morning. Though he was terrified, with a blaze streaming from the kirk, yet as it is a well-known fact that to turn back on these occasions is running by far the greatest risk of mischief, he prudently advanced on his road. When he had reached the gate of the kirk-yard, he was surprised and entertained, through the ribs and arches of an old gothic window which still faces the highway, to see a dance of witches merrily footing it round their old sooty blackguard master, who was keeping them alive with the powers of his bag-pipe. The farmer stopping his horse to observe them a little, could plainly descry the faces of many old women of his acquaintance and neighbourhood. How the gentle-man was dressed, tradition does not say; but the ladies were all in their smocks: and one of them happening unluckily to have a smock which was considerably too short to answer all the purpose of that piece of dress, our farmer was so tickled that he involuntarily burst out, with a loud laugh, 'Well luppen Maggy wi the short sark !' and recollecting himself, instantly spurred his horse to the top of his speed. I need not mention the universal known fact, that no diabolical power can pursue you beyond the middle of a running stream. Lucky it was for the poor farmer that the river Doon was so near, for notwithstanding the speed of his horse, which was a good one, against the odds he reached the middle of the arch of the bridge, and consequently the middle of the stream, the pursuing, vengeful, hags, were so close at his heels, that one of them actually sprung to seize him; but it was too late, nothing was on her side of the stream but the horse's tail, which immediately gave way to her infernal grip, as if blasted by a stroke of lightning; but the farmer was beyond her reach. However, the unsightly, tailless condition of the vigorous steed was to the last hour of the noble creature's life, an awful warning to the Carrick farmers, not to stay too late in Ayr mar-kets. . . . (Letter 401).

Tam O' Shanter: A Tale

First printed in *The Edinburgh Herald*, 18th March, 1791; then *The Edinburgh Magazine*, March 1791; followed by publication in Francis Grose's *Antiquities of Scotland*, Vol. II, April 1791 before inclusion in the Edinburgh edition, 1793.

Of Brownyis and of Bogillis full is this Buke.
GAWIN DOUGLAS.

	When chapman billies leave the street,	pedlar friends
	And drouthy neebors, neebors meet,	thirsty neighbours
	As market-days are wearing late,	
	An' folk begin to tak the gate;	road/go home
5	While we sit bousing at the nappy,	drinking, ale
	And getting fou and unco happy,	full/drunk, mighty
	We think na on the lang Scots miles,	not, long
	The mosses, waters, slaps, and styles,	bogs, pools, stiles
	That lie between us and our hame,	home
10	Whare sits our sulky sullen dame,	where
	Gathering her brows like gathering storm,	
	Nursing her wrath to keep it warm.	
	This truth fand honest *Tam o' Shanter*,	found
	As he frae Ayr ae night did canter,	from, one
15	(Auld Ayr, wham ne'er a town surpasses	who/that
	For honest men and bonie lasses).	pretty
	O *Tam!* had'st thou but been sae wise,	so
	As taen thy ain wife *Kate's* advice!	taken, own
	She tauld thee weel thou was a skellum,	told, well, rogue
20	A blethering, blustering, drunken blellum;	chattering, babbling, idle talker
	That frae November till October,	from
	Ae market-day thou was nae sober;	one, not
	That ilka melder, wi' the miller,	every meal grinding
	Thou sat as lang as thou had siller;	long, money
25	That ev'ry naig was ca'd a shoe on,	horse, shod
	The smith and thee gat roaring fou on;	got, full/drunk
	That at the Lord's house, even on Sunday,	
	Thou drank wi' Kirkton Jean till Monday.	
	She prophesied that late or soon,	
30	Thou would be found deep drown'd in Doon;	
	Or catch'd wi' warlocks in the mirk,	wizards, dark
	By *Alloway's* auld, haunted kirk.	old

Ah, gentle dames! it gars me greet,   makes, weep
To think how mony counsels sweet,   many
35   How mony lengthen'd, sage advices,   many
The husband frae the wife despises!   from

      But to our tale: — Ae market-night,   one
Tam had got planted unco right;   mighty
Fast by an ingle, bleezing finely,   fire, blazing
40   Wi' reaming swats, that drank divinely   foaming ale
And at his elbow, Souter *Johnny*,   cobbler
His ancient, trusty, drouthy crony;   drinking pal
Tam lo'ed him like a very brither —   loved, brother
They had been fou for weeks thegither!   full/drunk, together
45   The night drave on wi' sangs and clatter   drove, songs, chat
And ay the ale was growing better:
The landlady and *Tam* grew gracious,
Wi' favours, secret, sweet and precious:
The Souter tauld his queerest stories;   cobbler told
50   The landlord's laugh was ready chorus:
The storm without might rair and rustle,   roar
Tam did na mind the storm a whistle.   not

Care, mad to see a man sae happy,   so
E'en drown'd himsel amang the nappy: among, ale
55   As bees flee hame wi' lades o' treasure,   fly home, loads
The minutes wing'd their way wi' pleasure:
Kings may be blest, but *Tam* was glorious,
O'er a' the ills o' life victorious!

      But pleasures are like poppies spread,
60   You seize the flower, its bloom is shed;
Or like the snow falls in the river,
A moment white — then melts for ever;
Or like the borealis race,
That flit ere you can point their place;
65   Or like the rainbow's lovely form
Evanishing amid the storm. —
Nae man can tether time or tide;   no, hold/control
The hour approaches *Tam* maun ride;   must
That hour, o' night's black arch the key-stane,   -stone
70   That dreary hour he mounts his beast in;
And sic a night he taks the road in,   such, takes
As ne'er poor sinner was abroad in.

The wind blew as 'twad blawn its last;   it would have blown
The rattling showers rose on the blast;
75 The speedy gleams the darkness swallow'd;
Loud, deep, and lang, the thunder bellow'd: long
That night, a child might understand,
The Deil had business on his hand.   devil

Weel mounted on his gray mare, *Meg* —   well
80 A better never lifted leg —
Tam skelpit on thro' dub and mire,   rode fast, puddle
Despising wind, and rain, and fire;
Whyles holding fast his guid blue bonnet;   good
Whyles crooning o'er some auld Scots sonnet;   muttering, old
85 Whyles glow'ring round wi' prudent cares,   looking with fear
Lest bogles catch him unawares: bogies
Kirk-Alloway was drawing nigh,
Whare ghaists and houlets nightly cry. —   where ghosts, owls

By this time he was cross the ford,   burn
90 Whare in the snaw the chapman smoor'd;   where, snow, pedlar, smothered
And past the birks and meikle stane,   birches, big stone
Whare drunken *Charlie* brak's neck-bane;   where, broke his, -bone
And thro' the whins, and by the cairn,   gorse bushes
Whare hunters fand the murder'd bairn;   where, found, child
95 And near the thorn, aboon the well,   above
Whare *Mungo's* mither hang'd hersel. —   where, mother
Before him *Doon* pours all his floods;
The doubling storm roars thro' the woods;
The lightnings flash from pole to pole;
100 Near and more near the thunders roll:
When, glimmering thro' the groaning trees,
Kirk-Alloway seem'd in a bleeze;   blaze/lit up
Thro' ilka bore the beams were glancing;   every chink in the wall
And loud resounded mirth and dancing.

105 Inspiring bold *John Barleycorn!*
What dangers thou canst make us scorn!
Wi' tippenny, we fear nae evil;   cheap two penny ale, no
Wi' usquabae, we'll face the Devil! —   whisky
The swats sae ream'd in *Tammie's* noddle,   small beers, so, mind
110 Fair play, he car'd na deils a boddle.   cared not a farthing
But *Maggie* stood, right sair astonish'd,   sore
Till, by the heel and hand admonish'd,   spurred and slapped

She ventur'd forward on the light;
And, vow! *Tam* saw an unco sight!   strange/wondrous
115   Warlocks and witches in a dance;   wizards
Nae cotillion brent new frae *France*,   no, brand new from
But hornpipes, jigs, strathspeys, and reels,
Put life and mettle in their heels.
A winnock-bunker in the east,   window recess
120   There sat auld Nick, in shape o' beast;   old
A tousie tyke, black, grim, and large,   shaggy dog
To gie them music was his charge: give
He screw'd the pipes and gart them skirl,   made, blare
Till roof and rafters a' did dirl. —   ring/shake
125   Coffins stood round, like open presses,   cupboards
That shaw'd the dead in their last dresses;   showed
And by some devilish cantraip sleight,   magic trick
Each in its cauld hand held a light. —   cold
By which heroic *Tam* was able
130   To note upon the haly table,   holy
A murderer's banes, in gibbet-airns;   bones, -irons
Twa span-lang, wee, unchristen'd bairns;   two, -long, babies
A thief new-cutted frae a rape,   from, rope
Wi' his last gasp his gab did gape;   mouth, gasp
135   Five tomahawks wi' blude red-rusted;   axes, blood
Five scymitars wi' murder crusted;
A garter, which a babe had strangled;
A knife, a father's throat had mangled,
Whom his ain son o' life bereft,   own
140   The grey-hairs yet stack to the heft;[1]   stuck, handle
[Three Lawyers' tongues, turned inside out,
Wi' lies seamed like a beggar's clout;
Three Priests' hearts, rotten black as muck,
Lay stinking, vile, in every neuk].   corner

145   As *Tammie* glowr'd, amaz'd, and curious,   stared
The mirth and fun grew fast and furious:
The piper loud and louder blew;
The dancers quick and quicker flew;

1 After the word 'heft', most editors print 'Wi' mair of horrible and awefu', /
Which even to name wad be unlawfu'.' The original lines written by Burns
are placed in square brackets. They were effectively edited out of the 1793
Edinburgh edition on the advice of Alexander Fraser Tytler, who thought
them offensive to priests and lawyers.

	Text	Gloss
	They reel'd, they set, they cross'd, they cleekit,	clasped one another
150	Till ilka carlin swat and reekit,	every witch, sweated, steamed
	And coost her duddies to the wark,	cast off clothes, work
	And linket at it in her sark!	set to it, shirt
	Now *Tam*, O *Tam*! had thae been queans,	they, girls
	A' plump and strapping in their teens,	
155	Their sarks, instead o' creeshie flannen,	shirts, greasy flannel
	Been snaw-white seventeen hunder linen!	snow-, fine threaded linen
	Thir breeks o' mine, my only pair,	these breeches
	That ance were plush, o' guid blue hair,	once, good
	I wad hae gi'en them off my hurdies,	would have given, backside
160	For ae blink o' the bonie burdies!	one, pretty lasses
	But wither'd beldams, auld and droll,	hags, old
	Rigwoodie hags wad spean a foal,	tough, would, abort
	Louping and flinging on a crummock,	jumping, cudgel
	I wonder did na turn thy stomach.	not
165	But *Tam* kend what was what fu' brawlie,	knew, full well
	There was ae winsome wench and wawlie,	one comely, choice
	That night enlisted in the core,	
	(Lang after kend on *Carrick* shore;	long, known
	For mony a beast to dead she shot,	many
170	An' perish'd mony a bonie boat,	many, handsome
	And shook baith meikle corn and bear,	both much, barley
	And kept the country-side in fear).	
	Her cutty-sark, o' Paisley harn	short shirt, coarse cloth
	That while a lassie she had worn,	
175	In longitude tho' sorely scanty,	revealing
	It was her best, and she was vauntie. —	proud of it
	Ah! little kend thy reverend grannie,	knew
	That sark she coft for her wee Nannie,	shirt, bought
	Wi' twa pund Scots ('twas a' her riches),	two pounds
180	Wad ever grac'd a dance of witches!	would
	But here my Muse her wing maun cour;	must fold/curb
	Sic flights are far beyond her pow'r;	such
	To sing how Nannie lap and flang,	leaped, kicked
	(A souple jad she was, and strang),	supple lass, strong
185	And how *Tam* stood like ane bewitch'd,	one
	And thought his very een enrich'd;	eyes

Even Satan glowr'd, and fidg'd fu' fain,   stared, fidgeted excitedly
And hotch'd and blew wi' might and main: jerked
Till first ae caper, syne anither,   one, then another
190   *Tam* tint his reason a' thegither,   lost, together
And roars out, 'Weel done, Cutty-sark!'   well
And in an instant all was dark:
And scarcely had he *Maggie* rallied,
When out the hellish legion sallied.

195   As bees bizz out wi' angry fyke,   buzz, fret
When plundering herds assail their byke;   hive
As open pussie's mortal foes,   a hare's
When, pop! she starts before their nose;
As eager runs the market-crowd,
200   When 'Catch the thief!' resounds aloud;
So *Maggie* runs, the witches follow,
Wi' mony an eldritch skriech and hollow.   many, unearthly screech

Ah, *Tam*! ah, *Tam*! thou'll get thy fairin'!   reward/due
In hell they'll roast thee like a herrin'!
205   In vain thy *Kate* awaits thy comin'!
Kate soon will be a woefu' woman!
Now, do thy speedy utmost, Meg,
And win the key-stane of the brig;[2]   key-stone, bridge
There, at them thou thy tail may toss,
210   A running stream they dare na cross.   not
But ere the key-stane she could make,   -stone
The fient a tail she had to shake!   little of
For Nannie, far before the rest,
Hard upon noble *Maggie* prest,   pressed
215   And flew at *Tam* wi' furious ettle;   aim
But little wist she Maggie's mettle —   was
Ae spring brought off her master hale,   one, whole
But left behind her ain grey tail: own
The carlin claught her by the rump,   old witch caught
220   And left poor *Maggie* scarce a stump.

2 It is a well-known fact that witches, or any evil spirits, have no power to
follow a poor wight any farther than the middle of the next running stream. It
may be proper likewise to mention to the benighted traveller, that when he
falls in with bogles, whatever danger may be in his going forward, there is
much more hazard in turning back. R.B.

Now, wha this tale o' truth shall read,   who
Ilk man and mother's son take heed: each
Whene'er to drink you are inclin'd,
Or cutty-sarks run in your mind,   short shirts/skirts
225   Think! ye may buy the joys o'er dear —
Remember *Tam o' Shanter's* mare.

Tam O' Shanter, 'Burns's most sustained single poetic effort', as Daiches rightly comments, was written as a result of Burns being prompted to write a superstitious story for the English antiquarian Francis Grose, to accompany a sketch of Alloway Kirk in his forthcoming *Antiquities of Scotland*. From the prose evolved the poem, not in a day's work, as has been foolishly suggested, but over several months of composition and correction. Between the edition printed by Grose and the 1793 edition there are 59 noticeable differences in words and punctuation. An example of reworking is evident in a letter Mrs Dunlop wrote to Burns quoting back to him some lines of what is clearly an early draft:

Kings may be blest, but thou art glorious,
O'er a' the ills of life victorious;
As bees fly home laden with treasure,
By thee the moment's winged with pleasure.
But pleasure will not always last;
They're like the rainbow in the blast:
Awhile it shows its lovely form,
Then vanishes amid the storm. . .

The narrative tale behind the poem, given above to introduce the poem and explain its origin, reveals the poet's astonishing skill in translating prose into poetry. As Daiches notes (p. 251):

. . . showed him a master of verse narrative as no Scots poet had been since the fifteenth century. The speed and verve of the narration, the fine, flexible use of the octosyllabic couplet, the effective handling of the verse paragraph demonstrate a degree of craftmanship that few other users of this verse form have achieved.

Unlike Wordsworth, Burns was not given to narrative poetry of this kind – it is his only example. When, however, Wordsworth tried to get some of the story and comic feel of *Tam* into *The Waggoner* it was almost a complete flop. Edwin Muir commented aptly on the poem thus:

'It is the privilege of poetic genius' he [Wordsworth] said writing about *Tam O'Shanter*, 'to catch, under certain restrictions of which perhaps at the time of its being executed it is but dimly conscious, a spirit of pleasure wherever it can be found – in the walks of nature, and in the business of men'. Burns caught this 'spirit of pleasure', and in a poem in which there was not a weak line, not an uncertain intonation, rendered it with a vigour and pliancy which must have astonished himself. He painted corruption in colours so festive and at the time so objective, that his picture had not only a poetic, but a philosophic value (Muir, *Uncollected Scottish Criticism*, p. 186).

Probably the earliest criticism of *Tam* is still the most accurate. As early as March 1791, it was apparent to A.F. Tytler that in this tale Burns had ored the purest poetic gold:

Had you never written another syllable, [this poem] would have been sufficient to have tramsmitted your name down to posterity with high reputation. In the introductory part, where you paint the character of your hero, and exhibit him at the alehouse ingle, with his tippling cronies, you have delineated nature with an honour and naivete, that would do honour to Matthew Prior; but when you describe the unfortunate orgies of the witches' sabbath, and the hellish scenery in which they are exhibited, you display a power of imagination, that Shakespeare himself could not have exceeded (Currie, 1800, Letter CVI, 12th March 1791).

McGuirk's contextual and textual remarks on the poem in her *Selected Poems* and *Robert Burns and the Sentimental Era* are particularly cogent and stimulating.

On Seeing a Wounded Hare
limp by me, which a Fellow had Just Shot
First printed in the Edinburgh edition, 1793.

Inhuman man! curse on thy barb'rous art,
    And blasted be thy murder-aiming eye!
    May never pity soothe thee with a sigh,
Nor never pleasure glad thy cruel heart!

5   Go live, poor wanderer of the wood and field,
        The bitter little that of life remains:
        No more the thickening brakes and verdant plains
    To thee shall home, or food, or pastime yield.

    Seek, mangled wretch, some place of wonted rest,
10   No more of rest, but now thy dying bed!
        The sheltering rushes whistling o'er thy head,
    The cold earth with thy bloody bosom prest.

    Oft as by winding Nith I, musing, wait
        The sober eve, or hail the cheerful dawn,
15   I'll miss thee sporting o'er the dewy lawn,
    And curse the ruffian's aim, and mourn thy hapless fate.

This work was written during April of 1789, at Ellisland, after the
poet witnessed the shooting of a hare. He wrote to Alexander
Cunningham on 4th May 1789:

> One morning lately as I was out pretty early in the fields
> sowing some grass-seeds, I heard the burst of a shot from a
> neighbouring Plantation, & presently a poor little wounded
> hare came crippling by me. – You will guess my indignation
> at the inhuman fellow, who could shoot a hare at this season
> when they all of them have young ones; & it gave me no
> little gloomy satisfaction to see the poor injured creature
> escape him. Indeed there is something in all that multiform
> business of destroying for our sport individuals in the animal
> creation that do not injure us materially, that I could never
> reconcile to my ideas of native Virtue and eternal Right
> (Letter 336).

Later in the same letter Burns remarks 'I am doubtful whether it
would not be an improvement to keep out the last stanza but one,
altogether'. The dropped stanza develops the idea of the hare's 'little
nurslings' being left to fend for themselves alone, without 'That life
a mother only can bestow' (H & H, Vol. I, Notes, p. 443). Indeed,
the same early draft contains the line 'The cold earth with thy blood-
stain'd bosom warm', evoking a more graphic image of the dying
hare's blood, running warm into the earth. So, in a sense, the final
work is the less graphic and personal.

The sentiments expressed to Cunningham reveal again the im-
portance of the poet's holistic world view on his poetry: he judges all

creatures of creation as 'individuals' or creatures of God. This is
seen in poems such as *To A Mouse*,

> I'm truly sorry Man's dominion
> Has broken Nature's social union,
> And justifies that ill opinion
>   Which makes thee startle
> At me, thy poor, earth-born companion
>   And fellow mortal!

The real spark of indignation, though, is not that the hare has been
shot *per se*, but that it has been shot *out of season*. This is mentioned
specifically by Burns in the comment 'the inhuman fellow, who
could shoot a hare *at this season* when they all of them have young
ones'. There has always been a rural, country code of those who
shoot, that animals are not shot during the period when they are
having or rearing young ones. Such behaviour is generally con-
demned as it is so eloquently here.

Burns partly moderates his outrage when commenting on the poem
to Mrs Dunlop, merely to placate the hare-shooting, Major Dunlop:
'this set my humanity in tears and my indignation in arms. . . . please
read [it] to the young ladies. I believe you may include the Major too,
as whatever I have said of shooting hares I have not spoken one
irreverent word against coursing them' (Letter 330). Despite this, it is
evident that Burns was opposed to killing 'game' for mere *sport*. The
'slaughtering guns' of *Westlin Winds* remains a telling image.

Address, to the Shade of Thomson,
On Crowning his Bust at Ednam,
Roxburgh-Shire with a Wreath of Bays

First published in *The European Magazine*, November 1791, prior to
inclusion in the 1793 Edinburgh edition.

> While virgin Spring, by Eden's flood
>   Unfolds her tender mantle green,
> Or pranks the sod in frolic mood,
>   Or tunes Eolian strains between:

> 5   While Summer with a matron grace
>   Retreats to Dryburgh's cooling shade,
> Yet oft, delighted, stops to trace
>   The progress of the spikey blade:

While Autumn, benefactor kind,
10   By Tweed erects his aged head,
And sees, with self-approving mind,
     Each creature on his bounty fed:

While maniac Winter rages o'er
     The hills whence classic Yarrow flows,
15 Rousing the turbid torrent's roar,
     Or sweeping, wild, a waste of snows:

So long, sweet Poet of the Year!
     Shall bloom that wreath thou well has won;
While Scotia, with exulting tear,
20   Proclaims that *Thomson* was her son.

The occasion of this poem was to prove ill-fated. David Erskine, Earl of Buchan, was the elder brother of the more celebrated Henry and Thomas. He had the family egotism without perhaps the talent. His celebration of James Thomson was spoiled by the bust being shattered the night before the unveiling ceremony. Burns had been commissioned to write a poem but could not appear, allegedly because of harvest business. Burns had referred Buchan to Collins's *Ode on the Death of Mr. Thomson*, which he despaired of equalling. Burns's four seasonal stanzas neatly replicate the more prolix chronology of Thomson's best-known poem. The attempt in the last stanza to repatriate Thomson was foredoomed to failure. Complicit with the forces of agrarian capitalism and a propagandist for Anglo-British imperialism (he actually wrote *Rule Britannia* for his *Masque of Alfred*), Thomson had, a poetic pig in clover, absolutely no notion of returning to his austere native land. In political and social values he is almost Burns's antithesis which may in part account for Burns's creative hesitancy and non-appearance.

On the Late Captain Grose's Peregrinations
Thro' Scotland Collecting the Antiquities of that Kingdom
First printed in *The Edinburgh Evening Courant*, 11th August 1789, designated an *Address to the People of Scotland*, signed Thomas A Linn.

Hear, Land o' Cakes, and brither Scots,   oatcakes, brother
Frae Maidenkirk to Johnny Groat's! —   Kirkmaiden parish
If there's a hole in a' your coats,
     I rede you tent it: warn, attend
5 A child's amang you takin notes,   fellow's among
     And, faith, he'll prent it: print

If in your bounds ye chance to light
Upon a fine, fat, fodgel wight,   plump
O' stature short but genius bright,
10   That's he, mark weel — well
And wow! he has an unco sleight uncommon skill
    O' cauk and keel. chalk, pencil

By some auld, houlet-haunted biggin,[1] old, owl-, building
Or kirk deserted by its riggin, roof
15 It's ten to ane ye'll find him snug in one
    Some eldritch part, eerie/haunted
Wi' deils, they say, Lord safe' s! colleaguin' conferring
    At some black art. —

Ilk ghaist that haunts auld ha' or chamer, each ghost, old hall, chamber
20 Ye gipsy-gang that deal in glamour,
And you, deep-read in hell's black grammar, spells/magic
    Warlocks and witches;
Ye'll quake at his conjuring hammer,
    Ye midnight bitches.

25 It's tauld he was a sodger bred, told, soldier
And ane wad rather fa'n than fled; one who would, fallen
But now he's quat the spurtle-blade, quit, sword
    And dog-skin wallet,
And taen the — *Antiquarian trade*, taken
30   I think they call it.

He has a fouth o' auld nick-nackets: fund, old, nick-nacks
Rusty airn caps and jinglin jackets,[2] iron, metal armour
Wad haud the Lothians three in tackets, would hold, shoenails
    A towmont guid; twelvemonth good
35 And parritch-pats, and auld saut-backets, porridge-pots, old salt boxes
    Before the Flood.

Of Eve's first fire he has a cinder;
Auld Tubalcain's[3] fire-shool and fender; old, -shovel
That which distinguishèd the gender
40   O' Balaam's[4] ass;
A broomstick o' the witch of Endor[5],
    Weel shod wi' brass. well

1 Vide his Antiquities of Scotland. RB.
2 Vide his treatise on ancient armour and weapons. R.B.
3 Genesis, IV, 22.
4 Numbers, XXII, 21.
5 Samuel, I, XXVIII, 7.

	Forbye, he'll shape you aff fu' gleg	*besides, off full smartly*
	The cut of Adam's philibeg;	*kilt*
45	The knife that nicket Abel's craig	*cut, throat*
	He'll prove you fully,	
	It was a faulding jocteleg,	*folding clasp-knife*
	Or lang-kail gullie. —	*long cabbage knife*

	But wad ye see him in his glee,	*would*
50	For meikle glee and fun has he,	*much*
	Then set him down, and twa or three	*two*
	Gude fellows wi' him;	*good*
	And *port, O port!* shine thou a wee,	*for a little*
	And THEN ye'll see him!	

55	Now, by the Pow'rs o' Verse and Prose!	
	Thou art a dainty chield, O Grose! —	*fellow*
	Whae'er o' thee shall ill suppose,	*whoever*
	They sair misca' thee;	*sore miscall*
	I'd take the rascal by the nose,	
60	Wad say, Shame fa' thee.	*would, fall*

Francis Grose (1731–1791) was born at Greenford, Middlesex, the son of a jeweller who emigrated from Switzerland to England. After obtaining the rank of Captain in service to the Surrey Militia, he used his inheritance to follow an interest in the arts and became a travelling antiquarian, publishing the well-received *The Antiquities of England and Wales* (1773–87).

Various publications of this poem appeared in newspapers and journals throughout Britain after it first featured in the *Edinburgh Evening Courant* in August 1789, under the pen-name Thomas A. Linn, including appearing in the radical Irish newspaper, *The Northern Star*, issue April 14th–18th 1792. Scott Douglas mentions that it appears also in *The Kelso Chronicle*, 4th September, 1789. (Vol. 1, p. 360). The initial title by Burns was an *Address to the People of Scotland*.

Although the comic tone of the poem is added to by the deliberate naïveté of its point of view (ll. 29–30), Burns himself was influenced by the antiquarian, collecting tendencies of the late eighteenth century. Arguably antiquarianism bears a hidden anxiety that the past is not only different but retreating from us so that we need to preserve its artefacts. Burns was also well aware of the absurdity inherent in some forms of supposed preservation as in the brilliant send-up of Biblical bric-a-brac in ll. 37–48. For Tubalcain (l. 37), see *Gen*.iv.22.; Balaam's Ass, *Num*. xxii. 21ff; The Witch of Endor, 1 *Sam*. xxviii.7ff. Burns's deeply affectionate caricature of Grose in a letter to Mrs Dunlop is a small comic gem in itself. It also reveals his intense, admiring reading of the English eighteenth-century novel and its fundamental contribution to his sensibility as well as his own deep interest in local history of place. '. . . if you discover a chearful-looking gig of an old, fat fellow, the precise figure of Dr Slop, wheeling about your avenue in his own carriage with a pencil & paper in his hand, you may conclude, "Thou art the man!" (II *Samuel* 12:7).' It has also been suggested that 'Tubalcain' was Burns deliberately identifying a key word of Masonic ritual employed by both Grose and himself.

To Miss Cruickshank, a Very Young Lady
Written on the Blank Leaf of a Book,
presented to her by the Author
First printed in the Edinburgh edition, 1793.

Beauteous rose-bud, young and gay,
Blooming on thy early May,
Never may'st thou, lovely Flower,
Chilly shrink in sleety shower!
5   Never Boreas' hoary path,
Never Eurus' pois'nous breath,
Never baleful stellar lights,
Taint thee with untimely blights!
Never, never reptile thief
10   Riot on thy virgin leaf!
Nor even Sol too fiercely view
Thy bosom blushing still with dew!

May'st thou long, sweet crimson gem,
Richly deck thy native stem;
15   Till some evening, sober, calm,
Dropping dews and breathing balm,
While all around the woodland rings,
And ev'ry bird thy requiem sings;
Thou, amid the dirgeful sound,
20   Shed thy dying honours round,
And resign to parent Earth
The loveliest form she e'er gave birth.

This was composed for Miss Jean Cruikshank, the only daughter of William, a classics teacher at the High School Edinburgh and colleague of William Nicol (see Letters 142, 214, and 292 for Burns's correspondence to W. Cruikshank). The poem was probably written late in 1788, although dating the letter containing the poem to William Cruikshank is problematic, estimated for sometime in December 1788 or January 1789. Burns first describes the young girl as 'the sweet little Rose-bud' in March, 1788 (Letter 214). David Sillar of Irvine composed the music for these verses.

Anna Thy Charms
First printed in the London *Star*, 18th April, 1789.

Anna, thy charms my bosom fire,
    And waste my soul with care;
But ah! how bootless to admire,
    When fated to despair!

Yet in thy presence, lovely Fair,
    To hope may be forgiven;
For sure 'twere impious to despair
    So much in sight of Heaven.

This song is generally thought to have appeared first in the Edinburgh edition, 1793. It first publication, was, however, in a London newspaper. It is featured the day after *Ode on the Departed Regency Bill* in Peter Stuart's spurious *Star* (so named because another newspaper *The London Star* existed, the spurious Star being formed after Stuart led a breakaway from the main paper). It was copied and printed by *The London Gazetteer* a few days later, 20th April, 1789.

On Reading in a Newspaper, the Death of John M'Leod, Esq.
Brother to a Young Lady,
A Particular Friend of the Author's
First printed in the Edinburgh edition, 1793.

Sad thy tale, thou idle page,
    And rueful thy alarms;
Death tears the brother of her love
    From Isabella's arms.

5 Sweetly deckt with pearly dew
        The morning rose may blow;
    But cold successive noontide blasts
        May lay its beauties low.

    Fair on Isabella's morn
10   The sun propitious smil'd;
    But, long ere noon, succeeding clouds
        Succeeding hopes beguil'd.

    Fate oft tears the bosom chords
        That Nature finest strung:
15 So Isabella's heart was form'd,
        And so that heart was wrung.

    Dread Omnipotence, alone,
        Can heal the wound He gave;
    Can point the brimful grief-worn eyes
20   To scenes beyond the grave.

    Virtue's blossoms there shall blow,
        And fear no withering blast;
    There Isabella's spotless worth
        Shall happy be at last.

This is a poem of condolence to Miss Isabella McLeod, described
by Burns as 'Aunt to the young Countess of Loudon' near Kilmar-
nock (Letter 139). A copy of the poem was included in a letter to
Patrick Miller on 28th September 1787. John McLeod, the younger
brother of Isabella, died on 20th July 1787 and the poem was
composed shortly after Burns read of his death in an Edinburgh
newspaper.

The Humble Petition of Bruar Water,[1]
to the Noble Duke of Athole
First printed in the Edinburgh edition, 1793.

My Lord, I know, your noble ear
    Woe ne'er assails in vain;
Embolden'd thus, I beg you'll hear
    Your humble slave complain,

---

1 Bruar Falls, in Athole, are exceedingly picturesque and beautiful; but their
effect is much impaired by the want of trees and shrubs. – R.B.

5   How saucy Phoebus' scorching beams,   the Sun
        In flaming summer-pride,
    Dry-withering, waste my foamy streams,
        And drink my crystal tide.

    The lightly-jumping, glowrin' trouts,   staring/keen-eyed
10   That thro' my waters play,
    If, in their random, wanton spouts,   darts
        They near the margin stray;
    If, hapless chance! they linger lang,   long
        I'm scorching up so shallow,
15 They're left the whitening stanes amang,   stones among
        In gasping death to wallow.

    Last day I grat wi' spite and teen,   wept, vexation
        As Poet Burns came by,
    That, to a Bard, I should be seen
20   Wi' half my channel dry:
    A panegyric rhyme, I ween,   trust
        Ev'n as I was he shor'd me;   threatened/offered
    But, had I in my glory been,
        He, kneeling, wad ador'd me.   would have

25 Here, foaming down the skelvy rocks,   shelved
        In twisting strength I rin;   run/flow
    There high my boiling torrent smokes,
        Wild-roaring o'er a linn: a waterfall
    Enjoying large each spring and well
30   As Nature gave them me,
    I am, altho' I say't mysel,
        Worth gaun a mile to see.   going

    Would, then my noble master please
        To grant my highest wishes,
35 He'll shade my banks wi' towering trees,
        And bonie spreading bushes.   bonny
    Delighted doubly then, my Lord,
        You'll wander on my banks,
    And listen mony a grateful bird   many
40   Return you tuneful thanks.

The sober laverock, warbling wild,   lark
    Shall to the skies aspire;
The gowdspink, Music's gayest child,   goldfinch
    Shall sweetly join the choir:
45 The blackbird strong, the lintwhite clear,   linnet
    The mavis mild and mellow;
The robin pensive Autumn cheer
    In all her locks of yellow.

This, too, a covert shall ensure,
50   To shield them from the storm;
And coward maukin sleep secure,   hare
    Low in her grassy form: bed
Here shall the shepherd make his seat,
    To weave his crown of flowers;
55 Or find a sheltering, safe retreat,
    From prone-descending showers.

And here, by sweet, endearing stealth,
    Shall meet the loving pair,
Despising worlds with all their wealth,
60   As empty idle care:
The flowers shall vie in all their charms
    The hour of heaven to grace,
And birks extend their fragrant arms   birch trees
    To screen the dear embrace.

65 Here haply too, at vernal dawn,
    Some musing Bard may stray,
And eye the smoking, dewy lawn,
    And misty mountain, grey;
Or, by the reaper's nightly beam,
70   Mild-chequering thro' the trees,
Rave to my darkly dashing stream,
    Hoarse-swelling on the breeze.

Let lofty firs, and ashes cool
    My lowly banks o'erspread,
75 And view, deep-bending in the pool,
    Their shadows' wat'ry bed:
Let fragrant birks, in woodbines drest,   birches, dressed
    My craggy cliffs adorn;
And, for the little songster's nest,
80   The close embowering thorn.

So may Old Scotia's darling hope,
    Your little angel band,
Spring, like their fathers, up to prop
    Their honour'd, native land!
85   So may, thro' Albion's farthest ken,
       To social-flowing glasses,
The grace be — 'Athole's honest men
    And Athole's bonie lasses!'

This was composed during the first week of September 1787, when the poet was touring the Highlands. Writing from Inverness on 5th September, Burns sent a copy of the poem to Josiah Walker, tutor to the Duke of Atholl's son. He told Walker, 'I have just time to write the foregoing, and to tell you that it was, at least most part of it, the effusion of the half hour that I spent at Bruar. – I don't mean that it was extempore, for I have endeavoured to brush it up as well as Mr Nicol's chat and the jogging of the chaise would allow' (Letter 135). Walker replied by telling Burns how well his poem was received at Blair Atholl and that the family wished to see it in print. He responded to this idea: 'I would not like it published in any other newspaper than a magazine, nor there, but as if by chance, and "said" to be done by such a Man: but it is to me a matter totally indifferent: you are at perfect liberty to do as you please' (Letter 140). This final comment reveals how Burns instructed Walker on the manner in which the poem was to be printed and 'said' to be by him, a move that would, during this period, add some mystique to the publication and Burns would not be seen as a self-publicist. Of course, it was not an indifferent matter to him; all his poetic compositions were the 'offspring' of his Muse or creative genius and he would have been quietly delighted if the poem appeared in print. Later, Walker, appointed Professor at the University of Glasgow, looked back on the poet's visit to the castle at Blair Atholl, recording that it was 'ability alone that gave him [Burns] a title to be there' (Scott Douglas, Vol. I, p. 367).

    This work makes an interesting comparison to *On the Destruction of the Trees at Drumlanrig*, a poem presented to the world as a work of Burns, but then claimed by Henry Mackenzie, although he did not add it to *his* collected writings.

On Scaring Some Water-Fowl in Loch Turit,
A Wild Scene among the Hills of Oughtertyre
First printed in the Edinburgh edition, 1793.

Why, ye tenants of the lake,
For me your wat'ry haunt forsake?
Tell me, fellow-creatures, why
At my presence thus you fly?
5   Why disturb your social joys,
Parent, filial, kindred ties? —
Common friend to you and me,
Nature's gifts to all are free:
Peaceful keep your dimpling wave,
10   Busy feed, or wanton lave;
Or, beneath the sheltering rock,
Bide the surging billow's shock.

Conscious, blushing for our race,
Soon, too soon, your fears I trace:
15   Man, your proud usurping foe,
Would be lord of all below:
Plumes himself in Freedom's pride,
Tyrant stern to all beside.

The eagle, from the cliffy brow,
20   Marking you his prey below,
In his breast no pity dwells,
Strong Necessity compels.
But Man, to whom alone is given
A ray direct from pitying Heaven,
25   Glories in his heart humane —
And creatures for his pleasure slain.

In these savage, liquid plains,
Only known to wandering swains,
Where the mossy riv'let strays,
30   Far from human haunts and ways;
All on Nature you depend,
And life's poor season peaceful spend.

Or, if Man's superior might
Dare invade your native right,

35   On the lofty ether borne,
       Man with all his powers you scorn;
       Swiftly seek, on clanging wings,
       Other lakes and other springs;
       And the foe you cannot brave,
40   Scorn at least to be his slave.

A note by Burns in his Glenriddell Manuscript reads: 'This was a production of a solitary forenoon's walk from Ochtertyre-house. – I lived there, Sir William's guest, for two or three weeks, and was much flattered by my hospitable reception. – What a pity that the mere emotions of gratitude are so impotent in this world! 'Tis lucky that, as we are told, they will be of some avail in the world to come.' The poet met Sir William Murray of Ochtertyre (1705–1793), the Earl of Mansfield, when visiting Blair Atholl in the first week of September 1787 and later visited the old man at his home in Strathearn, where he composed this work in October 1787. Euphemia Murray, a young cousin of Sir William, and daughter of Mungo Murray of Lintrose, is the subject of the poet's song, *Blythe Was She*. Euphemia was known as the 'flower of Strathmore'. The poem is another example of Burns's preoccupation with man as bestial predator.

Verses Written with a Pencil
over the Chimney-Piece, in the Parlour of the Inn
at Kenmore, Taymouth

First printed in *The Edinburgh Evening Courant*, 6th September 1787.

       Admiring Nature in her wildest grace,
       These northern scenes with weary feet I trace;
       O'er many a winding dale and painful steep,
       Th' abodes of coveyed grouse and timid sheep,
5   My savage journey, curious, I pursue,
       Till fam'd Breadalbane opens to my view. —
       The meeting cliffs each deep-sunk glen divides,
       The woods, wild-scattered, clothe their ample sides;
       Th' outstretching lake, embosomed 'mong the hills,
10   The eye with wonder and amazement fills;
       The Tay, meandering sweet in infant pride,
       The palace, rising on his verdant side;
       The lawns, wood-fring'd in Nature's native taste;
       The hillocks, dropt in Nature's careless haste,
15   The arches, striding o'er the new-born stream;
       The village, glittering in the noontide beam —

Poetic ardors in my bosom swell,
Lone wand'ring by the hermit's mossy cell:
The sweeping theatre of hanging woods;
20   The incessant roar of headlong tumbling floods —

Here Poesy might wake her heaven-taught lyre,
And look through Nature with creative fire;
Here, to the wrongs of Fate half reconcil'd,
Misfortune's lightened steps might wander wild;
25   And Disappointment, in these lonely bounds,
Find balm to soothe her bitter rankling wounds:
Here heart-struck Grief might heavenward stretch her scan,
And injur'd Worth forget and pardon man.

When published in the *Edinburgh Evening Courant* these verses were
described as the work of the 'celebrated Ayrshire bard' and found by
an unknown person, who gives only their initials, 'O.B.', while on
visit to Taymouth, where the verses were found on a Hermitage
wall. Most editors guess that Burns himself sent the verses to the
newspaper. A further variant edition appears in *The Bee* magazine
on 9th May 1792, under the title *Verses Written on a Window in
Breadalbane*, by Mr Robert Burns. There are several textual
changes between the two versions. The copy in *The Bee* is probably
a textual improvement made by Burns taken from a manuscript sent
to a friend as there is no evidence that Burns visited Breadalbane on
a second tour. If this is the case, Burns appears to have reverted to
the earlier version when including the poem in his 1793 Edinburgh
edition.

Written with a Pencil Standing
by the Fall of Fyers, near Loch Ness

First printed in the Edinburgh edition, 1793.

Among the heathy hills and ragged woods
The roaring Fyers pours his mossy floods;
Till full he dashes on the rocky mounds,
Where, thro' a shapeless breach, his stream resounds,
5   As high in air the bursting torrents flow,
As deep recoiling surges foam below,
Prone down the rock the whitening sheet descends,
And viewless Echo's ear, astonished, rends.

Dim-seen through rising mists and ceaseless showers,
10 The hoary cavern, wide-surrounding, lours.
Still thro' the gap the struggling river toils,
And still, below, the horrid caldron boils —

This was composed around 5th September 1787, when Burns
travelled from Loch Ness to Foyers. In form and metre, this verse
follows on from the pastoral sketch of the previous work, on the
scenic view from Breadalbane.

On the Birth of a Posthumous Child,
Born in Peculiar Circumstances of Family-Distress
First printed in the Edinburgh edition, 1793.

Sweet flow'ret, pledge o' meikle love,   much
    And ward o' mony a prayer,   many
What heart o' stane wad thou na move,   stone would, not
    Sae helpless, sweet, and fair.   so

5   November hirples o'er the lea,   limps
    Chill, on thy lovely form;
And gane, alas! the shelt'ring tree,   gone
    Should shield thee frae the storm   from

May He who gives the rain to pour,
10   And wings the blast to blaw,   blow
Protect thee frae the driving show'r,   from
    The bitter frost and snaw!   snow

May He, the friend of Woe and Want,
    Who heals life's various stounds,   pangs/pains
15 Protect and guard the mother plant,
    And heal her cruel wounds.

But late she flourished, rooted fast,
    Fair on the summer morn:
Now, feebly bends she, in the blast,
20   Unsheltered and forlorn.

Blest be thy bloom, thou lovely gem,
    Unscath'd by ruffian hand!
And from thee many a parent stem
    Arise to deck our land.

The head-note to this poem, in the Glenriddell Manuscripts, reads: 'Extempore nearly – On the Birth of Monsr. Henri, posthumous child to a Monsr. Henri, a Gentleman of family and fortune from Switzerland; who died after three days illness, leaving his lady, a sister of Sir Thos. Wallace, in her sixth month of this her first child. – The lady and her Family were particular friends of the Author. – The child was born in November 1790'. James Henri married Mrs Dunlop's daughter Susan, but died 22nd June, 1790. Burns wrote to Mrs Dunlop, on hearing of the birth, 'I literally, *jumped for joy* . . . out skipt I among the broomy banks of Nith to muse over my joy by retail. – To keep within the bounds of prose was impossible. Mrs Little's is a more elegant, but not a more sincere Compliment to the sweet little fellow, than I extempore almost poured out to him in the following verses' (Letter 427).

N.B. The Whistle: A Ballad was the last work printed in the 1793 Edinburgh edition. It was first published in Johnson's fourth volume of the *Scots Musical Museum*, August 1792 and is therefore printed in the next section, songs published by Burns during his lifetime.

PART FOUR

The Songs of Burns
Published During His Lifetime

Young Peggy

Tune: The Last Time I came O'er the Moor
First printed in the S.M.M., Vol. 1, 22nd May, 1787.

Young Peggy blooms our boniest lass,
    Her blush is like the morning,
The rosy dawn, the springing grass,
    With early gems adorning:
5 Her eyes outshine the radiant beams
    That gild the passing shower,
And glitter o'er the crystal streams,
    And cheer each fresh'ning flower.

Her lips, more than the cherries bright,
10   A richer dye has grac'd them,
They charm th' admiring gazer's sight
    And sweetly tempt to taste them:
Her smile is as the ev'ning mild,
    When feather'd pairs are courting,
15 And little lambkins wanton wild,
    In playful bands disporting.

Were Fortune lovely Peggy's foe,
    Such sweetness would relent her,
As blooming Spring unbends the brow
20   Of surly, savage Winter.
Detraction's eye no aim can gain
    Her winning pow'rs to lessen;
And fretful Envy grins in vain,
    The poison'd tooth to fasten.

25 Ye Pow'rs of Honour, Love, and Truth,
    From ev'ry ill defend her;
Inspire the highly-favour'd Youth
    The destinies intend her;
Still fan the sweet connubial flame
30   Responsive in each bosom;
And bless the dear parental name
    With many a filial blossom.

Young Peggy was Margaret Kennedy (1766–95), daughter of Robert Kennedy of Daljarrock, where he worked as the factor to the Earl of Cassilis. The poet met Margaret because her father was Gavin Hamilton's brother-in-law. Burns sent a copy of the song in a letter to Miss Kennedy in the Autumn of 1785:

> Permit me to present you with the enclosed SONG, as a small tho' grateful tribute for the honour of your acquaintance. I have, in these verses, attempted some faint sketches of your PORTRAIT in the unimbellished, simple manner of descriptive TRUTH. Flattery I leave to your LOVERS; whose exaggerating Fancies may make them imagine you still nearer, if possible, to Perfection than you really are.
>
> . . . even the sight of a fine flower, or the company of a fine Woman (by far the finest part of God's works below), have sensations for the poetic heart that the HERD of Man are strangers to. . . . I am, as in many other things, indebted to Mr Hamilton's kindness in introducing me to you (Letter 20).

The aspirations of the last stanza are tragically ironic, given what happened to Margaret Kennedy nine years later, when, in 1794, she had an affair with a Captain Andrew McDoul, whose child she bore, resulting in a paternity row in which McDoul denied being the child's father. Young Peggy died before the £3000 award was made for the child's maintenance.

Johnson appears to have selected his own tune, *Loch Eroch Side*, when he printed the song. The poet was advised not to print the song in his Edinburgh edition (Letters 90 and 88) and decided to send it to the S.M.M.

Bonie Dundee

First printed in the S.M.M., Vol. 1, 22nd May, 1787.

'O whar did ye get that hauver-meal bannock?'   where, oatmeal
    O silly blind body, O dinna ye see;   do you not
I gat it frae a young, brisk Sodger Laddie,   got, from, soldier
    Between Saint Johnston and bonie Dundee.   Perth
5 O gin I saw the laddie that gae me't!   if, gave
    Aft has he doudl'd me up on his knee;   often, dandled
May Heaven protect my bonie Scots laddie,
    And send him hame to his babie and me.   home

'My blessin's upon thy sweet, wee lippie!   lips
10   My blessins upon thy bonie e'e brie!   eyebrow
Thy smiles are sae like my blythe Sodger   Laddie, so,
        Thou's ay the dearer and dearer to me!
But I'll big a bow'r on yon bonie banks,   build
        Whare Tay rins wimplin by sae clear;   where, runs, so
15 And I'll cleed thee in the tartan sae fine,   clothe, so
        And mak thee a man like thy daddie dear.'   make

This is an updated version of a traditional song. The first verse
is improved, the second is from Burns. The description 'hauver-
meal bannock' is a euphemistic reference to being pregnant and
showing it.

To the Weaver's Gin Ye Go

Tune: To the Weaver's Gin ye Go
First printed in the S.M.M., Vol. 2, 14th February, 1788.

My heart was ance as blythe and free,
        As simmer days were lang,   summer, long
But a bonie, westlin weaver lad   from the West
        Had gart me change my sang.   made, song

Chorus
5   To the weaver's gin ye go, fair maids,   if
To the weaver's gin ye go,   if
I rede you right, gang ne'er at night,   warn, go
To the weaver's gin ye go.   if

My mither sent me to the town   mother
10   To warp a plaiden wab;
But the weary, weary warpin o't
        Has gart me sigh and sab.   made, sob
To the weaver's &c.

A bonie, westlin weaver lad
        Sat working at his loom;
15 He took my heart, as wi' a net
        In every knot and thrum.
            To the weaver's &c.

I sat beside my warpin-wheel,
    And ay I ca'd it roun';   always, drove
And every shot and every knock,
20   My heart it gae a stoun.   gave, thump
      To the weaver's &c.

The moon was sinking in the west
    Wi' visage pale and wan,
As my bonie, westlin weaver lad
    Convoy'd me thro' the glen.
      To the weaver's &c.

25   But what was said, or what was done,
      Shame fa' me gin I tell;   fall on, if
But Oh! I fear the kintra soon   countryside
    Will ken as weel's mysel!   know, as well as
      To the weaver's &c.

This is based on an old song but the lyrics, bar the chorus, are from Burns. The poet comments:

> The chorus of this song is old, the rest of it is mine. Here, once for all, let me apologise for many silly compositions of mine in this work. Many beautiful airs wanted words; in the hurry of other avocations, if I could string a parcel of rhymes together anything near tolerable, I was fain to let them pass. He must be an excellent poet indeed, whose every performance is excellent.

This self-deprecatory remark should not be taken seriously. Burns had a phenomenal capacity to evolve lyrics from traditional music. Having brought him wool to weave, the girl finds herself caught not only in the rhythm of the shuttle but of the penis. The garment is made and she also finds herself pregnant.

I'm o'er Young to Marry Yet

Tune: I'm o'er Young to Marry Yet
First printed in the S.M.M., Vol. 2, 14th February, 1788.

I am my mammie's ae bairn,   one child
    Wi' unco folk I weary, Sir,   strangers
And lying in a man's bed,
    I'm fley'd it make me irie, Sir.   frightened/melancholy

Chorus
5   I'm owre young, I'm owre young,   *too*
      I'm owre young to marry yet;
   I'm owre young, 'twad be a sin
      To tak me frae my mammie yet.   *from*

   Hallowmass is come and gane,   *All Saints' Day, gone*
10   The nights are lang in winter, Sir;   *long*
   And you an' I in ae bed,   *one*
      In trowth, I dare na venture, Sir.   *truth, not*
      I'm o'er young, &c.

   Fu' loud and shrill the frosty wind   *full*
      Blaws thro' the leafless timmer, Sir;   *blows, timber/trees*
15   But if ye come this gate again,
      I'll aulder be gin simmer, Sir.   *older, come, summer*
      I'm o'er young, &c.

This is a traditional song re-written by Burns. He kept the original chorus and added new verses. The lyric plays on the subject of viginity with the promise that, come next summer, the young lass will let her suitor have his way. The female voices of these songs are constantly frank and honest about their sexual desires.

The Birks of Aberfeldey –
First printed in the S.M.M., Vol. 2, 14th February, 1788.

Now Simmer blinks on flow'ry braes,   *summer, hillsides*
And o'er the crystal streamlets plays;
Come let us spend the lightsome days
      In the birks of Aberfeldey. –

Chorus
5   Bonie lassie, will ye go,
   Will ye go, will ye go,
   Bonie lassie, will ye go
      To the birks of Aberfeldey?

   The little birdies blythely sing   *happily*
10   While o'er their heads the hazels hing,   *hang*
   Or lightly flit on wanton wing
      In the birks of Aberfeldey. –

The braes ascend like lofty wa's,   walls
The foaming stream, deep-roaring fa's   falls
15   O'er hung with fragrant-spreading shaws,   leaves
        The birks of Aberfeldey. –

The hoary cliffs are crown'd wi' flowers,
White o'er the linns the burnie pours,   waterfall, small burn/stream
And, rising, weets wi' misty showers   makes wet
20   The birks of Aberfeldey. –

Let Fortune's gifts at random flee,
They ne'er shall draw a wish frae me,   from
Supremely blest wi' love and thee
    In the birks of Aberfeldey. –

Composed during the poet's tour of the Highlands in 1787. Burns
has a predilection for rivers and streams as the essence of the spirit of
place.

McPherson's Farewell

Tune: McPherson's Farewell
First printed in the S.M.M., Vol. 2, 14th February, 1788.

Farewell, ye dungeons dark and strong,
    The wretch's destinie!
M'Pherson's time will not be long,
    On yonder gallows-tree.

Chorus
5   Sae rantingly, sae wantonly,   riotously
        Sae dauntingly gae'd he: went
    He play'd a spring, and danc'd it round   tune
        Below the gallows-tree.

O what is death but parting breath?
10   On many a bloody plain
    I've dar'd his face, and in this place
        I scorn him yet again!
            Sae rantingly, &c.

Untie these bands from off my hands,
  And bring to me my sword,
15 And there's no a man in all Scotland
  But I'll brave him at a word.
   Sae rantingly, &c.

I've liv'd a life of sturt and strife;   trouble
  I die by treacherie:
It burns my heart I must depart
20 And not avenged be.
   Sae rantingly, &c.

Now farewell, light, thou sunshine bright,
  And all beneath the sky!
May coward shame distain his name,
  The wretch that dares not die!
   Sae rantingly, &c.

This song immortalises James MacPherson (illegitimate son of a
gentleman to a gypsy woman), a cattle thief who robbed in Moray-
shire and was hanged on 7th November, 1700. While myth and
folklore enshrine Macpherson's memory, it does seem factually true
that he did play a fiddle tune of his own composition prior to his
execution and then, before the crowd, destroyed his fiddle. Burns, in
opposition to the original ballad of the early 1700s, which was a
'confessional and crudely moralistic' song (Low, *The Songs of
Robert Burns*, p. 232) warning others not to steal cattle, character-
istically presents Macpherson as a rebellious hero.

My Highland Lassie, O

Tune: McLauchlin's Scots-Measure
First printed in the S.M.M., Vol. 2, 14th February, 1788.

Nae gentle dames, tho' ne'er sae fair,   no, so
Shall ever be my Muse's care;
Their titles a' are empty show;
Gie me my Highland Lassie, O.   give

Chorus
5 Within the glen sae bushy, O,   so
 Aboon the plain sae rashy, O,   above, so rushy
 I set me down wi' right guid will,   good
 To sing my Highland Lassie, O.

O were yon hills and valleys mine,
10   Yon palace and yon gardens fine!
The world then the love should know
I bear my Highland Lassie, O.
    Within the glen &c.

But fickle Fortune frowns on me,
And I maun cross the raging sea;   *must*
15   But while my crimson currents flow,   *blood*
I'll love my Highland Lassie, O.
    Within the glen &c.

Altho' thro' foreign climes I range,
I know her heart will never change,
For her bosom burns with honor's glow,
20   My faithful Highland Lassie, O.
    Within the glen &c.

For her I'll dare the billows' roar;
For her I'll trace a distant shore;
That Indian wealth may lustre throw
Around my Highland Lassie, O.
    Within the glen &c.

25   She has my heart, she has my hand,
My secret troth and honor's band!
'Till the mortal stroke shall lay me low,
I'm thine, my Highland Lassie, O.

Final Chorus

Farewell, the glen sae bushy, O!   *so*
30   Farewell, the plain sae rashy, O!   *so*
To other lands I now must go
To sing my Highland Lassie, O.

This is an early work of Burns referring to Mary Campbell, so-called 'Highland Mary', whose premature death has provoked a myriad of largely pointless speculation. To some extent Burns himself in later life was responsible for this mythification of Mary Campbell; see, for example, Cromek's *Reliques* (1808), p. 237.

Though Cruel Fate

Tune: She Raise and Loot Me In *or* The Northern Lass.
First printed in the S.M.M., Vol. 2, 14th February, 1788.

Though cruel Fate should bid us part,
    Far as the Pole and Line,
Her dear idea round my heart
    Should tenderly entwine:

Though mountains rise, and desarts howl,
    And oceans roar between;
Yet dearer than my deathless soul
    I still would love my Jean.

This is signed as a work from Burns in Johnson's S.M.M. and unlike the songs marked only with an X or Z, it is original. It is essentially the progenitor of *Of A' The Airts*, written for Jean Armour.

Stay, My Charmer, Can You Leave Me

Tune: An Gille dubh ciar dhubh
First printed in the S.M.M., Vol. 2, 14th February, 1788.

Stay, my charmer, can you leave me?
Cruel, cruel to deceive me!
Well you know how much you grieve me:
    Cruel charmer, can you go!
5   Cruel charmer, can you go!

By my love so ill-requited:
By the faith you fondly plighted;
By the pangs of lovers slighted;
    Do not, do not leave me so!
10   Do not, do not leave me so!

Burns adored fiddle music, particularly sad, evocative and melodic slow airs. Accordingly, he wrote this lyric for a Highland air he heard during his tour of the Highlands in 1787. Scotland was, particularly after the 1745, fertile in tragic slow airs and defiant fast ones. Burns himself was defined as a 'home fiddler'; that is an amateur not good enough for public performance.

Strathallan's Lament

Tune: As song title.
First printed in the S.M.M., Vol. 2, 14th February, 1788.

Thickest night, surround my dwelling!
    Howling tempests, o'er me rave!
Turbid torrents wintry-swelling,
    Roaring by my lonely cave.
5 Crystal streamlets gently flowing,
    Busy haunts of base mankind,
Western breezes softly blowing,
    Suit not my distracted mind.

In the cause of Right engaged,
10   Wrongs injurious to redress,
Honor's war we strongly waged,
    But the Heavens deny'd success:
Ruin's wheel has driven o'er us,
    Not a hope that dare attend,
15 The wide world is all before us —
    But a world without a friend!

A haunting, evocative, and powerful Jacobite lyric, this elegiac monologue gives voice to the mourning of James Drummond, whose father, William, Viscount Strathallan, died at the battle of Culloden, 1746. The son fled, taking refuge in a cave, the setting of this first person lament. Unlike earlier commentators, Donaldson interprets this mythically rather than historically, believing it sung from the mouth of William Drummond, the dead father (pp. 80–1). The first stanza sets the scene and mood in poignant juxtaposition, nature's raw beauty contrasted with human desolation. The ferocious winter nightscape is, for a Jacobite, an appropriate metaphor for the complete destruction of his world.

A peculiar mirror image of this poem was collected by Scott Hogg in 1996 from *The Morning Chronicle*, August 1795 and considered by him as possibly by Burns. *Exiles* is written not about a Jacobite exile, but the exile of Thomas Muir, Fysche Palmer and the other radical martyrs of this period. Metrically and musically *Exiles* exactly fits *Strathallan's Lament*. The iconic, 'arm'd' Wallace is also compatible with Burns's newly discovered Bruce poems. It is difficult to imagine any specifically Scottish poem appearing in the *Chronicle* from any other source. It is also wholly characteristic of Burns to take a Jacobite theme and recontextualise it in a Radical context. It can also be read in its last two stanzas as an embryonic version of *Ode for General Washington's Birthday*.

Dark in misty horror glooming,
 Where the Southern Ocean roars
And the hoary Billows booming,
 Ceaseless lash barbaric shores,
5 Round the beach in deep emotion,
  Sternly rov'd a mournful train,
While along the expanse of Ocean
 Echoed far the Patriot strain.

 . . . Arm'd alone with Truth and Reason,
10 Mammon's venal slaves we dar'd;
  Short of triumph was the season: -
Virtue, view the base reward.

Doom'd among these wilds to languish,
 Exil'd from our native shore;
15 Friends bewail in bitter anguish,
  Victims they behold no more.
What the cause of our destruction?
  Tell th' astonish'd world around;
'Twas the combat with Corruption;
20 Britain feels her mortal wound!

Scotland, once our boast, our wonder,
 Fann'd by Freedom's purer gale,
When thy Wallace, arm'd with thunder,
 Bade the baffl'd TYRANT wail:
25 O, our Country! Vultures rend thee,
  Proudly riot on thy store;
Who deluded, shall befreind thee?
  Ah! do we thy lot deplore.

What Will I Do Gin My Hoggie Die

Tune: Moss Platt
First printed in the S.M.M., Vol. 2, 14th February, 1788.

What will I do gin my Hoggie die,	if, lamb
My joy, my pride, my Hoggie;	lamb
My only beast, I had nae mae,	no more
And vow but I was vogie. —	vain

5	The lee-lang night we watch'd the fauld,	live-long, fold
	Me and my faithfu' doggie;	
	We heard nocht but the roaring linn	nothing, waterfall
	Amang the braes sae scroggie. —	hillsides, so, scrub-covered

	But the houlet cry'd frae the Castle-wa',	owl, from, wall
10	The blitter frae the boggie,	snipe, from
	The tod reply'd upon the hill,	fox
	I trembled for my Hoggie.	lamb

	When day did daw and cocks did craw,	dawn, crow
	The morning it was foggie;	
15	An unco tyke lap o'er the dyke	strange dog, stone wall
	And maist has kill'd my Hoggie.	almost, lamb

Given his life long intimacy with and empathy for domestic and wild animals, this traditional song was particularly attractive to Burns.

Jumpin John

First printed in the S.M.M., Vol. 2, 14th February, 1788.

	Her Daddie forbad, her Minnie forbad;	
	Forbidden she wadna be:	would not
	She wadna trow't, the browst she brew'd	would not believe it
	Wad taste sae bitterlie.	would, so

Chorus
5	The lang lad they ca' jumpin John	long, call
	Beguil'd the bonie lassie,	
	The lang lad they ca' jumpin John	
	Beguil'd the bonie lassie.	

	A cow and a cauf, a yowe and a hauf,	calf, sheep & lamb
10	And thretty guid shillins and three;	thirty good
	A vera gude tocher, a cotter-man's dochter,	very good dowry, daughter
	The lass with the bonie black e'e.	eye
	The lang lad &c.	

Kinsley remarks 'Stenhouse says that this is "a fragment of the old humorous ballad, with some verbal corrections"; but the "ballad" has not been identified' (Vol. III, no. 199, p. 1263). Stenhouse clearly did not know the old song adapted by Burns which is

certainly *My Daddie Forbade* in Herd's Collection, beginning
'Though my Daddie forbade, and my Minnie forbade, /Forbidden
I will not be'. It is likely there never was an 'old humorous ballad'.

Up in the Morning Early

First printed in the S.M.M., Vol. 2, 14th February, 1788.

Cauld blaws the wind frae east to west,	cold, blows, from
The drift is driving sairly;	sorely
Sae loud and shill's I hear the blast,	so, shrill
I'm sure it's winter fairly.	

Chorus
5   Up in the morning's no for me,
      Up in the morning early;

When a' the hills are covered wi' snaw,	snow
I'm sure it's winter fairly.	

The birds sit chittering in the thorn,	
10 A' day they fare but sparely;	
And lang's the night frae e'en to morn,	long is, from
I'm sure it's winter fairly.	
Up in the morning's &c.	

The chorus of this is traditional, but the verses are by Burns.

The Dusty Miller

First printed in the S.M.M., Vol. 2, 14th February, 1788.

Hey the dusty Miller,
    And his dusty coat;
He will spend a shilling
    Or he win a groat:
5   Dusty was the coat,
    Dusty was the colour;
Dusty was the kiss

That I gat frae the Miller. —	got from

Hey the dusty Miller,
10   And his dusty sack;
Leeze me on the calling
    Fills the dusty peck:

Fills the dusty peck,
   Brings the dusty siller;   money/coins
15 I wad gie my coatie   would give
   For the dusty Miller.

A traditional song adapted slightly by Burns. See Kinsley's notes
(Vol. III, no. 201, p. 1264), where he quotes the earlier lines: 'O the
dusty miller, O the dusty miller, / Dusty was his coat, dusty was his
colour, / Dusty was the kiss I got frae the miller'.

The Young Highland Rover

Tune: Morag.

First printed in the S.M.M., Vol. 2, 14th February, 1788.

Loud blaw the frosty breezes,   blow
   The snaws the mountains cover;   snows
Like winter on me seizes,
   Since my young Highland rover
5   Far wanders nations over. —

Chorus
Where'er he go, where'er he stray,
   May Heaven be his warden;
Return him safe to fair Strathspey
   And bonie Castle-Gordon. —

10 The trees, now naked groaning,
   Shall soon wi' leaves be hinging,
The birdies dowie moaning   dolefully
   Shall a' be blythely singing,
   And every flower be springing.

Second Chorus
15 Sae I'll rejoice the lee-lang day,   live long
   When by his mighty Warden
My Youth's return'd to fair Strathspey
   And bonie Castle-Gordon.

This was written as a result of the poet's tour of the Highlands and
his visit to Castle Gordon in September 1787 to see the Duchess of
Gordon. Burns, keenly aware of Jacobite history, knew that Prince
Charles Edward Stuart visited Castle Gordon sometime before the
battle of Culloden.

The Winter It is Past

First printed in the S.M.M., Vol. 2, 14th February, 1788.

The winter it is past, and the summer's comes at last,
    And the small birds sing on ev'ry tree;
The hearts of these are glad, but mine is very sad,
    For my Lover has parted from me.

5   The rose upon the brier, by the waters running clear,
    May have charms for the linnet or the bee;
Their little loves are blest and their little hearts at rest,
    But my Lover is parted from me.

My love is like the sun, in the firmament does run,
10   For ever is constant and true;
But his is like the moon that wanders up and down,
    And every month it is new.

All you that are in love and cannot it remove,
    I pity the pains you endure:
15 For experience makes me know that your hearts are full of woe,
    A woe that no mortal can cure.

This is adapted from a lyric *The Love Sick Maid* published in 1765.
The original words tell the story of an Irish woman whose lover, a
highway robber, was hanged at the Curragh of Kildare, leaving her
to mourn. Mackay has dropped the final two stanzas, which appear
in S.M.M and most major editions, including Henley and Hender-
son and Kinsley.

I Dream'd I Lay

Tune: I Dream'd I Lay
First printed in the S.M.M., Vol. 2, 14th February, 1788.

I dream'd I lay where flowers were springing
    Gaily in the sunny beam,
List'ning to the wild birds singing,
    By a falling, chrystal stream;
5   Streight the sky grew black and daring,
    Thro' the woods the whirlwinds rave;
Trees with aged arms were warring,
    O'er the swelling, drumlie wave.   turbid

Such was my life's deceitful morning,
10   Such the pleasures I enjoy'd;
But lang or noon, loud tempests storming—   ere
        A' my flowery bliss destroy'd.
Tho' fickle Fortune has deceiv'd me,
        She promis'd fair, and perform'd but ill;
15   Of mony a joy and hope bereav'd me,   many
        I bear a heart shall support me still.

Burns wrote 'These two stanzas I composed when I was seventeen'.
Composition is therefore sometime in 1776. This provides another
example of the degree to which he was early, presciently haunted by
an ill-fated life.

Duncan Davison

First printed in the S.M.M., Vol. 2, 14th February, 1788.

There was a lass, they ca'd her Meg,   called
        And she held o'er the moors to spin;
There was a lad that follow'd her,
        They ca'd him Duncan Davison.   called
5   The moor was dreigh, and Meg was skeigh,   dull, fiery
        Her favour Duncan could na win;   not
For wi' the rock she wad him knock,   would
        And ay she shook the temper-pin.   speed regulator pin

As o'er the moor they lightly foor,   went
10   A burn was clear, a glen was green,
Upon the banks they eas'd their shanks,   rested limbs/legs
        And ay she set the wheel between:
But Duncan swoor a haly aith   swore, holy oath
That Meg should be a bride the morn;
15   Then Meg took up her spinnin-graith,   equipment
And flang them a' out o'er the burn.   threw

We will big a wee, wee house,   build
        And we will live like king and queen;
Sae blythe and merry's we will be,   so
20   When ye set by the wheel at e'en.   evening
A man may drink and no be drunk,
        A man may fight and no be slain:
A man may kiss a bonie lass,
        And ay be welcome back again.

Burns signed this with a 'Z' when published by Johnson to indicate that he had either made 'corrections, or additions' to a traditional work. The final lines have a natural flow indicative of Burns, as found in his version of *Logan Braes*.

Theniel Menzies' Bonie Mary

Tune: The Ruffian's Rant, or Roy's Wife
First printed in the S.M.M., Vol. 2, 14th February, 1788.

In comin by the brig o' Dye,   bridge
    At Darlet we a blink did tarry;   short while, stopped
As day was dawin in the sky   dawning
    We drank a health to bonie Mary. —

Chorus
5 Theniel Menzies' bonie Mary,
    Theniel Menzies' bonie Mary,
Charlie Grigor tint his plaidie   lost his plaid
    Kissin Theniel's bonie Mary. —

Her een sae bright, her brow sae white,   eyes so, so
10   Her haffet locks as brown's a berry,   temple
And ay they dimpl't wi' a smile,
    The rosy cheeks o' bonie Mary. —
    Theniel Menzies' &c.

We lap an' danc'd the lee-lang day,   jumped, live long
    Till Piper lads were wae and weary;   worn out
15 But Charlie gat the spring to pay   got
    For kissin Theniel's bonie Mary. —
    Theniel Menzies' &c.

The river Dye is near Stonehaven. The poet visited the area (where some of his relatives lived) with William Nicol on 10th September, 1787 during his tour of the Highlands. The music for the lyric is a strathspey known under the two titles listed above. Kinsley is probably right that the words are adapted from an original bawdy song.

Lady Onlie, Honest Lucky,
or A' the Lads o' Thorniebank
Tune: The Ruffian's Rant
First printed in the S.M.M., Vol. 2, 14th February, 1788.

A' the lads o' Thornie-bank
    When they gae to the shore o' Bucky,   go
They'll step in an' tak a pint   take
    Wi' Lady Onlie, honest lucky. —

Chorus
5 Lady Onlie, honest lucky,
    Brews gude ale at shore o' Bucky;   good
I wish her sale for her guid ale,   good
    The best on a' the shore o' Bucky. —

Her house sae bien, her curch sae clean,   so snug, kerchief
10   I wat she is a dainty Chuckie!   know, old darling
And cheery blinks the ingle-gleede   hearth-ember
    O' Lady Onlie, honest lucky. —

This is a traditional drinking song collected and brushed up by
Burns during his Highland tour in September 1787. 'Bucky' refers
to the small fishing town of Buckie. Lady Onlie is the old landlady.

The Banks of the Devon
Tune: Bhannerach dhon na chri
First printed in the S.M.M., Vol. 2, 14th February, 1788.

How pleasant the banks of the clear-winding Devon,
    With green-spreading bushes, and flow'rs
    blooming fair!
But the boniest flower on the banks of the Devon
    Was once a sweet bud on the braes of the Ayr.   hill sides
5 Mild be the sun on this sweet-blushing Flower,
    In the gay, rosy morn as it bathes in the dew;
And gentle the fall of the soft, vernal shower,
    That steals on the evening each leaf to renew!

O spare the dear blossom, ye orient breezes,
10   With chill, hoary wing as ye usher the dawn!
And far be thou distant, thou reptile that seizes
    The verdure and pride of the garden or lawn!

Let Bourbon exult in his gay, gilded Lilies,
   And England triumphant display her proud Rose;
15 A fairer than either adorns the green vallies
   Where Devon, sweet Devon meandering flows. —

This exquisite lyric celebrates Charlotte Hamilton (1763–1806), younger sister of Gavin Hamilton, Mauchline. Burns wrote to Gavin on 28th August, 1787, commenting – 'Yesterday morning I rode from this town [Stirling] up the meandering Devon's banks, to pay my respects to some Ayrshire folks at Harvieston [Clackmannanshire]. . . . Of Charlotte I cannot speak in common terms of admiration: she is not only beautiful, but lovely . . .' (Letter 132).

Weary Fa' You, Duncan Gray

Tune: Duncan Gray
First printed in the S.M.M., Vol. 2, 14th February, 1788.

WEARY fa' you, Duncan Gray,   fall
   Ha, ha the girdin o't,   horse girthing/ galloping
Wae gae by you, Duncan Gray,   woe go
   Ha, ha the girdin o't;
5 When a' the lave gae to their play,   remainder go
   Then I maun sit the lee-lang day,   must, live-long
And jeeg the cradle wi' my tae   rock, toe
   And a' for the bad girdin o't. —   girthing for galloping (copulation)

Bonie was the Lammas moon
10   Ha, ha the girdin o't,
Glowrin a' the hills aboon,   glowing, above
   Ha, ha the girdin o't;
The girdin brak, the beast cam down,   girthing broke, horse came
   I tint my curch and baith my shoon,   lost, kerchief, both, shoes
15 And Duncan ye're an unco loun;   strange rascal
   Wae on the bad girdin o't. —   woe

But Duncan gin ye'll keep your aith,   if, oath
   Ha, ha the girdin o't,
I'se bless you wi' my hindmost breath,   I'll
20   Ha, ha the girdin o't;
Duncan gin ye'll keep your aith,
   The beast again can bear us baith   horse, both
And auld Mess John will mend the skaith   old, Minister, damage
   And clout the bad girdin o't. —   patch

This is based on a traditional bawdy song somewhat cleaned up by
Burns, but left with happy overtones of horsy, sexual pleasure. The
original lyric changed by Burns is from the David Herd collection.

The Ploughman

First printed in the S.M.M., Vol. 2, 14th February, 1788.

The Ploughman he's a bony lad,
    His mind is ever true, jo,   *sweetheart*
His garters knit below his knee,
    His bonnet it is blue, jo.

Chorus
5 Then up wi't a', my Ploughman lad,   *with it*
    And hey, my merry Ploughman;
Of a' the trades that I do ken,   *know*
    Commend me to the Ploughman.

My Ploughman he comes hame at e'en,   *home, evening*
10   He's aften wat and weary: *often wet*
Cast aff the wat, put on the dry,   *off, wet*
    And gae to bed, my Dearie.   *go*
        Then up wi't a', &c.

I will wash my Ploughman's hose,
    And I will dress his o'erlay;   *necktie*
15 I will mak my Ploughman's bed,   *make*
    And chear him late and early.
        Then up wi't a', &c.

I hae been east, I hae been west,   *have*
    I hae been at Saint Johnston,   *Perth*
The boniest sight that e'er I saw
20   Was the Ploughman laddie dancin.
        Then up wi't a', &c.

Snaw-white stockings on his legs,   *snow-*
    And siller buckles glancin;   *silver*
A guid blue bonnet on his head,   *good*
    And O but he was handsome!
        Then up wi't a', &c.

25 Commend me to the Barn yard,
        And the Corn-mou, man;   corn stook
    I never gat my Coggie fou   got, (cup) *womb* full
        Till I met wi' the Ploughman.
            Then up wi't a', &c.

This is another traditional song worked over by Burns from the song
collection by David Herd. The second and third stanzas are from the
old song. The chorus is also old, leaving Burns's input as the first,
fourth, fifth and sixth stanzas.

Landlady, Count the Lawin
Tune: Hey Tuti Tatey –
First printed in the S.M.M., Vol. 2, 14th February, 1788.

    Landlady count the lawin,   bill
    The day is near the dawin,   dawning
    Ye're a' blind drunk, boys,
        And I'm but jolly fou. —   full/drunk

    Chorus
5   Hey tuti, tatey, How tuti, taiti,
    Hey tuti taiti, wha's fou now. —

    Cog an ye were ay fou,   drinking jug, always drunk
    Cog an ye were ay fou;
    I wad sit and sing to you,   would
10   If ye were ay fou. —
            Hey tuti, tatey &c.

    Weel may we a' be,   well, all
    Ill may ye never see!
    God bless the king
        And the Companie!
            Hey tuti, tatey &c.

This is a reworking of a traditional lyric. Like *Willie Brew'd A Peck
O Maut*, it is a drinking song to be sung as by a drunk. Given the
traditional tune and lyrics, it is certain the reference is to a Stuart not
a Hanoverian king.

Raving Winds around Her Blowing
Tune: McGrigor of Rora's Lament
First printed in the S.M.M., Vol. 2, 14th February, 1788.

Raving winds around her blowing,
Yellow leaves the woodlands strowing,
By a river hoarsely roaring
Isabella stray'd deploring.
5   Farewell, hours that late did measure
Sunshine days of joy and pleasure;
Hail, thou gloomy night of sorrow,
Cheerless night that knows no morrow.

O'er the Past too fondly wandering,
10   On the hopeless Future pondering;
Chilly Grief my life-blood freezes,
Fell Despair my fancy seizes.
Life, thou soul of every blessing,
Load to Misery most distressing,
15   Gladly how would I resign thee,
And to dark Oblivion join thee!'

This work was written in 1787 by Burns out of sympathy with Miss
Isabella McLeod, on the death of her sister, Flora McLeod, and her
sister's husband, the Earl of Loudon, who killed himself due to
financial debts.

Musing on the Roaring Ocean
Tune: Druimionn dubh
First printed in the S.M.M., Vol. 2, 14th February, 1788.

Musing on the roaring ocean
    Which divides my Love and me,
Wearying Heaven in warm devotion
    For his weal where'er he be;
5   Hope and Fear's alternate billow
    Yielding late to Nature's law,
Whispering spirits round my pillow,
    Talk of him that's far awa. —

Ye whom Sorrow never wounded,
10   Ye who never shed a tear,
Care-untroubled, joy-surrounded,
        Gaudy Day to you is dear:
Gentle Night do thou befriend me;
        Downy sleep the curtain draw;
15 Spirits kind again attend me,
        Talk of him that's far awa!

Burns records that he composed this song as a 'compliment to a Mrs McLachlan, whose husband is an officer in the East Indies' (See Low, no. 82, p. 257).

Blythe was She –
Composed at Auchtertyre on Miss Euphemia Murray of Lentrose
Tune: Andro and his Cuttie Gun.
First printed in the S.M.M., Vol. 2, 14th February, 1788.

By Oughtertyre grows the aik,   oak
        On Yarrow banks the birken shaw;   birch woods
But Phemie was a bonier lass   Miss Murray
        Than braes o' Yarrow ever saw. —   hillsides

Chorus
5 Blythe, blythe and merry was she,
        Blythe was she butt and ben: outside, inside
Blythe by the banks of Ern,   river Earn
        And blythe in Glenturit glen!

Her looks were like a flower in May,
10   Her smile was like a simmer morn,   summer
She tripped by the banks o' Ern
        As light's a bird upon a thorn. —
        Blythe, blythe &c.

Her bonie face it was as meek
        As ony lamb upon a lee;   any, pasture
15 The evening sun was ne'er sae sweet   never so
        As was the blink o' Phemie's e'e.   eye
        Blythe, blythe &c.

The Highland hills I've wander'd wide,
    As o'er the lawlands I hae been;   lowlands, have
But Phemie was the blythest lass
20   That ever trod the dewy green. —
      Blythe, blythe &c.

Written in the Autumn of 1787 at Auchtertyre on Miss Euphemia
Murray of Lentrose as Burns records in the extended title to this
song.

To Daunton Me –

Tune: To Daunton Me -
First printed in the S.M.M., Vol. 2, 14th February, 1788.

The blude-red rose at Yule may blaw,   blood-, blow
The simmer lilies bloom in snaw,   summer, snow
The frost may freeze the deepest sea,
But an auld man shall never daunton me. —   old, subdue

Chorus
5 To daunton me, to daunton me,
For an auld man shall never daunton me. —

To daunton me, and me sae young,   rule/subdue, so
Wi' his fause heart and flatt'ring tongue,   false
That is the thing you shall never see
10 For an auld man shall never daunton me. —   old

For a' his meal and a' his maut,   oatmeal, malt
For a' his fresh beef and his saut,   salt
For a' his gold and white monie,   money
An auld man shall never daunton me.   old
      To daunton me &c.

15 His gear may buy him kye and yowes,   wealth, cattle, ewes
His gear may buy him glens and knowes,   hillocks
But me he shall not buy nor fee,   hire
For an auld man shall never daunton me. —   old
      To daunton me &c.

He hirples twa-fauld as he dow,   limps, two-fold, able
20 Wi' his teethless gab and his auld beld pow,   mouth, old bald head
And the rain rins down frae his red-blear'd e'e,   runs, from, eye
That auld man shall never daunton me. —   old
To daunton me &c.

This is a song written in late 1787, adapted from an old Jacobite
song. It is rearranged by Burns to focus on the married mismatch of
age and youth with all its concomitant problems. The feisty female
voice records its triumph over both her husband's material posses-
sions and his tangible physical decay.

O'er the Water to Charlie –

First printed in the S.M.M., Vol. 2, 14th February, 1788.

Come boat me o'er, come row me o'er,
Come boat me o'er to Charlie;
I'll gie John Ross another bawbee   halfpenny
To boat me o'er to Charlie. —

Chorus
5 We'll o'er the water, we'll o'er the sea,
We'll o'er the water to Charlie;
Come weal, come woe, we'll gather and go,
And live or die wi' Charlie. —

I lo'e weel my Charlie's name,   love, well
10   Tho' some there be abhor him:
But O, to see Auld Nick gaun hame,   old Devil, going home
And Charlie's faes before him!   foes
We'll o'er the water, &c.

I swear and vow by moon and stars,
And sun that shines so early!
15 If I had twenty thousand lives,
I'd die as aft for Charlie. —   often
We'll o'er the water, &c.

An obvious Jacobite song, as Low remarks (see no. 85, p. 265), based
on a traditional work in *The True Loyalist* (1779), where the chorus
is adapted from another song in the same collection. Donaldson
notes that:

Burns matches the rhythmical impetus of the superb original
tune with subtly varied repetition and an unobtrusive pattern of
alliteration and internal rhyme to produce a heady evocation of
Jacobite exile with a distictly millenarian flavour (p. 81).

A Rosebud, by My Early Walk

First printed in the S.M.M., Vol. 2, 14th February, 1788.

A Rose-bud by my early walk,
Adown a corn-inclosed bawk,   unploughed rig end
Sae gently bent its thorny stalk
    All on a dewy morning. —

5   Ere twice the shades o' dawn are fled,
In a' its crimson glory spread,
And drooping rich the dewy head,
    It scents the early morning. —

Within the bush her covert nest
10 A little linnet fondly prest,
The dew sat chilly on her breast
    Sae early in the morning. —   so

She soon shall see her tender brood
The pride, the pleasure o' the wood,
15 Amang the fresh green leaves bedew'd,   among
    Awauk the early morning. —   awake

So thou, dear bird, young Jeany fair,
On trembling string or vocal air,
Shall sweetly pay the tender care
20   That tents thy early morning. —   tends

So thou, sweet Rosebud, young and gay,
Shalt beauteous blaze upon the day,
And bless the Parent's evening ray
    That watch'd thy early morning. —

The 'rosebud' of this song was Miss Janet (Jeany) Cruickshank,
daughter to Mr William Cruickshank, classics teacher, Edinburgh
High School. There are three extant letters from Burns to Mr
Cruickshank. On 8th October, 1787 Burns describes her as his 'dear

little Jeany' (Letter 142). In March 1788 he refers to her as a 'sweet little Rose-bud' (Letter 214). He sent the poem to Dr John Moore, February 1791.

To a Blackbird
or Revision for Clarinda
Tune: Scots Queen
First printed in the S.M.M., Vol. 2, 14th February, 1788.

Go on, sweet bird, and soothe my care,
Thy tuneful notes will soothe Despair;
Thy plaintive warblings void of art
Thrill sweetly thro' my aching heart.
5   Now chuse thy mate, and fondly love,
And all the charming transport prove;
While I a lovelorn exile live,
Nor transport or receive or give.

For thee is laughing Nature gay;
10 For thee she pours the vernal day:
For me in vain is Nature drest,
While Joy's a stranger to my breast!
These sweet emotions all enjoy;
Let love and song thy hours employ!
15 Go on, sweet bird, and soothe my care;
Thy tuneful notes will hush Despair.

This work was written by Clarinda, Agnes McLehose, then revised by Burns before publication. Ll. 8–14 are the contribution of Burns. Burns did not claim the song as his. It was published as 'By a lady'.

And I'll Kiss Thee Yet
Tune: Braes o' Balquhidder
First printed in the S.M.M., Vol. 2, 14th February, 1788.

Chorus
An I'll kiss thee yet, yet,
    An I'll kiss thee o'er again;
An I'll kiss thee yet, yet,
    My bonie Peggy Alison.

5 Ilk Care and Fear, when thou are near,   each/every
   I ever mair defy them, O;   more
 Young Kings upon their hansel throne newly obtained
   Are no sae blest as I am, O!   not so
    An I'll kiss &c.

 When in my arms, wi' a' thy charms,
10   I clasp my countless treasure, O!
 I seek nae mair o' Heav'n to share,   no more
   Than sic a moment's pleasure, O! such
    An I'll kiss &c.

 And by thy een sae bonie blue,   eyes, so
   I swear I'm thine forever O!
15 And on thy lips I seal my vow,
   And break it shall I never O!
    An I'll kiss &c.

The first verse does not appear in the S.M.M. but was included in a later manuscript. Burns notes in the Hastie MS: 'The chorus is the first, or lowest part of the tune – Each verse must be repeated twice to go through the high, or 2nd part – .' Burns signed this 'Z' to indicate the chorus is old; the verses his. Gilbert Burns and his sister Isobel tell differing stories of the possible heroine. As they cannot both be right, it is likely the name employed comes from the old song, not a woman Burns met.

Rattlin, Roarin Willie

First printed in the S.M.M., Vol. 2, 14th February, 1788.

 O Rattlin, roarin Willie,
   O he held to the fair,
 An' for to sell his fiddle
   And buy some other ware;   goods
5 But parting wi' his fiddle,
   The saut tear blin't his e'e;   salt, blinded, eye
 And Rattlin, roarin Willie,
   Ye're welcome hame to me.   home

 O Willie, come sell your fiddle,
10   O sell your fiddle sae fine;   so
 O Willie, come sell your fiddle,
   And buy a pint o' wine;

If I should sell my fiddle,
 The warld would think I was mad, world
15 For mony a rantin day many, jovial
 My fiddle and I hae had. have

As I cam by Crochallan came, the Fencibles' Club
 I cannily keekit ben, cautiously looked in
Rattlin, roarin Willie
20 Was sitting at yon boord-en', board-end/top of the table
Sitting at yon boord-en',
 And amang guid companie; among good
Rattlin, roarin Willie,
 Ye're welcome hame to me! home

The poet records in the Interleaved S.M.M. that only the final stanza of this song is his, the remainder being a traditional song. He states 'it was composed out of compliment to one of the worthiest fellows in the world, William Dunbar, Esq., writer to the Signet, Edinburgh, and Colonel of the Crochallan corps – a club of wits who took that title at the time of raising the fencible regiments'. There are seven letters between Burns and William Dunbar. See notes to *Where Wit May Sparkle*, a quatrain newly added to the canon, written by Burns to Dunbar.

Where, Braving Angry Winter's Storms

Tune: Neil Gow's Lament for Abercairny
First printed in the S.M.M., Vol. 2, 14th February, 1788.

Where braving angry Winter's storms
 The lofty Ochels rise, Ochil hills
Far in their shade, my Peggy's charms
 First blest my wondering eyes. —

5 As one who by some savage stream
 A lonely gem surveys,
Astonish'd doubly marks it beam
 With art's most polish'd blaze. —

Blest be the wild, sequester'd glade
10 And blest the day and hour,
Where Peggy's charms I first survey'd,
 When first I felt their pow'r. —

The tyrant Death with grim controul
   May seize my fleeting breath,
15 But tearing Peggy from my soul
   Must be a stronger death. —

This was one of two songs went to Gavin Hamilton's cousin, Margaret (Peggy) Chalmers (1763–1843) in the early winter of 1787. In a letter to her Burns gives considerable indication not only of the genesis of the song but the complex intensity of his attitude to Margaret Chalmers:

> I have just now read yours. The poetic compliments I pay cannot be misunderstood. They are neither of them so particular as to point *you* out to the world at large; and the circle of your acquaintances will allow all I have said. Besides, I have complimented you chiefly, almost solely, on your mental charms. Shall I be plain with you? I will; so look to it. Personal attractions, madam, you have much above par; wit, understanding and worth, you possess in the first class. This is a cursed flat way of telling you these truths, but let me hear no more of your sheepish timidity. I know the world a little. I know what they will say of my poems; by second sight I suppose; for I am seldom out in my conjectures; and you may believe me my dear madam, I would not run any risk of hurting you by an ill-judged compliment, I wish to show the world the odds between a poet's friends and those of simple prosemen. More for your information *both* the pieces go in' (Letter 150).

Margaret's resistance was partly successful. The more obviously identifiable *My Peggy's Face, My Peggy's Form* did not appear till 1803 (S.M.M., no. 501). Manifestly this is more than a quarrel about a private relationship being made artistically public. There is an insistent pressure in these letters to Margaret Chalmers, cultured, musical, that bespeak more intimate needs. Margaret Chalmers is alleged to have in later life told the poet Thomas Campbell that Burns had proposed marriage but that she was already engaged to a banker, Lewis Hay, whom she in fact married in December, 1788. Burns's letters to her exist only in transcript; the originals were deliberately destroyed. None of her letters to him survive. This correspondence was being carried on simultaneously with the inflammatory melodrama with Mrs McLehose who certainly did not like to hide the light of her creative intentions under a bushel.

O Tibby, I Hae Seen the Day

Tune: Invercauld's Reel
First printed in the S.M.M., Vol. 2, 14th February, 1788.

Yestreen I met you on the Moor	yesterday evening
Ye spak na, but gaed by like stoor	spoke not, went by, dust
Ye geck at me because I'm poor	scoff, or toss the head
But fient a hair care I. —	not

Chorus
5   Tibby I hae seen the day — have
Ye wadna been sae shy — would not, so
For laik o' gear ye lightly me — lack of possessions
    But trowth, I care na by — — truly, I care as little

When comin hame on Sunday last — home
10 Upon the road as I cam past
Ye snufft an' gae your head a cast — sniffed
    But trowth, I caretna by. — — truly, I care as little
       O Tibbie &c.

I doubt na lass, but ye may think — not, you
Because ye hae the name o' clink — you, have, money
15 That ye can please me at a wink
    Whene'er ye like to try. —
       O Tibbie &c.

But sorrow tak him that's sae mean — take, so
Altho' his pouch o' coin were clean
Wha follows onie saucy Quean, — any, girl
20   That looks sae proud and high. —
       O Tibbie &c.

Altho' a lad were e'er sae smart — ever so
If that he want the yellow dirt
Ye'll cast your head anither airt — another direction
    And answer him fu' dry. — — full
       O Tibbie &c.

25 But if he hae the name o' gear — has, wealth
Ye'll fasten to him like a breer — wild thorny brier
Tho' hardly he for sense or lear — learning
    Be better than the ky. — — cattle
       O Tibbie &c.

But, Tibbie, lass, tak my advice	take
30 Your daddie's gear maks you sae nice	wealth, haughty
The de'il a ane wad spier your price	devil, one, would ask
Were ye as poor as I. —	you
O Tibbie &c.	

There lives a lass beside yon park,
I'd rather hae her in her sark   have, shirt or dress
35 Than you wi' a' your thousand mark
     That gars you look sae high. —   makes
          O Tibbie &c.

An' Tibby I hae seen the day
Ye wadna been sae shy
An' for laik o' gear ye lightly me   scorn
40 But fien' a hair care I. —

In the *First Commonplace Book* an early draught of this song
appears, dated September 1784, although the poet records that
he began the song when about seventeen years old. 'Tibbie' is
believed to be Isabella Steven, who lived near Lochlie, where the
Burns family farmed from 1777. Scott Douglas mentions a Tibbie
Steen, as the heroine (Vol. 2, p. 235). The song is autobiographical,
revealing an early sign of Burns's chronic problem in relating to
socially superior women. Signed X in the S.M.M. where there are
only six verses printed, rather than the eight of the final song.

Clarinda

First printed in the S.M.M., Vol. 2, 14th February, 1788.

Clarinda, mistress of my soul,
     The measur'd time is run!
The wretch beneath the dreary pole,
     So marks his latest sun.

5 To what dark cave of frozen night
     Shall poor Sylvander hie,
Depriv'd of thee, his life and light,
     The Sun of all his joy.

We part — but by these precious drops,
10   That fill thy lovely eyes!
No other light shall guide my steps,
     Till thy bright beams arise.

She, the fair Sun of all her sex,
    Has blest my glorious day:
15 And shall a glimmering Planet fix
    My worship to its ray?

This was the poet's parting song to Mrs McLehose when he left
Edinburgh in early 1788. Sylvander was Burns's pen-name in his
epistlotary relationship with Clarinda (Mrs McLehose). Unlike *Ae
Fond Kiss*, this poem echoes the sentimental clichéd tone of their
letters.

Second Epistle to Davie

First printed in 1789 by David Sillar, in his own collection of poems.

AULD NIBOR,	old neighbour
I'm three times, doubly, o'er your debtor,	
For your auld-farrant, frien'ly letter;	old-fashioned
Tho' I maun say't, I doubt ye flatter,	shall/must
5 Ye speak sae fair;	so
For my puir, silly, rhymin' clatter	poor, noise
Some less maun sair.	must, serve
Hale be your heart, hale be your fiddle;	
Lang may your elbuck jink an' diddle,	elbow, move fast, jig
10 To cheer you thro' the weary widdle	struggle
O' war'ly cares,	worldly
Till bairns' bairns kindly cuddle	children's children
Your auld grey hairs.	old
But DAVIE, lad, I'm red ye're glaikit;	informed, careless/foolish
15 I'm tauld the MUSE ye hae negleckit;	told, have, neglected
An' gif it's sae, ye sud be lickit	if, so, should, beaten
Until ye fyke;	fidget
Sic hauns as you sud ne'er be faiket,	such hands, should, excused
Be hain't wha like.	spared
20 For me, I'm on Parnassus brink,	
Rivin the words to gar them clink;	tearing at, make, rhyme
Whyles daez't wi' love, whyles daez't wi' drink,	sometimes dazed
Wi' jads or masons;	lasses
An' whyles, but ay owre late, I think,	sometimes, always over
25 Braw sober lessons.	fine

Of a' the thoughtless sons o' man,
Commen' me to the Bardie clan;   commend
Except it be some idle plan
    O' rhymin clink,   noise
30 The devil-haet, that I sud ban,   -have it/should
    They never think.

Nae thought, nae view, nae scheme o' livin',   no,
Nae cares to gie us joy or grievin',   no, give
But just the pouchie put the nieve in,   pocket, hand/fist
35   An' while ought's there,
Then, hiltie, skiltie, we gae scrivin',   helter-skelter, go writing
    An' fash nae mair.   trouble/bother no more

Leeze me on rhyme! It's ay a treasure,   commend me to/give me
My chief, amaist my only pleasure,   almost
40 At hame, a-fiel', at wark or leisure,   home, in the field, work
    The Muse, poor hizzie!   hussy
Tho' rough an' raploch be her measure,   coarse
    She's seldom lazy.

Haud to the Muse, my dainty Davie: hold
45 The warl' may play you [monie] a shavie;   world, many, trick
But for the Muse, she'll never leave ye,
    Tho' e'er sae puir,   so poor
Na, even tho' limpan wi' the spavie   no, spavin/worn joints
    Frae door to door.   from

Although this first appeared courtesy of David Sillar it did not enter
the Burns canon until published by Dr James Currie in 1800.
Sillar's own volume appeared in 1789, but the poem by Burns is
generally dated to the 1785 period. It is a letter epistle in colloquial
language written to encourage a friend to keep writing poetry. See
the first *Epistle to Davie* for notes on David Sillar.

Grace Before Meat

First printed in *The Caledonian Mercury*, August 27th, 1789.

O Thou, who kindly dost provide
    For ev'ry creature's want!
We bless thee, God of Nature wide,
    For all Thy goodness lent:

And, if it please thee Heavenly guide,
    May never worse be sent;
But whether granted or denied,
    Lord, bless us with content!
        Amen!!!

Burns printed this and the following grace under his own name in *The Caledonian Mercury*, August 27th, 1789 but they were not included in the 1793 Edinburgh edition. They appear in Currie, 1800, then along with *Grace After Meat*, in Stewart, 1802.

Grace After Meat

First printed in *The Caledonian Mercury*, August 27th, 1789.

O Thou, in whom we live and move,
    Who mad'st the sea and shore,
Thy goodness constantly we prove,
    And grateful would adore.

And if it please Thee, Pow'r above,
    Still grant us with such store;
The *Friend* we *trust*, the *Fair* we *love*;
    And we desire no more.

Like the above grace, Burns printed this under his own name in *The Caledonian Mercury*, August 27th, 1789, but they did not enter the canon until 1800 (See notes above).

I Love My Love in Secret

First printed in the S.M.M., Vol. 3, 2nd February, 1790.

My Sandy gied to me a ring,	gave
Was a' beset wi' diamonds fine;	all
But I gied him a far better thing,	gave
I gied my heart in pledge o' his ring.	gave

Chorus
5 My Sandy O, my Sandy O,
    My bony, bony Sandy O!

Tho' the love that I owe to thee I dare na show,	not
Yet I love my love in secret, my Sandy O.	

My Sandy brak a piece o' gowd,   broke, gold
10   While down his cheeks the saut tears row'd;   salt, rolled
He took a hauf and gied it to me,   half, gave
        And I'll keep it till the hour I die.
            My Sandy O, &c.

The traditional text was a bawdy song cleaned up by Burns. In such
rural songs the name Sandy was a stock name of this period.

Tibbie Dunbar

Tune: Jonny McGill
First printed in the S.M.M., Vol. 3, 2nd February, 1790.

O wilt thou go wi' me, sweet Tibbie Dunbar;
O wilt thou go wi' me, sweet Tibbie Dunbar:
Wilt thou ride on a horse, or be drawn in a car,
Or walk by my side, O sweet Tibbie Dunbar. —

I care na thy daddie, his lands and his money;   not
I care na thy kin, sae high and sae lordly: not, family, so
But say that thou'lt hae me for better for waur, have, worse
And come in thy coatie, sweet Tibbie
        Dunbar. —

A traditional song renovated by Burns in his desire to put words to
and preserve an old tune by a Girvan fiddler, John McGill. During
the 19th century Hector MacNeil's lyrics, *Come Under My Plaidie*,
made the tune popular – a rare occasion of another poet upstaging
Burns's work.

Highland Harry Back Again

Tune: The Highlander's Lament
First printed in the S.M.M., Vol. 3, 2nd February, 1790.

My Harry was a gallant gay,
        Fu' stately strade he on the plain;   full, strode/walked
But now he's banish'd far awa,   away
        I'll never see him back again.

Chorus
5   O for him back again,
        O for him back again,
I wad gie a' Knockhaspie's land   would give all
        For Highland Harry back again.

When a' the lave gae to their bed,	all, rest, go
10 I wander dowie up the glen;	sad
I set me down, and greet my fill,	weep
And ay I wish him back again.	
O, for him &c.	

O were some villains hangit high,	hanged
And ilka body had their ain!	every, own
15 Then I might see the joyfu' sight,	
My Highland Harry back again.	
O, for him &c.	

The poet states in the Interleaved S.M.M. that he collected the chorus of this song from a woman's singing in Dunblane, 'the rest of the song is mine'. The Chambers–Wallace edition (p. 321) give two additional stanzas with sharper Jacobite lyrics, apparently not in the hand of the poet but in manuscript in the British Museum. Knock-haspie, l.7, refers, according to Cunningham, to a part of the farm land at Mossgiel. Kinsley accepts this (Vol. III, no. 164, p. 1241), but the chorus is not from Burns. The land referred to is more likely to be in Aberdeenshire where the original song and chorus come from.

The Taylor Fell thro' the Bed
Tune: Beware of the Ripells
First printed in the S.M.M., Vol. 3, 2nd February, 1790.

The Taylor fell thro' the bed, thimble an' a',	tailor
The Taylor fell thro' the bed thimble an' a';	
The blankets were thin and the sheets they were sma',	small
The Taylor fell thro' the bed, thimble an' a'.	

5 The sleepy bit lassie, she dreaded nae ill,	no
The sleepy bit lassie she dreaded nae ill;	
The weather was cauld and the lassie lay still,	cold, still
She thought that a Taylor could do her nae ill.	

Gie me the groat again, cannie young man,	give, fourpence
10 Gie me the groat again cannie young man;	
The day it is short and the night it is lang,	long
The dearest siller that ever I wan.	money, won

There's somebody weary, wi' lying her lane,	alone
There's somebody weary wi' lying her lane;	
15 There's some that are dowie, I trow wad be fain	sad, trust would
To see the bit Taylor come skippin again.	

The second and fourth verses are claimed by Burns in his notes to the Interleaved S.M.M., the remainder is traditional.

Ay Waukin O

First printed in the S.M.M., Vol. 3, 2nd February, 1790.

Simmer's a pleasant time,	summer's
Flowers of every colour;	
The water rins owre the heugh,	runs, cliff or crag
And I long for my true lover!	

Chorus
5 Ay waukin, O,   waking
   Waukin still and weary:
Sleep I can get nane,   none
   For thinking on my Dearie. —

When I sleep I dream,
10   When I wauk I'm eerie,   wake, restless
Sleep I can get nane,   none
   For thinkin on my Dearie. —
      Ay waukin, O, &c.

Lanely night comes on,   lonely
   A' the lave are sleepin: rest/remainder
15 I think on my bonie lad,
   And I bleer my een wi' greetin. —   blur, eyes, weeping
      Ay waukin, O, &c.

This deceptively simple, but profoundly moving song of tormented loss, is transformed by Burns from an original song. Some modern recordings regrettably omit the Scots word 'heugh' from the first verse, for which there is no adequate *sounding* translation in English.

Beware O' Bonie Ann

First printed in the S.M.M., Vol. 3, 2nd February, 1790.

Ye gallants bright I red you right,	advise/warn
Beware o' bonie Ann;	
Her comely face sae fu' o' grace,	so full
Your heart she will trepan.	ensnare/trap
5 Her een sae bright, like stars by night,	eyes so
Her skin is like the swan;	
Sae jimply lac'd her genty waist	so tightly, graceful
That sweetly ye might span.	

Youth, grace and love attendant move,
10   And Pleasure leads the van:
In a' their charms, and conquering arms,
   They wait on bonie Ann.

The captive bands may chain the hands,
　　But Love enslaves the man:
15　Ye gallants braw, I rede you a',　　　　　　advise, all
　　Beware o' bonie Ann.

Composed in 1788 on Miss Ann Masterton, daughter to the poet's Edinburgh friend, the school teacher Allan Masterton (composer of musical airs, inter alia, *Strathallan's Lament*).

The Gardener Wi' His Paidle

Tune: The Gardener's March
First printed in the S.M.M., Vol. 3, 2nd February, 1790.

When rosy May comes in wi' flowers
To deck her gay, green, spreading bowers;
Then busy, busy are his hours,
　　The Gardener wi' his paidle. —　　　　　hoe/spade

5　The chrystal waters gently fa';　　　　　　crystal, fall
　　The merry birds are lovers a';　　　　　　all
　　The scented breezes round him blaw,　　　blow
　　The Gardener wi' his paidle. —　　　　　hoe

When purple morning starts the hare
10　To steal upon her early fare;　　　　　　food
　　Then thro' the dew he maun repair,　　　must
　　The Gardener wi' his paidle. —

When Day, expiring in the west,
The curtain draws o' Nature's rest,
15　He flies to her arms he lo'es best,　　　loves
　　The Gardener wi' his paidle. —

This was unsigned by Burns on publication, but he states in the Interleaved S.M.M. that the title is old and the song his. This is a man who fertilises everything he and his 'paidle' touches.

On a Bank of Flowers

Tune: The Bashful Lover
First printed in the S.M.M., Vol. 3, 2nd February, 1790.

On a bank of flowers in a summer day,
　　For summer lightly drest,
The youthful blooming Nelly lay,
　　With love and sleep opprest.
5　When Willie wand'ring thro' the wood,
　　Who for her favour oft had sued;

He gaz'd, he wish'd, he fear'd, he blush'd,
     And trembled where he stood.

Her closed eyes like weapons sheath'd
10   Were seal'd in soft repose;
Her lips, still as she fragrant breath'd
     It richer dyed the rose.
The springing lilies sweetly prest,
     Wild, wanton kiss'd her rival breast;
15   He gaz'd, he wish'd, he fear'd, he blush'd,
     His bosom ill at rest.

Her robes light waving in the breeze,
     Her tender limbs embrace;
Her lovely form, her native ease,
20   All harmony and grace:
Tumultuous tides his pulses roll,
     A faltering, ardent kiss he stole;
He gaz'd, he wish'd, he fear'd, he blush'd,
     And sigh'd his very soul.

25   As flies the partridge from the brake
     On fear-inspired wings,
So Nelly starting, half-awake,
     Away affrighted springs.
But Willie follow'd, — as he should,
30   He overtook her in the wood;
He vow'd, he pray'd, he found the maid
     Forgiving all, and good.

This song is based on one of the same title printed in the *Tea Table Miscellany*, Volume 3, 1727. It is signed as from Burns in the S.M.M., suggesting that it is mostly new lyrics by Burns. On this type of lyrical romance Kinsley remarks 'The situation is a common one in Restoration and eighteenth-century pastoral' (Vol. III, no. 292, p. 1331). It could also be remarked that it is deeply pre-Keatsian.

My Love, She's but a Lassie Yet –
Tune: Miss Farquarson's Reel
First printed in the S.M.M., Vol. 3, 2nd February, 1790.

Chorus
     My love, she's but a lassie yet,
     My love, she's but a lassie yet;
     We'll let her stand a year or twa,   two
     She'll no be half sae saucy yet. —   so

5 I rue the day I sought her O,
  I rue the day I sought her O,
 Wha gets her needs na say he's woo'd,   who, not
  But he may say he has bought her O. —
   My love, she's &c.

  Come draw a drap o' the best o't yet, pour, drop
10 Come draw a drap o' the best o't yet:
 Gae seek for Pleasure whare ye will,   go, where
  But here I never misst it yet. —   missed
   My love, she's &c.

  We're a' dry wi' drinkin o't,
  We're a' dry wi' drinkin o't:
15 The minister kisst the fiddler's wife,
  He could na preach for thinkin o't. — not
   My love, she's &c.

This is another example of a song where Burns took the title from an old song and re-wrote the lyric: the first, repetitive lines of the chorus and the final 'half stanza' are old (See Scott Douglas, Vol. 1, p. 244 and Low, no. 133, p. 378). The tune is known as both the above title and *My Love, She's but a Lassie Yet.*

Jamie, Come Try Me

Tune: Jamie, Come Try Me.
First printed in the S.M.M., Vol. 3, 2nd February, 1790.

If thou should ask my love,
 Could I deny thee?
If thou would win my love,
 Jamie come try me.

Chorus
5 Jamie come try me,
  Jamie come try me,
 If thou would win my love
 Jamie come try me.

If thou should kiss me, love,
10 Wha could espy thee?
 If thou wad be my love,
  Jamie come try me.
   Jamie, come try &c.

Here Burns, as Low comments (no. 153), has composed lyrics for a tune printed in Oswald's 1742 collection of Scottish tunes, he wished to preserve.

My Bony Mary

Tune: The Secret Kiss
First printed in the S.M.M., Vol. 3, 2nd February, 1790.

Go fetch to me a pint o' wine,
 And fill it in a silver tassie;   cup/goblet
That I may drink, before I go,
 A service to my bonie lassie:
5 The boat rocks at the Pier o' Leith,
 Fu' loud the wind blaws frae the Ferry, full, blows, from
The ship rides by the Berwick-law,
 And I maun leave my bony Mary.   must

The trumpets sound, the banners fly,
10 The glittering spears are ranked ready,
The shouts o' war are heard afar,
 The battle closes deep and bloody.
It's not the roar o' sea or shore,
 Wad mak me langer wish to tarry, would, longer
15 Nor shouts o' war that's heard afar —
 It's leaving thee, my bony Mary!

Burns affirms that other than the first four lines, this song is his (Letter 586). The title in some editions is *The Silver Tassie*. On publication it was called *My Bony Mary,* so that title is given here. The 'Ferry' referred to is Queensferry. The Berwick-law, according to Chambers edition, is a hill near the shore on the Firth of Forth visible from Edinburgh, near Berwick; but it may refer to the Bass Rock.

The Lazy Mist

First printed in the S.M.M., Vol. 3, 2nd February, 1790.

The lazy mist hangs from the brow of the hill,
Concealing the course of the dark winding rill;
How languid the scenes, late so sprightly, appear,
As Autumn to Winter resigns the pale year.

5 The forests are leafless, the meadows are brown,
And all the gay foppery of Summer is flown:
Apart let me wander, apart let me muse,
How quick Time is flying, how keen Fate pursues.

How long I have liv'd — but how much liv'd in vain;
10 How little of life's scanty span may remain:
What aspects, old Time, in his progress has worn;
What ties, cruel Fate, in my bosom has torn.
How foolish, or worse, till our summit is gain'd!
And downward, how weaken'd, how darken'd, how pain'd!
15 Life is not worth having with all it can give,
For something beyond it poor man sure must live.

This is an original work of Burns. A copy was sent to Dr Blacklock from Mauchline on 15th November 1788. The final couplet carries the same sentiment as 'And a' the comfort we're to get,/ Is that ayont the grave, man' from *The Tree of Liberty* (ll. 71–2), without that later poem's sense of revolutionary, redemptive freedom achievable in this life.

The Captain's Lady
Tune: Mount Your Baggage
First printed in the S.M.M., Vol. 3, 2nd February, 1790.

When the drums do beat,
 And the cannons rattle,
Thou shalt sit in state,
 And see thy love in battle.

Chorus
5 O mount and go,
 Mount and make you ready,
O mount and go,
 And be the Captain's Lady.

When the vanquish'd foe
10 Sues for peace and quiet,
To the shades we'll go,
 And in love enjoy it.
  O, mount and go, &c.

Henley and Henderson suggest that a broadside called *The Liggar Lady* is probably the basis of this song (Vol. 3, p. 344). Kinsley also accepts this (Vol. III, p. 1332). The finished work differs significantly from the traditional one.

Of a' the Airts

Tune: Miss Admiral Gordon's Strathspey
First printed in the S.M.M., Vol. 3, 2nd February, 1790.

Of a' the airts the wind can blaw,		directions, blow
I dearly like the West,		
For there the bonie Lassie lives,		
The Lassie I lo'e best:		love
5 There 's wild woods grow, and rivers row,		roll
And mony a hill between;		many
But day and night my fancy's flight		
.Is ever wi' my Jean. —		
I see her in the dewy flowers,		
10 I see her sweet and fair;		
I hear her in the tunefu' birds,		
I hear her charm the air:		
There's not a bonie flower, that springs		
By fountain, shaw, or green;		woodland
15 There's not a bony bird that sings		
But minds me o' my Jean. —		

In the Interleaved S.M.M. Burns writes 'This song . . . I composed out of compliment to Mrs Burns'. The evocative strathspey was composed by William Marshall who worked for the Duke of Gordon. A music-seller in Edinburgh, John Hamilton, added two stanzas to this song, but they were never fully incorporated by Burnsians due to their mediocrity. Hamilton is probably responsible for some other fake lyrics attributed to Burns during the nineteenth century (See Chambers–Wallace, 1896, p. 270, footnote 1).

Carl and the King Come

First printed in the S.M.M., Vol. 3, 2nd February, 1790.

An somebodie were come again,		
Then somebodie maun cross the main,		must
And every man shall hae his ain,		have, own
Carl an the King come.		old man

Chorus
5 Carl an the King come,
Carl an the King come;
Thou shalt dance and I will sing,
  Carl an the King come.

I trow we swapped for the warse: trust, worse
10 We gae the boot and better horse;   gave
An that we'll tell them at the cross,
  Carl an the King come.

Coggie an the King come,   drinking jug
Coggie an the King come,
15 I'll be fou an thou'se be toom,   drunk, empty
  Coggie an the King come.

'Carl' , meaning old man, is a reference to Prince Charles Edward Stuart. A song of this title existed in Cromwellian times, but several variants appear as Jacobite songs in the eighteenth century. It is partly traditional, partly Burns.

Whistle o'er the Lave o't

Tune: Whistle o'er the Lave o't
First printed in the S.M.M., Vol. 3, 2nd February, 1790.

First when Maggy was my care,
Heaven, I thought, was in her air;
Now we're married — spier nae mair —   inquire no more
  But whistle o'er the lave o't. —   rest

5 Meg was meek, and Meg was mild,
Sweet and harmless as a child —
Wiser men than me's beguiled;
  Whistle o'er the lave o't. —   rest

How we live, my Meg and me,
10 How we love and how we gree;   agree
I care na by how few may see,   not
  Whistle o'er the lave o't. —

Wha I wish were maggots' meat,   who
Dish'd up in her winding-sheet;
15 I could write — but Meg wad see't —   would
  Whistle o'er the lave o't. —

These are Burns's new lyrics adapted considerably from a bawdy
song in the David Herd collection (1769). On the evidence of several
of Burns's songs, feminine submission was not, to say the least,
implicit in the eighteenth century matrimonial state.

O, Were I on Parnassus Hill

Tune: My Love is Lost to Me
First printed in the S.M.M., Vol. 3, 2nd February, 1790.

O were I on Parnassus hill;
    Or had o' Helicon my fill;
That I might catch poetic skill,
    To sing how dear I love thee.
5   But Nith maun be my Muses' well,   must
    My Muse maun be thy bonie sell,   must, self
On Corsincon I'll glowr and spell,   glower
    And write how dear I love thee.

Then come, sweet Muse, inspire my lay!
10   For a' the lee-lang simmer's day,   live-long summer
I couldna sing, I couldna say,   could not,
    How much, how dear, I love thee.
I see thee dancing o'er the green,
    Thy waist sae jimp, thy limbs sae clean,   so neat, so shapely
15 Thy tempting lips, thy roguish een —   eyes
    By Heaven and Earth I love thee!

By night, by day, a-field, at hame,   in a field
    The thoughts o' thee my breast inflame;
And ay I muse and sing thy name,
20   I only live to love thee.
Tho' I were doom'd to wander on,
    Beyond the sea, beyond the sun,
Till my last, weary sand was run;
    Till then — and then I love thee.

This song, as *The Vision*, has its inspiring domestic Muse in Jean
Armour. It is different, however, from that long poem and unchar-
acteristic of Burns, in that his native landscape is felt as inadequate
compared to that of the classical world. Helicon, the Greek river of
inspirational water, neatly plays off against Corsicon, a hill viewable
from Ellisland.

There's a Youth in this City
Tune: Neil Gow's Lament for his Brother
First printed in the S.M.M., Vol. 3, 2nd February, 1790.

There's a youth in this city, it were a great pity
That he from our lasses should wander awa';
For he 's bony and braw, weel-favor'd witha',   handsome, well-
An' his hair has a natural buckle an' a'. —   curl
5   His coat is the hue o' his bonnet sae blue;   so
His fecket is white as the new-driven snaw;   woollen waistcoat
His hose they are blae, and his shoon like the slae;   blue, shoes, sloe
And his clear siller buckles they dazzle us a'.   silver

For beauty and fortune the laddie's been courtin;
10   Weel-featur'd, weel-tocher'd, weel-mounted, an' braw;   (see notes)
But chiefly the siller, that gars him gang till her;   money, makes, go
The Pennie 's the jewel that beautifies a'. —
There 's Meg wi' the mailen that fain wad a haen him;   farm, gladly would
And Susie whase daddie was laird of the Ha',   whose, Hall
15   There 's lang-tocher'd Nancy maist fetters his fancy —   long-, most
But th' laddie's dear sel he loes dearest of a'. —   self, loves

Burns indicates in the Interleaved S.M.M. that the first 'half-stanza' is traditional and the remainder his own. He also states that the tune is by the famous fiddler Neil Gow. The explanation of the Scots hyperbole in l. 10 is too lengthy to be set in the right margin and is translated as follows: our hero is well endowed, rides a good horse, has money and is handsome, but, for all his show, as the final line suggests, he loves himself a little too much.

My Heart's in the Highlands
Tune: Failte na miosg
First printed in the S.M.M., Vol. 3, 2nd February, 1790.

Farewell to the Highlands, farewell to the North;
The birthplace of Valour, the country of Worth:
Wherever I wander, wherever I rove,
The hills of the Highlands for ever I love. —

Chorus
5 My heart's in the Highlands, my heart is not here;
My heart's in the Highlands a chasing the deer;
Chasing the wild deer, and following the roe;
My heart's in the Highlands, wherever I go. —

Farewell to the mountains high cover'd with snow;
10 Farewell to the Straths and green valleys below:
Farewell to the forests and wild-hanging woods;
Farewell to the torrents and loud-pouring floods. —
My heart's in the Highlands, &c.

The chorus of this song is taken from a broadside called *The Strong Walls of Derry* which narrates the forlorn love of a Highlander emigrating to Ireland to find his true love has married another. The remainder of the lyric is by Burns.

John Anderson My Jo

First printed in the S.M.M., Vol. 3, 2nd February, 1790.

John Anderson my jo, John,	
When we were first acquent;	darling/love
Your locks were like the raven,	acquainted
Your bonie brow was brent;	
5 But now your brow is beld, John,	unwrinkled
Your locks are like the snaw;	bald
But blessings on your frosty pow,	snow/white
John Anderson my Jo.	white head
	darling
John Anderson my jo, John,	
10 We clamb the hill thegither;	climbed, together
And mony a cantie day, John,	happy
We've had wi' ane anither:	one another
Now we maun totter down, John,	shall
And hand in hand we'll go;	
15 And sleep thegither at the foot,	together
John Anderson my Jo.	

This is surely Burns's best example of cleaning up an old bawdy song to create a soothing lyric about love in old age, sung in the feminine voice. A version of the original bawdy work is in the poet's M.M.C. collection.

Awa', Whigs, Awa'

First printed in the S.M.M., Vol. 3, 2nd February, 1790.

Our thrissles flourish'd fresh and fair,   thistles
    And bonie bloom'd our roses;
But Whigs cam like a frost in June,   came
    An' wither'd a' our posies.

Chorus
5 Awa' Whigs awa',
    Awa' Whigs awa',
Ye're but a pack o' traitor louns,   rogues
    Ye'll do nae guid at a'.   no good

Our ancient crown's fa'n in the dust;   fallen
10   Deil blin' them wi' the stoure o't,   devil, dust
An' write their names in his black beuk   book
    Wha gae the Whigs the power o't!   who gave
    Awa' Whigs awa', &c.

Our sad decay in church and state
    Surpasses my descriving:.   describing
15 The Whigs cam o'er us for a curse,   came
    And we hae done wi' thriving.   have
    Awa' Whigs awa', &c.

Grim Vengeance lang has taen a nap,   long, taken
    But we may see him waukin: awaken
Gude help the day when Royal heads   God
20   Are hunted like a maukin.   hare
    Awa', Whigs, awa', &c.

This is adapted from a song in Herd's collection (See Kinsley, no. 303, Vol. III, p. 1336) where Burns lifts the chorus. Wallace suggests that only verses two and four are from Burns, but three sounds like him also. It is a stereotypical Jacobite protest song which, as Donaldson remarks (p. 80), 'could have been written at almost any point in the eighteenth century'.

Ca' the Yowes to the Knowes

[First version]

First printed in the S.M.M., Vol. 3, 2nd February, 1790.

As I gaed down the water-side   went
There I met my Shepherd-lad,
He row'd me sweetly in his plaid,   wrapped
    And he ca'd me his Dearie. —   called

Chorus

5 Ca' the yowes to the knowes,   call, ewes, hillocks
Ca' them whare the heather grows,   call, where
Ca' them where the burnie rowes,   stream runs/flows
    My bonie Dearie. —

Will ye gang down the water-side   go
10 And see the waves sae sweetly glide   so
Beneath the hazels spreading wide,
    The moon it shines fu' clearly. —
    Ca' the yowes, &c.

I was bred up at nae sic school,   no such
My Shepherd-lad, to play the fool;
15 An' a' the day to sit in dool,   sorrow
An' naebody to see me. —   nobody
    Ca' the yowes, &c.

Ye sall get gowns and ribbons meet,   shall
Cauf-leather shoon upon your feet,   shoes
And in my arms ye'se lie and sleep,
20 An' ye sall be my Dearie. —   shall
    Ca' the yowes, &c.

If ye'll but stand to what ye've said,
I'se gang wi' you, my Shepherd-lad,   go
And ye may row me in your plaid,   wrap
And I sall be your Dearie.
    Ca' the yowes, &c.

25 While waters wimple to the sea;   meander
While Day blinks in the lift sae hie;   sky so high
Till clay-cauld Death sall blin' my e'e,   -cold, shall, eye
    Ye sall be my Dearie. —   shall
    Ca' the yowes, &c.

This is the poet's first version of this duet, adapted from a traditional work. He wrote to Thomson retrospectively in September 1794: 'When I gave it to Johnson, I added some stanzas to the song and mended others, but still it will not do for *you*' (Letter 636). Stanzas four and five are old. Stanza three is missing in the Mackay version (p. 299). The later version (printed in Posthumous Works), interweaves the local, Lincluden scenery.

Kissin My Kate

Tune: Lord Breadalbine's March
First printed in the S.M.M., Vol. 3, 2nd February, 1790.

O merry hae I been teethin a heckle,   have, flax-dresser's comb
    An' merry hae I been shapin a spoon: have
O merry hae I been cloutin a kettle,   have, mending
    An' kissin my Katie when a' was done.
5 O, a' the lang day I ca' at my hammer,   long, knock
    An' a' the lang day I whistle an' sing;   long
O, a' the lang night I cuddle my kimmer,   long, mistress
    An' a' the lang night as happy's a king.   long

Bitter in dool I lickit my winnins   sorrow, made the best
10   O' marrying Bess, to gie her a slave: give
Blest be the hour she cool'd in her linens,   shroud
    And blythe be the bird that sings on her
      grave!
Come to my arms, my Katie, my Katie,
    An' come to my arms, and kiss me again!
15 Drucken or sober, here's to thee, Katie!   drunken
    And blest be the day I did it again.

This is another adaption by Burns from an old song with the man ecstatically re-energised by replacing the loathed, deceased Bess with the beloved Katy. The phrase 'teethin a heckle' refers to putting teeth into a flax-dresser's comb.

Mrs Ferguson of Craigdarroch's Lamentation for the Death of her Son,
or A Mother's Lament
Tune: Finlayston House –
First printed in the S.M.M., Vol. 3, 2nd February, 1790.

'Fate gave the word , the arrow sped,'
    And pierc'd my Darling's heart;
And with him all the joys are fled,
    Life can to me impart. —

5 By cruel hands the Sapling drops,
    In dust dishonor'd laid:
So fell the pride of all my hopes,
    My age's future shade. —

The mother-linnet in the brake
10   Bewails her ravish'd young;
So I, for my lost Darling's sake,
    Lament the live day long. —

Death! oft, I've fear'd thy fatal blow;
    Now, fond, I bare my breast;
15 O, do thou kindly lay me low,
    With him I love at rest!

The title given here is the title Burns himself adopted when informing Mrs Dunlop of the song he had just written (Letter 275) on 27th September 1788. The title generally used is *A Mother's Lament*.

The Braes o' Ballochmyle
First printed in S.M.M., Vol. 3, 2nd February, 1790.

The Catrine woods were yellow seen,
    The flowers decay'd on Catrine lee,
Nae lav'rock sang on hillock green,   no lark
    But Nature sicken'd on the e'e.   eye
5 Thro' faded groves Maria sang,
    Hersel in beauty's bloom the while,   herself
And ay the wild-wood echoes rang —
    Fareweel the braes o' Ballochmyle.   farewell, hill sides

Low in your wintry beds, ye flowers,
10   Again ye'll flourish fresh and fair;
Ye birdies dumb, in with'ring bowers,
    Again ye'll charm the vocal air.
But here alas! for me nae mair   no more
    Shall birdie charm, or floweret smile;   bird
15 Fareweel the bonnie banks of Ayr,
    Fareweel, fareweel! sweet Ballochmyle!   farewell, hill sides

This song, in the voice of 'Maria', Mary Anne Whitefoord, Sir John Whitefoord's oldest daughter, laments the family loss of their country estate in Ayrshire when its finances were almost ruined by the collapse of the Ayr Bank. It was composed in 1785. The poet's Edinburgh friend Allan Masterton composed the music.

The Rantin Dog, the Daddie o't
First published in S.M.M., Vol 3, 2nd February 1790.

O wha my babie-clouts will buy,   who, -linen
O wha will tent me when I cry;   who, attend to
Wha will kiss me where I lie,   who
    The rantin dog, the daddie o't.   fun-loving, of it

5   O wha will own he did the faut,   who, fault
O wha will buy the groanin maut,   who, groaning/midwife's ale
O wha will tell me how to ca't,   name it
The rantin dog, the daddie o't.

When I mount the Creepie-chair,   stool of repentance
10 Wha will sit beside me there,   who
Gie me Rob, I'll seek nae mair,   give, no more
    The rantin dog, the daddie o't.

Wha will crack to me my lane;   converse, alone
Wha will mak me fidgin fain;   who, sexually excited
15 Wha will kiss me o'er again   who
    The rantin dog, the daddie o't.

Burns comments in the Interleaved S.M.M., 'I composed this song very early in life, and sent it to a young girl, a very particular friend of mine, who was at that time under a cloud'. The likely recipient was probably Elizabeth Paton, who bore a child to Burns, although

this is not certain. What is interesting is that this song, unlike several
other poems on the subject, gives voice not to the father but to the
unmarried mother.

Thou Lingering Star

Tune: Captain Cook's Death
First printed in the S.M.M., Vol. 3, 2nd February, 1790.

Thou ling'ring Star with less'ning ray,
    That lovest to greet the early morn,
Again thou usherest in the day
    My Mary from my Soul was torn.
5   O Mary! dear departed Shade!
    Where is thy place of blissful rest?
Seest thou thy Lover lowly laid?
    Hearest thou the groans that rend his breast?

That sacred hour can I forget,
10   Can I forget the hallow'd grove,
Where by the winding Ayr we met,
    To live one day of Parting Love?
Eternity cannot efface
    Those records dear of transports past;
15 Thy image at our last embrace,
    Ah, little thought we 'twas our last!

Ayr gurgling kiss'd his pebbled shore,
    O'erhung with wild-woods, thickening, green;
The fragrant birch, and hawthorn hoar,
20   'Twin'd, amorous, round the raptur'd scene:
The flowers sprang wanton to be prest,
    The birds sang love on every spray;
Till too, too soon the glowing west
    Proclaim'd the speed of winged day. —

25 Still o'er these scenes my mem'ry wakes,
    And fondly broods with miser-care;
Time but th' impression stronger makes,
    As streams their channels deeper wear:
My Mary, dear, departed Shade!
30   Where is thy place of blissful rest!
Seest thou thy Lover lowly laid!
    Hearest thou the groans that rend his breast!

On 13th December 1789 Burns expostulated to Mrs Dunlop, discussing who he might meet if there were an after-life: 'There should I, with speechless agony of rapture, again recognise my lost, my ever dear MARY, whose bosom was fraught with Truth, Honour, Constancy & LOVE' (Letter 374). He had already sent a copy of the song to Mrs Dunlop in November, but requotes his own lines in December. The identity of Mary or 'Margaret' Campbell has been an obsessive preoccupation with some Burnsians since the early nineteenth century, culminating in the recent macabre call to exhume a grave near Greenock and employ D.N.A. testing to answer the myth.

Eppie Adair

Tune: My Eppie
First printed in the S.M.M., Vol. 3, 2nd February, 1790.

By Love, and by Beauty;
By Law, and by Duty;
I swear to be true to
    My Eppie Adair!

Chorus
5 An O, my Eppie,
My Jewel, my Eppie!
Wha wadna be happy   who would not
    Wi' Eppie Adair!

A' Pleasure exile me;
10 Dishonour defile me,
If e'er I beguile thee,
    My Eppie Adair!
      An' O, my Eppie, &c.

This is another example of an old song reworked by Burns.

The Battle of Sherramuir

Tune: Cameronian Rant
First printed in the S.M.M., Vol. 3, 2nd February, 1790.

O cam ye here the fight to shun,   came
    Or herd the sheep wi' me, man,
Or were ye at the Sherra-moor,
    Or did the battle see, man.

5   I saw the battle sair and teugh,   sore, tough
     And reekin-red ran mony a sheugh,   bloody-red, ditch
     My heart for fear gae sough for sough,   gave, sigh, sigh
     To hear the thuds, and see the cluds   clouds
     O' Clans frae woods, in tartan duds,   from, clothes
10   Wha glaum'd at kingdoms three, man.   who grasped

     The red-coat lads wi' black cockauds   Hanoverian cockades
         To meet them were na slaw, man,   not slow
     They rush'd, and push'd, and blude outgush'd,   blood
         And mony a bouk did fa', man: carcase, fall
15   The great Argyle led on his files,
     I wat they glanc'd for twenty miles,   wot
     They hough'd the Clans like nine-pin kyles,   mowed, skittles
     They hack'd and hash'd while braid-swords clash'd, broad-
     And thro' they dash'd, and hew'd and smash'd,
20   Till fey men dee'd awa, man.   doomed, died

     But had ye seen the philibegs   kilts
         And skyrin tartan trews, man,   showy tight trousers
     When in the teeth they daur'd our Whigs,   dared
         And Covenant Trueblues, man;   Covenanter flag
25   In lines extended lang and large,   long
     When baiginets o'erpower'd the targe,   bayonets, shield
     And thousands hasten'd to the charge;
     Wi' Highland wrath they frae the sheath   from
     Drew blades o' death, till out o' breath
30   They fled like frighted dows, man.   doves

     O how deil Tam can that be true,   devil
         The chase gaed frae the north, man;   went from
     I saw mysel, they did pursue
         The horse-men back to Forth, man;
35   And at Dunblane in my ain sight   own
     They took the brig wi' a' their might,   bridge
     And straught to Stirling wing'd their flight,   straight
     But, cursed lot! the gates were shut
     And monie a huntit, poor Red-coat   hunted
40   For fear amaist did swarf, man.   almost swoon

     My sister Kate cam up the gate   came
         Wi' crowdie unto me, man;   oatmeal and water
     She swoor she saw some rebels run   swore
         To Perth and to Dundee, man:

45 Their left-hand General had nae skill;   no
    The Angus lads had nae gude will   no, good
    That day their neebours' blude to spill;   neighbours' blood
    For fear by foes that they should lose
    Their cogs o' brose, they scar'd at blows   wooden bowls of porridge
50   And hameward fast did flee, man.   homeward

    They've lost some gallant gentlemen
        Amang the Highland clans, man;   among
    I fear my Lord Panmure is slain,
        Or in his en'mies' hands, man:
55 Now wad ye sing this double flight,   would
    Some fell for wrang, and some for right,
    But mony bade the warld gudenight;   good-
    Say pell and mell, wi' muskets' knell
    How Tories fell, and Whigs to Hell
60   Flew off in frighted bands, man.

This is adapted by Burns from the broadside written by Rev. John
Barclay (1734–1798), founder of the Barclayites sect, which records
an alleged conversation between two shepherds on the day of the
battle of Sherriffmuir, *Dialogue Between Will Lick-Ladle and Tom
Clean-Cogue*. The battle occurred on 13th November 1715, when the
Duke of Argyll led the Hanoverian crown troops, the men in black
cockades (l. 11) against the white-cockaded Jacobites led by the Earl
of Mar in a quite indecisive encounter.

    Low follows Kinsley in commenting on the poem being composed
'in the manner of traditional battle poetry' but this is profoundly to
miss the tension between form and content because the poem's
reductive vision is the implicit chaotic incoherence of both the
perception and experience of battle. Stendhal remarked that 'L'un
des plus grandes poètes selon moi, aient paru dans ces derniers
temps, c'est Robert Burns'. He had probably not read this song, but
Burns's burlesquing manner in this mini-masterpiece prefigures
Stendhal's own brilliant analysis of the subjective experience of
battle in *The Charterhouse of Parma*. William Donaldson, remarking
on Burns's ability to sustain a 'narrative of breathless pace, a
headlong torrent of alliteration, assonance and internal rhyme',
finely adds:

This amazing verbal tour de force has many admirable quali-
ties: the effortlessly sustained illusion of eye-witness contem-
poraneity (we have to force ourselves to remember that the

events described happened more than thirty years before the
poet was born); the concentration upon the common man and
the human fallibility of the participants; the way in which the
conventionally heroic is both indulged and debunked through-
out.

This essentially reductive technique is seen at its clearest in
the fifth verse, where the timely retreat of the Angus lads is
attributed not only to the absence of military appetite, but to
the presence of an appetite of a ridiculously different kind.
Despite the dreadful strokes and rivers of blood, the overall
effect is deeply comic.

Burns's power of characterisation produces a picture rooted
in everyday realities, where the epic and mundane are ludi-
crously entangled and the proverbial cast of common speech is
wielded with ruthlessly deflationary effect . . . a burlesque of
the conventionally heroic, which, in its refusal to consider men
in the mass, dehumanised by uniforms or warlike array is
fundamentally humane (pp. 83–4).

Sandy and Jockie

Tune: Jenny's Lamentation
First printed in the S.M.M., Vol. 3, 2nd February, 1790.

TWA bony lads were Sandy and Jockie;	two
Jockie was lo'ed but Sandy unlucky;	loved
Jockie was laird baith of hills and of vallies,	both
But Sandy was nought but the King o' gude	good
fellows.	

Jockie lo'ed Madgie, for Madgie had money,	loved
And Sandy lo'ed Mary, for Mary was bony:	
Ane wedded for Love, ane wedded for treasure,	one
So Jockie has siller, and Sandy had pleasure.	money

The first two lines are traditional, the remainder is from Burns. It
expresses the poet's belief that natural, spontaneous love more than
compensated for wealth.

Young Jockie was the Blythest Lad

First printed in the S.M.M., Vol. 3, 2nd February, 1790.

Young Jockey was the blythest lad
    In a' our town or here awa;   *away/round about*
Fu' blythe he whistled at the gaud,   *while goading*
    Fu' lightly danc'd he in the ha'.
5   He roos'd my een sae bonie blue,   *praised, eyes, so*
    He roos'd my waist sae genty sma;   *praised, so, small*
An ay my heart cam to my mou,   *mouth*
    When ne'er a body heard or saw.

My Jockey toils upon the plain
10   Thro' wind and weet, thro' frost and snaw; *wet, snow*
And o'er the lee I leuk fu' fain   *look fondly*
    When Jockie's owsen hameward ca'.   *oxen homeward drive*
An ay the night comes round again,
    When in his arms he taks me a';   *takes, fully*
15 An ay he vows he'll be my ain   *own*
    As lang's he has a breath to draw.   *long as*

This is signed by Burns with a 'Z' in the S.M.M to indicate it is a traditional song he improved. Jockey (l. 3) was the leader of the plough-horses and carried a stick as a goad.

A Waukrife Minnie

First printed in the S.M.M., Vol. 3, 2nd February, 1790.

Whare are you gaun, my bony lass,   *where, going*
    Whare are you gaun, my hiney.   *where, going, darling*
She answer'd me right saucilie,
    An errand for my minnie.   *mother*

5   O whare live ye, my bony lass,   *where*
    O whare live ye, my hiney.   *darling*
By yon burnside, gin ye maun ken,   *if, shall know*
    In a wee house wi' my minnie.   *mother*

But I foor up the glen at e'en,   *went, evening*
10   To see my bony lassie;
And lang before the grey morn cam,   *long, came*
    She was na hauf sae saucey.   *not half so*

O weary fa' the waukrife cock,   woe befall, wakeful
    And the foumart lay his crawin!   polecat
15 He wauken'd the auld wife frae her sleep, wakened, old, from
    A wee blink or the dawin.   just before, dawn

An angry wife I wat she raise,   know
    And o'er the bed she brought her;
And wi' a meikle hazel rung   big, stick
20   She made her a weel-pay'd dochter. well-, daughter

O fare thee weel, my bonie lass!   -well
    O fare thee weel, my hinnie!   -well, darling
Thou art a gay and a bony lass,
    But thou has a waukrife minnie.   wakeful mother

Burns notes in the Interleaved S.M.M. that this song was sung to
him by a girl in Nithsdale. It is generally included among his songs
on the assumption that he, at least, improved the old song. Kinsley
gives two possible sources (Vol. III, no. 311, p. 1339).

Tho' Women's Minds
Tune: For A' that an' a' that.
First printed in the S.M.M., Vol. 3, 2nd February, 1790.

Tho' women's minds, like winter winds,
    May shift, and turn an' a' that,
The noblest breast adores them maist,   most
    A consequence I draw that.

Chorus
5 For a' that, an' a' that,
    And twice as meikle's a' that,   much as
My dearest bluid to do them guid,   blood, good
    They're welcome till't for a' that.

Great love I bear to all the Fair,
10   Their humble slave an' a' that;
But lordly WILL, I hold it still
    A mortal sin to thraw that.   question
        For a' that, an' a' that, &c.

In rapture sweet this hour we meet,
　　Wi' mutual love an' a' that,
15　But for how lang the flie may stang,　　　　*long, fly, sting*
　　Let inclination law that.
　　　　For a' that, an' a' that, &c.

Their tricks and craft hae put me daft,　　　*have, stupid*
　　They've taen me in an' a' that,　　　　　*taken*
But clear your decks, and here's the SEX!
20　I like the jads for a' that!　　　　　　*hussies*
　　　　For a' that, an' a' that, &c.

This is signed as the work of Burns in the S.M.M. It is an adapted extract from his cantata, *The Jolly Beggars*, namely *The Bard's Song*.

Killiecrankie

Tune: Killiecranckie
First printed in the S.M.M., Vol. 3, 2nd February, 1790.

Whare hae ye been sae braw, lad!　　　　*where have, so fine*
　　Whare hae ye been sae brankie O?　　　*strutting smartly*
Whare hae ye been sae braw, lad?
　　Cam ye by Killiecrankie O?　　　　　*come*

Chorus
5　An ye had been whare I hae been,　　　*where, have*
　　Ye wad na been sae cantie O;　　　*would not, so cheerful*
An ye had seen what I hae seen ,　　　　*have*
　　On the braes o' Killiecrankie O.　　　*hill slopes*

I faught at land, I faught at sea,
10　　At hame I faught my Auntie, O;　　　*home*
But I met the Devil and Dundee
　　On th' braes o' Killiecrankie, O.　　　*hill slopes*
　　　An ye had been, &c.

'The bauld Pitcur fell in a furr,　　　*bold, dep ditch*
　　An' Clavers gat a clankie, O;　　　*blow*
15　Or I had fed an Athole Gled　　　　*hawk*
　　On th' braes o' Killiecrankie, O.　　　*hill slopes*
　　　An ye had been, &c.

Although Burns visited the scene of this battle in the Autumn of 1787, during his Highland tour, it is uncertain how much of this song is his. He left no commentary and the remarks in the Interleaved S.M.M. are by Robert Riddell, who noted that the battle occurred on 27th July 1689 between the Jacobite forces of Graham of Claver-house (Bonnie Dundee) and the Hanoverian loyalists led by General Mackay. As Kinsley states, the song is written in the voice of 'one of Mackay's men saved only by the deaths, in pursuit, of Claverhouse and Haliburton of Pitcur' (Vol. III, no. 313, p. 1340).

Willie Brew'd a Peck o' Maut

First printed in the S.M.M., Vol. 3, 2nd February, 1790.

O, Willie brewed a peck o' maut,	malt
And Rob and Allan cam to see;	came
Three blyther hearts, that lee-lang night,	live-long
Ye wad na found in Christendie.	would not

Chorus
5 We are na fou, we're nae that fou,   not full/drunk, not drunk
  But just a drappie in our e'e;   droplet, eye
The cock may craw, the day may daw,   crow, dawn
  And ay we'll taste the barley bree.   -brew

Here are we met, three merry boys,
10   Three merry boys I trow are we;   pledge
And monie a night we've merry been,
   And monie mae we hope to be!   more
      We are na fou, &c.

It is the moon, I ken her horn,   know
  That's blinkin in the lift sae hie;   glinting, sky, high
15 She shines sae bright to wyle us hame,   so, lure, home
  But, by my sooth she'll wait a wee!   word, while
      We are na fou, &c.

Wha first shall rise to gang awa,   who, go away
  A cuckold, coward loun is he!   fool
Wha first beside his chair shall fa',   who, fall
20   He is the king amang us three!   among
      We are na fou, &c.

The music to this drinking song is by Allan Masterton, one of the poet's Edinburgh friends, who, with the poet, is alluded to in the first stanza. The brewer of this Bacchanalian song, Willie, is William Nicol, the Latin teacher at Edinburgh High School. The song celebrates a convivial evening when the three friends met in Moffat where Nicol was on holiday.

The Day Returns –
For Robert Riddell's Wedding Anniversary
Tune: Seventh of November
First printed in the S.M.M., Vol. 3, 2nd February, 1790.

The day returns, my bosom burns,
    The blissful day we twa did meet;   two
Tho' Winter wild in tempest toil'd,
    Ne'er simmer-sun was half sae sweet: so
5 Than a' the pride that loads the tide,
    And crosses o'er the sultry Line;
Than kingly robes, than crowns and globes,
    Heav'n gave me more — it made thee mine.

While day and night can bring delight,
10   Or Nature aught of pleasure give;
While Joys Above, my mind can move,
    For Thee and Thee alone I live!
When that grim foe of Life below
    Comes in between to make us part;
15 The iron hand that breaks our Band,
    It breaks my bliss — it breaks my heart!

This lyric was written by Burns to accompany a melody composed by his friend Robert Riddell of Glenriddell on his wedding anniversary, which fell on 7th November – hence the name of the tune. Burns was an intimate friend of the Riddells: 'At their fire-side I have enjoyed more pleasant evenings than at all the houses of fashionable people in this country put together . . . many of the happiest hours of my life' (quoted by Cromek, p. 269, from Burns's notes in the *Interleaved Scots Musical Museum*). The song is sung as from the lips of Robert Riddell to his wife. Ll. 7–8 are also politically apposite to Burns's relationship to Robert Riddell.

The Blue-Eyed Lassie

Tune: The Blathrie O' 't
First printed in the S.M.M., Vol. 3, 2nd February, 1790.

I gaed a waefu' gate, yestreen,	went, doleful, way, last night
A gate, I fear, I'll dearly rue;	
I gat my death frae twa sweet een,	got, from two, eyes
Twa lovely een o' bonie blue.	two, eyes
'Twas not her golden ringlets bright,	
Her lips like roses, wat wi' dew,	wet
Her heaving bosom, lily-white,	
It was her een sae bonie blue.	eyes so

She talk'd, she smil'd, my heart she wyl'd,	
She charm'd my soul I wist na how;	know not
And ay the stound, the deadly wound,	heart ache
Cam frae her een sae bonie blue.	came from, eyes so
But spare to speak, and spare to speed;	shy & inattentive
She'll aiblins listen to my vow:	maybe
Should she refuse, I'll lay my dead	
To her twa een sae bonie blue.	two eyes so

This was composed on Jean Jaffray (1773–1850), daughter of Rev. Andrew Jaffray, minister at Lochmaben, Dumfriesshire. The initial air by Robert Riddell was changed to *The Blathrie O' 't* in Thomson's version.

Tam Glen

Tune: Merry Beggars
First printed in the S.M.M., Vol. 3, 2nd February, 1790.

My heart is a breaking, dear Tittie,	sister
Some counsel unto me come len';	lend
To anger them a' is a pity,	
But what will I do wi' Tam Glen? —	

5	I'm thinking, wi' sic a braw fellow,	such, fine
	In poortith I might mak a fen':	poverty, shift
	What care I in riches to wallow,	
	If I mauna marry Tam Glen. —	may not

There's Lowrie the laird o' Dumeller,
10   'Guid day to you, brute' he comes ben: good, on
He brags and he blaws o' his siller,   boasts, money
       But when will he dance like Tam Glen. —

My minnie does constantly deave me,   mother, chide
       And bids me beware o' young men;
15 They flatter, she says, to deceive me,
       But wha can think sae o' Tam Glen. —   who, so

My Daddie says, gin I'll forsake him,   if
       He'd gie me gude hunder marks ten: give, good
But if it's ordain'd I maun take him,   must
20   O wha will I get but Tam Glen?   who

Yestreen at the Valentines' dealing,[1]   last night
       My heart to my mou gied a sten;   mouth gave, leap
For thrice I drew ane without failing,   one
       And thrice it was written, Tam Glen. —

25 The last Halloween I was waukin   waken/watching
       My droukit sark-sleeve, as ye ken;   drenched shirt-, know
His likeness came up the house staukin,   image, stalking
       And the very grey breeks o' Tam Glen!   trousers

Come, counsel, dear Tittie, don't tarry;   sister
30   I'll gie ye my bonie black hen,   give
Gif ye will advise me to Marry   if
       The lad I lo'e dearly, Tam Glen. —   love

Burns sent this original dramatic lyric to Johnson in November
1788. A characteristic theme of Burns's women's songs is the
matrimonial choice of love as opposed to wealth. Aided by the
psychic forces occassioned by the Valentine's lottery and the Hal-
loween rituals, the girl is not to be denied her materially poor lover.
'Brute' is restored in l. 10 as earlier editors suppressed this female
denunciation of a social superior.

1 An old custom of sweethearts being chosen by lot on St. Valentine's Day.
R.B.

The Banks of Nith

Tune: Robie donna gorach
First printed in the S.M.M., Vol. 3, 2nd February, 1790.

The Thames flows proudly to the sea,
    Where royal cities stately stand;
But sweeter flows the Nith, to me,
    Where Cummins ance had high command: once
5 When shall I see that honor'd Land,
    That winding Stream I love so dear!
Must wayward Fortune's adverse hand
    For ever, ever keep me here.

How lovely, Nith, thy fruitful vales,
10   Where bounding hawthorns gaily bloom;
And sweetly spread thy sloping dales
    Where lambkins wanton thro' the broom!
Tho' wandering now must be my doom,
    Far from thy bonie banks and braes,   hill slopes
15 May there my latest hours consume
  Amang my friends of early days!   among

This was, as Burns told Mrs Dunlop, his first compliment to the
river Nith, written on 20th August 1788. Cummins (l. 4) is Bruce's
rival, The Red Comyn.

Prologue Spoken at the Theatre of Dumfries
On New Year's Day Evening, 1790

First printed in *The St. James's Chronicle & British Evening Post*,
14th January, 1790.

No song nor dance I bring from yon great city,
That queens it o'er our taste — the more's the pity:
Tho' by the bye, abroad why will you roam?
Good sense and taste are natives here at home.
5 But not for panegyric I appear,
I come to wish you all a good New Year!
Old Father Time deputes me here before ye,
Not for to preach, but tell his simple story:
The sage grave Ancient cough'd, and bade me say,
10 'You're one year older this important day,'
If *wiser* too — he hinted some suggestion,
But 'twould be rude, you know, to ask the question;
And with a would-be-roguish leer and wink,
He bade me on you press this one word — 'THINK!'

15 Ye sprightly youths, quite flush with hope and spirit,
Who think to storm the world by dint of merit,
To you the dotard has a deal to say,
In his sly, dry, sententious, proverb way!
He bids you mind, amid your thoughtless rattle
20 That the first blow is ever half the battle;
That tho' some by the skirt may try to snatch him,
Yet by the forelock is the hold to catch him;
That whether doing, suffering, or forbearing,
You may do miracles by persevering.

25 Last, tho' not least in love, ye youthful fair,
Angelic forms, high Heaven's peculiar care!
To you old Bald-Pate smoothes his wrinkled brow,
And humbly begs you'll mind the important — Now!
To crown your happiness he asks your leave,
30 And offers, bliss to give and to receive.

For our sincere, tho' haply weak endeavours,
With grateful pride we own your many favours;
And howsoe'er our tongues may ill reveal it,
Believe our glowing bosoms truly feel it.

George Sutherland was manager of the Dumfries Theatre (the old theatre referred to here no longer exists, but the new theatre subscribed for during 1790 still stands). Burns got in touch with Sutherland, knowing the theatre was playing on New Year's Day, 1790, and enclosed an early draft of the above. The poet appears to have been in the audience that evening and wrote to his brother Gilbert on 11th January, 1790, remarking 'On Newyearday evening I gave him the following Prologue which he spouted to his Audience with great applause' (Letter 381).

Johnie Cope

First printed in S.M.M., Vol. 3, 1790.

Sir John Cope trod the north right far
Yet ne'er a rebel he cam naur,   near
Until he landed at Dunbar
Right early in the morning.

Chorus
5 Hey Johnie Cope are ye waulking yet,   wakened
Or are ye sleeping I would wit;
O haste ye get up for the drums do beat,
O fye Cope rise in the morning.

He wrote a challenge from Dunbar,
10 Come fight me Charlie an ye daur;   dare
     If it be not by the chance of war
     I'll give you a merry morning.
          Hey Johnie Cope &c.

     When Charlie look'd the letter upon
     He drew his sword the scabbard from —
15 'So Heaven restore me to my own,
     I'll meet you, Cope, in the morning'.
          Hey Johnie Cope &c.

     Cope swore with many a bloody word
     That he would fight them gun and sword,
     But he fled from his nest like an ill scar'd bird,
20 And Johnie he took wing in the morning.
          Hey Johnie Cope &c.

     It was upon an afternoon,
     Sir Johnie march'd to Preston town;
     He says, my lads come lean you down,
     And we'll fight the boys in the morning.
          Hey Johnie Cope &c.

25 But when he saw the Highland lads
     Wi' tartan trews and white cokauds,   cockades/white rose
     Wi swords and guns and rungs and gauds,   cudgels, goads
     O Johnie he took wing in the morning.
          Hey Johnie Cope &c.

     On the morrow when he did rise,
30 He look'd between him and the skies;
     He saw them wi their naked thighs,
     Which fear'd him in the morning.
          Hey Johnie Cope &c.

     O then he flew into Dunbar,
     Crying for a man of war;   ship
35 He thought to have pass'd for a rustic tar,   sailor
     And gotten awa in the morning.   away
          Hey Johnie Cope &c.

     Sir Johnie into Berwick rade,   rode
     Just as the devil had been his guide;
     Gien him the warld he would na stay'd   given, world, not
40 To foughten the boys in the morning.   fight
          Hey Johnie Cope &c.

Says the Berwickers unto Sir John,
O what's become of all your men,
In faith, says he, I dinna ken,   do not know
I left them a' this morning.
    Hey Johnie Cope &c.

45   Says Lord Mark Car, ye are na blate,   not shy
To bring us the news o' your ain defeat;   own
I think you deserve the back o' the gate,
Get out o' my sight this morning.
    Hey Johnie Cope &c.

This is the poet's reworked version of an old, popular Jacobite ballad, most of which is traditional. Johnie Cope was Sir John Cope, General of the Hanoverian army defeated at the battle of Prestonpans in 1745 by the Jacobites.

O Dear Minny, What Shall I Do?
First printed in S.M.M. Vol. 3, 1790.

O dear Minny, what shall I do?
O dear Minny, what shall I do?
O dear Minny, what shall I do?
Daft thing, doylt thing, do as I do. —   stupid

5   If I be black, I canna be lo'ed;   cannot, loved
If I be fair, I canna be gude;
If I be lordly, the lads will look by me:
O dear Minny, what shall I do. —
      O dear Minny, &c.

Burns adapted this woman's song from a lyric in Herd's 1769 collection.

I'll Make You be Fain to Follow Me
First printed in S.M.M. Vol. 3, 1790.
Tune: I'll Make You be Fain to Follow Me

As late by a sodger I chanced to pass,   soldier
I heard him a courtin a bony young lass;
My hinny, my life, my dearest, quo he,   darling

I'll mak you be fain to follow me.
Gin I should follow you, a poor sodger lad,   if
Ilk ane o my cummers wad think I was mad;   each, one, wenches, would
For battles I never shall lang to see,   long
I'll never be fain to follow thee.   glad

To follow me, I think ye may be glad,
A part o my supper, a part o my bed,
A part o my bed, wherever it be,
I'll mak you be fain to follow me.   glad
Come try my knapsack on your back,
Alang the king's high-gate we'll pack;   along
Between Saint Johnston and bony Dundee,   Perth
I'll mak you be fain to follow me.

This is a traditional ballad slightly improved by Burns. It was
unsigned in the S.M.M. It first appears as a work of Burns in
Barke, 1955.

The White Cockade
First printed in S.M.M., 1790.

My love was born in Aberdeen,
The boniest lad that e'er was seen,
But now he makes our hearts fu' sad,   full
He takes the field wi' his White Cockade.

Chorus
5   O, he's a ranting, roving lad,
He is a brisk an' a bonie lad;
Betide what may, I will be wed,
And follow the boy wi' the White Cockade.

I'll sell my rock, my reel, my tow,   flaxing gear, fibre
10   My guid gray mare and hawkit cow;   good, spotted
To buy mysel a tartan plaid,   full body kilt
To follow the boy wi' the White Cockade.
        O he's a ranting, &c.

This is Burns's reworked version of a song in Herd's collection (1769)
called *The Ranting Roving Lad*. It was unsigned in the S.M.M. The
white rose (cockade) is the flower and emblem of the Jacobites.

The Campbells are Comin

First printed in S.M.M., Vol. 3, 1790.

Upon the Lomonds I lay, I lay,
Upon the Lomonds I lay, I lay,
I looked down to bonie Lochleven,
    And saw three bonie perches play —   fish

5 The Campbells are comin, Oho, Oho!
The Campbells are comin, Oho, Oho!
The Campbells are comin to Bonie Lochleven,
    The Campbells are comin, Oho, Oho!

Great Argyle he goes before,
10 He makes his cannons and guns to roar,
Wi sound o trumpet, pipe and drum
    The Campbells are comin, Oho, Oho!

The Campbells they are a' in arms
Their loyal faith and truth to show,
15 Wi banners rattling in the wind
    The Campbells are comin, Oho, Oho!

The poet remarks in the *Interleaved Scots Musical Museum* that the
original lyric was 'Said to be composed on the imprisonment of
Mary Queen of Scots in Lochleven Castle'.

Craigie-burn Wood

First printed in Johnson's S.M.M., Vol. 4, 13th August 1792.

Sweet closes the evening on Craigie-burn Wood,
    And blythely awaukens the morrow;   awakens
But the pride o' the spring on the Craigie-
    burn Wood
    Can yield me naught but sorrow. —

Old Chorus
5 Beyond thee, Dearie, beyond thee, Dearie,
    And Oh to be lying beyond thee!
O sweetly, soundly, weel may he sleep,   well
    That's laid in the bed beyond thee. —

I see the spreading leaves and flowers,
10   I hear the wild birds singing;
But pleasure they hae nane for me   have none
    While care my heart is wringing.

I can na tell, I maun na tell,   not, shall not
   I daur na for your anger: dare not
15   But secret love will break my heart,
   If I conceal it langer.   longer

I see thee gracefu', straight and tall,
   I see thee sweet and bonie;
But Oh, what will my torment be,
20   If thou refuse thy Johnie!

To see thee in another's arms,
   In love to lie and languish:
'Twad be my dead, that will be seen,
   My heart wad burst wi' anguish!   would

25   But Jeanie, say thou wilt be mine,
   Say thou loes nane before me;   loves none
And a' my days o' life to come
   I'll gratefully adore thee.

This is the first of two versions of this song, the second, more dense
in Scots, was sent to Thomson. The lyric is original but the chorus is
old. The heroine is Jean Lorimer (1775–1831) who lived at Kem-
mishall a few miles south of Ellisland farm and is celebrated in
several works of Burns as his 'Chloris'. Burns wrote to Thomson
that 'you are indebted for many of your best songs of mine . . .
whenever I want to be more than ordinary *in song*; to be in some
degree equal to your diviner airs . . . I put myself on a regimen of
admiring a fine woman; and in proportion to the admirability of her
charms, in proportion you are delighted with my verses' (Letter
644). She was indeed Burns's Gravesian 'White Goddess': 'she is, in
a manner, what Sterne's Elza was to him – a Mistress, or Friend, or
what you will, in the guiltless simplicity of platonic love.'

Frae the Friends and Land I Love

Tune: Carron Side
First printed in Johnson's S.M.M., Vol. 4, 13th August 1792.

Frae the friends and Land I love,   from
   Driv'n by Fortune's felly spite,   deadly
Frae my best Belov'd I rove,   from
   Never mair to taste delight. —   more
5   Never mair maun hope to find   more shall
   Ease frae toil, relief frae care: from, from
When Remembrance wracks the mind,
   Pleasures but unveil Despair.

Brightest climes shall mirk appear,   *gloomy*
10   Desart ilka blooming shore;   *desert, every*
Till the Fates, nae mair severe,   *no more*
    Friendship, Love, and Peace restore. —
Till Revenge, wi' laurell'd head,
    Bring our Banish'd hame again;   *home*
15 And ilk loyal, bonie lad   *each*
    Cross the seas, and win his ain. —   *own*

Burns claims only the last four lines of this Jacobite song, asserting that the remainder is traditional. Most editors suspect the song is entirely his given that no earlier version has been traced. Although it is not of the same quality as *Strathallan's Lament*, it is probably correct that most of the song is his.

O John, Come Kiss Me Now –

First printed in Johnson's S.M.M., Vol. 4, 13th August 1792.

O some will court and compliment,
    And ither some will kiss and daut;   *other, caress*
But I will mak o' my gudeman,   *goodman*
    My ain gudeman, it is nae faute. —   *own, no fault*

Chorus
5 O John, come kiss me now, now, now;
    O John, my luve, come kiss me now;
O John, come kiss me by and by,
    For weel ye ken the way to woo. —   *well, know*

O some will court and compliment,
10   And ither some will prie their mou,   *other, kiss, mouth*
And some will hause in ithers arms,   *embrace, other's*
    And that's the way I like to do. —
    O John, come kiss &c.

Here Burns has created a version of an old popular song which Kinsley believes is anti-courtly and derived from a fragment preserved in Herd's collection. (Vol. III, p. 1358)

Cock Up Your Beaver

First printed in Johnson's S.M.M., Vol. 4, 13th August 1792.

When first my brave Johnie lad came to this town,
He had a blue bonnet that wanted the crown,
But now he has gotten a hat and a feather,
Hey, brave Johnie lad, cock up your beaver.　a hat

Cock up your beaver, and cock it fu' sprush;　full spruce
We'll over the border and gie them a brush;
There's somebody there we'll teach better
　behaviour,
Hey, brave Johnie lad, cock up your beaver.

Wallace believed this to be based on an old work 'ridiculing Scotsmen
who settled in London after the accession of James VI to the throne of
England' (1896, p. 523). Even if this were so, Burns has converted it
into a triumphalist assertion of émigré Scotsmen on the make.

My Tocher's the Jewel

First printed in Johnson's S.M.M., Vol. 4, 13th August 1792.

　O meikle thinks my Luve o' my beauty,　much
　　And meikle thinks my Luve o' my kin;　much
　But little thinks my Luve I ken brawlie,　know well
　　My tocher's the jewel has charms for him.　dowry
5　It's a' for the apple he'll nourish the tree;
　　It's a' for the hiney he'll cherish the bee;　honey
　My laddie's sae meikle in luve wi' the siller,　so much, money
　　He canna hae luve to spare for me.　cannot have

　Your proffer o' luve's an airle-penny,　bargain money
10　　My tocher's the bargain ye wad buy;　would
　But an ye be crafty, I am cunnin,
　　Sae ye wi' anither your fortune maun try.　so, another
　Ye're like to the timmer o' yon rotten wood,　trees
　　Ye're like to the bark o' yon rotten tree,
15　Ye'll slip frae me like a knotless thread,　from
　　An' ye'll crack ye're credit wi' mair nor me.　more

The second last couplet of the first stanza and the final two of the
second are old, the remainder is from Burns. This is another example
of the sceptical, tough-minded women's voices in these songs.

Then Guidwife, Count the Lawin

First printed in Johnson's S.M.M., Vol. 4, 13th August 1792.

Gane is the day and mirk's the night,	gone, gloomy
But we'll ne'er stray for faute o' light,	fault/lack
For ale and brandy's stars and moon,	
And blude-red wine's the rysin Sun.	blood-, rising

Chorus

5   Then, guidwife, count the lawin, the lawin,   goodwife, bill
      the lawin,
   Then guidwife count the lawin, and bring a
      coggie mair.   jug more

There's wealth and ease for gentlemen,	
And semple-folk maun fecht and fen';	simple, must fight
But here we're a' in ae accord,	one
10 For ilka man that's drunk 's a lord.	each
Then, guidwife, count the lawin, &c.	

My coggie is a haly pool,	jug, holy
That heals the wounds o' care and dool;	sorrow
And pleasure is a wanton trout,	lurking/ waiting
An ye drink it a', ye'll find him out.	
Then, guidwife, count the lawin, &c.	

The chorus of this is old but the verses are from Burns. The 'lawin' refers to the reckoning, or bill, an account to be paid at the end of the night's drinking – in modern colloquial Scots, the 'damage'.

The Whistle:
A Ballad
First printed in the S.M.M., Vol. 4, 13th August 1792.

Burns wrote the following introduction:

As the authentic Prose history of the WHISTLE is curious, I shall here give it. – In the train of Anne of Denmark, when she came to Scotland with our James the Sixth, there came also a Danish gentleman of gigantic stature and great prowess, and a matchless champion of Bacchus. He had a little ebony Whistle, which, at the commencement of the orgies, he laid on the table; and whoever was last able to blow it, every body else being disabled by the potency of the bottle, was to carry off the Whistle as a trophy of victory. – The Dane produced credentials of his victories, without a single defeat, at the Courts of Copenhagen, Stockholm, Moscow, Warsaw, and several of the petty courts in Germany; and challenged the Scots Bacchanalians to the alternative of trying his prowess, or else of acknowledging their inferiority. – After many overthrows on the part of the Scots, the Dane was encountered by Sir Robert Lowrie of Maxwelton, ancestor to the present worthy baronet of that name; who, after three days and three nights' hard contest, left the Scandinavian under the table, 'And blew on the Whistle his requiem shrill'.

Sir Walter, son to Sir Robert before mentioned, afterwards lost the Whistle to Walter Riddell of Glenriddell, who had married a sister of Sir Walter's. – On Friday, the 16th October, 1789, at Friar's-Carse, the Whistle was once more contended for, as related in the Ballad, by the present Sir Robert Lowrie of Maxwelton; Robert Riddell, Esq. of Glenriddell, lineal descendant and representative of Walter Riddell, who won the Whistle, and in whose family it has continued; and Alexander Ferguson, Esq. of Craig-darroch, likewise descended of the great Sir Robert, which last gentleman carried off the hard-won honours of the field. R.B

I sing of a Whistle, a Whistle of worth,
I sing of a Whistle, the pride of the North,
Was brought to the court of our good Scottish King,
And long with this Whistle all Scotland shall ring.

5   Old Loda¹, still rueing the arm of Fingal,
The god of the bottle sends down from his hall —
'This Whistle's your challenge, to Scotland get o'er,
And drink them to hell, Sir! or ne'er see me more!'

Old poets have sung, and old chronicles tell,
10   What champions ventur'd, what champions fell;
The son of great Loda was conqueror still,   the gigantic Dane
And blew on the Whistle their requiem shrill.

Till Robert, the lord of the Cairn and the Scaur²,
Unmatch'd at the bottle, unconquered in war,
15   He drank his poor god-ship as deep as the sea,
No tide of the Baltic e'er drunker than he.

1 See Ossian's *Caric-thura*. R.B.
2 Sir Robert Lawrie. The Cairn is a stream in Glencairn parish, where Maxwelton House is erected. The Skarr, likewise, runs into the Nith.

Thus Robert, victorious, the trophy has gain'd,
Which now in his house has for ages remain'd;
Till three noble chieftains, and all of his blood,
20   The jovial contest again have renew'd.

Three joyous good fellows with hearts clear of flaw;
Craigdarroch so famous for wit, worth, and law;
And trusty Glenriddel, so skilled in old coins;
And gallant Sir Robert, deep-read in old wines.

25   Craigdarroch began, with a tongue smooth as oil,
Desiring Glenriddel to yield up the spoil;
Or else he would muster the heads of the clan,
And once more, in claret, try which was the man.

'By the gods of the ancients!' Glenriddel replies,
30   'Before I surrender so glorious a prize,
I'll conjure the ghost of the great Rorie More[3],
And bumper his horn with him twenty times o'er.'

Sir Robert, a soldier, no speech would pretend.
But he ne'er turn'd his back on his foe — or his friend,
35   Said, Toss down the Whistle, the prize of the field,
And knee-deep in claret he'd die ere he'd yield.

To the board of Glenriddel our heroes repair,
So noted for drowning of sorrow and care;
But for wine and for welcome not more known to fame,
40   Than the sense, wit, and taste of a sweet lovely dame.

A Bard was selected to witness the fray,
And tell future ages the feats of the day;
A Bard who detested all sadness and spleen,
And wish'd that Parnassus a vineyard had been.

45   The dinner being over, the claret they ply,
And ev'ry new cork is a new spring of joy;
In the bands of old friendship and kindred so set,
And the bands grew the tighter the more they were wet.

---

3 See Johnson's *Tour to the Hebrides*. R.B.

Gay Pleasure ran riot as bumpers ran o'er;
50   Bright Phoebus ne'er witness'd so joyous a corps,   core
And vow'd that to leave them he was quite forlorn,
Till Cynthia hinted he'd see them next morn.

Six bottles a-piece had well wore out the night,
When gallant Sir Robert, to finish the fight,
55   Turn'd o'er in one bumper a bottle of red,
And swore 'twas the way that their ancestor did.

Then worthy Glenriddel, so cautious and sage,
No longer the warfare, ungodly, would wage;
A high ruling elder⁴ to wallow in wine!
60   He left the foul business to folks less divine.

The gallant Sir Robert fought hard to the end;
But who can with Fate and Quart Bumpers contend?
Though Fate said, a hero should perish in light;
So uprose bright Phoebus — and down fell the knight.

65   Next uprose our Bard, like a prophet in drink: —
'Craigdarroch, thou'lt soar when creation shall sink!
But if thou would flourish immortal in rhyme,
Come — one bottle more — and have at the sublime!

'Thy line, that have struggled for freedom with Bruce,
70   Shall heroes and patriots ever produce:
So thine be the laurel, and mine be the bay;
The field thou hast won, by yon bright god of day!'

Before inclusion in the poet's Edinburgh edition of 1793, this
ballad was printed in James Johnson's *Scots Musical Museum*, in
August 1792. There has been some controversy over whether or
not Burns witnessed this drinking contest, but it appears
that he did attend, without taking part, despite his undeserved
reputation for being a drunkard. While the alcohol consumed
here is abnormal, even by the standards of eighteenth-century
upper-class and professional Scotland, Burns was a moderate
drinker compared to many of his social superiors. Boswell, who

---

4 Robert Riddell was a Kirk Elder, representing the presbytery of Dumfries
at the Scottish Assembly from 1789–93.

became a hysterical loyalist under the impact of the French revolution, was a far heavier drinker. The reference to 'old coins' (l. 23) alludes to the fact that Riddell was, amongst other things, an antiquarian.

There'll Never be Peace till Jamie Comes Hame

First printed in Johnson's S.M.M., Vol. 4, 13th August 1792.

By yon castle wa' at the close of the day,	wall
I heard a man sing tho' his head it was grey;	
And as he was singing the tears down came,	
There'll never be peace till Jamie comes hame. —	home
5 The Church is in ruins, the State is in jars,	
Delusions, oppressions, and murderous wars:	
We dare na weel say't, but we ken wha's to blame,	not well, know, who's
There'll never be peace till Jamie comes hame. —	home
My seven braw sons for Jamie drew sword,	fine
10 But now I greet round their green beds in the yerd;	weep, graves, field
It brak the sweet heart o' my faithfu' auld Dame,	broke, old
There'll never be peace till Jamie comes hame. —	
Now life is a burden that bows me down,	
Sin I tint my bairns, and he tint his crown;	since, lost, kids, lost
15 But till my last moments my words are the same,	
There'll never be peace till Jamie comes hame. —	

Introducing this Jacobite inspired song to Alexander Cunningham, the poet wrote, 'When Political combustion ceases to be the object of Princes & Patriots, it then, you know, becomes the lawful prey of Historians & Poets' (Letter 441). This is a deliberately ambivalent remark. It does not necessarily mean that either history or poetry is a mere record of things irretrievably past, but that both have a disturbing, resurrectionary potential as a prelude to political action. Yeats would perhaps be the most tangible example of this sort of poetic influence.

What Can a Young Lassie Do wi' an Auld Man

First printed in Johnson's S.M.M., Vol. 4, 13th August 1792.

What can a young lassie, what shall a young lassie,
    What can a young lassie do wi' an auld man? old
Bad luck on the pennie, that tempted my Minnie mother
    To sell her puir Jenny for siller and lan'! poor, money & land

5 He's always compleenin, frae mornin to eenin, complaining, from, evening
    He hoasts and he hirpis the weary day lang: coughs, limps
He's doylt and he's dozin; his blude it is frozen, worn-out, dull, blood
    O, dreary's the night wi' a crazy auld man! old

He hums and he hankers, he frets and he cankers, fretful, peevish, crabbit
10 I never can please him, do a' that I can;
He's peevish, an' jealous of a' the young fallows,
    O, dool on the day I met wi' an auld man! sorrow, old

My auld auntie Katie upon me taks pity, old
    I'll do my endeavour to follow her plan;
15 I'll cross him, an' wrack him until I heartbreak him,
    And then his auld brass will buy me a new old money
      pan.

This is an original work by Burns, which he describes in the British Museum manuscript as having 'some merit' but 'miserably long' (See Wallace 1896, p. 370). Economically enforced May/September relationships in the world of eighteenth-century Scottish folk songs begin, never mind end, badly.

The Bonie Lad that's Far Awa

First printed in Johnson's S.M.M., Vol. 4, 13th August 1792.

O how can I be blythe and glad,
    Or how can I gang brisk and braw, go, fine
When the bonie lad that I lo'e best love
    Is o'er the hills and far awa. —

5 It's no the frosty winter wind,
    It's no the driving drift and snaw; snow
But ay the tear comes in my e'e , eye
    To think on him that's far awa. —

My father pat me frae his door,   put from
10   My friends they hae disown'd me a';   have
But I hae ane will tak my part,   have one
        The bonie lad that's far awa. —

A pair o' gloves he bought to me,
        And silken snoods he gae me twa,   hair-ribbons, gave, two
15 And I will wear them for his sake,
        The bonie lad that's far awa. —

O weary Winter soon will pass,
        And Spring will cleed the birken shaw: clothe, birch woods
And my sweet babie will be born,
20   And he'll be hame that's far awa.   home

Burns informed Thomson in October 1794 that this song 'is mine'
(Letter 644). It is partly modelled on an old fragment preserved by
Herd which begins 'How can I be blythe or glad, / Or in my mind
contented be'. Burns's poetry, as his world, was filled with harsh,
punitive separation with people either fiscally driven out or sucked
into the vortex of the French war. The winter pain of this woman,
bearing her illegitimate child, is, at least, lightened by anticipation
of Spring and return.

I Do Confess Thou art sae Fair —
First printed in Johnson's S.M.M., Vol. 4, 13th August 1792.

I do confess thou art sae fair,   so
        I wad been o'er the lugs in luve;   would, ears
Had I na found, the slightest prayer   not
        That lips could speak, thy heart could muve. —

5 I do confess thee sweet, but find,
        Thou art so thriftless o' thy sweets,
Thy favours are the silly wind
        That kisses ilka thing it meets.   every

See yonder rose-bud rich in dew,
10   Amang its native briers sae coy,   among, so
How sune it tines its scent and hue,   soon, loses
        When pu'd and worn a common toy!   pulled

Sic fate ere lang shall thee betide;   such, long, become
    Tho' thou may gayly bloom awhile,
15 And sune thou shalt be thrown aside,   soon
    Like onie common weed and vile. —   any

In the Interleaved S.M.M. Burns writes, 'This song is altered from
a poem by Sir Robert Ayton . . . I have improved the simplicity of
the sentiments, by giving them a Scots dress.'

Sensibility How Charming
Tune: Cornwallis Lament for Coln. Moorhouse
First printed in Johnson's S.M.M., Vol. 4, 13th August 1792.

Sensibility how charming,
    Dearest Nancy, thou can'st tell;
But Distress with horrors arming,
    Thou hast also known too well. —

5   Fairest flower, behold the lily,
    Blooming in the sunny ray.
Let the blast sweep o'er the valley,
    See it prostrate on the clay. —

Hear the woodlark charm the forest,
10   Telling o'er his little joys:
Hapless bird! a prey the surest
    To each pirate of the skies. —

Dearly bought the hidden treasure,
    Finer Feelings can bestow:
15 Chords that vibrate sweetest pleasure,
    Thrill the deepest notes of woe. —

In two separate letters (Letters 411 and 462) Burns informs both
Mrs Dunlop and Agnes McLehose that this work was written for
them, first as a condolence to Mrs Dunlop on the death of her son-
in-law and then as a compliment to his 'Clarinda': hence the
reference to 'Nancy', l. 2. This is probably due to the poet's desire
to comfort two close friends on separate occasions. Burns's under-
standing of the fact that hypersensitivity to pleasure necessarily,
dreadfully, entails hypersensitivity to pain, evoked a passionate
response among the English Romantic poets. Wordsworth, in

particular, saw Burns as symptomatic of this dire, manic depressive alternation of extreme emotional states. See, for example, *Resolution and Independence* (ll. 44–9):

> Of Him who walked in glory and in joy
> Following his plough, along the mountain-side:
> By our own spirits are we deified:
> We Poets in our youth begin in gladness;
> But thereof come in the end despondency and madness.

Yon Wild Mossy Mountains

First printed in Johnson's S.M.M., Vol. 4, 13th August 1792.

Yon wild, mossy mountains sae lofty and wide,   so
That nurse in their bosom the youth o' the Clyde;
Where the grouse lead their coveys thro' the heather to feed,
And the sheepherd tents his flock as he pipes on his reed.

5   Not Gowrie's rich valley, nor Forth's sunny shores,
To me hae the charms o' yon wild, mossy moors: have
For there, by a lanely, sequestered stream,   lonely
Resides a sweet Lassie, my thought and my dream. —

Amang thae wild mountains shall still be my path,   among those
10 Ilk stream foaming down its ain green, narrow strath;   each, own
For there wi' my Lassie, thy lang-day I rove,   long
While o'er us, unheeded, flee the swift hours   fly
    o' Love. —

She is not the fairest, altho' she is fair;
O' nice education but sma' is her share;
15 Her parentage humble as humble can be;
But I lo'e the dear Lassie because she lo'es me. —

To Beauty what man but maun yield him a prize,   must
In her armour of glances, and blushes, and sighs;
And when Wit and Refinement hae polish'd her darts,   have
20 They dazzle our een, as they flie to our hearts. —   eyes, fly

But Kindness, sweet Kindness, in the fond-sparkling e'e,   eye
Has lustre outshining the diamond to me;
And the heart beating love as I'm clasp'd in her arms,
O, these are my Lassie's all-conquering charms!

Burns writes in the Interleaved S.M.M. 'This tune is by Oswald: the song alludes to a part of my private history which it is of no consequence to the world to know' (quoted in Wallace, 1896, p. 372). It is, therefore, an original work although the identity of the romance is not known.

It is Na, Jean, Thy Bonie Face

Tune: The Maid's Complaint
First printed in Johnson's S.M.M., Vol. 4, 13th August 1792.

It is na, Jean, thy bonie face,   *not*
   Nor shape that I admire,
Altho' thy beauty and thy grace
   Might weel awauk desire. —   *well, awaken*

5 Something in ilka part o' thee   *each*
   To praise, to love, I find,
But dear as is thy form to me,
   Still dearer is thy mind. —

Nae mair ungen'rous wish I hae,   *no more, have*
10 Nor stronger in my breast,
Than, if I canna mak thee sae,   *cannot, so*
   At least to see thee blest.

Content am I, if Heaven shall give
   But happiness to thee:
15 And as wi' thee I wish to live,
   For thee I'd bear to die.

Although allegedly based on an old English song, which editorially still remains unlocated, this was written for Jean Armour. The ultimate rhyme of 'thee' and 'die' requires the Scots pronunciation *dee*.

Eppie Macnab –

First printed in Johnson's S.M.M., Vol. 4, 13th August 1792.

O saw ye my dearie, my Eppie McNab?
O saw ye my dearie, my Eppie McNab?
'She's down in the yard, she's kissin the Laird,
She winna come hame to her ain Jock Rab. — *will not, home, own*

5   O come thy ways to me, my Eppie McNab;
      O come thy ways to me, my Eppie McNab;
      What-e'er thou has done, be it late, be it soon,
      Thou's welcome again to thy ain Jock Rab. — own

      What says she, my dearie, my Eppie McNab?
10   What says she, my dearie, my Eppie McNab?
      She lets thee to wit that she has thee forgot,
      And for ever disowns thee, her ain Jock Rab.

      O had I ne'er seen thee, my Eppie McNab!
      O had I ne'er seen thee, my Eppie McNab!
15   As light as the air and as fause as thou's fair,   false
      Thou's broken the heart o' thy ain Jock Rab!

This is Burns's somewhat sanitised version of an old bawdy song
with its political as well as erotic implications.

Wha is That at My Bower Door?

First printed in Johnson's S.M.M., Vol. 4, 13th August 1792.

      Wha is that at my bower-door?   who, cottage
            O, wha is it but Findlay;
      Then gae your gate, ye 'se nae be here!   go, way, not
            Indeed maun I! quo' Findlay. —   must

5   What mak ye, sae like a thief?   so
            O, come and see, quo' Findlay,
      Before the morn ye'll work mischief;
            Indeed will I, quo' Findlay. —

      Gif I rise and let you in,   what if
10   Let me in, quo' Findlay;
      Ye'll keep me waukin wi' your din;   waken
            Indeed will I, quo' Findlay. —

      In my bower if ye should stay,
            Let me stay, quo' Findlay;
15   I fear ye'll bide till break o' day;
            Indeed will I, quo' Findlay. —

Here this night if ye remain,
    I'll remain, quo' Findlay;
I dread ye'll learn the gate again;   *come back*
20   Indeed will I, quo' Findlay. —

What may pass within this bower,
    Let it pass, quo' Findlay;
Ye maun conceal till your last hour;   *must*
    Indeed will I, quo' Findlay. —

This question and answer dialogue ballad is modelled on an old broadside *Who's that at my chamber door?* (Kinsley, Vol. III, no. 356, p. 1392).

The Bonny Wee Thing

First printed in Johnson's S.M.M., Vol 4, 13th August 1792.

Wishfully I look and languish
    In that bonie face o' thine;
And my heart it stounds wi' anguish,   *beats*
    Lest my wee thing be na mine. —   *not*

Chorus
5 Bonie wee thing, cannie wee thing,
    Lovely wee thing, wert thou mine;
I wad wear thee in my bosom,   *would*
    Lest my Jewel it should tine.   *be lost*

Wit, and Grace and Love, and Beauty,
10   In ae constellation shine;   *one*
To adore thee is my duty,
    Goddess o' this soul o' mine!
    Bonie wee thing, &c.

Deborah Duff Davies was a petite young Welshwoman who, especially from his letters to her (Letters 472A, 556A, 564) made, even by his inflammatory standards, an extraordinary impact on Burns. His erotic enthusiasm was further intensified by political approval. He met her as a friend of the Riddells at Woodley Park and, from the evidence of Letter 556A she shared his reformative radical passions: 'They talk of REFORM – My God! What a reform would *I* make among the Sons, & even the Daughters, of Men!' She died an early consumptive death.

Ae Fond Kiss

Tune: Rory Dall's Port
First printed in Johnson's S.M.M., Vol. 4, 13th August 1792.

Ae fond kiss, and then we sever;   one
Ae fareweel, and then forever!
Deep in heart-wrung tears I'll pledge thee,
Warring sighs and groans I'll wage thee. —

5 Who shall say that Fortune grieves him,
While the star of hope she leaves him:
Me, nae cheerfu' twinkle lights me;   no
Dark despair around benights me. —

I'll ne'er blame my partial fancy:
10 Naething could resist my Nancy: nothing
But to see her, was to love her;
Love but her, and love for ever. —

Had we never lov'd sae kindly,   so
Had we never lov'd sae blindly!
15 Never met — or never parted,
We had ne'er been broken-hearted. —

Fare-thee-weel, thou first and fairest!   -well
Fare-thee-weel, thou best and dearest!
Thine be ilka joy and treasure,   each/every
20 Peace, Enjoyment, Love and Pleasure! —

Ae fond kiss, and then we sever!
Ae fareweel, Alas, for ever!
Deep in heart-wrung tears I'll pledge thee,
Warring sighs and groans I'll wage thee. —

Kinsley has traced the source of this song to Dodsley:

One fond kiss before we part,
    Drop a Tear and bid Adieu;
Tho' we sever, my fond Heart
    Till we meet shall pant for you' (Vol. III, p. 1379).

If this is the ore, Burns has transmuted it into one of his most golden lyrics though Kinsley himself thinks the song's success depends on ll. 13–16.

Despite the over-heated artificiality of much of the relation-ship, Burns, because of his class, and Mrs MacLehose, because of her separated status, were, to a degree, outsiders in polite Edin-burgh society. Her decision to rejoin her husband who she, against her Edinburgh surgeon father's advice, had married when seventeen and, five years and three children later, had separated from, led her to take ship, ironically, to Jamaica. The song, then, is charged with a combination of sexual loss and foreign exile, bringing together two of Burns's dominant themes. The journey, too, led only to further humiliation for her. Her husband stayed with his mistress, refused to meet her and so she took the same ship home. She long outlived the poet and in 1831 recorded in her Journal: 'This day (6 December) I can never forget. Parted with Burns in the year 1791, never more to meet in this world. Oh, may we meet in Heaven!'

As I Was a Wand'ring

Tune: Rinn m'eudial mo mhealladh – a Gaelic air
First printed in Johnson's S.M.M., Vol. 4, 13th August 1792.

As I was a wand'ring ae midsummer e'enin,	one, evening
The pipers and youngsters were makin their game,	having fun
Amang them I spyed my faithless fause luver,	among, false
Which bled a' the wounds o' my dolour again. —	

Chorus

5	Weel, since he has left me, may pleasure gae wi' him;	well, go
	I may be distress'd, but I winna complain:	will not
	I'll flatter my fancy I may get anither,	another
	My heart it shall never be broken for ane. —	one

	I could na get sleepin till dawin, for greetin;	not, dawn, weeping
10	The tears trickl'd down like the hail and the rain:	
	Had I na got greetin, my heart wad a broken,	not, crying, would
	For Oh, luve forsaken's a tormenting pain!	
	Weel, since he has left me &c.	

	Although he has left me for greed o' the siller,	money
	I dinna envy him the gains he can win:	do not
15	I rather wad bear a' the lade o' my sorrow,	would, load
	Than ever hae acted sae faithless to him. —	have, so
	Weel, since he has left me &c.	

This is omitted by Mackay but accepted by Kinsley. Two versions
of this traditional song have been given as the work of Burns. On this
version, Kinsley asserts that only the last verse is by Burns. Kinsley
has repeated Scott Douglas's error. The latter printed Johnson's
text and asserted that only the final stanza came from Burns. The
original text from the S.M.M. should not be the one attributed to
Burns. This can be clearly seen if we compare the original text with
the revised Burns one above:

As I was walking ae May morning,
The fiddlers and youngsters were makin their game;
And there I saw my faithless lover,
And a' my sorrows returned again.

Chorus
5   Weel, since he's gane – may joy gae wi' him!
It's never be he that shall gar me complain:
I'll cheer up my heart, and I *will* get another,
I'll never lay a' my luve upon ane ane. –

I could na get sleepin' yestreen, for weepin,
10   The tears trickl'd down like showers o' rain;
And had I no got greetin, my heart wad ha' broken,
And O! but love's a tormenting pain!
    Weel, since he has gane &c.

Although he has left me for greed o' the siller,
I dinna envy him the gains he can win:
15   I rather wad bear a' the lade o' my sorrow,
Than ever hae acted sae faithless to him. –
    Weel, since he has gane &c.

Lovely Davies

Tune: Miss Muir
First printed in Johnson's S.M.M., Vol. 4, 13th August 1792.

O how shall I, unskilfu', try
    The Poet's occupation?
The tunefu' Powers, in happy hours,
    That whisper, inspiration,
5   Even they maun dare an effort mair   may, more
    Than aught they ever gave us,
Or they rehearse in equal verse
    The charms o' lovely DAVIES. —

Each eye it cheers, when she appears,
10   Like Phoebus in the morning,
When past the shower, and every flower
      The garden is adorning:
As the wretch looks o'er Siberia's shore,
      When winter-bound the wave is;
15 Sae droops our heart when we maun part   so, must
      Frae charming, lovely DAVIES. —   from

Her smile's a gift frae boon the lift,   from above, sky
      That maks us mair than princes;   more
A sceptred hand, a king's command,
20   Is in her darting glances:
The man in arms 'gainst female charms,
      Even he her willing slave is;
He hugs his chain, and owns the reign
      Of conquering lovely DAVIES. —

25 My Muse to dream of such a theme,
      Her feeble powers surrender;
The eagle's gaze alone surveys;
      The sun's meridian splendour:
I wad in vain essay the strain,   would
30   The deed too daring brave is;
I'll drap the lyre, and, mute, admire   drop/cease
      The charms o' lovely DAVIES. —

Letter 472A, which presumably accompanied this song, is a much
more astonishing piece of prose than his conventional song.

The Weary Pund o' Tow

First printed in Johnson's S.M.M., Vol. 4, 13th August 1792.

I bought my wife a stane o' lint,   stone in weight, flax
      As gude as e'er did grow;   good
And a' that she has made o' that
      Is ae poor pund o' tow.   one, pound string

Chorus
5 The weary pund, the weary pund,   pound
      The weary pund o' tow;   flax string
I think my wife will end her life,
      Before she spin her tow. —

There sat a bottle in a bole,   hole in a wall
10   Beyont the ingle lowe;   near, fireside flame
And ay she took the tither souk   another such
     To drouk the stourie tow. —   wet, dusty flax string
        The weary pund, &c.

Quoth I, for shame, ye dirty dame,
     Gae spin your tap o' tow!   go
15 She took the rock, and wi' a knock,   distaff
     She brake it o'er my pow. —   head
        The weary pund, &c.

At last her feet, I sang to see't,
     Gaed foremost o'er the knowe;   went, edge of hill
And or I wad anither jad,   wed another hussy
20   I'll wallop in a tow. —
        The weary pund, &c.

As Kinsley has rightly remarked (Vol. III, no. 360, p. 1395), this is based on a traditional English song, published in a collection *The Charmer* in 1782, beginning 'I bought my woman and my wife half a pound of tow'. As with other English songs, Burns has given this what he termed a *Scots dress*.

I Hae a Wife o' My Ain

First printed in Johnson's S.M.M., Vol. 4, 13th August 1792.

I hae a wife o' my ain,   have, own
     I'll partake wi' naebody;   nobody
I'll tak Cuckold frae nane,   take, from none
     I'll gie Cuckold to naebody. —   give, nobody

5 I hae a penny to spend,   have
     There, thanks to naebody;
I hae naething to lend,   have nothing
     I'll borrow frae naebody. —   from nobody

I am naebody's lord,
10   I'll be slave to naebody;
I hae a gude braid sword,   have good broad
     I'll tak dunts frae naebody. —   blows from

I'll be merry and free,
 I'll be sad for naebody;
15 Naebody cares for me,
 I care for naebody. —

This is adapted from an old simple Scots ballad on defiant self-sufficiency against poverty and was not composed by Burns just after his marriage as some editors have erroneously believed. If it had been Burns's own work he would have signed it in the S.M.M.

When She Cam Ben, She Bobbed

First printed in Johnson's S.M.M., Vol. 4, 13th August 1792.

O when she cam ben she bobbed fu' law, came in, bowed
O when she cam ben she bobbed fu' law;
And when she cam' ben she kiss'd Cockpen,
 And syne she deny'd she did it at a'. — later, at all

5 And was na Cockpen right saucy witha', not, everyone
And was na Cockpen right saucy witha',
In leaving the dochter o' a lord, daughter
 And kissin a Collier-lassie an' a'. —

O never look down, my lassie at a',
10 O never look down, my lassie at a';
Thy lips are as sweet, and thy figure compleat, complete
 As the finest dame in castle or ha'. — hall

Tho' thou hast nae silk and holland sae sma, no, so small
Tho' thou hast nae silk and holland sae sma,
15 Thy coat and thy sark are thy ain handywark shirt, own work
 And Lady Jean was never sae braw. so fine

This is an improved version of a traditional song about a Laird who had an affair with a common girl, printed in Herd's collection (Vol. 2, p. 206). The first two stanzas are almost unaltered while the last two are from Burns.

O, for Ane and Twenty, Tam

Tune: The Moudiewart
First printed in Johnson's S.M.M., Vol. 4, 13th August 1792.

They snool me sair, and haud me down,	snub, sore, hold
And gar me look like bluntie, Tam;	make, fool
But three short years will soon wheel roun',	round
And then comes ane-and-twenty, Tam.	one-

Chorus
5   An O, for ane and twenty, Tam!   one-
     And hey, sweet ane and twenty, Tam!
   I'll learn my kin a rattlin sang,   song
     An I saw ane and twenty, Tam.

A gleib o' lan', a claut o' gear,	piece, handful
10 Was left me by my Auntie, Tam;	
At kith or kin I needna spier,	need not ask
An I saw ane and twenty, Tam.	
An' O, for ane and twenty, &c.	

They'll hae me wed a wealthy coof,	have, fool
Tho' I mysel hae plenty, Tam;	have
15 But hear'st thou, laddie, there's my loof,	hand
I'm thine at ane and twenty, Tam!	one
An' O, for ane and twenty, &c.	

Although published anonymously in the S.M.M., Burns acknowl-
edges to George Thomson in October 1794 that this is his song, with
the remark ' "In summer when the hay was mawn", "An O for ane
and twenty Tam" are both mine' (Letter 644). Again, this is a song
of significant female defiance regarding an 'unsuitable' marriage
partner.

O Kenmure's on and Awa, Willie

First printed in Johnson's S.M.M., Vol. 4, 13th August 1792.

O Kenmure's on and awa, Willie,	
O, Kenmure's on and awa;	away
An' Kenmure's Lord's the bravest Lord	
That ever Galloway saw.	

5   Success to Kenmure's band, Willie!
      Success to Kenmure's band,
  There's no a heart that fears a Whig
      That rides by Kenmure's hand.

  Here's Kenmure's health in wine, Willie,
10   Here's Kenmure's health in wine,
  There ne'er was a coward o' Kenmure's blude,   blood
      Nor yet o' Gordon's Line.

  O Kenmure's lads are men, Willie,
      O Kenmure's lads are men,
15 Their hearts and swords are metal true,
      And that their faes shall ken.   foes, know

  They'll live, or die wi' fame, Willie,
      They'll live, or die wi' fame,
  But soon wi' sounding victorie
20   May Kenmure's lord come hame.   home

  Here's Him that's far awa, Willie,
      Here's Him that's far awa,
  And here's the flower that I lo'e best,   love
      The rose that's like the snaw!   snow/white cockade

Previous editors have assumed this is based on an old Galloway song, but no evidence of such an earlier work exists. It is not impossible that Burns converted a Highland Jacobite song (akin to *Up an Warn A' Willie*) so that Galloway becomes the location and Viscount William Gordon of Kenmure Castle, who led the Jacobite troops in the South of Scotland in 1715, becomes the hero. The poet and John Syme spent three days at Kenmure Castle (sadly now in ruins), near New Galloway village at the end of July, into August, 1793, on the poet's first tour of Galloway. The snow white rose is the Jacobite emblem (the white cockade) which even the Marxist McDiarmid writes of with considerable pathos. The song is original and carries overtones of *Here's A Health Tae Them That's Awa'*, a later song where Jacobite dissidents meet and merge with the radicalism of the 1790s.

Bessy and her Spinning Wheel

Tune: The Sweet Lass that Loves Me
First printed in Johnson's S.M.M., Vol. 4, 13th August 1792.

O leeze me on my spinnin-wheel,   *delight me with*
And leeze me on my rock and reel;   *distaff*
Frae tap to tae that cleeds me bien,   *from, head, toe, clothes, well*
And haps me fiel and warm at e'en!   *covers, well, evening*
5   I'll set me down, and sing and spin,
While laigh descends the summer sun,   *low*
Blest wi' content, and milk and meal,
O leeze me on my spinnin-wheel. —

On ilka hand the burnies trot,   *either, small burns run*
10 And meet below my theekit cot;   *thatched cottage*
The scented birk and hawthorn white   *birch*
Across the pool their arms unite,
Alike to screen the birdie's nest,
And little fishes' callor rest: *cool*
15 The sun blinks kindly in the biel'   *glimmers, shelter*
Where blythe I turn my spinnin-wheel. —

On lofty aiks the cushats wail,   *oaks, wood pigeons*
And Echo cons the doolfu' tale;   *woeful*
The lintwhites in the hazel braes,   *linnets, rows of*
20 Delighted, rival ither's lays:
The craik amang the claver hay,   *corncrake, clover*
The paitrick whirrin o'er the ley,   *partridge, grass land*
The swallow jinkin round my shiel,   *darting, sheiling*
Amuse me at my spinnin-wheel. —

25 Wi' sma to sell, and less to buy,   *little*
Aboon distress, below envy,   *above*
O wha wad leave this humble state,   *who would*
For a' the pride of a' the Great?
Amid their flairing, idle toys,
30 Amid their cumbrous, dinsome joys,
Can they the peace and pleasure feel
Of Bessy at her spinnin-wheel!

This song derives its title, if not its form and content from Ramsay's *The Loving Lass and Spinning Wheel*. The song is a eulogy to Elizabeth Burgess of Watcarrick in Eskdalemuir.

The song is a celebration of what were to become Wordsworthian pastoral, sessile virtues of economic and environmental content-ment, but with a personal, intimate, charming sense of specific character of which the English poet was arguably not capable.

My Collier Laddie

First printed in Johnson's S.M.M., Vol. 4, 13th August 1792.

Whare live ye, my bonie lass,		where
And tell me how they ca' ye?		what, call
My name, she says, is Mistress Jean,		
And I follow the Collier laddie.		
My name, she says, is Mistress Jean,		
And I follow the Collier laddie.		

5	See you not yon hills and dales		
	The sun shines on sae brawlie?		so finely .
	They a' are mine and they shall be thine,		
	Gin ye'll leave your Collier laddie.		if
	They a' are mine &c.		

	Ye shall gang in gay attire,		go/dress
10	Weel buskit up sae gaudy;		well dressed so splendidly
	And ane to wait on every hand,		one/servants
	Gin ye'll leave your Collier laddie.		if
	And ane to wait &c.		

	Tho' ye had a' the sun shines on,		
	And the earth conceals sae lowly;		so
15	I wad turn my back on you and it a',		would
	And embrace my Collier laddie.		
	I wad turn my &c.		

	I can win my five pennies in a day		
	An' spen 't at night fu' brawlie;		full/well
	And make my bed in the Collier's neuk,		corner
20	And lie down wi' my Collier laddie.		
	And make my bed &c.		

Loove for loove is the bargain for me,   love
    Tho' the wee Cot-house should haud me;   hold
And the warld before me to win my bread,   world
    And fair fa' my collier laddie!   blessings on
And the warld before &c.

A responsive female song of celebratory love for her collier husband, combined with economic hope. There was an embryonic Ayrshire coalfield by the 1790s, the Fife field was much older, but it remains uncertain to what degree this was a traditional song.

Nithsdale's Welcome Hame

Tune: The Country Lass
First printed in Johnson's S.M.M., Vol. 4, 13th August 1792.

The noble Maxwels and their powers
    Are coming o'er the border,
And they'll gae big Terreagles' towers   go build
    And set them a' in order:
5 And they declare, Terreagles fair,
    For their abode they chuse it;
There's no a heart in a' the land   not
    But 's lighter at the news o't. —

Tho' stars in skies may disappear,
10   And angry tempests gather;
The happy hour may soon be near
    That brings us pleasant weather:
The weary night o' care and grief
    May hae a joyfu' morrow,   have
15 So dawning day has brought relief,
    Fareweel our night o' sorrow. —   farewell

This song celebrates the return of Lady Winifred Constable-Maxwell to rebuild Terreagles, the family seat, which had been forfeited by the participation of her grandfather, William Maxwell, 5th Earl of Nithsdale, in the 1715 rebellion. Discussed in the Introduction, Lady Winifred (Letter 377) was the passionate object of Burns's still contentious claim of the mutual Jacobite history of their respective families.

The Country Lassie
or In Simmer, when the Hay was Mawn
First printed in S.M.M., Vol. 4, 13th August 1792.

In simmer, when the hay was mawn,		summer, mown
And corn wav'd green in ilka field,		every
While claver blooms white o'er the lea,		clover, grass lands
And roses blaw in ilka bield;		blow, shelter
5 Blythe Bessie, in the milking shiel		hut
Says, I'll be wed, come o't what will;		
Out spake a dame in wrinkled eild,		age
O' gude advisement comes nae ill.		good, no

Its ye hae wooers mony ane,		have, many a one
10 And lassie, ye're but young, ye ken;		know
Then wait a wee, and cannie wale,		while, cautious chose
A routhie butt, a routhie ben:		well-stocked kitchen, parlour
There Johnie o' the Buskieglen,		
Fu' is his barn, fu' is his byre;		full
15 Tak this frae me, my bonie hen,		take, from
It 's plenty beets the luver's fire.		fans

For Johnie o' the Buskieglen,		
I dinna care a single flie;		do not
He lo'es sae weel his craps and kye,		so well, crops, cattle
20 He has nae loove to spare for me:		no
But blythe's the blink o' Robie's e'e,		eye
And weel I wat he lo'es me dear;		well, know
Ae blink o' him I wad na gie		one, would not give
For Buskieglen and a' his gear.		possessions

25 O thoughtless lassie, life's a faught,		struggle
The canniest gate, the strife is sair;		prudent way, sore/harsh
But ay fu'-han't is fechtin best,		full-handed, fighting
A hungry care's an unco care:		heavy
But some will spend, and some will spare,		
30 An' wilfu' folk maun hae their will;		shall have
Syne as ye brew, my maiden fair,		while/thus
Keep mind that ye maun drink the yill.		must, ale

O gear will buy me rigs o' land,   wealth
    And gear will buy me sheep and kye;   cattle
35 But the tender heart o' leesome loove,   gladsome
    The gowd and siller canna buy: gold, coins cannot
We may be poor, Robie and I,
    Light is the burden Loove lays on;
Content and Loove brings peace and joy,
40   What mair hae queens upon a throne.   more have

Burns acknowledges authorship of this work in a letter to George
Thomson in October 1794, mentioning the song along with *An O for
Ane and Twenty Tam*, remarking they 'are both mine' (Letter 644).
Youthful feminine passion is, characteristically, wholly victorious
over aged prudence.

Fair Eliza

First printed in Johnson's S.M.M., Vol. 4, 13th August 1792.

Turn again, thou fair Eliza,
    Ae kind blink before we part;   one, glance
Rew on thy despairing Lover,   have pity
    Canst thou break his faithfu' heart!
5 Turn again, thou fair Eliza,
    If to love thy heart denies,
For pity hide the cruel sentence
    Under friendship's kind disguise!

Thee, sweet maid, hae I offended?   have
10   The offence is loving thee:
Canst thou wreck his peace for ever,
    Wha for thine wad gladly die!   who
While the life beats in my bosom,
    Thou shalt mix in ilka throe: every
15 Turn again, thou lovely maiden,
    Ae sweet smile on me bestow. —   one

Not the bee upon the blossom,
    In the pride o' sinny noon;   sunny
Not the little sporting fairy,
20   All beneath the simmer moon;   summer
Not the Poet in the moment
    Fancy lightens in his e'e,   eye
Kens the pleasure, feels the rapture,   knows
    That thy presence gies to me.   gives

It is assumed this song was the result of a promise by Burns to James Johnson that he would compose a love song for him on a lady: 'Have you never a fair Godess that leads you a wild-goose-chase of amorous devotion? . . . and I shall task my Muse to celebrate her' (Letter 258).

Ye Jacobites By Name

First printed in Johnson's S.M.M., Vol. 4, 13th August 1792.

Ye Jacobites by name, give an ear, give an ear;
  Ye Jacobites by name, give an ear;
    Ye Jacobites by name
      Your fautes I will proclaim,   faults
5   Your doctrines I maun blame,   will
      You shall hear. —

What is Right, and what is Wrang, by the law, by the law?
  What is Right, and what is Wrang, by the law?
    What is Right, and what is Wrang?
10   A short Sword, and a lang,   long
      A weak arm, and a strang
      For to draw. —

What makes heroic strife, fam'd afar, fam'd afar?
  What makes heroic strife, fam' d afar?
15   What makes heroic strife?
      To whet th' Assassin's knife,
      Or hunt a Parent's life
      Wi' bludie war. —   bloody

Then let your schemes alone, in the State, in the State,
20   Then let your schemes alone in the State,
    Then let your schemes alone,
      Adore the rising sun,
      And leave a Man undone
      To his fate. —

This song has generally been seen as a traditional Whig anti-Jacobite polemic. This would be an unusual viewpoint for Burns. Donaldson (pp. 85–6) produces a subtle, complex reading which reveals it as a Jacobite's renunciatory perception of the terrible, ideological violence that pervades *all* political systems.

The Posie

First printed in Johnson's S.M.M., Vol. 4, 13th August 1792.

O luve will venture in where it daur na weel be seen,   dare not well
O luve will venture in where wisdom ance hath been;   once
But I will doun yon river rove, amang the woods sae green,   down, so
    And a' to pu' a posie to my ain dear May. —   pull, own

5   The primrose I will pu', the firstling o' the year;
And I will pu' the pink, the emblem o' my Dear,
For she's the pink o' womankind, and blooms without a peer;
    And a' to be a posie to my ain dear May. —

I'll pu' the budding rose when Phoebus peeps in view,   the Sun
10   For it's like a baumy kiss o' her sweet, bonie mou;   mouth
The hyacinth's for constancy, wi' its unchanging blue,
    And a' to be a posie to my ain dear May. —

The lily it is pure, and the lily it is fair,
And in her lovely bosom I'll place the lily there;
15   The daisy's for simplicity and unaffected air,
    And a' to be a posie to my ain dear May. —

The hawthorn I will pu', wi' its locks o' siller gray,   silver
Where, like an agèd man it stands at break o' day;
But the songster's nest within the bush I winna tak away;   will not
20   And a' to be a posie to my ain dear May. —

The woodbine I will pu' when the e'ening star is near,
And the diamond draps o' dew shall be her een sae clear;   drops, eyes so
The violet's for modesty which weel she fa's to wear,   well has a right
    And a' to be a posie to my ain dear May. —

25   I'll tie the posie round wi' the silken band o' luve,
And I'll place it in her breast, and I'll swear by a' abuve,   above
That to my latest draught o' life the band shall ne'er remuve,   remove
    And this will be a posie to my ain dear May.

This beautiful lyric originates with Mrs Jean Burns, who rarely receives credit for her role in singing old and new songs to the poet – a valuable service to any songwriter. Burns was delighted with the song *There was a Pretty May, and A-Milkin' She Went* as sung to

him by Jean. He composed new lyrics for the song and wrote to
Thomson several years later that it was 'My composition . . . the old
words are trash' (Letter 644). *B.C.*, 1922, p. 9 gives the traditional
lyric.

Ye Flowery Banks o' Bonie Doon

Tune: Cambdelmore
First printed in Johnson's S.M.M., Vol. 4, 13th August 1792.

Ye flowery banks o' bonie Doon,
    How can ye blume sae fair;   bloom so
How can ye chant, ye little birds,
    And I sae fu' o' care!   so full

5 Thou'll break my heart, thou bonie bird
    That sings upon the bough;
Thou minds me o' the happy days
    When my fause luve was true.   false

Thou'll break my heart, thou bonie bird
10   That sings beside thy mate;
For sae I sat, and sae I sang,   so
    And wist na o' my fate.   knew nothing

Aft hae I rov'd by bonie Doon,   often have
    To see the wood-bine twine,
15 And ilka bird sang o' its luve,   each
    And sae did I o' mine.   so

Wi' lightsome heart I pu'd a rose   pulled
    Frae aff its thorny tree,   from off
And my fause luver staw my rose,   false, stole
20   But left the thorn wi' me.

Wi' lightsome heart I pu'd a rose,   pulled
    Upon a morn in June:
And sae I flourish'd on the morn,   so
    And sae was pu'd or noon!   so, pulled ere

This is essentially the first version of *Ye Banks and Braes*, set to a
different tune than the final version. The contrast between birds and
singer is simple but emotionally profound.

Ye Banks and Braes o' Bonie Doon

Tune: The Caledonian Hunt's Delight
First printed in Johnson's S.M.M., Vol. 4, 13th August 1792.

Ye banks and braes o' bonie Doon,	hill slopes
How can ye bloom sae fresh and fair;	so
How can ye chant, ye little birds,	
And I sae weary, fu' o' care!	so
5 Thou'll break my heart, thou warbling bird,	
That wantons thro' the flowering thorn:	
Thou minds me o' departed joys,	
Departed never to return. —	

Aft hae I rov'd by bonie Doon,	often have
10 To see the rose and woodbine twine;	
And ilka bird sang o' its Luve,	each
And fondly sae did I o' mine. —	so
Wi' lightsome heart I pu'd a rose,	pulled
Fu' sweet upon its thorny tree;	
15 And my fause Luver staw my rose,	stole
But, ah! he left the thorn wi' me. —	

Although a revision of the earlier lyric set to a different air, both were printed in the same volume by Johnson. This version brings the song to a perfect pitch.

Willie Wastle

Tune: The Eight Men of Moidart
First printed in Johnson's S.M.M., Vol. 4, 13th August 1792.

Willie Wastle dwalls on Tweed,	dwelt
The spot they ca' it Linkumdoddie.	called
A creeshie wabster till his trade,	weaver good
Can steal a clue wi' ony bodie:	any
He has a wife that's dour and din,	sulky, pale
Tinkler Madgie was her mither;	gypsy, mother
Sic a wife as Willie's wife,	such
I wadna gie a button for her. —	would not give

She has an e'e, she has but ane,   eye, one
    The cat has twa, the very colour;   two
Five rusty teeth, forbye a stump,   also
    A clapper-tongue wad deave a miller: would deafen
5   A whiskin beard about her mou,   mouth
    Her nose and chin they threaten ither;   each other
Sic a wife as Willie's wife,   such
    I wadna gie a button for her. —   would not give

She's bow-hough'd, she's hem-shin'd,   bandy-legged, splayed feet
10   Ae limpin leg a hand-bread shorter;   one, hand-breadth/size
She's twisted right, she's twisted left,
    To balance fair in ilka quarter: each
She has a hump upon her breast,
    The twin o' that upon her shouther;   shoulder
15 Sic a wife as Willie's wife,
    I wadna gie a button for her. —

Auld baudrans by the ingle sits,   old cat, fireside
    An' wi' her loof her face a washin;   paw
But Willie's wife is nae sae trig,   not so dainty
20   She dights her grunzie wi' a hushian: wipes, mouth, arm stockings
Her waly nieves like midden-creels,   big fists, byre baskets
    Her face wad fyle the Logan-water;   would foul
Sic a wife as Willie's wife,
    I wadna gie a button for her. —

A splendid exercise in the comic grotesque derived from the Scot-
tish flyting tradition and eighteenth-century cartoon caricature.
The word 'clue' (l. 4) is from 'clew', thread. Part of the craft must
have been a proficiency in stealing material. Linkumdoddie was
apparently once a village or hamlet five miles from Broughton, near
the Logan Water's confluence with the Tweed.

Lady Mary Ann

First printed in Johnson's S.M.M., Vol. 4, 13th August 1792.

O Lady Mary Ann looks o'er the castle-wa',   wall
She saw three bonie boys playing at the ba',   ball
The youngest he was the flower amang them a',
    My bonie laddie's young but he's growin yet. —

5   O Father, O Father, an ye think it fit,
We'll send him a year to the College yet,
We'll sew a green ribban round about his hat,   ribbon
    And that will let them ken he's to marry yet. —   know

Lady Mary Ann was a flower in the dew,
10 Sweet was its smell and bonie was its hue,
And the langer it blossom'd, the sweeter it grew,   longer
    For the lily in the bud will be bonier yet. —

Young Charlie Cochran was the sprout of an aik,   oak
Bonie, and bloomin and straucht was its make,   straight, like
15 The sun took delight to shine for its sake,
    And it will be the brag o' the forest yet. —   boast

The Simmer is gane when the leaves they were green,   summer, gone
And the days are awa that we hae seen,   away, have
But far better days I trust will come again,
20   For my bonie laddie's young but he's growin yet. —

This is adapted from an old song Burns may have heard sung. Hans
Hecht quotes the old words in *Songs From David Herd's Manu-
scripts* (1904, p. 145) – 'She looked o'er the castle wa', /She saw three
Lords play at the ba': /O the youngest is the flower of a', /But my
love is lang o' growing'. The difference in metre with the traditional
verse is due to Burns matching his revised lyric to a new tune.

Such a Parcel of Rogues in a Nation
First printed in Johnson's S.M.M., Vol. 4, 13th August 1792.

Fareweel to a' our Scottish fame,   farewell
    Fareweel our ancient glory;
Fareweel even to the Scottish name,
    Sae famed in martial story!   so
5 Now Sark rins o'er the Solway sands,   runs
    And Tweed rins to the ocean,   runs
To mark whare England's province stands,   where
    Such a parcel of rogues in a nation!

What force or guile could not subdue,
10   Thro' many warlike ages,
Is wrought now by a coward few,
      For hireling traitors' wages.
The English steel we could disdain,
      Secure in valour's station;
15 But English gold has been our bane,
      Such a parcel of rogues in a nation!

O would, or I had seen the day
      That Treason thus could sell us,
My auld grey head had lien in clay,   old, lain
20   Wi' BRUCE and loyal WALLACE!
But pith and power, till my last hour,
      I'll mak this declaration;
We're bought and sold for English gold,
      Such a parcel of rogues in a nation!

With his customary erudition, Kinsley has detected a group of popular anti-Union songs out of which this pristine national elegiac lyric has been distilled. Most of these are located in James Hogg's, *The Jacobite Relics of Scotland*, 1819, nos. xl-xlii and lxii. The most likely source found in Hogg, no xxxix, is *The Awkward Squad*, an attack on the 'Thirty-one Rogues', the Scottish Commissioners who allegedly sold the nation out in 1707:

    Shame fa' my een,
    If e'er I have seen
    Such a parcel of rogues in a nation.

From this memorable phrase, Burns creates a song which combines defiance and despair where his two great national heroes are entombed beyond resurrection. The song, thus, is the antithetical companion piece to *Scots Wha Hae*. Consciously or otherwise on the part of the modern poets, it prefigures poems like Muir's *Scotland's Winter* and MacDiarmid's *At Dunbar's Grave* which also enact burial rites for the Scottish spirit. The song was published unsigned partly because its political vision is the reverse of the soon to be wholly triumphal forces of pro-Union Scottish Toryism, most manifest in Walter Scott's writings.

Kellyburn Braes –

First printed in Johnson's S.M.M., Vol. 4, 13th August 1792.

There lived a carl in Kellyburnbraes,   *old man*
Hey and the rue grows bonie wi' thyme;
And he had a wife was the plague o' his days,
And the thyme it is wither'd and rue is in prime;
5 And he had a wife was the plague o' his days,
And the thyme it is wither'd and rue is in prime. —

Ae day as the carl gaed up the lang-glen,   *one, went, long*
Hey and the rue &c.
He met wi' the Devil, says how do you fen?   *fend/how are you*
10 And the thyme it is wither'd and rue is in prime;

I've got a bad Wife, sir, that's a' my complaint,
Hey and the rue &c.
For, saving your presence, to her ye're a saint,
And the thyme &c.

15 It's neither your stot nor your staig I shall crave, *bullock, colt*
Hey and the rue &c.
But gie me your wife, man, for her I must have,   *give*
And the thyme &c.

O, welcome most kindly! the blythe carl said;   *old man*
20 Hey and the rue &c
But if ye can match her — ye're waur than ye're ca'd, *worse, called*
And the thyme &c.

The Devil has got the auld wife on his back,   *old*
Hey and the rue &c.
25 And like a poor pedlar he's carried his pack,
And the thyme &c.

He's carried her hame to his ain hallan-door,   *home, own, front-*
Hey and the rue &c.
Syne bade her gae in for a bitch and a whore,   *go*
30 And the thyme &c.

Then straight he makes fifty, the pick o' his band,
Hey and the rue &c.
Turn out on her guard in the clap o' a hand,
And the thyme &c.

35   The carlin gaed thro' them like onie wud bear,   *went, any mad*
     Hey and the rue &c.
     Whae'er she gat hands on, cam ne'er her nae mair,   *got, no more*
     And the thyme &c.

     A reekit, wee devil looks over the wa',   *smoking devil, wall*
40   Hey and the rue &c.
     O help, Master, help!, or she'll ruin us a',   *master*
     And the thyme &c.

     The Devil he swore by the edge o' his knife,
     Hey and the rue &c.
45   He pitied the man that was ty'd to a wife,
     And the thyme &c.

     The Devil he swore by the kirk and the bell,
     Hey and the rue &c.
     He was not in wedlock, thank Heaven, but in Hell,
50   And the thyme &c.

     Then Satan has travell'd again wi' his pack,
     Hey and the rue &c.
     And to her auld husband he's carried her back,   *old*
     And the thyme &c.

55   I hae been a Devil the feck o' my life,   *have, most*
     Hey and the rue &c.
     But ne'er was in Hell till I met wi' a wife,
     And the thyme it is wither'd, and rue is in prime.
     But ne'er was in Hell till I met wi' a wife,
60   And the thyme it is wither'd, and rue is in prime.

This is signed by Burns in the S.M.M. It is partly based on an old
English song, *The Farmer's Old Wife*, but the body of the lyric is by
Burns. It has all the hallmarks of a traditional male drinking club
song combined with the wit of Burns, humorously lamenting the old
man's marriage to a wife who is so difficult to live with that even the
Devil returns her to him.

Jockey Fou and Jenny Fain

First printed in Johnson's S.M.M., Vol. 4, 13th August 1792.

[Ithers seek they kenna what,
Features, carriage, and a' that,
Gie me loove in her I court;
Loove to loove maks a' the sport.]

Let loove sparkle in her e'e;	love, eye
Let her loe nae man but me;	love, no
That 's the tocher gude I prize,	dowry, good
There the Luver's treasure lies. —	

The second stanza is by Burns and was written to accompany an old song he lifted from *The Tea-Table Miscellany* (1726) and printed by Johnson with the poet's additional stanza.

The Slave's Lament

First printed in Johnson's S.M.M., Vol. 4, 13th August 1792.

It was in sweet Senegal that my foes did me enthrall
    For the lands of Virginia-ginia O;
Torn from that lovely shore, and must never see it more,
    And alas! I am weary, weary O!
        Torn from &c.

5   All on that charming coast is no bitter snow and frost,
    Like the lands of Virginia-ginia O;
There streams for ever flow, and the flowers for ever blow,
    And alas! I am weary, weary, O!
        There streams &c.

The burden I must bear, while the cruel scourge I fear,
10   In the lands of Virginia-ginia O;
And I think on friends most dear with the bitter, bitter tear,
    And Alas! I am weary, weary O!
        And I think &c.

No less an authority than Maya Angelou has discovered in Burns, most specifically in this song, an empathy with the enslaved, brutalised quality of Black experience. Kinsley, however, would have absolutely no truck with such a relationship. Here is his dismissive treatment of the song:

> Burns's part in this song is uncertain. It is ascribed to him only on the evidence of the Hastie MS. There is nothing in the argument that it represents 29 [*The Ruined Farmer*] (Chambers–Wallace, IV, 355). It is related in form and theme, with some verbal correspondences, to the broadside *The Trapann'd Maid* (*Roxburghe Ballads*, ed. Ebsworth, vii 513). (Vol. III, p. 1405.)

Kinsley's peremptory rebutal of the Chambers-Wallace claim that the refrain from Burns's early song The Ruined Farmer , 'It's O fickle fortune O' has no resonance with 'And alas! I am weary, weary O!' is, at least, debatable. What is certain is that Kinsley had neither knowledge nor sympathy for the radical social context out of which this song emerged. Anti-slavery was the integrative factor in all the varied British radical and reform groupings in the latter eighteenth century. It was particularly strong in Scotland which had over sixty anti-slave societies. Further, the successful legal appeal by Joseph Knight, which particularly interested Dr Johnston, to repeal his slave status created a connection with the white Scottish colliers whose actual status was little better than that of plantation slaves. This enlightened Scottish impulse, of which Burns is the creative voice, to see history as an evolving process of the mass of humanity freeing itself from bondage is most cogently and powerfully dicovered in the writings of that great, now sadly submerged, figure of the Scottish radical Enlightenment, Glasgow University's Professor John Millar. Thus Millar on American slavery:

> It affords a curious spectacle to observe that the same people who talk in a high strain of political liberty, and who consider the privilege of imposing their own taxes as one of the unalienable rights of mankind, should make no scruple of reducing a great proportion of their fellow creatures into circumstances by which they are not only deprived of property, but of almost every species of right. Fortune perhaps never produced a situation more calculated to produce a liberal hypothesis, or to show how little the conduct of men is at the bottom directed by philosophical principles. (William C. Lehmann, *John Millar of Glasgow, 1735–1801*, C.U.P., 1960, p. 321).

The Song of Death
or Orananaoig – A Gaelic Air.
First printed in Johnson's S.M.M., Vol. 4, 13th August 1792.

Scene – A Field of Battle – Time of the day, evening – The wounded
and dying of the victorious army are supposed to join in this song.

Farewell, thou fair day; thou green earth; and ye skies,
    Now gay with the broad setting sun!
Farewell, loves and friendships, ye dear tender ties!
    Our race of existence is run.
5 Thou grim king of terrors, thou life's gloomy foe,
    Go frighten the coward and slave!
Go teach them to tremble, fell tyrant! but know,
    No terrors hast thou to the Brave.

Thou strik'st the dull peasant, he sinks in the dark,
10   Nor saves e'en the wreck of a name:
Thou strik'st the young hero, a glorious mark!
    He falls in the blaze of his fame.
In the field of proud honour, our swords in our hands,
    Our King and our Country to save,
15 While victory shines on Life's last ebbing sands,
    O, who would not die with the Brave?

As we saw in the Introduction, this poem was seized on by Robert
Nares, the governmental reviewer of *The British Critic*, as evidence
that Burns, particularly with l. 14's apparent patriotism, had seen
the gross error of his political ways. This poem was allegedly the
antidote to the seditious *Scots Wha Hae* with its connection of the
fourteenth-century Scottish Wars of Independence with the on-
going French Revolution. Nares further claimed that:

> In 1795 when we were first threatened with invasion, he
> appeared in the ranks of the Dumfries Volunteers and con-
> tributed to rouse the martial genius of his countrymen, by the
> following animated and almost sublime war-song.

Unfortunately for this conservative argument the song was written
as early as May 1791, a few years before Britain went to war with
France and at a time when many people in Britain still supported the
French experiment. Explaining the song to Mrs Dunlop he wrote:

I have just finished the following Song, which to a lady the descendant of Wallace, & many heroes of his truly Illustrious line: & herself the mother of several Soldiers, needs neither preface nor apology. . . . The circumstance that gave rise to these verses was – looking over with a musical friend, McDo-nald's collection of Highland airs, I was struck with one, an Isle of Skye tune, entitled 'Oran an Aoig' or 'The Song of Death', to the measure of which I have adapted my stanzas' (Letter 453).

This song is an elemental, post-Ossianic in mood, account of death in battle for both rich and poor. The peasant who dies, even his name is forgotten, but he who dies in battle, is through history, remembered as a hero. Sung from the lips of the dead and wounded soldiers of the victorious army, the 'king of terrors' (l. 5) and 'fell tyrant' (l. 7) not feared by the 'Brave' is Death itself.

Afton Water

First printed in Johnson's S.M.M., Vol. 4, 13th August 1792.

Flow gently, sweet Afton, among thy green braes,   *hill slopes*
Flow gently, I'll sing thee a song in thy praise;
My Mary's asleep by thy murmuring stream,
Flow gently, sweet Afton, disturb not her dream.

5 Thou stock dove whose echo resounds thro' the glen,
Ye wild whistling blackbirds in yon thorny den,
Thou green-crested lapwing, thy screaming forbear,
I charge you disturb not my slumbering Fair.

How lofty, sweet Afton, thy neighbouring hills,
10 Far mark'd with the courses of clear, winding rills;
There daily I wander as noon rises high,
My flocks and my Mary's sweet Cot in my eye.   *cottage*

How pleasant thy banks and green vallies below,
Where wild in the woodlands the primroses blow;
15 There oft, as mild ev'ning weeps over the lea,
The sweet-scented birk shades my Mary and me.   *birch trees*

Thy chrystal stream, Afton, how lovely it glides,
And winds by the cot where my Mary resides;
How wanton thy waters her snowy feet lave,   *clean*
20 As, gathering sweet flowerets she stems thy clear wave.

Flow gently, sweet Afton, among thy green braes,
Flow gently, sweet River, the theme of my lays;
My Mary's asleep by thy murmuring stream,
Flow gently, sweet Afton, disturb not her dream.

This fine song appears first on 5th February, 1789, in a letter from Ellisland to Mrs Dunlop: 'There is a small river, Afton, that falls into the Nith, near New Cumnock, which has some charming, wild, romantic scenery on its banks. – I have a particular pleasure in those little pieces of poetry such as our Scots songs, &c. where the names and landskip-features of rivers, lakes or woodlands, that one knows are introduced. – I attempted a compliment of that kind, to Afton, as follows' (Letter 310). The quotation found in the letter begins 'Flow gently, clear Afton . . .', not 'sweet Afton', suggesting it was re-drafted before publication. The spot described by Burns would appear to be Glen Afton, near New Cumnock.

My Bonie Bell

First printed in Johnson's S.M.M., Vol. 4, 13th August 1792.

The smiling Spring comes in rejoicing,
    And surly Winter grimly flies;
Now crystal clear are the falling waters,
    And bonie blue are the sunny skies.
5 Fresh o'er the mountains breaks forth the morning,
    The ev'ning gilds the Ocean's swell;
All Creatures joy in the sun's returning,
    And I rejoice in my Bonie Bell.

The flowery Spring leads sunny Summer,
10   The yellow Autumn presses near,
Then in his turn comes gloomy Winter,
    Till smiling Spring again appear.
Thus seasons dancing, life advancing,
    Old Time and Nature their changes tell,
15 But never ranging, still unchanging,
    I adore my Bonie Bell.

The metre and flow of this song is irregular and does not have the expected natural ease of Burns's best songs. It was found in transcript, not in the poet's holograph. It is, however, signed as from Burns in the S.M.M. It is not known for certain if it is an original work or a substantially updated traditional work. If the words 'are' and 'forth' were taken from lines 4, 5, and 6 – with further minor textual changes – it would read more like Burns. Whether Johnson modified lyrics we do not know given that their correspondence is incomplete. As it is signed as from Burns in print during his lifetime, there is little to question its authenticity.

The Gallant Weaver

Tune: The Weaver's March
First printed in Johnson's S.M.M., Vol. 4, 13th August 1792.

Where Cart rins rowin to the sea,	runs
By mony a flower and spreading tree,	many
There lives a lad, the lad for me,	
He is a gallant Weaver. —	

5	Oh I had wooers aught or nine,	eight
	They gied me rings and ribbans fine;	gave, ribbons
	And I was fear'd my heart wad tine	would break
	And I gied it to the Weaver. —	gave

	My daddie sign'd my tocher-band	dowry agreement
10	To gie the lad that has the land,	give
	But to my heart I'll add my hand	
	And give it to the Weaver. —	

	While birds rejoice in leafy bowers,	
	While bees delight in opening flowers,	
15	While corn grows green in simmer showers	summer
	I love my gallant Weaver. —	

Mackay affirms this is a 'reworking of a traditional ballad' (p. 464) but it is signed in the S.M.M. This suggests it is a substantial re-write of the old song. It is surprising that Burns allowed 'gied' in stanza 2 and 'give' in stanza 3 to stand, which, although incongruous, makes the ending of the song more English. The river Cart runs through Paisley, important to the weaving industry during the 1780s and '90s. The weaving community was definably politically radical.

Hey, Ca' Thro'
or The Carls of Dysart
First printed in Johnson's S.M.M., Vol. 4, 13th August 1792.

Up wi' the carls of Dysart,
 And the lads o' Buckhaven,
And the Kimmers o' Largo,
 And the lasses o' Leven.

Chorus
5 Hey ca' thro' ca' thro'   pull
 For we hae mickle ado,   have much to do
Hey, ca' thro' ca' thro'
 For we hae mickle ado.   have much to do

We hae tales to tell,   have
10 And we hae sangs to sing;   have songs
We hae pennies to spend,
 And we hae pints to bring.
  Hey ca' thro' &c.

We'll live a' our days,
 And them that comes behin',
15 Let them do the like,
 And spend the gear they win.   wealth
  Hey ca' thro' &c.

This is based on an old Fifeshire fishing song. It has been assumed that Burns collected this work when passing through Fife at the close of his Highland tour in the late Autumn of 1787. It is not certain that Burns improved the song but, on the assumption he did, it is placed in the canon. Given that many such old works are irregular in metre and uneven in quality, this song does appear to have been tightened up by Burns. The deceptively simple clarity of lyric would appear to be his handiwork.

Can Ye Labour Lea
First printed in Johnson's S.M.M., Vol. 4, 13th August 1792.

I fee'd a man at Martinmass,   hired
 Wi' airle-pennies three;   bargain money
But a' the faute I had to him,   fault
 He could na labour lea.   could not, till grass land

Chorus
5   O can ye labour lea, young man,
        O can ye labour lea;
    Gae back the gate ye came again,   go, way
        Ye'se never scorn me. —

    O clappin's gude in Febarwar,   caressing, February
10   An' kissin's sweet in May;
    But what signifies a young man's love,
        An't dinna last for ay.   does not, ever
            O can ye &c.

    O kissin is the key o' luve,
        An' clappin is the lock,   caressing
15 An' makin-of 's the best thing,
        That e'er a young Thing got. —
            O can ye &c.

This is based on an old song Burns heard his own mother sing. As
the original is unknown it is assumed Burns re-wrote the lyric. A
bawdy version collected by Burns is in the *Merry Muses*.

The Deuk's Dang o'er My Daddie

First printed in Johnson's S.M.M., Vol. 4, 13th August 1792.

    The bairns gat out wi' an unco shout,   child's got, great
    The deuk's dang o'er my daddie, O,   duck, beaten
    The fien-ma-care, quo' the feirrie auld wife,   devil-may-, lusty old
    He was but a paidlin body, O. —   wading/messsing about
5   He paidles out, an' he paidles in,   paddles
    An' he paidles late and early, O;
    This seven lang years I hae lien by his side,   seven, have lain
    An he is but a fusionless carlie, O. —   useless old man

    O haud your tongue, my feirrie auld wife,   hold, lustful old
10 O haud your tongue, now Nansie, O:
    I've seen the day, and sae hae ye,   so have
    Ye wad na been sae donsie, O. —   would not, so saucy
    I've seen the day ye butter'd my brose,   porridge/sexual connotations
    And cuddled me late and early, O;
15 But downa do's come o'er me now,   cannot perform, can't do has
    And, Oh, I find it sairly, O!

Although partly based on an old song this is signed in the S.M.M. indicating that it is substantially the work of Burns. This can be proven given the lines quoted by Charles Kirkpatrick Sharpe from the old song (see Wallace (1896), p. 382). This tragi-comic marriage dialogue is based on the old man's impotence.

She's Fair and Fause

Tune: The Lads of Leith.
First printed in Johnson's S.M.M., Vol. 4, 13th August 1792.

	She's fair and fause that causes my smart,	false
	I lo'ed her meikle and lang;	greatly, long
	She's broken her vow, she's broken my heart,	
	And I may e'en gae hang. —	go
5	A coof cam in wi' routh o' gear,	fool, plenty, money
	And I hae tint my dearest dear;	have lost
	But Woman is but warld's gear,	world's wealth
	Sae let the bonie lass gang. —	so, go
	Whae'er ye be that Woman love,	whoever
10	To this be never blind;	
	Nae ferlie 'tis tho' fickle she prove,	no wonder
	A Woman has't by kind:	
	O Woman lovely, Woman fair!	
	An angel form 's faun to thy share;	fallen
15	'Twad been o'er meikle to gien thee mair,	much, have given, more
	I mean an angel mind. —	

Editors prior to Kinsley have guessed this song was written about Alexander Cunningham's mistress Anna, who jilted him (See *Anna, Thy Charms*). There is no evidence to prove the claim. The song appears to be a traditional one improved by Burns. The tone of stanzas 1 and 2 is quite different: the first has a clumsy rhyme repitition on 'gear', indicative of an amateur poet. The second stanza flows naturally and is almost certainly, in sentiment, language and diction, from Burns. Since the original song cannot be traced this conclusion is conjectural. It is surprising that Burns did not also improve the first stanza.

The Deil's Awa wi' th' Exciseman

Tune: The Hemp-Dresser
First printed in Johnson's S.M.M., Vol. 4, 13th August 1792.

The Deil cam fiddlin thro' the town,   *devil, came*
    And danc'd awa wi' th' Exciseman;
And ilka wife cries, auld Mahoun,   *every, old*
    I wish you luck o' the prize, man.

Chorus
5   The deil's awa the deil's awa   *away*
    The deil's awa wi' th' Exciseman,
He's danc'd awa he's danc'd awa
    He's danc'd awa wi' th' Exciseman.

We'll mak our maut and we'll brew our drink,   *malt/whisky*
10   We'll laugh, sing, and rejoice, man;
And mony braw thanks to the meikle black deil, *fine, great, devil*
    That danc'd awa wi' th' Exciseman.
        The deil's awa &c.

There's threesome reels, there's foursome reels,
    There's hornpipes and strathspeys, man,
15 But the ae best dance ere cam to the Land   *one, came*
    Was, the deil's awa wi' th' Exciseman.
        The deil's awa &c.

Despite being unsigned in the S.M.M. the evidence in Letter 500 (to John Leven) indicates this is an original work by Burns. The notion Burns wrote the work extempore while waiting for reinforcements before boarding and taking the smuggling ship *Rosamond* on the Solway is probably myth. Burns may have thought of the song at that time but there is no definite proof of this folk tale.

Wandering Willie

Tune: Here Awa, There Awa
First printed in Thomson's *Select Collection*, May 1793.

Here awa', there awa' wandering Willie,   *away*
    Here awa', there awa', haud awa' hame;   *hold, home*
Come to my bosom, my ae only deary,   *one, dearie*
    And tell me thou bring'st me my Willie the same.

5   Loud tho' the Winter blew cauld on our parting,   *cold*
     'Twas na the blast brought the tear in my e'e: *not, eye*
   Welcome now Simmer, and welcome my Willie;   *summer*
     The Simmer to Nature, my Willie to me.   *summer*

   Rest, ye wild storms, in the cave o' your slumbers,
10   How your dread howling a lover alarms!
   Wauken, ye breezes! row gently, ye billows!   *waken*
     And waft my dear Laddie ance mair to my arms.   *once more*

   But oh, if he's faithless, and minds na his Nannie,   *not*
     Flow still between us, thou wide roaring main:
15   May I never see it, may I never trow it,   *pledge*
     But, dying, believe that my Willie's my ain!   *own*

This is based on an old song called *Thro' the Lang Muir*, which contains one stanza and a chorus, repeated with a variation (See Scott Douglas, Vol. 1, p. 377). The original is a competent Scots song – an additional stanza was added to the version printed in the S.M.M. in 1787 – but the song is significantly improved by Burns. It was written in early 1792, but redrafted for Thomson in March 1793 (Letter 543).

Braw Lads o' Galla Water

First printed in Thomson's *Select Collection*, May 1793.

   Braw, braw lads on Yarrow braes,   *fine, hill sides*
     Rove amang the blooming heather;   *among*
   But Yarrow braes, nor Ettrick shaws,   *woods*
     Can match the lads o' Galla water.

5   But there is ane, a secret ane,   *one, one*
     Aboon them a' I loe him better;   *above, love*
   And I'll be his, and he'll be mine,
     The bonie lad o' Galla water.

   Altho' his daddie was nae laird,   *no*
10   And tho' I hae na meikle tocher,   *have no big dowry*
   Yet, rich in kindest, truest love,
     We'll tent our flocks by Galla water.   *tend*

It ne'er was wealth, it ne'er was wealth,
  That coft contentment, peace, or pleasure; <small>bought</small>
15 The bands and bliss o' mutual love,
  O that's the chiefest warld's treasure!   <small>world's</small>

The original of this song is found in Herd's collection, although a
version appears in S.M.M. in 1788, with slight variations in text,
which might have been minor improvements by Burns. However,
the above is merely modified on the old song and is significantly
changed to make a superior song.

Auld Rob Morris

First printed in Thomson's *Select Collection*, May 1793.

There's Auld Rob Morris that wons in yon glen,   <small>dwells</small>
He's the king o' gude fellows and wale of auld men; <small>good, pick</small>
He has gowd in his coffers, he has owsen and kine, <small>gold, oxen, cattle</small>
And ae bonie lassie, his dawtie and mine.   <small>one, darling</small>

5 She's fresh as the morning, the fairest in May,
She's sweet as the e'enin amang the new hay;   <small>among</small>
As blythe and as artless as the lambs on the lea, <small>pasture</small>
And dear to my heart as the light to my e'e.   <small>eye</small>

But oh, she's an Heiress, auld Robin's a laird;   <small>old</small>
10 And my daddie has nocht but a cot-house and yard: <small>nothing, cottage</small>
A wooer like me maunna hope to come speed;   <small>must not, succeed</small>
The wounds I must hide that will soon be my dead. <small>death</small>

The day comes to me, but delight brings me nane; <small>none</small>
The night comes to me, but my rest it is gane: <small>gone</small>
15 I wander my lane like a night-troubled ghaist,   <small>alone, ghost</small>
And I sigh as my heart it wad burst in my breast. <small>would</small>

O had she but been of a lower degree,
I then might hae hop'd she wad smil'd upon me! <small>would have</small>
O, how past descriving had then been my bliss,   <small>describing</small>
20 As now my distraction no words can express!

This is based on a traditional dialogue song between a mother and
daughter printed in the *Tea-Table Miscellany*, but only a couplet or
so of the original are kept by Burns. He struggled with the pedantic

Thomson to maintain an air of rustic simplicity in the song. He told Thomson, 'There is a naivete, a pastoral simplicity, in a slight intermixture of Scots words and phraseology, which is more in unison . . . than any English verses whatever. – For instance, in my Auld Rob Morris, you propose instead of the word 'descriving', to substitute the phrase 'all telling', which would spoil the rusticity, the pastoral, of the stanza' (Letter 535). The theme once again is the juxtaposition of love and wealth in a feudal social order. The rhyme at lines 15–16 of 'ghaist' and 'breast' relies on the west of Scotland Scots pronunciation of *breast* as *braist*. A version of this song appears in the *Scots Magazine*, July 1797, p. 479.

Open the Door to Me, Oh
Tune: Open the Door Softly
First printed in Thomson's *Select Collection*, May 1793.

Oh, open the door, some pity to shew,
    If love it may na be, Oh;   not
Tho' thou hast been false, I'll ever prove true,
    Oh, open the door to me, Oh.

5 Cauld is the blast upon my pale cheek,   cold
    But caulder thy love for me, Oh: colder
The frost, that freezes the life at my heart,
    Is nought to my pains frae thee, Oh.   from

The wan moon sets behind the white wave,
10   And Time is setting with me, Oh:
False friends, false love, farewell! for mair
    I'll ne'er trouble them, nor thee, Oh.

She has open'd the door, she has open'd it wide,
    She sees his pale corse on the plain, Oh: corpse
15 My true love! she cried, and sank down by his side,
    Never to rise again, Oh.

The old song Burns has used here is Scottish, set to an Irish air. Thomson printed it with the headnote 'Altered by Robt. Burns' and placed rewritten lyrics for the same song by Dr John Wolcot (Peter Pindar) suggesting that Thomson thought Pindar's more English version as good as Burns's, which it is not. It was sent to Thomson in April 1793.

The Sodger's Return

Tune: The Mill, Mill O

First printed in Thomson's *Select Collection*, May 1793.

	When wild War's deadly blast was blawn,	blowing
	And gentle Peace returning,	
	Wi' mony a sweet babe fatherless,	many
	And mony a widow mourning:	many
5	I left the lines, and tented field,	
	Where lang I'd been a lodger,	long
	My humble knapsack a' my wealth,	
	A poor and honest sodger.	soldier
	A leal, light heart was in my breast,	loyal
10	My hand unstain'd wi' plunder;	
	And for fair Scotia, hame again	home
	I cheery on did wander.	
	I thought upon the banks o' Coil,	
	I thought upon my Nancy,	
15	And ay I mind't the witching smile	always, remembered
	That caught my youthful fancy.	
	At length I reach'd the bonny glen,	
	Where early life I sported;	
	I pass'd the mill and trysting thorn,	meeting place
20	Where Nancy aft I courted:	often
	Wha spied I but my ain dear maid,	who, own
	Down by her mother's dwelling!	
	And turn'd me round to hide the flood	
	That in my een was swelling.	eyes
25	Wi' alter'd voice, quoth I, sweet lass,	
	Sweet as yon hawthorn's blossom,	
	O! happy, happy may he be,	
	That's dearest to thy bosom:	
	My purse is light, I've far to gang,	go
30	And fain wad be thy lodger;	would
	I've serv'd my king and country lang,	long
	Take pity on a sodger!	soldier

Sae wistfully she gaz'd on me,   so
    And lovelier was than ever;
35 Quo' she, a sodger ance I lo'ed,   loved
    Forget him shall I never:
Our humble cot, and hamely fare,   homely food
    Ye freely shall partake it,
That gallant badge, the dear cockade,   Jacobite white rose
40   Ye're welcome for the sake o't.

She gaz'd — she redden'd like a rose —
    Syne pale like ony lily,   then, any
She sank within my arms, and cried,
    Art thou my ain dear Willie? —   own
45 By Him who made yon sun and sky,
    By whom true love's regarded,
I am the man — and thus may still
    True lovers be rewarded!

The wars are o'er, and I'm come hame,   home
50   And find thee still true-hearted;
Tho' poor in gear, we're rich in love,
    And mair, — we'se ne'er be parted!   more
Quo' she, my grandsire left me gowd,   gold
    A mailen plenish'd fairly;   piece of arable land
55 And come, my faithfu' sodger lad,   soldier
    Thou 'rt welcome to it dearly!

For gold the merchant ploughs the main,   sea
    The farmer ploughs the manor;
But glory is the sodger's prize,   soldier
60   The sodger's wealth is honour;
The brave poor sodger ne'er despise,
    Nor count him as a stranger;
Remember, he's his country's stay
    In day and hour of danger.

This was the final song Burns sent to Thomson for inclusion in his Volume going to press in April for May 1793. Thomson's arrogance as an editor of song lyrics compelled him to change the lines 'Wi' monie a sweet babe fatherless /And monie a widow mourning' to the dull 'And eyes again with pleasure beam'd, /That had been blear'd wi' mourning'. According to Thomson, Burns's original lines did not suit the music. Characteristically this alleged aesthetic improvement was, in reality, an act of political censorship. Thomson is smoothing over the patently obvious anti-war connotations of the song, resonant at that time since Britain was currently at war with France (see notes to *Logan Braes* for a similar censorial act). It is probably due to the editorial changes made by Thomson that Burns printed his song in *The Glasgow Courier* in September 1793, in order to see a corrected version in print. The theme of the poet's song is found in one of Ramsay's works, *Beneath a Green Shade I Fand a Fair Maid*, in the *Orpheus Caledonius*, 1733, where the soldier returns from Flanders to find his true love. Given that the word 'sodger' is used through the song – soldier would not rhyme with 'lodger' – it seems incongruous to title the song *The Soldier's Return*. The title given here is therefore the Scots *The Sodger's Return*.

A Red, Red Rose

Tune: Major Graham
First printed in Urbani's selection of Scots Songs, Edinburgh, 1794.

O my Luve 's like a red, red rose,
  That 's newly sprung in June;
O my Luve 's like the melodie
  That 's sweetly play'd in tune. —

5 As fair art thou, my bonie lass,
  So deep in luve am I;
And I will luve thee still, my Dear,
  Till a' the seas gang dry. —   go

Till a' the seas gang dry, my Dear,   go
10 And the rocks melt wi' the sun:
I will luve thee still, my dear,
  While the sands o' life shall run. —

And fare thee weel, my only Luve!   well
  And fare thee weel, a while!
15 And I will come again, my Luve,
  Tho' it were ten thousand mile!

This exquisite love song epitomises a central dilemma with the poet's song output. Almost all of the phrases and images employed here have been traced to various traditional songs. For example, these old words are given in Kinsley:

Her cheeks are like the Roses
    That blossom fresh in June,
O, she's like a new-strung instrument
    That's newly put in tune;

/ . . . Altho' I go a thousand miles
    I vow thy face to see,
Altho' I go ten thousand miles
    I'll come again to thee, dear Love,
I'll come again to thee . . .
    The Day shall turn to Night, dear Love,
And the Rocks melt wi' the Sun,
    Before that I prove false to thee. (Vol. III, pp. 1454–5.)

Since frequently the seam cannot be detected between folk-song and Burns's verse, there exists an insoluble critical problem as to original compositon. With regard to this poem, Kinsley oddly remarks that: 'We may, however, be doing an injustice to oral tradition in regarding [this] even as a reconstruction by Burns.' Burns himself would be the last person to deny that, if his lyrics were golden, it was because of the quality of the traditional ore. On the other hand, he rightly feared the parochial, sentimental verse which would be written in his name.

Sonnet: On the Death of Robert Riddell Esq. of Glenriddell,
April 1794
This first appears in *The Dumfries Journal*, 22nd April, 1794.

No more, ye warblers of the wood, no more,
    Nor pour your descant grating on my soul!
    Thou young-eyed Spring, gay in thy verdant stole,
More welcome were to me grim Winter's wildest roar.

5   How can ye charm, ye flowers, with all your dyes?
    Ye blow upon the sod that wraps my friend:
    How can I to the tuneful strain attend?
That strain flows round th' untimely tomb where Riddell lies.

Yes, pour, ye warblers, pour the notes of woe,
10   And sooth *the Virtues* weeping o'er his bier.
The *Man of Worth* — and 'as not left his peer —[1]
Is in his 'narrow house' for ever darkly low.[2]

Thee, Spring, again with joy shall others greet,
Me, mem'ry of my loss will only meet.

Robert Riddell (1755–94), died on 20th April, 1794, aged 39 years. The sonnet which appeared under the poet's name in *The Dumfries Journal* was also sent to the London *Star*, and printed on 30th April, then subsequently copied by the *Morning Chronicle, 5th May*, and in the May issue of *The Gentleman's Magazine*. The newspaper obituary on Riddell is also thought to be by Burns, although it has never been formally credited. Burns commented on Robert Riddell of Glenriddell, who lived at Friars Carse, near Ellisland farm, that 'At their fire-side I have enjoyed more pleasant evenings than at all the houses of fashionable people in this country put together . . . many of the happiest hours of my life' (Cromek, p. 269, from the *I.S.M.M*). He is, therefore, a crucial, but still not fully-known player in the Burns story.

Kinsley omits the most important factor about Riddell, that he was a leading radical Whig, known throughout Britain (Vol. III, p. 1274). As we have seen, he wrote the pro-reform essay printed under the pen-name 'Cato' which Burns posted to *The Edinburgh Gazetteer* (Letter 530). Several of his essays feature in *The Glasgow Journal*; they fiercely debate with Edmund Burke the question of imported manufactures and the India question relating to the trial of Warren Hastings. Riddell was thus a key radical Whig of the period (See our notes to *On Glenriddell's Fox Breaking its Chain*). Professor Werkmeister cogently remarks that Burns's allowing his name to be associated with Riddell was: '. . . a courageous resolve, for, since Riddell was no friend of Government, a "tribute" to him had to be regarded as political and hence publishable only in an Opposition newspaper' (*Robert Burns and the London Daily Press, Modern Philology*, LXIII, 1966, p. 326).

The sonnet sets a deliberate parallel between Burns and Riddell and the profound loss felt by Milton when his friend Edward King was drowned, as lamented in *Lycidas*, hence the quote (l. 11).

---

1 Adapted from Milton's *Lycidas*.
2 Gray's *Elegy*, '. . . in his narrow cell for ever laid'.

Wilt Thou Be My Dearie?

Tune: The Sutor's Dochter
First printed in *The Morning Chronicle*, 10th May, 1794.

Wilt thou be my dearie?
When Sorrow wrings thy gentle heart,
    O, wilt thou let me cheer thee?
By the treasure of my soul —
5   That's the love I bear thee —
I swear and vow that only thou
    Shall ever be my dearie!
Only thou, I swear and vow,
    Shall ever be my dearie!

10 Lassie, say thou lo'es me,   *loves*
    Or, if thou wilt na be my ain,   *will not, own*
    Say na thou'lt refuse me!   *not*
If it winna, canna be,   *will not, cannot*
    Thou for thine may choose me,
15 Let me, lassie, quickly die,
    Trusting that thou lo'es me!
Lassie, let me quickly die,
    Trusting that thou lo'es me!

This appears first in the London Whig Opposition paper *The Morning Chronicle*, two days after the unsigned publication of *Scots Wha Hae*. It was signed as the work of Burns. It is not a controversial work, so there was no problem about his name being printed. Most editors assume the heroine of the song is Janet Miller, daughter of the poet's former landlord at Ellisland, Patrick Miller of Dalswinton. This is not known for certain. Both Kinsley and Mackay err in their notes to this work by going on to assert that Patrick Miller offered Burns a job with *The Morning Chronicle* in April 1794, when in fact it is known that the offer of removal for full time journalistic work in London was rejected by Burns in mid-March, 1794. Miller merely conveyed the offer from James Perry, the paper's editor.

O Wat Ye Wha's in Yon Town

Tune: We'll Gang Nae Mair to Yon Town
First printed in *The Glasgow Magazine*, September 1795.

NOW haply down yon gay green shaw   wood
    She wanders by yon spreading tree;
How blest ye flow'rs that round her blaw,   blow
    Ye catch the glances o' her ee.   eye

Chorus
5 O wat ye wha's in yon town,   know, who's
    Ye see the e'enin Sun upon,   evening
The dearest maid's in yon town,
    That e'enin Sun is shining on.

How blest ye birds that round her sing,
10   And welcome in the blooming year,
And doubly welcome be the Spring,
    The season to my Jeanie dear.
      O wat ye wha's &c.

The sun blinks blyth on yon town,
    Amang the broomy braes sae green;   among, hill slopes so
15 But my delight in yon town,
    And dearest pleasure, is my Jean.
      O wat ye wha's &c.

Without my Fair, not a' the charms
    O' Paradise could yield me joy;
But gie me Jeanie in my arms,   give
20   And welcome Lapland's dreary sky.
      O wat ye wha's &c.

My cave wad be a lover's bow'r,   would
    Tho' raging Winter rent the air;   rend
And she a lovely little flower,
    That I wad tent and shelter there.   would tend
      O wat ye wha's &c.

25 O sweet is she in yon town,
    The sinkin Sun's gane down upon: gone
A fairer than's in yon town
    His setting beam ne'er shone upon.
      O wat ye wha's &c.

If angry Fate is sworn my foe,
30   And suff'ring I am doom'd to bear;
I careless quit aught else below,   *ought*
      But spare me, spare me Jeanie dear.
        O wat ye wha's &c.

For while life's dearest blood runs warm,
      Ae thought frae her shall ne'er depart,   *one, from*
35 And she — as fairest is her form,
      She has the truest, kindest heart.
        O wat ye wha's &c.

Burns started this work when snow-bound in the village of Eccle-
fechan on the evening of 7th February, 1795. It was finished and
sent to Thomson in April (Letter 661). It is a modification of the
poet's own song *I'll Ay Ca' in by Yon Town* which had been sent to
Johnson.

The Dumfries Volunteers

Tune: Push About the Jorum
First published in *The Edinburgh Courant*, 4th May, 1795.

Does haughty Gaul invasion threat,
      Then let the loons beware, Sir!   *fools*
There's WOODEN WALLS upon our seas
      And VOLUNTEERS on shore, Sir:
5 The *Nith* shall run to *Corsincon*[1],
      And *Criffel* sink in *Solway*[2],
Ere we permit a Foreign Foe
      On British ground to rally!

O let us not, like snarling curs,   *dogs*
10   In wrangling be divided,
Till, slap! come in an *unco loun*,   *strange fool*
      And wi' a rung decide it!   *cudgel*
Be BRITAIN still to BRITAIN true,
      Amang oursels united: *among ourselves*
15 For never but by *British hands*
      Maun *British wrangs* be righted.   *shall, wrongs*

1 A high hill at the source of the Nith. R.B.
2 A high hill at the confluence of the Nith and the Solway Firth. R.B.

The *kettle* o' the Kirk and State,
    Perhaps a *clout* may fail in't;   patch
But Deil a *foreign* tinkler loon
20   Shall ever ca' a nail in't.   hammer
Our FATHERS' BLUDE the *kettle* bought,   blood
    And wha wad dare to spoil it,   who would
By Heav'ns! the sacrilegious dog
    Shall fuel be to boil it!

25 The wretch that would a *Tyrant* own,
    And the wretch, his true-sworn brother,
Who would set the Mob above the *Throne*,
    May they be damn'd together!
Who will not sing God Save The KING
30   Shall hang as high 's the steeple;
But while we sing God Save The KING,
    We'll ne'er forget THE PEOPLE!

After publication in *The Edinburgh Evening Courant* on 4th May 1795 this song appeared in *The Dumfries Journal* on 5th May, *The Caledonian Mercury* on 7th May and was copied in *The Northern Star*, Belfast, 29th October–2nd November 1795 issue. It was printed by Currie in 1800 and features in S.M.M., no. 546, 1803.

A first draught, which has not survived and was probably destroyed, contained a satirical attack on a 'ci-devant Commodore' which the poet later omitted. The reason Burns dropped the satirical lines is explained to Mrs Dunlop: 'Miss Keith will see that I have omitted the four lines on the ci-devant Commodore which gave her so much offence. Had I known that he stood in no less connection than the Godfather of my lovely young Friend, I would have spared him for her sake' (*Robert Burns and Mrs Dunlop*, edited by W. Wallace, London, 1898, p. 419). The fact that this song originally contained a satirical attack on a high ranking military officer is missed by previous editors who distort the song into a statement of the poet's loyalty to the Pitt government and hence, a cessation of his radical values. This is far from the case. Indeed, the message of the song is unequivocally in *support* of reform, that is, placing the practice of politics back on a footing according to the principles of the Constitution, a sentiment clearly echoed in the lines:

Be Britain still to Britain true,
    Amang oursels united!
For never but by British hands
    Maun British wrangs be righted!

A cleverly balanced criticism of the Pitt government hints that there are indeed problems that should be addressed and resolved. Extremes are exposed as no solution in themselves – the 'tyrant' and 'mob' – echoes his earlier line, 'Be Anarchy cursed and Tyranny damned'. It would be naïve to read the reference to singing 'God Save the King' as a statement of loyalism, given that it is Burns, as he does on many occasions, giving ironic assent to what he is actually attacking and preparing the song to end on a final and loudly emphasised phrase 'We'll ne'er forget THE PEOPLE!' The appearance of 'loyalty' is, in reality, a sleight of hand that refers more to an abstract loyalism to the higher ideal of reforming politics and placing into practice the ideals of the British constitution. By early 1795 the radical French leader Marat had been assassinated and the French Revolution had strayed far from its original ideals and was at this time in the hands of an oligarchy hell-bent on Empire building and the reactionary imperial cult of the young officer, Napoleon Bonaparte. It is therefore no contradiction and entirely consistent with the radical views of Burns that he would oppose a French invasion of Britain, given that their revolution had metamorphosed to being a tyrannical power. Hence, Burns could oppose a French invasion but at the same time still agree with the original principles of the French Revolution. Moreover, this song allowed him the breathing space of *appearing* to be a loyal subject, but one who actually opposed the political leadership of Pitt and Dundas. As he remarked to Mrs Dunlop in mid-January 1795, he looked forward to the day when a person might be able to criticise 'Billy Pitt' without being judged an enemy (all reformers were branded Jacobins at this time) of his country.

Given Burn's expurgation of the poem's specific satirical target combined with an understandably, fear-induced political tracks-disguising over-subtlety, Burns's legion of conservative enemies, from the outset, seized upon this poem as absolute, final evidence, despite the overwhelming mass of his politically contrary poetry, of his loyal, wholly anti-revolutionary, pro-Hanoverian stance. Fearfully living throughout the nineteenth century in the shadow of the French Revolution, almost all institutionalized, *published* Burns criticism followed this line. The radical Burns of the Chartist Movement and subsequent proto-socialism existed at a working class, oral level. (See William Power, 'The Song of Friendship', in *Robert Burns and Other Essays and Sketches* (London & Glasgow, 1926, p. 48). In the economically fraught, politically turbulent Scotland of the aftermath of the First World War, this political division became more extreme. Burns was, albeit simplistically, the poet-prophet of Red Clydeside and the ILP. The opposing bour-

geois populism of the Burns Federation was of a decidedly reac-
tionary, pro-Unionist order. Hence, for example, Duncan
McNaught's account of Burns's politics as expressed in *The Dum-
fries Volunteers* in B.C. (No. 34, 1925), pp. 61–5:

> From the way in which Burns is quoted on political platforms
> and by the huge army of open-air preachers of social reform, one
> can only conclude that the intention of the orators is to represent
> Burns as the outstanding extremist of his generation. In some of
> his earlier poems, as, for instance 'Epistle to Davie', the case for
> Labour is put in the strongest of lights, and enforced with much
> the same arguments as the Socialist of today has rendered us so
> familiar with; but the whole volume of his poetry and prose will
> be searched in vain for a single line that expresses the slightest
> sympathy with the doctrines of the Bolshevism, Communism,
> and Socialism which are now so loudly proclaimed from the
> housetops. Burns's philosophy was on a higher plane; his opi-
> nions were founded on the axioms of political ethics which apply
> to all parties alike, and which have been subscribed to by all
> sensible men who have thought seriously on the subject. A short
> compendium of his political creed, written the year before his
> death, will be found in 'Does Haughty Gaul', a composition
> which effectually disposes of the mythical tradition that he was a
> disloyal subject and a Revolutionist.

Sadly, however, misinterpretation was not exlusively the pre-
rogative of wilful reactionaries. The publication of *The Dumfries
Volunteers* led to a back-lash against Burns by his erstwhile Ulster
supporters who saw it as an act of apostasy akin, as Liam McIl-
vanney has pertinently pointed out ('Robert Burns and the Ulster-
Scots Literary Revival of the 1790s', *Bullán: An Irish Studies
Journal*, Vol. IV, No. 2, pp. 124–44), to the betrayal that the
younger English radicals felt for Wordsworth. This led to the
publication of this *Song* in the republican *Northern Star* (29 Octo-
ber–2 November, 1795):

> O Scotia's Bard! my muse alas!
> For you in private blushes!
>   You've dipt i' th' dish wi' slee D[unda]s
> An' prie'd the Loaves and Fishes!
>   When *bare-foot* owre the Ayr-shire hills,
> A rustic ye ran chanting,
>   Ye wadna took a score o' gills
> To hae deav'd us wi' sic ranting.

SONGS PUBLISHED IN HIS LIFETIME 421

The *kettle* o' your *kirk* and *state*
For which your dads contended,
    Has been sae ding'd and spoil'd of late,
I fear it can't be mended!
    And if a British Tinkler dare
But shaw his bag and nails, man;
    O bid the meddling loun beware
O' shaving and South-Wales man.

    There Muir and Palmer, tinklers good
As ever Scotia rear'd, man,
    Were banish'd owre the foaming flood,
For daring to repair man.
    Then sith ye canna mak' it staunch,
Swith fling it out of doors, man.
    Ye'll get a new ane frae the F——h
Ane worth a score o' yours, man.

    But tent me, much revered Bob,
You err, and unco far man,
    For *those*, you Burke-like, call the *mob*,
The very PEOPLE are man.
    So now I sing, God Save the King,
And the Queen to keep him warm, sir;
    But may he high as Haman hing,
Who dares oppose – REFORM, sir.

That this specific charge was untrue has to be set against the general truth that Scotland did fail Ireland at its hour of need. See John Brims's very fine 'Scottish Radicalism and the United Irishman' in *The United Irishmen, Republicanism, Radicalism and Rebellion* (Dublin: 1993), pp. 151–66.

PART FIVE

Anonymous and Pseudonymous Works

Lines on Seeing the Royal Palace at Stirling in Ruins

First printed in *The Edinburgh Evening Courant*, 5th October, 1787.

> Here Stewarts once in triumph reign'd,
> And laws for Scotland's weal ordain'd;
> But now unroof'd their Palace stands,
> Their sceptre's fall'n to other hands;
> 5 Fallen indeed, and to the earth,
> Whence grovelling reptiles take their birth. —
> The injured STEWART-line are gone,
> A Race outlandish fill their throne;
> An idiot race, to honour lost;
> 10 Who know them best despise them most. —
>
> R.B.

These anti-Hanoverian lines were inscribed anonymously on a window in Stirling by Burns during his first tour into the Highlands in August 1787. They reappeared in *The Edinburgh Evening Courant*, 5th October 1787, thinly disguised by the poet's initials 'R.B.' If the author's identity was not patently obvious at this point, it was made public knowledge by James Maxwell, an elderly mediocre Paisley poet, deeply envious of the young bard's success who published the lines and named Burns as the author. Maxwell used the opportunity to attack the poet in a pamphlet, *Animadversions on Some Poets and Poetasters* (Paisley, 1788). While accustomed to a degree of notoriety, at least in Ayrshire, this episode proved to be a mini-rehearsal of the graver trouble waiting ahead for Burns due to his bent for controversy. He wrote to Mrs McLehose on 27th January 1788: 'I have almost given up the Excise idea. I have been just now to wait on a great Person . . . Why will Great people not only deafen us with the din of their equipage, and dazzle us with their fastidious pomp, but they must also be so very dictatorially wise? I have been question'd like a child about my matters, and blamed and schooled for my Inscription on Stirling window' (Letter 189).

During the early nineteenth century Motherwell tried to omit these controversial lines from the canon by suggesting they were written by the bard's touring companion, William Nicol. The poet's somewhat vague title in the Glenriddell manuscript, *Written by Somebody in the Window of an Inn at Stirling* gave some credence to those who wished to deny his authorship. By 1834, as McGuirk remarks, Cunningham was too timid to publish the final anti-Hanoverian couplet. Acting as censor, Cunningham justifed his action thus: 'What was improper in the days of Burns is not proper now' (McGuirk, p. 245). Ll. 5–6 were added in the Glenriddell Manuscript and were probably not inscribed on the Stirling window.

Elegy on the Year 1788

First printed in *The Caledonian Mercury*, 10th January, 1789, under the pen name Thomas A. Linn.

	For Lords or kings I dinna mourn,	do not
	E'en let them die — for that they're born!	
	But oh! prodigious to reflect,	
	A *Towmont*, Sirs, is gane to wreck!	12 months, gone
5	O *Eighty-Eight*, in thy sma' space	small
	What dire events hae taken place!	have
	Of what enjoyments thou hast reft us!	taken from
	In what a pickle thou hast left us!	
	The Spanish empire's tint a head,	lost, leader
10	An' my auld teethless Bawtie's dead;	old, dog
	The toolzie's teugh 'tween Pitt and Fox,	struggle's tough
	An' our gudewife's wee birdie cocks;	goodwife's, small
	The tane is game, a bluidy devil,	one, bloody
	But to the *hen-birds* unco civil;	very
15	The tither's dour, has nae sic breedin',	other's is stubborn, no
	But better stuff ne'er claw'd a midden!	scratched, open dung heap
	Ye ministers, come mount the pupit,	pulpit
	An' cry till ye be haerse an' roupet;	hoarse, husky
	For *Eighty-Eight* he wished you weel,	well
20	An' gied ye a' baith gear an' meal;	gave, both, goods, food
	E'en mony a plack, an' mony a peck,	coin, sack of oats
	Ye ken yoursels, for little feck!	know, return

Ye bonie lasses, dight your een, *wipe, eyes*
For some o' you hae tint a frien'; *have lost, friend*
25 In *Eighty-Eight*, ye ken, was taen *know, taken*
What ye'll ne'er hae to gie again. *have, give*

Observe the vera nowte an' sheep, *very, cattle*
How dowff an' dowie they creep; *dull, weary*
Nay, even the yirth itsel' does cry, *earth*
30 For Embro' wells are grutten dry. *Edinburgh, wept*

O *Eighty-Nine*, thou's but a bairn, *child*
An' no owre auld, I hope to learn! *over old*
Thou beardless boy, I pray tak care,
Thou now has got thy Daddy's chair,
35 Nae hand-cuff'd, mizzl'd, half-shackl'd *Regent*, *no, muzzled*
But, like himsel, a full free agent.
Be sure ye follow out the plan
Nae war than he did, honest man! *no worse*
As muckle better as ye can. *much*

This was written on 1st January, 1789 and published in *The Caledonian Mercury*, January 1789, under the pen-name, Thomas A. Linn (probably taken from the song *Tam Linn*). It was also printed anonymously in *Lloyd's Evening Post*, on 12th–14th January, 1789, where it may have been copied, as was common practice, by that paper.

This is politically a wickedly reductive little poem, salted with sexual slyness. A panorama of 1788, where 'great' events (the death of Charles III of Spain (l. 9) and the Regency Bill Crisis) are brought down to the vernacular earth of Burns's farmyard animals. Ll. 11–16 allude not only to the intensity of the quarrel between the still-favoured Pitt and Fox over the regency question but their utterly disparate sexuality. L. 30 alludes to the restriction of Edinburgh's water supply due to the severe frost of the winter of 1788–9. Even by the standards of Burns's anti-Hanoverianism, ll. 31–39 are stunning in that they brilliantly transpose the image of the metaphorically shackled Prince of Wales into the actual physical restraints now restraining his temporarily insane father.

Ode to the Departed Regency Bill

First printed in the London *Star*, 17th April, 1789, signed Agricola,
Edinburgh.

Daughter of Chaos' doting years,
Nurse of ten thousand hopes and fears;
Whether thy airy, unsubstantial Shade
(The rights of sepulture now duly paid)
5   Spread abroad its hideous form
On the roaring Civil Storm,
Deafening din and warring rage
Factions wild with factions wage;
Or underground, deep-sunk, profound,
10   Among the demons of the earth,
With groans that make the mountains shake,
Thou mourn thy ill-starred, blighted birth;
Or in the uncreated Void,
Where seeds of future-being fight,
15   With lightened step thou wander wide,
To greet thy Mother — Ancient Night,
And as each jarring, monster mass is past,
Fond recollect what once thou wast:
In manner due, beneath this sacred oak,
20   Hear, Spirit hear! thy presence I invoke!
By a Monarch's heaven-struck fate!
By a disunited State!
By a generous Prince's wrongs!
By a Senate's strife of tongues!
25   By a Premier's sullen pride,
Louring on the changing tide!
By dread Thurlow's powers to awe,[1]
Rhetoric, blasphemy and law!
By the turbulent ocean,
30   A Nation's commotion!
By the harlot-caresses
Of borough-addresses!
By days few and evil!
Thy portion, poor devil!

1 Edward, Lord Thurlow (1731–1806). Lord Chancellor for the Fox–North
Coalition in 1778, who was asked to return to this post by Pitt.

35 By Power, Wealth, Show! the Gods by men adored!
      By Nameless Poverty! their Hell abhorred!
         By all they hope! by all they fear!
            Hear!!! And Appear!!!

      Stare not on me, thou ghastly Power;
40   Nor grim with chained defiance lour:
   No Babel-structure would *I* build
         Where, Order exil'd from his native sway,
   Confusion may the REGENT-sceptre wield,
         While all would rule and none obey:
45   Go, to the world of Man relate
         The story of thy sad, eventful fate;
      And call Presumptuous Hope to hear,
      And bid him check his blind career;
      And tell the sore-prest Sons of Care,
50   Never, never to despair. —

   Paint CHARLES'S speed on wings of fire,
         The object of his fond desire;
         Beyond his boldest hopes, at hand:
   Paint all the triumph of the Portland Band:[2]
55 Mark! how they lift the joy-exulting voice;
   And how their numerous Creditors rejoice:
   But just as hopes to warm enjoyment rise,
   Cry CONVALESCENCE! and the vision flies. —

   Then next pourtray a dark'ning twilight gloom
60   Eclipsing sad, a gay, rejoicing morn,
   While proud Ambition to th' untimely tomb
         By gnashing, grim, despairing fiends is borne:
   Paint Ruin, in the shape of high Dundas
         Gaping with giddy terror o'er the brow;
65 In vain he struggles, the Fates behind him press,
         And clamorous Hell yawns for her prey below:
   How fallen That, whose pride late scaled the skies!
   And This, like Lucifer, no more to rise!
         Again pronounce the powerful word;
70 See Day, triumphant from the night, restored. —

2 Whigs led by William Cavendish Bentick (1738–1809), the 3rd Duke of
Portland. He had been the First Lord of the Treasury under the Fox–North
Coalition.

Then know this truth, ye Sons of Men!
  (Thus ends thy moral tale)
Your darkest terrors may be vain,
  Your brightest hopes may fail. —

This parodic, pacey Pindaric ode satirises the clashing rhetoric of manoeuvring politicians as they vied for position during the constitutional Regency crisis of 1788–9. When he sent the first complete version of the poem to Mrs Dunlop, Burns knew the risk he was taking: 'I have this moment finished the following political Squib, and I cannot resist the temptation of sending you a copy of it – the only copy indeed that I will send to anybody except perhaps anonymously to some London Newspaper. — Politics is dangerous ground for me to tread on, and yet I cannot for the soul of me resist an impulse of anything like Wit' (Letter 326). Thurlow (l. 27) refers to Edward Lord Thurlow (1731–1806). Portland (l. 54) is the Duke of Portland, who led an exodus of influencial Whigs to the Conservatives when Britain went to war with France in 1793. Dundas (l. 63) refers to Henry Dundas, Viscount Melville (1742–1811) whose power over Scottish affairs during this period was near total. Burns here displays his dislike of Dundas in a similar style to that which Shelley later used so well to satirise Lord Castlereagh. Charles (l. 51) is Charles James Fox, leader of the Whigs, who supported the Prince of Wales taking the throne from his father after George III was declared insane in late 1788. William Pitt favoured severe restrictions on the monarchy, fearing that the Prince, who supported the Whigs, would be placed on the throne. The King eventually recovered and continued his reign, bar certain aberrations, such as his speech about unparalleled peace and tranquillity in December 1792 when in reality the government tightened the sedition laws and declared Martial Law in a panic at the rise of reform societies throughout Britain. In a chaotic mixture of ambition and vanity, this episode provoked Burns burlesques from the supposed loyal subjects of George III as they clashed over who would benefit by the Prince's succession.

    The consequence of London publication is explained in Professor Lucylle Werkmeister's *Robert Burns and the London Newspapers*, in the *Bulletin of the New York Public Library* (Oct. 1961, Vol. 65, no. 8). Werkmeister quotes the *Star*'s editor Stuart's introductory note:

    As the following fanciful verses contain the genuine energy and commanding spirit of POETRY, the printer is happy in communicating them to the PUBLIC, and he assures his readers, notwithstanding they appear under a fictitious signature, that they are the product of a GENIUS who ranks very highly in the REPUBLIC of LETTERS.

The same issue of Stuart's *Star* boasted in notes 'TO CORRESPON-DENTS' they would print a 'Love Sonnet by Mr. Burns, the Darling Poet of Caledonia, to-morrow'. Werkmeister goes on to quote Burns who was, at this juncture, unaware that Stuart had meddled with the poem to suit his own political views:

> I have had my usual luck in receiving your paper. – They have all come to hand except the two which I most wanted, the 17th and 18th, in which I understand my verses are. – So it has been with me always. – A damned Star has almost all my life usurped my zenith, and squinted out the cursed rays of its malign influences (Letter 339).

As Werkmeister remarks, the 'damned star' was the editor himself. Differing in politics from Burns, Stuart re-wrote some passages he did not agree with and deleted other passages. What Burns did not know was that the Portland Whigs were subsidising Stuart so that he amended the poem to serve their cause. Thus, for example, in ll. 51–4 Fox became Pitt and the Portland Band became the Tories. To hide his deceit, he stopped Burns from receiving a copy for 17th April. This was, as Werkmeister explains, the same newspaper that printed the ridiculous verse on the Duchess of Gordon's dancing and attrib-uted them to Burns, knowing full well they were not his composition. (Werkmeister totally discredits the notion that they were written by the semi-literate Henry Dundas and suggests that they were the work of someone on Stuart's staff in order to ridicule Dundas.) Stuart managed to stay on the right side of Burns by accident, since a friend of Burns misled him into believing that the guilty newspaper was the *London Gazetteer*, which innocently copied the nonsense from Stuart's *Star*. Burns eventually found out that the Ode had been considerably changed ('mangled', Letter 379) from the text he sent to London. While the image 'Daughter of Chaos' derives from Pope's *The Dunciad*, I, ll. 11–16, the language and sentiment is influenced more by Milton's *Paradise Lost*, II, ll. 894–7.

The pen-name 'Agricola', revealingly and perhaps deliberately so, means a farmer. Burns may have also picked this name given that the Roman general Agricola is supposed to have encamped a few miles to the north of Ellisland prior to the building of Hadrian's wall. The poem, on publication, was printed as a work sent from an Edinburgh poet, not a Dumfries one.

Ode, Sacred to the Memory of Mrs. Oswald Of Auchencruive

First printed in the London *Star*, 7th May, 1789, under the name Tim Nettle.

Dweller in yon dungeon dark,
Hangman of creation, mark!
Who in widow weeds appears,
Laden with unhonoured years,
5   Noosing with care a bursting purse,
Baited with many a deadly curse?

Strophe

View the wither'd beldam's face —
Can thy keen inspection trace
Aught of Humanity's sweet melting grace?
10   Note that eye, 'tis rheum o'erflows,
Pity's flood there never rose.
See those hands, ne'er stretch'd to save,
Hands that took — but never gave.
Keeper of Mammon's iron chest,
15   Lo, there she goes, unpitied and unblest,
She goes, but not to realms of everlasting rest!

Antistrophe

Plunderer of Armies! lift thine eyes,
(A while forbear, ye torturing fiends),
Seest thou whose step, unwilling, hither bends?
20   No fallen angel, hurl'd from upper skies;
'Tis thy trusty *quondam Mate*,
Doom'd to share thy fiery fate,
She, tardy, hell-ward plies.

Epode

And are they of no more avail,
25   Ten thousand glittering pounds a year?
In other worlds can Mammon fail,
Omnipotent as he is here?
O, bitter mockery of the *pompous bier*!
While down the wretched *vital part* is driven!
30   The cave-lodged beggar, with a conscience clear,
Expires in rags, unknown, and goes to Heaven.

The subject of this Ode, Mrs Oswald, was a Mary Ramsay who married Richard Oswald of London. He purchased Auchencruive estate, Ayrshire, in 1764, but died in 1784. The widow moved back to London thereafter. She died 6th December, 1788 and was brought to Ayrshire for burial. Burns explained the background in detail to Dr Moore:

> I spent my early days in her neighbourhood, and among her servants and tenants I know that she was detested with the most heart-felt cordiality . . . in the particular part of her conduct, which roused my Poetic wrath, she was much less blameable. In January last, on my road to Ayrshire, I had put up at Bailie Whigham's in Sanquar, the only tolerable Inn in the place. The frost was keen, and the grim evening and the howling wind were ushering in a night of snow and drift. My horse and I were both much fatigued with the labors of the day, and just as my friend the Bailie and I, were bidding defiance to the storm over a smoking bowl, in wheels the funeral pageantry of the late great Mrs Oswald, and poor I, am forced to brave all the horrors of the tempestuous night, and jade my horse, my young favourite horse whom I had just christened Pegasus, twelve miles further on, through the wildest moors & hills of Ayrshire, to New Cumnock, the next Inn. Suffice it to say that when a good fire at New Cumnock had so far recovered my frozen sinews, I sat down and wrote the enclosed Ode (Letter 322).

That an aristocrat could still be more important as a corpse than a living human being, thrown into the teeth of winter, is the spark that kindled Burns's poetic indignation.

Although first published under the name Tim Nettle in a London newspaper, this work was included in the 1793 Edinburgh edition. On both occasions, Mrs Oswald's identity was dashed out, to preserve anonymity. Burns's letter to Stuart, editor of the London *Star*, introduced the poem. Burns begins by pretending he does not know who the author of the poem is:

Mr Printer

> I know not who is the author of the following poem, but I think it contains some equally well-told and just compliments to the memory of a matron who, a few months ago, much against her private inclination, left this good world and twice five good thousands per annum behind her . . .
>
> . . . I dislike partial respect of persons, and am hurt to see the

public make such a fuss when a poor pennyless gipsey is consigned over to Jack Ketch [the hangman], and yet scarce take any notice when a purse-proud Priestess of Mammon is by the inexorable hand of death prisoned in everlasting fetters of ill-gotten gold . . .

Tim Nettle (Letter 338).

Due to the chicanery of Peter Stuart, a personal letter Burns sent him was, unknown to Burns, published beneath the Ode. This act of betrayal, according to Lucylle Werkmeister, might have had appalling consequences for Burns:

It is therefore incredible that, immediately below the letter from Tim Nettle . . . Stuart should have printed the whole of Burns's personal letter to him, altering, it appears, only the salutation, which now read 'Mr PRINTER', and the name of the author, which was now in capital letters. Not only did this letter identify Mrs Oswald as subject of the 'Ode' and Burns as its author, but it reached back to identify him as the author of the 'Ode to the Departed Regency Bill' as well. A copy of this number of the newspaper, one can be certain, was also not sent to Burns (Werkmeister, *Robert Burns and the London Newspapers*, *Bulletin of the New York Public Library*, Vol. 65, 1961, p. 496).

It is surprising, therefore, that the poet's Excise employers did not caution or discipline Burns at this juncture for his insurrectionary social satire, although it is likely they would have been notified of his publication.

It is not the least of Burns's many formal jokes that he borrows the nomenclature and structure of this poem from Collins's *Ode to Mercy*. Kinsley, always ready to agree with nineteenth century denial of the poet's radical values, describes this as a 'savage satire in the quite unsuitable Pindaric form' (Vol. III, p. 1292). On the contrary, the Pindaric form succeeds, moving crisply from the delivery of the deceased to the Devil (the hangman of Creation), to the atmospheric cadence of the *Strophe*, examining the subject for any trace of humanity, to the awakening of her dead husband, also in hell, in the *Antistrophe*. In the final *Epode*, Burns reveals the art of his dark painting, '. . . down the wretched vital part is driven', meaning the loss of her soul (the vital part) in life and its transport to Hell. It is excessive wealth and her oppressive nature that has, in life, destroyed the woman's soul and condemned her to her fate. The line 'Plunderer of Armies!' refers to Mrs Oswald's husband whose 'war-profiteering' had earned their fortune.

A New Psalm for the Chapel of Kilmarnock on the Thanksgiving-Day for His Majesty's Recovery –

First printed in the London *Morning Star*, 14th May, 1789, signed Duncan M'Leerie.

O, sing a new Song to the Lord!
    Make, all and every one,
A joyful noise, ev'n for the king
    His Restoration. —

5   The Sons of Belial in the land
        Did set their heads together;
    Come, let us sweep them off, said they,
        Like an o'erflowing river. —

They set their heads together, I say,
10   They set their heads together:
On right, and left, and every hand,
    We saw none to deliver. —

Thou madest strong two chosen Ones,
    To quell the Wicked's pride:
15   That Young Man, great in Issachar
    The burden-bearing Tribe. —

And him, among the Princes chief
    In our Jerusalem,
The Judge that's mighty in thy law,
20   The Man that fears thy name. —

Yet they, even they, with all their might,
    Began to faint and fail;
Even as two howling, ravening wolves
    To dogs do turn their tail. —

25   Th' Ungodly o'er the Just prevail'd,
    For so thou hadst appointed,
That thou might'st greater glory give
    Unto thine own Annointed. —

And now thou hast restored our State,
30   Pity our kirk also,
For she by tribulations
         Is now brought very low! —

Consume that High-Place, PATRONAGE,
         From off thine holy hill;
35   And in thy fury burn the book
         Even of that man M'GILL. —

Now hear our Prayer, accept our Song,
         And fight thy Chosen's battle:
We seek but little, Lord, from thee,
40   Thou kens we get as little.   knows

This was written to commemorate the day of public thanksgiving
declared when King George III recovered from his bout of insanity.
Burns describes his feelings on this occasion to Mrs Dunlop: 'As I
am not devoutly attached to a certain Monarch, I cannot say that my
heart run any risk of bursting . . . God forgive me for speaking evil
of dignities! But I must say that I look on the whole business as a
solemn farce of pageant mummery. The following are a few Stanzas
of new Psalmody for that 'Joyful Solemnity' which I sent to a
London Newspaper' (Letter 335). The poem appeared in the Lon-
don *Star* (not the *Edinburgh Star*, as Mackay suggests (p. 354), since
no such paper existed) with the indication that it was written at
Kilmarnock on the 25th April. It was signed under the pen name
Duncan M'Leerie. The note with the song suggested it had been
sung 'devoutly' in a chapel in Kilmarnock on the 23rd past. Burns
openly acknowledged to Mrs Dunlop in the same letter that Stuart,
the publisher of the London *Star* was 'an old acquaintance of mine,
and as I am a little tinctured with Buff & Blue myself, I now and
then help him to a Stanza' (Letter 335). This is another example of
how Burns protected his Excise career by employing a pen name and
printing the song as though it was written other than in Dumfries.
This was a procedure he was forced to extend in the darker political
years ahead.

    The 'Young Man' (l. 15) refers to William Pitt; while 'chief' (l.
17) alludes to Lord Thurlow (See footnote 1, *Ode to the Departed
Regency Bill*). Rev. McGill (l. 36) is Rev. Dr McGill (1732–1807) of
Ayrshire who was persecuted for his liberal views on religious
doctrine, published in his text *A Practical Essay on the Death of
Jesus Christ* (1786) and *The Benefits of the Revolution* (1789) in

which he defended his views against the illiberal attack by Dr Peebles, Kirk minister at Newton-upon-Ayr (See Vol. III, Kinsley, pp. 1306–7). Burns boasted to Mrs Dunlop that he would hunt down the persecutors of Dr McGill like wild prey (Letter 148). See also notes to *The Kirk's Alarm*.

The song is written in the style of the Presbyterian metrical psalms, paraphrasing in the first line from *Psalms*, CXLIV, line 9, 'I will sing a new song unto thee, O God'. Kinsley lists several biblical allusions from, inter alia, *Deuteronomy* and *Judges*. They are employed to mock the farcical new 'Jerusalem' of Pitt. Although printed during the poet's lifetime pseudonymously, this work did not feature in the canon until Hately Waddell's edition (1867), almost a century after its first appearance.

The Kirk's Alarm
or The Kirk of Scotland's Garland
Tune: Push about the Brisk Glass
First printed in 1789 as an anonymous broadside sheet.

Orthodox, Orthodox, wha believe in John Knox,   who
    Let me sound an alarm to your conscience;
A heretic blast has been blawn i' the West —   blown, West
    That what is not Sense must be Nonsense, Orthodox
5   That what is not Sense must be Nonsense. —

Doctor Mac,[1] Doctor Mac, ye should streek on a rack,   stretch
    To strike Evildoers wi' terror;
To join FAITH and SENSE upon ony pretence   any
    Was heretic, damnable error, &c.

10 Town of Ayr, Town of Ayr, it was rash, I declare,
    To meddle wi' mischief a brewing;
Provost John[2] is still deaf to the Church's relief,
    And Orator Bob[3] is its ruin, &c.

1 Rev. Doctor McGill, Ayr. R.B.
2 Provost John Ballantine. R.B.
3 Mr [Bob] Aitken. R.B.

D'rymple[4] mild, D'rymple mild, tho' your heart 's like a child,
15   And your life like the new-driven snaw;   snow
Yet that winna save ye, auld Satan maun have ye,   will not, shall
    For preaching that three 's ane and twa, &c.   one, two

Calvin's Sons, Calvin's Sons, seize your sp'ritual guns —
    Ammunition you never can need;
20 Your HEARTS are the stuff will be POWTHER enough,   powder
    And your SCULLS are store-houses o' LEAD, &c.

Rumble John,[5] Rumble John, mount the steps with a groan,
    Cry, the BOOK is wi' heresy cramm'd;
Then lug out your ladle, deal brimstone like aidle,   pull, cow's piss
25   And roar every note o' the DAMN'D, &c.

Simper James,[6] Simper James, leave the fair Killie dames,   Kilmarnock
    There 's a holier chase in your view:
I'll lay on your head that the PACK ye'll soon lead,
    For PUPPIES like you there 's but few, &c.

30 Singet Sawnie,[7] Singet Sawnie, are ye herding the PENNIE,   money
    Unconscious what danger await?
Wi' a jump, yell, and howl, alarm every soul,
    For the Foul Thief is just at your gate, &c.

Poet Willie,[8] Poet Willie, gie the Doctor a volley,   give
35   Wi' your 'Liberty's chain' and your wit:
O'er Pegasus' side ye ne'er laid a stride,
    Ye but smelt, man, the place where he shit, &c.

Andro' Gowk,[9] Andro Gowk, ye may slander the BOOK,
    And the Book not the waur, let me tell ye: worst
40 Ye are rich and look big, but lay by hat and wig —
    And ye'll hae a CALF'S-HEAD o' sma' value, &c.   have

4 Dr Dalrymple, Ayr. R.B.
5 John Russel, Kilmarnock. R.B.
6 James McKindlay, Kilmarnock. R.B.
7 A. Moodie, Riccartoun. R.B.
8 William Peebles in Newton upon Ayr, a Poetaster, who among many other things, published an Ode on the Centenary of the Revolution in which was this line – 'And bound in liberty's endearing chain'. R.B.
9 Dr Andrew Mitchel, Monkton. R.B.

Barr Steenie,[10] Barr Steenie, what mean ye, what mean ye?
 If ye'll meddle nae mair wi' the matter,   no more
Ye may hae some pretence, man, to havins and sense,
45 Wi' people wha ken ye nae better, &c.   who know

Jamie Goose,[11] Jamie Goose, ye hae made but toom roose   empty
 In hunting the wicked Lieutenant;   speculation
But the Doctor's your mark, for the Lord's haly ark   holy
 He has cooper'd and ca'd a wrang pin in, &c.   nailed, wrong

50 Davie Rant,[12] Davie Rant, in a face like a saunt,   saint
 And a heart that would poison a hog;
Raise an impudent roar, like a breaker lee-shore,
 Or the Kirk will be tint in a bog, &c.   lost

Cessnock-side,[13] Cessnock-side, wi' your turkey-cock pride,
55 O' manhood but sma' is your share;
Ye've the figure, it's true, even your faes maun allow,   foes must
 And your friends daur na say ye hae mair, &c.   dare not, have more

Muirland Jock,[14] Muirland Jock, whom the Lord made a rock
 To crush Common Sense for her sins,
60 If ill-manners were Wit, there's no mortal so fit
 To confound the poor Doctor at ance, &c.   once

Daddie Auld,[15] Daddie Auld, there's a tod i' the fauld, fox
 A tod meikle waur than the CLERK: much worse
Tho' ye do little skaith, ye'll be in at the death,   damage
65 For if ye canna bite ye may bark, &c.   can not

Holy Will,[16] Holy Will, there was wit i' your skull,
 When ye pilfer'd the alms o' the poor;
The timmer is scant, when ye're taen for a saunt,   wood, taken, saint
 Wha should swing in a rape for an hour, &c.   who, rope

10 Stephen Young, [of] Barrr. R.B.
11 James Young in New Cumnock, who had lately been foiled in an
ecclesiastic prosecution against a Lieutenant Mitchel. R.B.
12 David Grant, Ochiltree. R.B.
13 George Smith, Galston. R.B.
14 John Shepherd, Muirkirk. R.B.
15 Rev. William Auld, Mauchline. R.B.
16 An Elder in Mauchline. R.B. [See *Holy Willie's Prayer*.]

70 Poet Burns, Poet Burns, wi' your priest-skelping turns,
        Why desert ye your auld native shire?
    Tho' your Muse is a gipsey, yet were she ev'n tipsey,
        She could ca' us nae waur than we are, Poet Burns,   call, no worse
        She could ca' us nae waur than we are. —

POSTSCRIPTS
Afton's Laird,[17] Afton's Laird, when your pen can be spar'd,
    A copy of this I bequeath,
On the same sicker score as I mention'd before,   safe/confidential
    To that trusty auld Worthy, Clackleith,[18] Afton's Laird,
    To that trusty auld Worthy, Clackleith.

Factor John,[19] Factor John, whom the Lord made alone,
    And ne'er made another thy peer,
Thy poor servant, the Bard, in respectful regard,
    Presents thee this token sincere, Factor John,
    Presents thee this token sincere. —

The Kirk's Alarm first appears as an anonymous song under the title
*The Ayrshire Garland, an Excellent New Song; Tune – The Vicar and
Moses.* The first version contained only thirteen stanzas, compared
to the complete song's twenty. The song is a stalwart defence of the
Rev. Dr William McGill (1732–1807) against his persecution by the
Synod of Glasgow and Ayr (See our notes for *A New Psalm for the
Chapel of Kilmarnock*). This is made vividly clear by Burns as early
as November 1787: '. . . if the prosecution which I hear the Erebean
Fanatics are projecting against my learned and truly worthy friend,
Dr McGill, goes on, I shall keep no measure with the savages, but
fly at them with the faulcons of Ridicule, or run them down with the
bloodhounds of Satire, as lawful game, wherever I start them'
(Letter 124). On the opponents of McGill, listed in the poem,
Burns goes on, in July 1789, just after completing the ballad:
'Several of these reverend lads, his opponents, have come thro'
my hands before, but I have some thoughts of serving them up
again in a different dish. . . . I have just sketched the following
ballad . . . I am thinking to throw off two or three dozen copies at a
Press in Dumfries, & send them as from Edinburgh to some
Ayrshire folks on both sides of the question' (Letter 352). Mrs
Dunlop advised him not to do this but he disregarded her. The

17 John Logan. R.B.
18 James Johnson. R.B.
19 John Kennedy. R.B.

original broadside was probably paid for and circulated by Burns himself.

The work also appears in *Songs and Poems* by Alexander Tait (Paisley, 1790, pp. 170–3), under the bizzare and malicious pen-name 'Composed by Plotcock, the Foul Thief's Exciseman'. Tait's version matches the broadside text. He published the Burns poem as an occasional piece to set up his own reply, *The Answer to Plotcock*, an inferior work satirising Burns's work. He does not give away the poet's identity, although he knew Burns was the author. Sandy Tait was the author of three unpleasantly frivolous poems on Burns and his family, *Burns in His Infancy, Burns in Lochly* and *Burns's Hen Clockin in Mauchline*. The poem itself did not appear as a work by Burns until Stewart's edition, 1801.

Kinsley rightly remarks that the poetic form is common to drinking songs (the tune picked by Burns is that of a drinking song) and political squibs before Burns. Henderson and Henley point out that the immediate model may have been a pro-Pitt attack on Charles James Fox printed in *The Glasgow Mercury*, 23rd–30th December 1788 (See Kinsley, Vol. III, p. 1308). This is formally similar to *The Kirk's Alarm*:

> Mr. Fox, Mr. Fox,
> Thou'rt knock'd down like an Ox
> By honest Will Pitt's argumentum:
> 'Twas a cruel mistake, &c.

Kinsley, who lifts his quote from H–H, misquotes the text of the newspaper poem, with 'argumentation' instead of 'argumentum'. Burns made several copies of the song; adding and modifying several verses; hence there are several variant readings. This is a rogues' gallery of ecclesiastics previously satirised by Burns, the 'auld lichts' whose interpretation of the 1688 revolutionary celebrations in 1788 differed markedly from the liberal McGill. The late eighteenth century did not differentiate theology and politics as we do.

Verses Written upon a Blank Leaf
in COWPER's POEMS Belonging to a Lady
First printed in *The Gentleman's Magazine*, April 1789.

Let dear Eliza pass the gliding hours,
By culling sweets from choice poetic flowers!
Of all those various beauties form'd to please,
There's none more choice, and none more sweet than these:

5   For truth with elegance is here display'd;
       Descriptive Nature beauteously array'd:
       Whether he trip, by Luna's silver sheen,
       Whether bright Pheobus gild with genial ray
       The blushing morning of the coming May;
10   Whether pourtray'd the shrub, or fragrant flower;
       His soft, his lively portraits, you'll admire.
       With gentle Thomson tracing wood and grove,
       He paints recesses, sweet for heaven-born love;
       Pope's softest numbers harmonize each line,
15   The fire of Dryden, Milton's thoughts sublime,
       The lash of Churchill, Waller's warbling lays,
       Sing loud their merit, loudly chant their praise.
       Describ'd the humble cot, proud city's tower
       The cloud-capt hill, the lovely vale or bower,
20   Still guided by the radiant son of Jove,
       In Nature's walks, behold his fav'rite rove!

                                                    R.B.

Verses Written upon a Blank Leaf in COWPER's POEMS Belonging to a Lady was printed in the April 1789 issue of *The Gentleman's Magazine* (p. 353). It was recently brought to light after the discovery of a known Burns work in the same journal in 1794, *also* printed under his initials, 'R.B.' An abridged version of *A Winter Night* was printed under a new title, *Humanity: An Ode*. Given that the publication of this work had never before been recorded and no search of the journal for missing work by Burns ever documented, the magazine was consequently scanned for such a possibility. The above poem and an epigram on the death of Dr Adam Smith (signed under the known Burns pen name, Agricola) were the result.

The controversial *Lines on Seeing the Royal Palace at Stirling in Ruins* were first printed by Burns in a newspaper signed, 'R.B.' So, we know he employed his initials in this manner. The case for Burns being the author of *Humanity: An Ode* needs little argument because it is obviously a modified variant of *A Winter Night*, printed in the 1787 Edinburgh edition. Indeed, if *A Winter Night* had not already been in print, there could be no absolute certainty Burns wrote *Humanity: An Ode*; despite the fact that we could not trace another active poet employing these initials in that period.

During 1789 Burns, still farming Ellisland, was the neighbour of Robert Riddell. Riddell was a contributor to *The Gentleman's*

Magazine as an antiquarian long before he met Burns. It is quite probable that Riddell, a subscriber to the magazine, suggested Burns seek publication in it.

While not a poem of any great literary significance, the verse is reasonably competent in its limited task of impressing a lady that the author is familiar with the poetry of Cowper. In contrasting Cowper with so many other, well-known English poets and the Scottish Thomson, it is slightly exhibitionist. Burns was, by 1789, fond of Cowper verse, with a particular liking for the popular long poem, *The Task*, as glowingly mentioned to Mrs Dunlop (Letter 605). Indeed, the first literary comparison made in the poem (l. 12) is between Cowper and James Thomson, author of *The Seasons*. Burns compares these two poets in September 1788, in a letter to William Dunbar – '. . . Cowper's *Poems*, the best poet out of sight since Thomson' (Letter 274). Burns owned a copy of *The Lives of the English Poets* edited by Dr Johnson and was well acquainted with the poets listed (ll. 14–16). The poem rightly mentions the variegated literary influences of Thomson, Pope, Dryden, Churchill and Waller (ll. 12–16) in Cowper's verse. Having been so influenced himself, it is no surprise that Burns liked Cowper's somewhat evangelical-influenced poetry and in particular his stance against the slave trade which heavily permeated the popular radical press. Cowper, as Baird reveals, was an admirer of Burns. He told Samuel Rose, after poring over the Edinburgh edition:

> I think them on the whole a very extraordinary production. He is, I believe, the only poet these islands have produced in the lower rank of life since Shakespeare, (I should rather say since Prior,) who need not be indebted for any part of his praise to a charitable consideration of his origin, and the disadvantages under which he has laboured (John D. Baird, 'Two Poets of the 1780s: Burns and Cowper' in *Critical Essays on Robert Burns*, ed. Donald Low, (Routledge, London, 1975, p. 108).

It would be frivolous to speculate on the identity of the unknown young lady ('Eliza') but it suffices that Burns knew of several such ladies, one being Elizabeth Burnett mentioned in *Address to Edinburgh*. The missing line after l. 7 may be the result of a printer's error.

Epitaph: On Robert Fergusson
On the Tombstone in the Canongate Churchyard
Born Sept. 5th, 1750 Died Oct. 17th, 1774
First printed in *The Edinburgh Advertiser*, 7th–11th August, 1789.

By special Grant of the Managers to Robert Burns, who erected this
Stone, this Burial Place is to remain for ever sacred to the Memory
of ROBERT FERGUSSON.

No sculptur'd Marble here, nor pompous lay,
  'No storied Urn nor animated Bust;'
This simple stone directs pale SCOTIA'S way
  To pour her sorrow o'er the POET'S dust.

5 [She mourns, sweet tuneful youth, thy hapless fate:
    Tho' all the powers of song thy fancy fir'd,
Yet Luxury and Wealth lay by in State,
    And, thankless, starv'd what they so much admir'd.

This humble tribute with a tear he gives,
10   A brother Bard, he can no more bestow:
But dear to fame thy Song immortal lives,
    A nobler monument than Art can show.]

Only the first of these stanzas, written in early 1787, was printed in
The Edinburgh Advertiser of early August 1789; then subsequently
featured in Currie, 1800. The final stanzas were entered in the *SCB*.
They did not enter the canon until the notebook surfaced in the
1870s. Burns's headstone to Fergusson was not erected until August
1789. The newspaper printed the lines after the stone was erected. It
was inscribed on Burns's behalf by an Edinburgh architect named
Robert Burn. The dedicatory inscription on the stone is given as the
subtitle.

    The quote from Gray's *Elegy in a Country Churchyard* (l. 2) is
not always so identified by previous editors. Given that the poet
waited two years for the work to be finished, he deliberately took
two years to pay for the headstone, costing £5. 10 shillings (See
Letters 81 and 495). Fergusson died, apparently insane, in the
Edinburgh asylum.

On the Late Death of Dr Adam Smith

First printed in *The Gentleman's Magazine,* September 1790.

Death and *Hermes* of late in Elysium made boast,
That each would bring thither what earth valued most:
Smith's *Wealth of Nations Hermes* stole from his shelf;
DEATH just won his cause – he took off Smith himself.

Agricola.

This epigram which was recently found in *The Gentleman's Magazine,* September 1790, p. 843, is given here as a probable work of Burns for several reasons. The same pen-name (meaning a farmer) was employed by Burns the year previous in his *Ode on the Departed Regency Bill.* There is no other occurrence of this pen-name by any poet during the entire 1780–1800 period. Contextually the evidence points to Burns. As his letters show, he was well read not only in Smith's *The Theory of Moral Sentiments* but also *The Wealth of Nations.* The epigram reveals a mixture of respect and irony. Hermes, the God of commerce and communication thinks Smith's best-known book is the greatest thing on earth but Death goes one step further and whisks off Smith himself.

Epigram on Captain Francis Grose,
the Celebrated Antiquary

First printed in *The Belfast Newsletter,* 18th May 1792.

The Devil got notice that GROSE was a-dying,
So whip! at the summons, old Satan came flying;
But when he approach'd where poor FRANCIS lay moaning,
And saw each bed-post with its burthen a-groaning,
Astonish'd! confounded! cry'd Satan, by God,
I'll want 'im, ere take such a damnable load. —

This was written at Ellisland in 1789 when the pendulous Grose was alive not, as implied by Mackay, after the death of Grose in 1791 at Dublin. After appearing in *The Belfast Newsletter* it was subsequently printed by Stuart, Glasgow, 1801.

Extempore –
On Some Late Commemorations of the Poet Thomson
First published in *The Edinburgh Gazetteer*, 23rd November, 1792.

DOST thou not rise, indignant Shade,
    And smile wi' spurning scorn,
When they wha wad hae starved thy life,   who would have
    Thy senseless turf adorn? —

5   They, wha about thee mak sic fyke   make such fuss
    Now thou art but a name,
Wad seen thee damn'd ere they had spar'd   would have
    Ae plack to fill thy wame. —   one farthing, belly

Helpless, alane, thou clamb the brae,   alone, climbed, hillside
10   Wi' meikle, honest toil,   much
And claucht th' unfading garland there,   clutched
    Thy sair-won, rightful spoil. —   sore-

And wear it there! and call aloud,
    This axiom undoubted —
15   'Wouldst thou hae Nobles' Patronage?'   have
    First learn to live without it!!!

'To wham hae routh, more shall be given'   have plenty
    Is every Patron's faith;
But he, the friendless, needful wretch,
20   Shall lose the mite he hath. —

The above text is from *The Edinburgh Gazetteer* where it was printed under the pseudonym Thomas A. Rhymer. Despite appearing first in the Edinburgh newspaper in November 1792, it did not enter the canon until the 1820s.

Kinsley suggests that the poem was written at the same time as the previous English tribute to Thomson. The only reference to the poem comes in a panic-stricken letter to Robert Graham of Fintry of 5th January, 1793, where Burns tried desperately to disassociate himself from the political implications of his relationship with the soon-to-be incarcerated Captain Johnston, editor of the dissident *Edinburgh Gazetteer*:

Of Johnston, the publisher of the *Edinburgh Gazetteer*, I know nothing. – One evening in company with four or five friends, we met with his prospectus which we thought manly and inde-pendent; & I wrote to him ordering his paper for us. If you think that I act improperly in allowing his Paper to come addressed to me, I shall immediately countermand it. – I never, so judge me, God! wrote a line of *prose* (our italics) for the Gazetteer in my life. – An occasional address, spoken by Miss Fontenelle on her benefit-night, here which I called, the Rights of Woman, I sent to the Gazetteer; as also some extempore stanzas on the Commemoration of Thomson: both of these I will subjoin for your perusal. – You will see that they have nothing whatever to do with Politics. – At the time I sent Johnson one of these poems, but which one I do not remember, I inclosed at the request of my warm & worthy friend, Robt. Riddell Esq: of Glendriddel, a prose Essay, signed Cato, written by him, & addressed to the delegates for the Country Reform, of which he was one for this Country. – With the merits or demerits, of that Essay I have nothing to do, farther than transmitting it in the same Frank, which Frank he had procured me (Letter 530).

In fact, on ordering *The Edinburgh Gazetteer*, Burns was driven by rampant enthusiasm for the edition he had acquired and, on behalf of four or five friends, suggests he will pay his subscription via Peter Hill, his Edinburgh bookseller friend. His enthusiasm for the newspaper is telling: 'Go on, Sir! Lay bare with un-daunted heart & steady hand that horrid mass of corruption called Politics & State-Craft!' (*Letter*, 515). As we shall see, he did not stop contributing.

Nor is this bitter little poem devoid of political comment. It has little or nothing to do with Thomson, who, happily exiled, waxed fat in southern pastures. It is a compound of memories of Robert Fergusson's and his own grim Parnassian uphill struggle. The life of the true poet is seen as a particularly acute example of an aristocratic society gripped by injustice towards the poor. The last stanza pertinent to this theme echoes *Matthew* xiii.12; cf. *Mark* iv.25 and *Luke* viii.18. Further, the poem's retarded entry into the canon in the 1820s suggests a significant dissident content.

The Rights of Woman
An Occasional Address Spoken on her Benefit Night, Nov. 26th, 1792, at Dumfries, by Miss Fontenelle
First published in *The Edinburh Gazetteer*, 30th Nov. 1792

WHILE Europe's eye is fix'd on mighty things,
The fate of Empires and the fall of Kings;
While quacks of State must each produce his plan,   doctors
And even children lisp, The Rights of Man;
5   Amid the mighty fuss, just let me mention,
THE RIGHTS OF WOMAN merit some attention. —

First, in the Sexes' intermix'd connexion,
One sacred Right of Woman is PROTECTION.
The tender flower, that lifts its head, elate,
10   Helpless, must fall before the blasts of Fate,
Sunk on the earth, defac'd its lovely form,
Unless *your Shelter* ward th' impending storm.

Our second Right — but needless here is caution —
To keep that Right inviolate's the fashion:
15   Each man of sense has it so full before him,
He'd die before he'd wrong it — 'tis DECORUM!
There was, indeed, in far less polish'd days,
A time, when rough, rude Man had naughty ways:
Would swagger, swear, get drunk, kick up a riot,
20   Nay, even thus invade a Lady's quiet. —
Now, thank our Stars! these Gothic times are fled;
Now, well-bred men — and you are all well-bred —
Most justly think (and we are much the gainers)
Such conduct neither spirit, wit, nor manners. —

25   For Right the third, our last, our best, our dearest:
That Right to fluttering Female hearts the nearest,
Which even the Rights of Kings, in low prostration,
Most humbly own — 'tis dear, dear ADMIRATION!
In that blest sphere alone we live and move;
30   There taste that life of life — Immortal Love!
Smiles, glances, tears, sighs, fits, flirtations, airs;
'Gainst such an host, what flinty savage dares —
When awful Beauty joins with all her charms,
Who is so rash as rise in rebel arms?

35   But truce with Kings, and truce with Constitutions,
With bloody armaments and Revolutions;
Let MAJESTY your first attention summon:
Ah! ça ira! THE MAJESTY OF WOMAN!!!   thus shall it go/let it go

This was printed anonymously in *The Edinburgh Gazetteer*, 30th November, 1792 next to a political essay written by Robert Riddell. The text is from the Edinburgh newspaper. The original publication contains a minor spelling error, giving Miss Fontenelle's name as Foftenelle. Miss Louisa Fontenelle was a London actress who moved to the Theatre Royal, Edinburgh and played provincial theatres in Scotland. She was a favourite of Burns's (See *Occasional Address*, December 1794 and *On Seeing Miss Fontenelle in A Favourite Character*, same date). This, superficially, is an equally light-weight, even frivolous piece. Its implications are, however, of deeper political import and its performance and reception were to have far-reaching consequences for Burns.

Burns was fascinated by the actress as this belt and braces compliment suggests: 'To you Madam, on our humble Dumfries boards, I have been more indebted for entertainment, than ever I was in prouder Theatres.—Your charms as a woman would insure applause to the most indifferent Actress, and your theatrical talents would secure admiration to the plainest figure . . . Will the forgoing lines be of any service to you on your appearing benefit night? . . . They are nearly extempore . . .' (Letter 519). The poem was revised and sent to Mrs Graham of Fintry on 5 January, though Burns still describes it as 'this little poem, written in haste on the spur of the occasion, & therefore inaccurate; but a sincere Compliment to that Sex, the most amiable of the works of God . . .' Kinsley, while noting this, fails to remark that Mrs Graham received this a mere five days after Burns's semi-hysterical denial of revolutionary tendencies to her husband in which he had denoted *The Rights of Woman* as quite apolitical. This was evidently the frivolously anodyne evidence being offered to Fintry by way of his wife. Certainly the references in it to (l. 4) Paine's enormously popular *Rights of Man* (1792) and Mary Wollstonecraft's *The Rights of Woman* (1793) seem merely playful. There was correspondence between Wollstonecraft and Burns which, like so much else, has vanished forever. Certainly if Mary Wollstonecraft had read this poem she would have loathed it as it is replete with the kind of condescension to women that prevented them from occupying a creative, professional and intellectual level with men. Thus, for example, she could write: 'Taught from their infancy that beauty is woman's sceptre, the mind shapes itself to the body, and roaming around its gilt cage, only seeks to adore its prison (*Vindication of the Rights of Woman* (London, 1975), p. 197). The fact that the sexually predatory 'Gothic' age is passed would have been small consolation to her. Burns may also have been politically ironic in asserting this. Kinsley notes that 'Burns's lines are an ironical allusion to the annual saturnalia of the Caledonian Hunt at Dumfries' (Chambers–Wallace, iii.361). Cf Burns to Mrs Dunlop, 29 October 1794: 'We have had the Caledonians here for this bypast fortnight; and of course, we have the roar of Folly and Dissipation' (Letter 645).

The notion that the priapic Burns, the only rooster in the barn-yard, would have any affiliation to women's rights seems not credible. He was, however, more complex than that. His friendship with Maria Riddell was based on a common radicalism. Part of the extreme tension within that relationship derived from the fact that, because of her social position, she was able to articulate political ideas about which he had to keep his mouth shut. Through the Riddell connection, however, he met another young, apparently radically inclined Welshwoman, Deborah Duff Davies. Writing to her on April 6th, 1793, less than a year after the Dumfries perfor-mance we get this tormented letter written in the wake of the Sedition Trials as Burns rages at the impotence not only of his own radical values but the cost to this for even more depressed and suppressed women. Catherine Carswell, politically empathetic to Burns, believed that he was, because of his non-appearance in Edinburgh among The Scottish Friends of the People, guilt-driven as well as manifestly confined by his office and his alert enemies. Thus he writes:

> Good God, why this disparity between our wishes & our powers!— . . . I know that your hearts have been wounded by the scorn of the Proud whom accident has placed above you, or worse still, in whose hands, perhaps, are placed many of the comforts of your life: but, there! ascend that rock of Indepen-dance, & look, justly, down on their littleness of soul.—Make the Worthless tremble under your indignation, & the Foolish sink before your contempt; & largely impart that happiness to others which I am certain will give yourselves so much pleasure to bestow!
> . . . Why, amid my generous enthusiasm, must I find myself a poor, powerless devil, incapable of wiping one tear from the eye of Misery, or of adding one comfort to the Friend I love!— Out upon the world! say I; that its affairs are administered so

ill!—They talk of REFORM—My God! what a reform would *I* make among the Sons, & even the Daughters of men!

Down, immediately, should go FOOLS from the high places where misbegotten CHANCE has perked them up, & through life should they sculk, ever haunted by their native insignificance, as the body marches accompanied by its shadow.—As for a much more formidable class, the knaves, I am at a loss what to do with them.—Had *I* a world, there should not be a knave in it: & on the other hand, Hell as our Theologians paint it, particularly an eternal Hell, is a deeper damnation than I could bear to see the veriest scoundrel in earth plunged into.— But the hand that could give, I would liberally fill: & I would pour delight on the heart that could kindly forgive, & generously love.—

Still, the inequalities of life are, among MEN, comparatively tolerable: but there is a DELICACY, a TENDERNESS, accompanying every view in which one can place lovely WO-MAN, that are grated & shocked at the rude, capricious distinctions of Fortune.— Woman is the BLOOD-ROYAL of life: let there be slight degrees of precedency among them, but let them be all sacred.—

Whether this last sentiment be right, or wrong, I am not accountable: it is an original, component feature of my mind.— I remember, & 'tis almost the earliest thing I do remember, when I was quite a boy, one day at church, being enraged at seeing a young creature, one of the maids of his house, rise from the mouth of the pew to give way to a bloated son of Wealth & Dullness, who waddled surlily past her.— Indeed the girl was very pretty; & he was an ugly, stupid, purse-proud, money-loving, old monster, as you can imagine (Letter 556A).

This is marked by the trauma of failure of revolutionary anticipations, reiterated cries of despair found in the late Burns comparable in quality and intensity to those prevailing in William Hazlitt's prose. In 1792 all still seemed possible so that the actual performance of *The Rights of Woman* in the agitated Dumfries theatre, as reported by Scott Douglas, seems quite probable:

At the Dumfries Theatre, under the management of Mr. Sutherland, a pretty young actress—Miss Fontenelle—formed one of the company during the winter of 1792, and also of the year following. The local newspapers announced her benefit-night for 26th November, 1792, and that after the play—The Country Girl—she would 'deliver an occasional address, written by Mr. Robert Burns, called *The Rights of Woman.*' At that period the government of this country was in great alarm regarding the spread of what were termed liberal or revolutionary opinions. Paine had produced his 'Rights of Man,' and Mary Wollstoncroft was advocating the 'Rights of Woman,' and many thought that the line, 'Truce with kings, and truce with constitutions'— the fourth from the end in this Address, was by far too bold, and that the finishing-stroke, *ça ira!* was intolerable.

Chambers records, that a lady with whom he once conversed, 'remembered being present in the theatre of Dumfries, during the heat of the Revolution, when Burns entered the pit somewhat affected by liquor. On God save the King being struck up by the band, the audience rose as usual—all except the intemperate poet, who cried for *ça ira!* A tumult was the consequence, and Burns was compelled to leave the house.' (Vol. II, p. 156)

Burns's denial that the words of the great, inflammatory song of the Revolution ('Ça ira,/La liberté s'établira,/Malgré les tyrans tout réussira') ever exclusively left his lips in his letter to Fintry is a mini-masterpiece of self-defensive comic irony:

I was in the playhouse one night, when Ça ira was called for.—I was in the middle of the pit, & from the Pit the clamour arose.—One or two individuals with whom I occasionally associate were of the party, but I neither knew of the Plot, nor joined in the Plot; nor ever opened my lips to hiss, or huzza, that, or any other Political tune whatever.—I looked on myself as far too obscure a man to have any weight in quelling a Riot; at the same time, as a character of higher respectability, than to yell in the howlings of a rabble.—This was the conduct of all the first Characters in this place; & these Characters know, & will avow, that such was my conduct (Letter 530).

He repeats this denial to Mrs Dunlop with another variation of what happened in the theatre with the audience divided over the English national anthem and the French song of revolution but implies his poem was not that night's cause of disturbance:

We, in this country, here have many alarms of the reform, or rather the Republican spirit, of your part of the kingdom.— Indeed, we are a good deal in commotion ourselves, & in our Theatre here, 'God save the king' has met with some groans and hisses, while Ça ira has been repeatedly called for.—For me, I am a *Placeman*, you know; a very humble one indeed, Heaven knows, but still so much so as to gag me from joining in the cry.—What my private sentiments are, you will find out without an Interpreter.—In the mean time, I have taken up the subject in another view, and the other day, for a pretty Actress's benefit-night, I wrote an Address, which I will give on the other page, called *The Rights of Woman* (Letter 525).

Even if Burns believed that Mrs Dunlop lived in a 'republican' Ayrshire, it is extraordinary that he could, given she had sons fighting the French, have so misjudged her political sympathies as to believe she would continue to act as his political confidante. In fact, she broke off all connection with him till just before his death as a consequence of his revealed revolutionary sentiments to her. This reaches its climax in his extraordinary letter to her of December 31st of 1792 of which two three-quarter-page sections have been cut away as part of the largely unsystematic but catastrophic destruction of political evidence that has been such a curse for subsequent understanding, scholarly and otherwise. This is the real situation about both his beliefs and the tormentingly hostile environment in which he held them:

> —I have corresponded with Commissr. Graham, for the Board had made me the subject of their animadversions; & now I have the pleasure of informing that all is set to rights in that quarter.—Now, as to these inquisitorial Informers, Spies, Persecutors, &c. may the d-vil & his angels be let loose to— but hold! I was praying most fervently in my last sheet, & I must not so soon fall accursing in this.—
>
> Alas! how little do the wickedly, or wantonly, or idly, offi- cious, think what mischief they do by their malicious insinua- tions, indiscreet impertinence, or thoughtless blabbings.— What a difference there is, in intrinsic worth; Candour, Bene- volence, Generosity, Kindness—in all the Charities & all the Virtues; between one class of human beings & another!—[*three words deleted*] For instance, the amiable circle I so lately mixed with in the hospitable hall of Dunlop,—their gentle, generous hearts; their uncontaminated, dignified minds; their informed &

polished understandings what a contrast, when compared—if such comparing were not downright sacrilege—with the prostituted soul of the miscreant wretch, who can deliberately & diabolically plot the destruction of an honest man who never offended him; & with a hellish grin of satisfaction can see the unfortunate man, his faithful wife, & prattling innocents, turned over to Beggary & Ruin.—Can such things be? Oui! telles choses se font! Je viens d'en faire une épreuve maudite.—(By the way, I don't know whether this is French; & much would it go against my soul, to mar anything belonging to that gallant people: though my real sentiments of them shall be confined alone to my [letters (*deleted*)] correspondence with you.) (Letter 529)

On the Commemoration
of Rodney's Victory
King's Arms, Dumfries, 12th April, 1793
First printed in *The Edinburgh Advertiser*, issue 16th–19th April, 1793.

Friday last, being the Anniversary of the late Admiral Rodney's glorious victory, a party of gentlemen desirous to commemorate the day, dined together in the King's Arms, Dumfries. Many loyal and suitable toasts were drunk on the occasion, and several naval songs were sung: the following EXTEMPORE by BURNS, when it was his turn to sing, ought not to be omitted:

Instead of a song, boys! I'll give you a toast;
Here's the *Mem'ry of those on the twelfth that we lost*!
We lost! did I say? no, by Heav'n, that we found!
For their fame it shall live while the world goes round.
5   The next in succession I'll give you the KING.
And *who* would betray him, on high may *he* swing!
And here's the grand fabric, OUR FREE CONSTITUTION
As built on the base of THE GREAT REVOLUTION!
And, longer with Politics not to be cramm'd —
10   *Be Anarchy curs'd — and be Tyranny d[amn]'d;*
And *who* would to Liberty e'er prove disloyal,
May his son be a *hangman*, and *he* his first trial!!

Admiral George Brydges Rodney (1718–92) won a victory over the French navy at Dominica on 12th April, 1782, securing British control of the Atlantic. It was a major naval engagement, the 'Battle of the Saints', where 36 British engaged 34 French ships.

The headnote is taken from *The Edinburgh Advertiser* where the verse was first printed. Given that there is no extant manuscript, this newspaper entry is the only evidence of the poet's authorship. Despite J.W. Egerer's dismissal of the poem as 'doggerel' Burns did not write (See Kinsley, Vol. III, p. 1425), it is obviously authentic. Kinsley accepts it into the canon, recording that it appears in the *Advertiser*, although he does not specify which *Advertiser* and clearly did not check the original source. The use of italics and capitals, not given in most editions, is vividly that of Burns in the newspaper copy, as printed above. The poem is not printed in the usual poetry section of the newspaper but presented as a news item.

Burns had a very good reason for seeing it printed in *The Edinburgh Advertiser*, Scotland's most loyal, governmental newspaper. He had been instructed formally by the Excise to keep out of radical politics. So, the introduction to the fragment suggests it was sent to the newspaper by someone *other* than Burns. The habitual stylistic stressing of the poem in the newspaper version could only have been copied from a manuscript. A manuscript could only have come from Burns himself, or someone to whom he gave a copy. If Burns acted with complicity in seeing the poem deliberately printed in a pro-government newspaper, then we are probably looking at a precursor to *The Dumfries Volunteers*, where Burns's verse appears in public to present him as a loyal subject of the King. If this is a correct assumption, it was intended to delight critics of the poet's radical politics who probably thought he had changed his views. While Burns might have set out deliberately to appease his Edinburgh Excise masters who would certainly have seen this song, it is apparent from his emphatic use of capitals that the Great Revolution, the Constitution and particularly Liberty (for radicals this meant reform) were still uppermost in his mind. The irony here is that most of the loyalist government supporters were avowed enemies of 'Liberty', seen at this time as the key principle of French Republicanism. Hence, in these few lines the politically chastened Burns disarms his critics by toasting the King, then drinks a toast to Liberty, declaring that those who would betray 'Liberty' should be hung by their own offspring. Admiral Rodney's victory was a convenient opportunity to do so. Indeed, it may have been sent to the loyalist newspaper to parry further accusations of being the author of works such as *The Dagger*. If questioned or accused of writing further radical work Burns could refer his employers to this 'loyal' song in *The Edinburgh Advertiser*. Werkmeister preceded us in identifying the 'decoy' strategy.

Kinsley's view that the lines were given in 1793 at a meeting of the Dumfries Volunteers is incorrect for the simple reason that the Volunteers were not yet established. Kinsley guesses that differences in printed texts suggest that a manuscript must have been seen by some editors, but he was unaware that Scott Douglas meddled with the text. The original was probably lost among the papers of *The Edinburgh Advertiser*.

The Dagger

First printed in *The Edinburgh Gazetteer*, 16th May, 1793.

When a' the people thick an' thrang	crowded
Disclose their minds sae fully,	so
Permit me here to sing a sang	song
Of Paddy and his gully;	knife/dagger
5 (For Paddy's e'en a dainty chiel;	fellow
Glib gabbed an' auld farran;	smooth-tongued, old-fashioned
An' can busk up a tale as weel	well
As onie Lord or Baron)	any
I trow this day.	pledge
10 Had ye but seen him in his glee,	
When he drew out his gully,	dagger
Ye maist wad swear that he should be,	most would
The House o' Commons bully:	
For when he's warmed in argument,	
15 An' wants to be a bragger,	
He handles weel the instrument —	well
The all-convincing DAGGER,	
On onie day.	any
The DAGGER mode that's been brought in	
20 By this Hibernian shaver,	Irish joker
Has rais'd indeed an unco din,	lots of noise
And muckle clishmaclaver,	great gossip
An' been a topic o' discourse	
To ilka lass and laddie;	every
25 While mony jokes are pass'd in course;	
But fient a hair cares Paddy	not a
For that this day.	

For tho' wi' aspect like a Turk,
    Demosthenes or Tully
30 Had tried an argument wi' Burke,
    An' gi'en him but his gully;   *given, dagger*
In spite o' a' their eloquence,
    Their rhetoric and logic,
Their Lettres Belle and Common Sense,
35   'Twad been a fruitless project.
        For them this day.

For tho' a man can speak wi' grace,
    That matters na a spittle —   *not a drop*
Can onie man haud up his face,   *any, hold*
40   An' argue wi' a whittle?   *knife*
An' Paddy, should the DAGGER fail,
    Before he will knock under,
Can neist apply (to back his tale)   *next*
    A twa and forty pounder,   *two (cannon)*
45   Wi' birr some day.   *vigour*

But trouth I fear the Parliament
    Its ancient splendour fully,
When chiels man back an argument   *fellows must*
    By waving o' a gully: *dagger*
50 Yet some there are, wi' honest heart,
    (Whose courage never swaggers)
Will ne'er the public cause desert,
    For cannons or for daggers,
        By night or day.

55 Now Paddy be nae langer rude,   *no longer*
    But lay aside your storming;
And shew the 'Swinish Multitude'
    The folly o' reforming.
Convince them that their cause is wrang,   *wrong*
60   An' tell how sair they grieve ye;   *sore*
But swine are ay sae damned headstrang,   *always so, headstrong*
    They'll aiblins no believe ye   *maybe not*
        In that this day.

May peace and plenty bless our isle —
65   May placemen ne'er oppress us —
May Grey and Erskine's gracious smile
        O' grievances redress us.
May Fox and brave McLeod exert
        Their power with due attention;
70 And never from our cause depart
        For sake o' post or pension,
                Like some this day.

God bless our King, lang may he reign
        Owre subjects free and happy —
75 May ilka loyal British swain   every
        Toss off his health in nappy —   beer
May War be banish'd from our land,
        Wi' a' its dreadfu' thunder; —
And may our Constitution stand
80   The warld's pride and wonder   world's
                Ilk coming day.   each
                        Ane O' The Swine.   One of

This burlesque, in the eight-line stanza of *The Holy Fair*, targets Edmund Burke's speech in the House of Commons debate on the Alien Bill in late December 1792 when he brandished a dagger, declaring that the radicals in Britain would eventually rise in bloody rebellion. Burke is reported in *The Edinburgh Gazetteer*, 1st January 1793, saying 'every man in France has murder in his heart and in his face'. Even his colleagues laughed at these overwrought expostulations. The poem uses this incident to develop a brilliant satire on the wider campaign for parliamentary reform which dominated British politics during the winter of 1792–3.

The person behind the campaign to raise a subscription for daggers to assist the French revolutionary troops was the poet's (future) doctor, William Maxwell. Burns boasted of his friend's radical past to Mrs Dunlop, 'the Doctor Maxwell whom Burke mentioned in the House of Commons about the affair of the daggers' (Letter 638). Mentioning Maxwell to George Thomson, he wrote 'the identical Maxwell whom Burke mentioned in the House of Commons' (Letter 637). The *Sun* of 8th October, 1792 included an article entitled 'English Jacobins. No. I. Doctor Maxwell.' Maxwell was reputed to have dipped a handkerchief in the blood of the guillotined French King. Not only does the poem mention Maxwell's daggers, but links daggers and cannons ('For cannons or for daggers', l. 53) to praise those who would help the French republicans. This is a startling reference, given Burns's own attempt covertly to send four carronade cannons captured in his semimilitary customs duties from the smuggling ship *The Rosamond* which he subsequently purchased. Hence the full force of the line bringing his and Maxwell's treasonable activities together. It was not public knowledge at this time that Burns had tried to get the cannons to France. So, if a poet other than Burns were to write such a line, it would be a remarkable coincidence.

The target of ferocious radical satire and cartoon caricature for his derogatory description of the French masses as the 'swinish multitude', Burke's infamous remark was well known to Burns. To Mrs Dunlop, writing on food shortages in Dumfries, Burns ironically wrote 'How long the *Swinish Multitude* will be quiet, I cannot tell: they threaten daily' (Letter 688). Burns certainly detested Burke. This is clear in his epigram:

Oft have I wonder'd that on Irish ground
No poisonous reptile has ever been found:
Revealed the secret stands of great Nature's work:
She preserved her poison to create a Burke!

Further, the ex-Glasgow University rector, Burke, had previously disputed in the letter columns of *The Glasgow Journal* with the poet's intimate friend Robert Riddell, who wrote several pieces under the pen-name Cato.

Also revealing for the context of Burns's attitude to Burke in general and *The Dagger* in particular, is the fact that the Irishman had also been provoked by Dr William Maxwell's political print activities. Burns most probably had knowledge of the advertisement Maxwell had placed in *The Morning Chronicle* for 7th September, 1792 in which he referred to 'the present combination of Despots against the Rights of Human Nature'. In writing to no less than Henry Dundas on the urgent matter of charity for French loyalist refugees Burke ended thus:

But perhaps the temper of the common people may best be seen in the event of the late advertisement by Dr. Maxwell for the support of the Jacobins, and the maintenance of a war against the allies of this country, the Emperor and the King of Prussia; whom he had at the same time the insolence to revile in the coarsest language. (*The Correspondence of Edmund Burke, Vol. VII, 1792–4*, ed. Marshall and Woods (Cambridge University Press, 1968) p. 217).

Already inflamed against Maxwell, the matter of the dagger utterly enraged him. There is a quite fascinating letter reprinted again in Volume VII of Burke's correspondence for 16th January, 1793 from James Woolley of Birmingham, 'Manufacturer of all Kinds of Swords, Sword-hilts, Bayonets, Ram-rods, Matchets &c.', regarding both the volme (3,000) and nature of the weapons ordered. They were, in fact, to be fair to Burke, brutal foot-long blades designed for the sans culottes to eviscerate the horses of their mounted opponents. The editors conclude the letter with this fascinating footnote:

> Burke read this letter to the House of Commons on 4 March [*Parliamentary History*, XXX, 554]. Two days later William Maxwell wrote to him complaining of 'Certain Slanders' which 'have been Countenanced by a Speech of your's in the house of Commons' [Ms at Sheffield]. Burke is reported to have given Maxwell an interview in which his behaviour was 'more temperate' than it had been in the House [*Morning Post*, 16 March]. Shortly afterwards Maxwell seems to have fled to France, where he had obtained an appointment in the French Army [*The Despatches of Earl Gower*, ed. Browning, p. 260].

Nor were Riddell and Maxwell the only intimates of Burns to lock horns with Burke; William Roscoe of Liverpool was also centrally involved. Roscoe wrote perhaps the most famous pro-French/radical song of that decade. It haunted Hazlitt for the rest of his life as a bitter elegy rather than a celebratory anthem. Roscoe wrote 'O'er the vinecover'd hills and gay regions of France' in 1791. On his death a copy of the song was found in Burns's hand among his papers. This copy was returned by Maria Riddell to Roscoe. These are the relevant lines:

> Let Burke like a bat from the splendour retire,
>   A splendour too strong for his eyes;
>   Let pedants and fools his effusions admire,
> Entrapt in his cobwebs like flies
> Shall insolent Sophistry hope to prevail
>   When Reason opposes her weight.

The 'cobweb' image of the great Irish spider was arguably to provoke Burns to one of his most complex political poems, *The Cobweb*, the penultimate poem in this section. (For the highly relevant conflict between Roscoe and Burke, see *The Writings and Speeches of Edmund Burke, Vol. IX*, ed. R.B. McDowell, Oxford, Clarendon Press, 1991, pp. 24–5).

Also highly important is the fact that Burns is the only poet of the period to describe Burke on the basis of his Irish origins, as 'Paddy Burke', in *When Guilford Good*. *The Dagger* also describes Burke as 'Paddy'. Also, the earlier poem rhymes 'Burke' with 'Turk' in the same fashion as *The Dagger* (ll. 27–9). Ll. 5–9 are echoed in Burns's *The Author's Earnest Cry and Prayer*:

> Dempster, a true blue Scot I'se warran
> Thee, aith detesting, chaste Kilkerran;
> An' that glib-gabbet Highland baron,
> The Laird o Graham;
> An' ane, a chap that's damn'd auldfarran,
> Dundas his name.

These old Scots words, 'glib-gabbet' and 'auldfarran' are uncommon among other Scottish radical poets of the period, a point emphasised by McGuirk in an American review of *Robert Burns: The Lost Poems* where she lists 'dainty chiel', 'fient a hair', 'Demosthenes or Tully', the rhyming of 'happy' with 'nappy', 'rhetoric and logic', 'clishma-claver', 'honest heart' and the repeated image of 'gullies' and 'whit-tles' – daggers' as stock-in-trade language of Burns (*Eighteenth Century Scottish Studies Newsletter*, 1997, *Books in Review*, pp. 14–15). In fact, *The Dagger* is without doubt the work of a poet steeped in the *œuvre* of Scots song, as Burns certainly was.

The burlesque of 'Now Paddy be nae langer rude,/ But lay aside your storming' (ll. 55–63) is echoed in Burns's *The Ordination*:

> Now Roberston, harangue nae mair
> But steek your gab for ever;
> Or try the wicked town of Ayr,
> For there they'll think you clever;
> Or, nae reflection on your lear,
> You may commence a shaver.

The notion of Burke trying and failing to 'shew the Swinish Multitude' the 'folly o' reforming' politics is similar to a line of prose written by Burns to George Thomson. Burns wrote '& shew the swinish multi-tude that they are but beasts & like beasts must be led by the nose & goaded in the backside' (Letter 632). For this Burke too, the masses or 'swine are ay sae damned headstrang, /They'll aiblins no believe ye'.

The pantheon of contemporary radical icons, Colonel McLeod, Thomas Erskine, Charles James Fox and Charles Grey are praised in Burns's *Here's A Health tae Them That's Awa*. While any radical lyricists might applaud these Scottish and English politicians, close reading of the newspaper and printed songs of the period rarely, if ever, mention classical radical icons Demosthenes and Tully (Cicero), as mentioned in *The Author's Earnest Cry and Prayer,* 'Whom auld Demosthenes or Tully,/ Might own for brithers'. Burns, having previously and singularly grouped these radicals together, classical *and* modern, appears to have done so again.

The final burlesque on Burke is that no matter how loud the public laughs at his extremism, the more he rants, oblivious to 'Common Sense', which, in *The Holy Fair* was off and up the 'Cowgate', but here, is simply lost to Burke. Not only does the poem end with such Burns-like rhymes as 'nappy' and 'happy', but its closing sentiment dovetails with his known sentiments concerning the British constitution: he inscribed a copy of De Lolme's *The British Constitution,* 'Mr Burns presents this book to the Library, & begs they will take it as a creed of British Liberty – untill they find a better'. Ll. 83–5 of *The Dagger* reads 'And may our Constitution stand / The warld's pride and wonder, / Ilk coming day'. The final point which convinced McGuirk of the poem's provenance is Burns's peculiar skill, clear in the final stanza, of 'providing ironic assent to a position he really is attacking'. (See McGuirk, op cit, p. 15.) Daiches too, in conversation with the editors, emphasised this characteristic poetic device evident in *The Dagger.*

Robert Burns and Robert the Bruce

Of the following cluster of three 'Bruce' poems now presented, the middle and long-known one was anonymously published in *The Morning Chronicle* on 8th May, 1794 though from a letter of Burns to George Thomson of late August 1793 we know it was composed around that date. Burns's explanation of the creative impulsion for that poem is also wholly relevant to the other two poems, published pseudonymously in *The Edinburgh Gazetteer,* despite the fact that their resonance is not that of Scottish vernacular poetry but of Miltonic blank verse:

> I do not know if the old Air, 'Hey, tuttie taitie', may rank among this number; but well I know that . . . it has often filled my eyes with tears. There is a tradition . . . that it was Robert Bruce's March at the Battle of Bannockburn. This thought in my yesternight's evening walk, warmed me to a pitch of enthusiasm on the theme of Liberty & Independence which I threw into a kind of Scots Ode . . . that one might suppose to be

the gallant ROYAL SCOT'S address to his heroic followers on
that eventful morning . . .

. . . I had no idea of giving myself any trouble on the Subject,
till the accidental recollection of that glorious struggle for
Freedom, associated with the glowing ideas of some other
struggles of the same nature, *not quite so ancient*, roused my
Rhyming Mania (Letter 582).

After quoting the poem, Burns adds: 'So may God ever defend the
cause of TRUTH and LIBERTY, as he did that day!—Amen!' The
other two blank verse poems are, literally, the answer to this prayer
as the solder/saint victor, rather than the martyred Wallace, returns
as visionary upholder of Scotland's endangered freedom. How
endangered it was can be gauged that these poems were written
at the nadir of reformist, radical fortunes with the terrible impact of
the Sedition Trials and Braxfield running fast and loose with a
Scottish legal system inherently inadequate in itself regarding the
definition of treason.

While Bruce never quite occupied the place of Wallace in Burns's
soul, the seeds of his devotion to him were early sown in this self-
dramatising account of an early visit to Bannockburn:

. . . two hours ago, I said a fervent prayer for old Caledonia
over the hole in a blue-whin-stone where Robert de Bruce
fixed his Royal Standard on the banks of Bannockburn
(Letter 131).

Further, the intrusion of spiritual aid at a moment of a dark night
for the *national* soul had also appeared in *The Vision*. As McGuirk
(p. 208) suggests, Burns derived this from a Ramsay forgery also
titled *The Vision* which deals with the national crisis caused by
John Balliol's appeasement of the English king. If Ramsay's lines
influenced *The Vision*, they resonate even more deeply in the two
Bruce poems:

Quhilk held a thistle in his paw,
And round his collar graift I saw
    This poesie pat and plain,
Nemo me impune lacess
–et: —In Scots Nane sall oppress
    Me, unpunist with pain.
Still schaking, I durst naithing say,
    Till he with kynd accent

Sayd, 'Fere let nocht thy hairt affray,
    I cum to hier thy plaint;
        Thy graining and maining
        Hath laitlie reikd myne eir,
        Debar then affar then
        All eiryness or feir.'

(*Ever Green*, 1724; reprinted in *Longer Scottish Poems*, Vol. 2, ed. Crawford, Hewitt, and Law, Edinburgh: Scottish Academic Press, 1987, p. 33.)

The Ghost of Bruce

First printed in *The Edinburgh Gazetteer*, 16th July, 1793.

As late I stroll'd through Bannockburn's proud field,
At midnight hour, close by the *Bore Stene* stood
A Form Divine illumin'd round with fire,
In ancient armour spendidly array'd:
5   'Stop passenger,' he said; 'art thou a Scot?
Does Caledonian blood flow in thy veins?
Art thou a friend or foe to Freedom's cause?'
A friend, aghast I said of Scottish blood.
'Then fear not,' he said; 'the Ghost of Bruce
10   Four hundred years and more, in quiet rest,
The shade of Bruce has silent kept the tomb,
But rest no longer can his Spirit have:
His country is in danger; chains anew
Are forging fast t' enslave his Native Land.
15   Go forth, my Son, for every Scot is mine
Whom brave unconquer'd Caledonia owns;
Go tell my Country that the Shade of Bruce
Is risen to protect her injur'd Rights; —
To reinstate in splendour, as before,
20   Her Liberty near lost — bid her not fear —
The time approaches fast when Brucian fire
Shall slash destruction on her perjur'd foes.
My Broad Egeant Shield shall guard my Sons,
My Arm shall bring them Victory and Peace,
25   And Happiness shall crown their honest toils.'
Thus spake the Ghost — and in a flame flew south:
Night seiz'd her mantle — and I heard no more.

Agrestis: April 16th 1793. Banks of Bannockburn.

Given that (see *To Robert Graham of Fintry*) Burns had under severe Excise scrutiny lied about his connection to Captain Johnston's *Edinburgh Gazetteer*, there is no reason to disbelieve that he would not subsequently pursue a course of pseudonymous publication in that newspaper. He continued such activity in *The Morning Chronicle*. See, for example, the following key 1794 poem *Bruce's Address to His Troops at Bannockburn*. The name 'Agrestis' is hardly a heavy disguise given its farming allusion and its obvious connection to the 'Agricola' pseudonym which he had used in *Ode on The Departed Regency Bill* and *Epitaph for Dr. Adam Smith*.

Burns's use of Miltonic resonant blank verse is ambivalent. On the one hand, it is a medium with which he would not be normally associated. His use of the medium was desultory and insignificant. Like his poetic generation, however, Burns was haunted by the shadow of the great republican poet. Leaving historical accuracy aside, if a Scottish King is to become manifest, it should be within a democratic, heightened tone and form. There is, given spiritual intrusion into the political realm, another distinctly Miltonic touch, to be echoed in the other poem, in the fact that the work is deliberately dated 16th April, 1793 which was Easter Sunday. The resurrected Christ/Bruce is to rise in an act of desperately needed national salvation. There are in the text several other Burnsian 'fingerprints'.

The question 'Art thou a Scot?' is taken from William Hamilton's *The Life and Heroic Actions of Sir William Wallace*, a work Burns not only knew but adapted two lines from for *Scots Wha Hae*. Abbreviating the world 'to' to merely the 't'' is common in the poetry of Burns but is exceptionally rare in the general poetry of this era, as in the above example, 'Are forging fast t' enslave his Native Land'. In Bruce's personal description of 'brave unconquer'd Caledonia' there is a remarkable echo of Burns's earlier song *Caledonia* which reads 'Bold, independent, *unconquer'd* and free'. The fact that Scotland was 'unconquered' under Bruce was evidently a key historical point for Burns and this point is stressed from the mouth of Bruce himself. If we add to this accumulative evidence the somewhat minor observation that the final 'e' from 'unconquer'd' is dropped by Burns in his song and is dropped from pronunciation in *The Ghost of Bruce*, this type of consistency is surely expected if Burns is the author. Such practice was not commonplace typography among newspaper printers. The powerful image of historical Scottish martial resistence to tyranny, evoked here by the return of Bruce's 'Shade' to address the poet, is reminiscent in tone and language of the lines Burns wrote in *Prologue Spoken by Mr. Woods*:

. . . to shield the honour'd land!
Strong may she glow with all her ancient fire;
May every son be worthy of his Sire;
Firm may she rise, with generous disdain
At Tyranny's, or dire Pleasure's chain;
Still self-dependent in her native shore,
Bold may she brave grim Danger's loudest roar,
Till Fate the curtain drops on worlds to be no more!

Robert Bruce's Address to His Troops at Bannockburn –
or Scots Wha Hae
Tune: Hey Tutti Taitie
First printed anonymously in *The Morning Chronicle*, 8th May, 1794.

Scots, wha hae wi' WALLACE bled, who have
Scots, wham BRUCE has aften led, whom, often
Welcome to your gory bed, —
  Or to victorie. —

5 Now's the day, and now's the hour;
See the front o' battle lour;
See approach proud EDWARD'S power,
Chains & Slaverie. —

Wha will be a traitor-knave?
10 Wha can fill a coward's grave?
Wha sae base as be a Slave? — so
  Let him turn, & flie. —

Wha for SCOTLAND'S king & law, who
Freedom's sword will strongly draw,
15 FREE-MAN stand, or FREE-MAN fa', fall
  Let him follow me. —

By Oppression's woes & pains!
By your Sons in servile chains!
We will drain our dearest veins,
20 But they *shall* be free!

Lay the proud Usurpers low!
Tyrants fall in every foe!

LIBERTY 'S in every blow!
   Let US DO — or DIE!!!

The exact date and place of composition is unknown. There is, however, evidence to suggest that the lyric was radically reworked. A MS. of the song, sold by Puttock and Simpson in London in 1862, contains this early version:

> Do you hear your children cry
> 'Were we born in chains to lie?'
> No! come Death or Liberty!
> Yes, they shall be free!

MacDiarmid's early insistence of the superiority of vernacular Scots to standard English is certainly, in this instance, borne out by the evolved, final song. As we have seen Burns's whole intention was to draw analogies with Scottish freedom past and Scottish freedom present. Even more riskily, he was alluding to contemporary French struggles. The last line of the poem, 'Let US DO—or DIE!!!' is, triple exclamatory, the tennis court oath of the French revolutionaries. Hence discussing his sending it to Perry's *Morning Chronicle*, he wrote to Patrick Miller Jnr. in mid-March 1794: 'they are most welcome to my Ode; only let them insert it as a thing they have met with by accident & unknown to me'. When Perry did publish it on 8th May, 1794, he did preserve the poet's anonymity:

> If the following warm and animating Ode was not written near the time to which it applies, it is one of the most faithful imitations of the simple and beautiful style of the Scottish bards we ever read, and we know of but one living Poet to whom to ascribe it.

This complimentary but, surely for Burns, frighteningly transparent description, was followed by a weird printing error which read 'Scene-Lewis Garden' rather than 'Tune-Lewie Gordon'. This was corrected in the *Chronicle* of 10th May, 1794. Why there was a nine-month delay in the song's publication is unknown, but, as the least seditious of the three Bruce pieces, it is entirely possible that its publication in, for example *The Edinburgh Gazetteer* would have alerted authorities to link him with the other Bruce poems. The song did, however, reappear in *The Chronicle* with Burns's name attached a few months after he was safely dead.

As we saw in the Introduction, government critics were well able to discern the seditious nature of the song: 'So complete and deplorable was his delusion, that he thought he was doing honour to the ancient heroes of his native land, when he confounded them with the slaves of Robespierre, whom he thought the soldiers of liberty! and on whose arms he implored the benediction of God' (Low, p. 156). The song reappeared in Thomson's 1803 collection, not 1799 as Scott Douglas indicated. With Burns dead, Thomson had no compunction in impertinently perverting its political meaning into an *anti-French* song in a manner symptomatic of the whole nineteenth-century tendency in 'domesticating' the poet to Anglo-Scottish tribal pieties:

> By changing *wha* into who, *hae* into have, *aften* into often, and *sae* into so, the following song will be English; and by substituting *Gallia* for *Edward*, and Britain for *Scotland*, it will be adapted to the present time.

One could hardly think of a more direct linkage of linguistic and political emasculation. Not only of Burns himself, but of the Scottish tradition in that Burns had informed Thomson that he had adapted two lines from William Hamilton of Gilbertfield's epic poem on William Wallace to compose his own final stanza: 'A false usurper sinks in every foe/ And liberty returns with every blow' (Book VI, chapter 2, ll. 92–3). With his customary eclecticism, however, there is also a Scottish translation, noted by Hogg, from Shakespeare's *Julius Caesar* (Act III, scene ii) where Brutus asks the gathered crowds 'Who is here so base as would be a bondsman?' which turns into 'Wha sae base as be a slave?'

So powerful was the democratic impulse of the song that John Mayne, in his *A Patriotic Address to the Inhabitants of the United Kingdom* (1799), attempted by means of turgid verses to invert its meaning:

> English, Scots and Irishmen,
> All that are in Valour's ken! . . .
> . . . Now's the day, and now's the hour,
> Frenchmen wou'd the Land devour—
> Will ye wait till they come o'er
> To give ye Chains and Slavery?
> Who wou'd be a Frenchman's slave?
> Who wou'd truckle to the knave?
> Who wou'd shun a glorious grave?

The Ghost of Bruce

First printed in *The Edinburgh Gazetteer*, 24th September, 1793.

I WHO erewhile the Ghost of far fam'd Bruce
Bade aft the dread and eke the joy to see,
Alone went wandering through his laurel'd field
The other night, revolving all the ills,
5   Our Country has endur'd from P[it]t, D[unda]s,
And all their Pension'd Slaves – Curse of our Isle.
O'erwhelm'd with grief, and bursting into tears,
I cried, Indignant, 'Oh! dear Native land!'
'My country!' 'Is there not some chosen curse,
10   Some hidden thunder in the stores of Heaven,
Red with uncommon wrath to blast the men
Who owe their greatness to their Country's ruin!'
Scarce had I spoke, when, thick, involv'd in mist,
More awful and more grand than former fire,
15   The Chief of Men, great minded Bruce appear'd.
'Cheer up your heart, my Son; why grieve you so:
Your Country in her breast still carries Bruce,
And ne'er shall be enslav'd. Trust me (he said)
So far you've done your duty as I bade,
20   To warn my Country what she had to fear —
And what she had to hope for from my arm.
The time is now arriv'd, when all that's dear
To Briton's shall arouse them from their sleep —
To sleep no more, till each brave Briton's free:
25   But still it much imports each Patriot Scot
To act with prudence, keen and still reserve.
Their foes are wringing out their dying pangs
On Virtue; — but the strife will soon be o'er —
Bid all my Sons be firm; and when the storm
30   Shall gather thickest, boldly show their front,
United as in One. The work is done'.
He only added, When the clouds should burst,
That awful hover'd over Britain's Isle,
He would again appear to stay the hand
35   Of Vengeance, and bid Mercy take her place.

Agrestis – September 6th, 1793

This poem is a very close variation on the first 'Bruce' poem but is more dangerously outspoken in that (l. 5) Pitt and Dundas are named. It also opens with a specific echo of Milton in the first line of *Paradise Regained*: 'I who erewhile the happy garden sung'. Hence the concept of Bruce as risen, redemptive figure is re-emphasised in the first line. The Miltonic 'feel' of the two poems, a world penetrated by supernatural entities, is also as close to Blakean Milton influenced mytho-poetry as Burns ever came. 'When the clouds should burst/ That awful hover'd over Britain's Isle' could, indeed, come directly from Blake's *America*. Even more telling in identifying Burns as author is the fact that four lines from Addison's *Cato* are adapted and integrated into the poem. As Liam McIlvanney's forthcoming study shows, Addison, in particular, and eighteenth-century republican literature were the deliberate Murdoch selected texts in Masson's reader used in Burns's schooling. *Cato* is also mentioned four times in Burns's letters. The lines in question are those spoken by Marcus, Cato's son, to his brother Portious:

Oh Portious! Is there not some chosen curse,
Some hidden thunder in the store of Heav'n,
Big with uncommon vengeance to blast the men
Who owe their greatness to their country's ruin.

These lines are adapted and quoted by Burns/Agrestis. Addison was the first poet to inspire Burns to write poetry in his youth when he read his *Vision of Mirza*. Burns quotes Addison in his autobiographical letter to Dr Moore, stating that his lines 'for though in dreadful whirls we hung, / High on the broken wave', were 'music to my boyish ears'. There are 22 references to Addison in the poet's letters, more than for Fergusson, Ramsay, Young or Milton. A further Burns–Addison–Robert the Bruce link occurs. Burns wrote to Captain Patrick Miller enclosing a copy of *Scots Wha Hae* and casually quotes Addison's poem *Letter from Italy to Lord Halifax*, 'O Liberty—, / Thou mak'st the gloomy face of Nature gay, / Giv'st beauty to the sun, & pleasure to the day' (Letter 613). Addison was not the most popular poet in Scotland at this time, so the notion that another poet *other than Burns* would link Addison's poetry with the story of Bruce in the context of a critique on contemporary politics in the way that Burns does in relation to *Scots Wha Hae, at this exact time* is, in the face of the textual evidence almost bizarre. The language of liberty might have been ubiquitous during the 1790s, but an association between Addison, Robert the Bruce and contemporary political problems in Scotland at this time is a triangle pointing one way, towards Burns.

In his explanatory letter to George Thomson, quoted earlier,

Burns refers to composing *Scots Wha Hae* during his yesternight's evening walk when he linked Bruce's fight for freedom and liberty with the modern struggle for the same ideals. This same experience, linking Bruce to contemporary political tumult, is woven into and narrated in this version of the second Bruce poem. How coincidental that Agrestis was, like Burns, wandering alone *the other night*, contemplating the 'ills' of contemporary Scotland, thinking of King Robert De Bruce. Agrestis, it would appear, was able not only to read the poet's mind, but his letters also.

Hogg also reveals in *The Lost Poems* that *The Ghost of Bruce* switches from the general use of 'Britons' to 'each patriot Scot' in ll. 22–5, a change of emphasis echoed by Burns in his earlier prose '. . . let every Briton, and particularly every Scotsman' (Letter 283). The phrase 'thick mists obscure involv'd me round', from *Lament for James, Earl of Glencairn*, is very akin to the image of Bruce appearing 'thick, involv'd in mist'. In such a tight description one would not expect three words to be repeated in this similar imagery, 'thick', 'involv'd' and 'mist'. The words 'thick' and 'mist' are commonplace and predictable, but 'involv'd' is the unexpected and quite improbable repetition in both examples, once again suggesting one author. Even the description of Bruce as the 'Chief o' Men' can be traced to the first version of *A Man's A Man*, where Burns wrote 'The honest man, tho' e'er sae poor, / Is chief o' men for a' that'. Not only is this exact phrase employed here, prior to the composition of the democratic anthem, but when Burns changed the phrase 'chief o' men' in *A Man's A Man*, he switched the word 'king' for 'chief': 'Is king o' men for a' that'. Having described King Robert the Bruce as a 'chief', the change in *A Man's A Man* from 'chief' to 'king' would appear to be almost a natural, subconscious word association. Furthermore, the image of the battle louring in *Scots Wha Hae* — 'See the front of battle lour' — that is, the enemy coming towards the Scottish troops like an ominous, dark and angry cloud, is one developed in more detail by Agrestis in *The Ghost of Bruce*, ll. 29–33.

Another trope in Burns, a powerful man given to the practice of explosive shot-putting (he left his shot-putt at Ellisland farm), is that of the sometimes vengeful, justice-giving arm. It is found, for example, in *A Birthday Ode* when in an analogous political situation, he envisages the return of the Stuarts and the overthrow of the present royal family:

So Vengeance's arm, ensanguined, strong
Shall with resistless might assail
   Usurping Brunswick's head shall lowly lay,
And Stewart's wrongs and yours with tenfold weight repay.

It is highly significant that this poem does not call for a similar act of restorative violence but rather for fortitude and patience till the nightmare political hurricane blows itself out. L. 31, with the phrase 'United as in One', may also be deeply relevant as not derived from history but contemporary radical rhetoric. Consider this passage from *Address from the Society of United Irishmen in Dublin, 1792* which was designed to provoke the Convention of Friends of the People in Scotland into action:

> We have told you what our Situation was, what it is, what it ought to be; our End, a National Legislature; our Means, an Union of the whole People. Let this Union extend throughout the Empire. Let all unite for all, or each Man suffer for all. In each country let the People assemble in peaceful and constitutional Convention. Let Delegates from each country digest a Plan of reform, best adapted to the Situation and Circumstances of their respective Nations, and let the Legislatures be petitioned at once by the urgent and unanimous Voice of England, Scotland and Ireland.

This radical vision of the enlightened end of history with each democratically united nation in a consequent equal, pacific union with nations similarly inclined, hence an end to both Anglo-British imperialism and Irish religious self-division, is to reappear in one of Burns's most important political poems, *Ode on General Washington's Birthday* in the posthumous section. This poem, however, is one that, with American exceptionalism, is of the British Isles as the scene of tri-national tragedy. The above quotation is taken from Appendix II of Elaine W. McFarland's indispensable *Ireland and Scotland in the Age of Revolution* (Edinburgh, 1994).

An Unpublished Letter on Robert the Bruce

As a natural appendix to these 'Bruce' poems, we add the following hitherto unpublished letter by Burns. This letter remained with its recipient Dr Hughes until his death in 1843 and was sold later in the century to a New York collector, Mr John Kennedy. In January 1928, the Hereford Burns Club published the letter with its history. A copy of this is available in the Mitchell Library, Glasgow and a facsimile of the letter is displayed in the Burns Room of the Murray Arms Hotel, Gatehouse of Fleet, in Galloway. Why the letter has not been included in the poet's collected letters is unknown. It is certainly genuine. It was written as an explanation to *Bruce's Address to His Troops at Bannockburn* and dated 1795:

> This battle was the decisive blow which put Robert the First, commonly called Robert de Bruce, in quiet possession of the Scottish throne. It was fought against Edward the Second, son to that Edward who shed so much blood in Scotland in consequence of the dispute between Bruce and Baliol.
>
> Apropos, when Bruce fled from London to claim the Scottish crown, he met with the Cummin, another claimant of the crown, at Dumfries. At the altar, in the Priory there they met, and it is said that Bruce offered to Cummin – 'Give me your lands and I'll give you my interest in the crown', or vice versa.
>
> What passed nobody knows, but Bruce came in a flurry to the door and called out to his followers – 'I am afraid that I have slain the Cummin'. 'Are you only afraid!' replied Sir Roger de Kilpatrick (ancestor to the present Sir James Kilpatrick of Closeburn), and ran into the Church and stabbed Cummin to the heart; and coming back said, showing a bloody dagger, 'I've sicker'd him!' – that is in English, I have secured him. Until lately this was the motto of the Closeburn family, but the late Sir Thomas changed it into 'I make sure' – the crest still is the bloody dagger. R.B.

The Scotian Muse:
An Elegy.

First printed in *The Edinburgh Gazetteer*, 1st October 1793.

The Muse unwilling leaves the sacred shore,
    Where every virtue held its peaceful reign —
Hangs with regret on scenes she lov'd before;
    The last sad wand'rer from the pensive plain.

5   She views where once the Sons of Freedom stray'd
    Whose hard misfortunes claim the sigh sincere:
She saw fair Genius fly his native shade,
    And pour'd the parting tribute of a tear.

But why, sweet maid, so fondly dost thou cling
10   To rugged rocks, where no soft verdure grows,
While climes more grateful court the tuneful string,
    And point to vales of pleasure and repose?

Haply thou lov'st to soothe th' afflicting smart
    That tears the breast, by misery doom'd to mourn;
15 To gild the gloom around the *victim's* heart;
    Or bend with *pity* o'er the *patriot's* urn.

Or haply, where beneath the iron hand
    Of stern *Oppression*, youth's fair flow'rets fade,
Kindly, with *Sympathy's* endearing band,
20   And bright-ey'd *Hope*, thou cheer'st the dungeon's shade.

For him, who warm'd by *Freedom's* genial fire,
    With soul unfetter'd, drags the *Despot's* chain,
Perhaps thy hand attunes the living lyre
    To soothe his woes by music's magic strain.

25 And thou, gay *Fancy*, bless his languid hours!
    Each flattering phantom let thy care bestow;
To strew his lonely path with fairy flowers,
    And pluck the noxious nettles as they grow.

Say (and, ye *Powers of Truth*, accordant join!)
30   'The time will come — that *Fate* has fix'd the doom —
'The *Friends of suffering virtue* shall combine,
    'And hurl each blood-stained Despot to the tomb!'

                         Lysander.

This appears in the *Edinburgh Gazetteer* a few weeks after the second *Ghost of Bruce*. The subject of the lament is the injustice of the transportation sentences to Botany Bay served upon the radical lawyer Thomas Muir and the Rev. Fysche Palmer on charges of sedition. The theme of the lament is the spirit of 'Freedom' departing Scotland in sorrow, but that the essential spirit of Scottish poetry, incarnated in Burns himself, gives them constant succour. This is in harmony with the bard's plaintive language, 'Where is the soul of freedom fled? / Immingled with the mighty dead' from the *Ode to General Washington on His Birthday*, written shortly after *The Scotian Muse*. The title is echoed in the first line of *To Miss Graham of Fintry* by Burns, 'Here, where the Scottish Muse immortal lives'. The language of this work is found in many verses by Burns, such as *Elegy on Captain Matthew Henderson*, 'Where haply, Pity strays forlorn'; and in *A Dedication to Gavin Hamilton*, 'The last, sad mournful rites bestow'. The lamentation is similar to *On the Death of Lord President Dundas*, 'Sad to your sympathetic glooms I fly' where the expression 'grim Oppression' is also found. There are other echoes in Burns's *Elegy on the Death of Sir*

James Hunter-Blair, 'I saw fair Freedom's blossoms richly blow', and 'Her form majestic droop'd in pensive woe', which compare to the *Scotian Muses*'s 'She saw fair Genius fly his native shade'. In *The Scotian Muse* the description an 'iron hand / Of stern Oppression' (ll. 17–18) is echoed in *A Winter Night*, 'See stern Oppression's iron grip'. L. 15's 'gild the gloom' is also found in Burns's *The Lament*. While it may be argued that these similarities are the result of contemporary standardised elegiac language, the high number of Miltonic lexical similarities point to Burns's hand. As in the *Gazetteer* 'Bruce' poems, this is absolutely the only Scottish published radical poetry derived from high Miltonic style.

There is, however, in this poem and the two rediscovered Bruce poems a similar pattern of a sense of the nightmare darkness of oppression before the final dawn of freedom. This is very similar to the patttern found in Shelley's response to the terrible events of 1819. Compare, for example, these stanzas from *The Revolt of Islam*, at the end of Canto ix:

> The seeds are sleeping in the soil: meanwhile
>   The Tyrant peoples dungeons with his prey,
> Pale victims on the guarded scaffold smile
>   Because they cannot speak; and, day by day,
> 5   The moon of wasting Science wanes away
> Among her stars, and in that darkness vast
>   The sons of earth to their foul idols pray,
> And gray Priests triumph, and like blight or blast
> A shade of selfish care o'er human looks is cast.
>
> 10   This is the winter of the world; – and here
>   We die, even as the winds of Autumn fade,
> Expiring in the frore and foggy air. —
>   Behold! Spring comes, though we must pass, who made
> The promise of its birth, — even as the shade
> 15   Which from our death, as from a mountain, flings
>   The future, a broad sunrise; thus arrayed
> As with the plumes of overshadowing wings,
> From its dark gulf of chains, Earth like an eagle springs.

The pen-name Lysander (echoing Sylvander?) may well be derived from Burns's early schooling. As Liam McIlvanney's forthcoming *The Radical Burns* will show, Burns's school-reader, an anthology of liberal sentiment, *Masson's Collection of Prose and Verse from the Best English Authors for the Use of School* had both a seminal and persistent influence on Burns. Lysander features in the book as an exemplary English gentleman of fine feeling and good works.

New Song
or A Wet Day at Walmer Castle
First published in *The Morning Chronicle*, 9th September, 1793.

O! Willy is a wanton wag,	reckless joker
The blythest lad that ere I saw	
And has so well the gift of *gab*,	conversation
He makes *John Bull* his purse-strings draw.	the British public
5 He can armies raise and navies,	
He can venture on a war;	
Men and money how he levies —	
His like is neither near nor far.	
For *Catskins* when he went to fight,	
10 Of insults offer'd loud did bawl,	
And honest John, who thought him right,	John Bull
At last agreed to pay for all.	
But Willy then was in a passion,	
Swore he'd give John, *Nootka Sound*;	
15 Yet by his fam'd Negotiation	
John got ne'er an inch of ground.[1]	
With *Russia* then he would be fighting,	
For *Oczakow*, to please the *Turks*;	
But John not much in war delighting,	
20 Fox soon *exposed his humbug works*.[2]	
For Willy's *Plans* are always droll,	
Nor saw he *Poland* in his map;	
All *Liberty* from Pole to Pole,	
He threw in Kate's *voracious lap*.[3]	

1 'The Convention with Spain of October 28, 1790, which resolved the dispute over Nootka Sound and which the Opposition regarded as a great humiliation for Pitt. The dispute had begun in 1789, when Spain seized a British trading station on Nootka Sound and some English vessels. Pitt seemed determined to go to war over what the Opposition maintained was only a seizure of 'Catskins'.

2 Russia had seized Oczakow in 1788, but Pitt ignored the seizure until 1791, when he demanded that Catherine restore the town to Turkey. She refused, but there were so many petitions against the war that Pitt was compelled to forget the matter.

3 The second partition of Poland, which Pitt had not anticipated and which was an additional embarrassment to the government.

25 And now he's gone to war with France,[4]
        Where men and money he must send:
    In short he leads John such a dance,
        That God knows when his wars may end.
    From East to West, from South to North,
30   O'er all Europe the sword he'll draw,
    And not content, he'll still hold forth,
        And quarrel with *America*.[5]

    As he can *drink*, and not be *drunk*,
        As he can *fight*, and not be *slain*,
35 As he can *speak* and strike the *trunk*,
        That never dar'd to *strike again*;
    Then what cares he for thousands lost,
        Or what cares he for thousands slain?
    What cares he what wars may cost,
40   For *Widows tears*, or *Mother's pain*!

    And so for Sport he's gone to Dover,
        With D[undas], R[eeves], and L[ong],[6]
    Tho' bad at *dashing into cover*,
        They say he can do nothing wrong.
45 And they're a set of *wanton wags*,   reckless jokers
        The *blythest lads* that e'er we saw;
    While o'er their bottle Harry brags,
        That honest John must pay for a'.   all

These footnotes are derived from Professor Lucylle Werkmeister who first attributed the song to Burns in her seminal essay *Robert Burns and the London Daily Press*, published in *Modern Philology* (1966). Werkmeister explains the appearance of the poem:

> In September, 1793, Burns reminded George Thomson: 'For Willie was a wanton wag' – you have a song made on purpose,

4 The announcement that Britain was now officialy at war with France was made on 1st February, 1793.
5 The new quarrels with America were just beginning. They were settled by 'Jay's Treaty' of 1794.
6 Dundas, who headed an army of spies and informers; John Reeves, organiser of the Association for Protecting Liberty and Property against Republicans and Levellers; and Charles Long (later Baron Farnborough), Secretary of the Treasury, who assisted in the subversion of the press. These three were regarded as the principal warmongers and conspirators against democratic liberties.

also by Hamilton, which you will find in Ramsay's [Tea-table] Miscellany, beginning 'Willy, ne'er enquire what end'. Supposedly Burns did not intend to write such a 'song' himself, and yet there is a political version of it in *The Morning Chronicle* of September 9 1793, which was certainly not provided by any of the Chronicle's usual contributors. The subject is sinecures and wars, and 'Willy' is the Prime Minister, William Pitt. In August 1792, Pitt had made himself Lord Warden and Admiral of the Cinque Ports and Governor of Dover Castle . . . on August 27 he and his intimate, Henry ('Harry') Dundas, Secretary of State for the Home Department, had gone to Dover to take possession of Walmer Castle. There they had remained for several 'wet' days, both of them being addicted to port wine. Since this was the choicest of the sinecures, assuring the holder of six country houses and an income of £4000 a year for life, Pitt's seizure of it was still a newspaper issue in 1793 and it had often enough been charged by Fox, Sheridan, and other Opposition leaders that Pitt had deliberately involved England in a war in order to safeguard this and other emoluments (p. 324).

Unaware of her work, it was recently re-attributed to Burns in Scott Hogg's *The Lost Poems*, where Werkmeister's research procedures and results were frequently replicated. The poem appears first in *The Morning Chronicle*, but a copy was also sent to *The Edinburgh Gazetteer* where it appears within a week of the London paper. Werkmeister goes on to argue:

Since by 1793 the *Morning Chronicle* was the principal Opposition newspaper, 'An Excellent New Song' would have attracted some attention. But there was no sequel, and three days later (12 September, 1793) the Ministerial *Public Advertiser* published 'LINES, On the BIRTH of a posthumous CHILD; Born in Peculiar Circumstances of Family Distress. By ROBERT BURNS'. The heading 'For the Public Advertiser' made it clear that Burns had submitted the poem himself, and he had evidently also authorized the use of his name. If there had been any suspicion that he was responsible for 'An Excellent New Song' these lines in the Ministerial *Public Advertiser* would have dispelled it . . . (p. 325).

She illustrates the fact that it was a customary tactic for Burns regularly to submit radical material to the Opposition press, while at the same time, sending non-radical verse under his own name to the pro-government Ministerial newspapers.

Not only do we see here Burns's unparalleled skill in turning old Scots lyrics into contemporary radical song, but his remarkable ability to compress a range of historical events into six condensed stanzas, always hitting the prime targets with satirical wit. *When Guilford Good Our Pilot Stood* is the perfect case in point, which meticulously chronicles the key events of the American-British war.

The chief satirical victims here are William Pitt and his deputy Henry Dundas (l. 42), who was in charge of the Home Office spy network which existed throughout Britain and successfully infiltrated many groups such as The Friends of the People in Scotland and monitored the London Corresponding Society, the leading intellectual and propaganda arm of British radicalism. John Reeves (l. 42) set up the Association for Protecting Liberty and Property against Republicans and Levellers, a propaganda arm of government supporters which rallied 'men of rank' to support the King and Constitution against the fear of invading Jacobins and their supporters at home. Charles Long (l. 42) was Secretary to the Treasury and through paying the pro-government press to speak the ministerial line, he was made a Baron. As Werkmeister comments, there is no evidence that these 'wanton wags' visited Walmer Castle at this time (1794) for a weekend's drinking session, so this visit may be poetic licence. It was, though, common knowledge that when announcing Britain's involvement in the war against Revolutionary France, both Pitt and Dundas were drunk; the latter falling and faltering at the despatch box. Burns would have been wholly aware of Dundas's public reputation for heavy drinking. Coleridge, accordingly, called him 'brazen faced' and Dr Walcot (Peter Pindar) and Professor Richard Porson also emphasised this issue in their satires on him.

Werkmeister did not feel the need to strengthen her case with textual comparison. A few examples, though, are persuasive. The echo of Burns's song *Duncan Davidson*, ll. 5–8 is apparent:

A man may drink, and no be drunk;
 A man may fight, and no be slain;
A man may kiss a bonie lass,
 And ay be welcome back again!

The *New Song* (ll. 33–36) has virtually the same text, suitably adapted. The similarity is striking. The same poetic sentiment, mourning the death caused by war; the 'widow's tears, the orphan's cry', is found in the final stanza of *Logan Braes*. A further description employing the Scots-derived 'Kate' for 'Catherine', referring to Catherine the Great, is also found in Burns's *Why Should Na Poor Folk Mowe*, 'Auld Kate laid her claws on poor Stanislaus,/ And Poland has bent like a bow'.

The textual similarities cannot, however, be explained by another poet's imitation of *Duncan Davison* and *Logan Braes*: the fomer was printed anonymously and the latter was yet to be published.

Moreover, the poem contains a stylistic peculiarity of Burns, evident in his Kilmarnock edition (where he acted as publisher): an excessive use of italics, compared to other contemporaneous poetry. It is probably no coincidence that a month after Burns mentioned *Willie is A Wanton Wag* to George Thomson that a political version of it appeared in *The Morning Chronicle*. Thomson had already poured scorn on Burns's anti-war *Logan Braes* and his squeamish, at best apolitical views would have warned Burns never to send him another overtly political piece.

In recent research on interactive British radical poetry of the 1790s, we are beginning to understand not simply English-Scottish interaction, but how Burns influenced the dissenting Ulster poets. This example, signed 'Paddy Burns', possibly written by John Orr, shows not simply radical Ulster's assimilation of Burns's poetic form (as in *The Holy Fair*) but also the Scottish poet's radical subject matter. Here, for example, are the first two stanzas of *An Address to Mr Pitt, In Guid Braid Scotch*:

Dear Billy, I'm right wae for you;
    Ye're in a hobble warse and warse:
Ye bred it a' your sell I trow,
    By pickin' quarrels like an Ass;
    'Bout Nooska-Sound ye made a faird,
Ye wadna want the Spotet Cats;
    Trouth ye might your three millions spared,
    An' let them rin, and catch the Rats
        For mony a day.

'Bout Oszacow ye fine advis'd;
    Nane maun posses't but wha ye like:
But Kate your meddlin' gaits despis'd,
    An' sent you hame wi trailin' pike.
In sullen mood ye broodin' sat,
    Watchin' whar ye might hae a chance,
To breed a scrape: at last ye gat,
    A thick dust kicket up wi' France
        Ae luckless day.

We are not only indebted to Dr Liam McIlvanney's archival retrieval of this particular poem, but to his innovative awareness of the influence of Burns's political poetry in Ulster in the 1790s. As McIlvanney notes: 'The common vogue for Burns's poems is itself a symptom of this shared political culture. Burns's egalitarian and democratic sentiments, his outspoken pro-Americanism, and his

depiction of the Westminster government as a 'system of corruption
all endeared him to an Ulster Presbyterian audience, and to poets
like Orr and Campbell, who were to participate in the 1798 Rising'.
('Robert Burns and the Ulster–Scots Literary Revival of the 1790s',
Bullán, Vol. IV, No. 2, pp. 125–43).

Lines on Ambition

First published in *The Edinburgh Gazetteer*, 31st December, 1793.

As Caesar once perus'd the warlike page,
    Frought with the acts of Macedonia's Chief,
Discordant passions in his bosom rage,
    And sudden tears declare his inward grief.
5 And when his anxious friends, who round him stood,
    Ask'd, what disturb'd the quiet of his breast —
While yet his eyes distill'd a briny flood,
    The future tyrant thus his cares express'd —
'[. . . text unreadable . . .] my years attain'd,
10 His triumphs round the earth's wide orb were spread;
And [. . . text unreadable . . .] seat the hero gain'd,
    And Conquest twin'd her laurels round his head.
While I remain unnotic'd and unknown,
    A novice yet among the sons of Fame,
15 Where are the trophies I can call my own?
    What spoils of victory can Caesar claim?'
Thus Julius, burning with Ambition's fire,
    At length, thro' Roman blood, to empire rose —
But henceforth may that wretch accurs'd expire,
20   Whose glory on his country's ruin grows.
May fortune always their endeavours bless,
    Who struggle to defend their country's cause,
May victory crown their labours with success,
    Who fight for Freedom, and for Patriot Laws.
25 But those who dare a People's rights invade,
    Who millions, for dominion would enslave;
May all their toils with infamy be paid,
    Not *tears* – but *curses* visit them to the grave.
In deep oblivion may their acts be hid,
30   That none their despot victories may lead;
As Greece her sons, to sound *his name* forbid,
    Who, to be known, perform'd a villain's deed.[1]

                             A. Briton

1 The last two lines refer to Erestrates, who, to perpetuate his name, set fire
to the temple of Diana, to Esphus. As well as this specific footnote, there is
also an apparently unspecified footnote in the newspaper: '*See Plutarch's Life
of Caesar.*'

This is attributed to Burns in Hogg's *The Lost Poems* (1997). The crucial pen-name 'A. Briton' was first used by Burns in his anti-Hanoverian letter in *The Edinburgh Evening Courant* of November 1788 (Letter 283). We know from his personal correspondence that he was the author of this seditious letter. We are now confronted in this section with two recently discovered poems and a political essay which use this pseudonymn. Checking of the *Dictionary of Anonymous and Pseudonymous Literature* showed no other usage of 'A. Briton' other than the Burns *Courant* letter during this period and mentions an obscure booklet of 1819 on bank coins, signed A. Briton. We then embarked on a sustained textual scansion of period newspapers and journals in order to discover this pen-name anywhere other than in *Lines on Ambition*, *The Cob-Web* and the political essay from Burns's main London radical outlet, *The Morning Chronicle*. No other usage was found. As we shall see, regarding the new essay, Burns was particularly keen to emphasise to *The Morning Chronicle* that he was, indeed 'a Briton'. Further, in the late eighteenth century, this pseudonym does not precede Burns's usage and also disappears after his death.

Textually, the new poem is strikingly similar to lines written by Burns during mid-1793 in John Syme's copy of *The British Album*, a volume of the Della Cruscan poets led by Robert Merry:

> PERISH their names, however great or brave,
> Who in the DESPOT's cursed errands bleed!
> But who for FREEDOM fill a hero's grave,
> Fame with a Seraph-pen, record the glorious deed!

These lines not only read as though they were embryonic of *Lines on Ambition* but could easily be inserted in the final part of the poem. Although the first part of the poem is rather cumbersome, Burns did compose very similar lines during mid-1793.

That the subject of 'Ambition' might be a topic for the poet's pen is evident if a letter to Thomson, written in June 1793, is considered:

> Have you ever, my dear Sir, felt your bosom ready to burst with indignation, on reading of, or seeing, how these mighty villains who divide kingdom against kingdom, desolate provinces & lay Nations waste out of the wantonness of Ambition, or often from still more ignoble passions? (Letter 566).

Moreover, the notion that Burns might curse the leaders of Britain for involving the country in a war against France (ll. 19–20, ll. 25–8), is clearly seen in a letter to Peter Hill in 1793: 'O! may the wrath & curse of all mankind, haunt and harass these turbulent, unprincipled misc[reants] who have involved a people in this ruinous business!!!' (Letter 553).

There is no evidence to suggest this poem was copied from an English newspaper or was the work of an English poet. It does not appear in English radical newspapers. It was almost certainly sent to *The Edinburgh Gazetteer* by Burns, who had previously employed the pen-name.

Indeed, the poet's primary educational text, under his influential tutor Murdoch, that is Arthus Masson's *A Collection of Prose and Verse from the Best English Authors*, carries a powerful essay 'The Twelve Caesars' which dwells on the corrupt abuse of power by the ambitious, beginning with the reign of Julius Caesar.

Remember the Poor

First printed in *The Glasgow Advertiser*, 27th January 1794.

	Frae Greenland's snawie mountain high,	snowy
	(Whare sleaks o' ice tumult'ous lye,	lie
	An' dismal scenes appear)	
	Bauld Boreas, wi' his surly train,	bold North Wind
5	Rides howling thro' the mirk domain,	dark
	An' leads and guides the weir: –	war of elements
	Nae mair the gowany field leuks gay,	no more, looks
	Nor flow'r-bespangled green,	
	To tempt our waunrin' feet to stray,	wandering
10	Or charm our rovin' een;	eyes
	Mair dowie they grow ay,	more woeful
	An' wither in the blast,	
	I'm vext now, perplext now,	
	To think their beauty's past.	
15	Happy are they, wha, without dread,	who
	Can hear the storm blaw owre their head,	blow over
	Nor danger needs to fear: –	
	Blest are ye, highly favour'd Great,	
	Wha coshly rest on beds o' state,	comfortably
20	Crown'd wi' ilk dainty chear; –	each
	Enrag'd ay whan I do compare	when
	Your blythsome lives wi' mine,	
	(For mine's a life opprest wi' care,	
	An' drudgery an' pine.)	
25	I snarl an' quarrell	
	Wi' Fortune, that blind wh – re,	whore
	That leuks down, an' does frown	looks
	On me, and hauds me poor:	holds, keeps

Reflect sae wretched's they maun be   *so, must*
30 That's doom'd tae pinchin' poverty   *to*
  And stern Misfortune's blows;
An' O! thy pittance do thou grant –
'Twill banish their ilk' care an' want,   *every*
  An' rid them o' their woes:
35 Wi' sauls quite liberal an' free   *souls*
  Your charity extend;
Now is the time, – an' credit me
  Ye'll no' miss't in the end.
   Mak' haste then, nor waste then
40   Your siller on ought ill;   *money*
   Ease their need wi' a' speed
    Lest hunger does them kill.

Hail ye wha ha'e wi' open heart   *who have*
Come forth o' late, an' ta'en their part –   *taken*
45 A noble gen'rous deed!
Is there, whate blude rins in his viens,   *what blood runs*
A wretch, wha's cash, an' yet refrains   *who's*
  Tae join ye wi' a speed –
(Uwordy's he to see the light   *not worthy*
50 O' day, that e'er wad scan,   *would*
An', for the sake o' riches, slight
  His fellow-creature, Man) –
   May his gear thro' ilk year   *possessions, each*
    Ay mair an' mair decrease,   *always, more*
55   Wha'll no join wi' his coin   *who'll not*
    To help fowks in distress.   *folks*

Lang may ye live, Sirs, to defend   *long*
An' stand the poor man's constant friend
  In ilka time o' need;   *every*
60 Syne, whan Death at your doors does ca',   *then, when, call*
An' lays ye lifeless, ane an' a',   *one and all*
  Amang the silent dead,   *among*
Fame on her trump your praise will soun',   *sound*
  An' mark ye in her pages,
65 That your deeds may be handed down
  Unto the latest ages; –
   An' may 't be your decree –
    'Throughout an' endless day,
   'T' inherit by merit
70   'The ever-sproutin' bay'.

  Jan 1794, JOB.

This poem was first ascribed to Burns in Hogg's *Robert Burns: The Lost Poems* (1997). It appears in *The Glasgow Advertiser* of 27th January, 1794. It was composed after a public plea for charity to feed the hungry in and around areas of Glasgow during the harsh winter of 1793–4. To launch the initial call for public charity Burns's poem *The Cottar's Saturday Night* was reprinted in Dr James Anderson's magazine *The Bee*, where the charity appeal originated in December 1793. Burns knew Anderson and added (Letter 426) a few friends' names to Anderson's subscriber list. By the time *Remember the Poor* was printed, over a month after the appeal went public, *The Bee* had been forcibly closed down in Edinburgh for its part in serialising the ferocious political critique on government by James Thomson Callender, *The Political Progress of Britain*. Hence perhaps, the poem's appearance in *The Glasgow Advertiser*.

There are several reasons to suggest this work is by Burns. He would have known *The Cottar's Saturday Night* was part of the charity appeal and his egalitarian sentiments were such that he would have surely wished to contribute. On several occasions Burns remarks that the only 'coin' a poet can pay with is *rhyme* (Letter 571). As we see in the Introduction, *The Book of Job* is compulsively present in Burns's poetry and letters (Letters 248, 362, 446). This identification of his own and his father's suffering with that of Job would make this an obvious choice of pen-name.

In addition, it is now known that Burns not only published prose in *The Glasgow Advertiser* but its subject was *poverty*. Here is the full text from the newspaper on 29th April–2nd May, 1791:

FRAGMENT – ON POVERTY

POVERTY! Thou half-sister of Death! Thou cousin-german of Hell! Where shall I find force of execration equal to thy demerits? – By thee, the venerable Ancient, though, in thy invidious obscurity, grown hoary in the practice of every virtue under Heaven, now laden with years and wretchedness, implores from a stony-hearted son of Mammon, whose sun of prosperity never knew a cloud, a little, little aid to support his very existence, and is by him, derided and insulted. – By thee, the man of sentiment, whose heart glows with Independence and melts with sensibility, [only – error] inly pines under the neglect, or wreathes [writhes] in bitterness of soul under the contumely, of arrogant, unfeeling Wealth. – By thee, the man of Genius, whose ill-starred ambition plants him at the tables of the Fashionable and Polite, must see, in suffering silence, his remark neglected and his person despised, while shallow greatness in his idiot attempts at wit, shall meet with countenance and applause. – Nor is it only the family of worth to have reason to complain of thee. – The children of Folly and Vice, tho' in common with thee, the offspring of evil, smart equal[ly] under thy rod. – Owing to thee, the man of unfortunate disposition and neglected education, is condemned as a fool for his dissipation; despised and shunned as a needy wretch, when his follies, as usual, have brought him to want, and when his unprincipled necessities drive him to dishonest practices, he is abhorred as a miscrent [miscreant], and perishes by the justice of his country. – But far otherwise is the lot of the Man of family and Fortune. – His early extravagance and folly are fire and spirit; his consequent wants are the embarassments of an Honest Fellow; and when, to remedy the matter, he sets out with a legal commission to plunder distant provinces and massacre peaceful nations, he returns laden with the spoils of rapine and murder – lives wicked and respected – and dies a Villian and a Lord. – Nay, worst of all, alas! For hapless Woman – the needy creature who was shivering at the corner of the street, waiting to earn the wages of casual prostitution, is ridden down by the Chariot wheels of the CORONETED RAPE – hurrying out to the adulterous assignation – She, who, without the same necessities to plead, riots nightly in the same guilty trade!!!

Although anonymous, this flyting critique on poverty and social oppression, bar a few minor textual and typographical differences, is found in a letter by Burns to Peter Hill, Edinburgh, dated for 17th January, 1791, some three months prior to appearing in the Glasgow publication (see Letter 430). Given the poet's habit of making fair copies of many of his letters and his tendency to repeat himself, it is pretty certain he sent this material to the *Advertiser*. The only known manuscript is without address and unsigned. Hence, here is now definitive proof that Burns covertly published prose in *The Glasgow Advertiser* during 1791.

The first stanza of the poem is its best. The winter scene is set within a powerful image of the god of the North Wind riding, 'howling', through icy Greenland with an elemental power so wild that they have decimated, as far away as Scotland, any flowers that might have survived. This confidently flowing image is reminiscent of Burns's characteristic painting of a winter scene to create a mood fit for the human despair and loss in the ensuing verses. The description of 'Bauld Boreas, wi' his surly train' is echoed in Burns's 'Cauld Boreas, wi' his boisterous crew' from *The Fête Champêtre*, which was published posthumously. The phrase 'Bauld Boreas' is found only in Ramsay's (1686–1758) *The Nipping Frost and Driving Sna'*. The description 'the mirk domain, / And leads and guides the weir' (ll. 5–6) is adapted from Fergusson's '. . . bleak domain / And guides the weir', *The Daft Days*, stanza 3. Also, the phrase (l. 10) 'Or charm our rovin' een' is partly adapted from Fergusson's *Leith Races*, 'To charm our rovin' een'. Such echoes of Ramsay and Fergusson are everywhere in Burns.

A further distinct feature of Burns in poetry and prose is his constant attack on the 'great folk' or 'highly favour'd Great', as seen here. Or in *Elegy on the Death of Captain Matthew Henderson*, 'Go to your sculptur'd tombs, ye Great, / In a' the tinsel trash o' state'. Ll. 15–20 read like a condensed version of the social and economic oppression suffered by the poor in *A Winter Night*, 'Oh ye! who, sunk in beds of down, / Feel not a want but what yourselves create, /Think, for a moment, on his wretched fate, / Whom friends and fortune quite disown!' This type of comment in Burns is found along with his motif of despair for the poor in general and himself in particular, his personal angst, suffering at the hands of 'Fortune' , as seen at ll. 21–8, a passage which is autobiographical as in Burns's: 'snarl an' quarrell / Wi' Fortune, that blind wh—ore'. The anonymously published prose by Burns, given above from *The Glasgow Advertiser* is a perfect example of Burns 'enrag'd' at the effects of poverty. (Further examples of this sentiment expressed in poetry and prose are found in *Lines Written on a Banknote*, *My Father Was A Farmer*, *The Creed of Poverty*, comments in the *FCB* and Letters 244, 335, 358, 347, 510 319, 605 and 638). As he wrote to Mrs Dunlop, 'Poverty, is to be my attendant to the grave' (Letter 638). Ll. 15–28 are a self-portrait of a poet unable to give cash to the charity plea who is deeply indignant at the semi-feudal economic structure which is implicitly blamed as the cause of poverty.

To Messrs Muir, Palmer, Skirving and Margarot

First printed in *The Edinburgh Gazetteer*, 15th January, 1794.

Among innumerable false – unmov'd,
Unshaken, unseduced, unterrify'd. – Milton.

Friends of the Slighted people – ye whose wrongs
From wounded FREEDOM many a tear shall draw
As once she mourn'd when mock'd by venal tongues
Her SYDNEY fell beneath the form of law.

5   O had this bosom known poetic fire
    Your names, your deeds, should grace my votive songs
    For Virtue taught the bard's far-sounding lyre
    To lift the PATRIOT from the servile throng.

    High o'er the wrecks of time *his* fame shall live
10 While proud Oppression wastes her idle rage.
    His name on history's column shall revive
    And wake the genius of a distant age.

    It shines – the dawn of that long promised day
    For eager Fancy bursts the midnight gloom
15 The patriot's praise, the grateful nations pay
    And tears the trophy from the oppressor's tomb.

    Yet what the praise far distant times shall sing
    To that calm solace Virtue *now* bestows.
    Round the dire bark She waves her guardian wing;
20 She guides her exiles o'er the trackless snows:
    With Joy's gay flowers She decks the sultry wild
    And sheds the beam of Hope where Nature never smil'd.

Whereas the most beautiful gem stones are the result of the raw
geological power in the vortex of Earth's volatile central core, the
genesis of this poetic gem is the intense crucible of political antagon-
ism that came to a head in December 1793 and January 1794 in
Edinburgh. Continuing the theme of *The Scotian Muse*, it laments
the oppression of radical activists and in particular, those convicted of
sedition and sentenced to transportation to the penal colony of
Botany Bay, namely Thomas Muir, the Rev. Fysche Palmer, William
Skirving and Maurice Margarot. It also accords Muir the honour
of being compared to the great hero-martyr of the Whig tradition
Algernon Sydney (1622–83), the English statesman, who was an icon
of the French as well as British radical movement at this period.
    Having tried and convicted Muir and Palmer for sedition and
served upon them sentences of 14 years' and 7 years' transportation
respectively, the Scottish Friends of the People branches – those
'Friends of the Slighted people' (l. 1) – were galvanised and grew,
despite the key Edinburgh branch, central to organisation of the
Scottish radicals, being infiltrated by the cousin of James Boswell,
Claude Irvine Boswell, Depute Sheriff of Fife. Another government
spy, P. Moir, described the Rev. Fysche Palmer bizarrely as a
bankrupt butcher from Birmingham paid by Joseph Priestley's

radical group (see RH 2/4/70/f.48, dated 8th March, 1793). The government moved to arrest William Skirving and Maurice Margarot when they were about to convene a meeting of the National Convention of the Friends of the People in Edinburgh near the end of 1793. The government feared the setting up of a Jacobin-derived government. Robert Dundas (nephew to Henry) wrote in early January 1794:

> You may believe that the present state of madness here, engrosses all our attention . . . if we take decided and strong measures against those Rebels, we shall be supported. . . . It is the only system that will have effect or, otherways, an Insurrection will be the consequence. (RH 2/4/74/f.76).

Political anxiety was running at such a pitch that at one point, it was thought Glasgow radicals were tunnelling from Glasgow to the Edinburgh Tolbooth to liberate Thomas Muir (such a crazy alarm is described in *The Edinburgh Gazetteer* October 1793). Prior to the arrests there were reports that 'Paisley & its neighbourhood' were in a 'state of tumult and unrest' (RH 2/4/74/f.76). Even worse, reports came in from a Charles Ogilvie of the Customs in Greenock that local people were supplying provisions to French naval ships at the town docks (RH 2/4/74/f.95). Edinburgh Supporters of the accused gathered at Calton Hill, Edinburgh as the trial went on. Scott, the Fiscal, ordered 'to have people on the watch' and list who was in attendance (Laing II, 500, f.533). In the following week, legal action against the editor of *The Edinburgh Gazetteer* was successful and it was forcibly closed. Being charged with sedition, James Thomson Callender (1758–1803), author of the savage critique on political corruption, *The Political Progress of Britain*, fled the country and was declared a fugitive. (See Michael Durey, *With the Hammer of Truth. James Thomson Callender*, University of Virginia, 1990.) Amid such tumult, upwards of '10,000' people helped take Maurice Margarot in a carriage to parliament square in Edinburgh on the opening of his trial: all 'well wishers . . . where we were received with such a universal shout . . . entered into the court & having taken my seat at the Bar between two soldiers with drawn bayonets' the court was adjourned due to a 'sudden illness of the Lord Advocate [Robert Dundas]' (TS 11/959/3505: Margarot to Thomas Hardy, LCS, London, January 1794). Despite their varied and eloquent defences, expressed in Enlightenment concepts and Biblical allusion, the accused were all found guilty of sedition. As a result, this and later political suppression of radicalism put back the cause of British democratic progress for over a generation. Burns, watching from Dumfries, was conscious of these events and wrote wryly in *From Esopus to Maria*, that 'his heresies in Church and State, / Might well award him Muir and Palmer's fate'.

The introductory quotation from Milton is an apt description of Burns's personal predicament in Dumfries, where his relationship with, inter alia, John Syme, was strained. He cast a keen glance at the London treason trials during early 1795, as he remarked to Mrs Dunlop:

> Thank God, these London trials have given us a little more breath, & I imagine that the time is not far distant when a man may freely blame Billy Pit[t], without being called an enemy to his Country (Letter 649).

It is evident from the extent of censorship outlined in our Introduction that Burns almost certainly had his say on these matters and that missing letters to Mary Wollstonecraft, William Roscoe, William Masterton, William Smellie and others, probably contained commentary and/or poetry on the Scottish sedition trials.

The language employed here is seen in the elegiac style of *Elegy on the Death of Sir James Hunter-Blair*, where the Muse of Caledonia loudly laments:

> I saw my sons resume their ancient fire,
>   I saw fair Freedom's blossoms richly blow;
> But ah! How hope is born but to expire,
>   Relentless fate has laid their guardian low.
>
> My patriot falls, but shall he die unsung,
>   While empty Greatness saves a worthless name?
> No: every Muse shall join her tuneful tongue,
>   And future ages hear his glowing fame.

Indeed, these stanzas might almost be placed within the new poem and read with natural continuity, despite the fact that the poems were written some four years apart.

What makes this a typical Burnsian political poem is that, despite his creative anxieties of being worthy of his theme, the poet's metaphorical darkness precedes a radical dawn. Thus, the poem ends with the beautiful image of poetry itself succouring the sea-borne exiles. The feel is akin to Coleridge and, indeed, we might here recall the first lines of Coleridge's sonnet, *To the Honourable Mr [Thomas] Erskine* which also deals with the exiled Scots:

When British Freedom for an happier land
  Spread her broad wings, that flutter'd with affright,
  ERSKINE! thy voice she heard, and paus'd her flight
Sublime of hope, for dreadless thou didst stand

(Thy censer glowing with the hallow'd flame)
  A hireless Priest before the insulted shrine,
  And at her altar pour the stream divine
Of unmatch'd eloquence . . .

Coleridge's sonnet appeared in *The Morning Chronicle* at the end
of the same year, 1794. As well as demonstrating poetic affinity
between the two men, it records the enormous impact the Scottish
Sedition Trials had on British radical consciousness.

The Ewe Bughts

First printed in *The Morning Chronicle*, 10th July, 1794.

'Will you go to the Ewe-bughts, Marian,	sheep pens
'And wear in the sheep wi' me?	bring
'The mavis sings sweetly, my Marian,	song thrush
'But not sae sweetly as thee'.	so
5 These aft were the words of my Sandy,	often
As we met in the how of the glen,	hollow
But nae mair shall I meet wi' my Sandy,	no more
For Sandy to Flanders is gane.	gone
How can the trumpets loud clarion	
10 Thus take a' the shepherds afar?	
Oh could na' the Ewe-bughts and Marian	not, sheep fold/pen
Please mair than the horrors of war?	more
But, oh, tis the fault o' them a', Sirs,	all
In search of gowd and of fame,	gold
15 The lads daily wander awa', Sirs,	away
And leave their poor lasses at hame.	home
Not a plough in the land has been ganging,	moving
The owsen hae stood in the sta',	oxen have, stall
Nae flails in our barns hae been banging,	no
20 For mair than this towmond or twa.	more, 12 months, two
Ilka Laird in the Highlands is rueing,	each
That he drove his poor tenants away,	
For naething is seen here but ruin,	nothing
As the haughs are a' lying in lay.	fertile lands, all

25 There's gowd in the garters of Sandy,   gold
        And silk in his blue-bonnet lug,   flap of a cap/bonnet
    And I'm not a kaerd nor a randy,   gypsy, rude person
        Nor a lass without blanket or rug;
    Then why should he fight sae for riches,   so
30   Or seek for a sodger's degree,   soldier's commission
    Or fling by his kilt for the breeches,   throw, trousers
        And leave the dear Ewe-Bughts and me?

This appears anonymously in *The Morning Chronicle*, 10th July, 1794. It was first ascribed to Burns by Professor Lucylle Werkmeister in her 1966 paper *Robert Burns and the London Daily Press* (*Modern Philology*, LXIII, p. 328). Werkmeister does not provide a textual argument for her case, but a formally contextual one as we shall see in notes to the immediately following 'A Cabinet Dinner'. It was subsequently ascribed to Burns in Scott Hogg's *The Lost Poems* (1997).

Textually, the song is based on an old song named *Will Ye Go to the Ewe Bughts, Marion* and its tune of the same name, which melody Burns had already set to *Will Ye Go to the Indies, My Mary*. This new version is significantly adapted from Allan Ramsay's earlier *Ewe Bughts, Marion*. Like Burns's treatment of *Logan Braes*, the new lyric has been transformed into a war-broken love song. The simple language and style is enhanced by the evocative use of the feminine voice; a characteristic trait of Burns's lyrics. Ramsay's version is written in the male voice. No poet of the eighteenth century possessed Burns's skill in employing the female voice in song.

L. 20 is almost straight from Burns's *The Ronnals of the Bennals*, which reads 'For mair than this towmond, or twa'. Burns employs the name 'Sandy' (l. 5) on many occasions; it was a stock-in-trade name within pastoral narrative or dialogue during the century (See Burns's *Sandy and Jockie*). Moreover, he sent a copy of *Ewe Bughts Marion* to James Johnson in 1795, commenting 'Another song – "Ewe Bughts Marion" – a quite different set from the one you have already published' (Letter 684). He also mentions it to Thomson (Letter 511) and in his reply to Burns, Thomson commented, 'What you say of The Ewe Bughts is just . . . All I requested was that you would try your hand on some of the inferior stanzas' (Currie, 1800, Correspondence, Letter VII, p. 191). Burns was aware that at least two older versions existed and wrote of the earliest text that he was 'not sure if this old and charming air be of the South, as it is commonly said, or of the North of Scotland. There is a song apparently as ancient as "Ewe Bughts Marion", which sings to the same time, and is evidently of the North' (Hogg, *The Lost Poems*, 1997, p. 158). The Ramsay collected version reads:

Will ye go to the ewe-bught, Marion,
    And wear in the sheep wi' me?
The sun shines sweet, my Marion,
    But nae half sae sweet as thee.
5   O Marion's a bonie lass,
    And the blyth blinks in her e'e;
And fain wad I marry Marion,
    Gin Marion wad marry me.

There's gowd in your garters, Marion,
10   And silk on your white hause-bane;
Fu' fain wad I kiss my Marion,
    At e'en when I come hame . . .

/I'm young and stout, my Marion;
    Nane dances like me on the green:
15   And gin ye forsake me, Marion,
    I'll e'en gae draw up wi' Jean . . .

This is clearly the model for the new radical text. Such a radical revision would not have been sent to Thomson given his prudish slight on Burns's anti-war *Logan Braes*. The obvious outlet, given the demise of *The Edinburgh Gazetteer* in January 1794, was *The Morning Chronicle*. After all, as already shown, he did promise to send them such pieces. McGuirk describes *The Ewe Bughts* as a jewel among the recently recovered poems, stating it has 'the strongest claim' to be one of the 'previously unknown poems by Robert Burns' (*Books in Review, Eighteenth Century Scottish Studies Newsletter*, 1997, p. 15).

A Cabinet Dinner

Printed in *The Morning Chronicle* with *The Ewe Bughts*, 10th July, 1794.

'How shall we save the loaves and fishes;
    Where safely shall we hide 'em?
To keep them from the Gallic meshes,'
    Says Loughb'rough, *'let's divide 'em'*.

'Ah! should they fail in savage hand,
    You know how they would treat 'em!
As friends, then, to our native land,
    'Tis better *we should eat 'em*'.

This was, as Professor Werkmeister comments in her 1966 paper,
Robert Burns and the London Daily Press, printed next to *Ewe Bughts
Marion*, 'paired but unsigned' (p. 328). On this basis she argues it is
by the same author as *Ewe Bughts Marion* and ascribes it to Burns. It
was the newspaper custom to pair poems or songs, set them out next
to each other without a line across the page to indicate they are by
the same author. In the second *Heron Ballad* (1. 76). Burns also
refers to 'the fishes and loaves'. Loughborough (1. 4) was Alexander
Wedderburn, the Lord Chancellor.

The 'loaves and fishes' reference is, of course, a brutally ironic
inversion of Christ's miraculous feeding of the poor. This *anti-*
Christian governing class is predatorily grabbing everything for
itself. It is a bitter double irony, and complete confirmation of
Werkmeister's suggestion of Burns's authorship, that in 1795 an
Ulster poet, believing, on the sole evidence of *The Dumfries Vo-
lunteers*, that Burns had betrayed the democratic cause, wrote these
lines:

    O Scotia's Bard! my muse alas!
    For you in private blushes!
        You've dipt i' th' dish wi' slee Dundas
    An prie'd the Loaves and Fishes.

For a full account of this Ulster context see Liam McIlvanney,
'Robert Burns and the Ulster-Scots Literary Revival of the 1790s',
Bullán, Vol. IV, No. 2, pp. 125–43.

Humanity: An Ode

First printed in *The Gentleman's Magazine*, August 1794.

Blow, blow, ye winds! with heavier gust!
And freeze, thou bitter-biting frost!
Descend, ye chilly, smothering snows!
Not all your rage, united, shews
5   More hard unkindness, unrelenting,
Vengeful malice, unrepenting,
Than heav'n-illumin'd *Man* on brother *Man* bestows! —

　　　See stern Oppressions iron lip,
　　　　　See mad Ambition's gory hand,
10　Sending like blood-hounds from the slip,
　　　　　Woe, Want and Murder, o'er a land![1]
　　　Even in the peaceful, rural vale,
　　　Truth, weeping, tells the mournful tale,
　　　How Luxury, with Flattery by her side,
15　The parasite, empoisoning her ear,
　　　With all the servile wretches in the rear,
　　　Looks o'er proud Property extended wide;
　　　And eyes the simple, lowly hind,
　　　Whose toil upholds the glittering show,
20　A creature of another kind,
　　　Some coarser substance, unrefin'd,
　　　Plac'd for her Lordly use thus vile below!
　　　Where, where, is Love's fond, tender throe,
　　　With lordly Honour's lofty brow,
25　The powers you proudly own?
　　　Is there, beneath Love's noble name,
　　　Can harbour, dark, the selfish aim,
　　　　　To bless himself alone? —
　　　Mark Maiden-Innocence, a prey
30　　　To love-pretending snares:
　　　This boasted honour turns away,
　　　Shunning soft Pity's rising sway,
　　　Regardless all of tears, and unavailing prayers.
　　　Perhaps this hour, in misery's squalid nest,
35　She strains your infant to her joyless breast,
　　　And with a mother's fears shrinks at the rocking blast!

　　　　　O ye! who sunk in beds of down,[2]
　　　Feel not a want but what *yourselves create*,

1 '– In our world, Death deputes
Intemperance to the work of age!
And, hanging up the quiver Nature gave him,
As flow of execution, for despatch
Sends forth imperial butchers; bids them slay
Their sheep [the silly sheep they fleec'd before]
And toss him twice ten thousand at a meal.' Young's *Consolation*. R.B.

'Cry havoc, and let slip the dogs of war.' Shakespeare. R.B.

2 'Ah, little think the gay, licentious proud,
Whom pleasure, power, affluence surround . . .' Thomson. R.B.

Think, for a moment, on his hapless fate,
Whom friends and fortune quite disown!
Ill-satisfy'd keen Hunger's clamorous call,
Stretched on his straw he lays himself to sleep,
While through the ragged roof, and chinky wall,
Chill, o'er his slumbers, falls the drifty heap!
Think on the dungeon's grim confine,
Think on the terrors of the mine,
Where Guilt and poor Misfortune pine!
Guilt, erring Man, relenting view!
Nor let thy legal rage pursue
The wretch, already beaten low
By dire *Misfortune's* undeserved blow!
Afflictions sons are brothers in distress;
A brother then relieve, and God the deed shall bless.

R.B.

Several major poems by Burns are recorded with variant stanzas or lines, depending on whether the poem was drafted on several occasions and modified significantly before publication, or changed after publication. The poem given here does not fall into the category of being merely a variant reading of *A Winter Night*, first published in 1787. It is an updated version, published by Burns himself in August 1794 also in *The Gentleman's Magazine,* some three months after *Sonnet on the Death of Robert Riddell*. Robert Riddell was a subscriber and contributor to the journal and would have made the poet familiar with its pages during their meetings at Friar's Carse. The poem *Humanity: An Ode* is not found in manuscript. It does not feature in any previous edition of Burns and lay undiscovered until Scott Hogg's 1997 research.

The main, obvious difference between the new version and *A Winter Night* is that the body of the poem is no longer presented as a *voice* heard at night by the poet. The opening stanzas of *A Winter Night* in Standard Habbie format are cut away and the consolatory ending is dropped. What remains is an exclusively dissident text expressing the humanitarian sentiment of the poem, hence the new title, *Humanity: An Ode*. There are, on close examination, several minor textual changes from the 1787 version to this final work, including new lines and a new ending to the poem. The differences are: 'as now' is dropped from the line 'Not all your rage, [as now] united, shews'; 'iron grip' is modified to 'iron lip'; 'Or mad Ambition's gory hand' becomes 'See mad Ambition's gory hand'; 'How pamper'd Luxury' is changed to 'How Luxury, with Flattery by her side'; 'rustic hind' becomes 'lowly hind'; 'thus far' is omitted from 'Plac'd for her Lordly use [thus far,] thus vile below!'; 'Regardless of the tears' is changed to 'Regardless all of tears . . .'; 'wretched fate' is changed to 'hapless fate'; 'piles the drifty heap!' becomes 'falls the drifty heap!' A new line, adding emphasis is given, 'Think on the terrors of the mine.' The question 'But shall thy legal rage pursue' is dropped for the more direct and forceful, 'Nor let thy legal rage pursue.' The phrase 'crushed low' is now 'beaten low'. The final section of the question ending with 'By cruel Fortune's undeserved blow?' is altered to the indignant expression 'By dire Misfortune's undeserved blow!' The poem concludes with a new, improved ending:

Afflictions sons are brothers in distress;
A brother then relieve, and God the deed shall bless.

The structural and stylistic changes made to the poem serve to sharpen the moral outrage of the values expressed. The rhythmical strophes of *A Winter Night,* lines supposedly heard by the narrator, are now presented as the unequivocal voice of the poet. While the original head quotation from *King Lear* has been left out, the new, additional footnotes add to the increased energy of the piece within the wholly new context of Britain's mendacious involvement in the European conflagration. Condemnation of war and its concomitant desolation of human affairs is given a new impetus in a 1794 context, where 'stern Oppression' and 'mad Ambition's gory hand' were responsible for unleashing 'Woe, Want and Murder, o'er a land!' Burns reinforces this by reference to Young's 'imperial butchers', implying criticism on contemporary warmongers, surrounded by indulgent 'pleasure' and 'power' from Thomson's ironic couplet. The Shakespearean debt of *Humanity: An Ode* (see notes to *A Winter Night*) is re-emphasised by the footnote 'Cry havoc, and let slip the dogs of war' (*Julius Caesar*, Act III. Sc. I, 1. 273) alluding to an earlier state overwhelmed with bloody civil strife. Battle had also been joined with France.

At Dumfries Theatre

First published in *The Morning Chronicle*, 7th February, 1795.

KEMBLE, thou cur'st my unbelief
    Of Moses and his rod: –
At YARICO's sweet Notes of Grief
    The rock with tears had flow'd.
        R.B.

This was not, as is generally accepted, first published by Stuart, Glasgow, 1801, but appears in *The Morning Chronicle* on 7th February, 1795, designated by the poet's initials. These lines are further proof Burns was, as promised, sending material to the Opposition press in London. Mrs Stephen Kemble (1763–1841), wife of Stephen Kemble the manager of the Edinburgh theatre, appeared at Dumfries theatre on 21st October, 1794, in the part of Yarico in the drama *Inkle and Yarico* by George Colman. With its potent anti-slave-trade sentiments, it was a popular drama among radicals of the period. Accordingly, these lines are an indirect political statement by Burns. They were written just after the performance. Kinsley, while drawing attention to the allusion to Exod. xviii, does not mention this political context.

The Heron Ballads
First Heron Ballad
Tune: For a' That and a' That
First printed as an anonymous broadside, 1795.

	Wham will we send to London town,	who
	To Parliament, and a' that,	
	Wha maist in a' the country round,	who most, all
	For worth and sense may fa' that. —	be up to/do
5	For a' that and a' that,	
	Thro' Galloway and a' that,	
	Where is the Laird, or belted Knight,	
	That best deserves to fa' that?	do

	Wha sees Kirrouchtree's open yett,	who, gate
10	And wha is 't never saw that,	who
	Wha e'er wi' Kirrouchtree met,	who ever
	That has a doubt of a' that?	
	For a' that and a' that,	
	Here's Heron yet for a' that;	
15	The independent Patriot,	
	The Honest Man, and a' that.	

	Tho' wit and worth, in either sex,	
	Saint Mary's Isle[1] can shaw that;	show
	Wi' Lords and Dukes let Selkirk mix,	
20	For weel does Selkirk fa' that.	well, do

1 The seat of the Earl of Selkirk, home of the poet's friend Lord Daer.

For a' that and a' that,
    Here's Heron yet for a' that;
An independent Commoner
    Maun bear the gree and a' that.   *shall win the day*

25 To paughty Lordlings shall we jeuk,   *insolent, bow*
    And it against the law, that:
For even a Lord may be a gowk,   *fool/cuckoo*
    Tho' sprung frae kings and a' that.   *from*
For a' that and a' that,
30   Here's Heron yet for a' that;
A Lord may be a lousy loon,   *idiot*
    Wi' ribban, star, and a' that. —   *ribbon*

Yon beardless boy comes o'er the hills,[2]
    Wi's uncle's gowd, and a' that: *with his, gold*
35 But we'll hae ane frae 'mang oursels   *have one from*
    A man we ken, and a' that. —   *know*
For a' that and a' that,
    Here's Heron yet for a' that;
We are na to the market come,   *not*
40   Like nowt and naigs and a' that. —   *cattle, horses*

If we are to be knaves and fools,
    And bought and sauld and a' that,   *sold*
A truant callan frae the schools   *lad, from*
    It 's ne'er be said did a' that.
45 For a' that and a' that,
    Here's Heron yet for a' that;
And Master Dicky, thou shalt get
    A gird and stick to ca' that.   *hoop, call*

Then let us drink, the *Stewartry*,
50   Kirrouchtree's Laird, and a' that,
Our Representative to be,
    For weel he's worthy a' that.   *well*
For a' that and a' that,
    Here's Heron yet for a' that;
55 A House of Commons such as he,
    They wad be blest that saw that.   *would*

2 Thomas Gordon of Balmagie, the Tory candidate. His wealthy 'uncle' was James Murray of Broughton.

The election for the Stewartry of Kirkcudbright, a significant part of Galloway, took place in the Spring of 1795. Burns decided to give unqualified support to his friend and new found patron Patrick Heron (1736–1803), the Whig candidate, from Kirroughtree (this is now the accepted spelling), near Newtown Stewart (then named Newtown Douglas). Burns had probably met Heron prior to this either at Edinburgh or the Caledonian Hunt races in Dumfries, but in June 1794 he was Heron's guest at Kirroughtree. The song *The Banks of Cree* was written for Lady Elizabeth Heron. The Tory candidate opposing Heron was Thomas Gordon of Balmagie; he, and almost all of his local aristocratic supporters are lampooned in the four Heron ballads.

In a letter to Patrick Heron, Burns admits to circulating this and the second ballad as printed broadsides: 'I have privately printed a good many copies of both ballads, and have sent them among friends all about the country' (Letter 660). They were written as ephemeral verse, specific to one purpose; to assist the return of Heron to Parliament. Burns boasted to Heron, his satire would:

> . . . pillory on Parnassus the rank reprobation of character, the utter dereliction of all principle, in a profligate junto which has not only outraged virtue, but violated common decency; which, spurning even hypocrisy as paltry iniquity below their daring; – to unmask their flagitiousness to the broadest day – to deliver such over to their merited fate, is surely not merely innocent but laudable; is not only propriety, but virtue. – You have already, as your auxiliary, the sober detestation of mankind on the heads of your opponents; and I swear by the lyre of Thalia to muster on your side all the votaries of honest laughter, and fair, candid ridicule (Letter 660).

More potent, more potentially treasonable anti-Pitt words, were not spoken by the Botany Bay bound radicals Thomas Muir, Rev. Fysche Palmer, William Skirving or Maurice Margarot. But Burns, without the protection of the influential (deceased) Lord Glencairn, saw in Heron a potential ally, a powerful friend who might be of some use to him in the future. He spells this out to Heron, wishing that one day he might gain promotion in the Excise to the level of Collector, where richer, he would have free time to pursue literary activities:

> I am on the supervisor's list, and as we come on there by precedency, in two or three years I shall be at the head of that

list, and be appointed, *of course*. Then, a FRIEND might be of service to me in getting me into a place in the kingdom which I would like. A supervisor's income varies from about a hundred and twenty, to two hundred per year; but the business is an incessant drudgery, and would be nearly a complete bar to every species of literary pursuit. The moment I am appointed supervisor, in the common routine, I may be nominated on the collector's list; and this is always a business purely of political patronage. A collectorship varies much, from better than two hundred a year to near a thousand. . . . besides a handsome income, a life of compleat leisure. A life of literary leisure with a decent competence, is the summit of my wishes (Letter 660).

However regrettable that this wish was never fulfilled, Burns may have won one partly influential friend with his Heron Ballads, but the Whigs were in Opposition and although Burns told Richarld Oswald of Auchincruive he had lately 'come forward with my services, as poet laureate' to the Whig Party (Letter 662), they were impotent to repay his services.

It mattered little that all of the individuals in the ballads had their names partly dashed out in the original publication, leaving only one or two letters as a hint of the satirical target. It was obvious who the individuals were, given the naming of places associated with the Tory candidate and his supporters. After the eulogy to Heron (ll. 1–24) as a somwhat idealised independent patriot, ll. 25–32 are a biting attack on Tory Landlordism, sharper in tone than the revolutionary *A Man's A Man*, particularly the treasonable 'For even a Lord may be a gowk, / Tho' sprung frae kings and a' that'. Giving voice to the voiceless peasant, ll. 39–42 hit on the brutal inequalities of the rural feudal system 'We are na to the market come,/ Like nowt and naigs and a' that. —/ If we are to be knaves and fools, / And bought and sauld and a' that'. It was probably evident to many readers that Burns was the author, despite his apparent loyalty to King and country in *The Dumfries Volunteers*. The Heron Ballads represent Burns's deliberate political intervention in an election, albeit cloaked in anonymity, which would have lost him both his liberty, his job as an Excise officer and his family income if he was discovered as the author and, accordingly, found guilty on a charge of sedition.

This ballad first entered the canon with Hogg and Motherwell, 1834, then the same year, in Cunningham.

SECOND HERON BALLAD:

The Election – A New Song
Tune: Fy, Let Us a' to the Bridal
First printed as an anonymous broadside, 1795.

Fy let us a' to Kirkcudbright,   now, go
    For there will be bickerin there;   a scrimmage
For Murray's *light horse* are to muster,[1]
    And O, how the heroes will swear!
5   And there will be Murray commander,
    An' Gordon the battle to win;[2]
Like brothers they'll stan' by each other,   stand
    Sae knit in alliance and kin.   so

And there'll be black-nebbit *Johnie*,[3]   -nosed
10   The tongue o' the trump to them a';   Jew's harp/spokesman
An he get na Hell for his haddin,   not, dwelling
    The Deil gets nae justice ava.   devil, no, at all
And there'll be *Kempleton's* birkie,[4]   lively fellow
    A boy no sae black at the bane;   not so, bone
15 But as to his fine *Nabob* fortune,
    We'll e'en let the subject alane.   even, alone

An' there'll be *Wigton's* new *Sheriff*,[5]
    Dame Justice fu' brawly has sped;   bravely
She's gotten the heart of a *Bushby*,
20   But Lord! what's become o' the head?
An' there'll be *Cardoness*, ESQUIRE,[6]
    Sae mighty in *Cardoness'* eyes;
A wight that will weather damnation,
    The Devil the prey will despise.

1 James Murray of Broughton.
2 Thomas Gordon of Balmagie, Tory candidate.
3 John Bushby, sheriff clerk, Dumfries.
4 William Bushby, John's brother.
5 Maitland Bushby, John's son.
6 David Maxwell of Cardoness, hit at in satire by Burns in the Galloway
epigrams.

25 And there'll be *Douglasses* doughty,[7]
    New-christening towns far and near;
Abjuring their democrat doings
    By kissing the arse of a *Peer*.
An' there'll be *Kenmure* sae gen'rous,[8]   so
30   Whase honour is proof to the storm;   who's
To save them from stark reprobation,
    He lent them his name to the *Firm*.

But we winna mention *Redcastle*,[9]   will not
    The *body*, e'en let him escape:
35 He'd venture the gallows for siller,   money
    An' 'twere na the cost o' the rape.   rope
An' whare is our King's *Lord Lieutenant*,[10]   where
    Sae famed for his *gratefu'* return?   so
The billie is gettin his questions,   lad
40   To say in *St. Stephen's* the morn.   Westminster, tomorrow

An' there will be Lads o' the gospel,
    Muirhead, wha's as *gude* as he's *true*:[11]   who is, good
An' there'll be *Buittle's Apostle*,[12]
    Wha's mair o' the *black* than the *blue*;   who is more
45 An' there'll be Folk frae *Saint MARY's*,[13]   from
    A *house* o' great merit and note;
The deil ane but honours them highly,   devil a one/no-one
    The deil ane will gie them his vote.   give

An' there'll be wealthy young *RICHARD*[14]—
50   Dame Fortune should hing by the neck   hang
For prodigal thriftless bestowing —
    His merit had won him respect.
An' there'll be rich brither *Nabobs*,[15]

7 Sir William Douglas & James Douglas. Newtown Douglas was later renamed Newton Stewart.
8 John Gordon, of Kenmure.
9 Walter Sloan Lawrie of Redcastle.
10 George Stewart, Lord Garlies.
11 Rev. James Muirhead, minister of Urr, near Castle Douglas.
12 Rev. George Maxwell, minister at Buittle.
13 The Earl of Selkirk's family home, St Mary's Isle, near Kirkcudbright.
14 Richard Oswald, Auchincruive.
15 Wallace's edition records this as a reference to the Hannay family of Sorbie tower. Mackay states 'D & J Anderson'. It was probably the Hannays, still an important Galloway family.

Tho' *Nabobs*, yet men o' the first:
55 An' there'll be *Collieston's* whiskers,[16]
    An' Quinton — o' lads no the warst.[17]   not, worst

An' there'll be *Stamp-office Johnie*,[18]
    Tak tent how ye purchase a dram: be careful
An' there'll be gay *Cassencarry*,[19]
60   An' there'll be gleg *Colonel Tam*;[20]   quick-witted
An' there'll be trusty KIRROUCHTREE,[21]
    Whase honour was ever his law;
If the VIRTUES were packt in a parcel
    His WORTH might be sample for a'.   all

65 And can we forget the auld MAJOR,[22]
    Wha'll ne'er be forgot in the *Greys*;
Our flatt'ry we'll keep for some other,
    Him only it's justice to praise.
And there'll be maiden *Kilkerran*,[23]
70   And also *Barskimming's* gude Knight;[24]   good
And there'll be roaring *Birtwhistle*,[25]
    Yet, luckily roars in the right.

And there frae the *Niddlisdale* border,   from
    Will mingle the *Maxwells* in droves;
75 Teugh *Jockie*, Staunch *Geordie*, and *Walie*,[26]   tough
    That girns for the fishes and loaves.   cries
An' there'll be *Logan M'Doual*,[27]
    Sculdud'ry — an' he will be there;   skulduggery
An' also the *Wild Scot o' Galloway*,
80   Sogering, gunpowther *Blair*.[28]   soldiering, gunpowder

16 William Copeland of Colieston.
17 Quinton McAdam of Graigengillan.
18 John Syme, distributor of Stamps, Dumfries – the poet's friend.
19 Colonel McKenzie of Cassencarry.
20 Colonel Thomas Goldie of Goldielea.
21 Patrick Heron, the Whig candidate.
22 Major Basil Heron, brother of the Whig candidate.
23 Sir Adam Ferguson of Kilkerran.
24 Sir William Miller of Barskimming.
25 Alexander Birtwhistle, Provost of Kirkcudbright.
26 John Maxwell of Terraughty; George Maxwell of Carruchan; Wellwood Maxwell of the Grove.
27 Captain Andrew McDoul of Logan, Rhins of Galloway.
28 Major Blair of Dunskey near Portpatrick, Rhins of Galloway.

Then hey the *chaste Interest o Broughton,*
   And hey for the blessin 'twill bring;
It may send *Balmaghie* to the Commons,[29]
   In *Sodom* 'twould mak him a King.
And hey for the sanctified *Murray,*[30]
   Our land wha wi' Chapels has stor'd: who
He founder'd his horse among harlots,
   But gied the auld naig to the Lord!   gave old horse

For the original context of this ballad, see notes to the first Heron
ballad. This, the second Heron ballad, is based on an old song *The
Blythesome Wedding* which Burns probably saw in *The Orpheus
Caledonius* (1733). Henderson and Henley record that a broadside
copy of this ballad exists in the British Museum, marked 'Printed
for private distribution by James Hill, Esq., W.S., 1795' (Vol. II,
p. 402). This ballad first entered the canon in 1834, printed in
Hogg and Motherwell, followed the same year by Cunningham's
edition.

Unlike the oblique slight at the idle gentry's 'whoring' and
squandering money playing cards, subtly interwoven in the dialogue
of *The Twa Dogs,* these blatant acerbic verses probably had the
effect of indiscriminate machine gun fire among Pittite Tory sup-
porters throughout Galloway. The various personal failings, idio-
syncrasies and hypocrisy of local Tory aristocrats are mocked in this
broadside of biting polemical satire, which rings out not the titled
but colloquial names for the landed families, thus reducing their
importance to the level of local inn gossip. It exposes, then attacks
the closed-shop alliance of political, economic and legal power
controlled by landed families in the south west. That birth was
the prerequisite to position and power in semi-feudal Scotland,
profoundly irritated Burns, not primarily because he was envious of
his so-called social superiors, but because it bred nepotism and
corruption and allowed many people of rank into places of power
their intellect or ability did not merit. This process, most radicals
believed, acted as a barrier to social, economic and political pro-
gress. Political reform, though was not enough for Burns, as he
commented to Deborah Duff Davies:

DOWN, immediately, should go FOOLS from the high
places where misbegotten CHANCE has perked them up,

29 The Tory candidate.
30 Murray of Broughton.

& through life should they sculk, ever haunted by their native insignificance, as the body marches accompanied by its shadow . . . But the hand that could give, I would liberally fill (Letter 556A).

While the underlying egalitarian values of Burns were often his impetus to satirical verse, an apologia for the Heron Ballads might argue that his hopes for a better, more enlightened society were destroyed by the disintegration of political freedom under Pitt's oppressive government.

There is, though, no substantive evidence that Burns was widely known to be the author of these verses during his lifetime, nor is it known how widely they penetrated the local peasant or aristocratic culture of Galloway during the election. What is known is that the Rev. James Muirhead (l. 42; footnote 11) replied in verse. His reply branded Burns a '. . . shabby son of a whore' and a '. . . rhymster, gauger, pimp'. Speaking as one of the dominant Tory hierarchy then ruling Galloway, Muirhead's libel became part of the black Tory gossip that marred Burns's character *before* and after his death. The lines which probably stung Muirhead, the minister at Urr near Castle Douglas, are in the fourth Heron Ballad (ll. 29–32), where Burns compares him unfavourably to a sour crab apple. The personal and political virulence of the backlash against Burns can be gauged from The Young Ms. in Edinburgh University. Alexander Young of Harben was a student friend of James Currie and Heron's Tory lawyer. His memoir in the form of a commentary on Currie's biography is reprinted in Professor Robert Fitzhugh's *Robert Burns, his Associates and Contemporaries* (Chapel Hill, N.C., 1943).

THIRD HERON BALLAD:

John Bushby's Lamentation
Tune: Babes o' the Wood
First printed in 1834 in Hogg and Motherwell, then Cunningham.

'Twas in the seventeen hunder year	hundred
O' Christ and ninety-five,	
That year I was the waest man	saddest
Of ony man alive. —	any

5 On March, the three and twentieth morn,
      The sun raise clear and bright,   rose
  But Oh, I was a waefu' man   woeful
      Ere toofa' o' the night. —   nightfall

  Earl Galloway lang did rule this land   long
10   With *equal* right and fame,
  Fast knit in *chaste* and *haly* bands   holy
      With Broughton's noble name. —[1]

  Earl Galloway's man o' men was I,
      And chief o' Broughton's host:
15 So twa blind beggars on a string,   two
      The faithfu' tyke will trust. —   dog

  But now Earl Galloway's sceptre's broke,
      And Broughton's wi' the slain;   with
  And I my ancient craft may try,
20   Sen honestie is gane. —   since, gone

  'Twas on the bonie banks o' Dee,
      Beside Kirkcudbright's towers,
  The Stewart and the Murray there
      Did muster a' their powers. —

25 The Murray on the auld grey yad,   old mare
      Wi' *wingèd spurs,* did ride;[2]
  That auld grey yad, a' Nidsdale rade, old mare all, rode
      He lifted by Nidside.   alighted

  [An' there had na been the Earl himsel, not
30   O there had been nae play;   no
  But Garlies was to London gane,[3]
      And sae the kye might stray. —] so, cattle

  And there was Balmaghie, I ween,[4] pledge
      I' th' front rank he wad shine;   would
35 But Balmaghie had better been
      Drinkin Madeira wine. —

1 The Earl's daughter, Lady Euphemia Stewart, wed Murray of Brought-
on's son Alexander.
2 An allusion to the winged spur crest of the Johnstone family, given that
Murray had eloped with a lady of that family.
3 George Stewart, Lord Garlies.
4 The Tory candidate.

And frae Glenkens cam to our aid[5]   from
     A Chief o' doughty deed:
In case that WORTH should wanted be,
40   O' Kenmure we had need. —

And by our banners march'd Muirhead,
     And Buittle was na slack,[6]   not
Whase haly Priest-hoods nane could stain,   whose holy, none
     For wha can dye the BLACK. —   who

45 And there, sae grave, Squire Cardoness,[7]   so
     Look'd on till a' was done:
Sae, in the tower o' Cardoness   so
     A howlet sits at noon. —   owl

And there led I the Bushby clan;
50   My *gamesome* billie WILL,[8]   friend
And my son Maitland, *wise* as *brave*,[9]
     My footsteps follow'd still. —

The DOUGLAS and the HERON'S name
     We set nought to their score:
55 The DOUGLAS and the HERON'S name
     Had felt our might before. —[10]

But DOUGLASSES o' weight had we,[11]
     The pair o' lusty lairds,
For building cot-houses sae fam'd,   so
60   And christening kail-yards. —   kitchen-gardens

And there Redcastle drew the sword[12]
     That ne'er was stain'd wi' gore;
Save on a wand'rer, lame and blind,
65   To drive him frae his door. —   from

5 Gordon of Kenmure Castle. Burns visited the Gordons during his first
Galloway tour in 1793.
6 Rev. James Muirhead, of Urr, near Castle Douglas, and Rev. George
Maxwell, of Buittle.
7 David Maxwell of Cardoness.
8 William Bushby, John's brother.
9 James Maitland, Earl of Lauderdale, was a Whig and friend of Burns.
10 This is a potent allusion to the failure of the Douglas and Heron Bank in
1773, placing the blame firmly at the door of the Galloway Tory families,
particularly the Bushby clan.
11 Sir William Douglas and Sir James Douglas.
12 Walter Sloan Lawrie.

And last cam creepin Collieston,[13]   came
   Was mair in fear than wrath: more
Ae KNAVE was constant in his mind —   one
   To keep that KNAVE frae scathe. —   from harm

In this, the third Heron Ballad, Burns places the lament in the mouth of John Bushby, one of the leading supporters of the Tory candidate Thomas Gordon of Balmagie. Bushby was the former manager of the Dumfries branch of the defunct Douglas, Heron and Co. Bank. In the middle of this piece, Burns places the blame for the fall of the bank on the Bushby family and by implication, their family connections among Galloway's powerful aristocracy. He was Sheriff Clerk to the county of Dumfries when Burns knew him. We have included ll. 29–32, given in brackets above, missed by Kinsley but printed by Mackay. It was probably circulated as a broadside, like the other ballads.

FOURTH HERON BALLAD:

Buy Braw Troggin:
An Excellent New Song
Tune: Buy Broom Besoms
First printed as an anonymous broadside, 1796.

Wha will buy my Troggin,   who, misc. items sold by vagrants
   Fine ELECTION WARE;
Broken trade o' BROUGHTON,[1]
   A' in high repair.   all

Chorus
5   Buy braw Troggin,   fine
   Frae the banks o' DEE!   from
Wha want Troggin,   who
   Let them come to me.

Here's a noble Earl's
10   Fame and high renown,
For an auld sang —   old song
   It's thought the Gudes were stown.[2]   goods, stolen
   Buy braw Troggin &c.

13 William Copeland of Collieston.
1 James Murray of Broughton.
2 Earl of Galloway. An allusion to the loss of the Scottish parliament in 1707.

Here's the Worth o' BROUGHTON,
   In a *needle's e'e*:   eye
15 Here's a reputation
     Tint by BALMAGHIE.[3]   lost
        Buy braw Troggin &c.

Here's an HONEST CONSCIENCE,
   Might a Prince adorn,
Frae the *Downs o' Tinwald*,   from
20   — So was never worn.
        Buy braw Troggin &c.

Here's its Stuff and Lynin,
   Cardoness's Head;[4]
Fine for a Soger,   soldier
   A' the wale o' lead.   boast/choice
        Buy braw Troggin &c.

25 Here's a little Wadset —   mortgage
   Buittle's scrap o' TRUTH,[5]
Pawn'd in a gin-shop,
   Quenching haly drouth.   holy thirst
        Buy braw Troggin &c.

Here's Armorial Bearings,
30   Frae the Manse o' Urr: from
The crest, an auld *crab-apple*, old
   Rotten at the core.[6]
        Buy braw Troggin &c.

Here is Satan's Picture,
   Like a bizzard-gled,   buzzard kite
35 Pouncing *poor Redcastle*,[7]
   Sprawlin like a tade.   toad
        Buy braw Troggin &c.

3 The Tory candidate, Gordon of Balmaghie.
4 David Maxwell of Cardoness.
5 Rev. George Maxwell of Buittle.
6 Rev. James Muirhead of Urr, near Castle Douglas.
7 Walter Sloan Lawrie of Redcastle.

Here's the Font where *Douglas*
    Stane and mortar names;   stone
Lately used at *Caily*,[8]
40   Christening *Murray's* crimes.
    Buy braw Troggin &c.

Here's the Worth and Wisdom
    Collieston can boast;[9]
By a *thievish Midge*
    They had been nearly lost.
    Buy braw Troggin &c.

45 Here is *Murray's* Fragments
    O' the Ten Commands;
Gifted by BLACK JOCK[10]
    — To get them aff his hands.   off
    Buy braw Troggin &c.

Saw ye e'er sic Troggin?   such
50   If to buy ye're slack,   slow
HORNIE'S turnin Chapman,   the Devil
    He'll buy a' the *Pack*!   all
    Buy braw Troggin &c.

Buy braw Troggin,   fine
    Frae the banks o' DEE!   from
55 Wha want Troggin,   who
    Let them come to me.

For introduction, see notes to the first and second Heron ballads. During the 1796 election Patrick Heron's opponent was the son of the Earl of Galloway, Montgomery Stewart. This propaganda song was composed sometime in May or early June, 1796. One of Burns's last radical works, it is further evidence of his anonymous, underground support for the Opposition cause until his death. It displays remarkable brevity without losing its pointed satirical effect, employing the image of a trogger to reduce the Tory candidate to that of a travelling packman, or hawker, peddling election promises like worthless goods. One of its many satirical barbs alludes to the Earl

8 Cally House at Gatehouse of Fleet. This is an allusion to plunders of war.
9 William Copeland of Collieston.
10 John Bushby.

of Galloway's role (1. 12) in selling out the Scottish parliament in 1707, while the Laird of Cardoness, David Maxwell is the straw man of the Tory show. The Rev George Maxwell, of Buittle (1. 26) is castigated as a gin addict and the Rev. James Muirhead (1. 30) of Urr, near Castle Douglas, a sour faced crab-apple. These palpable hits were, probably developed from gossip circulating among radicals within Galloway. It was probably with an eye to the Heron Ballads that Burns told Maria Riddell in June 1796, '. . . if I must write, let it be Sedition, or Blasphemy' (Letter 697). A broadsheet was printed in 1796, probably by Burns himself. A copy of the broadsheet was sold in 1939 and now exists in the Spoor Library, Lot 107. It is further proof of his radical involvement on behalf of the Whig Opposition. This Heron Ballad was first included in the canon by Cunningham, 1834.

A Man's a Man for a' That
Published anonymously in *The Glasgow Magazine*, August, 1795.

Tune: – For a' That, and a' That.

Is there, for honest Poverty		
That hings his head, an' a' that;	hangs
The coward-slave, we pass him by,		
We dare be poor for a' that!		
5 For a' that, an' a' that,		
Our toils obscure, an' a' that,		
The rank is but the guinea's stamp,		
The Man 's the gowd for a' that.	gold

What though on hamely fare we dine,	homely foods
10 Wear hoddin grey, an' a' that?	coarse woollen cloth
Gie fools their silks, and knaves their wine,	give
A Man's a Man for a' that.		
For a' that, an' a' that,		
Their tinsel show, an' a' that;		
15 The honest man, tho' e'er sae poor,	so
Is king o' men for a' that.		

Ye see yon birkie ca'd a lord,	fellow called
Wha struts, an' stares, an' a' that,		
Tho' hundreds worship at his word,		
20 He's but a coof for a' that.	fool/lout
For a' that, an' a' that,		

His ribband, star, an' a' that,
The man o' independent mind,
He looks an' laughs at a' that.

25 A Prince can mak a belted knight,
        A marquis, duke, an' a' that!
    But an honest man's aboon his might —   above
        Guid faith, he mauna fa' that!   good, must not be like
    For a' that, an' a' that,
30   Their dignities, an' a' that,
    The pith o' Sense an' pride o' Worth
        Are higher rank than a' that.

    Then let us pray that come it may,
        As come it will for a' that,
35 That Sense and Worth o'er a' the earth
        Shall bear the gree an' a' that.   win the day
    For a' that, an' a' that,
        It's comin yet for a' that,
    That Man to Man the warld o'er   world
40   Shall brithers be for a' that.   brothers

The first version of *A Man's a Man*, printed anonymously during
the poet's life, differs textually from the final version given above.
Rather than containing five, it has only four stanzas, beginning with
what became the second:

What tho' on hamely fare we dine,
    Wear hodden grey, and a' that:
Gie fools their silk, and knaves their wine,
    A man's a man for a' that.
For a' that, and a' that,
    Their tinsel shew, and a' that;
An honest man, tho' ne'er sae poor,
    Is Chief o' men for a' that.

It was this early version, printed in the *Glasgow Magazine*, August
1795 that was copied by the radical Belfast-based *The Northern
Star*, 19th–22nd October, 1795. A more sinister publication oc-
curred just prior to the poet's death, when the first Glasgow
version re-appeared in the pro-government London *Oracle*, 2nd
June 1796, but this time, disturbingly, with Burns's name as
author. Professor Werkmeister remarks on this: 'Considering the
character of the poem, one doubts even so that Burns had author-

ized it over his signature. The poem was copied by *The Star* on
June 3.' (*Robert Burns and the London Daily Press, Modern Philol-
ogy* 1966, p. 329). There can be little doubt that the governmental
spy network would have taken notice of the song and judged it as
seditious. While there is no mention that the song was published
under his name in surviving letters, it is certain to have caused
some considerable anxiety for Burns, given his Excise post. That
his employers took no action against him, or enquired formally into
the matter, is perplexing. With hindsight, it may be that the poet's
illness was well known to his Excise superiors and the Commis-
sioners in Edinburgh that they chose not to take action against him.
Either way, Burns not only feared imprisonment, being pursued
for the debt owed for his Dumfries Volunteers uniform, but must
have known about this named publication which could have had
him arrested at any moment from 2nd June, 1796 onward and
charged with sedition.

Another, hitherto undocumented version was printed in 1798 by
Professor Peter Urbani, Edinburgh. It too begins with what became
the second stanza. Its second stanza is the one Burns eventually
reworked to become the final version's first stanza:

> Wha wad for honest poverty,
> Hang down their heads an' a' that?
> The coward slave we pass him by
> And dare be poor for a' that.
> >   For a' that and a' that,
> >   Their purse-proud looks and a' that,
> >   In ragged coats ye'll often find
> >   The noblest hearts for a' that.

Kinsley mentions a 1793 songbook edited by Peter Urbani, but not
the more important 1798 publication containing version two of *A
Man's A Man*. Henley and Henderson are dismissive of variant lines
in another version they found, published by Brash and Reid (1801)
in Glasgow which is similar to the 1798 text, mentioning 'purse-
proud looks'. They refer to the 'absurd version of this half stanza,
apparently the invention of the ingenious Reid' (Vol. 3, p. 490)
unaware that it occurs in the 1798 Urbani version and they display
their ignorance of Burns's letters, where the phrase 'purse-proud'
occurs several times. Their commentary is mixed with obvious
political loathing and they appear unaware that the song had been
re-drafted several times by Burns. The second version has five
stanzas, not the four of the first edition.

Henley and Henderson were not perceptive enough to see the genesis of the final lyric, from the original publication, through Urbani's 1798 text to the intermediate Brash and Reid text, printed at Glasgow, *circa* 1801. The Brash and Reid print contains many of the peculair typographic stresses employed by Burns, evident among his manuscripts and it is the first publication to have the famous first verse in place as it is now known, although the text is rather more Scottish than the final version:

Wha wad for honest poverty,
   Hing down his head an' a' that?
The coward slave we pass him by
   And dare be poor for a' that.

For a' that, and a' that,
   Our toils obscure, and a' that,
The RANK is but the GUINEA stamp,
   The MAN's the GOWD for a' that.

In self-deprecatory mood Burns described the lyric to George Thomson as '. . . no Song; but will be allowed, I think, to be two or three pretty good *prose* thoughts, inverted into rhyme' (Letter 651). He did not hide his authorship to Thomson, but probably trusted the song collector implicitly not to pass copies around. When Thomson eventually printed the song in 1805, it had been in Currie's 1800 edition and was well known as a work of Burns, having surfaced in *The Morning Chronicle*, in late 1796 with the poet's name ascribed. Even then, Thomson felt compelled to make a few of his own meddling changes to the text. The many variant texts are ample proof that Burns considered this one of his best songs and the final draft was the result of considerable textual re-appraisal.

For Daiches, the merits of this song, dedicated to the worthiness of 'honest poverty' and democratic rights, is apparent:

It is a rhetorical poem, testifying to the effect on Burns of the French revolution and its ideological currents, and it owes its popularity to its effectiveness as a series of slogans . . . it represents a legitimate and in its way impressive use of the poetic medium . . . The poem has a well contrived structure, moving from the generalization about 'honest poverty' through specific illustrations of the difference between virtue and social rank to a final climactic generalization which is at once a prayer and a prophecy (pp. 302–3).

Crawford rightly refers to the 'revolutionary yearning for fraternity that underlies' the song, with its theme, 'a spontaneous and passionate democratic humanism'. Crawford quotes the introduction to Marshak's *Robert Burns in Translation*, Moscow, 1957: 'He was able to describe the finest and most truly human feelings and experiences of the simple people . . . not as a critic, but as a brother and friend' (Crawford, p. 337). Interestingly, Crawford shows specific influences on the song from Thomas Paine's *The Rights of Man* (Crawford, p. 365).

Due to the different texts of this marching revolutionary anthem it is certain that Burns produced the first text probably very late in 1794 and considering that the anonymous publication in August 1795 is of the first draft, he must have worked on the piece well into 1795 and possibly touched it up again early in 1796. Hence, the final draft would have been improved well *after* the composition of *The Dumfries Volunteers*.

A Prose Essay by Burns
To the Editor of The Morning Chronicle.
Printed 1st January, 1795.

It is a melancholy reflection, that in an age when the theory of Government and legislation has been so well developed by a long succession of celebrated writers, mankind still struggle with the imperfections experienced in more unenlightened days.

The People of France in endeavouring to unshackle themselves from the oppression of their Government, and trusting to the theories of philosophers, have fallen a prey to an oligarchy, who hold unbalanced every branch of government; this they have undergone, although theory has often said that the same persons must not be Legislators and Judges, and the dread occasioned by the misfortunes of that country, induced the people of this to fall into the opposite extreme – the adoration of Regal Power.

The Alarmists have cried down all Reform in Parliament as dangerous, and Parliament has given into the hand of the Crown our dearest rights. Nothing now remains, but to renew that act of Henry VIII by which the King's Proclamation may have the force of an Act of Parliament; for as the majority of our House of Commons is not elected by a majority of the People, nor by a majority of those, who, under the present system have a right to vote, we have no security for its speaking the sense of the People; and, like the Romans in the days of Augustus Caesar, are insulted, with the forms of a free Government, while, in some of the most important parts, the substance is lost.

To tell us that Reform is dangerous, is to say, my children, be good and don't complain, you will have all you desire granted you at a more convenient time. Will anyone who knows the history of mankind assert, that any liberty or privilege we shall have lost, will be ever spontaneously restored, even by the wisest and best of Kings? During the prosperous reigns of Nerva, Trajan, and the Antonines, the Roman world was governed with wisdom and equity; but those Emperors, although they knew the miseries which the People had suffered under their predecessors, never put one bar on the omnipotence of their own authority; and the succession of Commodus shews, that though a good Prince need not be shackled, those shackles ought to exist, as no Sovereign, let him be ever so good and just, can become immortal but in the page of history.

It therefore is proper, that every man who has a love for his King and country, should wish to see the Government brought back to the spirit of its institution: because every free man should hold his privileges dear; and because, when he sees ministers endeavouring, under insidious pretexts, to increase the power of the Crown at the expense of those privileges, he should forsee the most terrible consequences; for either the Government must become absolutely despotic, or the bulk of mankind, not properly sensible of the fine texture, and intrinsic value of our Constitution, may one day join in a general cry against Kings, and overturn the regal part of the Government.

The present time seems to be the crisis which is to determine whether England is to remain a free country or not. At this moment you and I are subject to be seized and confined without having a right to demand a trial; for when a Minister can send his *marechausée*[1] into your house, and take you in silence to a dungeon, what security can you have against a transportation to some distant region? This has not been the case as yet, but what does the annihilation of your dearest privileges tend to but this; will not our children, perhaps, be subject to such an iron sceptre?

---

1 French for *mounted policeman*. Burns knew French well and might have heard this phrase from Dr William Maxwell who spoke fluent French, or Maria Riddell.

This prospect of our future condition, whether we be over-whelmed by tyranny, or become the victims of anarchy, is alarming to men who value, and who understand the British Constitution. Ministers continually warn us to dread innovations, while we daily see the encroachments made on the free part of the Government, which, although they have not yet been called by that name, are not to be stopped by having the word innovation retaliated on them. I will briefly declare what reflection I have made on the subject of our Government, and if I am guilty of errors, shall hope to stand corrected through the medium of your paper.

The spirit of the British Constitution seems to consist in this: That the House of Commons are the deputies of the separate districts of this island, who meet to deliberate for the common good; while the House of Peers, forming the Aristocratical part of the Constitution, may be a check on the Tribune of the People, and, at the same time, constitute the highest Court of Judicature; from the Crown, we are insured in the quick execution of our laws, and we blend with the advantages of a Republic, all those of a Monarchy. But when the servants of the Crown are at the same time permitted to be Tribunes of the People; when the vassals of Nobles enjoy the same pre-eminence, on what do the bulk of this nation rest the bulwark of their liberty? The same parliament that has continued the suspension of the Habeus Corpus may establish a Committee of the House of Commons to take cognizance of cases of High Treason; the Tribunal of the Star Chamber may be renewed; and should that be the case, how are we to help ourselves, when so great a military force exists in these kingdoms.

Our present situation is critical: we are involved in a war without properly knowing why! Do we propose ourselves to re-establish the regal authority in France? That were a vain hope, all our Allies have nearly abandoned us. Do we wish to defend Holland? The Dutch are better disposed towards France than towards us. What object do we propose by the war? the Minister acquires great patronage, and he is thus enabled to keep his place, at the public expense, and by the lives of his fellow-subjects. How many have already been the victims of his ambition; and he tranquilly holds his place, though he knows that his countrymen daily bleed to keep him there? This might, one would think, better become a Rober-spierre; but before we feel abhorrence at the cruelty of the Convention, let us ask ourselves, Whether those who vote for the continuance of the war be not as unfeeling? What signifies it to the sufferers, whether they fall by the guillotine of Roberspierre, or by the massacres which the Great Catherine and the King of Prussia have committed for the sake of good order, Religion, &c. Will Poland feel any better effects from those, than France from the former? Does not the same hold good with regard to the subjects we daily lose on the Continent?

The true medium between anarchy and tyranny ought to be strictly kept in view, for extremities touch; and therefore, so far from its being dangerous to reform our Parliament, we ought to rouse from the present infatuation, and before it is too late, before every trace of our Constitution be effaced, bring it back to those principles on which it is established: that is, make the theory and practice tally better together.

A. Briton

Burns promised to send radical material to the London Whig newspaper *The Morning Chronicle* in a letter of mid-March 1794. Replying to an offer of full-time work on the literary staff of this, the main Whig Opposition newspaper, conveyed to him on behalf of James Perry, the editor, by Captain Patrick Miller Jnr., Burns promised to supply not only occasional poetry, but:

> . . . little Prose Essays, which I propose sending into the world through the medium of some Newspaper; & should these be worth his while, to these Mr. Perry shall be welcome; & all my reward shall be, his treating me with his Paper, which, by the bye, to any body who has the least relish for Wit, is a high treat indeed (Letter 620B).

A thorough search of *The Morning Chronicle* archives, looking specifically at anonymous and pseudonymous prose, has revealed this essay as being in all probability the result of his promise.

The essay appears in *The Morning Chronicle*, 1st January, 1795, printed over the pen-name 'A. Briton', a signature we know Burns exclusively employed in 1788 (See notes for *Lines on Ambition*). There are, also, contextual pointers which suggest this is his composition.

Wishing not to miss any issues of the paper, Burns, revealingly, wrote to the newspaper sometime in January 1795, to complain that specific copies of the newspaper had not been sent to him. The January 1795 letter begins:

> You will see by your subscribers' list, that I have now been about nine months one of that number. – I am sorry to inform

you, that in that time, seven or eight of your Papers either have
never been sent me, or else have never reached me. – To be
deprived of any one Number of the first Newspaper in Britain,
for information, ability & independence, is what I can ill brook
and bear; but to be deprived of that most admirable oration of
the Marquis of Landsdowne, when he made the great, though
ineffectual attempt, (in the language of the Poet, I fear too true)
'to save a SINKING STATE' – this was a loss, which I neither
can, nor will forgive you. That paper, Gentlemen, never
reached me; but I demand it of you. – I am a BRITON;
and must be interested in the cause of LIBERTY: I am a
MAN and the RIGHTS OF HUMAN NATURE cannot be
indifferent to me. . . . that humble domicile in which I shelter
my wife and children, is the CASTELLUM of a BRITON . . .
(Letter 654).

It was roughly nine months since Burns requested a free subscrip-
tion, in exchange for poetry or prose. Letter 620B is dated approxi-
mately for mid-March 1794 and Letter 654 is dated roughly for
January 1795. So, if Burns had kept his side of the bargain, it
appears he was disappointed to have missed several issues of the
newspaper. Yet, the letter is far more than merely a reader's request
for missed issues. Burns almost scolds the editor, demanding that he
receive a back copy of the newspaper. He does not tell the editor
which issue he wants, that is, the date or dates of the daily news-
paper(s) he missed. What jumps out of the page is the fact that Burns
tells the Editor quite categorically that he is 'a BRITON', a
description that occurs twice for emphasis and is spelt out in large,
bold letters. 'A. Briton' is, of course, the signature employed under
the new essay.

The newspaper demanded by Burns is one containing a speech by
the Marquis of Landsdowne. Landsdowne, a Whig, spoke in the
House of Lords on 30th December, 1794. The debate is covered on
31st December, 1794 and 1st January, 1795 in *The Morning Chronicle*.
The debate in the House of Lords and the House of Commons
centred on the King's speech. William Wilberforce added an
amendment to the debate, moving a motion to negotiate peace with
the French. The Marquis's speech is elaborate, powerful and anti-
war; it dwells on the increased losses of British troops on the
Continent and the fact that the allies arraigned against France were
in disarray. The final note on the debate refers to 'the abstract of the
operations of the French Armies, read by the Marquis of Lands-
downe'. Biographical studies have missed the fact that Burns

praised and aligned himself with the Marquis's passionate anti-war, anti-Pitt speech. Moreover, the political views outlined by Landsdowne are found in a more developed, elaborate and lucid essay under the psedonymn 'A. Briton' *in the same newspaper*. So, in Letter 654 Burns, declaring himself loudly to be 'a BRITON' demanded a copy of the newspaper in which the actual 'A. Briton' essay appeared, 1st January, 1795.

When Letter 654 appeared in Cromek in 1808, it was supposedly left unsigned. Finding the fair copy of the letter Cromek guessed it was not sent by Burns to London, neglecting the fact that Burns often made copies of his letters. Indeed, Cromek further estimated that the letter must have been written on behalf of a Dumfries friend, unaware that the poet had joined the free subscription list nine months previous. There is no reason to doubt the recorded letter is both *by* Burns and *from* Burns. The original was probably forwarded to the London newspaper. It remains unknown if the issue for 1st January, 1795 was sent to Burns. Contextual evidence, therefore, before examining textually the new prose essay, suggests that Burns is probably the author.

A textual examination of the new prose essay finds many echoes in the letter Burns wrote in April 1793, to Erskine of Mar:

> Does any man tell me, that my feeble efforts can be of no service; & that it does not belong to my humble station to meddle with the concerns of a PEOPLE? – I tell him, that it is on such individuals as I, that for the hand of support and the eye of intelligence, a Nation has to rest . . . the titled, tinsel Courtly throng may be its feathered ornament, but the number of those who are elevated enough in life, to reason & reflect; yet low enough to keep clear of the venal contagion of a Court; these are a Nation's strength (Letter 558).

He goes on to pinpoint flaws in the British body politic:

> I would say that there existed a system of corruption between the Executive Power & the Representative part of the Legislature, which boded no good for our glorious Constitution; & which every patriotic Briton must wish to see amended (Letter 558).

The phrase 'every patriotic Briton' might be expected from an author who had already signed his name 'A. Briton', but such a description is also central to the radical legacy inherited by Burns from Addison and other writers of the Commonwealth school. That such were still his views in the Spring of 1793 is important in considering the sentiments and the pen-name of the new 1795 essay. To Erskine, Burns went on in a vein similar to the new prose:

> I have three sons, whom, I see already, have brought with them into the world souls ill qualified to inhabit the bodies of Slaves . . . the little independent Britons in whose veins runs my own blood? (Letter 558).

Here, even the poet's sons are 'independent *Briton*s'. Burns's fear is that if political oppression steadily increases or conversely, liberties are further eroded, his children might eventually suffer. The new essay comments on this topic 'will not our children, perhaps, be subject to such an iron sceptre?' An early manuscript of *Scots Wha Hae* expresses this very sentiment 'Do you hear your children cry / Were we born in chains to lie?' The letter to Erskine thus displays the poet's determination not to be silenced by his employers and asserts his right to be independent in his views.

Further textual similarities occur. Having described the calculated manoeuvring of Pitt and his colleagues as '*invidious* powerful individuals . . . *under insidious pretexts* to subvert' [our italics] political opponents, in a letter of February 1789, signed John Barleycorn (Letter 311), we find this same language blaming 'ministers endeavouring, *under insidious pretexts* [our italics], to increase the power of the Crown' in the new prose. Also in setting out his case in the first newspaper letter he signed 'A. Briton', Burns is didactic and succinct, 'The simple state of the case, Mr. Printer, seems to me to be this' (Letter 283) which is very like the language of the new letter which reads 'The spirit of the British Constitution seems to consist in this: That the House of Commons are . . .'. While there were obviously various conventions expected in writing a letter to the press during this period, it is quite evident that his piece does contain many of the stylistic mannerisms and nuances of Burns's prose.

The essay's concluding argument contrasts anarchy and tyranny, 'The true medium between anarchy and tyranny ought to be strictly kept in view'. This is precisely the view expressed emphatically in italics by Burns in his 1793 newspaper published poem, *On The Commemoration Of Rodney's Victory*, '*Be Anarchy curs'd — and be Tyranny d[amn]'d*'. A further similarity exists with the same poem, where it is argued that reform is necessary before 'our Constitution be effaced, bring it back to those principles on which it is established: that is, make the theory and practice tally better together'. The poem records 'And here's the grand fabric, OUR FREE CONSTITUTION / As built on the base of THE GREAT REVOLUTION!' In both examples it is 'our constitution', not simply 'the consititution'. The poet's handwritten note within John Syme's copy of Jean Louis De Lolme's book on the British Consitution, indicating sarcastically that it would suffice until a better was created, is resonant in this last remark. That Burns was deeply read in Constitutional matters, as was Robert Riddell, his closest aristocratic friend during the Dumfries years, and acutely aware of political developments at this time, only makes it more plausible that he would compose such an essay.

It is now known after the appearance of *Ode for General Washington's Birthday*, that Burns wrote, in controlled rage, of England as a country in the grip of political tyranny. Most radical commentators saw the suspension of Habeas Corpus as a significant shift towards futher erosion of individual rights. The possibility seemed real that unaccountable and dictatorial rule by a 'Star Chamber' was to be the next step in Pitt's campaign of terror to crush radical dissent. The current essay asks the question whether or not England can remain a free country, answering in the negative, similar to the manner in which *The Tree of Liberty* deals with the same topic:

> But seek the forest round and round,
>   And soon 'twill be agreed, man,
> That sic a tree can not be found
>   'Twixt London and the Tweed, man.

Between London and the river Tweed, is of course, England, not Britain. Burns does not condemn the political violence that occurred in revolutionary France in his song, nor is it condemned in the essay. Indeed, the massacres by Catherine the Great and the King of Prussia, in the name of law and order, are mentioned as greater crimes. What is seen as an equal crime to anything perpetuated by the French is the act of those British politicians who voted for the continuation of the war. They are blamed as being as unfeeling as a Roberspierre. Moreover, it would be expected that Burns would hit at Pitt's receipt of further patronage due to the war (See *A New Song, or A Wet Day at Walmer Castle*) and his increase in despotic powers, not only over the nation's purse by additional taxation, but, driven by ambition, the deeper urge to be remembered in the pages of history. (This of course, is the theme of *Lines on Ambition*, also signed 'A. Briton' and already ascribed to Burns in this edition.) If

The Tree of Liberty was written during early January 1795, its reformist sentiments – its concluding prayer that 'Auld England' may eventually plant the 'far-famed tree' of liberty, meaning reform, is consistent with the new political essay.

General acceptance of the new prose work is of essential importance to Burnsian studies. If, as we believe it to be Burns's last public commentary on wider British politics and the European scene, it not only maps out precisely what he thought of the Pitt government, and its involvement against France, but it answers emphatically the nineteenth- and twentieth-century notion that Burns was confused on political matters. Indeed, it not only reveals his passionate democratic reformism, his intellectual involvement with current affairs, his depth of knowledge in political theory and historical allusion, in particular Roman history, but a sharp ability to argue a case cogently, and logically, with a poet's eye to penetrate acidly that somewhat intangible, hidden aspect of a nation's history, the motive and ambition of its leading politicians. One can, from the vantage point of the twenty-first century, begin to see that in an unjust, socially and economically rigid hierarchical society, dominated by an oligarchy of aristocratical privilege, a critical thinking, democratic national poet, unable to accept his inferior social position, unable to keep 'silent and obedient', was, in a sense, the ruling élite's worst nightmare.

Without manuscript authority, the provenance of the new prose cannot be proven beyond doubt, but the evidence, contextual and textual, convincingly says Burns. That he would deliver on a promise should be no surprise. If correct, we finally have his last, emphatic political statement proving beyond doubt he was a committed democratic reformer.

The Cob Web – A Song

First printed in *The Morning Chronicle*, 22nd August, 1795.

The sweets of a blessing
Are had by possessing,
Hail! Britons! the cause is your own;
You are wonderful great,
5   You have Princes and State,
And the wisest and best on a Throne!

What a contrast is France,
Where is now the gay dance,
They are no way so happy as we;
10   We have flourishing Trade,
Plenty, beer, meat, and bread!
While madly they starve to be free!

It was once so for us,
Indeed it was thus,
15   Like them we once swore to maintain,
The blessing that God,
Sent to cheer man's abode,
And preserve free from blemish or stain.

Thus, they might suppose,
20   To be led by the nose,
Was not for a People, like them;
That we being free,
Should with freemen agree,
Nor those who sought freedom condemn.

25   But there they was wrong,
We have alter'd our song,
Resolv'd to have nothing to do —
With a good, full of evil,
Devis'd by the Devil,
30   That freedom for which the French rue.

Yet, lest it be thought,
We lov'd self to a fault,
We offer'd Court blessings to treat them;
Ah! could you expect
35   This they would reject,
And force us, unwilling, to beat them.

First a King, good as may be,
We made of a Baby,
Then demanded they'd fawn on the Child!
40   But, so wicked were they,
That they would not obey,
But beat us! for being so wild.

We brib'd to divide them,
Tried all arts to chide 'em,
45   To starve them, made a great fuss;
When, some Demon of Hell,
Inverting the spell,
Turn'd the picture of Famine on us!

So great is the blessing
50   We got by redressing
Each nation's faults but our own;
To destroy them, their Trade,
We, their country invade,
While our own is cut up to the bone.

55   But courage my Friends
We may yet gain our ends,
Perhaps in a circle they'll meet:
When, nine out of ten
They've kill'd of our men,
60   And the rest are left something to eat.

A. Briton

As an introduction to this song, the political prose essay signed 'A. Briton' is printed first, in chronological order. Both appear in *The Morning Chronicle* during 1795, and are signed under the same name. While it may not automatically follow that one author wrote both, evidence suggests that this is highly probable. The prose by 'A. Briton' employs the ironic description 'the wisest and best of Kings', while the song, written several months later, contains the lexically similar, ironic 'And the wisest and best on a Throne!' If, as already argued, Burns is the author of the prose, then, there is a strong case to argue that the song, too, is his.

This work was provisionally ascribed to Burns in Hogg's *The Lost Poems* (1997). There are several factors which suggest it may be from Burns. He, as we have seen, promised to send radical work to *The Morning Chronicle* (Letter 620B). For discussion of this crucial pen-name, see notes to *Lines on Ambition*. As also mentioned in the case for the new radical essay, Burns wrote to *The Morning Chronicle* in January 1795 and emphasised that he was 'a Briton' (Letter 654).

The song is almost certainly by a Scot, given the rhyme of 'trade' and 'bread' (ll. 10–11) where the latter is pronounced *braid*. More important, the song contains a peculiar, deliberate ungrammatical use of 'was' (rather than *were*) for colloquial effect, 'But there they was wrong' (l. 25). After an exhaustive check of period poetry scanning the eighteenth-century Poetry Database, and printed works, only one poet appears out of the crowd who employed this language quirk, Burns. His non-grammatical 'was' is found, inter alia, in *John Barleycorn*, 'There was three Kings unto the east'.

Textually, the song begins with ironic assent, setting up the target of attack by appearing to praise everything British, in constrast to the apparently monstrous French. In reality, the poem is a brillaintly ironic attack on the anti-French war policy of William Pitt. The notion that Britain has 'the wisest and best' on a 'throne' is absurd, given the madness of King George III and the public knowledge that Pitt and Dundas were behind almost every Royal Proclamation printed in the daily newspaper during the 1790s. In truth, King George remained a background puppet, in the shadow of Pitt's increasingly overt abuse of power.

The theme of the song is of Britons being caught in Pitt's political 'cob-web' of ambition and deceit. Burns's favourite contemporary radical song at this period, which he copied out in his own hand and quoted to Mrs Dunlop in January 1795, *The Vine Cover'd Hills and Gay Regions of France*, by William Roscoe, refers to the British people 'caught in his [Pitt's] cob-web like flies'. This song, the Burns-copied manuscript of which was presented to Roscoe by Maria Riddell after Burns's death, is probably the progenitor of the new song's title. Britain was being brought to its knees. Hunger and at times, famine, occurred in parts of England and Scotland, as reported in the press during the winter of 1794–5. Ll. 47–52 allude to this, suggesting that the Pitt government's early plan of starving the French into submission had backfired and was having such an effect at home. This point, far from being poetic fantasy, is eloquently put by the great Glasgow radical, Professor John Millar, a year later in *The Scots Chronicle*, September 2nd, 1796:

> We thought of no less than uniting all the states of Europe, whether great or small, against the French Republic; and we expected to employ successfully the two great engines of *force* and *famine* for affecting our purposes What a dreadful reverse of fortune we have sustained!

In these years destitution and famine are omnipresent in radical writing, culminating in Coleridge's Macbeth-derived incantational attack on Pitt, *Fire, Famine and Slaughter*.

While we know Burns personally experienced food shortages in the first three months of 1796, when he complained of his family going for days without food, his was not an isolated example. Dumfries witnessed food shortage problems in 1795 when this radical song was composed. David Staig wrote to Robert Dundas, Lord Advocate, on 4th February, 1795 requesting help due to extreme shortages of oatmeal in Dumfriesshire: 'The enclosed memorial was handed to me this morning by our Magistrates . . . under this alarm of scarcity . . . it is impossible for me as Collector of the Customs, to give the wished for relief.' (RH 2/4/ 78/f.25). A pamphlet by Dumfries bakers and grain dealers complains that grain from the area was being shipped out of Scotland and not enough was available to them to make a living or feed the local people (RH 2/4/78/f.27–28). Although there are no newspaper accounts of food riots in Dumfries during early 1795, there did exist a serious food problem, partly caused by exorbitant prices and exportation of grain and oatmeal from the area to London. (RH 2/ 4/79/f.3).

One critic has suggested *The Cob Web* might be the work of Dr Alexander Geddes, a radical Scot living in London. Granted Geddes was a prolific pro-Fox poet but he did not employ this pen-name. The entire canon of Geddes is extant in Chelmsford at the Essex County Record Office and the Scottish Catholic Archive in Edinburgh: both were examined. It is not among his papers. Not one of Geddes's radical works is known ever to have been destroyed. His complete poetic jottings and journals are extant, and they contain many of his favourite works copied out at least twice. Textually, there is no example among his poems where he employed the colloquial, common-language usage of 'was' in place of 'were'. Nor does he display the Burnsian skill of ironic assent to what he is actually attacking so evident here. Given this circumstantial and stylistic evidence, the song is attributed to Burns. Without definitive manuscript evidence, the attribution cannot be made with absolute certainty, but considering the evidence for the new political essay and its lexical similarity with *The Cob Web*, it appears that the same 'A. Briton' composed both prose and song.

Along with the poem's comic, sophisticated dramatic inversion, there are two other elements which strongly suggest Burns. First, as in *Ode on General Washington's Birthday*, the notion of a degenerate England betraying her libertarian heritage in order to destroy France. Second, his capacity for integrating on-going political events into his poetry. What ll. 37–9 refer to is the English support for solving the French crisis by returning the Dauphin to the throne as Child-King. This was mooted in 1791 when he was ten but the intended Louis XVII died on June 8, 1795 just prior to this poem's composition. Implicit in the poem (ll. 13–18) is the promise of freedom sent by God through the true child-king, Jesus Christ, as opposed to the false, worldly child-king. Burns did, indeed, belong to that category of writers defined by Herman Melville as those 'who breathe that unshackled democratic spirit of Christianity in all things'.

John Anderson My Joe

First printed in *The Morning Chronicle*, 5th December, 1795.

John Anderson my Joe, John,
    I wonder what you mean,
Approving of the Bills, John
    The Bills you ne'er had seen!
5 'Twas surely very foolish, John,
    And how could you do so?
Pray haud your tongue and say nae mair,   hold, no more
    John Anderson my Joe!

The story of the Phaeton, John,   high carriage
10   Was but an auld wife's saw,   old, tale
And like another Phaeton, John,
    You'll surely have a fa':   fall
This talking will undo you, John,
    And lack of truth much mo' —   more
15 You've neither brains nor gift o' Gab;   conversation
    John Anderson my Joe!

Hogg, *The Lost Poems*, pp. 189–90, attributed this poem to Burns. Burns had already adapted the traditional *John Anderson, My Jo* in a sexually expurgated, personal version. It is characteristic of him to use a traditional song for political purposes. John Anderson is the Scottish John Bull (see *New Song* or *A Wet Day at Walmer Castle*). Simplistic and sycophantic, he toes the Tory line by paying excessive war taxes and basking in a national glory not his own. The use of 'phaeton' is double-edged, being in Burns's usage, both mythological and contemporary. Ll. 9–12 allude to the fable of the son of Helios (the sun god), who rode his chariot too close to the earth, causing Zeus to strike him with a thunderbolt to prevent his incendiary danger to the planet. The contemporary meaning for 'phaeton', for Burns, as in his *To the Hon. Mr. Wm. R. Maule of Panmure on his High Phaeton*, is this sort of carriage as a sign of social vanity and fiscal iniquity.

By 1795, the vinegar on the sponge for heart-broken radicals was their inability to carry the common people with them in their programme of anti-establishment reform. Hazlitt bitterly summed it up thus.

> There is something in the human mind, which requires an object for it to repose on; and driven from all other sources of pride and pleasure, it falls in love with misery and grows enamoured of oppression. It gazes after the liberty, the happiness, the comfort, the knowledge, which have been torn from it by the unfeeling gripe of wealth and power, as the poor debtor gazes with envy and wonder at the Lord Mayor's show. Thus is the world by degrees reduced to a spital or lazar house, where the people waste away with want and disease, and are thankful if they are only suffered to crawl forgotten to their graves. ('*The Times Newspaper*. On the Connexion between Toad-Eaters and Tyrants', *The Selected Writings of William Hazlitt*, Vol. 4, Political Essays, ed. by Duncan Wu, Pickering & Chatto, 1998, p. 139).